Strategies for Reading and Arguing about Literature

MEG MORGAN

KIM STALLINGS

JULIE TOWNSEND

PEARSON

Prentice
Hall

Upper Saddle River, New Jersey 07458

Library of Congress Cataloging-in-Publication Data

Morgan, Meg.
  Strategies for reading and arguing about literature / Meg Morgan, Kim Stallings,
Julie Townsend.
    p. cm.
  ISBN 0-13-093853-X
  1. English language—Rhetoric—Problems, exercises, etc. 2. Criticism—Authorship—
Problems, exercises, etc. 3. Literature—History and criticism—Theory, etc. 4. Persuasion
(Rhetoric)—Problems, exercises, etc. 5. College readers. I. Stallings, Kim. II. Townsend,
Julie. III. Title.
  PE1479.C7M67 2007
  808'.0668—dc22

                                                                2005036546

Editorial Director: Leah Jewell
Acquisitions Editor: Vivian Gaicia
Editorial Assistant: Christina Volpe
Marketing Assistant: Vicki DeVita
Production Liaison: Fran Russello
Permissions Supervisor: Mary Dalton-Hoffman
Manufacturing Buyer: Christina Amato
Cover Design: Kiwi Design
Cover Image Credit: Mimi Jensen, "Slow Dance" copyright 2002, oil on canvas, Triptych, each 36×24,
  Courtesy Hespe Gallery, San Francisco, CA
Director, Image Resource Center: Melinda Reo
Manager, Rights and Permissions: Zina Arabia
Interior Image Specialist: Beth Boyd-Brenzel
Cover Image Specialist: Karen Sanatar
Photo Researcher: Kathy Ringrose
Image Permission Coordinator: Cathy Mazzucca
Composition/Full-Service Project Management: Mike Remillard/Pine Tree Composition
Printer/Binder: RR Donnelley & Sons Company
Cover Printer: RR Donnelley & Sons Company

Credits and acknowledgments borrowed from other sources and reproduced, with permission, in this textbook appear on pages 645–650.

Pearson Education LTD. London
Pearson Education Singapore, Pte. Ltd
Pearson Education, Canada, Ltd
Pearson Education–Japan
Pearson Education Australia PTY, Limited

Pearson Education North Asia Ltd
Pearson Educación de Mexico, S.A. de C.V.
Pearson Education Malaysia, Pte. Ltd
Pearson Education, Upper Saddle River, New Jersey

10 9 8 7 6 5 4 3 2

ISBN: 0-13-093853-X

Contents

CASEBOOK TWO GROWING UP AND OLDER: HIS AND HERS—RITES OF PASSAGE 279

CASEBOOK THREE THE TIES THAT BIND: RELATING AND RELATIONSHIPS 353

CASEBOOK FOUR   LAND OF THE FREE, HOME OF THE BRAVE: DEFINING AMERICA(NS)   421

CASEBOOK FIVE (HU)MAN/NATURE: EXPLORING THE NATURE OF HUMANITY AND THE HUMANITY OF NATURE 541

Chapter Literature Selections

Chapter Practices and Writing Assignment Suggestions

Preface

Strategies for Reading and Arguing About Literature is designed to bring together the often divergent studies of argumentation and literature. Argumentation has become an important part of most college and university English programs—especially second-semester freshman writing courses—but it is typically taught with a focus on social issues and real-world events. Our approach does something a little different. Understanding that literature is the traditional cornerstone of all English programs, we have created a textbook that teaches the art of academic argumentation through a focus on classic and contemporary literature.

Divided into five major sections, *Strategies for Reading and Arguing About Literature* accomplishes the following goals:

1. Students will learn, practice, and master:
   - critical reading strategies.
   - critical writing and research strategies.
   - the essentials of academic argumentation.
   - basic literary theory as it relates to the development of an argument.
2. Students will explore and appreciate a variety of literature ranging from the classical to the contemporary in a variety of genres.
3. Students will be exposed to critical analyses of literary works.

Part One is an introduction to argument and arguing about literature. Students will begin to think of literary texts as arguments and to talk about the function of argumentation in the academic community. They will investigate argument structure and strategies for creating arguments with a focus on the Toulmin philosophy of argumentation.

Part Two focuses on reading strategies. Students will develop a repertoire of critical reading tools to understand the surface meaning of a literary text, tools to explore and understand their own responses to a literary text, and tools to place any given text within appropriate contexts.

Part Three incorporates traditional literary theory as a tool for exploring literature and generating arguments about literature. We have developed an approach that first asks students to turn in toward a work of literature and explore meaning through the text alone. Then, students are asked to turn out from a work of literature and explore meaning through various critical lenses (literary theories).

Part Four guides students in the exploration of writing strategies: planning, drafting, revising, editing, and researching. We have also included an extensive section of MLA documentation instruction and examples.

Finally, Part Five is the anthology portion of our textbook and contains five thematic casebooks. Each casebook contains a balance of classical literature and contemporary literature, poetry, short stories, and plays. We have also included a more focused section at the end of each casebook to look closely at a body of related works. Titled "A Closer Look," these mini-casebooks present an interview with an author, one or more literary works by that author, and a critical essay written about one of those literary pieces.

Within each of the main chapters, we have included a variety of practice exercises (some individual and some collaborative) designed for students to practice various critical thinking, reading, and writing strategies as they move through the textbook. Each chapter concludes with two larger writing assignment suggestions—typically essay assignments. Though we have provided some student models within the textbook, additional models for each practice and writing assignment may be found—along with instructional commentary—in the on-line Instructor's Manual supplement.

We are always on the lookout for excellent student models, so we invite you and your students to submit essays to us for consideration. We also welcome your thoughts on various aspects of this textbook, your experiences using the book in your classroom, your reflections, and suggestions for future editions of the book (including literature selections).

We would like to thank the following reviewers: Denise Rogers, University of Louisiana at Lafayette; Lucille M. Schultz, University of Cincinnati; Margaret Lindgren, University of Cincinnati; David D. Esselstrom, Azusa Pacific University; Matt Turner, Cy-Fair College; Francie Quaas-Berryman, Cerritos College; Carol Marion, Guilford Technical Community College; and Joanna Johnson, University of Texas-Arlington.

Thank you. We look forward to hearing from you.

Meg Morgan
Kim Stallings
Julie Townsend

PART ONE

Introduction to Argument and Arguing About Literature

CHAPTER 1

Text as Argument—Argument as Text

Why Argue About Anything?

People may deny that they like to argue, but many often enjoy the verbal and intellectual struggle with ideas that characterizes argument. Some will argue just for the heck of it and proudly claim that they are only "playing devil's advocate." Perhaps you have argued with friends about the best university to attend, or about who will make it to the Super Bowl, or about the value of the war in Iraq. Argument is so strong a tradition in Western culture that public argument was often the way business got done in Greek society twenty-five hundred years ago. When men argued in Athens, they spoke in public places, so their argument was oral, and their audience was before them and a response to their position immediate. Obviously, the best speaker often won, regardless of the "truth," so men had to learn to argue well. Then, like today, formal arguments typically occurred within three circumstances or situations:

- **Guilt or innocence in the law courts.** In Athens, all free men (but no slaves or women) could participate in the courts of law, serving on juries that decided the guilt or innocence of the accused. Today, in the American judicial system, arguments set forth by a defender or prosecutor attempt to convince the jury of a particular outcome (the guilt or innocence of the accused). Famous cases dominate the news. Recent trials of two snipers who terrorized the Washington, D.C., area were argued based on the alterations made to the defendants' car that enabled them to shoot out of its trunk.
- **Alternative courses of public action.** The great arguers in Athens delved into political debates, asking questions such as "Should we go to war?" "Should we go to war now or wait for a better time?" "Do tax rebates help build the economy?" Today, if you listen to the radio, watch the news or talk shows on TV, or read the local or national newspapers, you see that these issues are still being debated. As in the academic arena, the public and civic arenas favor argument as the way to debate and even perhaps decide important issues.
- **The goodness or badness of a person, often as a way to convince listeners of a person's fitness or unfitness to become a senator, or a general, or a public leader.** If you look at any campaign for public office, you can understand the importance of being able to argue for the quality of a person's record or character. Today, as in ancient Athens, people's reputations are formed and changed based on public

3

argument. Sometimes this argument is based on fact, sometimes on gossip and hearsay. Regardless of the quality of the argument, a person's reputation still may be enhanced or diminished as a result.

When we argue, we are following in the footsteps of a historic tradition—a tradition that we will practice and enhance in this textbook. However, in *this* textbook we do something different. We do not argue about public issues; instead, we argue about issues as they arise in works of literature. Throughout the next ten chapters, we look at literary works as arguments themselves or as instruments for raising potential arguments. Often we consider how the issues presented in literary works relate to our own lives and the lives of those around us.

Why We Can Argue About Literature

We look at a text—whether verbal, visual, or multimedia (some combination of verbal, visual, and electronic)—as an artifact of contemporary culture or of a more remote (in time or place) culture. Scholars have always argued about texts. For many centuries, they have questioned the authorship of Shakespeare's plays (whether William Shakespeare was a man or a woman, whether the same man authored all of the literary works assigned to Shakespeare, for example). Anything that can be questioned can be argued, and we can question literary works because they are imaginative texts written within a particular time and place, often to record how a single writer sees that time and place. They do not claim to be true in any factual sense of the word, nor do they prescribe a code of behavior. They are not historical texts: generally, they do not claim to record events. Although many literary texts occur within a seemingly accurate historical period, many occur in a mostly unrecorded past (such as the tales of King Arthur) or in an equally unverifiable, often scary, future. Writers create a world for us, inviting us to step outside of our lives and crawl into someone else's. We can love or hate characters, visit exotic places, experience complicated situations by simply turning a page.

Yet, literary texts are not completely imaginative. They touch something real in us—something we can connect with, which is why we can argue about them. Don't forget that the writer of an imaginative text has interacted in a culture and has learned something about human and cultural behavior from that interaction. A writer was not born yesterday into a world brushed clean like the proverbial blank slate, but was born into a family—a poor or rich family; an Asian, African, European, or American family; an immigrant or indigenous family; a Catholic, Buddhist, Muslim, or atheist family. He or she learned from the family and community what to do and not to do, what is good or evil, what is valuable or disposable. In addition to individual life experience, a writer may bring into his or her work research about the subject in that work. All of the writer's experience and knowledge comes together in the creation of a work of literature. The bottom line: a writer has opinions (based on experience and knowledge) that appear in his or her work; a writer has a view about art and carries it into his or her artistic expression.

Because literary texts are present in and important to our own culture, we can argue about them to learn more, to clarify positions, to influence others. Literature is there to teach us—not scientific or verifiable truth but how some people or characters can behave under certain circumstances and under the control of a writer who creates situations and manages the outcomes. Because it is imaginative, literature can entertain us, and we do not have to feel any obligation to do anything except think and feel as we read and enjoy a text. But literature *can* inspire us—to achieve a level of moral behavior, to think new thoughts or old thoughts in different ways, to write artistically, to argue. In all of its many forms, literature is there for us to use as we see fit.

In this text, we use literature to argue in an attempt to understand it in new ways: why and how it influences us; why and how it "works"; why and how some literary pieces have had such profound effects on human behavior and even public policy.

What About Literature Is Arguable?

Literature involves argument in two ways, which are reinforced throughout this text. First, we can argue about the literary work itself—how it works, and what it means regardless of any external conditions. Often when we argue in this manner, we are trying to understand what the text communicates about such topics as love, death, hope, despair, failure, relationships, work, and so on. Second, we can argue that a work of literature represents, in a particular way, a social, historical, or political world outside the text—that it makes a connection between itself (the world created in the text) and an external condition. We can argue *both* ways from the same text: we can say that a text makes statements about its own world of ideas or abstractions and also makes statements about the outside world.

Let's examine these two perspectives in more detail, using the following poem by Gwendolyn Brooks for our example:

WE REAL COOL

The Pool Players. Seven at the Golden Shovel.

We real cool. We
Left school. We

Lurk late. We
Strike straight. We

Sing sin. We
Thin gin. We

Jazz June. We
Die soon.

First, we can argue about **the meaning of the literary work itself regardless of external conditions** (the world outside the text of the poem). For this type of argument, we look *in* the text for evidence about its meaning. In an argument about "We Real Cool," we might claim that the poem suggests *meaningless deaths follow meaningless lives.* To support this position, we could look to the form of the poem—the short, almost empty sentences; the line lengths; the clipped, broken sentences that begin on one line and end on the next—to show how form mirrors, enhances, and/or creates meaning. We might even look to the first person pronoun, "We," to argue that the narrators speak for a group or class of people, not just an individual. We could also say that the activities described in the poem portray situations that lead to an early death or that the poem is about bad choices that lead to an early death. We do not have to step outside of the poem to make and support these assertions; instead, our support comes from the words and the form of the poem itself.

Second, we can argue that **a work of literature makes a statement beyond itself using information outside the text.** Literary texts often create arguments about the culture we live in. In any text, the author is making a claim about the "truth" of the world around her. This claim is based on three things: first, personal experiences with what an individual sees as reality (her truth); second, a writer's cultural experiences, including encounters with families, religious authorities, and government/national authorities; and third, the cultural, religious, and historical questions a writer might have asked during the process of research. With this in mind, let's return to "We Real Cool."

What is the writer of this text, Gwendolyn Brooks, saying about the world or environment outside this poem? Certainly, the poem suggests the irrelevance of education to these men (the seven at the Golden Shovel) and perhaps others like them; it suggests the lack of choice they feel and the despair in their lives, which seem so unimportant that imminent death is accepted and acceptable. From this reading, we could make a claim about the relationship between human beings and the social worlds they live in—outside the text. We could even use the same claim we used above—*meaningless deaths follow meaningless lives*—but now, instead of looking only to the poem to support the claim, we look at evidence outside the poem: what we know about Brooks and what we know about social and material conditions of urban Blacks, especially African American men in the 1960s.

To begin with, we might look outside the text at the author's life and experience. Brooks, an African American poet, spent many years in Chicago. In an interview, Brooks said that one day she was passing by a pool hall and noticed young men, who should have been in high school, playing pool. From this experience, she wrote the poem, which reflects the culture of those young men, one that does not value formal education and offers little motivation to do much more than "Lurk late," and "Sing sin." We might use this information to support our claim.

In addition to knowledge of the author's life and experiences, it may be important to know that this poem was written in the 1960s and popularized in the early 1970s, after the Civil Rights Movement, after the death and destruction of the urban riots of 1967 and 1968, after the deaths of Malcolm X and Martin Luther King, Jr. Based on this knowledge, and to support our position (*meaningless deaths follow meaningless lives*), we must do research outside the text: we must look at the effects on African American men of the post–Civil Rights activities, of the deaths of two powerful black leaders, of the urban education system, and of the economy and employment opportunities.

Additionally, we may have to find a good definition of meaningless/meaningful. We might have to look at sociology research, educational research, economic research, and employment and suicide statistics. We could even use this poem to comment on conditions of urban African American males today: Does the social system still segregate the haves and the have-nots? Or we could point to the improvements in similar material conditions and argue that the poem no longer presents a "true" picture of urban, African American male culture. Moving outside the text of the poem, the possibilities for developing arguments become rich, exciting, as well as complex and demanding.

Notice the difference between how we approach the two claims we've just explored. When we argue the first claim, we seem to be arguing that this poem expresses a timeless theme—meaningless deaths follow meaningless lives in a universal way. The statement could be made about many literary works. In the second instance, while we are arguing the same claim, we are arguing that this poem is about these young men and their meaningless lives, men who will end up dead and forgotten because they are of a certain class and race in a certain country and at a certain time in history. There is no timelessness here but rather a specific cultural tragedy tied to the historical moment the poem records.

This difference may seem to be splitting hairs, but the distinction between the two claims is important for several reasons:

- The first exists solely within the "imaginary" world of the text; the second suggests the relationship of the text to the world outside the text.
- The kinds of assumptions that the arguer and the readers might share will vary. For example, the arguer of the first claim might assume that meaning exists within the text. The second arguer assumes that poems make social and cultural commentary verified externally by consulting historical, political, and social documents.
- The kinds of evidence that an arguer might use to "prove" the claims are very different: proving the first claim requires evidence within the text; proving the second claim requires evidence outside the text.

Our perception of a claim, therefore, shapes and is shaped by many forces.

Turning In—Turning Out

What we have just explored is the guiding framework for the remainder of this textbook: turning in and turning out. In the following chapters, we look at various pieces of literature by turning in toward the text and by turning out away from the text to the world at large. Turning in, we argue the meaning of a given piece of literature by examining the world of the text itself: its words, phrases, sentences, stanzas, paragraphs, and overall form—how these elements exist and play off of one another and what they come together to show us within the structure of a specific text. Turning out, we may look beyond a given text and show the connections between a work of literature and various aspects of a culture.

PRACTICE 1-A

In Casebook Four, *Land of the Free, Home of the Brave: Defining America(ns),* read the poem "In Response to Executive Order 9066." Answer the following questions in a notebook or journal and bring the answers to class for discussion:

1. How is this poem about a "truth" within the text? What, for example, does the poem say about prejudice, about heroism, about patriotism, about war? How are these truths universal?
2. How is the text about a historical, social, or cultural event? If you don't know the historical event that prompted this poem, find and read Franklin D. Roosevelt's Executive Order 9066.
3. In the same casebook, find another example of a story or poem that turns in and turns out. Discuss how that text says something about a universal truth separate from the time and situation that prompted the work. Look for support for your ideas from the text only. Then discuss how the writer extends the claim into the world beyond the text. What evidence from the text can you find to support that opinion? Do you agree with the writer's assertions?
4. Consider this: Since September 11, 2001, how have American attitudes changed toward Middle Eastern males? What, if any, conditions have occurred that might prompt a literary response to those changes?

Why Should We Be Concerned About Argument?

Argument is one of the preferred purposes of writing in college, and your teacher will expect you to argue well, using many of the same tools Athenian philosophers and scholars used over twenty-five hundred years ago. To argue well, you must identify and analyze a situation that suggests an argument. Here are some questions you might ask to identify and analyze a potential writing situation:

-   What is the urgency that prompts an argument? Is it the right time and place to argue?
-   Who are you trying to influence?
-   What are some possible audience responses to the argument, and what barriers may the audience create to resist the argument? How forceful must the argument be to influence the audience?
-   What are some constraints or limitations within which the arguer must work?

Now, let's examine each question as it relates to arguing about literature.

What Is the Urgency That Prompts an Argument?

When public situations arise, the urgency that inspires argument appears from a combination of circumstances. A crime is committed, a person is arrested, and a trial determines legal guilt or innocence. In the civic arena, a situation arises—such as the question of whether a community needs more schools, a new highway, or a new shopping center—and making the issue public enables the community to know what's happening.

As a student of literature, you will learn that many lives are influenced by literature. One famous example is a letter written by Martin Luther King Jr., called "A Letter from a Birmingham Jail," which helped shape the course of the Civil Rights Movement. There are many other examples. In the 1920s, for instance, a novel written by D. H. Lawrence, *Lady Chatterley's Lover,* forced the New York Supreme Court to redefine obscenity laws, and that redefinition opened the door to a more expanded interpretation of freedom of speech in this country, an interpretation that is being felt today as the courts decide what is allowed on the Internet and who can access it. So, arguments in literature and about literature often become public policy issues. However, works of literature don't always carry with them this immediate sense of urgency. Yet in every literary work, whether it is a poem, play, novel, essay, or short story, there is an argument being made, and that argument is waiting for someone to reveal its subtleties, its meaning, and its issues to an audience.

Who Are You Trying to Influence?

The purpose of an argument is to influence an audience to one degree or another. In the best of circumstances, an argument will influence an audience to rethink a given issue, to see and understand it in a particular way, or to take a recommended action. More often, the best we can hope for is to influence an audience to listen, to consider an opinion that might differ from their own. Your academic writing has several audiences: teachers, peers, and other readers.

TEACHER AS AUDIENCE

In the academic environment, the audience is often the teacher, and in many cases, the teacher as audience is often a "fiction" created by her students. Arguing about literature is no different. Your audience will often be an expert in the study of literature. To be a successful reader of your argument about literature, your teacher may suspend her level of expert knowledge about the text, playing instead the role of your peer or a general reader when she reads your argument.

PEERS AS AUDIENCE

The teacher may not be the only audience for a classroom-based argument. Many students imagine writing to their peers—other members of their class. In many ways, using your classmates as readers makes the writing situation easier: you can assume that your peers are like you in the type and level of knowledge they possess about a subject. In fact, because you have researched or studied the work in depth, you may assume that you are the expert and they are the novice readers. Writing from a position of expertise provides a level of confidence you may not possess if you write to the teacher only. Yet, thinking of your classmates as readers has its own problems. First, this readership can often morph into the notion of "general reader," partly because there is so much variety among classmates: they may differ significantly in age, race, ethnicity, level of reading ability, and experience with kinds of texts. The one commonality of belonging to the same community of learners within the same classroom may not be enough to offset the perhaps vast differences among them. Second, the classroom situation may be highly competitive, at least in the minds of many students. If you perceive your classmates as competing for grades, for attention, for approval, you may place on yourself as a writer certain hardships that, in fact, may or may not exist. Writing under these hardships may constrain you in harmful ways. (We'll get to other kinds of constraints later in this chapter.) Finally, although you may perceive your classmates as your readers, unless they are going to assign your final grades for the course—and this is possible—you may not be able to get past the idea that your teacher is your reader. What you may be doing is setting up multiple readers (and this is not all bad) for whom you may have to juggle even more alternatives.

OTHER READERS

Your teacher may choose to create a context in which your task is to argue for a particular position relative to a particular literary work. For example, you may be encouraged to write a review about a new novel, then send your essay to your local or college newspaper for possible publication.

What Are Some Possible Audience Responses?

In arguing about literature, you may expect a range of audience response to a text. Individual readers may respond to the ideas and events presented in a literary work enthusiastically, with indifference, or with outright hostility. "The Holocaust Party" by Robin Hemley, reprinted on the following pages, is an example of the type of work that is likely to evoke the full range of audience responses. For those who are open and accommodating, your argument may clarify something they already accept, or it may stir up some hidden issues. Fun! Perhaps with this audience, only the lightest touch is necessary. For those who are indifferent, not only must you convince them of the reasonableness of your case, but you must also get past their indifference. Those who are angry or resistant present the most difficult task. Sometimes the best that you can hope for is a reduction in their anger or resistance so that their minds are more open to your ideas.

What Barriers May the Audience Create to Resist the Argument?

You can use three tools, in varying degrees of strength, to work with audience resistance: *logos, pathos,* and *ethos.* Although they all come from classical argument theory, they still work today. Logos is the appeal to an audience's reason, pathos is the appeal to an audience's emotions or values; ethos is used to convince readers of our integrity, goodwill, and intelligence.

Say you want to argue that "because of the decline of the stock market, there is now a greater gap between the rich and the poor." An open and accommodating audience might agree with this statement without any evidence because it seems reasonable. The decline of the stock market affects the wealth of citizens. Poor people may become poorer because, in the wake of the decline, companies might lay off workers, increasing the number of unemployed. Often, lower-status workers get laid off first, although this may not be so in certain industries. For the accommodating audience, this claim seems to contain enough truth that many people might not question its plausibility. However, what appears to be obvious or self-evident to one audience might be challenged by a resistant audience. For example, those who resist the statement about the stock market might point out that the gap may be narrower because it is mostly rich and middle-income people who have enough money in the stock market to affect their incomes. Thus, those who might have been wealthy because of owning stocks might now be poorer because of the decline in the value of their stocks. The opposite conclusion might very well be true—that the gap is smaller because of the decline in the stock market.

What you need, of course, are facts (such as what historically has happened to the gap when the stock market dropped), statistics, expert opinion (economists' predictions), and examples (international precedents) to offer as evidence. The more resistant your audience, the stronger your facts, statistics, expert opinion, and examples must be. While one or two experts may convince an indifferent or agreeable audience, you need either more experts or a kind of consensus of experts to convince a resistant audience. And you may never convince every reader. (But we argue, anyway, because one day, they may change their minds.)

But because this textbook is about writing literary arguments and a literature example is pertinent here, we now examine in detail a short story that, when you read it, might evoke a range of responses. It is a story about bigotry, innocence, and guilt, among other things. We use this story to illustrate audience response and the concepts of logos, pathos, and ethos in this chapter. We use it again throughout the text to illustrate types of claims and evidence. Please read this story before you read the rest of the chapter.

The Holocaust Party

by ROBIN HEMLEY

"We've invited a Holocaust survivor to our house, Joel," Amy announced, halfway to Edina, like this was some game show and I'd won the grand prize.

"Excuse me," I said. "A what?"

"A Holocaust survivor," she said in that same tone. "My parents thought that since you're, gosh, Jewish, you'd be interested." She had a hard time saying Jewish. She'd even asked me once if Jew was a dirty word. I was horrified by her ignorance, but that's all it was. Just ignorance, not malice. I've always believed that people can be educated.

Growing up in the Midwest in towns where there weren't many Jews besides my family, I'd learned to be tolerant. I didn't have much choice if I wanted friends. Besides, Amy was intelligent in other ways. We'd met in college. She'd had a double major in drama and French. I'd seen her in most of our school productions—*Sexual Perversity in Chicago, The Pajama Game, The Apartment.* She complained about always being cast as the ingenue. She tried to act cynical, but she really was the ingenue type. She'd been a twirler in high school and had won a Little Miss pageant. Her parents were rock-bottom conservatives carved out of Midwestern limestone. Her dad belonged to the John Birch Society. Her mom was a homemaker, nasal-spray addict, and retired child abuser. Now Amy worked in Edina at Laura Ashley in the Galleria, selling dresses her mother approved of and dating a news anchor for KARK who wasn't ready for marriage but liked showing her off at TV station picnics. Still the ingenue.

What I was doing at the time in St. Cloud, I'm not proud of. But after college I needed a job, and landed one through a family connection at Minnesota Biological Services. We handled animals, cats mostly. It was a job.

But I was glad to take breaks from it, so when Amy called and asked if I wanted to go to a Christmas get-together at her family's house, I said sure. I didn't know how to drive so Amy had to pick me up. And it wasn't a short drive either, all the way from St. Cloud to Edina. I didn't care that it was a Christmas party, but what was I supposed to do with a Holocaust survivor? Jump for joy at the prospect of meeting one? Say, "Oh, you shouldn't have. How thoughtful of you"? In my family, this was not a theme one organized a party around.

Or a holiday. I imagined myself in a box beneath the Christmas tree—alone, in the dark, someone coming by and shaking the box next to their ear: "Sounds like a Jew!"

"I wish you'd told me."

"Don't worry, Joel. She's really very nice. She was my kindergarten teacher. She's the sweetest woman in the world. And her story's amazing."

"That's not the point," I said. "I don't invite Catholics to tell you stories of martyrdom."

Snow started falling and the road became patchy. But Amy didn't slow down in that time capsule of hers from the seventies, an old Cadillac her dad had given her, complete with a CB that wasn't hooked up and a defunct eight-track player. The seat belts had been cut off and the blue vinyl seat had slashes across it. Amy drove as though it were the middle of summer, at least seventy miles an hour. I gripped the door handle and pretended I had a brake on my side.

Trees with snow-covered branches arched over the unlit driveway. The house was a Swiss-chalet type, and from the front looked small, not much more than a garage and a peaked roof. But the place went back a ways, sprawling out over the river. Amy's mother greeted us at the door. She was a copy of Amy, aged twenty-five years, with a too-smooth face, tight, pulled-back hair, and a toothy smile. She was dressed in a Laura Ashley flower print with a white lace collar. I didn't trust her because of what Amy had told me about her. She had a habit of knocking Amy around, though rarely now that Amy was no longer a child.

Amy's dad was in the kitchen reading some magazine, the title of which I didn't want to know. *Armageddon Quarterly,* no doubt. But these people seemed pleasant, and offered me punch and Christmas cookies, and we went to sit down in the living room, which looked like something out of an Andy Williams Christmas Special: a fireplace with roaring fire, Christmas stockings, popcorn strings, a tree with presents underneath. Amy's dad looked a little like Andy Williams, except that he was completely bald. He wore an Andy Williams kind of wool sweater, though he didn't sing but glowered. Andy Williams wouldn't have lasted a season if he'd glowered like that. He would have shaken his guests' hands, offered them punch, and stared. His guests would have felt menaced.

Also in the living room was a roly-poly woman in her sixties, the guest of honor. One of the first things I noticed about her was the pewter cross she wore around her neck. As crosses go, it was elaborate, with the curves and flourishes of a family crest, a fleur-de-lis. I hadn't expected the woman to be Christian. Other than this cross, she dressed plainly, in a brown skirt and dull red top that had faded from washing. She was in her stocking feet, and had her legs curled beneath her on the couch.

"You must excuse me," she said when we were introduced. "My feet are frozen solid." Her accent sounded French. The only other Holocaust survivor I'd known was Rose, my great-aunt by marriage. She bleached her hair blonde and spoke with a thick Eastern European accent. The tattoo was visible on her wrist, but this woman had no tattoo.

Amy's mother fiddled with her pulled-back hair and smiled at me from the hallway entrance. Amy's father stood by the fireplace and poked at it, sending sparks up the chimney.

"Amy, honey," her mother said. "Make sure our guests are comfortable. Why don't you bring in more cookies for them?"

"Sure, Mom," said Amy, bounding into the kitchen as though overjoyed with the task. You never would have known these two had problems.

That left me alone, more or less, with the woman, whose name was Mrs. Isabel. Amy's dad didn't count. He stood frozen by the fireplace, holding his poker near the flames but not in them. Mrs. Isabel patted a place on the sofa and smiled up at me like she was my aunt Rose. I sat down with my knees close together and my arms in my lap, and smiled with my mouth closed. It was a meek smile. If my smile had been my fist, I could describe it as a glancing blow.

Amy bounded back into the room with the tray of cookies just at the moment it looked like Mrs. Isabel was going to start to talk to me. I would have said something to her, but of the two topics that came to mind, one was too trivial and the other too immense: the snow and the Holocaust.

Before turning to look at the cookie tray, Mrs. Isabel gave me one last steady look. Her smile had no pretense in it like the smile of Amy's mom. It was the kind of smile that shows joy that other people exist, not only oneself. I remembered my aunt Rose smiling that way when I visited her, and I wondered if I'd ever smile like that in my life.

Then Mrs. Isabel turned to Amy and darted her finger at a scroll-like cookie.

"May I have one of those?" she asked, as if it were an extraordinarily precious object.

"Sure," Amy said. "You can have as many as you want."

"Oh, don't say that!" Mrs. Isabel said, touching Amy's wrist lightly and breaking into a singsong laugh. Amy laughed and I laughed, too. For a moment, I laughed because I wanted to laugh, but then I had to spoil it with my self-consciousness. Thinking again of Mrs. Isabel's smile, I wondered if my laughter was, or ever could be, as genuine as hers. And of course, that brought a little strain to my laugh and a snort came out of my nose.

Amy and Mrs. Isabel both glanced at me and I reached for a cookie, the same scroll-like kind as Mrs. Isabel's. It crumbled in my hand.

I must have looked grief-stricken because Amy gave me a sympathetic look, her head slightly tilted, and said, "Don't worry, Joel. It's only a cookie."

I blew a little air through my nose like I thought that was funny and took another cookie.

Amy's mother returned to the room and hovered by her husband at the fireplace. She sniffled slightly and dabbed at her nose with a balled-up tissue. She must have seen me studying her because she looked straight at me and said, "It's a little damp in here, isn't it?"

I gave her my same meek smile, the one that meant I really had no opinions. Amy set her tray of cookies on the coffee table and sat down beside me. Her dad sat on a stool by the fireplace, the same kind Andy Williams might sing a Christmas song from, and held the poker at his side. Amy's mother sat in a rocker and smiled at me in a way that made me jump up and reach for another cookie. As soon as I sat down again, I took a bite, but felt like I was chewing too loudly, so I held the cookie in my lap and bowed my head. The room was quiet except for popping from the logs in the fire and the creaking of the rocker Amy's mother sat in. Outside, I could hear the buzzing of snowmobiles on the river. For a moment, I thought we were going to say a prayer.

"I've told Joel about your story, Mrs. Isabel," Amy said abruptly. "I think he'd really like to hear it, wouldn't you, Joel?"

I nodded and smiled. Part of me did want to hear it. At least I was more interested than I'd been when Amy had sprung this on me. But I didn't want to hear it in this situation. I was the one in the monkey house, not Mrs. Isabel.

She didn't take much prodding. Amy's asking her to tell the story was just a formality. Telling her story was her reason for being here. Mine was to listen. Maybe if this worked out, we could take it on the road. Bill it as "See the Holocaust Survivor Tell Her Tale! See the Jew React!"

Mrs. Isabel uncurled her feet and sat back, taking us all in and smiling like she was about to tell a Bible story to her Sunday school class.

"I live in Liege," she said. "I am only seventeen when the German invades Belgium, not much younger than you." She had her eyes closed, but I knew that she meant Amy and me. She had a disconcerting habit of speaking in the present tense, as though she weren't an old woman, as though these events were now unfolding around her and her fate might go either way. And the only article she ever used was the, which made everything seem absurdly singular.

"By then, the German is spreading himself across Europe, and he needs the workers for the factories because most of the young men are off in our countries, and the German woman is making the war material. So he says that all of us between the age sixteen and twenty must go to Germany to work. And like that, I disappear.

"He puts me on the train with hundreds and sends me to Stuttgart, and he puts me in the factory doing metal work—too dangerous, he says, for the German. I hate it, of course, but there's nothing really I can do. I am in his country. He is in mine. My paper says I am the guest worker, but of course I am not the guest. Many of us stay together in a . . ." She fumbled for a word, and opened her eyes, as though one of us owned the word she searched for. "Hotel?" she asked, not pronouncing the h. "No, not hotel," she said.

"Barracks," Amy's dad said authoritatively. "That's what you mean."

"Okay," she said. "If you say." She closed her eyes again. "I stay in the barracks and cannot come out at night. The only times I come out is walking from the town to the factory. He doesn't guard me then because where do I go, even with the papers? After all, I am just the stupid Belgian young person and he is arrogant." Mrs. Isabel laughed, and touched her cross.

"He tells me he is paying the wages, but I never see this money because he says I have to pay for the food and . . . barracks, which are so crowded and I am starving most of the time. I work twelve hours a day, every day of the week."

"But of course, I know I am better off than the Jew, who is guarded all of the time. I see him working every day by the side of the road. The German has him there for me, so I can see I am not as miserable as he. I cannot go near, and he is beaten if he stops work. I feel pity for him, but there is nothing I can do. Only once I am able to walk near without being shot. I have nothing with me, but I go up to the old man I see every day. I just want to talk to him."

Mrs. Isabel paused. I realized I had my eyes closed, and opened them now, but Mrs. Isabel hadn't opened hers. In my mind, they were skinny men and boys, all ages, but with the same sunken faces and flimsy patches of hair.

Mrs. Isabel's mouth was open as though a word were stuck there and couldn't be dislodged. Amy's dad stood and replaced the poker by the fireplace. He looked at Mrs. Isabel impassively, then padded across the living room in his burgundy slippers, and went off down the hall. Neither Amy nor Amy's mom paid attention to him, but just getting up in the middle of Mrs. Isabel's story seemed incredibly rude and insensitive to me. A door closed down the hall. Amy and her mother were leaning back in their seats, identical smiles on their lips, like people at a movie who know what comes next and are just dying to tell you.

Mrs. Isabel waved her hand, and the old man beside the road was left behind. I wanted to know what had happened, but of course I couldn't ask. Obviously, she found the memory tough. Had he collapsed? Or stared at her without understanding? Or continued to work without acknowledging her?

Maybe none of these. Maybe she was making it up. She could have just wanted my sympathy.

"One day, my friend Renée and I are working in the field outside of Stuttgart," Mrs. Isabel continued. I closed my eyes again. "We are through with the labor and so we begin to walk home. On the way, we pass the orchard where the apples look red. They are so ripe that they bend down the branches and many have fallen to the ground. My God, apples. It has been so long since I have tasted the fruit. I say to Renée, 'Wouldn't it be nice to have the apple?'

"'No,' she says. She is such a coward. 'We will get into trouble,' she says.

"'Not if we only take a few apples that have fallen already to the ground. Surely, the farmer will not miss these apples.'

"After some time, I am able to convince Renée to follow me, and we run through the orchard picking the fallen apples. We are so happy we don't know what we are doing. We pick up the apple, take a bite, and throw it down. Then we pick up the other. 'This one is too soft,' I say.

"'This one is too firm,' she says, laughing, and hurrying on to the next apple.

"We say we will go home when we are full, before we are missed. We pick up six more apples each to bring with us and start again on our way. Then we hear the voice behind us, the man. He says, 'I hope you are enjoying my apples.'

"We turn around and see the farmer with the rifle pointing at us. He is the old man with the frowning mouth and he instructs us not to throw down the apples we have collected. He says he is going to turn us in to the constable and use the apples for the proof. "Of course, Renée begins to cry, but the farmer isn't moved. He marches us into town, pointing the gun at us as we carry the apples in our smocks, and Renée begs the farmer for her life the whole way.

"When we reach the police station, I try to tell the constable the side of the story that is ours. I say we are willing to pay for the apples and we took them only because we were starving.

"'Six apples,' I say. 'Only six, twelve in all for the both of us. And they were all fallen, with wormholes.'

"The constable is understanding and he tries to make the farmer see the reason, but he won't. So the constable must do something. He tells us he must make a decision about what will be done with us, and he sends us back to our . . . hotel?"

"Barracks," Amy's mother corrected.

"Or dormitory," Amy said.

I didn't see what difference it made. We all knew it wasn't a hotel.

I heard a toilet flush down the hall, and then Amy's father must have opened the bathroom door because the flushing sound grew louder. He padded back through the living room like an apparition. He was no longer wearing his Andy Williams sweater, but a red flannel Pendleton shirt, a brighter red than his burgundy slippers. He went into the kitchen, where I heard him open the refrigerator, and then he coughed. Amy didn't pay him any attention, but her mother followed his every step with a dark look. She sniffled again and dabbed her nose with her balled-up tissue.

"Later that night," Mrs. Isabel continued, "we approach the guard of our barracks and ask if we may walk. He says we must stay inside, but I say, 'All we want is the short walk. You have our identity papers. After all, we're only two Belgian girls.'

"'You have a point,' he says, and lets us out.

"Of course, we go right away to the train station. We know our chances are not good, but we also know our chances are much worse if we stay. We are sure they will send us to the concentration camp.

"After we are going, we sneak on the train. Renée worries they will catch us, but I tell her I will kill her myself if she starts to cry. We have no money, no identity papers. But I trust God to see us through.

"We spend most of the time on the train trying to avoid the conductor. When he comes, we hide in the bathroom or the dining car. And then we meet the French family who help us by taking away the conductor's attention when he comes near.

"Finally, we reach the border. The German orders everyone out from the train. It is night and we stand outside looking across the border to the lights of a few houses. The train stays there on the German side and the passenger walks one by one through the gate in the fence, where the guard checks their papers. The train starts moving slowly across the border and Renée and I stay back at the end of the line. We have no idea what to do."

Amy's dad returned from the kitchen just then with a beer bottle, holding it by its long neck as if it were some dead game bird. Then he went back to his stool and stared into the fire again. I waited for him to pick up the poker, but he didn't. Instead, he started flicking a finger at his bottle, repeatedly hitting the same high note, which sounded like the warning bell at a railroad crossing.

Mrs. Isabel had been smiling serenely the whole time Amy's dad was going through his routine. He seemed oblivious to the fact that other people were around, much less guests, and he seemed completely unmoved by Mrs. Isabel. I could tell Amy's mom was upset by his banging about, and Amy seemed nervous, eyes darting between her parents, wearing a thin smile. Only Mrs. Isabel seemed unperturbed.

He slowed down the tapping until, finally, the sound grew fainter, and faded completely.

"I notice another gate, closer to the train," Mrs. Isabel continued. "This gate is shut, but there is the space between the fence and the gate, big enough for two skinny girls to squeeze through. Another guard stands by this gate. He is walking back and forth on the Belgian side. So I grab Renée by the arm and we make the way to the gate. When the guard is walking the other direction, Renée sneaks through. Then she calls to the guard as I have told her to do. He approaches her with the smile because she is the very pretty girl and he asks her what trouble she is having. Then while she is talking, I also slip through. But at that moment, the guard turns around and sees me.

"I don't panic. I'm not sure if he does see me slip through the gate. So I think he does not. The large valise sits beside the tracks and I tell him I need assistance.

"'The valise is too big for my sister and me to carry,' I say to him. 'Could you assist us?'

"'Certainly,' he says and he calls over two more guards. The three of them together lift the valise, which is huge, and put it on the train. We thank them for their help and board the train ourselves. I have no idea whose valise that was, but it is lucky it was there.

"In this way, we make our path back to Belgium. When we arrive, we find the friends and the family who help us with the identity papers.

"I pass the war in this same way, working and surviving. Times are difficult and there is never enough of the food. I go to the train station at night and climb to the top of one of the cars carrying the vegetables. I gather as much as possible to bring home. Everything goes fine for a while. One day, I climb to the top of the car with the potatoes. But before I am through, explosions happen from the other trains at the station.

"The whole place becomes crawling with the German. He shines lights all around the station. He fires the guns. And then he spots me on top of the potatoes. He does not shoot—a miracle. He thinks, naturally, I am one of the saboteurs.

"He tells me to climb down. He orders me to say the names of my collaborators. I try to tell him I am stealing the potatoes, not blowing up the trains.

"Of course, he doesn't believe me and he locks me in the box, with only the tiny hole to see and breathe. He promises to shoot me in the morning. The German always does everything quick, but he likes to wait until the morning. I don't know why. Maybe he must start the days cruelly in order to continue this. Maybe it is easier to do this after he has slept and fed himself.

"The whole night I pray. I can see nothing, but I hear the shouts and the running feet and more explosions and the guns. At dawn, I hear the yelling closer and I shout, 'What is it?'

"It is the Allies. They have captured Liege and I am saved."

With that, I opened my eyes, and saw that Mrs. Isabel's eyes were still closed. Then she opened them, smiled, and looked at me. Amy and her mother were also looking at me.

"Isn't that remarkable?" Amy asked.

What could I say? It was remarkable, amazing in fact. I was impressed, but anything I might say seemed trite, though necessary, just as all major events—births, marriages, deaths—need to be attended by words. But before I could say anything, Amy's father spoke up.

"What about Renée?" he said. "You never said what happened to her."

There was hostility in his voice, and I wondered what his problem was. This guy was definitely touched, whacked out. Amy blushed and her mother stared politely at the rug, but Mrs. Isabel hardly seemed to notice.

She shook her head and pointed at the ceiling. "She is killed by the bomb," she said. "We are sitting at the café when the air-raid sirens occur. Everyone runs in whatever direction, but as I cross the street, a fat man steps on my toe and breaks it. Renée helps me across the street, but . . . she does not get there."

We were silent, and I thought about Renée begging for her life in the orchard, and the way Mrs. Isabel had portrayed her as silly and innocent and cowardly. I imagined this thin young woman, nineteen or twenty, forever moored to those awful years of the war.

I was startled by Mrs. Isabel's singsong laugh. "This toe is the only thing I am left with from the war. You see, I do not go to the doctor because I do not think it is serious. Then it swells up so big, and the woman whose house I am living in sees it and says, 'My God, we must take you to the doctor.' But by then, it is too late and the doctor must remove the toe. But I know I will survive. My faith in God has seen me through, and why would He let me survive so many bad happenings only to kill me from the broken toe?"

I didn't know. It wasn't a question I could answer, but I thought about it.

Then Amy's dad stood up. He was holding his poker again. "That must have hurt a lot," he said. "I bet it still hurts."

"Roger," Amy's mother said.

"What?" he said. "I'm just saying that losing your goddamn toe would smart."

He placed the poker beside the fireplace and it brushed his beer bottle. The bottle tipped over the fireplace ledge and onto the floor, where it rolled with a clatter to the edge of the rug. Beer foamed out of the bottle.

He stormed out of the living room and out the front door into the snow. He didn't bother to put on any outdoor clothing, not his Andy Williams sweater or an overcoat. All he had on was his red Pendleton shirt, his thin brown slacks, and his burgundy slippers.

Mrs. Isabel and I pretended nothing had happened. She looked in her purse for something, pulled out a pack of gum, and offered me a piece. "The mouth gets so dry," she said, "when I talk so much."

Amy's mother was already in the kitchen, getting something to wipe up the spill with, I assumed. She poked her head around the corner, a roll of paper towels in her hand, and said, "Amy, will you come here a moment?"

"Sure," Amy said, and smiled at me like her father hadn't just gone balmy and run out the front door.

I took a piece of gum from Mrs. Isabel and thanked her. The two of us sat there chewing our gum, looking at the fire, which had started to fade.

"That was an amazing story," I said.

"Yes, life is strange," she said, as though this is what I had remarked on. She didn't seem to be sitting beside me. She still seemed to be back in the war. "I am sure that God is watching over me. This is how I survive."

Then she turned to me and she seemed back in the present. "I am glad though the German never gives me the blood test," she said.

"A blood test?" I said. "Why's that?" I laughed, thinking this might be some kind of joke. What did blood tests have to do with anything?

"My grandfather," she said, "is Jewish. I look Jewish. If the German gives me the blood test, he will know."

"Excuse me?" I said.

"The Jewish blood," she said. "It is thinner than the normal blood."

"Excuse me?" I said, or I think I said it. Maybe I didn't say anything at all.

Maybe I just sat back and wondered if I'd heard her correctly.

In any case, she didn't answer me. She just closed her eyes and hummed a note. "Mmm, good gum," she said.

Suddenly, I was afraid of something, but I didn't know what. For some reason, I saw the animals at the lab.

I wondered where Amy was, and why her mother had called her aside. Things were too quiet. I imagined Amy's mother pinning her to the wall, slapping her across the face, saying that her father's outburst was all Amy's fault. It didn't make sense, but that kind of abuse never did.

"Excuse me," I said to Mrs. Isabel. I stood up and walked through the kitchen, but Amy and her mother weren't there. The paper towels sat on the counter.

I found Amy and her mother in the hallway. At first, they didn't see me. They were talking softly, anxiously, but they were separated by a few feet. As far as I could tell, Amy's mom hadn't touched her, had hardly been near her. Then Amy turned and saw me, and Amy's mom saw me a moment later. Amy's mother smiled and walked toward the bathroom. Amy approached me and took me by the arm.

"Sorry about Dad," she said. "He was in the war, too. He spent it in a Japanese camp in the Philippines."

I only half-heard her. I was still trying to make sense of what Mrs. Isabel had said, how someone who had gone through so much could say something as ignorant as what she had told me, that she could believe this Nazi lie for nearly fifty years.

"Are you all right, Joel?" Amy asked.

"Sure," I said. "I'm just trying to take in Mrs. Isabel's story."

Amy shook her head. "It's amazing, isn't it?"

"Amazing."

"I guess you probably need to head back now," Amy said.

"Early day at work tomorrow," I said. "But thanks for inviting me."

Amy smiled sadly at me. "Okay, I'll be right out. I just want to make sure my mom's all right. She says it's getting harder and harder to live with him."

Amy went off after her mother and I went outside and stood by the car in the snow. I didn't want to say good-bye to Mrs. Isabel and I didn't care if she thought I was rude. Amy's dad stood at the end of the driveway by the mailbox. He was looking out at the road. The snow shifted around him, swirling into a small drift by his feet. Maybe I had judged him harshly. Maybe people are more complicated than simply what they've read, what they've experienced, even what they've survived.

I saw a woman once on TV who had shot her own children, shot them—only no one knew at the time that she had done it. She'd shot herself in the wrist, too, to cover up the crime. But when she talked, she seemed concerned only about her own flesh wound, and talked flippantly about the whole incident, though one of her children was dead, another paralyzed, and another ravaged by a stroke.

What I'd told Amy was a lie. I didn't have to be at work early in the morning because I wasn't going back there again. Even so, I had worked there for six months, and that can never be erased, no matter what. But I know one thing. I'm never going to talk about it.

LOGOS

Logos is the appeal to the audience's reason—its sense of what makes sense, of what seems plausible. In our culture, creating an argument using logos generally requires using one or more types of evidence in support of a claim: *facts, statistics, expert opinion,* and *examples.* The type, amount, and "truthfulness" of the evidence you present depend on the willingness of the audience to accept your claim.

As we mentioned, writing arguments about the "The Holocaust Party" may evoke a range of audience responses. We could state, for example, that this story is about the bigotry that exists in people you would never expect to be bigots. This is a very uncontroversial statement about this story, not one that will evoke much resistance from an audience. Mrs. Isabel clearly has suffered because of the bigotry of the Nazis, so we might not expect her to be a bigot. Thus, her statement at the end about Jews surprises us. We would have to present evidence, of course, to convince the reader that this story is about unexpected bigotry, but few people would have problems with that assertion. We would probably want to present two kinds of evidence to argue this point: an *expert* definition of "bigot" cited from a credible source (not a dictionary) and *examples* from the text to show Mrs. Isabel's bias against Jews.

On the other hand, what if we also used Joel, the Jewish protagonist, as an example of a bigot? We might find more resistance from our audience, especially if it is primarily students. Joel is a young person (like many college students), he is the narrator of the story (we tend to sympathize with narrators), and he is a Jew (and we tend to support the oppressed). To persuade the opposite of what people usually believe, an appeal to reason (logos) must be stronger: we need better evidence. Perhaps we need a more expert source for a definition (a sociological dictionary, for example), more examples from the short story, and experts to testify that young members of oppressed minorities can harbor strong prejudices (religious, ethnic, political, or generational). The more resistance expected from an audience, the stronger the evidence in support of a claim must be.

PATHOS

Often arguments seem to be centered on emotions or values rather than facts. When we make such a claim, we must appeal not only to reason but also to the emotions and values of a given audience. Argument in the academic community is almost always based on reason (logos) because members of that community value reason. At least we like to think so. However, there may be times when we need to construct an argument based on pathos. A pathos-based argument is made about literature when, in addition to appealing to reason, we want to affect people's emotional needs or values. To argue in this way often triggers deeply held feelings. For example, we may make a statement about "The Holocaust Party" that calls upon the reader to agree to the value of that story. We could state that "The Holocaust Party" reveals that unconscious prejudices are more dangerous than conscious prejudices. We may have to use emotional appeal to argue this statement, showing through examples from both in the text and outside the text that unconscious bigotry is often more dangerous. Evidence of unconscious bigotry in the text is easy to find: Mrs. Isabel, even though part Jewish, believes that Jewish blood is thinner than Gentile blood. She does not see her own prejudice. However, Joel is an even more unconscious bigot. We can point to examples from the text: his ideas about Amy's father are based only on his own prejudices against old men who belong to religious and political groups he does not agree with. We then have to show how both these characters are dangerous, but that Joel's prejudice is more dangerous than Mrs. Isabel's, perhaps a harder sell.

We can point to examples from ancient and current "good" texts. The play, "The Laramie Project," in Casebook Four, is based on the true story of a young gay man—Matthew Shepard—beaten and left to die along a road in Wyoming. The bigotry revealed in this play belongs to the young men who committed this violent and appalling act, and it also belongs to many of the residents of Laramie, Wyoming, who were interviewed after the fact—people who managed to hide their true feelings for most of their lives. We can probably think of many other examples of people who seem perfectly normal (like Joel and Mrs. Isabel) but hold onto hidden bigotry. To argue using such examples that appeal to our emotions, in this case our revulsion toward heinous acts against humanity, is using the emotional (pathetic) appeal.

Remember—readers might be hostile to ideas that threaten their belief systems. The stronger we can make the appeal to their emotions, therefore, the stronger our argument will be. In this argument, it is not enough to show that "The Holocaust Party" is about unconscious prejudice, but that unconscious prejudice is dangerous to all. That's not so obvious, and we must work hard to show this.

The appeal to emotions may not always make a very strong argument: it often does not use facts, statistics, or expert testimony as evidence. Often the arguer may misjudge the strength of the readers' emotions or the areas of strength. All readers have values and beliefs—our task is to tap into their strongest beliefs and argue from that position. Of course, readers are often reluctant to give up deeply held beliefs, just as you might be reluctant to give up yours. Arguments based on pathos often result in mutual respect if not a complete change of mind.

ETHOS

A third way to argue is to convince readers of our integrity, goodwill, and intelligence; however, few arguments are won on ethos alone. Ethos usually convinces readers that logos-based arguments are credible. However, a lack of ethos may raise doubts about the validity of any argument we would make, even a good one. For example, a well-written argument handed in late will diminish the credibility of a student's logos because the lateness raises questions about his or her goodwill. Poorly cited sources raise questions about an author's integrity, and a poorly edited argument raises questions about intelligence. There are ways to prove that we have those characteristics and ways to further enhance them. However, using our own ethos as the major line of argument for a good grade ("This paper deserves an 'A' because I worked hard on it") is probably not the best strategy.

Let's talk about integrity in academic argument. One way to prove integrity is by demonstrating intellectual honesty: to avoid choosing only the information that supports our position, we should acknowledge that others may have interpreted information differently or that other studies raise further questions about the studies we have chosen. Students often think that bringing in and refuting opposing opinions weakens their argument. Quite the opposite: refuting other opinions strengthens an argument because it creates and reinforces the honesty and integrity needed to argue from ethos.

Goodwill is the second leg of this appeal to ethos. It is closely connected to integrity, but may manifest itself more obviously in the tone of an argument. When we read arguments, we can usually tell how the writer feels about the subject and the readers. We want to convince our readers that we are passionate about the subject and that we respect them and their opinions. Thus, name-calling and sarcasm are not effective argumentative strategies, especially when the digs are directed toward an audience or toward people whom they respect.

Intelligence in our writing is closely connected to the kinds of strategies we use to persuade readers. If we decide to argue using logos, the quality of the evidence—its breadth, specificity, pertinence, credibility—will help to convince an audience of a writer's intelligence. Irrelevant, outdated, or too-general evidence will convince readers that an author doesn't have a clue about his or her topic. Intelligence can also be implied by written presentation. Neatly typed, error-free text with all evidence carefully cited increases the ethos (intelligence factor) of an argument. The opposite also is true. When readers encounter poorly worded thoughts, questionable grammar, or typographical errors, they also doubt the writer's ability to think and to conduct good research. This is true for professionals and students alike, although students are perhaps more vulnerable to criticism.

What Are Some of the Constraints Within Which You Must Work?

No one writes with complete freedom. All writers operate within certain boundaries, which we shall call writing *constraints* or *limitations.* In this section, we discuss some of the constraints we may encounter as we write arguments about literature.

KNOWLEDGE OF THE CULTURAL, SOCIAL, AND HISTORICAL CONTEXT

In many cases, we may be reading literature that culturally, socially, and historically falls outside our lived experience. Even works written in the late twentieth century, for a traditional college-aged student, may be written and placed in a context more familiar to his or her parents or grandparents. Gwendolyn Brooks's poem "We Real Cool" may be set within a cultural context and genre unfamiliar to many of us: perhaps we were not yet living in the 1960s; some of us are not male, African American, or urban; we did not leave school; and we may have never stepped into a pool parlor. Thus, unfamiliarity with certain cultural knowledge may constrain effective arguments. However, just because we have not lived an experience doesn't mean we cannot know and understand it—if this were true, learning would be impossible. So, an effective argument requires some background reading, possibly to gather evidence for an argument and certainly for our own knowledge and academic credibility.

KNOWLEDGE OF AN AUDIENCE

We don't argue in a vacuum. Our audience members for any argument will also have cultural, social, historical, and religious contexts from which they read and interpret information. We must recognize that *their* contexts can prove to be constraints on *our* arguments. For example, we might make different arguments about Joel's reaction to Mrs. Isabel's story in "The Holocaust Party" if we knew in advance that our readers were Jewish—or Catholic. Understanding our readers' cultural knowledge and cultural assumptions, the strengths and limitations of that knowledge, what readers and writers have in common, and what common assumptions writers, readers, and a text share is the task of any good arguer.

KNOWLEDGE OF LITERARY GENRES

Another constraint that we must face is the extent to which both we and our readers know the genre within which we are working. What makes a poem? A short story? An essay? A screenplay? What are our expectations of the genre? Must a poem always have meter, metaphor, or visual images? Must a short story always have conflict or dialogue? If we or our readers disagree on the definition of poetry or story, we may not have the common ground necessary to argue. For example, we might believe that fiction has an obligation to call attention to evil or good in a culture (similar to the argument we made about

"The Holocaust Party"), while our readers might believe that literature has no such obligation, that its only obligation is an artistic one: to speak of or to the imagination and artistic truth rather than factual or cultural truth. Given this basic difference regarding the
purposes of fiction, we may find making a credible argument difficult. We might also believe that while fiction has the moral obligation to teach, poetry does not. Different genres may themselves hold different meanings for us—and for our readers.

KNOWLEDGE OF LITERARY ARGUMENT

In addition to knowing about literary genres, we need to know something about how to
create arguments about literature. We need to know what constitutes a reasonable claim,
how to identify assumptions that we and our audience hold about literature, and what
type of evidence is valued. If we do not know how to make such an argument, we are seriously disadvantaged.

At the end of the course for which you are reading this textbook, you will know about
literary arguments. You will be adept at understanding the purposes of argument, and you
will know how to determine the strength and weakness of different kinds of evidence.

KNOWLEDGE OF READING AND WRITING PROCESSES

Many students think that they should know everything there is about a text by just sitting down and reading it. They blame themselves (sometimes) if this sitting-down strategy doesn't work; sometimes they blame the text for being "too hard" or the teacher for
being "unfair." Reading literature is not easy; it requires a different kind of reading than
the kind we do when we read a textbook, an e-mail message, or something from a Web
page. Later in this textbook, we discuss some strategies for reading more effectively.

The same is often true with writing: many students think that being able to write is
a gift—either you have it or you don't. Some students become better writers than others because they may have been read to as children, they may have a reason to write (to a pen pal
or a sister in the Peace Corps), and they may like to write the way others like to play tennis or design computer programs. Doing something a lot usually makes you get good at it.
We also give you writing strategies to help you become a better writer if you work at it.

KNOWLEDGE OF RESEARCHING

All argument requires research, and if we do not know how to "do" research, we come up
against another constraint of the rhetorical situation. In literary research, we make arguments by looking for representative examples from a primary text (the actual literary
work), by reading experts in the field to see what they have to say, and sometimes by
going outside the discipline (to philosophy, history, theology, or psychology, for example)
for some theoretical idea that can be used to frame a literary work. While we need to
know what kind of information is valued in the discipline of literary studies so we properly develop evidence for an argument, we also need to know how to *do* the nuts and
bolts of researching. How do we find the experts who have opinions about the literature?
How do we find the disciplinary theories from outside English that may help our read-

ers understand the point we are making about a text? How do we learn about the cultural, historical, religious, and other contexts that will enable us to connect with our readers? Learning proper research techniques will minimize our rhetorical constraints. In Chapter 10 we discuss ways to do research.

KNOWLEDGE OF THE ASSIGNMENT

Some of the most serious constraints you will encounter while using this textbook are the assignments your teacher gives you in this class and the expectations she may have of you as a writer and arguer. In addition to knowing how to research and write the argument, you may have to deal with length, type of documentation, type size, font, format (margins, cover page), use of visuals, and pagination. When a teacher asks for a six-page argument, does she mean six full pages, or does she mean that any number of words might appear on page six—say one or two—or does she mean six pages and maybe a few lines on page seven? Does she even care? She may or may not. Would she care if you used APA documentation instead of MLA? (Probably.) Would she care if you copied in blue ink instead of the standard black? (Who knows?) The answer to all of these questions: you should find out.

Finally, there are conventions of writing that are usually nonnegotiable. Most teachers do not accept disorganized arguments in which readers cannot follow your logic. You must demonstrate that you know how to order evidence, how to use transitions, and how to write correctly. Teachers like arguments that contain no spelling errors, especially those that could be caught by a simple run through spell-checking software. However, even those easy-to-miss errors (*is* for *it*, or *an* for *and*, or *it's* for *its*) may meet with various degrees of acceptance, depending on the teacher, or the time in the semester, or whether the teacher has already noted such errors on your previous draft. Grammatical errors, such as subject-verb agreement, pronoun agreement, and misplaced modifiers, meet with considerable disapproval. Nonstandard English expressions, such as the use of localisms or slang, often are met with disapproval. Your knowledge of the conventions of academic English functions as a constraint in academic writing.

PRACTICE 1-B

Let's go back to the poem we explored in the previous practice from Casebook Four, *Land of the Free, Home of the Brave: Defining America(ns),* "In Response to Executive Order 9066."

Try writing individual responses to each of the following questions, and then share your ideas with one another in small groups or as a whole class.

1. Read the poem again. What is the urgency that would prompt the creation of an argument about this poem?
2. Who is your audience for such an argument? What do you know about your teacher, your classmates? What do they know about literature in general,

(continued)

PRACTICE 1-B *(continued)*

poetry, and more specifically, this poem and the historical circumstances surrounding it?

3. What are some possible audience responses to an argument about this poem? How would you use logos as a strategy to create an argument about this poem? Pathos? Ethos?

4. Take an inventory of the constraints you might face in creating an argument about this poem. What do you know about the cultural, social, and historical context for the poem? What does your audience know? What do you know about this literary genre? What do you know about the creation of literary arguments? What is your current reading strategy—how do you read a text such as this poem? What is your current writing process—how do you move from assignment, to idea, to draft, to finished product? What do you know about research in general and researching literary arguments specifically? What do you know about the type of assignments you might receive in this course? What are your teacher's expectations? How would you overcome each of these constraints?

Conclusion

Let's just say that writing academic arguments is one of the most challenging tasks you will undertake as an undergraduate. The juggling metaphor comes to mind: as writer/juggler, you have to keep many balls in the air, and dropping one may lead to dropping another . . . and another. That's why it's important to understand the nature of argument, the nature of the rhetorical situation, and the processes you can come to understand as you learn to write. Jugglers are made, not born; writers are made, not born. Both get better with practice. But writing is more important to your future—inside and outside the academic setting—than juggling might be to anyone but the juggler.

Writing Assignment Suggestions

1. Review our juggling metaphor in the conclusion. Then, create your own metaphor for the importance of writing and the writing process. What is writing like for you? What is the writing process like? Practice extending the metaphor by writing a one-page explanation that is both detailed and descriptive. Share your metaphor with your classmates.

2. Write a brief essay in which you describe your experience with argument in daily life. What are some situations in which you have found yourself engaging in argumentation about real-life events? Compare the arguments you typically encounter day to day with argumentation in an academic setting. How are these forms of argument similar? How are they different?

CHAPTER 2

Argument Structure and Strategies

Argument Structure

In Chapter 1, we introduced you to arguing about literature and showed you how such arguments can *turn in* to examine the literary text or *turn out* to examine the connection between the literary text and the world. We explained that argument often occurs as the result of some sense of urgency, that audience shapes your argument, and that effective arguers adhere to and address with specific strategies certain limitations or constraints. We used the words *claim* and *evidence,* but we did not define them for you. In this chapter, we focus on additional concepts that help you analyze an argument, whether it is yours or someone else's. We introduce you to a specialized argument vocabulary, defining and explaining important terms. To begin with, we present and discuss these components in a general way, and then we turn once again to our specific focus on arguments about literature.

As you remember from Chapter 1, formal oral argument first became important in ancient Athens. Oral argument required a structure that would help orators find and remember what they were going to say and how and when they wanted to say it. Today, we use almost the same structure, which, once you learn it, can help you find and organize content for your arguments; it can also help you analyze other arguments. Today, we think of an argument as having six components that may occur in any order and that may occur more than once within a single argument: *claim, claim qualifier, evidence, warrants, backing,* and *refutation.*

- **Claim.** Your claim is the statement or assertion you are making about your subject; it is what you wish to prove to be true. A claim gives your argument a focus. It is always stated as a declarative sentence (see Chapter 9): for example, "Students who use the Internet regularly in their academic research are more inclined to plagiarize than are students who do not." In previous writing classes, your teachers may have called this a *thesis statement.* But claims are different from thesis statements because a claim must be arguable and a thesis statement need not be. A thesis statement could be "The use of the Internet in the United States has increased over the past fifteen years." The difference is clear. Few people would disagree over the recent and meteoric rise of the Internet in this country, but they may disagree about its contribution to plagiarism, which is why the first example meets our definition of a claim. Claims do not have to be "true." A claim is a statement about the *possible* or *probable* existence of a truth, not a statement of an absolute truth.

- **Claim qualifier.** Most claims have to be qualified in some way. Of the several ways to qualify a claim, the most common is to limit its subject with the use of such words as *most, many, some, few, sometimes,* and so on. Another way is to restrict the statement, for example, by time or place. We could qualify our claim about the Internet and plagiarism by writing "*College* students who use the Internet regularly in their academic research are more inclined to plagiarize than are students who do not." By adding the word *college* to our statement, we have restricted our argument to a specific group of students. This makes the claim more focused, more manageable, and more easily accepted by an audience. Qualifying a claim also helps us to avoid illogical statements called *fallacies.* We return to that concept later in this chapter.

- **Evidence.** In order for readers to accept your claim, you must present them with evidence: reasons and support. It is not enough to just assert a position; you have to state why you believe it and then document your reason(s) with evidence. Take our Internet example: if you are asserting that there is a rise in student plagiarism because of the Internet, you must explain your reasoning by showing the link between student use of the Internet and the rise in plagiarism. For example, "Students who use the Internet regularly in their academic research are more inclined to plagiarize than are students who do not because students often do not see that information on the Internet 'belongs' to anyone." You might need to produce some statistics to show that Internet use and the incidence of plagiarism rose at the same rate. You may wish to cite college or high school teachers' comments about the kind of plagiarism that's occurring: students cutting and pasting whole paragraphs and not citing the source, students buying or downloading whole papers from Internet sites, and so on. Most important, you must document that students see Internet information as belonging to no one. To do this, you may have to interview lots of students and find research already done on this phenomenon. Chapters 6 and 7 discuss at length the kinds of support you will use when making a claim about a literary text.

- **Warrants or assumptions.** Warrants or assumptions are what your readers must believe before they can accept your claim and evidence. Think of a road with a fork ahead. If you have traveled with someone down the road and shared experiences and points of view on certain issues (warrants or assumptions), when you come to the fork (the claim), it is easier to discuss those differences with a common understanding. If you begin the journey at the fork without that common understanding, it is much harder to come back together. So, when you argue, you must understand the assumptions held by your readers and where those assumptions may diverge from yours. As an arguer, you must try to get all readers' assumptions going in the same direction. For example, in our claim about the Internet and plagiarism, in order to accept that claim, you would have to agree that it is possible for one human behavior to cause another. If you cannot agree on human causality, you probably can't convince any readers that your claim is true, even if it is.

- **Backing warrants or assumptions.** Because dealing with warrants is crucial to convincing an audience to accept your claim, you may have to supply evidence for your warrants, just as you provide evidence for your claims. This evidence is called *backing.* Continuing with our Internet example, if your audience does not naturally accept the possibility of human causality, you will have to provide backing for that warrant. You will have to gather evidence that one human behavior (similar to Internet usage) has caused another human behavior (similar to plagiarism). In some arguments, the backing for the warrant may be the heart of your argument.

- **Refutation.** There are two ways to look at what we call *refutation.* There might be conditions under which your claim is not true (the Internet might not affect plagiarism if students do not have Internet access at home). Refutation can also mean that you present the reader's position, admit where it may be valid, and then point to ways in which your position is superior. Showing another (opposing) side to an argument, or admitting a weakness in your own argument, may result in lessening opposition to your position.

Claims

As already discussed, claims are statements about an issue. They are arguable: there are *at least* two sides to a claim. Although claims make different statements about reality, for the sake of simplicity, we will say that the type of claim is wholly dependent on the *form* that it takes. Based on its form, there are least three different types of claims, although there are subtypes within each: *claims of fact, claims of value,* and *claims of policy.* One claim is not truer or more worthwhile than another. An analogy to explain types of claims might help. Cars come in different types: sedans, convertibles, minivans, station wagons. They are all cars; they just take different *forms.* They also make different statements about the driver's condition of life. The same is true of claims. The form that the claim takes (whether of fact, value, or policy) is based on what condition or perspective you want to a take on an issue. Let's discuss each in some detail.

CLAIM OF FACT

Claims of fact assert that a situation or condition exists, and thus the form the claim takes is a sentence that looks, well, factual. Again, just because you state that something exists does not necessarily mean that the statement is true. We could say that the sun rises in the west. Although stated as a claim of fact, the claim is obviously not true. "Students who use the Internet regularly in their academic research are more inclined to plagiarize than are students who do not" is a claim of fact. The claim asserts that a situation exists, in this case a relationship between use of the Internet and the rise of plagiarism; it is your job to produce evidence to show that this is true. In terms of arguing about literature, in Chapter 1, we stated that the poem "We Real Cool" is about the relationship between life and death in the form of a claim of fact: *meaningless deaths follow meaningless lives.*

There are three kinds of claims of fact: claims that argue from a particular definition, claims that argue for a similarity, and claims that argue for a cause-and-effect relationship. Let's look at each briefly.

CLAIMS OF FACT THAT ARGUE FROM A DEFINITION. Sometimes it is necessary to argue that a thing is something by definition. There are two ways to go here. First, you could create a definition and argue from it. Second, you could argue from an already established definition and show how a certain act falls under that definition. In arguing about literature, you will usually argue using the latter strategy: that a literary work or an aspect of a literary work belongs in one previously defined category.

There are many types of claims of fact in a literary argument. Sometimes we want to argue that a work belongs to a particular genre or that it reflects a particular literary theory. We may want to argue that a character is a certain type. We've already argued that Mrs. Isabel is a bigot. We could argue that "The Holocaust Party" is an autobiographical piece—it belongs to the genre of autobiographical fiction. To prove this claim, we would have to define autobiographical fiction and show that significant aspects of the story are connected to aspects of Robin Hemley's life. If we wanted to argue that "The Holocaust Party" can reflect a feminist literary approach, we would have to define "feminist literary approach" and find examples from the text that fit into that definition. There are many ways to create literary arguments based on definition.

CLAIMS OF FACT THAT ARGUE FOR A RESEMBLANCE. Some claims of fact base their argument on comparing similarities or contrasting differences between two or more things. However, it's not enough to just compare or contrast two things—we must explore resemblance purposefully. For example, we can argue that both Mrs. Isabel and Joel are bigots—they are similar in many ways to what we think of as a bigot. In another argument, we can claim that while Mrs. Isabel is a bigot, Joel is not. Note that in these claims we must go back to a definition of the word *bigot* as well as compare or contrast the traits of two specific characters. When creating this type of claim of fact, we also must show why noting the similarities or differences is important in coming to some sort of understanding of the story.

CLAIMS OF FACT THAT ARGUE FOR A CAUSE-EFFECT RELATIONSHIP. Claims of fact that argue for a cause-effect relationship are quite common, even though direct causality is difficult to prove. The previously stated claim about the Internet and plagiarism is a causal claim of fact because it implies (although it does not explicitly state) that use of the Internet causes students to plagiarize. While causality is possible to prove in science, it is almost impossible to prove in the study of human behavior because there simply are too many variables and they cannot be controlled as they can in scientific experiments. So, "cause and effect" becomes more a statement of causes and effects.

Use of the Internet may be one cause of the increase in plagiarism. But there could be others. Perhaps teachers are not teaching ethical uses of source texts in elementary school; perhaps students have lower ethical standards in general; perhaps they are not rewarded for ethical behavior; or perhaps they feel pressure to get good grades in high school in order to get into a prestigious college and that pressure overrides ethical considerations. All of these "causes" may also have other effects, not just an increase in plagiarism. Suicide is the third-highest-ranking cause of death in young adults after traffic accidents and homicide. Are the "causes" of plagiarism also affecting the suicide rate?

In the study of literary texts, claims of fact using cause and effect (1) make some connection between the outside world and the genesis of the text; (2) make some connection between a reading of the text and a subsequent event, situation, or condition in the outside world; or (3) make causal connections between or among elements within the text. For example, you could claim that Gwendolyn Brooks was horrified by the lack of community concern for young black males, and her horror "caused" her to write "We Real Cool." Alternatively, you could argue that the homicide rate among young black males or an experience she had at a local pool hall caused her to write the poem. In each case, you would be claiming a cause-effect relationship between Brooks's life and her outside environment and the poem, suggesting motivation on her part. You *might* also argue that reading the poem "We Real Cool" inspired a group of people in Chicago to create a non-profit organization to target young men like those at the Golden Shovel and that others who read the poem might be inspired in much the same way to become activists in their communities. Or you might also claim cause-effect relationship within a work. In "We Real Cool," you could argue a causal connection, as does the writer, between the pool players described in the poem, their lifestyles described in the poem, and the threat of their imminent deaths as described in the poem. In other words, you could attribute causality *within* the text.

PRACTICE 2-A

In arguing about literature, many of your claims will be claims of fact. You might claim that a story's theme is X. You might claim that a writer's life experiences produced story Y or that the major symbol in a poem is Z.

Read carefully the poem "The Bean Eaters" by Gwendolyn Brooks in Casebook Three, *The Ties That Bind: Relating and Relationships.* For this poem, generate one of each of the three types of claims of fact discussed in this chapter. For example, you might claim: "The simplicity of eating beans contrasting with the richness of memories means that the poem is about treasuring the immaterial over the material." This is a claim of fact that argues by contrasting differences. The evidence to support this claim would come from inside the text.

Identify each type of claim you make. Also determine if the evidence to support the claim must come from outside the text or from within the text.

CLAIMS OF VALUE

A *claim of value* states that something has value, that it is either good or bad, right or wrong, beautiful or ugly, moral or immoral, and so on. It differs from a claim of fact in its purpose: rather than proving the *existence* of a condition or situation, it asserts the worth of an already existing condition or situation. It is similar to a claim of fact in that there is a sequence involved in making both types of claims: you must prove (or state if it does not need proof) something exists before you can evaluate its quality.

Claims of value are common in literary arguments. Book reviews are good examples. The local reviewer reads a book and then writes an essay that evaluates the quality of the book. In the academic literary community, claims of value are also very common.

Sometimes you will want to argue for the quality of one story, play, or poem against another. You may want to argue that the movies based on *The Lord of the Rings* trilogy are better than the books, or that *The Color Purple* was both an incredible movie as well as a meaningful novel, or that an early book by Stephen King is better than his latest book. Each of these claims of value requires that you discover and state the purpose of the work, the character, or the genre, that you define criteria that describe what makes the thing (or group) good, and that you measure your subject against this set of criteria.

In this section, we discuss claims of value by using "The Laramie Project," a play about the 1998 murder of Matthew Shepard in Laramie, Wyoming. "The Laramie Project," which appears in Casebook Four, provides a good topic for a claim of value because it deals with ethical, moral, and aesthetic topics. For instance, you could argue this claim of value: "The Laramie Project" is a *good example* of a socially relevant play.

Every claim of value states or implies three acts:

- **Knowing and stating why something exists (its purposes or goals).** The purpose of a socially relevant play is to call attention to conditions in order to create a change in society. Thus, "The Laramie Project" is more than a work of art; its goal is to make a change in the actions or behaviors of the society it depicts.
- **Stating the *standards* or *criteria* necessary for that thing to achieve its goal.** Standards or criteria are evaluative characteristics. They state what conditions a thing must meet to be good, effective, excellent, and so on—to achieve a defined goal. Thus, you could state that a good, socially relevant play portrays contemporary issues, underscores the complexity of life, and questions the status quo.
- **Being able to *measure* the target against the criteria.** You have to argue whether, given its purpose or goal and the criteria that determine its worth or value, the thing is indeed working as it should—thus it is either good or bad, moral or immoral, beautiful or ugly, workable or not workable, and so on. For example, referring to "The Laramie Project," you could argue that this socially relevant play is good because it meets or exceeds the standards that you have set up (portrays contemporary issues, underscores the complexity of life, and questions the status quo, etc.).

If you argue this claim, you would *turn in* to examples from the text to prove your claim: How well does the play portray a contemporary issue? How well does it underscore the complexity of life? And so on.

You could also write a claim that *turns out:* for example, "The Laramie Project" is a good play because it demonstrates how art can have an effect on society. To prove this claim, you would have to generate criteria related to art and its effect on life. Such criteria might include statements that assert that art must directly cause changes in public policy, politics, or human behavior to be considered a good example. To prove the claim that "The Laramie Project" has influenced public policy, politics, or human behavior, you could examine changes in local, state, or federal laws as a result of this play. You might look at the changes in rates of hate crime in Wyoming (this would be public policy in the form of reporting and prosecuting hate crimes as well as human behavior in the form of reducing the crimes actually committed). If you saw changes and could connect them to "The Laramie Project," you would have an effective argument.

Claims of value always measure something against a set of criteria. You could measure one thing (the text of "The Laramie Project," as we did above) or you could measure several things. For example,

- the text-based play and the documentary measured against a set of criteria
- the play on the stage and the made-for-TV movie measure against a set of criteria
- any or all of the above measured against a set of criteria.

Obviously, the more measuring you do, the more difficult your argument.

Claims of value are particularly hard to argue because they are often based on deeply held values or preferences. Often the assumptions or warrants for a claim of value are steeped in religious or moral upbringing, political beliefs, or firmly entrenched habits. If we return to our metaphor of the fork in the road, the Y-shaped road, the values in a claim of value are the leg of the Y, and that part of the road may be bumpy and potholed, so much so that the travelers have to negotiate very carefully if they are to successfully reach the end. Take "The Laramie Project." The play criticizes the biblical view of homosexuality. If you accept that view, you may be offended by a claim that argues for the effectiveness of this play because it changes public opinion toward homosexuality. A claim of value, because it depends so heavily on agreement over issues of value, depends on both logical and emotional support.

PRACTICE 2-B

1. The following articles review performances of "The Laramie Project." They are claims of value because they present or suggest standards or criteria and then measure the performance against them. Try to answer these questions based on these play reviews:
    - What does the reviewer say is the purpose of the play?
    - What are the criteria for such a play? Based on this review, how would we know a good performance from a bad one?
    - How does this performance exceed or fall short of those criteria, according to the reviewer?

REVIEW 1

A Curtain Up Review: The Laramie Project

BY ELYSE SOMMER

Eight people stand behind plain wooden straight-backed chairs. They are actors, and very good ones at that. The story they are about to enact for us does

(continued)

PRACTICE 2-B *(continued)*

not come from a script written in a playwright's study. It is instead a group effort in which Moisés Kaufman's unique troupe participated as research journalists, interviewing the characters they would eventually portray. The result is a play of forceful but never showy dramatic impact, its seriousness leavened with laughter.

On the surface *The Laramie Project* is a docudrama about a particular and particularly horrendous 1998 hate crime, the brutal and fatal beating of a gay college senior named Matthew Shepard in Laramie, Wyoming—population 26,687. The world-wide media coverage turned Shepard (like Oscar Wilde in Kaufman's previous journalistic drama, *Gross Indecency: The Three Trials of Oscar Wilde*) into a martyr symbolizing random acts of violence.

But this is not a rehash of a widely publicized crime. Instead, that single event is reexamined within the framework of a portrait of Laramie, its citizens and their reactions to the tragedy and the effect of being in the eye of a media storm. Mr. Kaufman and his colleagues have thus used the power of theater to force us to face the unsettling questions about the potential for violence in even the most ordinary corners of the American landscape.

Unlike *Gross Indecency* the victim whose story drives *The Laramie Project* is never on stage. The emphasis is on the effect of that victim's violent death on the town which transforms his premature exit from life into every parent's and every town's nightmare.

The story unfolds with deceptive simplicity. The eight actors explain how they became participants as interviewers during the company's six visits to Laramie. They set the scene for Shepard's fatal ride with his two attackers by giving us a bird's eye view of the erstwhile ranch and railroad town: its mores, its open spaces, its neighborly everybody knows everybody atmosphere on one hand and division between the working class and university populace on the other. As the actors take on the personae of the characters, types become identifiable individuals with opinions and attitudes that shed some light on THE EVENT that, as one person puts it, "defined the town by an accident."

The naturalness with which the actors move back and forth between their roles as visiting journalists and the multiple characters in this human collage give *The Laramie Project* its dramatic muscle. The script yields few memorable lines and the company's determined sensitivity to the fact that these people are still living with this story makes for a somewhat homogenized overall image of a modern-day Grovers Corners—with Wal-Mart and some town and gown tensions. However, these shortcomings are more than offset by the superb portraiture and cinematic but spare staging.

All the actors play at least a half a dozen characters and often themselves, as well as being part of ensemble scenes. Stephen Belber delivers bull's eye portrayals of Matt Galloway, the bartender who last saw Shepard alive; the limo driver who asks only "how much?" of those headed for the distant gay bar life unavailable in Laramie; the co-perpetrator Russell Henderson's Mormon spiritual adviser and a Kansas zealot who disrupts Shepard's funeral yelling "God hates fags!" Andy Paris is equally impressive as, among others, the doctor who keeps the hungry media informed about Shepard's condition and as theater student whose always supportive parents won't come to see his audition-winning performance in *Angels In America*. Greg Pierotti and John McAdams round out the male gallery with a dozen other memorable characters.

The women in the cast are also outstanding. Amanda Gronich is terrific as the feisty "live and let live" Marge Murray. Mercedes Herrero is fine as her daughter Reggie, the police officer who was exposed to Shepard's HIV infection when she untied Matthew from the fence to which he had been bound and left for dead (her account of that event is one of the play's more harrowing scenes). Barbara Pitts displays truly amazing versatility as a gay university professor, the grandmother of one of the killers and most incisively as a Muslim student who thinks the idea of a play "weird." It is this girl who voices the harsh truth that while this may be a town that doesn't raise children who commit murder, this is in fact the town where it happened.

Obviously, this is just a sampling of the bravura acting on display and the people who give definition to the company's portrait of this modern-day Grovers Corners.

The design team is a powerful ally in emphasizing the mood and theatricality of Kaufman's direction. The black brick wall underscores the somberness of the events being reenacted. A simple sliding wall reveals a screen on which the doctor's reports during the vigil before Shepard's death are projected. At the height of the media feeding frenzy, a half a dozen TV sets tumble down the wall showing the actors as reporters bringing the Laramie tragedy to viewers all over the world. Peter Golub's original music synchronizes every shift in mood.

In his ability to parlay factual research into a work of high-voltage theatricality, Moisés Kaufman has repeated what he successfully did with *Gross Indecency: The Three Trials of Oscar Wilde*. Having moved from a Victorian scandal linked to the uptight mores of a past era to a recent event that left a blemish on the American self-image of decency and open-mindedness, the playwright-director has also ventured into an exciting new direction by making his actors part of the playmaking process.

The grim subject matter and absence of hopeful answers to the questions raised may make *The Laramie Project* a tough sell to audiences looking for summer entertainment. Yet it's a play that will reward all interested in innovative and invigorating contemporary theater.

(continued)

REVIEW 2

(Mostly) Harmless Theatre Production: The Laramie Project

BY STEVE CALLAHAN

Take one of the most sensational murders in recent years, fold in a large scoop of sexual politics, let the media and the activists whip it to a froth and you've laid the groundwork for the kind of evening presented by the (Mostly) Harmless Theatre. It's *The Laramie Project,* a review of the events and reactions surrounding the 1998 death of Matthew Shepard, a young homosexual who was beaten by two rednecks, tied to a fence and left to die.

Brutal murders are all too common in this land of ours, and most of them get no more than a few lines in the police column. But the press sensed something in this—the boy was gay and the physical circumstances suggested an easy analogy to crucifixion, so the media hordes came down "like the wolf on the fold" and nearly flattened Laramie, Wyoming, in their scramble. Gay rights activists, of course, leapt to the bait and quickly transformed Shepard into a bona fide martyr.

The Tectonic Theatre Project, a group of genuine New York actors, visited Laramie six times over the subsequent eighteen months. This alone demonstrates their courage and commitment, for Laramie, on most New Yorkers' maps, is a backwater somewhere between terra incognita and "here there be monsters." (Their writing, by the way, never quite escapes this geographical perspective.) The troupe interviewed scores of people and documented their emotional reactions to the crime. The resulting script has a nominal author, one head writer, three associate writers and seven (count them)—SEVEN dramaturgs. So by golly it ought to be a real zinger! (Think what Chekhov could have done if he'd had that much help!)

Director Robert Neblett has assembled almost all the elements of a winning piece of theatre—ten of the best actors in St. Louis, truly fine scenery and lighting by veterans Bruce Bergner and Glenn Dunn, and beautiful evocative string quartet music composed by Adam Rosen. But here, as in Solla Salew, there's just one little problem.

Dare I say it? When some in the audience were standing to applaud the Emperor's wardrobe, how could I think that I saw him starkers? Dare I suggest in the face of all its compassion and political correctness that *The Laramie Project* is simply really bad theatre?

It's a tried and true concept. The Federal Theatre Project, in the 30s, produced a number of so-called "living newspapers"—plays addressing various current social problems and based on real-life events. They were done with large casts in many brief scenes and were the work of huge teams of otherwise unemployed actors and writers. But *The Laramie Project* fails for several reasons. Not just because the interviewers lacked objectivity (those Federal Theatre plays were as propagandistic as can be), but because, like most modern journalists, they focused on emotionalism. (You know, the "How did you FEEL about that, Mrs. Lincoln?" kind of interview.)

And the words they recorded were, for the most part, not the speech of real life, but the predictable utterances of people who have a microphone thrust into their faces and say the things they think they are expected to say. The result is generally maudlin and moralizing. Look at the preachers, for example. The good preacher never speaks but in a homily. The bad ones are simply demonized—which is never very interesting dramatically.

Moreover the interviewers intrude themselves into the presentation so that often the focus becomes not the murder and the residents of Laramie, but the interviewing team itself. They do this for two reasons: first because they feel their effort is so noble it deserves attention, and secondly to telegraph to us what the correct emotional response should be to the various interviews. They're like "Judas goats" leading us in for the emotional kill. One interviewer is so offended by comments from the really BAD preacher that she simply stops listening. But even this sensitive team can't always pass emotional muster: when they make their pilgrimage to the now holy site of the murder one member is properly overwhelmed with grief, but another shamefully admits that she "couldn't bring herself to cry."

So the script, with its pervasive air of condescension, is not good theatre. It's not theatre at all. And at nearly three hours it's self-indulgently overlong.

But the evening does indeed have some fine performances (though there is an occasional tendency to overact in reaching for the "aw shucks" regionalisms). There were two actors who impressed me most: David Schroeder is utterly convincing and engaging as a young drama student, and Elizabeth Watt really triumphs as the police officer who was called to the scene of the crime.

2. As a class project, read "The Laramie Project" together, then watch the movie and measure your own response about "The Laramie Project" by writing about the differences in watching the made-for-TV movie (HBO 2002) and reading the play.
3. Think back to the poem covered in Chapter 1, "In Response to Executive Order 9066." Consider the work's purpose and criteria for evaluating whether it accomplishes its purpose. Try writing a claim of value about that poem.

CLAIMS OF POLICY

The third type of claim is a *claim of policy* in which you argue for a change in a situation or condition. The claim of policy is often seen as a problem/solution argument with three parts: (1) you argue for the existence of a problem, then (2) you pose one or more solutions, and finally (3) you evaluate those solutions and argue for the best. If you unpack a claim of policy, you will see that it contains both a claim of fact (the *existence* of a problem) and a claim of value (one solution is *better* than another). A claim of policy is a statement about future action—a recommendation for what should be done to solve a perceived problem. One of the distinguishing hallmarks of a claim of policy is the form of the claim: it is always stated in a sentence that contains "should" or "ought" or "must." Thus, the statement *To help eliminate hate crime in high schools, "The Laramie Project" should be required reading in every American high school* would be a claim of policy.

Let's take a closer look at the three parts of this type of claim:

- **Argue for the existence of the problem.** You have to convince your readers that your chosen problem exists—like a claim of fact. If your readers do not recognize that a problem exists, there is no point in posing solutions. Thus, your first job is to determine whether your readers believe that your stated problem even exists. If readers admit to the problem, you have less of an argument to make; if they do not, you have to make a stronger argument. Using the above claim—*To help eliminate hate crime in high schools, "The Laramie Project" should be required reading in every American high school*—before doing anything else, you would have to convince your readers that hate crimes exist in high schools.
- **Pose one or more solutions.** After you have succeeded in convincing your readers of the existence of the problem, you have to pose one or more solutions. Workable solutions should solve the problem without creating a bigger one. Most solutions should be feasible, not overly costly, and not change the nature of the work being examined. You will have to research this part of the claim of policy unless you are very familiar with the situation. Again, with the above claim, once your readers agree that hate crimes exist and are a problem in American high schools, you would have to present solutions to the problem: expelling students who perpetrate them; requiring courses in tolerance; imposing community service projects on students who commit hate crimes; requiring students to read "The Laramie Project."
- **Evaluate proposed solutions and recommend the best one.** In a claim of policy, it is not enough to just propose solutions; you also must measure them against a set of criteria. Many students neglect this part of the argument, thinking that they have completed the task by just presenting solutions. Not so. Finally, you have to argue for the best solution. It is important that you make your strongest arguments here because others who have researched the same problem might be arguing for alternate solutions.

To argue for the best solution, you have to do what you did with claims of value: state goals, set criteria, and measure your proposed solution against the set of criteria. If the goal of the claim is to "eliminate hate crimes in high schools," and if one criterion is to be proactive, not reactive, then only setting up courses on tolerance and requiring reading "The Laramie Project" will meet the criterion. If another criterion is "financially feasible," then only reading "The Laramie Project" works because requiring a course will also require hiring or reassigning teachers—a very expensive proposition.

Although common in social or public discourse, in writing arguments about literature, claims of policy are unusual unless you are writing about a public issue and how it relates to a work of literature. However, one of the more interesting possibilities for a literary claim of policy might be suggesting a change to an existing story or poem because what exists is problematic for one reason or another. The most common instance of such alteration occurs when a book is adapted to a film—screenwriters often change elements of a story to make it work more effectively in the new medium or to make it more acceptable to a wider audience. In such cases, the film's creators, for example, might have to convince the author that there is a problem with the ending of the book and propose several alternate endings and recommend a particular alternative because it creates a more realistic conclusion or it resonates more honestly with readers.

PRACTICE 2-C

1. Sometimes, when reading poems or stories, you may become dissatisfied with the author's choices and wish to substitute your own. For example, several semesters ago, our classes read the novel *Cold Mountain* by Charles Frazier, a story about a Confederate soldier's journey westward across North Carolina to be with the woman he loved who lived in the Appalachian mountains. Readers go through many trials with Inman, the soldier: they see him beaten, starving, almost buried alive, taken care of by a young war widow, and hunted by one of the vigilante groups trying to find deserters. Within ten pages of the end, he dies. Students were outraged. They thought that reading the book was a waste of their time if this man who suffered so much, and whose suffering they experienced, dies without achieving his goals. So, they set about to rewrite the ending. They made him kill the young vigilante, marry his love, and successfully hide from bounty hunters until the end of the war. The students were much happier, although Charles Frazier might not be.

    In Casebook Four, read Shirley Jackson's short story "The Lottery." Propose an alternative ending to this story in a claim of policy. Define the problem as you see it with the current ending, propose one or more solutions, and argue for the best solution according to a set of criteria you have devised. Share your proposal with the class.

2. One of the most famous literary claims of policy is "A Modest Proposal," a satire written by Jonathan Swift in the eighteenth century. Swift, an Irishman, saw the effects of the English occupation of Ireland on the Irish economy—that many people were poor, starving, and without hope—and he

(continued)

PRACTICE 2-C *(continued)*

posed a unique solution. Note that Swift presents his satire in the form of a *proposal,* a common form for claims of policy.

Read Swift's "A Modest Proposal." What problem does he identify? How does he argue for its existence? Given that his readers are British nobility occupying Ireland, what obstacles does he have to overcome to convince them of the existence of the problem? What solution does he propose? Does he offer alternative solutions? How does he examine their advantages and disadvantages? In your opinion, does Swift successfully argue that his chosen solution is in fact the *best* one? What evidence from the text supports your opinion?

Propose an alternate solution to the problem presented by Jonathan Swift in "A Modest Proposal." Without necessarily attempting to imitate Swift's writing style or satirical tone, defend your solution on the basis of the facts as Swift presents them.

Share your proposed changes with your class. As a group, evaluate your solution in terms of (1) how well it solves the problem Swift identifies, (2) how well it meets the claim of policy criteria discussed in this text, and (3) how closely it adheres to the conditions and facts of the problem as Swift states them.

A Modest Proposal

For preventing the children of poor people in Ireland from being a burden to their parents or country, and for making them beneficial to the public.

It is a melancholy object to those who walk through this great town or travel in the country, when they see the streets, the roads, and cabin doors, crowded with beggars of the female sex, followed by three, four, or six children, all in rags and importuning every passenger for an alms. These mothers, instead of being able to work for their honest livelihood, are forced to employ all their time in strolling to beg sustenance for their helpless infants: who as they grow up either turn thieves for want of work, or leave their dear native country to fight for the Pretender in Spain, or sell themselves to the Barbadoes.

I think it is agreed by all parties that this prodigious number of children in the arms, or on the backs, or at the heels of their mothers, and frequently of their fathers, is in the present deplorable state of the kingdom a very great additional grievance; and, therefore, whoever could find out a fair, cheap, and easy method of making these children sound, useful members of the commonwealth, would deserve so well of the public as to have his statue set up for a preserver of the nation.

But my intention is very far from being confined to provide only for the children of professed beggars; it is of a much greater extent, and shall take in the whole number of infants at a certain age who are born of parents in effect as little able to support them as those who demand our charity in the streets.

As to my own part, having turned my thoughts for many years upon this important subject, and maturely weighed the several schemes of other projectors, I have always found them grossly mistaken in the computation. It is true, a child just dropped from its dam may be supported by her milk for a solar year, with little other nourishment; at most not above the value of two shillings, which the mother may certainly get, or the value in scraps, by her lawful occupation of begging; and it is exactly at one year old that I propose to provide for them in such a manner as instead of being a charge upon their parents or the parish, or wanting food and raiment for the rest of their lives, they shall on the contrary contribute to the feeding, and partly to the clothing, of many thousands.

There is likewise another great advantage in my scheme, that it will prevent those voluntary abortions, and that horrid practice of women murdering their bastard children, alas! too frequent among us! sacrificing the poor innocent babes I doubt more to avoid the expense than the shame, which would move tears and pity in the most savage and inhuman breast.

The number of souls in this kingdom being usually reckoned one million and a half, of these I calculate there may be about two hundred thousand couple whose wives are breeders; from which number I subtract thirty thousand couples who are able to maintain their own children, although I apprehend there cannot be so many, under the present distresses of the kingdom; but this being granted, there will remain a hundred and seventy thousand breeders. I again subtract fifty thousand for those women who miscarry, or whose children die by accident or disease within the year. There only remains one hundred and twenty thousand children of poor parents annually born. The question therefore is, how this number shall be reared and provided for, which, as I have already said, under the present situation of affairs, is utterly impossible by all the methods hitherto proposed. For we can neither employ them in handicraft or agriculture; we neither build houses (I mean in the country) nor cultivate land: they can very seldom pick up a livelihood by stealing, till they arrive at six years old, except where they are of towardly parts, although I confess they learn the rudiments much earlier, during which time, they can however be properly looked upon only as probationers, as I have been informed by a principal gentleman in the county of Cavan, who protested to me that he never knew above one or two instances under the age of six, even in a part of the kingdom so renowned for the quickest proficiency in that art. I am assured by our merchants, that a boy or a girl before twelve years old is no salable commodity; and even when they

(continued)

PRACTICE 2-C *(continued)*

come to this age they will not yield above three pounds, or three pounds and half-a-crown at most on the exchange; which cannot turn to account either to the parents or kingdom, the charge of nutriment and rags having been at least four times that value. I shall now therefore humbly propose my own thoughts, which I hope will not be liable to the least objection.

I have been assured by a very knowing American of my acquaintance in London, that a young healthy child well nursed is at a year old a most delicious, nourishing, and wholesome food, whether stewed, roasted, baked, or boiled; and I make no doubt that it will equally serve in a fricassee or a ragout.

I do therefore humbly offer it to public consideration that of the hundred and twenty thousand children already computed, twenty thousand may be reserved for breed, whereof only one-fourth part to be males; which is more than we allow to sheep, black cattle or swine; and my reason is, that these children are seldom the fruits of marriage, a circumstance not much regarded by our savages, therefore one male will be sufficient to serve four females. That the remaining hundred thousand may, at a year old, be offered in the sale to the persons of quality and fortune through the kingdom; always advising the mother to let them suck plentifully in the last month, so as to render them plump and fat for a good table. A child will make two dishes at an entertainment for friends; and when the family dines alone, the fore or hind quarter will make a reasonable dish, and seasoned with a little pepper or salt will be very good boiled on the fourth day, especially in winter.

I have reckoned upon a medium that a child just born will weigh 12 pounds, and in a solar year, if tolerably nursed, increaseth to 28 pounds.

I grant this food will be somewhat dear, and therefore very proper for landlords, who, as they have already devoured most of the parents, seem to have the best title to the children. Infant's flesh will be in season throughout the year, but more plentiful in March, and a little before and after; for we are told by a grave author, an eminent French physician, that fish being a prolific diet, there are more children born in Roman Catholic countries about nine months after Lent than at any other season; therefore, reckoning a year after Lent, the markets will be more glutted than usual, because the number of popish infants is at least three to one in this kingdom: and therefore it will have one other collateral advantage, by lessening the number of papists among us.

I have already computed the charge of nursing a beggar's child (in which list I reckon all cottagers, laborers, and four-fifths of the farmers) to be about two shillings per annum, rags included; and I believe no gentleman would repine to give ten shillings for the carcass of a good fat child, which, as I have said, will make four dishes of excellent nutritive meat, when he hath only some particular friend or his own family to dine with him. Thus the squire will learn to be a good landlord, and grow popular among his tenants; the mother will have eight shillings net profit, and be fit for work till she produces another child.

Those who are more thrifty (as I must confess the times require) may flay the carcass; the skin of which artificially dressed will make admirable gloves for ladies, and summer boots for fine gentlemen.

As to our city of Dublin, shambles may be appointed for this purpose in the most convenient parts of it, and butchers we may be assured will not be wanting; although I rather recommend buying the children alive, and dressing them hot from the knife, as we do roasting pigs.

A very worthy person, a true lover of his country, and whose virtues I highly esteem, was lately pleased in discoursing on this matter to offer a refinement upon my scheme. He said that many gentlemen of this kingdom, having of late destroyed their deer, he conceived that the want of venison might be well supplied by the bodies of young lads and maidens, not exceeding fourteen years of age nor under twelve; so great a number of both sexes in every country being now ready to starve for want of work and service; and these to be disposed of by their parents, if alive, or otherwise by their nearest relations. But with due deference to so excellent a friend and so deserving a patriot, I cannot be altogether in his sentiments; for as to the males, my American acquaintance assured me, from frequent experience, that their flesh was generally tough and lean, like that of our schoolboys by continual exercise, and their taste disagreeable; and to fatten them would not answer the charge. Then as to the females, it would, I think, with humble submission be a loss to the public, because they soon would become breeders themselves; and besides, it is not improbable that some scrupulous people might be apt to censure such a practice (although indeed very unjustly), as a little bordering upon cruelty; which, I confess, hath always been with me the strongest objection against any project, however so well intended.

But in order to justify my friend, he confessed that this expedient was put into his head by the famous Psalmanazar, a native of the island Formosa, who came from thence to London above twenty years ago, and in conversation told my friend, that in his country when any young person happened to be put to death, the executioner sold the carcass to persons of quality as a prime dainty; and that in his time the body of a plump girl of fifteen, who was crucified for an attempt to poison the emperor, was sold to his imperial majesty's prime minister of state, and other great mandarins of the court, in joints from the gibbet, at four hundred crowns. Neither indeed can I deny, that if the same use were made of several plump young girls in this town, who without one single groat to their fortunes cannot stir abroad without a chair, and appear at playhouse and assemblies in foreign fineries which they never will pay for, the kingdom would not be the worse.

(continued)

PRACTICE 2-C *(continued)*

Some persons of a desponding spirit are in great concern about that vast number of poor people, who are aged, diseased, or maimed, and I have been desired to employ my thoughts what course may be taken to ease the nation of so grievous an encumbrance. But I am not in the least pain upon that matter, because it is very well known that they are every day dying and rotting by cold and famine, and filth and vermin, as fast as can be reasonably expected. And as to the young laborers, they are now in as hopeful a condition; they cannot get work, and consequently pine away for want of nourishment, to a degree that if at any time they are accidentally hired to common labor, they have not strength to perform it; and thus the country and themselves are happily delivered from the evils to come.

I have too long digressed, and therefore shall return to my subject. I think the advantages by the proposal which I have made are obvious and many, as well as of the highest importance. For first, as I have already observed, it would greatly lessen the number of papists, with whom we are yearly overrun, being the principal breeders of the nation as well as our most dangerous enemies; and who stay at home on purpose with a design to deliver the kingdom to the Pretender, hoping to take their advantage by the absence of so many good protestants, who have chosen rather to leave their country than stay at home and pay tithes against their conscience to an episcopal curate.

Secondly, The poorer tenants will have something valuable of their own, which by law may be made liable to distress and help to pay their landlord's rent, their corn and cattle being already seized, and money a thing unknown.

Thirdly, Whereas the maintenance of an hundred thousand children, from two years old and upward, cannot be computed at less than ten shillings a-piece per annum, the nation's stock will be thereby increased fifty thousand pounds per annum, beside the profit of a new dish introduced to the tables of all gentlemen of fortune in the kingdom who have any refinement in taste. And the money will circulate among ourselves, the goods being entirely of our own growth and manufacture.

Fourthly, The constant breeders, beside the gain of eight shillings sterling per annum by the sale of their children, will be rid of the charge of maintaining them after the first year.

Fifthly, This food would likewise bring great custom to taverns; where the vintners will certainly be so prudent as to procure the best receipts for dressing it to perfection, and consequently have their houses frequented by all the fine gentlemen, who justly value themselves upon their knowledge in good eating: and a skilful cook, who understands how to oblige his guests, will contrive to make it as expensive as they please.

Sixthly, This would be a great inducement to marriage, which all wise nations have either encouraged by rewards or enforced by laws and penalties. It would increase the care and tenderness of mothers toward their children, when they were sure of a settlement for life to the poor babes, provided in some sort by the public, to their annual profit instead of expense. We should see an honest emulation among the married women, which of them could bring the fattest child to the market. Men would become as fond of their wives during the time of their pregnancy as they are now of their mares in foal, their cows in calf, their sows when they are ready to farrow; nor offer to beat or kick them (as is too frequent a practice) for fear of a miscarriage. Many other advantages might be enumerated. For instance, the addition of some thousand carcasses in our exportation of barreled beef, the propagation of swine's flesh, and improvement in the art of making good bacon, so much wanted among us by the great destruction of pigs, too frequent at our tables; which are no way comparable in taste or magnificence to a well-grown, fat, yearling child, which roasted whole will make a considerable figure at a lord mayor's feast or any other public entertainment. But this and many others I omit, being studious of brevity. After all, I am not so violently bent upon my own opinion as to reject any offer proposed by wise men, which shall be found equally innocent, cheap, easy, and effectual. But before something of that kind shall be advanced in contradiction to my scheme, and offering a better, I desire the author or authors will be pleased maturely to consider two points. First, as things now stand, how they will be able to find food and raiment for an hundred thousand useless mouths and backs. And secondly, there being a round million of creatures in human figure throughout this kingdom, whose whole subsistence put into a common stock would leave them in debt two millions of pounds sterling, adding those who are beggars by profession to the bulk of farmers, cottagers, and laborers, with their wives and children who are beggars in effect: I desire those politicians who dislike my overture, and may perhaps be so bold as to attempt an answer, that they will first ask the parents of these mortals, whether they would not at this day think it a great happiness to have been sold for food, at a year old in the manner I prescribe, and thereby have avoided such a perpetual scene of misfortunes as they have since gone through by the oppression of landlords, the impossibility of paying rent without money or trade, the want of common sustenance, with neither house nor clothes to cover them from the inclemencies of the weather, and the most inevitable prospect of entailing the like or greater miseries upon their breed for ever.

I profess, in the sincerity of my heart, that I have not the least personal interest in endeavoring to promote this necessary work, having no other motive than the public good of my country, by advancing our trade, providing for infants, relieving the poor, and giving some pleasure to the rich. I have no children by which I can propose to get a single penny; the youngest being nine years old, and my wife past child-bearing.

Claim Qualifiers

As we noted earlier in this chapter, *qualifiers* limit a claim. Using qualifiers affects an argument in three ways: first, qualifiers affect the kind of evidence you need to collect; second, they affect the tone of the argument; third, they prevent some forms of illogical thinking or fallacies.

Claims with qualifiers that state "most" or "many" require more evidence than claims with such qualifiers as "some" or "few." Let's look at the claim we made early in this chapter, changing it just a bit: "Students who use the Internet regularly in their academic research will plagiarize more than will students who do not." This claim states that ALL students WILL plagiarize; it is not qualified in any way, and thus it might be difficult to prove. Unqualified, this statement is illogical. It creates a fallacy of *sweeping generalizations* (applying characteristics of a select few in a broad manner to a larger group). However, you can moderate or qualify a statement to keep its controversial edge but still make it easier to prove and avoid illogical generalizations. For example, you could say: "Students who use the Internet regularly in their academic research are *more inclined* to plagiarize than are students who do not." *More inclined* is an example of a qualifier that significantly limits the claim and eliminates the possibility of creating an unsupportable logical fallacy. There are other possibilities. For instance, you could moderate the statement by qualifying the subject, students: "*Most* students who use the Internet regularly in their academic research will plagiarize more than will students who do not." Or you could state that "some" or "many" are inclined to plagiarize. The more you qualify, the easier it may be to prove your statement true.

Claim:

Gwendolyn Brooks should have revised her vision of black males in the poem "We Real Cool" to present them facing the future with more hope.

Reason:

Black males at the time of the Civil Rights Movement were struggling mightily against many forms of oppression and as a group would have benefited more by having a major writer give them hope rather than reinforce their despair.

Support:

Examples from other poets and poems showing black Americans persevering and overcoming despair; examples from contemporary news sources; first-person accounts.

Obviously, a claim may be true for many reasons. For each reason, you would have to produce some kind of evidence in support. Reasons are helpful because they focus your search for support. Without reasons, there may be no such focus, and you may fall into providing irrelevant data to support a claim (as discussed in the next section). Reasons also tell readers that you have some justification, some rational plan behind the claim, that it is not simply your personal opinion (although that may also be true).

Kinds of Support

Support is quite different from reasons. In most arguments, there are four types of support: *facts, statistics, expert opinion,* and *examples.* In a general argument, you would use all four kinds of support; however, in a literary argument, you will probably rely most heavily on facts, expert opinion, and examples. However, let's review all four kinds.

FACTS

Merriam-Webster's Collegiate Dictionary defines a fact as "something that has actual existence . . . a piece of information presented as having objective reality." Facts are often observable phenomena or primary source data. If you go out to the campus parking lot and note that there are no parking spaces available at 9:05 a.m., you have made an observation that turns into a fact: There are no parking spaces at 9:05 a.m. in the campus parking lot. Primary source data are often documents, such as a budget, a report from a committee, medical records, police reports, or court transcripts. Visual displays, such as pictures, photographs, even some charts and graphs, are factual documents. (Note that while the existence of the document itself is factual, its content may not be. Proving the truth of your supporting facts may become necessary to your argument. More about this as we continue.) In an argument about literature, source data would include biographical information, background historical information, an interview with the author, and previous works that may have influenced the author and the text in question.

STATISTICS

Statistics show relationships among sets of numbers. When we read that 60 percent of the students attending a college or university are female, we are reading a statistic. Statistical reports are types of factual documents. Like other source documents, statistics may not necessarily be true or reported accurately. Those compiling or interpreting the statistics may skew the data or may bring bias into the presentation, knowingly or unknowingly. In addition, the numbers may not have been gathered in a valid way. If you want to poll your schoolmates to see if they have trouble parking, it would not be valid to poll only those students who drive and have classes beginning at 10:00 a.m. It would not be valid to poll only females, or males, or seniors. You would need to poll all commuter students and poll them randomly.

In a literary argument, you would seldom generate statistics; however, you might very well research statistics. If, for example, you want to use statistics to support the Gwendolyn Brooks claim made previously, you might gather data on African American mortality rates and rates of attendance and completion of higher education for the years before, during, and after the height of the Civil Rights Movement.

EXPERT OPINIONS

There are good opinions and bad opinions: good opinions are not those we agree with and bad those we disagree with. Instead, good opinions come from reliable, knowledgeable sources, and bad opinions do not. Opinions are interpretations of data, either facts or statistics. We need people to interpret. But humans interpret and humans make mistakes. Eyewitness accounts are good examples of interpretations (opinions) about facts. Although eyewitnesses are the mainstay of trials and court cases, they are notoriously unreliable, influenced by such matters as age, gender, race, place, and time. Opinions used as evidence must never come from a single source, must always come from a reliable and capable opinion-maker, and must always be supported in their own right. In writing arguments about literature, you can find credible opinions in any published source, any book or journal article written by a literary scholar. You can also find credible sources in primary materials, such as letters, diary entries, or original manuscripts of works. Evidence in literary argument may also come from other disciplines, such as history or anthropology, or from published works in other fields. Chapter 10 explores the credibility of opinion in depth, and Chapter 7 discusses making arguments when you look outside the text to support your claims.

EXAMPLES

Examples in an argument can be drawn from personal experience or from primary or secondary sources. Examples drawn from personal experience, in certain situations, may not be strong support and may not be convincing without other evidence. In a literary argument, your support often will be based on examples from the text. Even when you write an argument that depends on expert opinion from outside the text, the conventions of arguing about literature will require that you find and cite examples from within the text. If we go back to our claim that the character Joel in "The Holocaust Party" is a bigot, one of our main sources of support will be *examples* from the story to show that Joel made value judgments about other characters based on his preconceptions.

In literary argument, facts, expert opinion, and examples are the primary forms of support. Depending on your claim, you might choose to research primary sources (such as diaries or autobiographies); you might want to examine secondary sources (books and articles written by literary scholars); and, most assuredly, you will use examples from the texts in question.

Characteristics of Support

One of the most helpful ways to judge whether your evidence will adequately support your claims is to evaluate it using STAR, described in *Teaching the Argument in Writing* by Richard Fulkerson. He writes that the evidence used in an argument can be measured "against four ideal traits" (p. 44): sufficiency, typicality, accuracy, and relevance.

S   *Sufficiency*. Quantity is the key consideration in sufficiency. You must determine whether you have enough—sufficient—evidence to support your claim. Do you have enough examples from the text to prove your claim? Have you gotten enough support from experts? You will have to make that determination, realizing that 300 examples or opinions may be too many and three may be too few (and vice versa on rare occasions).

T *Typicality.* Are the examples you are using typical of the whole, or do they present a skewed sample somehow? To use our Internet and plagiarism example, if we made our claim solely in interviews with students who admit plagiarism, we would not be getting a representative sample of all students using the Internet for research. If you are going to argue about a literary work, are the expert opinions you have cited typical of the field, or have you selected the few oddballs? Have you chosen typical passages from the text, or are your selected passages atypical in some way?

A *Accuracy.* Accuracy is often difficult to assess because in many cases we have to depend on other people for verification of accuracy. In a literary argument, for example, you have to trust that the printer or publisher has not made mistakes in typesetting the text or that the expert was quoted accurately in the first place. So, to some extent, while you can verify almost everything under your immediate control, you have to trust others to be accurate as well.

R *Relevance.* We have seen this trait violated on many occasions. Students have a good claim and they have good evidence, but the evidence has little or nothing to do with the claim. When you gather evidence, you must be certain that it will support your claim. It is, however, unethical only to gather evidence that supports your claim, rejecting all other evidence.

Think about STAR as you set out to research your claims about literature. In fact, in the next two chapters, we explore particular types of evidence that you can use when you make an argument about literature. If your argument *turns in* on the text and is about the text itself, you will use mostly examples from the text, examples that you will surface after a close reading and careful examination. You will interpret these examples in the light of your claim, so, in some ways, you will be the expert with your own opinion in interpretation. However, even when relying on evidence from inside the text, you can use expert opinion from literary scholars. When you are trying to argue a claim about the text's relationship to the world, when you *turn out* from the text, your evidence may include all three types used in literary argument: facts, expert opinion, and examples from the text.

Warrants

Warrants are perhaps the most difficult aspect of argumentation to recognize because they may be deeply embedded in our cultural habits and ways of thinking. Warrants are the general assumptions that link our claim to our support and control how the claim and support are reasoned. Without agreement between writer and readers on an underlying warrant or assumption, readers will not be inclined to accept the claim, no matter how expertly it is reasoned and supported. All warrants are more abstract and general than the claims they support, and a single warrant can often apply to many different arguments. Again, we are thankful to Richard Fulkerson for his information on lines of argument and for the acronym that makes these lines easy to remember: GASCAP (generalization, analogy, sign, cause and effect, authority, and principle.)

G *Generalization.* When we argue, we often believe that if we cite sufficient evidence out of a whole, our readers will in turn believe that our whole is true. Thus, we are generalizing from parts to the whole. However, if readers do not believe that the number is sufficient, they will not be convinced, no matter how persuasive we might be otherwise. The warrant of generalization is a major warrant in literary arguments because examples from the text are important to proving your claim. Your readers will have to believe that your examples generalize into your "truth" statement. They will need to believe that using examples is a solid way to argue your case. Because using examples is expected in literary argument, you seldom have to surface or defend this warrant.

A *Analogy.* Arguing by analogy is arguing by comparison. Your reader must accept that comparisons can be made between X and Y. The more similar the things being compared, the more inclined the reader will be to accept the argument. Literary arguments are often based on this warrant. You could claim that "poet Joy Harjo is similar to poet N. Scott Momaday because they are both Native Americans." (Both of these poets appear in Casebook Five, (Hu)Man/Nature.) However, comparisons work only if the similarities are close in significant ways. For example, although both Harjo and Momaday write about aspects of nature, they do so in very different ways; most obviously, Harjo writes about an eagle and Momaday writes about a bear—two very different animals with very different characteristics used to symbolize very different aspects of the human condition. Readers who know about both poets would not accept that they are similar, even though you provide many examples, because the warrant of analogy does not work in an important way. To use analogy for the main claim, you first might have to argue that the symbolic differences between the two poets are insignificant, an argument the readers are not likely to accept.

S *Sign.* When you argue from sign, you are asking readers to accept the existence of something they can't see on the basis of something they can see. The warrant of sign is very common in literary argument, so you will seldom have to support this warrant. We almost take for granted that certain words stand for other words and that things are not exactly as they appear on the page. We use the warrant of sign in literary arguments when we argue that the visible words in a poem or story point to an invisible reality; symbols are a good example. In the poem "We Real Cool," for example, you could argue that the words "Jazz June" represent youthful spontaneity for life. The verb "jazz" would mean something like "live for the day" (and you would need to research the meaning of this word to verify your definition). June is the month (especially in Chicago where Brooks lived) of growth and youthful flowering before the fullness of summer. You might assert that Jazzing June suggests a youthful exuberance. The signs are the words Jazz and June; to believe the argument that Jazz June represents youthful spontaneity, readers would have to accept your warrant that poetry uses such signs and that the words "Jazz" and "June" represent what you say they do.

C   *Cause and Effect.* Cause and effect is the major warrant when we make a causal claim of fact. Readers must believe that cause and effect is possible in the situation you describe before they will believe your claim. Often they are rightfully cautious of causality when dealing with human motivation. For example, we would have a difficult time proving our previously suggested claim that "Gwendolyn Brooks wrote the poem 'We Real Cool' because she was horrified by the lack of community concern for young black males" because we are arguing one cause to one effect. Readers might accept that her horror was one of the causes, but certainly the warrant of cause and effect would prohibit us from accepting that this single cause led to the single effect of authorship.

A   *Authority.* Readers accept arguments from authority on the basis of the credibility of the persons used as sources. If, for example, you are arguing about hate crimes using the text "The Laramie Project," and you cite as your only authority your neighbor who was harassed at work because he attached a sign on his office door commemorating the 1996 AIDS Memorial Quilt display in Washington D.C., you probably will not meet the warrant of authority. Your neighbor is likely neither an expert in literary studies (unless he is a professor harassed in an English department) nor an expert on hate crimes. Again, your claim and your evidence—perhaps examples from the text—may be sound, but because your authority is questionable, your readers may not believe your argument. **Because authority is one of the major warrants in academic writing, any researched project's credibility depends on the credibility of its sources.**

P   *Principle.* The warrant of principle is usually the primary warrant in a claim of value. For example, excellence is a value; that excellence is preferable to a lesser standard is a principle derived from that value. Warrants of principle hold in literary arguments if you argue that a work is or is not good because it does or does not meet standards of excellence (such as with a book review). Readers must accept your standards (and you may have to argue for your warrant as well as for your claim) before they will accept your claim.

As we said earlier, warrants may be difficult to detect. However, if you keep GASCAP in your head as a reminder, you may be able to identify not only general warrants (warrants of principle, generalization, etc.) but also the specific warrant under examination.

Backing

Backing for warrants is like evidence for claims. Some warrants seem obvious and do not appear to require support; others may need to be backed. If you are using a warrant of analogy, you may need to explain why you chose the two things you compare. If you are using a warrant of generalization, you may need to explain how you gathered your examples and show that they meet STAR. In other words, you will need to back your warrant if it is at all controversial or unclear to your reader. The same acronym applies to backing as to support: STAR.

Refutation

Many students misunderstand refutation, taking one of two positions. First, they think that in any discussion of issues, the writer has to present all sides, to have a "balanced" presentation of the issue. However, in this case, it is hard to discover where the writer stands—what position the writer prefers or is advocating. Second, students sometimes think that any mention of an opposing or alternative position weakens an argument. Instead, a weak argument is strengthened, and a strong argument made stronger, by recognizing and using alternative positions to advance your own. This rhetorical tool is called *refutation.*

Refutation requires that you, the writer, present all sides of the issue for the following reasons:

- **To win over resistant, even hostile, readers who are deeply committed to a position.** Your audience is much more likely to be open to your ideas if you first let them know that you understand and respect their ideas.
- **To concede that the opposing view has some legitimate points in the argument.** In all arguments, your opponent will have legitimate points because no issue is perfectly clear-cut—all good on one side, all bad on the other. (If it were, there would not be an issue, and we wouldn't be arguing about it.) So, in any refutation, it is a good strategy, especially with resistant readers, to concede legitimate opposing positions.
- **To argue against the opposing position.** It is not enough to just acknowledge and describe the opposing position; you have to argue against it. To raise alternative positions is "balanced"; to argue against them is advancing your own position.

If you return to the claim "College students who use the Internet regularly in their academic research are more inclined to plagiarize than are students who do not," you can see people who might not agree with this position on several levels:

- They might not agree that the assertion is true.
- They might not agree that this statement applies only to college students.
- They might not agree that non–Internet users plagiarize less.
- They might not agree that Internet use for research is a valid determining factor.

You could note their objections and then respond, showing, for example, that limiting your claim to college students is valid by citing credible statistical sources. You could show how easy and thus tempting it is to find online and download previously published work. Finally, perhaps through example interviews, you could show that students who seldom use the Internet for research are correspondingly less motivated to search out and copy other people's work. In other words, you would have to design a full-scale argument against your opponent's position.

Refutation can be an effective tool for creating a whole argument as long as the various sides are real and public. For example, if someone else were to make this claim about relating Internet use to plagiarism, you could refute with your own reasons and evidence. You would not be initiating an argument; instead, you would be responding to another's. However, to respond effectively, you would seldom introduce new issues that may be unknown to the opponent just to have something to refute, such as the existence of Web sites that exist solely to collect and sell previously written student work to other students. To do so would give your reader a new set of things to argue about.

PRACTICE 2-D

1. Following is an argument essay on the poem by Gary Soto, "Oranges," written by a student, Lindsay Franklin. You may find this poem in Casebook Two, *Growing Up and Older: His and Hers—Rites of Passage.* Using a set of colored highlight markers (yellow, green, blue, pink, and orange, for instance), indicate in different colors
   - the argument's claim, identifying the type of claim and marking the qualifying statement
   - the "because" clauses or reasons
   - the support for the reasons
   - the refutation
   - the warrants that connect the claim and support

   Share your analysis with one another in small groups or as a whole class. How does your reading and understanding of this essay compare to your classmates'?

"Oranges": A Glimpse at a Boy's Life Truly Lived

Henry Drummond once said, "You will find as you look back upon your life that the moments when you have truly lived are the moments when you have done things in the spirit of love." "Oranges" is a poem written about a young boy's first walk with a girl. Drummond's quote applies to this poem because the author is remembering a moment in his life that he did something "in the spirit of love." Filled with imagery and feeling, this was an important event in the boy's life which he chooses to portray to the world through a poem. Even

(continued)

PRACTICE 2-D *(continued)*

though it was written many years later, it is clearly shown through the poem that the images of what happened are indeed very vivid in the poet's mind. The reader can see very plainly everything that happened and can also feel what must have been going through the boy's mind as the couple was taking their first walk together. Poets commonly use events from their own lives and their lessons learned as the themes of their poems. Sometimes they use painful memories to warn the people who read them to avoid the hurtful event that the poet went through and sometimes they use life-changing, joyful events to share with the readers of their work. Gary Soto chooses the latter to depict this distinctive experience from his childhood. The poem "Oranges" is a reflection of a fond memory from Soto's past that had a profound effect upon his life while simultaneously grasping a great historical significance.

Commonly in literature writers use flashbacks or memories from their childhood to explain a position that they claim to support or to share an important part of their lives. For example, Maya Angelou, a very popular African American writer, explores a theme that she returns to often: her inability to understand the ways of the white people in her hometown, Stamps, Arkansas, and their inability to understand her. In "Finishing School," a chapter from *I Know Why the Caged Bird Sings,* she reminisces about an experience that she had as a young girl working for a woman in her town, Mrs. Cullinan, and the things she learned about being a "proper" woman. Soto's poem looks back to his first walk with a girl when he was twelve years old. There are a few reasons why he may have decided to write about this obviously significant event in his early life. Since Soto writes a lot about growing up as a Mexican American, he probably wrote the poem to give his account of what it was like for him to go out with a girl alone for the first time.

One reason that he decides to write about this may have been that he misses the innocence of such a young relationship. He is nostalgic about the past and his first experience being alone with a girl. Just going for a walk on a date and buying a chocolate for a girl instead of taking her out to dinner and a movie may be the kind of simple existence that he wants now that he is an adult with a wife and family of his own. Another reason why he chooses to relive this memory in a poem may be that this event is a turning point in the lives of all boys. This kind of first walk was certainly an important event in his young life. The girl he walked with could have been someone that he fell in love with, or she even could have been his first love. Most people remember the first person that they fell in love with, especially the earliest times that they spent together. Soto probably wanted to add his own story to the compilation of everyone else's. The girl he took the walk with may have even turned out to be the only love of his life, the woman he married. Though there are some speculations as to why this could have been a turning point, it surely is one because of the fact that he had to work up the courage to ask the girl for a walk, and that is a hard thing for a twelve-year-old boy to do. It is clear that he had been noticing this girl for a while because the poem describes, "Her house, the one whose / Porch light burned yellow / Night and day in any weather" (9–11). This observation implies that he had been interested in this girl's life for quite some time because he has at least glanced at her house during the night and day for several seasons. It probably took him a long time to summon the nerve to talk to her and ask her on a walk and he was surely very proud of himself when he finally did.

The imagery Soto uses within "Oranges" suggests that he fondly recalls this moment. He describes himself and his surroundings with bright, warm images that are associated with happiness rather than dreary colors and feelings of coldness. The image of the girl's face "bright / With rouge" (14–15) and the "Light in her eyes" (28) contribute to the blissful memory etched in his mind of her. The orange is another bright image. When he peels it, the orange "was so bright against the gray of December . . . someone might have thought / I was making a fire in my hands" (52–56). He is also fond of this walk because of the kindness of the woman at the counter in the store who let him help to pay for the chocolate with one of his oranges. She was sympathetic towards the boy for wanting to give the girl a better gift than he could afford to pay for with coins. Her kindness showed when, "The lady's eyes met [his], / And held them, knowing / Very well what it was all / About" (39–42), and she lets him use his orange instead of another nickel. The kindness of the woman helped him to have a good evening with his walking companion.

Although in general the walk was a great experience for the boy, there may have been a painful aspect to it. He may have felt bad that he could not pay for the girl's chocolate because he lacked the money he needed. It may have been an embarrassing part of his early life to not have had much, if any, money at all. This fact was probably a painful part of his young life. The only thing "cold" about the poem is the fact that they were walking during December in the nighttime. The outside world is dark and cold when the boy is by himself, but all of the warm images have to do with the couple themselves. For example, this observation is shown in the beginning of the poem when the boy is walking to greet his companion alone. Here, there is "Frost cracking / Beneath my steps, my breath / Before me, then gone" (5–7). He is cold without her, but they are warm, bright, and happy together in the frigid December night. Another example is apparent when they are walking together outside. It is dark along with "Fog hanging like old / Coats between the trees" (45–46). The scary-looking street does not seem to bother the two of them as they hold hands, absorbed in each other and their walk. The world around them disappears except for the "Someone" (55) watching them confusedly as he saw the boy "making a fire" (56) in his hands.

(continued)

===== **PRACTICE 2-D** *(continued)* =====

The historical setting is a relatively important part in the poem because of the things that are going on around the couple, and the couple's actions are affected by the setting of time and place. Soto is known for writing about his own life. In an interview he says, "A lot of my work seems autobiographical, because I write a lot about growing up as a Mexican American. It's important to me to create and share new stories about my heritage. It's a huge part of my life." Therefore, it can be assumed that this poem is actually based on his actual experience. Soto was born in 1952 so this event probably occurred in 1964, since Soto would have been twelve at this time. In 1964, lives of people were much simpler than the lives of Americans today.

Although some simplicity exists in American homes today, back then people did not have as much to worry about from the media, for example. The fact that life was different is perceptible for several reasons. First of all, the opening line implies that just taking a walk with a girl was as important then as a boy's first date is now. In essence the two "firsts" are equally important events in the lives of young men growing up in different decades. Also, the fact that a piece of chocolate can be bought with only a dime (a significant amount of money for a twelve-year-old in the 1960s) shows that the cost of living was much lower then. It is also worth noticing that the boy, lacking the extra five cents required to buy the chocolate, can pay for it using a nickel and one of the oranges he was carrying in his pocket. This would be a very uncommon happening during the late 20th or 21st centuries.

The setting is important because the time and place that this poem is set in was significant to him and his young life. He took a walk with a girl through the city and could therefore take her to buy something, while if they were in the country they would have probably taken a stroll through fields or the woods and noticed wildlife instead of the fog hanging from the trees planted along the sidewalk. The imagery in the poem would certainly be different. The time setting is also apparent because of the "few cars hissing past." The couple could not have been walking very late at night because of their ages. They were probably walking at about six o'clock at night when the winter darkness has just settled. In the present, around six, there are usually many cars out. People driving around seeing friends after school, returning from or going to work, shopping, and doing many other things. There are definitely more than a "few" cars out at this time of day.

Soto's poem "Oranges" was written to show his readers what it was like for him to take his first walk with a girl and how significant the event had been to him. Through his vivid imagery and his specific details of the innocent experience, he illustrates how important his first stroll with a girl was. The historical setting also adds to the imagery so the reader can obtain a very clear picture of what the couple must have been thinking, and how the two pre-teens related to each other. The endearing story of Soto's is a wonderful account of a principle happening from his young life.

2. Read the poem "Oranges" and make an outline of an argument you might try to make in response. What claim would you make? Identify the type of claim. What reasons and support would you offer? What is the warrant behind your claim? Would it need backing? Share your ideas with your classmates. Notice the many, many different claims that might be generated in response to one text.

Conclusion

This chapter presented in some detail the components of a formal argument. We discussed the structure of argument—claims, claim qualifiers, evidence, warrants, backing, and refutation. We also discussed in detail types of claim, evidence, and warrants, and the conditions under which you would use refutation in your argument. These components can be used when you argue in the public arena or when you write academic arguments about literature. We have tried to be somewhat generic here, using examples from both the public world and the academic world. In the next two chapters, you will learn what is special about making literary arguments, especially about gathering and presenting evidence.

Writing Assignment Suggestions

1. Read (or reread) the poem by Gary Soto, "Oranges," then read (or reread) the student essay "'Oranges': A Glimpse at a Boy's Life Truly Lived" in the section "Refutation" in this chapter. Write a brief response essay in which you explain your initial understanding of the poem and compare and contrast it with Lindsey's understanding. How do you account for these similarities and differences? Then exchange your response essays with a classmate. Read your classmate's essay and write a second response in which you compare and contrast your views.

2. Write a brief (one- or two-page) essay in which you consider the similarities and differences in arguing about social issues in the public world and arguing about literary works in the academic world. What are the benefits of each type of argumentation? What are the drawbacks? Share your essay with your classmates.

Works Cited

Fulkerson, Richard. *Teaching the Argument in Writing.* Urbana: NCTE, 1996.
Merriam-Webster's Collegiate Dictionary, 10 ed. Springfield, MA: 1999.

PART TWO
Reading Strategies
Overview: Why Are You Reading?

◆―――――――◆

Some books are to be tasted, others to be swallowed, and some few to be chewed and digested.

—FRANCIS BACON

There is nothing quite like curling up on a comfy couch with a book. Just throw a blanket over your feet, sip from a cup of your favorite beverage, and settle into a story. It's wonderful! Reading for pleasure is a great escape into limitless worlds of the imagination. Literature allows us to briefly step into someone else's skin and experience anything—live or relive any emotion, be and become anyone at any time or place in history. With fiction or poetry, we can travel to another town, another state, another country, another time in history, or another galaxy far, far away. Reading transports and transforms us. But we do not always read for pleasure—as students (in college or students of life) we read to keep up with what's going on in the world, to learn and—let's face it—to fulfill the requirements of an academic assignment. So it is important to make the distinction between *leisure reading* and *academic reading*—to have a clear understanding of how these experiences are different.

To begin with, the literature we read for pleasure is often (but not always) different from the literature we read for academic assignments. Leisure reading seldom includes poetry or short stories; most often, we choose novels to read in our spare time, and beyond that, we choose a particular kind of story. We typically choose a Tom Clancy rather than an Isaac Asimov, a Mary Higgins Clark rather than an Edgar Allen Poe, or a Danielle Steele rather than a Virginia Wolff.

Now, that does not mean that the literary texts we read as academic assignments are excruciating devices of mental torture. Reading for academic purposes can still be a pleasurable experience. What it does mean is that what we hope to gain from reading for pleasure is different from what we hope to gain when reading for an academic assignment.

For instance, we may read a novel by John Sandford—like *Mortal Prey*—to enjoy the exciting world of Detective Lucas Davenport and to slip safely into the mind of a criminal and become a part of a police investigation into her violent crime spree, but we may read a novel by Anna Quindlen—like *Black and Blue*—to explore the complex psychological workings and emotional consequences of a dysfunctional and violent relationship between a policeman/husband and his wife. **Our purposes for reading are different, so our processes—our behaviors and practices—must also be different.**

READING FOR PLEASURE VERSUS READING FOR AN ACADEMIC ASSIGNMENT

When reading for pleasure, we can get lost in the story. Reading for pleasure does not require a strategy other than a quiet, comfortable place to settle down and fall effortlessly into a great adventure or mystery or romance. When reading for an academic assignment, however, we may not get lost in the story. Most academic assignments require us to read for understanding and for meaning. This is an experience that requires a specific level of *active engagement* from us as readers.

Many, many students complain that they cannot remember the details of a story when they read, or that they read a poem and their mind wanders—so they find themselves reading the same lines and stanzas over and over again. This makes reading a very frustrating and unrewarding experience. These students are having difficulties because they have confused reading for pleasure with reading for an academic assignment; *they are being passive readers.*

> **READING FOR AN ACADEMIC ASSIGNMENT REQUIRES THAT WE READ ACTIVELY RATHER THAN PASSIVELY. WE MUST ACTIVELY ENGAGE IN CRITICAL THINKING AND REFLECTION AS WE READ.**

Academic reading is a *process* that involves first climbing into a story or poem and becoming familiar with that particular literary landscape, then stepping back

- to explore our reaction to that landscape, and
- to explore how that landscape has been influenced by history, culture, and other literary texts.

Active reading allows us to slowly peel back layers of text, response, and context in order to reveal something significant *about* the text, about ourselves, about humanity in general or the world around us. It is a process of discovery, analysis, and reflection. And each part of this process requires strategy. Before beginning an academic reading assignment, it is necessary to understand *why* we are reading and then have a *plan* to achieve that purpose.

Sometimes our academic reading begins (and ends) with the **primary text** (the original piece of fiction or the poem). We read for a *basic understanding* of what is happening within the text, we *explore our personal response* to the text, and we *construct meaning* based on the intersection between what is happening in the text and our response. The strategies we use for reading the primary text are designed to help us achieve these purposes. But literary study does not end within the confines of fiction or poetry. Many times our academic inquiry leads us outside of the primary text and into an exploration of various **secondary texts**—literary criticism or other cultural or historical artifacts and information—in order to situate the text in some larger cultural context as we construct meaning.

The strategies we use when reading primary and secondary texts are similar in many ways but require different levels of engagement. Reading to understand the surface action of a text, for instance, requires a different level of critical thinking than reading to respond requires. Reading to respond requires the use of strategies that reading to analyze a text as a representation of a particular culture does not necessarily require. Yet these various aspects of the reading process are not mutually exclusive—they are all connected—one feeding directly into the next and then giving back to and enriching the part of the process that came before.

In the following chapters, we begin by experimenting with several first-reading strategies—strategies we use when we are reading to understand what is happening in a text. Next, we practice various approaches for reading to understand your response—what you think and feel about what is happening in the text. Then, we look outside of the text and explore and discuss reading to understand literature in a particular context—historical, cultural, and textual. Finally, we explore how all of these strategies, when brought together, create a framework for interpretation so that we may fulfill our ultimate purpose and answer the question; *What is the meaning of this text?*

CHAPTER 3

Reading to Understand the Text

What's Going on Here?

The first time we read any piece of literature, our primary goal is to absorb and comprehend the *who, what, where,* and *when* of the story or poem. This type of reading answers the question, *What is happening?* and describes the surface level of a text. A careful *first reading* helps us to build a framework for later discovery. We do not spend a great deal of time and energy pondering the why or the how of the story or poem the first time we read it; we simply concentrate on *following what is happening—the surface action.*

When reading a story, for instance, we follow the **plot** (what happens as the story begins, progresses through the climax, and ends), we learn about the **characters,** their relationships to one another, and we focus on the **setting**—where and when the story takes place. When reading a poem, we often have to decode in order to follow the surface action—to restate what is happening in the poem in our own words—and through this process, we begin to form questions and make connections that will lead us to the construction of meaning.

> IN ALL OF OUR INITIAL READINGS, WE ARE ACTIVE PARTICIPANTS—ENGAGED
> IN A CONVERSATION WITH THE TEXT WITH PEN IN HAND AND PAPER NEARBY.

There are many useful strategies to help us achieve a surface understanding of a literary text before we move on in our search for a deeper meaning. Some of these strategies are informal and flexible, and some are more formal and structured. Some will work better for one reader, and some will work better for another; some will work better with one genre than another; and some will work fabulously with one assignment and not at all with another assignment. Try them all, experiment, and learn *what works best for you.* Develop an inventory of strategies from which to choose when your purpose is *reading to understand.*

Annotation

Annotation is perhaps the easiest and most commonly used strategy for reading to understand: *as you read, you take notes in the margins of a text.* These notes may be brief summaries of what is happening in the text, commentary (what you think about what is happening, or what you feel), your response to some aspect of the text (a particular word or phrase, a metaphor, a character, or some sort of action that is taking place), or questions about the plot, characters, or setting or a specific word or phrase. When annotating, you may also highlight or underline significant passages in the text.

The secret to successful annotation is to *be selective*. Don't comment on every happening in the text; don't underline every interesting word or phrase. The notes you make during a first reading will serve as references for later exploration and reflection. Because these notes are meant to help you process and recall what is happening in the text, as well as your initial response, they should be brief.

Following is the text to "Say I" by lyricists Scott Stapp and Mark Tremonti. A portion has been annotated as a model. The words, phrases, and images in verse are so concise and compact that we must use a tool—like annotation—for unpacking (almost translating) those images in order to understand the text—even on a surface level.

SAY I

Something has disturbed the dust but is settled now—the dust is remains of humans or humanity *Dust = dry, lifeless remains*	← The dust has finally settled on the field of human clay → *field = nature where humans grow humans are formed, shaped from this clay (which is earth)*
light = knowledge or understanding	← Just enough light has shown through
vision is still unclear *vision = understanding* *understanding is hazy—can only see and understand extremes (night vs. day)*	← To tell the night from the day
We = humans	← We are incomplete and hollow → *unfinished— something is missing on the inside*
the artist who shaped the clay/humans has abandoned them	← For our maker has gone away

← Who is to blame?

looking for some-one to blame—to understand the in-completeness, the abandonment

← We'll surely melt in the rain →

"surely"seems to carry a tone of fear

ironic—rain in a dry climate would normally be life-giv-ing—here it is destructive there is no protection from the rain (goes back to abandon-ment—inability to take care of ourselves)
rain = tears?

← (Say I)

Who is "I"? Is this a command? Or is it an answer to "who is to blame"? or does it imply knowledge? or is it an affirmation?

The stillness is so lifeless with no spirit in your soul
Like children with no vision do exactly what they're told
Being led into the desert
For your strength will surely fade

Who is to blame?
We'll surely melt in the rain

(Say I)
Frantic, faction, focus
The world breathes
And out forms this misconception we call man
But I don't know him
No I don't know him
Because he lies
(Say I)

Visually, it is immediately apparent that a conversation between the reader and the text is taking place through annotation. Our initial marginal notes on "Say I" include comments, questions, personal responses, and associations. This variety of notations may help us not only to understand what is happening in the text but also to com-plete many different types of assignments as we move on to subsequent readings of the text.

PRACTICE 3-A

Complete the annotation for "Say I." In small groups, exchange your work with your classmates. What similarities do you notice in your marginal notations? What differences? Does everyone find this strategy to be helpful? Why, or why not? Share your ideas with one another.

When used conservatively, annotation is an excellent strategy as you begin reading to understand poetry as well as works of fiction. However, you may prefer a more controlled strategy.

Skeleton Outline

Because annotation is often quite messy and therefore hard to make sense of afterwards, you may prefer to use a more organized strategy for reading to understand what is happening in a text. A good strategy is a skeleton outline. *A skeleton outline is a brief, sketchy overview started in the margins of a text and often transferred to outline form.* Normally, the idea of an outline is a turn-off for many students—the traditional I, II, III, a, b, c outline is simply too structured and often recalls the nightmare of term papers on boring topics about which the student had absolutely no interest. A skeleton outline is different from a traditional outline in that it is less formal, and it is used as a reading strategy rather than a tool for planning.

To create a skeleton outline, as you read, paragraph by paragraph (or stanza by stanza or line by line when reading poetry—whichever works for you), make very brief notes in the margins to summarize what is happening in that portion of the text. Limit your notes to a paraphrase of the surface action of a text.

Once you have finished reading a text, make an outline on a separate piece of paper beginning with the first paragraph and the basic ideas covered in that paragraph (or the first stanza or line) and moving through the story or poem to the conclusion. After creating a skeleton outline, you should be able to go back to that text at a later time and know at a glance what happened in each part of the text—beginning, middle, and ending.

As an example, we have modeled the marginal notations of a skeleton outline for a portion of the story "Black Elvis" by Geoffrey Becker. Note that the overall effect is more orderly than annotation.

Black Elvis

At five p.m. precisely, Black Elvis began to get ready. First, he laid out his clothes, the dark suit, the white dress shirt, the two-tone oxfords. In the bathroom, he used a depilatory powder to remove

¶1 *Black Elvis dresses and prepares to go out.*

the stubble from his face, then carefully brushed his teeth and gargled with Lavoris. He applied a light coating of makeup, used a liner to deepen the effect of his eyes. They were big eyes, the color of old ivory, and examining them in the mirror, he had to remind himself once again whose they were.

At the bus stop, his guitar precariously stowed in a clipboard case held together by a bungee cord, he was watched by two shirtless boys on a stoop, drinking sodas.

¶2 Black Elvis takes his guitar to the bus stop.

Their young, dark torsos emerged out of enormous dungarees like shoots sprouting.

"Yo," one of them called. "Let me see that."

Black Elvis stayed where he was, but tightened his grip on the case. The boys stood and walked over to him. The sun hung low in the sky, turning the fronts of the row houses golden red.

He meets two boys. They want to see his guitar, but he doesn't show it to them.

"Are you a Muslim, brother?" asked the smaller of the two. His hair was cornrowed, and one eye peered unnaturally to the side.

¶3 The boys think BE is a Muslim.

Black Elvis shook his head. He wondered how hot it still was. Eighty, at least.

"He's a preacher," said the other one. "Look at him." This boy, though larger, gave the impression of being less sure of himself. His sneakers were untied and looked expensive and new.

¶4 Then they ask if he's a preacher.

"Singing for Jesus, is that right?"

"No," said Black Elvis.

"For who, then?" said the smaller one.

"For an audience, my man. I have a gig." He knew this boy. Sometimes he drew pictures on the sidewalk with colored chalk.

¶5 He tells them he sings for an audience.

"Yeah?" The boy trained his one useful eye on the guitar case, the other apparently examining something three feet to the left. "Go on and play something, then."

¶6 The boys ask him to play.

"I'm a professional. No professional going to play songs at no bus stop."

"When the bus come?"

Black Elvis examined his watch. "Any time now."

"You got time. Play us something."

He refuses. Says a professional won't play at the bus stop.

"Was I talking to this here lamppost? Black Elvis don't play no bus stops."

"Black *what?*" said the bigger of the two boys.

"Elvis."

"Dude is tripping *out.*"

"Yo. Black Elvis. Why don't you help us out with a couple of dollars? Me and my boy here, we need to get some things at the store."

¶7 The boys persist— he continues to refuse—his name slips out. The boys are amused.

¶8 The boys ask him for money.

He considered. He had bus fare and another eight dollars on top of that, which he intended to use for beer at Slab's. In case

¶9 He thinks through how much money he has.

of emergency, there was the ten-dollar bill in his shoe, under the Air-Pillo Insole. He dug into his pocket and pulled out two ones.

"All right, then," he said, and handed them the money.

The smaller one leaned very close as he took it. He was about the same size as Black Elvis, and he smelled strongly of underarm.

"You crazier than shit, ain't you?"

"You take that two dollars," Black Elvis said calmly as the bus pulled in, "go on over to Kroger's, and get yourself some Right Guard."

At Slab's, the smell of grilled meat permeated the walls and the painted windows that advertised ribs, beer, and live music, and extended well out into the parking lot. The dinner rush had

> *The boys call him crazy. He ignores the comment and tells them to take the money and buy deodorant.*

already started, and there was a good-sized line of people waiting to place orders. Larry was working the register, grizzled white stubble standing out against his nut-brown skin, grease flames shooting up from the grill behind him as slabs and half slabs were tossed onto the fire. If hell had a front desk, he looked like he was manning it.

Butch, who ran the blues jam, was at his usual front table near the stage, finishing a plate of ribs, beans, and slaw. "Black Elvis," he said, with enthusiasm. He wiped his mouth with a napkin, then smoothed his goatee. His pink face glistened with a thin layer of sweat. "What is up?"

"Oh, you know, same old, same old. You got me?"

"I got you, man, don't worry." He tapped a legal pad with one thick finger. "Wouldn't be the blues jam without Black Elvis."

"I know that's right."

"You heard about Juanita?"

"No."

"Oh, man. She died last night. In her sleep. Put in her regular shift, just sassing people like she always did, you know. Didn't seem like anything was wrong with her at all. But I guess she had a bad ticker. She was a little overweight."

"She was, at that." He thought about Juanita's huge butt and breasts, how she more waddled than walked. But dead? How could that be?

"Yeah, it's a sad thing," said Butch. "Kind of makes you realize how fragile it all is, for all of us."

He watched as the drummer hauled the house snare drum out from the women's bathroom, where it was stored, up next to the stage. The wall behind the stage was painted to look like Stone Mountain, but instead of Confederate generals, the faces looking down at the crowd were those of B.B. King, Muddy Waters, Robert Johnson, and someone else who Black Elvis could never be quite sure about. Whoever had done the painting wasn't much of an artist.

"Hey, you want a beer?" Butch poured the remainder of the pitcher on the table into what looked like a used glass. "Go on, man, on the house."

Black Elvis picked up a napkin and ran it carefully around the rim of the glass. "Thanks," he said.

He found himself a seat next to a table of rich white folks who had been to some movie and were arguing about whether the actress in it had had her breasts enlarged. It had been a long time since Black Elvis had been to the movies, although he sometimes watched the ones they had running back in the video department of the Kroger's, where he cut meat. They mostly looked the same to him, flickering postage stamps of color. They ought never to have gone to color, he thought. A picture ought to be in black and white. He remembered going to a picture with his father years ago that had pirates in it and Errol Flynn. His father wouldn't buy him popcorn, said it was a waste of money. He must have been about eight. The war was over. There were ships and sword fighting and men with long hair, and suddenly his daddy was pressing a hard-boiled egg into his hand, and saying, "Go on, boy, take it." He ate the egg, shucking it carefully into his hand and placing the shells into the pocket of his shirt, while all around him he smelled the popcorn he really wanted.

He looked up. They'd asked him something, but he could not be sure what.

"Napkins?"

He pushed the dispenser toward them. He'd drifted someplace, it seemed. He took a swallow of beer. He needed something inside him, that was all—some weight to keep him from floating away. He was Black Elvis. He had a show to put on.

He'd been doing the jam now for four years. Everyone knew him. They relied on him. Sometimes he changed his repertoire around a little bit, threw in "Can't Help Falling in Love" or something else unusual—he had a version of "You Were Always on My Mind," but it just never sounded right to him—but for the most part he was a Sun Sessions man. "That's All Right, Mama" for an opener. "Hound Dog." "All Shook Up." "Milkcow Blues Boogie." If there was a band, he'd play with them—he liked that—but it didn't matter; he could do his songs by himself, too. He twisted his lip, stuck out his hip, winked at the ladies. Two years ago, *Creative Loafing* had done an article on Slab's, and his picture appeared next to it, almost as if his face were an addition to the mural, and he kept this taped to the wall next to his bed.

There were moments he'd tucked away in his mind the way people keep photos in their wallets, ones that stood out from the succession of nights of cigarettes and pork-grease smell, of cold beers and loud music. The time he'd explained to a fine young blonde-haired girl, whose boyfriend had come down to show off his rock-and-roll guitar playing, that it was Elvis who had said, "I'd rather see you dead, little girl, than to be with another man," in "Baby, Let's Play House," and not the Beatles, and the way she'd looked at him then, and said, "You mean they *stole* it?" and he smiled, and said, "That's exactly what I mean." Or the time a young white man in a suit gave him a fifty-dollar tip, and said, "You're the best dang thing I've seen in this whole dang town, and I been here one year exactly come Friday."

He should have been the first one called. That was usual. That was the way things went on blues jam night. But that wasn't what happened. Instead, Butch played a few songs to open—"Let the Good Times Roll" and "Messin' with the Kid"—then stepped to the microphone and looked right past Black Elvis.

"We got a real treat here tonight," he said. "Let's all give it up for Mr. Robert Johnson. I'm serious, now, that's his real name. Give him a nice hand."

From somewhere in the back, a person in an old-fashioned-looking suit and fedora worked his way up through the crowded restaurant, holding a black guitar case up high in front of him. Trailing out from the back of the hat was a straight black ponytail. When he reached the stage he opened the case and took out an antique guitar. He turned around and settled into a chair, pulling the boom mike down and into place for him to sing, while Butch arranged another mike for the instrument. Black Elvis just stared.

The man was Chinese.

"Glad to be here," said Robert Johnson. "I only been in Atlanta a week, but I can tell I'm going to like it a lot already." He grinned a big, friendly grin. His voice sounded southern. "Just moved here from Memphis," he said. "First thing I did, I said, 'Man, where am I gonna get me some decent ribs in this town?'" He plucked at the guitar, made a kind of waterfall of notes tumble out of it. "I can tell I'm going to be putting on some weight around here." There was laughter from the crowd.

Black Elvis drank some more beer and listened carefully as Robert Johnson began to play the Delta blues. He was good, this boy. Probably spent years listening to the original recordings, working them out note for note. Either that, or he had a book. Some of those books had it like that, exact translations. But that wasn't important. What was important was on the *inside.* You had to *feel* the music. That just didn't seem likely with a Chinese man, even one that came from Memphis.

He did "Terraplane Blues." He did "Sweet Home Chicago" and "Stones in My Pathway." He played "Love in Vain." Black Elvis felt something dark and opiate creeping through his blood, turning harder and colder as it did so. On the one hand, it should have been him up there, making the crowd love him. But the more he watched, the more he was convinced that he simply could not go on after Robert Johnson. With his pawn shop guitar and clumsy playing, he'd just look like a fool.

He watched Butch's face and saw the enjoyment there. He'd never seen the crowd at Slab's be so quiet or attentive to a performer. Robert Johnson *did* feel the music, even if he was Chinese. It was strange. Black Elvis glanced toward the front door and wondered if there were any way at all he might slip unnoticed through the crowded tables and out.

When Robert Johnson finished his set, people applauded for what seemed like hours. He stood and bowed, antique guitar tucked under one arm. Black Elvis felt he was watching the future, and it was one that did not include him. But that was negative thinking. You couldn't let yourself fall into that. He'd seen it happen to other people his age, the shadows who walked around his neighborhood, vacant-eyed, waiting to die. Esther, who lived in 2C, just below him, who watched television with the volume all the way up and opened the door only once a week for the woman from Catholic Social Services to come deliver her groceries. That woman had stopped up to see Black Elvis, but he'd sent her away. Ain't no Catholic, he'd said. That's not really necessary, she told him. So he told her he carried his own groceries, and got a discount on them, too. And as she was leaving he asked her if she knew what God was, and when she didn't answer, he told her: "The invention of an animal that knows he's going to die."

They were talking to him again, those people at the next table. He shook his head and wondered where he'd gone. His mind was like a bird these days.

"You're up," they told him. "They want you."

He brought his guitar up onto the stage. Robert Johnson had taken a seat with Butch, and they were talking intently about something. Butch had out a datebook and was writing in it. Butch also booked the music for Slab's on the other nights, the ones where the performers got paid. Robert Johnson's Chinese eyes squinted as tight as pistachio nuts when he smiled.

"Black Elvis," someone shouted. He heard laughter.

"I'm going to do something a little different," he said into the microphone. "A good person passed last night. Some of you probably heard about it by now. Juanita—" He struggled to find her last name, then heard himself say "Williams," which he was certain was wrong, but was the only name he could come up with. "Juanita was, you know, family for us here at Slab's, and we loved her. So I'd like to dedicate this song to Juanita. This one for you, baby."

He played a chord and was not surprised when his fourth string snapped like an angry snake striking. Ignoring this, he began to sing.

"Amazing grace, how sweet the sound . . ."

He didn't know if the next chord should be the same, or different, so he just played E again. It wasn't right, but it wasn't that wrong.

"That saved a wretch like me . . ."

He remembered his mother singing this. He could see her on the porch, stroking his sister Mae's head, sitting in the red metal chair with the flaking paint, the smell of chicken cooking in the kitchen flowing out through the patched window screen. His own voice sounded to him like something he was hearing at a great distance.

"I once was lost, but now I'm found . . ."

The people were staring at him. Even Larry had stopped ringing up sales and was watching, the fires continuing to dance behind him.

"Was blind, but now I see."

He lowered his head and hit a few more chords. He felt like he was in church, leading a congregation. He looked up, then nodded somberly and went back to his chair.

"That was beautiful man," said Butch, coming over to him. "Just fucking beautiful."

Robert Johnson offered to buy him a beer.

"All right," said Black Elvis. "Molson's."

"Molson's, it is." He was gone a few minutes, then returned with a pitcher and two glasses. "I like a beer with flavor," he said. "Microbrews and such."

"I like beer that's cold," said Black Elvis. "I like it even better if it's free."

"Hard to argue with that, my man." He filled the glasses. "I'm sorry to hear about your friend."

Black Elvis stared at him.

"Juanita?"

"That's right. Tragedy. They say she had a bad ticker. She *was* a little overweight, now." He thought again about her. She'd had a lot of facial hair, he remembered that. And she used to wear this chef's hat.

"This is a nice place," said Robert Johnson, looking around. The next group was setting up on stage. "Real homey."

"This is the best place for ribs and blues in Atlanta. Don't let no one tell you different." He peered at Robert Johnson's round, white face. "So, you from Memphis, huh?"

"That's right."

"Memphis, China?"

Robert Johnson laughed. "I'm Korean, not Chinese. Well, my parents are. I was born here. But I've always loved black music. I grew up around it, you know."

"What kind of guitar that is you play?"

"Martin. *1924 00-28* Herringbone. I wish I could tell you I found it in an attic or something, but it's not that good a story. I paid a lot for it. But it's got a nice sound, and it fits with the whole Robert Johnson act, you know?" He adjusted his tie. "I've learned that it's not enough to just be good at what you do, you have to have a marketing angle, too."

"Marketing, you say."

"I've got me a gig here already for next weekend."

Black Elvis was quiet for a moment. "You been to Graceland?"

"Graceland! Well, of course I've been to Graceland. Everyone in Memphis has been to Graceland."

"What's it like?"

"What's it like?" He gave a silver ring on his middle finger a half turn. "Tacky. In some ways, it feels like holy ground, but at the same time, you also feel like you're at the amusement park. The Jungle Room is pretty cool, I guess."

"Sun Studios?"

"They have tours, but I've never done one. If you're so interested, you ought to go."

"You think so?"

"Sure. Why not?"

"You got connections there? Like who could get me a gig?"

Robert Johnson considered this. Black Elvis realized that he'd done exactly what he'd wanted not to do, which was to put this person in a position where he had power over him. But he couldn't get it out of his head that there was something about this meeting that was more than chance. He had a feeling Robert Johnson was someone he was *supposed* to meet, if only he could determine why.

"I don't think so. I mean, if you're going to do an Elvis thing, you're probably better off just about anyplace *but* Memphis. Of course, that's just my opinion."

"I'll bet they don't have no black Elvises."

"Are you kidding? Black, Chinese, Irish, Jewish, you name it. You think fat white men in hairpieces have the market cornered on Elvis impersonations? I know a place where they have a dwarf who sings 'Battle Hymn of the Republic' every evening at ten while two strippers give each other a bath, right onstage."

For a moment, he imagined a big stage—an opera house—with hundreds of Elvises of all shapes and colors pushing and shoving each other to get to the front. The thought made him shiver. "Don't matter. I'm an original."

"No doubt. If you don't mind my asking, what made you decide to start doing this?" He looked at Black Elvis with admiration. "I love your hair, incidentally. I mean, if I looked like you, Jesus. I'd be working all the time. You must have that natural blues man look. You could be John Lee Hooker's cousin or something."

"I don't care much for blues music," said Black Elvis. He sniffed. "Never have."

"Really?"

"I like that rock and roll."

"Well, whatever makes you happy." Robert Johnson made a move to get up.

"No, wait," said Black Elvis, suddenly anxious. "Tell me something. Is that what you think? Have I gotten it wrong all this time? Should I be doing something else? You play good, you sing good, you know about marketing. Just tell me, and I'll listen. I don't have that much time left."

Robert Johnson stood up and adjusted his fedora. He looked slightly embarrassed. "I gotta go talk to a young woman over there," he said. "She's been staring at me ever since I got here. I'm sure you understand." He picked up a napkin and held it out. "You got a little nosebleed going."

Black Elvis took the napkin and held it tight against his nose.

When he got home, Juanita was waiting for him in the living room, wearing her chef's hat and a stained serving apron, her wide body taking up half the sofa.

"You late," she said. "Did you have a good time?"

"Good time?" he said. He thought about this. He didn't really go to the blues jam for a good time. He went because it gave him a purpose, a place to be, and because by now it just seemed that if he *didn't* go, all hell might break loose. The sun might not come up in the morning. "I sang you a song," he said.

"That right? What you sing? One of them Elvis songs?"

"Amazing Grace."

"Well, that's nice. You've got blood on your shirt, you know."

"Mmmm-hmmmm." He pulled up a chair and sat opposite her. He had not turned on any lights, and her figure was shadowy and evanescent, like a glimpse of a fish below the surface of a flat stream. "You supposed to be dead, now."

"Supposed to be."

"Bad ticker, huh?"

"Just stopped on me."

"Hurt?"

"Shit yes. For a second it felt like someone hit me in the chest with a sledgehammer. Now, tell me the truth, how come you singing songs for me? You know I don't care for you much at all. I'd have thought the feeling was mutual."

"Let me turn on a light."

"Don't do that. I like it better in the dark. Come on, now, what's with the song?"

Black Elvis closed his eyes for a moment. "There was a man there, a Chinese man. He took my spot."

"And so you go all churchy? You just nothing but a hypocrite. Just a big old faker."

"I don't believe in you," said Black Elvis. "And I'm turning on the light."

"I don't believe in you, either," said Juanita. "Go ahead."

He cut on the light, and she was gone, as he'd suspected she would be. From the street below, he heard shouting and laughter. He went over to the window and pulled back the curtains just far enough to see.

The two boys he'd seen earlier were out in the middle of the street. One had a spray can of paint and was walking slowly back and forth, while the other, the bigger one, watched and occasionally shouted encouragement. At first, he couldn't tell what the image was, but then the lines began to come together and he realized that it was him the boy was painting, Black Elvis, spray-painted twenty feet high down the center of the street. He watched in amazement as the details took shape, his pompadour, the serious eyes, sideburns, pouting lips.

"Believe in me," he said. "Stupid woman."

The nature of your assignment may play a role in determining which strategy you choose at this stage of the reading process, but the genre you are reading may have something to do with your choice of strategy, too. Annotation works equally well for both poetry and fiction, but skeleton outlines are often better suited for fiction.

PRACTICE 3-B

Read the entire text of "Black Elvis" and complete the skeleton outline. Copy your outline onto another sheet of paper, and in small groups, exchange work with your classmates. What similarities do you notice in your outlines? What differences? Does everyone find this strategy to be helpful? Why, or why not? Share your ideas with one another.

The annotation or skeleton outline helps to decode or translate the surface meaning of the text, and through associations, a pattern of ideas begins to emerge (something that will help us later as we construct meaning for the text). That pattern of ideas will help us complete the next step in the reading process, the summary.

Summary

Summary as a reading strategy works best with short stories and fiction, though it can be used with poetry, as well. *A summary is an objective restatement of the main ideas presented in a text.* A good summary is concise and covers only the main ideas (staying clear of any supporting details and examples and evaluative or responsive commentary). The length of a summary depends upon the length of the original text, but most summaries are anywhere from a single line to a paragraph or a full page.

Summary is an excellent tool to test your understanding of a text, and it is best used in conjunction with annotation or the skeleton outline (where—hopefully—the main ideas of a text have already been distilled but not explored or explained). Summary is neat and orderly and becomes a natural part of the writing process, as we often use summary to one extent or another when writing about literary texts.

Here is a summary of "Say I," which we previously annotated. Note that this summary is quite brief—stating only the main ideas covered in the original text—and it is objective (no effort has been made to explore or explain the text at this point).

> *"Say I" contemplates the condition of humans as incompletely formed creations abandoned by their maker and brought to life by the world.*

It is difficult to objectively summarize a poem. Because so much of the text of a poem is coded in symbols and metaphors, all of which are heavy with personal and cultural significance, *denoting* a poem (restating the literal meaning of the text) is difficult without hedging into *connotation* (the associated meaning of the words that make up a lyrical text). Summarizing a short story or a novel is somewhat easier.

An annotation of a short story looks similar to the annotation of a poem (though perhaps not as dense), but the summary of a short story is a bit more detailed than a summary of a poem (still sticking with the main ideas of a story and avoiding any descriptive details or examples).

Here is a summary of the short story we used to model a skeleton outline, Geoffrey Becker's "Black Elvis":

> *Geoffrey Becker's "Black Elvis" tells the story of a typical night in the life of a lonely guitar player in Atlanta. Black Elvis works days in the meat department of Kroger but lives for his weekly performances at Slab's blues jam. It is there that he meets Robert Johnson, a Korean blues guitarist. This chance encounter and the sudden death of a young woman who worked at the club cause Black Elvis to reflect with some desperation on the meaning of his life and the path he has chosen to take.*

Note that the main ideas of the text are covered, but supporting details (descriptions, dialogue, and examples) are not included. Also note that the summary is objective—no personal commentary is offered (for interpretation, analysis, or evaluation).

PRACTICE 3-C

Read the following poem or short story or both. Practice both annotation and creating a skeleton outline. Which strategy works better for you? Why? Do you find one strategy to be more effective for a particular genre?

Practice writing a summary of the poem or short story or both. Remember to be concise and to stick to the main ideas of the text.

Exchange summaries with a partner or in small groups. How are your summaries similar? How are they different? Even if your wording is different, have you conveyed essentially the same information?

How does being actively engaged in the reading process help you to better understand the text?

Why is it important to have a good understanding of what is happening in the text before trying to understand your response to the text?

(continued)

PRACTICE 3-C *(continued)*

"Call It Fear"

BY JOY HARJO

There is this edge where shadows
and bones of some of us walk
                       backwards.
Talk backwards. There is this edge
call it an ocean of fear of the dark. Or
name it with other songs. Under our ribs
our hearts are bloody stars. Shine on
shine on, and horses in their galloping flight
strike the curve of ribs.
                    Heartbeat
and breathe back sharply. Breathe
                           backwards.
There is this edge within me
                I saw it once
an August Sunday morning when the heat hadn't
left this earth. And Goodluck
sat sleeping next to me in the truck.
We had never broken through the edge of the
singing at four a.m.
                  We had only wanted to talk, to hear
any other voice to stay alive with.
                    And there was this edge—
not the drop of sandy rock cliff
bones of volcanic earth into
                Albuquerque.
Not that,
        but a string of shadow horses kicking
and pulling me out of my belly,
           not into the Rio Grande but into the music
barely coming through
                Sunday church singing
from the radio. Battery worn-down but the voices
talking backwards.

"The Welcome Table"

BY ALICE WALKER

For Sister Clara Ward

I'm going to sit at the Welcome table
Shout my troubles over
Walk and talk with Jesus
Tell God how you treat me
One of these days!
—Spiritual

The old woman stood with eyes uplifted in her Sunday-go-to-meeting clothes: high shoes polished about the tops and toes, a long rusty dress adorned with an old corsage, long withered, and the remnants of an elegant silk scarf as head rag stained with grease from the many oily pigtails underneath. Perhaps she had known suffering. There was a dazed and sleepy look in her aged blue-brown eyes. But for those who searched hastily for "reasons" in that old tight face, shut now like an ancient door, there was nothing to be read. And so they gazed nakedly upon their own fear transferred; a fear of the black and the old, a terror of the unknown as well as of the deeply known. Some of those who saw her there on the church step spoke words about her that were hardly fit to be heard, others held their pious peace; and some felt vague stirrings of pity, small and persistent and hazy, as if she were an old collie turned out to die.

She was angular and lean and the color of poor gray Georgia earth, beaten by king cotton and the extreme weather. Her elbows were wrinkled and thick, the skin ashen but durable, like the bark of old pines. On her face centuries were folded into the circles around one eye, while around the other, etched and mapped as if for print, ages more threatened again to live. Some of them there at the church saw the age, the dotage, the missing buttons down the front of her mildewed black dress. Others saw cooks, chauffeurs, maids, mistresses, children denied or smothered in the deferential way she held her cheek to the side, toward the ground. Many of them saw jungle orgies in an evil place, while others were reminded of riotous anarchists looting and raping in the streets. Those who knew the hesitant creeping up on them of the law saw the beginning of the end of the sanctuary of Christian worship, saw the desecration of Holy Church, and saw an invasion of privacy, which they struggled to believe they still kept.

Still she had come down the road toward the big white church alone. Just herself, an old forgetful woman, nearly blind with age. Just her and her eyes

(continued)

PRACTICE 3-C *(continued)*

raised dully to the glittering cross that crowned the sheer silver steeple. She had walked along the road in a stagger from her house a half mile away. Perspiration, cold and clammy, stood on her brow and along the creases by her thin wasted nose. She stopped to calm herself on the wide front steps, not looking about her as they might have expected her to do, but simply standing quite still, except for a slight quivering of her throat and tremors that shook her cotton-stockinged legs.

The reverend of the church stopped her pleasantly as she stepped into the vestibule. Did he say, as they thought he did, kindly, "Auntie, you know this is not your church?" As if one could choose the wrong one. But no one remembers, for they never spoke of it afterward, and she brushed past him anyway, as if she had been brushing past him all her life, except this time she was in a hurry. Inside the church she sat on the very first bench from the back, gazing with concentration at the stained-glass window over her head. It was cold, even inside the church, and she was shivering. Everybody could see. They stared at her as they came in and sat down near the front. It was cold, very cold to them, too; outside the church it was below freezing and not much above inside. But the sight of her, sitting there somehow passionately ignoring them, brought them up short, burning.

The young usher, never having turned anyone out of his church before, but not even considering this job as *that* (after all, she had no right to be there, certainly), went up to her and whispered that she should leave. Did he call her "Grandma," as later he seemed to recall he had? But for those who actually hear such traditional pleasantries and to whom they actually mean something, "Grandma" was not one, for she did not pay him any attention, just muttered, "Go 'way," in a weak sharp *bothered* voice, waving his frozen blond hair and eyes from near her face.

It was the ladies who finally did what to them had to be done. Daring their burly indecisive husbands to throw the old colored woman out they made their point. God, mother, country, earth, church. It involved all that, and they knew it. Leather bagged and shoed, with good calfskin gloves to keep out the cold, they looked with contempt at the bloodless gray arthritic hands of the old woman, clenched loosely, restlessly in her lap. Could their husbands expect them to sit up in church with *that?* No, no, the husbands were quick to answer and even quicker to do their duty.

Under the old woman's arms they placed their hard fists (which afterward smelled of decay and musk—the fermenting scent of onionskins and rotting greens). Under the old woman's arms they raised their fists, flexed their muscular shoulders, and out she flew through the door, back under the cold blue sky. This done, the wives folded their healthy arms across their trim middles and felt at once justified and scornful. But none of them said so, for none of them ever spoke of the incident again. Inside the church it was warmer. They sang, they prayed. The protection and promise of God's impartial love grew more not less desirable as the sermon gathered fury and lashed itself out above their penitent heads.

The old woman stood at the top of the stairs looking about in bewilderment. She had been singing in her head. They had interrupted her. Promptly she began to sing again, though this time a sad song. Suddenly, however, she looked down the long gray highway and saw something interesting and delightful coming. She started to grin, toothlessly, with short giggles of joy, jumping about and slapping her hands on her knees. And soon it became apparent why she was so happy. For coming down the highway at a firm though leisurely pace was Jesus. He was wearing an immaculate white, long dress trimmed in gold around the neck and hem, and a red, a bright red cape. Over his left arm he carried a brilliant blue blanket. He was wearing sandals and a beard and he had long brown hair parted on the right side. His eyes, brown, had wrinkles around them as if he smiled or looked at the sun a lot. She would have known him, recognized him, anywhere. There was a sad but joyful look to his face, like a candle was glowing behind it, and he walked with sure even steps in her direction, as if he were walking on the sea. Except that he was not carrying in his arms a baby sheep, he looked exactly like the picture of him that she had hanging over her bed at home. She had taken it out of a white lady's Bible while she was working for her. She had looked at that picture for more years than she could remember, but never once had she really expected to see him. She squinted her eyes to be sure he wasn't carrying a little sheep in one arm, but he was not. Ecstatically she began to wave her arms for fear he would miss seeing her, for he walked looking straight ahead on the shoulder of the highway, and from time to time looking upward at the sky.

All he said when he got up close to her was "Follow me," and she bounded down to his side with all the bob and speed of one so old. For every one of his long determined steps she made two quick ones. They walked along in deep silence for a long time. Finally she started telling him about how many years she had cooked for them, cleaned for them, nursed them. He looked at her kindly but in silence. She told him indignantly about how they had grabbed her when she was singing in her head and not looking, and how they had tossed her out of his church. A old heifer like me, she said, straightening up next to Jesus, breathing hard. But he smiled down at her and she felt better instantly and time just seemed to fly by. When they passed her house, forlorn and sagging, weatherbeaten and patched, by the side of the road, she did not even notice it, she was so happy to be out walking along the highway with Jesus.

She broke the silence once more to tell Jesus how glad she was that he had come, how she had often looked at his picture hanging on her wall (she hoped

(continued)

PRACTICE 3-C *(continued)*

he didn't know she had stolen it) over her bed, and how she had never expected to see him down here in person. Jesus gave her one of his beautiful smiles and they walked on. She did not know where they were going; someplace wonderful, she suspected. The ground was like clouds under their feet, and she felt she could walk forever without becoming the least bit tired. She even began to sing out loud some of the old spirituals she loved, but she didn't want to annoy Jesus, who looked so thoughtful, so she quieted down. They walked on, looking straight over the treetops into the sky, and the smiles that played over her dry wind-cracked face were like first clean ripples across a stagnant pond. On they walked without stopping.

The people in church never knew what happened to the old woman; they never mentioned her to one another or to anybody else. Most of them heard sometime later that an old colored woman fell dead along the highway. Silly as it seemed, it appeared she had walked herself to death. Many of the black families along the road said they had seen the old lady high-stepping down the highway; sometimes jabbering in a low insistent voice, sometimes singing, sometimes merely gesturing excitedly with her hands. Other times silent and smiling, looking at the sky. She had been alone, they said. Some of them wondered aloud where the old woman had been going so stoutly that it had worn her heart out. They guessed maybe she had relatives across the river, some miles away, but none of them really knew.

Writing Assignment Suggestions

1. Write a response essay to the following quotation of Francis Bacon: *Some books are to be tasted, others to be swallowed, and some few to be chewed and digested.* What does this quotation mean to you? Illustrate your response with examples that are both detailed and descriptive.

2. One of the examples in this chapter, "Say I," is a song lyric read here as if it were a poem. How are poems similar to song lyrics? How are they different? Write a brief essay in which you compare and contrast these two art forms. Use examples from your favorite songs and poems to illustrate.

CHAPTER 4

Exploring Your Response to a Text

What's Happening Within the Reader?

Immediately following our first reading of a text, it is important to note our initial response to the literature—*what is happening within us* as we read and respond to the text. A response is a reaction—we read, *the text acts on us* in a particular way, and *we react*—we think our individual thoughts and experience our own unique feelings about the plot, the characters, and the setting of the story and the images and metaphors in a poem *on the basis of what we bring to the experience of reading.*

Our thoughts and feelings—our responses to the texts we read—ultimately shape and influence our understanding of these texts. By recording our initial reactions, we can look back later as we work to develop an interpretation, and we can proceed with a more informed awareness of what we as readers bring to the search for meaning.

ANOTHER WORD ABOUT ANNOTATION

We introduced annotation in Chapter 3, a brilliant method for carrying on a conversation with a text as you read. We have already practiced annotation when reading to understand what is happening in the short story, novel, or poem— a type of annotation often limited to summarizing the surface action in a text. But annotation, carried a step further, may also include *commentary* (what you think about what is happening or what you feel), *response* to some aspect of the text (a particular word or phrase, a metaphor, a character or action that is taking place), *questioning* aspects of the work as well as connections and associations between aspects of the text and elements of your own life and experience.

When reading to understand *your own reaction* to a text rather than just to understand the text itself, it is important to explore your response, to have a clear picture in your own mind of what you "see" as significant in the poem, short story, or play. We often leave a text with a vague mental picture or generalized feelings (sadness, fear, joy). These impressions are difficult to articulate. In this chapter we introduce you to various reading strategies designed to help you explore your response to reading.

Photo Collage

A good reading strategy you can use to explore your initial impressions is to create a *photo collage—a visual representation of your response to the verbal text.* This is a very simple activity, probably familiar to many of you. Once you have read and annotated a text, make a list (brainstorm or bubble web) of your impressions: What images, actions, or events stand out for you? What do you feel? What is the overall mood created by the text? Then, once you have those responses, gather supplies to create your collage: blank construction paper, typing paper or a piece of cardboard or poster paper, old (already read and okay for destruction) magazines, scissors, and tape or glue. With your list of responses close by for reference, go through the magazines and cut out photos and pictures and words or phrases that remind you of your response. Then, before creating your collage, reread the text. With a fresh impression in mind, arrange and then tape or glue the cut-out words and visuals on a page to form a collage of images that represent your impressions of the text.

Briefly, here's how this strategy works:

Let's return to the poem we discussed in Chapter 1, "We Real Cool" by Gwendolyn Brooks. First, we complete an initial reading of the poem using annotation as a reading strategy to understand the text:

WE REAL COOL	⇒	*Not standard English—"real" cool—the real thing—as well as "very" cool*
The Pool Players. ***Seven at the Golden Shovel.***	⇒	*No names—just "Seven"*
We real cool. We	⇒	*lines are broken with emphasis on "we"—the group*
Left school. We	⇒	*they are their actions—how they're defined*
Lurk late. We	⇒	*everything they are/do is rebellious—"lurk"*
Strike straight. We	⇒	*don't mess with them—they strike back*
Sing sin. We	⇒	*they celebrate sin*
Thin gin. We	⇒	*gin straight up?—they're thin?*
Jazz June. We	⇒	*music—youth—again, celebration*
Die soon.	⇒	*but they celebrate—knowing they will die soon*

Next, we complete a bubble web of our impressions:

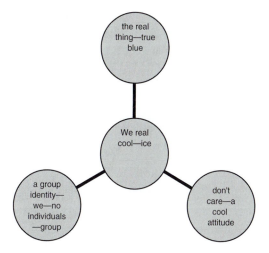

Figure 4.1

Then we look for images to represent the impressions we gathered from the poem. For instance, "real" in the title and first line could mean "authentic." But from the rest of the poem, we do not get the sense that these young men are authentic—they seem to have adopted an attitude and a lifestyle as almost a mask to escape the "real." So we might represent "real" in an ironic way with an image like this:

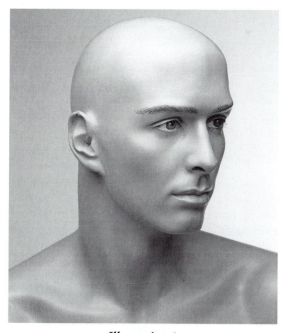

Illustration 1

Or to make more of a statement, this picture of a puppetlike mannequin body with a fea-
tureless head (as faces provide us with a unique and immediate physical identity) might
better illustrate the irony of "real":

Illustration 2

We would continue to gather images that represent our various impressions of the poem,
and then put them together in the form of a collage (see the examples of completed collages in Practice 4-A).

The results of this activity are often surprisingly revealing. Not only can they provide insights for you and others with whom you share your creations, but photo collages
often become works of art in and of themselves.

PRACTICE 4-A

1. Read "Diving Into the Wreck" by Adrienne Rich in Casebook Two,
   Growing Up and Older: His and Hers—Rites of Passage. Then look at the following collage created in response to the poem. To what images from the
   poem is the student responding? Can you determine the student's feelings
   about the poem from the collage?

Illustration 3

2. A student also created a collage in response to Alice Walker's short story "The Welcome Table" presented in Chapter 3. Read this story (if you have not already) and see if you can figure out this student's response to this story. Does the collage reveal anything about the story you did not see when you first read it?

(continued)

PRACTICE 4-A *(continued)*

Illustration 4

3. Read a work in one of the casebooks and create a photo collage in response. Share your collage with your classmates. How are your collages similar? How are they different? After viewing your collage, can your classmates tell what impressions you had of the poem or short story? What do you learn through sharing? Do you gain any insights into the texts your classmates chose to respond to?

Dialogue

One of the most useful reading strategies to encourage a thorough interaction with the text is the *dialogue* or *double-entry journal. A dialogue records quotations from the text and pairs them with the reader's response in the form of a two-column list.* Visually, this technique resembles a question and answer format: the text questions, the reader answers (or visa versa). A dialogue is actually an in-depth interview with a text, a conversation. It is an excellent tool to use when gathering information for support in an essay.

This type of strategy is also particularly useful when reading a secondary (and perhaps difficult) text for research purposes.

To complete a dialogue with a text, draw a vertical line down the center of a piece of paper forming two columns. At the top of the page on the left-hand side, write Quotes from the Text. At the top of the page on the right-hand side, write My Response. When you come across something significant in the text to which you would like to respond, copy the text (word for word) in the left-hand column of your paper. (Be sure to record the page number or paragraph number for later reference.) In the right-hand column, record your response to that quote.

Following is the full text of the poem "Aborted Fetus" by Christopher Davis, followed by a portion of a dialogue/double-entry journal created in response to that poem.

ABORTED FETUS

Now that I'm gone, my pale boy-body near
your ear, my skull-white forehead used

up, out beyond the lamplight, a Cain
trembling on tiptoe, desperate, mute

in shadows, yearning down to hear you
read aloud from your stuffed armchair,

I'd die to point to the art print
lifted from a motel wall on the move

west, hanged again over cold ash, above
the mantle's crucifix and musket—a

dusty redcoat landscape of a
sunset slicing clouds of woolen mutton-fat

open, the silver rains cornered, the gold
blade harrowing in over the wild field,

dubbing the bent spine in a shepherd's
burlap shroud, his wingless shoulders

quivering, his nape bent down, eye turned
from us, his slowing heart trans-

fixed on shock.
Lambs chew his feet.

Quotes from the Text	My Response
"Aborted Fetus" (title)	The title—is this a literally aborted fetus, or is this a metaphor for a child or unfinished being who is abandoned? Not just abandoned—but killed (some part of the being killed or destroyed—made so it cannot grow)? This title sounds so clinical and cold.
Now that I'm gone (line 1)	"I'm"—the speaker is the fetus? So this is not someone who is literally dead—the death is metaphorical somehow?
my pale boy-body near / your ear (line 1/2)	This description—pale seems to indicate unhealthy—and boy-body of course indicates a small person or a child . . . why is the body near someone's ear? Who is the "you" (your) in the poem? Why would someone be listening to a body? Listening for a heartbeat? To see if someone is alive or dead?
out beyond the lamplight, a Cain (line 3)	Cain—as in the biblical Cain of Cain and Abel? What could this intentional allusion mean? I am not very familiar with the story of Cain and Abel. Is it important in order to understand this poem? Was it Cain who killed Abel? If that is the story, then this does seem important and somehow related to the "aborted" fetus the title suggests.

As we mentioned earlier, this strategy works quite well when the ultimate goal is the creation of an essay, and it is necessary to pull specific quotations from a source to be used as evidence in support of an interpretation. For this reason (to avoid the risk of plagiarism), as you create a dialogue, it is important to *quote precisely* from the original text, and it is important to *note the paragraph or page number from which the quote is taken*.

PRACTICE 4-B

Reread "Aborted Fetus" and annotate as you read. Then go back and create a dialogue with the text. Exchange dialogues with a classmate.

Draw a third column beside "My Response" and label it "Peer Reaction." It should look something like this:

Quotes from the Text	My Response	Peer Reaction

As you read through your partner's dialogue, write your own reactions in that column. Note how the dialogue becomes even more like a conversation.

What do you learn from this experience?

Identifying Patterns of Response

The next step in the reading process is to use your photo collage or dialogue exercises to enable you to begin to *identify patterns:*

- particular aspects of the text to which you reacted with feeling
- characters or plot elements to which you were drawn
- similar words or phrases or metaphors that seem connected and that you associated with aspects of your own life and experience.

Identifying patterns of response helps you to locate significant themes within a piece of literature, and those themes and your reactions to them provide a framework as you begin to construct meaning from the text. There are two kinds of patterns you should look for: **patterns of repetition** and **patterns of opposition.**

Look back through what you have written and identify *patterns of repetition*. In the form of a list, group together the similar aspects of the text to which you have responded that seem to repeat in some manner. For example, after an initial reading of "Aborted Fetus," several patterns of repetition emerged for our student Carol. She made lists of the images to which she was drawn:

aborted	*fetus*	*Cain*	*musket*
gone	*boy-body*	*crucifix*	*redcoat*
skull-white	*on tiptoe*	*lambs*	*woolen mutton-fat*
I'd die to	*read aloud*		*shepherd*
shroud			*burlap*
slaying heart			

Carol's biggest list contained images of death, such as *aborted, gone,* and *shroud.* She was also drawn to the childlike images, religious images, and images that recall Colonial New England. At this point, it is unclear just what these various patterns mean within the poem, but recognizing them will serve as a framework for future readings as she moves toward an interpretation.

The second kind of pattern to explore is *patterns of opposition.* Look back over your responses and the text to see if you can determine any oppositions in the text that might create tension. One of the most obvious oppositions in "Aborted Fetus" is the opposition between the apparently dead narrator ("Now that I am gone. . .") and the fact that this dead person is telling a story as if alive. Another opposition is the apparently "live" scene of the person in the armchair and the picture hanging over the mantle.

Once you have identified patterns, before moving on, explore those patterns and your response to them. Why are you drawn to those aspects of the text? Are they important to you on a personal level for any reason? Do you associate those aspects of the story or poem with something significant in your own life? Try writing a free-response as you explore your answers to those questions. Then go back and reread the story or poem with those patterns and your self-exploration in mind.

How do the patterns work within the text as a whole? What overall impression is created? What does that impression mean to you? The answers you formulate to these questions provide you with the beginnings of an interpretation of the text—your next step in the reading process and your first step in the process of writing an argumentative essay.

PRACTICE 4-C

Read the following short story, poem, or both. Practice one of the strategies for *reading to understand what is happening in a text* (annotation or skeleton outline) and then write a summary. Then reread the story or poem (or both) and practice one or more of the strategies for *reading to understand your response to a text* (photo collage or dialogue).

Once you have completed your response, look back through what you have written and identify *patterns of repetition or opposition.* (Have you responded to a particular pattern of images—such as images associated with death or life, warmth or cold? Have you responded to a particular aspect of the plot, a particular character?) Group the similar aspects of the text to which you have responded. Then answer the following questions:

- Why are you drawn to those aspects of the story?
- Are they important to you on a personal level for any reason?
- Do you associate those aspects of the story or poem to something significant in your own life experience?

Try writing a free-response as you explore your answers to those questions. Now go back and reread the story or poem (or both) with those patterns in mind. Answer the following questions:

- How do the patterns work within the text as a whole?
- What overall impression is created?
- What does that impression mean to you?

Heartbeats

BY MELVIN DIXON

Work out. Ten laps.
Chin ups. Look good.

Steam room. Dress warm.
Call home. Fresh air.

Eat right. Rest well.
Sweetheart. Safe sex.

Sore throat. Long flu.
Hard nodes. Beware.

Test blood. Count cells.
Reds thin. Whites low.

Dress warm. Eat well.
Short breath. Fatigue.

Night sweats. Dry cough.
Loose stools. Weight loss.

Get mad. Fight back.
Call home. Rest well.

Don't cry. Take charge.
No sex. Eat right.

Call home. Talk slow.
Chin up. No air.

Arms wide. Nodes hard.
Cough dry. Hold on.

Mouth wide. Drink this.
Breathe in. Breathe out.

No air. Breathe in.
Breathe in. No air.

Black out. White rooms.
Head hot. Feet cold.

No work. Eat right.
CAT scan. Chin up.

(continued)

PRACTICE 4-C *(continued)*

Breathe in. Breathe out.
No air. No air.

Thin blood. Sore lungs.
Mouth dry. Mind gone.

Six months? Three weeks?
Can't eat. No air.

Today? Tonight?
It waits. For me.

Sweet heart. Don't stop.
Breathe in. Breathe out.

Riding the Whip

BY ROBIN HEMLEY

The night before my sister died, a friend of my parents, Natalie Ganzer, took me and her niece to a carnival. I couldn't stand Natalie, but I fell in love with the niece, a girl about fifteen, named Rita. On the ferris wheel Rita grabbed my hand. On any other ride I would have thought she was only frightened and wanted security. But this ferris wheel was so tame and small. There was nothing to be afraid of at fifty feet.

When we got down and the man let us out of the basket, I kept hold of Rita's hand, and she didn't seem to mind.

"Oh, I'm so glad you children are enjoying the evening," said Natalie. "It's so festive. There's nothing like a carnival, is there?"

Normally, I would have minded being called a child, but not tonight. Things were improving. There was nothing to worry about, my mother had told me over the phone earlier that evening. Yes, Julie had done a stupid thing, but only to get attention.

Still, there was something wrong, something that bugged me about that night, where I was, the carnival and its sounds. I was having too much fun and I knew I shouldn't be. Already, I had won a stuffed animal from one of the booths and given it to Rita. And usually I got nauseated on rides, but tonight they just made me laugh. Red neon swirled around on the rides and barkers yelled at us on the fairway. Popguns blew holes in targets, and there were so many people screaming and laughing that I could hardly take it in. I just stood there feeling everyone else's fun moving through me, and I could hardly hear what Rita and Natalie were asking me. "Come on, Jay," shouted Rita. My hand was being tugged. "Let's ride The Whip." The whip. That didn't make any sense to me. A whip wasn't something that you rode. It was something that hurt you, something from movies that came down hard on prisoners' backs and left them scarred.

"You can't ride a whip," I shouted to her over the noise.

She laughed and said, "Why not? Don't be scared. You won't get sick. I promise."

"Aren't you having fun, Jay?" Natalie asked. "Your parents want you to have fun, and I'm sure that's what Julie wants, too."

I didn't answer, though I was having fun. Things seemed brighter and louder than a moment before. I could even hear a girl on the ferris wheel say to someone, "You're cute, did you know that?" One carny in his booth stood out like a detail in a giant painting. He held a bunch of strings in his hand. The strings led to some stuffed animals. "Everyone's a winner," he said.

The carnival was just a painting, a bunch of petals in a bowl, which made me think of Julie. She was an artist and painted still lifes mostly, but she didn't think she was any good. My parents had discouraged her, but I bought a large painting of her once with some paper money I cut from a notebook. A week before the carnival, she came into my room and slashed the painting to bits. "She's not herself," my mother told me. "You know she loves you."

Now we stood at the gates of The Whip. Rita gave her stuffed animal to Natalie, who stood there holding it by the paw as though it were a new ward of hers. The man strapped us into our seat and Rita said to me, "You're so quiet. Aren't you having fun?"

"Sure," I said. "Doesn't it look like it?"

"Your sister's crazy, isn't she?" asked Rita. "I mean, doing what she did."

I knew I shouldn't answer her, that I should step out of the ride and go home.

"She just sees things differently," I said.

"What do you mean?" Rita asked. She was looking at me strangely, as though maybe I saw things differently too. I didn't want to see differently. I didn't want to become like my sister.

"Sure she's crazy," I said. "I don't even care what happens to her."

Then the ride started up and we laughed and screamed. We moved like we weren't people anymore, but changed into electrical currents charging from different sources.

In the middle of the ride something grazed my head. There was a metal bar hanging loose along one of the corners, and each time we whipped around it, the bar touched me. It barely hit me, but going so fast it felt like I was being knocked with a sandbag. It didn't hit anyone else, just me, and I tried several

(continued)

PRACTICE 4-C *(continued)*

times to get out of the way, but I was strapped in, and there was no way to avoid it.

At the end of the ride I was totally punch-drunk and I could barely speak. Rita, who mistook my expression for one of pleasure, led me over to Natalie.

"That was fun," said Rita. "Let's go on The Cat and Mouse now."

My vision was blurry and my legs were wobbling a bit. "I want to go on The Whip again," I said.

Natalie and Rita looked at each other. Natalie reached out toward my head, and I pulled back from her touch. "You're *bleeding,* Jay," she said. Her hand stayed in mid-air, and she looked at me as though she were someone in a gallery trying to get a better perspective on a curious painting.

I broke away from them into the crowd and made my way back to The Whip. After paying the man I found the same seat. I knew which one it was because it was more beat up than the rest, with several gashes in its cushion, as though someone had taken a long knife and scarred it that way on purpose.

Writing Assignment Suggestions

1. Select a poem, a short story, or a play. Read your selection and practice both strategies to help you understand and respond to the text. Then write an unsupported opinion essay in which you explain your understanding of the text and your response.

2. Select a poem, a short story, or a play from one of the casebooks in this text. Read your selection and practice both strategies to help you understand and respond to the text. Then write a response to the text in another genre (for example, if the original text is a short story, write your response in the form of a poem). Be sure to convey your understanding of the text through this new literary form. Share your creations with your classmates. See if you can guess the original text based on your response texts.

CHAPTER 5

Understanding a Text in Context

What Is the Framework for This Text?

Once we have a clear understanding of what is happening in a text and we have explored our response, the next question to ask as we move toward the development of an interpretation of that text is, *What has influenced the creation of this text?* Meaning is created through the intersection of what is happening on a surface level, a reader's response, and the *context in which the literature exists.* We have explored surface descriptions of text and reader response, but what is context? The context of a work of literature is *a framework that supports the creation of the text and our reading and understanding of the text. It is the world **outside of the text** that influences or impacts the literature and ultimately shapes its content and meaning.*

Though we can certainly develop an interpretation based solely on our response to a text, in order to create a rich and informed interpretation, it is necessary to explore and understand not only the aspects of our lives and experiences that shape our personal re-action to a text but the cultural elements that shape the creation of and our understanding of a text. No text exists within a vacuum. Every work of fiction or poetry is influenced in some way by the author and his or her life experience, the culture in which a text exists, and the history of that culture. So in order to truly understand the meaning communicated by a text, we must understand its cultural context.

Depending on the piece of literature and our own backgrounds as readers, students, and citizens within a given culture, we may have a great deal of knowledge about its context, or we may have little or no knowledge at all. So as we read, sometimes we will not have to do much exploration outside of the primary text, and sometimes we will have to kick our research skills into high gear and fill in gaps in our understanding of context. The following are three contextual categories we might explore as we seek a thorough understanding of a text and strategies for filling in the gaps in our knowledge of those categories.

Personal Inventory

We have already spent a great deal of time exploring our response to a text, but sometimes it is necessary to take that exploration to a deeper level and look at the origins of our re-sponses—why we think what we think, why we feel what we feel. What we see as signif-icant in a text and how we respond depend largely on what we as readers bring to that text—from our culture and from our life experiences, including our experiences with, knowledge of, and expectations of other previously read texts.

We read any text in the context of our own unique life experience—our beliefs and values, our personal knowledge related to the subject matter covered by the text, or our lack of knowledge. What we like and dislike about life, people, places—all of this baggage comes along with us as information and assumptions that typically exist on an unconscious level and becomes a kind of personal inventory. When searching for or creating meaning about a text, however, it is necessary to recognize, analyze, and reflect upon this inventory and how it may influence our understanding of the text.

Our personal inventory may be seen as a part of our personal ideology—our system of beliefs—and recognizing this ideology may help to explain how and why a text challenges us and inspires a particular reaction within us.

A good way to identify and explore your personal inventory of beliefs and assumptions is to conduct an interview—with yourself. Look into what aspects of the text challenge or confirm your beliefs and values, ask where your beliefs and values originate, and why or how the text challenges or confirms those beliefs and values. Ask how the beliefs and values expressed by the text are different from or like yours, and how that challenge or confirmation affects your response to the text. The purpose of this interview is to identify and express your understanding of your response to a text. Understanding the origins of your response and articulating and explaining your understanding will help you as you begin to dig deeper into the issues that emerge from the text. This kind of reflection is essential to the formulation of any sound argument.

As an example, let's follow one student's exploration of the short story by Kurt Vonnegut, "Harrison Bergeron," included in Casebook One, *Me, Myself, and I: Exploring Identity.*

Our student completed an initial reading of the story using annotation as her reading strategy. To better focus, she began by completing a small free-response paragraph to summarize her initial thoughts and feelings about the story:

My initial response to Harrison Bergeron was not a positive one. I did not like the story the first time I read it. It made me feel uncomfortable. Everything about the story was troublesome—the idea of a government that devised implements of torture to make people equal by handicapping the gifted or above-average, the dismal, emotionless existence experienced by all of the characters, the complete lack of mental stimulation, the horror of Harrison Bergeron himself and his fleeting attempt to be free. I did not like anything about this world of 2081, because I cannot stand the idea of being that limited, that controlled—unable to think my own thoughts or feel my own feelings. Every aspect of the lives of these characters was controlled and limited—like a prison. I did not want to be a part of that world for a minute.

She then returned to the story and completed a personal inventory in response to the following questions:

Where do these beliefs originate in my life experience? How might they be different from a particular character's experience?

My belief in freedom of will, emotion, and thought stems from being raised in a country that claims to be "the land of the free, the home of the brave." Since childhood, I have been raised to think of America and my life here in these terms. We are "free"—in many ways. My experience has been founded on the principal of freedom. I have free will that I must exercise responsibly. I am free to feel whatever I need to feel—the full range of emotions—and to express my feelings (again, responsibly). I am free to think—and to learn—and to make decisions and to change my mind. I am free to use my thoughts however I feel I should—responsibly. And the government that runs my country is (supposedly) elected by the people, for the people (though this time my candidate did not win the election). In my country and in my experience here, as long as I act responsibly, I am free to be me (a somewhat privileged white woman). I am taught that I can do and be whatever I want (even if that is an "ideal" and not exactly reality). If these ideas do not come from childhood and my home, the media provides many examples of freedom— the media IS an example of freedom. I grew up studying the Constitution, listening to Helen Reddy sing, "I am woman, hear me roar" and reading essays by Gloria Steinem and the poetry of Anne Sexton and the stories of Alice Walker. Every year we celebrate July 4th—Independence Day. Freedom has always been a part of my consciousness. But it was not always a part of my life experience. I have experienced the pain of oppression. So I think I react to this story too because I know how it feels to be oppressed. At a very young age, I became involved with and married an abusive man. I had no freedom—he restricted every part of my life. And he used violence to control me. Eventually, it was very hard to think or feel anything. I spent my days just surviving. I was so conditioned by this abuse that I could not see my experience as abnormal. Somehow, like Harrison Bergeron, I realized I had to break free, and I did. Unlike Harrison, after a great deal of struggle, I found my way to freedom. I won and my oppressor lost.

What aspect of the text challenges or confirms your beliefs and values?

There are so many aspects of this text that challenge my beliefs: The limiting of freedom, free will, emotions, and free thought, the failure of the human spirit to rise above oppression and adversity, a government steeped in power and out of control. I believe in freedom, in the strength of emotions and the power of the human mind. But most of all I believe in the resilience of the human spirit. Oh—and I am afraid of big government. In this story, no one is free—except maybe the Handicapper General and her agents. And none of the characters is capable— for one reason or another— of experiencing real emotions and forming thoughts, developing, and acting on what they think. And the one character to fight back against the oppressive governmental control is shot down and killed—he does not succeed—and as a result of his uprising—NOTH-ING CHANGES. The oppressor wins—and that goes against everything I believe and value. Call me idealistic, but this is what I believe and what I value—that the good guys can win—that we can all be free. Oh—and there's that big, out of control government. Tyrannical oppression at the hands of Diana Moon Glampers.

So there are many aspects of this text that challenge my beliefs, but I think my negative reaction stems from the aspects of the story that confirm my beliefs. I am afraid of the world in this story, because I believe there is some truth there. It is exaggerated, to be sure—but it is a truth nonetheless—a possibility. There are people in this world who deny freedom of will, emotion, and thought to someone every day. There are people who try every day in many ways to stamp out the human spirit. And there are governments at work that oppress people—all over the world. I know that these horrors exist, and I hate them—I am afraid of this possibility for cruelty.

Why does this aspect of the text challenge me?

*The text challenges my belief in freedom because the characters in the text are not free. An oppressive government controls them. And the one man who breaks free is killed just as he has a taste of freedom. The good guys don't win in the world of Harrison Bergeron. But because this text is such an exaggeration, I think Vonnegut really does confirm my beliefs. I do not think he created a world like this in support of oppression—I think he created this world to show us something about **our** world—and about the importance of freedom and small government.*

How does this exploration help me to come to a better understanding of the story and my initial response?

Because the text challenged my beliefs, I was turned off to it at first. I did not want to think about it. It made me feel uncomfortable—and it reminded me of experiences in my past that were painful. My personal experience distanced me from the text.

I'm not sure what made me come back to it and take another look—maybe because there were aspects of this story that I liked? Or because I had read other stories by Vonnegut and loved them—and I wanted to like this one, too? Or maybe I wanted to read it again in the hopes that I would find some, well, HOPE that I had somehow missed the first time around. I don't find any hope in this story—but after reading it, I look around at my world and feel a sense of urgency to protect the freedoms that mean so much to me.

PRACTICE 5-A

Look back at your response to one of the short stories or poems in Chapter 4. Ask yourself:

- Where do these beliefs originate in my life experience?
- How might they be different from a particular character's experience?
- What aspect of the text challenges or confirms my beliefs and values?
- Why does this aspect of the text challenge me?
- How does this exploration help me to come to a better understanding of the story and my initial response?

Author Inventory

Although many authors downplay the influence of their personal experiences on the creation of literature, it is difficult to deny the impact that every moment of our life experience has on what we create in some way. This is not to say that every piece of literature is biographical in nature—it is not. It *is* to say, however, that an artist's background shapes the creation of his or her art just as it shapes any other aspect of life. So it is often useful, as we attempt to understand the meaning of a short story or poem, to have some knowledge of the author's background.

Filling in the gaps of understanding for this or any other inventory of knowledge we discuss in this chapter is all about asking questions and seeking answers. As you study a piece of literature, ask yourself:

- What do you know about the author?
- What do you know about the author's childhood, his family, and where he was raised? Understanding, for instance, that an author grew up in rural South Carolina, the fourth child in a family of twelve, rather than in Southern California, the only child of two wealthy politicians, may be important as we construct meaning. Some knowledge of the level of education achieved by an author, or the type of education, may explain early textual influences that impacted the author's development.
- What were some significant factors in the author's adult life? Did the author stay close to her family as an adult? Did she remain close to home, or did she travel the world and move away from her childhood home?
- What might be important aspects of the author's personal relationships with parents, spouses, or significant others?

In addition to any biographical information we may uncover about an author, it is also interesting and informative to investigate what an author has said about a particular text in interviews and essays. Knowledge of an author's intentions can often shed light on the meaning of a text. For instance, as we discussed in previous chapters, knowing that Gwendolyn Brooks lived in Chicago and wrote "We Real Cool" after encountering a group of young men in a pool hall one day helps us to understand the reality of the poem, the real urgency behind its creation.

Finally, what else has the author written? Where does this particular text fit within the author's own canon of literature? Once you have explored these aspects of the author's inventory, ask yourself how this inventory may relate to the text. How does it explain anything about the text? How does it influence your understanding of the text?

PRACTICE 5-B

Each casebook in this text contains a section titled, "A Closer Look" that explores a related selection of work in greater depth and from several angles. Each one includes a brief biographical sketch of the author, an interview with the author, one or more of the author's works, and a critical essay on that work.

As a class, working in small groups, or working individually, select one of the "A Closer Look" sections from a casebook in this text. Beginning with the brief biographical information provided, do an author search in the library or on the Internet. Look for articles or essays that discuss the author's life. Then, using the reading strategies covered in chapters 3 and 4, read the interview included in the casebook. Write a brief report on the author's background and answer the following questions:

- What do you know about the author?
- What do you know about the author's childhood, his family, and where he was raised?
- What were some significant factors in the author's adult life? Did the author stay close to her family as an adult? Did she remain close to home, or did she travel the world and move away from her childhood home?
- What might be important aspects of the author's personal relationships with parents, spouses, or significant others?
- What has the author said about a particular text in interviews and essays?
- What else has the author written? Where does this particular text fit within the author's own canon of literature?

Finally, with the author's background in mind, read the literary piece included in the "A Closer Look" section. Does your author's inventory help to explain anything about the text? Write a paragraph or two and explore your discoveries and insights. Share your report with the class.

Cultural/Historical Inventory

Just as our families and childhood experiences shape our lives and perspectives, the culture in which we are raised also influences us. Culture is like an extension of family and is such a part of who we are, what we do, and how we think that we do not often recognize its influence, much less step back to critically examine the impact culture has on our lives.

Culture is more than geography, though that is certainly a part of culture; culture is also history—events that shape the world around us. It is the same for literature. Where and when a piece of literature is created has much to do with shaping its meaning. For instance, a story about family life in America will be very different from a story about family life in Asia. A story about family life in America in Alabama will be very different from a story about family life in America in New York. A story about family life in America in Alabama in 1995 will be very different than a story about family life in American in Alabama in 1965. And if the story were written by a Caucasian, it would be very different than a story written by an African American. So place and time in history have an impact on what is told, what is not told, and how it is told.

You can learn much by investigating when and where a piece of literature was created. The publication date is usually included with any text, but discovering where the text was created and looking into what was happening in the world at the time will take a bit of searching. When you read a text, you might want to ask what was going on in the world for the ten or so years before it was written. How is this cultural history reflected in the text? Does this inventory help to explain anything about the text? Does it change your understanding of the text in any way?

PRACTICE 5-C

1. Return to the section "A Closer Look" that you explored in Practice 5-B and research the culture of the literary text:
   - Find out when and where the text was created.
   - What was going on in the world at the time it was created?
   - What important events had transpired within the ten or so years before it was written?

   Then reread the text and ask:
   - How does this cultural history relate to the text?
   - Do you see anything in the text that reflects this culture and history?
   - Does this inventory help to explain anything about the text?
   - Does it change your understanding of the text in any way?

2. Read either the short story or poem that follows. Complete a reading strategy to understand (Chapter 3), then complete a reading strategy to explore your response (Chapter 4). Then take inventory. First explore your personal inventory. Then conduct any necessary research and create an author inventory and a cultural/historical inventory. Now reread the story or poem and ask yourself:
   - What does this mean to you?
   - How do all of the elements you explored come together to create meaning?

   Discuss your findings in small groups or as a whole class. How do your individual experiences influence your understanding of a text?

   (continued)

PRACTICE 5-C *(continued)*

At an Intersection

BY CHRIS DAVIS

From his limousine
the tyrant guessed into the
eyes of a laundry woman
and wept not for what he could not be
but less,
all he'd promised he would be.
The next morning all the blood was washed
out of his bathtub.
Now few remember him.
No one remembers the laundry woman
who crossed the street and went
home to live a little more easily, though in the end the same
upholstery killed her. I remember
finding a skeletal piglet outside a pigpen on a hot day; grass
was knitting the bones into the sun.
Flies singing
everywhere, sparrows in the grass
cool mud-stink from the barn
and the stare of the grunting black boar we called our king.
That's how it feels where our ribs touch.
I will never put my hand over my eyes.
I'll keep loving all I'm given to
love, there's no other revenge.

A Good Man Is Hard to Find

BY FLANNERY O'CONNOR

The Grandmother didn't want to go to Florida. She wanted to visit some of her connections in east Tennessee and she was seizing at every chance to change Bailey's mind. Bailey was the son she lived with, her only boy. He was sitting on the edge of his chair at the table, bent over the orange sports section of the *Journal.* "Now look here, Bailey," she said, "see here, read this," and she stood with one hand on her thin hip and the other rattling the newspaper at his bald head. "Here this fellow that calls himself The Misfit is aloose from the Federal

Pen and headed toward Florida and you read here what it says he did to these people. Just you read it. I wouldn't take my children in any direction with a criminal like that aloose in it. I couldn't answer to my conscience if I did."

Bailey didn't look up from his reading so she wheeled around then and faced the children's mother, a young woman in slacks, whose face was as broad and innocent as a cabbage and was tied around with a green head-kerchief that had two points on the top like rabbit's ears. She was sitting on the sofa, feeding the baby his apricots out of a jar. "The children have been to Florida before," the old lady said. "You all ought to take them somewhere else for a change so they would see different parts of the world and be broad. They never have been to east Tennessee."

The children's mother didn't seem to hear her but the eight-year-old boy, John Wesley, a stocky child with glasses, said, "If you don't want to go to Florida, why dontcha stay at home?" He and the little girl, June Star, were reading the funny papers on the floor.

"She wouldn't stay at home to be queen for a day," June Star said without raising her yellow head.

"Yes and what would you do if this fellow, The Misfit, caught you?" the grandmother asked.

"I'd smack his face," John Wesley said.

"She wouldn't stay at home for a million bucks," June Star said. "Afraid she'd miss something. She has to go everywhere we go."

"All right, Miss," the grandmother said. "Just remember that the next time you want me to curl your hair."

June Star said her hair was naturally curly.

The next morning the grandmother was the first one in the car, ready to go. She had her big black valise that looked like the head of a hippopotamus in one corner, and underneath it she was hiding a basket with Pitty Sing, the cat, in it. She didn't intend for the cat to be left alone in the house for three days because he would miss her too much and she was afraid he might brush against one of the gas burners and accidentally asphyxiate himself. Her son, Bailey, didn't like to arrive at a motel with a cat.

She sat in the middle of the back seat with John Wesley and June Star on either side of her. Bailey and the children's mother and the baby sat in front and they left Atlanta at eight forty-five with the mileage on the car at 55890. The grandmother wrote this down because she thought it would be interesting to say how many miles they had been when they got back. It took them twenty minutes to reach the outskirts of the city.

The old lady settled herself comfortably, removing her white cotton gloves and putting them up with her purse on the shelf in front of the back window.

(continued)

PRACTICE 5-C *(continued)*

The children's mother still had on slacks and still had her head tied up in a green kerchief, but the grandmother had on a navy blue straw sailor hat with a bunch of white violets on the brim and a navy blue dress with a small white dot in the print. Her collars and cuffs were white organdy trimmed with lace and at her neckline she had pinned a purple spray of cloth violets containing a sachet. In case of an accident, anyone seeing her dead on the highway would know at once that she was a lady.

She said she thought it was going to be a good day for driving, neither too hot nor too cold, and she cautioned Bailey that the speed limit was fifty-five miles an hour and that the patrolmen hid themselves behind billboards and small clumps of trees and sped out after you before you had a chance to slow down. She pointed out interesting details of the scenery: Stone Mountain; the blue granite that in some places came up to both sides of the highway; the brilliant red clay banks slightly streaked with purple; and the various crops that made rows of green lace-work on the ground. The trees were full of silver-white sunlight and the meanest of them sparkled. The children were reading comic magazines and their mother had gone back to sleep.

"Let's go through Georgia fast so we won't have to look at it much," John Wesley said.

"If I were a little boy," said the grandmother, "I wouldn't talk about my native state that way. Tennessee has the mountains and Georgia has the hills."

"Tennessee is just a hillbilly dumping ground," John Wesley said, "and Georgia is a lousy state too."

"You said it," June Star said.

"In my time," said the grandmother, folding her thin veined fingers, "children were more respectful of their native states and their parents and everything else. People did right then. Oh look at the cute little pickaninny!" she said and pointed to a Negro child standing in the door of a shack. "Wouldn't that make a picture, now?" she asked and they all turned and looked at the little Negro out of the back window. He waved.

"He didn't have any britches on," June Star said.

"He probably didn't have any," the grandmother explained. "Little niggers in the country don't have things like we do. If I could paint, I'd paint that picture," she said.

The children exchanged comic books.

The grandmother offered to hold the baby and the children's mother passed him over the front seat to her. She set him on her knee and bounced him and told him about the things they were passing. She rolled her eyes and screwed up her mouth and stuck her leathery thin face into his smooth bland one. Occasionally he gave her a faraway smile.

They passed a large cotton field with five or six graves fenced in the middle of it, like a small island. "Look at the graveyard!" the grandmother said, pointing it out. "That was the old family burying ground. That belonged to the plantation."

"Where's the plantation?" John Wesley asked.

"Gone With the Wind," said the grandmother. "Ha. Ha."

When the children finished all the comic books they had brought, they opened the lunch and ate it. The grandmother ate a peanut butter sandwich and an olive and would not let the children throw the box and the paper napkins out the window. When there was nothing else to do they played a game by choosing a cloud and making the other two guess what shape it suggested. John Wesley took one the shape of a cow and June Star guessed a cow and John Wesley said, no, an automobile, and June Star said he didn't play fair, and they began to slap each other over the grandmother.

The grandmother said she would tell them a story if they would keep quiet. When she told a story, she rolled her eyes and waved her head and was very dramatic. She said once when she was a maiden lady she had been courted by a Mr. Edgar Atkins Teagarden from Jasper, Georgia. She said he was a very good-looking man and a gentleman and that he brought her a watermelon every Saturday afternoon with his initials cut in it, E. A. T. Well, one Saturday, she said, Mr. Teagarden brought the watermelon and there was nobody at home and he left it on the front porch and returned in his buggy to Jasper, but she never got the watermelon, she said, because a nigger boy ate it when he saw the initials, E. A. T.! This story tickled John Wesley's funny bone and he giggled and giggled but June Star didn't think it was any good. She said she wouldn't marry a man that just brought her a watermelon on Saturday. The grandmother said she would have done well to marry Mr. Teagarden because he was a gentleman and had bought Coca-Cola stock when it first came out and that he had died only a few years ago, a very wealthy man. They stopped at The Tower for barbecued sandwiches. The Tower was a part stucco and part wood filling station and dance hall set in a clearing outside of Timothy. A fat man named Red Sammy Butts ran it and there were signs stuck here and there on the building and for miles up and down the highway saying, TRY RED SAMMY'S FAMOUS BARBECUE. NONE LIKE FAMOUS RED SAMMY'S! RED SAM! THE FAT BOY WITH THE HAPPY LAUGH. A VETERAN! RED SAMMY'S YOUR MAN!

Red Sammy was lying on the bare ground outside The Tower with his head under a truck while a gray monkey about a foot high, chained to a small chinaberry tree, chattered nearby. The monkey sprang back into the tree and got

(continued)

PRACTICE 5-C *(continued)*

on the highest limb as soon as he saw the children jump out of the car and run toward him.

Inside, The Tower was a long dark room with a counter at one end and tables at the other and dancing space in the middle. They all sat down at a board table next to the nickelodeon and Red Sam's wife, a tall burnt-brown woman with hair and eyes lighter than her skin, came and took their order. The children's mother put a dime in the machine and played "The Tennessee Waltz," and the grandmother said that tune always made her want to dance. She asked Bailey if he would like to dance but he only glared at her. He didn't have a naturally sunny disposition like she did and trips made him nervous. The grandmother's brown eyes were very bright. She swayed her head from side to side and pretended she was dancing in her chair. June Star said play something she could tap to so the children's mother put in another dime and played a fast number and June Star stepped out onto the dance floor and did her tap routine.

"Ain't she cute?" Red Sam's wife said, leaning over the counter. "Would you like to come be my little girl?"

"No I certainly wouldn't," June Star said. "I wouldn't live in a broken-down place like this for a million bucks!" and she ran back to the table.

"Ain't she cute?" the woman repeated, stretching her mouth politely.

"Aren't you ashamed?" hissed the grandmother.

Red Sam came in and told his wife to quit lounging on the counter and hurry up with these people's order. His khaki trousers reached just to his hip bones and his stomach hung over them like a sack of meal swaying under his shirt. He came over and sat down at a table nearby and let out a combination sigh and yodel. "You can't win," he said. "You can't win," and he wiped his sweating red face off with a gray handkerchief. "These days you don't know who to trust," he said. "Ain't that the truth?"

"People are certainly not nice like they used to be," said the grandmother.

"Two fellers come in here last week," Red Sammy said, "driving a Chrysler. It was a old beat-up car but it was a good one and these boys looked all right to me. Said they worked at the mill and you know I let them fellers charge the gas they bought? Now why did I do that?"

"Because you're a good man!" the grandmother said at once.

"Yes'm, I suppose so," Red Sam said as if he were struck with this answer.

His wife brought the orders, carrying the five plates all at once without a tray, two in each hand and one balanced on her arm. "It isn't a soul in this green world of God's that you can trust," she said. "And I don't count nobody out of that, not nobody," she repeated, looking at Red Sammy.

"Did you read about that criminal, The Misfit, that's escaped?" asked the grandmother.

"I wouldn't be a bit surprised if he didn't attack this place right here," said the woman. "If he hears about it being here, I wouldn't be none surprised to see him. If he hears it's two cent in the cash register, I wouldn't be a tall surprised if he ... "

"That'll do," Red Sam said. "Go bring these people their Co'-Colas," and the woman went off to get the rest of the order.

"A good man is hard to find," Red Sammy said. "Everything is getting terrible. I remember the day you could go off and leave your screen door unlatched. Not no more." He and the grandmother discussed better times. The old lady said that in her opinion Europe was entirely to blame for the way things were now. She said the way Europe acted you would think we were made of money and Red Sam said it was no use talking about it, she was exactly right. The children ran outside into the white sunlight and looked at the monkey in the lacy chinaberry tree. He was busy catching fleas on himself and biting each one carefully between his teeth as if it were a delicacy.

They drove off again into the hot afternoon. The grandmother took cat naps and woke up every few minutes with her own snoring. Outside of Toombsboro she woke up and recalled an old plantation that she had visited in this neighborhood once when she was a young lady. She said the house had six white columns across the front and that there was an avenue of oaks leading up to it and two little wooden trellis arbors on either side in front where you sat down with your suitor after a stroll in the garden. She recalled exactly which road to turn off to get to it. She knew that Bailey would not be willing to lose any time looking at an old house, but the more she talked about it, the more she wanted to see it once again and find out if the little twin arbors were still standing. "There was a secret panel in this house," she said craftily, not telling the truth but wishing that she were, "and the story went that all the family silver was hidden in it when Sherman came through but it was never found ... "

"Hey!" John Wesley said. "Let's go see it! We'll find it! We'll poke all the woodwork and find it! Who lives there? Where do you turn off at? Hey Pop, can't we turn off there?"

"We never have seen a house with a secret panel!" June Star shrieked. "Let's go to the house with the secret panel! Hey Pop, can't we go see the house with the secret panel!"

"It's not far from here, I know," the grandmother said. "It wouldn't take over twenty minutes."

Bailey was looking straight ahead. His jaw was as rigid as a horseshoe. "No," he said.

(continued)

PRACTICE 5-C *(continued)*

The children began to yell and scream that they wanted to see the house with the secret panel. John Wesley kicked the back of the front seat and June Star hung over her mother's shoulder and whined desperately into her ear that they never had any fun even on their vacation, that they could never do what THEY wanted to do. The baby began to scream and John Wesley kicked the back of the seat so hard that his father could feel the blows in his kidney.

"All right!" he shouted and drew the car to a stop at the side of the road. "Will you all shut up? Will you all just shut up for one second? If you don't shut up, we won't go anywhere."

"It would be very educational for them," the grandmother murmured.

"All right," Bailey said, "but get this: this is the only time we're going to stop for anything like this. This is the one and only time."

"The dirt road that you have to turn down is about a mile back," the grandmother directed. "I marked it when we passed."

"A dirt road," Bailey groaned.

After they had turned around and were headed toward the dirt road, the grandmother recalled other points about the house, the beautiful glass over the front doorway and the candle-lamp in the hall. John Wesley said that the secret panel was probably in the fireplace.

"You can't go inside this house," Bailey said. "You don't know who lives there."

"While you all talk to the people in front, I'll run around behind and get in a window," John Wesley suggested.

"We'll all stay in the car," his mother said. They turned onto the dirt road and the car raced roughly along in a swirl of pink dust. The grandmother recalled the times when there were no paved roads and thirty miles was a day's journey. The dirt road was hilly and there were sudden washes in it and sharp curves on dangerous embankments. All at once they would be on a hill, looking down over the blue tops of trees for miles around, then the next minute, they would be in a red depression with the dust-coated trees looking down on them.

"This place had better turn up in a minute," Bailey said, "or I'm going to turn around."

The road looked as if no one had traveled on it in months.

"It's not much farther," the grandmother said and just as she said it, a horrible thought came to her. The thought was so embarrassing that she turned red in the face and her eyes dilated and her feet jumped up, upsetting her valise in the corner. The instant the valise moved, the newspaper top she had over the basket under it rose with a snarl and Pitty Sing, the cat, sprang onto Bailey's shoulder.

The children were thrown to the floor and their mother, clutching the baby, was thrown out the door onto the ground; the old lady was thrown into the front seat. The car turned over once and landed right-side-up in a gulch off the side of the road. Bailey remained in the driver's seat with the cat—gray-striped with a broad white face and an orange nose—clinging to his neck like a caterpillar.

As soon as the children saw they could move their arms and legs, they scrambled out of the car, shouting, "We've had an ACCIDENT!" The grandmother was curled up under the dashboard, hoping she was injured so that Bailey's wrath would not come down on her all at once. The horrible thought she had had before the accident was that the house she had remembered so vividly was not in Georgia but in Tennessee.

Bailey removed the cat from his neck with both hands and flung it out the window against the side of a pine tree. Then he got out of the car and started looking for the children's mother. She was sitting against the side of the red gutted ditch, holding the screaming baby, but she only had a cut down her face and a broken shoulder. "We've had an ACCIDENT!" the children screamed in a frenzy of delight.

"But nobody's killed," June Star said with disappointment as the grandmother limped out of the car, her hat still pinned to her head but the broken front brim standing up at a jaunty angle and the violet spray hanging off the side. They all sat down in the ditch, except the children, to recover from the shock. They were all shaking.

"Maybe a car will come along," said the children's mother hoarsely.

"I believe I have injured an organ," said the grandmother, pressing her side, but no one answered her. Bailey's teeth were clattering. He had on a yellow sport shirt with bright blue parrots designed in it and his face was as yellow as the shirt. The grandmother decided that she would not mention that the house was in Tennessee.

The road was about ten feet above and they could see only the tops of the trees on the other side of it. Behind the ditch they were sitting in there were more woods, tall and dark and deep. In a few minutes they saw a car some distance away on top of a hill, coming slowly as if the occupants were watching them. The grandmother stood up and waved both arms dramatically to attract their attention. The car continued to come on slowly, disappeared around a bend and appeared again, moving even slower, on top of the hill they had gone over. It was a big black battered hearse-like automobile. There were three men in it.

It came to a stop just over them and for some minutes, the driver looked down with a steady expressionless gaze to where they were sitting, and didn't speak. Then he turned his head and muttered something to the other two and they got out. One was a fat boy in black trousers and a red sweat shirt with a silver stallion embossed on the front of it. He moved around on the right side of

(continued)

them and stood staring, his mouth partly open in a kind of loose grin. The other had on khaki pants and a blue striped coat and a gray hat pulled down very low, hiding most of his face. He came around slowly on the left side. Neither spoke.

The driver got out of the car and stood by the side of it, looking down at them. He was an older man than the other two. His hair was just beginning to gray and he wore silver-rimmed spectacles that gave him a scholarly look. He had a long creased face and didn't have on any shirt or undershirt. He had on blue jeans that were too tight for him and was holding a black hat and a gun. The two boys also had guns.

"We've had an ACCIDENT!" the children screamed.

The grandmother had the peculiar feeling that the bespectacled man was someone she knew. His face was as familiar to her as if she had known him all her life but she could not recall who he was. He moved away from the car and began to come down the embankment, placing his feet carefully so that he wouldn't slip. He had on tan and white shoes and no socks, and his ankles were red and thin. "Good afternoon," he said. "I see you all had you a little spill."

"We turned over twice!" said the grandmother.

"Once," he corrected. "We seen it happen. Try their car and see will it run, Hiram," he said quietly to the boy with the gray hat.

"What you got that gun for?" John Wesley asked. "Whatcha gonna do with that gun?"

"Lady," the man said to the children's mother, "would you mind calling them children to sit down by you? Children make me nervous. I want all you all to sit down right together there where you're at."

"What are you telling US what to do for?" June Star asked.

Behind them the line of woods gaped like a dark open mouth. "Come here," said their mother.

"Look here now," Bailey began suddenly, "we're in a predicament! We're in ... "

The grandmother shrieked. She scrambled to her feet and stood staring. "You're The Misfit!" she said. "I recognized you at once!"

"Yes'm," the man said, smiling slightly as if he were pleased in spite of himself to be known, "but it would have been better for all of you, lady, if you hadn't of reckernized me."

Bailey turned his head sharply and said something to his mother that shocked even the children. The old lady began to cry and The Misfit reddened.

"Lady," he said, "don't you get upset. Sometimes a man says things he don't mean. I don't reckon he meant to talk to you thataway."

"You wouldn't shoot a lady, would you?" the grandmother said and removed a clean handkerchief from her cuff and began to slap at her eyes with it.

The Misfit pointed the toe of his shoe into the ground and made a little hole and then covered it up again. "I would hate to have to," he said.

"Listen," the grandmother almost screamed, "I know you're a good man. You don't look a bit like you have common blood. I know you must come from nice people!"

"Yes mam," he said, "finest people in the world." When he smiled he showed a row of strong white teeth. "God never made a finer woman than my mother and my daddy's heart was pure gold," he said. The boy with the red sweat shirt had come around behind them and was standing with his gun at his hip. The Misfit squatted down on the ground. "Watch them children, Bobby Lee," he said. "You know they make me nervous." He looked at the six of them huddled together in front of him and he seemed to be embarrassed as if he couldn't think of anything to say. "Ain't a cloud in the sky," he remarked, looking up at it. "Don't see no sun but don't see no cloud neither."

"Yes, it's a beautiful day," said the grandmother. "Listen," she said, "you shouldn't call yourself The Misfit because I know you're a good man at heart. I can just look at you and tell."

"Hush!" Bailey yelled. "Hush! Everybody shut up and let me handle this!" He was squatting in the position of a runner about to sprint forward but he didn't move.

"I prechate that, lady," The Misfit said and drew a little circle in the ground with the butt of his gun.

"It'll take a half a hour to fix this here car," Hiram called, looking over the raised hood of it.

"Well, first you and Bobby Lee get him and that little boy to step over yonder with you," The Misfit said, pointing to Bailey and John Wesley. "The boys want to ast you something," he said to Bailey. "Would you mind stepping back in them woods there with them?"

"Listen," Bailey began, "we're in a terrible predicament! Nobody realizes what this is," and his voice cracked. His eyes were as blue and intense as the parrots in his shirt and he remained perfectly still.

The grandmother reached up to adjust her hat brim as if she were going to the woods with him but it came off in her hand. She stood staring at it and after a second she let it fall on the ground. Hiram pulled Bailey up by the arm as if he were assisting an old man. John Wesley caught hold of his father's hand and Bobby Lee followed. They went off toward the woods and just as they reached the dark edge, Bailey turned and supporting himself against a gray naked pine trunk, he shouted, "I'll be back in a minute, Mamma, wait on me!"

"Come back this instant!" his mother shrilled but they all disappeared into the woods.

(continued)

PRACTICE 5-C *(continued)*

"Bailey Boy!" the grandmother called in a tragic voice but she found she was looking at The Misfit squatting on the ground in front of her. "I just know you're a good man," she said desperately. "You're not a bit common!"

"Nome, I ain't a good man," The Misfit said after a second as if he had considered her statement carefully, "but I ain't the worst in the world neither. My daddy said I was a different breed of dog from my brothers and sisters. 'You know,' Daddy said, 'it's some that can live their whole life out without asking about it and it's others has to know why it is, and this boy is one of the latters. He's going to be into everything!'" He put on his black hat and looked up suddenly and then away deep into the woods as if he were embarrassed again. "I'm sorry I don't have on a shirt before you ladies," he said, hunching his shoulders slightly. "We buried our clothes that we had on when we escaped and we're just making do until we can get better. We borrowed these from some folks we met," he explained.

"That's perfectly all right," the grandmother said. "Maybe Bailey has an extra shirt in his suitcase."

"I'll look and see terrectly," The Misfit said.

"Where are they taking him?" the children's mother screamed.

"Daddy was a card himself," The Misfit said. "You couldn't put anything over on him. He never got in trouble with the Authorities though. Just had the knack of handling them."

"You could be honest too if you'd only try," said the grandmother. "Think how wonderful it would be to settle down and live a comfortable life and not have to think about somebody chasing you all the time."

The Misfit kept scratching in the ground with the butt of his gun as if he were thinking about it. "Yes'm, somebody is always after you," he murmured.

The grandmother noticed how thin his shoulder blades were just behind his hat because she was standing up looking down on him. "Do you ever pray?" she asked.

He shook his head. All she saw was the black hat wiggle between his shoulder blades. "Nome," he said.

There was a pistol shot from the woods, followed closely by another. Then silence. The old lady's head jerked around. She could hear the wind move through the tree tops like a long satisfied insuck of breath. "Bailey Boy!" she called.

"I was a gospel singer for a while," The Misfit said. "I been most everything. Been in the arm service, both land and sea, at home and abroad, been twict married, been an undertaker, been with the railroads, plowed Mother Earth, been in a tornado, seen a man burnt alive oncet," and he looked up at the children's mother and the little girl who were sitting close together, their faces white and their eyes glassy; "I even seen a woman flogged," he said.

"Pray, pray," the grandmother began, "pray, pray ..."

"I never was a bad boy that I remember of," The Misfit said in an almost dreamy voice, "but somewheres along the line I done something wrong and got sent to the penitentiary. I was buried alive," and he looked up and held her attention to him by a steady stare.

"That's when you should have started to pray," she said. "What did you do to get sent to the penitentiary that first time?"

"Turn to the right, it was a wall," The Misfit said, looking up again at the cloudless sky. "Turn to the left, it was a wall. Look up it was a ceiling, look down it was a floor. I forget what I done, lady. I set there and set there, trying to remember what it was I done and I ain't recalled it to this day. Oncet in a while, I would think it was coming to me, but it never come."

"Maybe they put you in by mistake," the old lady said vaguely.

"Nome," he said. "It wasn't no mistake. They had the papers on me."

"You must have stolen something," she said.

The Misfit sneered slightly. "Nobody had nothing I wanted," he said. "It was a head-doctor at the penitentiary said what I had done was kill my daddy but I known that for a lie. My daddy died in nineteen ought nineteen of the epidemic flu and I never had a thing to do with it. He was buried in the Mount Hopewell Baptist churchyard and you can go there and see for yourself."

"If you would pray," the old lady said, "Jesus would help you."

"That's right," The Misfit said.

"Well then, why don't you pray?" she asked trembling with delight suddenly.

"I don't want no hep," he said. "I'm doing all right by myself."

Bobby Lee and Hiram came ambling back from the woods. Bobby Lee was dragging a yellow shirt with bright blue parrots in it.

"Thow me that shirt, Bobby Lee," The Misfit said. The shirt came flying at him and landed on his shoulder and he put it on. The grandmother couldn't name what the shirt reminded her of. "No, lady," The Misfit said while he was buttoning it up, "I found out the crime don't matter. You can do one thing or you can do another, kill a man or take a tire off his car, because sooner or later you're going to forget what it was you done and just be punished for it."

The children's mother had begun to make heaving noises as if she couldn't get her breath. "Lady," he asked, "would you and that little girl like to step off yonder with Bobby Lee and Hiram and join your husband?"

"Yes, thank you," the mother said faintly. Her left arm dangled helplessly and she was holding the baby, who had gone to sleep, in the other. "Hep that lady up, Hiram," The Misfit said as she struggled to climb out of the ditch, "and Bobby Lee, you hold onto that little girl's hand."

(continued)

PRACTICE 5-C *(continued)*

"I don't want to hold hands with him," June Star said. "He reminds me of a pig." The fat boy blushed and laughed and caught her by the arm and pulled her off into the woods after Hiram and her mother.

Alone with The Misfit, the grandmother found that she had lost her voice. There was not a cloud in the sky nor any sun. There was nothing around her but woods. She wanted to tell him that he must pray. She opened and closed her mouth several times before anything came out. Finally she found herself saying, "Jesus. Jesus," meaning, Jesus will help you, but the way she was saying it, it sounded as if she might be cursing.

"Yes'm," The Misfit said as if he agreed. "Jesus thown everything off balance. It was the same case with Him as with me except He hadn't committed any crime and they could prove I had committed one because they had the papers on me. Of course," he said, "they never shown me my papers. That's why I sign myself now. I said long ago, you get you a signature and sign everything you do and keep a copy of it. Then you'll know what you done and you can hold up the crime to the punishment and see do they match and in the end you'll have something to prove you ain't been treated right. I call myself The Misfit," he said, "because I can't make what all I done wrong fit what all I gone through in punishment."

There was a piercing scream from the woods, followed closely by a pistol report. "Does it seem right to you, lady, that one is punished a heap and another ain't punished at all?"

"Jesus!" the old lady cried. "You've got good blood! I know you wouldn't shoot a lady! I know you come from nice people! Pray! Jesus, you ought not to shoot a lady. I'll give you all the money I've got!"

"Lady," The Misfit said, looking beyond her far into the woods, "there never was a body that give the undertaker a tip."

There were two more pistol reports and the grandmother raised her head like a parched old turkey hen crying for water and called, "Bailey Boy, Bailey Boy!" as if her heart would break.

"Jesus was the only One that ever raised the dead," The Misfit continued, "and He shouldn't have done it. He thown everything off balance. If He did what He said, then it's nothing for you to do but thow away everything and follow Him, and if He didn't, then it's nothing for you to do but enjoy the few minutes you got left the best way you can by killing somebody or burning down his house or doing some other meanness to him. No pleasure but meanness," he said and his voice had become almost a snarl.

"Maybe He didn't raise the dead," the old lady mumbled, not knowing what she was saying and feeling so dizzy that she sank down in the ditch with her legs twisted under her.

"I wasn't there so I can't say He didn't," The Misfit said. "I wisht I had of been there," he said, hitting the ground with his fist. "It ain't right I wasn't there because if I had of been there I would of known. Listen lady," he said in a high voice, "if I had of been there I would of known and I wouldn't be like I am now." His voice seemed about to crack and the grandmother's head cleared for an instant. She saw the man's face twisted close to her own as if he were going to cry and she murmured, "Why you're one of my babies. You're one of my own children!" She reached out and touched him on the shoulder. The Misfit sprang back as if a snake had bitten him and shot her three times through the chest. Then he put his gun down on the ground and took off his glasses and began to clean them.

Hiram and Bobby Lee returned from the woods and stood over the ditch, looking down at the grandmother who half sat and half lay in a puddle of blood with her legs crossed under her like a child's and her face smiling up at the cloudless sky.

Without his glasses, The Misfit's eyes were red-rimmed and pale and defenseless-looking. "Take her off and thow her where you thown the others," he said, picking up the cat that was rubbing itself against his leg.

"She was a talker, wasn't she?" Bobby Lee said, sliding down the ditch with a yodel.

"She would of been a good woman," The Misfit said, "if it had been somebody there to shoot her every minute of her life."

"Some fun!" Bobby Lee said.

"Shut up, Bobby Lee" The Misfit said. "It's no real pleasure in life."

Writing Assignment Suggestions

1. After completing an inventory of a poem or short story, write a response essay in which you explain your expectations and your response and show how the inventory resulted in some sort of discovery for you.

2. Write an essay in which you explain how one type of inventory reveals the most significant information about a text. Explain what is discovered through the particular inventory and how it helps to explain something significant about the text.

PART THREE
Tools and Techniques for Argument

CHAPTER 6

Contextualizing Claims and Evidence: Turning In

Making and Supporting Claims About Literature

As we explored in previous chapters, after we read and analyze a text, we formulate a claim to explain the meaning of an aspect of that text. We make an interpretation. Then we work to support that interpretation by gathering appropriate evidence. There are two ways to gather evidence to support a claim about literature—one is to *turn in* and examine the components that make up the short story, novel, poem, play, or essay (for example, imagery, figurative language, and various meanings of words and phrases). Another is to *turn out* and seek evidence from an external source or sources as support (facts, examples, expert opinion, statistics). In this chapter, we discuss how to turn in to a literary text to make and support a claim about that text.

The type of claim we make (claim of fact, value, or policy) does not determine the kind of evidence we will use; the evidence is dictated by the *content* of the claim—what we want to "prove" about the text. If we want to prove something about the components of the text itself and how those components work to create meaning, then our evidence will come from within the text. If we want to prove something about the text's relationship to culture, human behavior, history, or society, then our evidence will come from outside sources. As usual, we must consider both the assumptions behind our claim and the reader's needs when gathering and presenting evidence.

When we gather and present evidence to support any claim, we seek information from appropriate and credible sources—just the right example from the text or information from experts in a given field of study, for example. To determine whether evidence should come from inside or outside the text, we have to identify the type of evidence necessary to support the claim we wish to advance. To do this, we have to look closely at what we are trying to prove and identify the scholarly focus most closely related to the claim.

Although the lines between claims that turn in to the text for support and claims that turn out from the text for support sometimes overlap, just as fields of academic study sometimes overlap, we can think of each focus as a lens through which to view the text, a particular way of making meaning, of understanding and explaining various aspects of literature. Such lenses are known as *literary theories.*

Literary theories are ideas regarding the nature and meaning of literature, its functions, and the relationship of a text to its author, to its audience, to language, to society, to culture, and to history. Literary theories are not judgments or interpretations

119

on their own; they are *frameworks* for judgment and interpretation, tools for us to use as we explore literature for meaning.

Literary theories become especially useful *when used to contextualize arguments and when applied to the activity of research.* In creating arguments about literature, literary theories help to clarify the focus of a claim and to refine and direct research for supporting information. Looking through the lens of a particular literary theory, our vision becomes narrow and focused, our purpose clarified, and our attention drawn to a specific field of inquiry as we gather evidence and develop an argument.

There are many different theories used to study literature, each one detailed and complex enough to be the sole focus of an entire chapter (or a book or series of books). But for our purposes, we need only a working understanding of these theories—and not even all of these theories, just a few of the most common and generally useful. In this chapter, we introduce you to tools from two major literary theories, **deconstruction** and **new criticism.**

Deconstruction theory presumes that within a single work are several, often contradictory, stories that often cannot be resolved, and that in reading any work of literature the reader encounters gaps in understanding, some of which can be filled by using a technique called *close reading.* For instance, in "The Holocaust Party," there are at least two opposing stories. The obvious ones are the opposing stories of Mrs. Isabel and Amy's father, who have two very different versions of the war. However, there is also Joel's story, a story quite different from Amy's. When we read closely, we look for patterns of repetition and patterns of opposition in a text (you may recall that we briefly explored these strategies in Chapter 4).

Our second theoretical lens, new criticism theory, also expects close reading; however, a new critical reading analyzes imagery and symbolism, figurative language (such as metaphor and simile), denotation and connotation, and form in a text to help reveal its meaning. In many ways, these two theories overlap, especially in their mutual concern for the careful and close reading of a text.

Tools for Turning In: Deconstruction

The different genres of literature often appear complicated and difficult to analyze. For example, many people don't "get" poetry. They think that it is mysterious and that they need some special powers to interpret it. In our chapters on the reading and writing processes, we give you some tools to help you read literary texts and write arguments. In those chapters, our goals are to help you develop these abilities and especially to help you relate the text *to your own experiences.* The techniques presented in this chapter will help you gather evidence from the text for your argument; you will not consciously and necessarily be trying to make a connection between the text and yourself as a reader. Although, of course, you are always present as you read, for our purposes here, your personal response takes the proverbial back seat to the text.

Once you have read and responded to a poem, short story, or other text, to come to a fuller understanding of the text, you have to look at how its various elements are connected and how they work together. These smaller units of a text will point to the bigger units of **theme** (the meaning or dominant idea that emerges from a work of literature).

A theme provides a unifying point around which the plot, characters, setting, point of view, symbols, and other elements of a text are organized. It is important not to mistake the theme for the subject of the work; the theme refers to an abstract concept that is developed through the images, characterization, and action of the text. You can focus on these smaller units either unsystematically or systematically. There's not much to learn in an unsystematic analysis: you notice what pops out at you. Systematic analysis of literary texts, in contrast, can reap rewards of insight and understanding.

Our first set of techniques guides you in an exploration of patterns of repetition and opposition in a text. Although sometimes authors do not use opposition and repetition, most do, and here we begin by looking at the work at this very basic level. Our example text is the poem "Ethics" by Linda Pastan:

ETHICS

In ethics class so many years ago	1
our teacher asked this question every fall:	2
if there were a fire in a museum	3
which would you save, a Rembrandt painting	4
or an old woman who hadn't many	5
years left anyhow? Restless on hard chairs	6
caring little for pictures or old age	7
we'd opt one year for life, the next for art	8
and always half-heartedly. Sometimes	9
the woman borrowed my grandmother's face	10
leaving her usual kitchen to wander	11
some drafty, half-imagined museum.	12
One year, feeling clever, I replied	13
why not let the woman decide herself?	14
Linda, the teacher would report, eschews	15
the burdens of responsibility.	16
This fall in a real museum I stand	17
before a real Rembrandt, old woman,	18
or nearly so, myself. The colors	19
within this frame are darker than autumn,	20
darker even than winter—the browns of earth,	21
though earth's most radiant elements burn	22
through the canvas. I know now that woman	23
and painting and season are almost one	24
and all beyond saving by children.	25

REPETITION

When we analyze patterns of repetition, we examine the text or parts of the text for words or phrases that repeat—sometimes with variation (we might find within a poem many words associated with, for instance, darkness—*night, black, starless, stormy,* and so on. These are different words, but they all imply the same thing, so we say the image of darkness is repeated with variation). Writers repeat images, metaphors, and words for a purpose: not just because they could not think of a better word, but because they want the reader to notice something—to think of it as important to what they want us to learn from the text. Words that repeat shout at us: *Pay attention to me, I'm important.*

In "Ethics," Pastan has set up several potentially significant repetitions:

- year/years (lines 1, 6, 8, 13)
- fall/autumn/season (lines 2, 17, 20, 24)
- real (lines 17, 18)
- woman/grandmother/old woman (lines 5, 10, 14, 18, 23)
- dark/darker/winter (lines 20, 21)
- earth (lines 21, 22)
- fire/radiant/burn (lines 3, 22)
- save/saving (lines 4, 25)

Some of these repetitions are pretty self-evident and don't seem to require too much analysis: on one level, the poem is clearly about an old woman who is part of a question posed by a teacher (line 5) and an old woman who might very well be the poet (lines 17–18). This repetition moves the poem from the past to the present, as do many of the other ideas in the poem. The same might be true for the word *year* that repeats itself in four lines. However, what about the variant repetition of the words *fire, radiant,* and *burn?* Does the meaning in the word *fire* repeat itself in *burn,* or is there a change from one use to the other that, if we analyzed it, might give us something new to think about? How is this change affected or reflected by the word *radiant?* Let's consider these questions.

The word *fire* (line 3) is a noun and may be taken literally: a hypothetical fire in a hypothetical museum in a real question posed by a real teacher (within the world of the poem). The verb *burn* (line 22) may not mean a literal burning; instead, it may connect to the word *radiant* on line 22, and it may mean to show brightly or to diffuse heat or light. Or *burn* may be read as "burn through" (lines 22–23), meaning to penetrate something or to see through something (in this case to penetrate the canvas and to see through the art or the past, to develop some sort of insight or understanding).

As we explore these words that are repeated with variation, we begin to notice that some have positive connotations and some have negative connotations. Though the words are similar in terms of literal meaning, this difference in connotations may influence our interpretation in subtle ways. For example, whereas the words *burn* and *fire* can be seen as negative within the poem, something destructive, *radiant* seems to have a positive meaning (we use the word positively when we refer to a person's face as radiant—a light comes from within to reveal something beautiful and valuable on the face). So, in this poem, we might pause at the uses of *fire* and *radiant* and *burn* to question how they are similar and different and how these similarities and differences may actually tell us something we didn't know about the poem and its theme.

Again, a shift in use of the same or similar words happens with the words *save* and *saving*. At the beginning of the poem, the word *save* shows up in the teacher's question and seems to have the literal meaning of "to rescue"—from a fire in this case. However, when we look at the use of the word *saving* or the phrase *beyond saving* in the last line of the poem, we might suspect that the meaning has changed, and the word no longer simply means rescue as from a fire, but perhaps has some more abstract moral, ethical, or spiritual meaning. We know this because we are asked to consider how "woman and painting and season" are "beyond saving." We know that seasons cannot really be saved, so we know that *saving* must have another meaning for this poet.

Another word that repeats itself in this poem is not so obvious: the word *and*. The words we tend to notice in a close reading are nouns, verbs, and adjectives, but we can't overlook the repetition of other parts of speech. As a conjunction, *and* often denotes relationships or ideas that have equality or equal weight; this is significant in affecting our understanding of the poem as a whole.

Within this poem, the conjunction *and* appears four times, first in line 9 to join *life, art,* and *half-heartedly,* and then again in lines 23 and 24 to join *woman* and *painting* and *season.* In the first use of *and* in line 9, the mind-set of the students in the ethics class is reflected; *and* shows the relationship between their choice between life and art as arbitrary and their experience of that choice as half-hearted. For the students, saving one is no more important than the other. Then in lines 24 and 25, Pastan uses *and* to demonstrate a relationship among *woman* and *painting* and *season.* These three things appear to be equal in weight, and as they age and move toward "darker than autumn, / darker even than winter," they cannot be either separated or saved. So how does this repetition and creation of relationships add meaning to the poem?

If ethics is about making choices between similar things, those things must be able to be separated or distinguished—must be unequal in some way so a choice can be made. But the end of this poem points in another direction through the conjunction *and:* these things cannot be separated because they are equal ("almost one"); so how can one choose among them? They all must live and die together. Again, this is kind of a fancy analysis of the repetitions in this poem, but it is an analysis that is hardly beyond the range of any careful reading.

PRACTICE 6-A

Reread the poem "Ethics," this time focusing on some of the other repetitions previously noted, such as *year* and *years, fall* and *autumn, woman, grandmother,* and *old woman.* Which repetitions seem most significant? Identify the literal meaning of each word; then identify the connotation (or connotations) for each word. Are they similar? Different? How do these similarities and differences affect your understanding of the text? If the connoted meaning changes, do you recognize a pattern in that change? If so, how does the pattern affect your understanding of the text as a whole?

OPPOSITION

Another analytical tool that can help us to find meaning in a text is an exploration of patterns of opposition—words or phrases that seem to suggest opposites or to be in conflict somehow. These words or phrases could indicate opposing directions, like in/out, up/down. They might be opposites of time (then/now; before/after) or place (North/South or America/Europe). They might be opposites in relationship (I/you; we/they; mother/daughter/son; young/old). They may not be true opposites (like North/South or young/old), but the way that they are discussed or placed in the text may suggest an opposition that might not normally exist.

Let's read "Ethics" again, this time looking for patterns of opposition. Here is what we find:

- our teacher (line 2) and we / I (lines 8, 13)
- years ago (line 1) and this fall (line 17)
- restless on hard chairs (line 6) and I stand (line 17)
- painting (line 4) and pictures (line 7)
- old woman, life (lines 5, 8) and Rembrandt painting, art (lines 4, 8)
- half-imagined (line 11) and real (lines 17, 18)
- old woman, old age, grandmother, woman (lines 5, 7, 10, 14, 18, 23)
- Linda / children (lines 15, 25)
- darker / browns (lines 20, 21) and radiant (line 22)
- most (line 21) and nearly / almost (lines 19, 24)
- save (line 4) and beyond saving (line 25)
- fall / autumn (lines 2, 20) and winter (line 21)

As we can see from this list, there are many opposites or pseudo-opposites in this poem, and they present several pictures of the way life might exist for this speaker. She opposes the classroom, the teacher, and the hypothetical question ("if there were" . . . "would" with the museum that is "real" and grounded: "I stand"). She also poses the supposed opposites—*life* and *art*—in the voice of a teacher who is ungendered and to children who refuse to make a choice between them. In this way, the teacher who lives in the world of the hypothetical is opposed to the students who reject that world by taking the easy way out and opting "one year for life, the next for art / and always half-heartedly." So, through these oppositions we see two worlds from the eyes of the poet: one world occupied by an adult who tries to involve students by asking a question about a hypothetical (not real) situation and another occupied by students who refuse to answer in the expected way—in fact, who refuse to get involved at all.

Another important apparent opposition in the poem, of course, is that between the student Linda and the same person, now "nearly" old. As readers, we expect that she would have changed in those intervening years, and, in fact, she has. Instead now of *refusing* to make a choice "eschew[ing] the burdens of responsibility," she is *unable* to make one, because she sees that such a choice is impossible: the "woman / and painting and season are almost one." It might be some wisdom that comes with old age, with the approach of the darkness of winter, or something that is "darker even than winter," with a oneness that might very well be reflected in the "browns of earth." So, we see in this poem a movement toward both the dark and the radiant, a joining of opposites.

Now we must come to some kind of thematic statement about what this poem means. In order to do this, to move toward articulating meaning, we have to look closely at the words and phrases we have found in our lists of repetitions and oppositions.

After a careful reading of this poem and an equally careful review of our lists, we might generate the following claim:

> *The poem "Ethics" represents both youthful denial and indifference and an appreciative acceptance of the value of life that comes with age.*

Let's analyze this claim by unpacking its components, its warrant, and the evidence required as support.

CLAIM. This claim has at least two parts. First of all, we are arguing that aspects of the poem represent (stand for or embody) "youthful denial" of or "indifference" to the value of life. We are also arguing that the poem represents "an appreciative acceptance of the value of life that comes with age."

WARRANT. To accept this claim, the reader must accept the warrants. When we enter the world of a poem (or short story or play), we enter into an unspoken agreement with the conventions of the genre, and to a degree with the conventions of all imaginative literature. We agree, to a certain extent, to suspend our disbelief and to accept the world of the poem as it is—separate and distinct from the world outside of the poem. So, a common warrant, common in imaginative literature, is the warrant of sign (refer back to Chapter 2 for a discussion of different kinds of warrants). We accept that the poem's words represent various things outside of the poem: that they function as metaphors and symbols. This warrant assumes that the audience accepts and understands how language can be used to signify aspects of the human experience. This warrant probably does not have to be surfaced as we develop our argument; it is understood.

Another warrant common in literary argument is generalization. We made a list of all the words that repeat and oppose. When we argue using these words as evidence, readers believe that citing a certain number of words is representative of the whole and these examples can be generalized to the meaning of the poem.

EVIDENCE. The evidence to support this claim comes entirely from *turning in* to the poem itself, from the analysis of repetition and opposition. We are arguing about how various aspects of the poem generate a particular message in and of themselves without referencing anything in the world outside of the text. We would have to show where *in the poem* we see a representation of youthful denial (such as the behavior of the students in the ethics class "half-heartedly" opting to save the old woman one year, the painting the next). Then we would have to show the appreciative acceptance of life and perhaps of death demonstrated by the speaker's own realizations later in life as she views the painting and sees a connection between the art, her life, and the seasons depicted on the canvas. In any case, all of our examples would come from within the text of the poem and require our clear explanation of what we see, where we see it, and how all of this comes together to create meaning.

Let's look at another claim we might make based on our reading of "Ethics":

In "Ethics," both art and human life are valuable because they repre-sent age and experience; however, art is more valued and studied by so-ciety while human life in the form of an old woman is not. This suggests a criticism in the poem of how society treats old women.

CLAIM. The claim we suggest here has three parts: "Ethics" asserts (1) that human life and art are valuable; (2) that art is valued more by society; and (3) that the poem implicitly criticizes how society treats old women. We will have to prove from words in the text all three parts of this claim.

WARRANT. To accept this claim, readers must believe that poetry uses metaphor (one thing standing for another): art and human life *can represent more abstract ideas,* such as age and experience. This is a warrant of analogy. But the fact that concrete words can rep-resent more abstract ideas is a common warrant in any argument about literature, so this warrant will not have to be surfaced in our argument.

EVIDENCE. As before, support for this claim will come entirely from the text of the poem. First of all, we must show with examples that human life and art within this particular text are both valuable. The teacher's question suggests that they are valuable through the oppositions of Rembrandt and the old woman, although the qualifier "who hadn't many / years left anyhow?" may also suggest a differentiation between the two: art more valuable. We would show how art is represented in the poem (the Rembrandt painting, the description of the colors of the painting at the end of the poem), and then we would show how human life is represented through those same aspects of the poem.

The poem sets up an obvious comparison between art and life through the ques-tion posed by the teacher in the ethics class—save the painting or save the old woman? The question assumes that they can be separated and ranked in value. But the two ob-jects (the painting and the woman) become one by the end of the poem when the speaker is examining the colors of the painting. She stands "before a real Rembrandt, old woman,"—the two become "almost one" here, side by side on the line of poetry. And within the frame that holds the picture, this view of the two-as-one causes her to notice colors that describe more than the scene in the painting; they describe the process of aging—"darker than autumn, / darker even than winter—the browns of earth, / though earth's most radiant elements burn / through the canvas." The seasonal description of the colors ("darker than autumn"—autumn often suggests middle age, "darker even than winter"—winter often suggests old age or death) and the painting (where the subject is undefined) describe a life lived, time passed, but a life that continues to radiate, to have value. The poem closes with the line, "I know now that woman / and painting and sea-son are almost one." This is perhaps the strongest piece of evidence to support the claim that life is art within this poem and that if one ("painting") has value, then all have value, even the life ("woman") in winter ("season").

The second part of the claim, that old art is valued while old age is not, may not be supported by this poem if we mean that the *poet* suggests that position. However, if we can argue that the teacher (who may represent society, or at least an important part of it), in asking the question, separates "art" from "old age," we may argue that the poet poses that possibility but resolves it through the eyes of the woman at the end. Here, we might turn not only to the opposition between teacher and students but also to the opposition between hypothetical and real and the repetition of the conjunction *and*. Also, because there seems to more sympathy for the "I" in the poem (both as a student and as a "nearly" old woman), we can argue that art can't be more valuable than human life because they are "almost one," and that's what the woman sees at the end of the poem.

The point is, again, all of our evidence comes from within the text of the poem. If we cannot show evidence to support our ideas from the text, then we cannot make and prove our claim.

Before moving on, let's look at one more claim based on the same poem:

> *The poem "Ethics" creates meaning that functions on two levels. On one level, the literal, the poem examines an ethical dilemma posed by a teacher and contemplated by a former student years later. On another level, the poem implies the "real" ethical dilemma of aging and the aged and suggests that the strength and beauty of life that shines (often unrecognized or unappreciated) even as it wanes.*

CLAIM. This claim seeks to prove that the poem works on a literal level and a figurative level and that different meanings are created through an examination of each level.

WARRANT. To accept this claim, our audience must understand that the same words and phrases may have more than one meaning—a literal meaning and an implied meaning (or even more than one implied meaning) and that words and phrases can signify aspects of our life and experience in concrete and abstract ways. Again, backing for this warrant may not be necessary, or it may be that it is something intrinsic to the evidence introduced as support for the claim.

EVIDENCE. Again, supporting this claim involves a close examination of the poem at the level of words and phrases and their meaning. First we would argue that the poem functions at a literal level. This is much like summary (discussed as a reading strategy in Chapter 3 of this text). A literal reading would describe the action of the poem—exactly what it said, perhaps pointing to the obvious movements between teacher and students, between student (Linda) and old woman. This literal argument is easier said than done when it comes to poetry because so many poems work more on a figurative level than on a literal level. Nonetheless, once we have explained the literal meaning of the text, we would walk the reader through another reading that explores what is implied or suggested through the patterns of words and phrases. For instance, we would look at *fire* and *burn* ("fire in a museum") and all of the things that they represent (such as heat, energy, danger, and destruction on the literal level but also the implication of passion and life force on the figurative). Then we might look at the word *museum;* at the literal level, it's a place to house old, antique, valuable pieces of art; a place of culture and refinement for many people; a place where you cannot be lively and expressive but must be quiet, reserved, *contained.* However, it is contrasted with a classroom and even a kitchen, and thus it exists also on a figurative level. We would continue this practice throughout the poem, finishing with a summation of what the implied reading communicates to the audience.

An argument based on *deconstruction* requires that we look at patterns of opposition and repetition for meaning. An interpretation of these patterns requires that we are open to nuances of language and aware of cultural meanings. We may have to inquire about aspects of cultural knowledge. (For example, we may not know that the word *winter* has a long history of symbolizing a life near death, a death that could itself be metaphorical.) But the words of the text provide the raw material for that interpretation.

PRACTICE 6-B

1. Select a poem from one of the casebooks in this text. Complete an initial reading of the poem using the strategies we covered in Chapters 3, 4, and 5—take particular care to identify patterns of repetition and opposition throughout the text.

    Based on your observations, create several possible claims you might make regarding the theme of the poem. Then "unpack" those claims. Identify the aspects of each claim, the warrant or warrants, and the types of evidence needed as support.

2. As a class or in small groups, select a poem from one of the casebooks. Working individually, complete a reading of the poem. Then work together to identify and list on the blackboard patterns of repetition and opposition appearing throughout the text. Generate a list of possible claims, and work together to unpack those claims (identifying the aspects of each claim that must be addressed, the warrants, and the types of evidence needed as support).

Tools for Turning In: New Criticism

We began this chapter by briefly defining and discussing literary theory in general terms. We noted that there are many different literary theories and that for our purposes we define our chosen theories as lenses—tools for clarifying various claims we might make about literature and focusing our search for supporting evidence to prove those claims. Then we looked at two important deconstruction tools for exploring a work of literature: repetition and opposition. We also created and unpacked a few claims about the poem

"Ethics." Throughout the first part of this chapter, our focus was on the text and how various aspects of the text may generate meaning. This type of inquiry into literature involves the use of close reading, a technique used by our framework of literary theories, deconstruction and new criticism. In this section, we turn to other tools to examine literary texts, techniques closely associated with new criticism.

New criticism is a lens that views meaning as a product of the text itself. Proponents of new criticism also believe that the meaning of a short story, novel, poem, or play can be revealed only through a close reading of the text. The author's thoughts, feelings, and intentions, the world outside of the text—none of this has any bearing on meaning at all. Meaning is derived solely from the words on the page. Of course, it is immediately clear that this theory is a bit artificial. It seems to imply that if the text is the only source of meaning, there would be one correct meaning clear to all audiences. But we know this is not the case. There are many different ways to read and understand a single text because we, as readers, bring to the text a lifetime of unique experiences—we are, ourselves, lenses through which the text is filtered. What we see or do not see in a text has everything to do with what we have seen or what we have not seen and experienced in our lives. And this changes as *we* change and have more experiences that we bring with us to a text. What you see in the poem "Ethics" during a reading at age nineteen will be very different from what you see at age thirty-five or fifty. So we have to keep in mind that any claims of objectivity are slightly artificial (no matter how much the original new critics want to believe otherwise).

Understanding that we *always* view a text through the lens of our experience, we can then approach new criticism with the knowledge that meaning is created and supported by a close reading of the text, and there are multiple interpretations to be made through a close reading. We can make many meaningful claims about a text and support each solely with evidence from the text.

Within this theory there are several lenses (techniques) we might use to argue about and understand a text (and we need to be clear that, though we have used poetry as an example in this chapter, all of these lenses may be used to explore any kind of literary text—short stories, novels, plays, and essays). Deconstruction uses patterns of opposition and repetition to examine a text; new criticism also focuses on words and phrases through these lenses:

- imagery and symbolism
- simile and metaphor
- connotation and denotation

Remember, by looking through any of these lenses and also utilizing the tools of repetition and opposition, your vision becomes focused, your purpose clear, and your attention drawn to specific aspects of a text.

IMAGERY AND SYMBOLISM

When we make claims about a piece of literature that look at descriptions or descriptive details, particularly when details signify something or imply a range of meanings beyond the thing or emotion being described, we are looking through the lens of imagery and symbolism. Imagery and symbolism are sometimes talked about as separate entities, but we discuss them as two interconnected parts of a whole. Here's why: imagery is created through the descriptive details in a piece of literature—we sometimes call these details "mental pictures." Those pictures by themselves may not reference anything beyond the literal, but when a writer uses an image to refer to something more abstract or complex than the literal, the image becomes symbolic. For example, in Western culture, spring is often used to symbolize life. In contrast, as we see in the poem "Ethics," autumn may symbolize aging, and winter *really* old age or even death. When we see those seasonal words in an environmental report, they are not usually symbolic. However, when we see them in a story or poem, they usually are. Imagery can exist without symbolism (a description of a wide-open space, of rolling hills covered in green grass in an environmental report, for instance), and symbolism without imagery. The Christian cross, for example, signifies something beyond the object itself—but as stated here, it is an object, not a literary image. But many times imagery—especially if repeated, even with variation in a text— becomes symbolic: **the imagery represents more than what it appears to and contributes to understanding the meaning of the text under examination.**

In literature, authors often use imagery and symbolism to create an impression, to show readers something rather than tell them in more literal terms, and to reflect a particular theme. Imagery and symbolism are often culturally determined; in some countries or cultures, for example, spring may not symbolize life. However, most literary works written originally in English use images that evoke particular culturally accepted and understood symbolic meanings. For instance, a pattern of images in a text that describes darkness in one way or another may create the impression of foreboding and danger; these images may draw the reader's attention to something that is happening in the text at the level of plot or character, or they may ultimately work to support the development of a theme such as murder and revenge. Among the different images of darkness in a text, an author might make repeated references to the setting sun, often a symbol for imminent death. In any case, however they are used, images and symbols can create an emotional effect for readers who understand their intent. They are powerful literary tools and provide a useful lens with which to understand and argue about a text.

Let's begin by looking at the imagery and symbolism within the poem "Ethics." The first clear image is in line 3, "a fire in a museum." This is a visual detail—a mental picture of flames burning in a building that houses valuable artwork. To generate an understanding of meaning, we ask, Is this a descriptive detail to be taken only on a literal level—the description of a building on fire like we might read in a newspaper article— or is this an image with more than concrete meaning—a *sign* that *signifies something* that *signifies something else?*

First of all, this is a poem and not a newspaper article, so we expect meaning to go beyond a surface-level reading. But several aspects of this description are mentioned in different ways later in the poem—for example, the Rembrandt painting (housed in a museum), and the "radiant" canvas described at the end of the poem—so this description seems part of a larger message, something more than surface detail, that it is imagery symbolizing something beyond the literal. To unpack this image we have to ask,

What do the aspects of this image represent? What are they trying to show? For instance, recall that an image is a sign that signifies something that signifies something else. So the fire may be understood as a *sign,* a detail that signifies the mental picture of a real fire. That mental picture of a real fire in turn signifies something else for us. What does fire represent? Literally, it is a natural element that is hot; it burns; it provides energy and consumes whatever it comes in contact with. Fire is a useful element—when contained—but it is dangerous when it is out of control. Its heat gives us energy and life, but its flames destroy. So, beyond the literal, fire represents for us both life and death. Fire represents life when it is contained and its energy is directed; it represents death when it is uncontained, undirected—when it is running loose in a building such as a museum.

Now, what might the museum represent? A museum is a sign for a building that holds usually valuable artwork. It is a quiet place to study and appreciate certain aspects of our culture. But not everyone enjoys museums; some people find them boring. Beyond the literal, a museum represents culture, things timeless and priceless, which grow more valuable the older they get. Now, when we bring these two images together, on a literal level, we have fire burning a museum. On a symbolic level, we have a force (fire) that, uncontained, represents death destroying a place that holds a valued (invaluable) part of our culture. So, based on this imagery we might begin to write a claim that this poem is about the destruction of something valuable. While this claim seems vague, it is a beginning of an idea based on looking at just the first image in this poem.

Let's look back at the first claim we made in this chapter:

The poem "Ethics" represents both youthful denial and indifference and an appreciative acceptance of the value of life that comes with age.

The language of our claim itself tells us that we are talking about one thing *represented* as something else—a thing or an idea or a feeling *signifying another* thing or idea or feeling. The very act of one thing representing another is the creation of imagery and symbolism. So what we are looking for within the poem to support our claim is imagery that represents or symbolizes youthful denial and indifference and imagery that represents appreciation and acceptance as we age.

How might the image of the painting at the end of the poem and our unpacking of that image be used to support this claim? We are attempting to prove that "Ethics" represents (through images and symbols, among other things) youthful indifference and an appreciation that comes with age. Youthful indifference is represented by the image of the students "restless on hard chairs." This is a clear mental picture; we see in our mind the restless, wiggling students, anxious to get up from the wooden chairs in the classroom and escape the question posed by the teacher. Later in the poem, the speaker—one of these restless students—stands "before a real Rembrandt." She is no longer restless and sitting, casually, "half-heartedly" deciding whether to save a painting or an old woman; she is standing in front of a painting, thinking deeply about what she sees and what it means to her. This image is in stark contrast to the earlier one. There is a stillness of reflection as the poem closes.

Within the text of the poem itself we will find everything we need to support our claim. We take evidence in the form of examples from the poem and explain and connect our evidence to our claim so that the reader may follow our line of reasoning.

PRACTICE 6-C

As a whole class or in small groups, select a poem or short story from one of the casebooks at the end of this textbook. Read your selection using one or more of the strategies covered in chapters 3, 4, and 5 to make your reading more productive. Then, working with your classmates, brainstorm two or three possible claims you could make about the poem or story. Keeping in mind that images are descriptions and descriptive details that have a range of meaning beyond the literal, identify images and symbols that support one or more of your claims. Together, practice unpacking those images. What do they signify? How does this signification work to create meaning within the poem or story? If you find it helpful, use this guide to organize your thoughts:

- A Word/Sign:
- Signifies Something:
- That Signifies Something Else:

SIMILES AND METAPHORS

We use comparisons every day in ordinary conversations. In fact, it's very hard to talk about anything for very long without making some sort of comparison between one thing and another, one experience and another. Similes and metaphors are literary comparisons. Trying to talk without using them is like trying to run on water; writing without figurative language is drowning in a colorless ocean. The first clause in the preceding sentence contains a simile; the second is a metaphor. *Similes* compare two distinctly different things using the word *like* or *as*. My love is like a rose. This book is as sweet as candy. *Metaphors* go farther than a simple comparison; they merge two distinctly different things without asserting a comparison so that one essentially becomes the other. My love is a rose. This book is candy. Often such language creates patterns in a text that shape meaning.

Similes and metaphors provide us with another lens to understand even subtle meaning in a text. For instance, in the example from the preceding paragraph, if we read either *my love is like a rose* or *my love is a rose,* we get an image of an emotion—love—existing with the same characteristics as a rose. Most roses are red, a vibrant color—so we see love as red. Roses start out small and closed up as buds but blossom into luscious blooms as they grow—so we see love as something that starts out small and closed up but opens into a bloom as it grows. Roses are beautiful, but many have thorns and can hurt us if they prick our skin—so we see love as something that is beautiful but that has the potential to hurt, as well. Figurative associations add depth and layers of meaning to a short story, poem, or play.

Let's look at another claim about "Ethics," a slightly revised one from earlier in the chapter:

> *In the poem "Ethics," life is art, and art (Rembrandt) and old age (the old woman) both represent life and living and experience.*

We begin this claim with a metaphor: life is art. To support this claim, we might find different words or phrases in the poem used as similes or metaphors to support this assertion. To identify a simile is easy; we look for comparisons using the word *like* or *as*. There are no similes in the poem "Ethics." So we move on to look for metaphors.

In order to identify a metaphor, we look for anything described as a distinctly different kind of thing or action. We quickly find that there are no easily identifiable metaphors where one thing is clearly described as or named as another. Normally, metaphors are relatively easy to identify (my love is a rose), but in this poem the metaphors are mostly *implicit* or unstated. For instance, in the phrase "colors darker than autumn," because the concept "autumn" itself has no color, we suspect that the language may be metaphoric. If we enact a cultural notion that autumn means aging, the phrase "darker than autumn" becomes a metaphor for something worse than ("darker than") aging. Another example: "earth's most radiant elements" might be an implicit metaphor for energy of life. "Radiant" suggests light or brightness in a state of motion, "earth" and "elements" suggest something very basic—perhaps life itself. Also, "burn through the canvas" (supported by the adjective radiant) might be an implicit metaphor for something that is living rather than something that is dead or dying. As with imagery and symbolism, similes and metaphors add depth and layers of meaning to a text.

Reading the text through this lens reveals many possibilities of support for our claim. But to use a metaphor as support, we must unpack it just as we unpacked our claim by identifying the aspects of the claim, the warrant behind the claim, and the evidence needed as support. Whereas unpacking imagery involves reading first its literal meaning then connecting that meaning symbolically, unpacking a metaphor involves what is almost a translation of the figurative into the literal.

Let's refer to the example "colors . . . darker than autumn":

Colors (appearances)
  darker than (worse—bleaker or more depressing)
    Autumn (age—a time late in life when youth is passed)

Viewed side by side with the literal meaning, this unpacked metaphor clearly adds richness to the text with its visual elements and multiple abstract implications. The scene depicted in the painting becomes more than a record of a season; it becomes a message—that aging appears bleak, but (for the speaker in this poem) it is not. Rembrandt, with such colors, has survived; a "nearly" old woman, connected metaphorically by color to this work of art, will also survive. In addition, not only does the painting survive but positive energy ("earth's most radiant elements") actually "burns through the canvas." As the painting provides a conduit for this energy, so does life in old or nearly old age.

■ PRACTICE 6-D ■

Sometimes authors use characters' names as metaphors. Look again at one of the short stories you have read—either in the main text of this book (such as "Black Elvis" or "A Good Man Is Hard to Find") or one of the casebooks. What characters' names seem metaphoric? Try unpacking a few of these metaphors now. Do you see any connections between the characters and their names, between the names and the theme of the story? Do you see any patterns emerging that might hint to a theme for the story?

CONNOTATION AND DENOTATION

As we have already seen, words have meaning on more than one level. Another way to look at the complexity of words is to discover their *denotation* or dictionary definition (fire: a chemical change accompanied by the emission of heat and light, and often flame) and *connotation,* its associated meaning (fire: life through heat and light, death through burning and destruction). Looking at a poem through this lens, a study of single words can bring rich understanding to our reading of a text. It can provide us with evidence to support many different types of claims.

When we study word choice in a work of literature, we speak primarily of connotation, the suggested or implied meanings of words. Some words are symbols in and of themselves—signs created through a combination of letters from our alphabet that represent a concrete thing or an abstract idea or feelings. The direct connection between the sign and the concrete object or abstract idea represents the literal meaning of a word. But all words are ascribed meaning through our personal and cultural experiences, too.

In "Ethics," the narrator imagines her grandmother "leaving her kitchen." Let's look at the word *grandmother* and possible associations connected with it. Many of us have grandmothers and so have personal associations. As children, if our grandmother speaks softly in a sing-song voice, showers us with hugs and kisses, bakes cookies, and bandages our scraped knees, we come to associate the experience of being taken care of, of being and feeling loved, with the word grandmother. If, on the other hand, our grandmother often yells or speaks sternly, is not particularly affectionate, doesn't allow sweets in the house, or tells us to get up, dust ourselves off and get over it when we fall down, then the feelings we associate with the word grandmother are not so positive. So the particular shades of meaning we bring to the understanding of even individual words can be powerful and unique to each person. However, many connotations are culturally determined and exist even beyond individual experiences. Despite our example of the cold and uncaring grandmother, culturally this word usually connotes loving feelings and memories. So when we read in the poem "Ethics" that the old woman "borrowed my grandmother's face," we connect the ethical dilemma posed in the poem to something personal and/or cultural, someone aging we care about, and our understanding of it changes. The grandmother in the poem borrows the face of *our* grandmother (personal and/or cultural). This association makes the poem more meaningful.

PRACTICE 6-E

Take a moment to define the word *grandmother* according to your experience. What is the connotation of this word for you? Share your responses with your classmates. What similarities do you notice? What differences?

Let's take a look at the third claim we explored earlier in this chapter:

> *The poem "Ethics" creates meaning that functions on two levels. On the literal, the poem examines an ethical dilemma posed by a teacher and contemplated by a former student years later. On another, the poem implies the "real" ethical dilemma of aging and suggests the unappreciated strength and beauty of life that shines even as it wanes.*

A brief summary of what is happening on the surface level of the poem—in the denotation of the text—will support the first part of our claim regarding the ethical dilemma. But we must move more carefully through the poem—line by line, word by word (though not every word)—to prove the second part of our claim. To do this, we look at some of the individual words in the poem and show how they connote for an audience the value of aging and the aged, the strength of life, the beauty of life, and how they—value and strength and beauty—are often unappreciated. We would then unpack the connotations of those words just as we unpacked the imagery and metaphors earlier in this chapter.

We might look closely, for instance, at the word *grandmother,* as we did previously. We might explore the literal meaning of the word and then describe and explain its implied meaning and how that implied meaning demonstrates the value of aging and the aged. We might look for words that show the strength and life—"fire"—or words that represent beauty—"Rembrandt." The example of Rembrandt is interesting. Some people associate this type of painting with beauty, and some people do not find Rembrandt's work beautiful at all. But everyone understands that a Rembrandt painting is considered valuable, even priceless. We understand, even if we do not find this type of painting attractive personally, that this is something we should value or at least respect because others do. Looking closely at this association, we can see a connection to the complexities of the dilemma raised in the ethics class, and we can begin to formulate some sort of interpretation using our study of the words as support. Meaning in a poem lies somewhere between the literal and the figurative, the denotation and the connotation.

PRACTICE 6-F

1. As a whole class or in small groups, select and read a short story in one of the casebooks. Record the repetitions of important words in the story. What pattern of repetition emerges when you take this careful look? Suggest how this pattern of repetition points to a theme of the story. Share your ideas with your classmates.

2. Select a poem or short story from one of the casebooks at the end of this text. Read your selection and make a list of repetitions and oppositions. Then pay attention to imagery and symbolism, similes and metaphors, and denotation and connotation. What claims can you make about your selection that might be supported through a close reading of the text?

3. We have included a draft of a student's argument, which was created using the turning in strategies covered in this chapter. Monica's draft includes some of her planning work—her reading strategies. Her poem appears in Casebook Four, *Land of the Free, Home of the Brave: Defining America(ns)*. First read Gwendolyn Brooks's poem "The Second Sermon on the Warpland," using your choice of reading strategies. Then read Monica's essay. How did she employ the strategies covered in this chapter in her analysis of the poem? Do you agree with her interpretation? Why, or why not? Do you see something in the poem that Monica did not see? Share and discuss your observations with your classmates.

New Criticism Turning In of "The Second Sermon on the Warpland"

Quotes	My Response
This	Ambiguous subject of poem
urgency	Sense of movement for mass/a need: direct object of the verb is
Live	Subject and verb (mass should live not just one person)
bloom in	Mass compared to flower/beauty/prodigious growth
in the noise of the whirlwind	Noisy whirlwind suggests chaos and energy—mass of people/energetic
Salve, salvage, spin	Alliteration, hissing, singing sound of the letter "s", sound of words out of reader's mouth, give sound to whirlwind
splendor, splashes	Alliteration: greatness, beauty of the movement, beauty of the people moving
flawed utility	Opposition: utility = basic but flawed, not perfect
prop a malign or failing light	Move any negatives out of the light, light grows flowers: flowers bloom = mass
whirlwind is out commonwealth	Whirlwind benefits all: commonwealth = wealth of the mass

Easy man, jumbo brigand, pet bird of poets/shall straddle	These people stand on outside of the mass: not moving/ straddle the fence in indecision
Nevertheless	Even though these people are in the way of the whirlwind— keep pushing
All about (lines 13–15): cold places/pushmen/ jeopardy	Repetition to reiterates everywhere there are negative forces
stormers, scramblers	Alliteration: allude to the sound
Fear	Capital "f" bigness of the fear: personifies the fear
medicate	Why medicate if there is urgency to live/medicate sounds like control, confinement by the status quo
time cracks (lines 20–21)	Explosion of time/urgency of living
furious flower	Alliteration: personifies the flower with an emotion: chose flower to represent time versus sand
face/grace (lines 21–22)	Rhyme to link the action of the flower
sways in wicked grace	In the face of adversity the living (the mass) dances (sways) gracefully—alludes to people of color musical in bad times
tom-tom	Drum, war drum to add rhythm to the whirlwind: repetition—ultra Uncle Tom
bearing oranges and boom	Alludes to Trojan Horse/bearing gifts in war
bells for orphans	Death tolls for those that have lost
red and shriek and sheen	Refers to the boom of the explosion as the mass nears victory
garbageman is dignified as any diplomat	Refers to Dr. Martin Luther King's speech to be the best garbageman that one can be (BAM movement)
bigly	To what degree Big Bessie's feet hurt
under the unruly, scrutiny, stands	Alliteration and opposition; unruly things do not stand still under the scrutiny—adds character to Big Bessie and her aching feet: dignity
wild weed/wild weed (lines 32–33)	Repetition: makes the wild weed larger, more -underscores the importance of Big Bessie standing there in the middle of chaos bearing scrutiny
We are the last of the loud	Identifies the mass as a we instead of some ambiguous "this": pioneers have gone before and this may be the last time to speak out
Conduct your blooming in the noise and the whip of the whirlwind (lines 38–39)	Blooming of flowers, is quiet but the blooming of a people as beautiful like a flower with cohesiveness of a whirlwind: because a mass should be noisy in the jubilation/beauty of growth/tears up the resistance in its pathway

TURNING IN: AN EXPLORATION OF "THE SECOND SERMON ON THE WARPLAND"

Gwendolyn Brooks' "The Second Sermon on the Warpland" is a battle cry that reiterates the poet's contribution to the Black Arts Movement of the 1960s. The poem is directed to a black audience with the intention of helping them feel the need to move out of complacency, as a unit, into a stronger sense of being. She uses repetition of phrases, alliteration of the letter "s" and personification of the flower to underscore this need to move forward. To the listener's ears the words chosen for the poem are like the whirlwind that Brooks suggest that African-Americans join together to create a whirlwind of change.

When Gwendolyn Brooks chooses words to describe the whirlwind that is the "living" of blacks, she uses alliteration. In the second stanza, lines 3–4, she uses the words "salve, salvage, spin . . . splendor or splashes" to add a sound to the whirl. A listener of the poem notes the hiss and slide of the words that reiterates Gwendolyn Brooks' "noise of the whirlwind" (line 2). The alliteration of the letter "s" also plays a part in an oppositional image that Gwendolyn Brooks uses to describe a resisting force to the whirlwind. In lines 10–11, "sweetest sonnet / . . . shall straddle" is used adjectivally to describe those things/people that have not committed to "the movement." The sweetest sonnet that is referred to in this line is the response of Edgar Alan Poe's raven in his poem "The Raven." Unlike those that straddle the whirlwind, the raven in Poe's poem cries unwaveringly "nevermore" to every question asked of him. There is no question as to the conviction of the raven in his responses, the bird never changes his countenance or his answer regardless of what the narrator asks him, ergo Brooks' "sweetest sonnet."

Contrary to this, Brooks states that the easy man and the jumbo brigand "shall straddle the whirlwind" (line 11). By straddling the whirlwind, Brooks alludes to the fact that one foot is on the side of convention while the other is in need of being part of the whirlwind. The "easy man/jumbo brigand" (lines 8, 9) are mentioned in the same stanza as part of the description of the whirlwind but it is in opposition of the "salve, salvage" (line 3) and "splendor splashes" (line 4) that becomes the growing whirlwind. A salve is a healing balm. Its use here is meant to soothe/salvage a wound and for the poem's symbolism, salvage the dissonance that the straddling of the easy man and the jumbo brigand create. The oppositional force of these straddlers would malign or dim the fervor of the mass if the whirl of unity was not so strong—"a commonwealth" (line 7). As the force of the whirlwind gathers strength, repetition becomes apparent in the poem. The repetition serves as a chant/mantra to push the force along.

There are three significant instances of this repetition that occur in the poem. The first example is the word "live." The word is found in each of the four stanzas in lines 1, 12, 17, and 37 respectively. Each time that the word "live" is used it reiterates the directive of the poem. In line 1, "live" occurs after a colon. Alone this one word becomes both a verb and an adjective. As a verb, the word "live" tells the audience to thrive, get up and feel the urgency of the time. As an adjective, "live" describes the whirlwind that comes from the vibrancy of a living being—it is alive. In line 12, "nevertheless live" can be seen as a reiteration of the directive. Brooks provides a litany of people/objects that could stand in the way of the whirlwind. Even though these people are there to impede, the whirlwind must keep pushing on, not allowing them to straddle the fence of indecision.

In stanza 3, line 17, "Live and go out" serves to push the mass over the "Fear" of line 16, thus furthering the point of using "live" as a directive. The fear in this line is a living thing and Brooks' choice to capitalize the letter "f" lends importance. It is not enough for the mass to just live while overlooking impedance, now it must move—"go out" (line 17). The whirlwind must go out and seek more life to propel the fury over the roadblocks of the brigand and the easy man. The last occurrence of "live" occurs in the fourth stanza, line 37—"nevertheless live." Here Brooks speaks directly to the audience, not about the whirlwind but about facing adversity and pushing forward. It appears that this last in the trilogy of "live" is more a plea instead of a war cry or directive as Brooks mentions that yes it is "lonesome / for we are the last of the loud" (line 36). The plea is for the individual, not the noisy mass. The individual should recognize the need for preservation of this "last group of the loud" and that they still live (verb).

The second occurrence of repetition occurs in lines 13, 14, 15 at the beginning of each line—"all about are the cold places / all about are the pushmen and jeopardy, theft—/ all about are the stormers and scramblers." Brooks uses repetition here to reiterate the very presence of cold places, stormers, scramblers and the whirlwind must "medicate" (line 19) against the malingers to protect the motion and the growth of the mass(es). By repeating "all about," Brooks creates a sense of being unable to escape the negatives; they are everywhere.

The final point of repetition occurs in the fourth stanza lines 32–33—"in the wild weed / In the wild weed." Here Big Bessie stands in wild weeds and is described as a "citizen / . . . a movement of highest quality; admirable" (lines 34–35). The weeds would choke out Big Bessie's spirit if they were noticed. In nature, weeds choke out living plants. They grow prolifically around the flowers that are blooming much like the blooming whirlwind that bolsters Big Bessie and the "blooming in the noise" found in lines 23 and 38. The whirlwind must continue to bloom in both noise from the mass and the "bigness—bigly" (line 31) of Big Bessie. Out of the weeds of a choking society, the whirlwind is compared to a flower.

Magically, the flower image appears to be personified in the poem and shows decidedly feminist characteristics. Brooks uses the flower as a symbol of time. It is personified when the flower cracks "into furious flower / lifts its face / all unashamed. And sways in wicked grace" (lines 21–22). Time is not marked in the standard dribble of grains of sand but in a malevolent flower that "cracks." A flower normally would just be fragrant and pretty, lifting its face to the sun, but Brooks' flower lifts its face with a feeling of being unashamed and sways in the tail wind in a wicked grace. These words go far beyond describing a dainty force—the flower has feelings and fights against being "good." To describe that the flower has a wicked grace connotes sensuality to the movement of time and the movement of the swirling frenzy in which the commonwealth must stand up and live. The sensuality of the movement adds texture and personality to the whirlwind. The words chosen to personify this flower allude to a woman, a woman with a temper that is not ashamed to crack furiously. Gwendolyn Brooks fills this poem with imagery of a flower and a sense of urgency to move.

The word choice that she uses serves to lend sound to the whirlwind by using alliteration of words that begin with the letter "s"—salve, salvage/splendor, splashes/shall straddle/ and stormers, scramblers. She chose to repeat the word "live" interchanging the word's meaning by using it as both a verb and an adjective. The word becomes a mantra/chant for the people in the whirlwind to repeat as they move forward. Brooks repeats phrases like "all about" and "wild weed" to highlight the location of negative forces and a choking society. The repetition used here suggests the size and wildness of these things.

Brooks' whirlwind blooms with the progression of the poem until it culminates with nearly the same sentence that she used in the beginning of the poem—"blooming in the noise." Something so delicate as a flower now represents such grand concepts as time and a mass of people that must overcome negative force by the sound of the "last of the loud," lift its face to the sun and sway in wicked grace.

Writing Assignment Suggestions

1. Select a poem, short story, or play from one of the casebooks in this textbook. Read your selection using appropriate strategies covered in chapters 3, 4, and 5; then, write an essay in which you turn in toward the text using the tools of deconstruction: repetition and opposition. Make sure that your essay has all of the components of a strong argument: a claim, reasons, and supporting evidence.

2. Select a poem, short story, or play from one of the casebooks in this textbook. Read your selection using appropriate strategies covered in chapters 3, 4, and 5; then write an essay in which you turn in toward the text using one or more of the tools of new criticism: imagery and symbolism, simile and metaphor, denotation and connotation. Make sure that your essay has all of the components of a strong argument: a claim, reasons, and supporting evidence.

CHAPTER 7

Contextualizing Claims and Evidence: Turning Out

Looking Outside the Text

In Chapter 6 we considered making an argument based on a claim that links the text's meaning directly to evidence *from within* the text. To support this kind of claim, the writer does not have to go outside the text but instead uses the tools of deconstruction or new criticism to discover evidence. In this chapter, we do something different: we look at ways to discover evidence *from outside the text*. It is important to remember that the *types* of claims you make when arguing about literature (claims of fact, value, or policy) do not determine where to look for evidence; instead, the evidence comes from the *content* of the claim—what you want to "prove" about the text. As usual, the writer will have to consider the assumptions behind the claim and the audience's needs while gathering and presenting evidence.

Turning outside of the text in order to make an argument is in some ways more difficult, more demanding than staying within the world of the text itself. The world inside the text is more manageable because it is confined to a limited amount of information in a well-defined space. The world outside of the text is not so easily managed. It is, in fact, *enormous*. You may feel overwhelmed when faced with the task of locating just the right piece of evidence to use as support for your argument. One way to make this task more manageable is to focus your search for information. In order to do this, you have to have a clear understanding of the kind of information you seek—the area of academic inquiry you need to pursue with experts who are devoted to gathering that type of information.

Seeking information from credible sources—from experts in a given field of study—often requires you to identify a specific field of study. To do this, you have to look closely at what you are trying to prove and identify the scholarly focus most closely related to the claim. As we stated in the previous chapters, although the lines between various fields of study overlap in many ways, you can think of each scholarly focus as a lens through which to view the world, a particular way of making meaning, of understanding and explaining various aspects of life. As we discussed in the previous chapter, in the field of English, those lenses are known as *literary theories*.

For review, literary theory is the process of understanding what the nature of literature is, what functions it has, what the relation of text is to an author, to an audience, to language, to society, to culture, and to history. It is not a judgment but a framework

141

for judgment and interpretation. Literary theories—like theories in any discipline—are quite complex. They become useful, however, when you use them to contextualize and explain your argument. *Literary theories can help to explain the subject of your claim and to refine and direct your search for supporting information.* Looking through the lens of a particular type of literary theory, your vision becomes narrow and focused, your purpose clear, and your attention drawn to a specific field of inquiry.

There are many different theories used to study literature, each one detailed and complex enough to be the sole focus of an entire chapter (or book or series of books). But for the purpose of showing how you can use a theory to explain and direct your inquiry, we address just four of the most common and generally useful: gender studies, psychological theory, historicism, and new historicism. (Note: You may decide on your own to explore some other literary theories—such as reader response, Marxist, or archetypal), or your teacher may introduce some alternative theories or direct you to sources that cover additional theories. A good source for basic information on literary theories is *Literary Theory: A Very Short Introduction* by Jonathan D. Culler. You might also consult *Handbook to Literature* by William C. Harmon and Hugh Holman.)

Turning Out with a Focus on Gender Studies

When you make claims that explore aspects of gender, you are looking through the lens of what is known as *gender studies*. Largely influenced by the philosophical inquiries of Michel Foucault concerning communication, power, and the ways in which ideas of what is "normal" are formed, gender studies is a relatively new lens for literary theory. An offshoot of feminist theory, gender studies focuses not just on women and their experiences in a male-dominated society but the on similarities and differences in the experiences of *both* men *and* women, as well as how men and women relate to one another within the framework of a given culture.

To illustrate, we might want to generate the following claim from "The Holocaust Party," a story we explored earlier that involves the differences between Mrs. Isabel and Amy's father, especially as they deal with their experiences during World War II:

> *Mrs. Isabel represents a traditional or stereotypical "feminine" approach to experience and people (she shares her life with others); Amy's father, on the other hand, represents a traditional or stereotypical "masculine" approach to experience: he keeps it to himself.*

Let's try to analyze this claim according to the structure we discussed in the previous chapter.

CLAIM. The claim is that these two different people represent traditional or stereotypical approaches to feminine and masculine communication styles: the woman discloses and the man does not.

WARRANT. The warrant is that Mrs. Isabel and Amy's father have these two different communication styles, a warrant of sign. To back this warrant, you might have to cite some examples from the text; however, this difference between them is so clear from the text that you might not have to address this warrant at all. No one who has read the story and understands it even a little would deny that Mrs. Isabel speaks and Amy's father does not.

EVIDENCE. What we are claiming—that Mrs. Isabel and Amy's father represent gender-based communication styles—we cannot prove from the story alone. There is nothing in the story that discusses these different styles. So, to try to base this argument on the text alone is fruitless. Instead, we have to go outside the text to find evidence that will make this argument.

If we follow the lines of reasoning presented in this claim—that there is such a thing as a masculine or feminine style of communication—we may have to ask ourselves, ultimately, this question: Is this style genetic or learned? Is it inevitable that Mrs. Isabel will tell her story *because she is female,* and is it inevitable that Amy's father will not tell his story *because he is male?* An exploration of communication styles and the origins of those styles will lead us into the disciplines of communication and psychology (maybe biology if we think there is a possibility that behavior is genetically determined), but we also said that we would look for, within those disciplines, how different *genders* communicate. This brings us to the area of gender studies.

Gender studies, in terms of literature, focuses on the linguistic differences between men and women, and thus it is particularly important and applicable to literary studies. Sometimes it looks at aspects of language and communication that are associated with feminine characteristics as opposed to male characteristics. Sometimes the studies focus on how young girls and boys are taught to speak differently and how those differences affect future relationships. Through the lens of gender studies, the above claim might also lead to a study of discourse and power—does a feminine communication style empower or disempower? It might also investigate the question of what is "traditional" feminine or masculine discourse and how such labels have emerged. These possibilities would be particularly relevant to "The Holocaust Party." (Note that gender studies often is based on research done in other disciplines: in communication studies, psychology, etc. Within those disciplines, you would look for studies of gender difference.)

Therefore, to support our claim, there are several ideas we may want to explore here. To begin with, that women and men have different communication styles has been the subject of recent research, most notably through the writings of Deborah Tannen, a professor of linguistics at Georgetown University. A cursory search of a university database using the keywords "communication + styles" will probably surface her name or the notion of gender-based communication styles. This same search will probably reveal other sources about communication style, and a more thorough search using keywords such as "communication + styles + tragedy" or some other similar combination of terms may even surface ways that men and women discuss personal tragedy.

There might be other aspects of the story that could be viewed from the perspective of gender: for example, the movement and posturing of the characters in the story. Mrs. Isabel sits on the sofa and never moves from it, while Amy's father separates himself from others and sits on a stool above them. Mrs. Isabel tucks her feet under her; Amy's father walks or stands during much of the story. Again, the point would be, What are the behavioral differences between Mrs. Isabel and Amy's father? Are these differences related to gender? What might those differences mean? Your inquiry might even lead into research on the topic of gender-based body types and kinesiology in the discipline of physiology, but the lens through which you view this information is that of gender studies.

PRACTICE 7-A

Working as a whole class or in small groups, select a poem from one of the case-books at the end of this text. Read the poem utilizing one of your favorite reading strategies; then take another look through the lens of gender studies. What gender-related questions are raised for you? How might those questions be addressed using the lens of gender studies as a guide? What sources outside of the text might you consult in order to answer those questions? Share and discuss your ideas with your classmates.

Turning Out with a Focus on Psychological Theory

If the claims we make about a literary work have to do with aspects of behavior, personality, and mental or emotional functions, then we are looking through the lens of *psychological theory*. In terms of literature, psychological theory (closely related to psychoanalytical theory) views literature as a deliberate staging of psychic (mental and emotional) tensions just as dreams are an involuntary staging of those tensions. Through the various aspects of the text, these tensions are expressed or "worked out" in some way.

Born of the ideas of Sigmund Freud and Carl Jung and expanded by contemporary scholars, psychological theory traditionally focused on the piece of literature as a reflection of *the author's* state of mind or personality—the "working out" of the author's mental or emotional tensions. More recently, psychological theory has extended to include an examination of aspects of a text that represent the human psyche in broader terms. Today we use psychological studies to explore aspects of a text influenced by both the deliberate and involuntary mental and emotional functions of the human mind.

Let's take another example from "The Holocaust Party":

Amy's father's repressed anger is a consequence of his experiences as a Japanese prisoner of war. In some ways, his anger at Mrs. Isabel is a projection of the anger he feels toward all people who have not suffered in the same way he has.

With this claim, we are trying to prove that the anger repressed, held inside, unexamined, and unexpressed by Amy's father is the involuntary mental and emotional tension resulting from his experiences during World War II. In other words, this is an inquiry into the psychology of Amy's father (or people like Amy's father who have shared a similar experience). The content of our claim—emotional experience and resulting behavior—leads us to the field of psychology. Another clue is the language of our claim: *repressed* is a common psychological term used in the discussion of emotional tensions and behavior.

So, based on the content and language of this claim, we know we are looking for meaning through the lens of psychological theory. This knowledge will focus our search for evidence on sources dealing with aspects of psychology, specifically the repression or expression of emotions after a traumatic experience. We might look for professional psychological journals as outside sources of information or turn to credible organizations such as the American Psychological Association, statistics, and expert testimony on topics like posttraumatic stress disorder. We might also look to journals in other disciplines that explore aspects of behavior and its consequences. Like gender studies, psychological theory overlaps with many other disciplines as they connect to mental or emotional functions, such as linguistics, kinesiology, and history. You will inevitably discover that some of the scholarly lines between the disciplines blur.

Let's unpack this claim and explore the argument in more depth.

CLAIM. This is a claim of fact with four subclaims: (1) that Amy's father's anger is repressed; (2) that this repressed anger is a consequence of his experiences as a prisoner of war; (3) that he is angry at Mrs. Isabel; and (4) that this anger is a projection of the anger he feels toward all people who have not suffered in the same way he has.

WARRANT. The warrant seems to be that Amy's father is angry, a warrant of sign. To support that warrant, we would have to assume that his behavior is that of an angry person, and we would then have to show examples of his behavior from the text. This is easy enough. Joel observes that the father "glowered" and the *American Heritage Dictionary* defines glower as "to look or to stare angrily or sullenly." So, at least to Joel, Amy's father is angry. Later, Joel's words again seem to point to anger: "hostility," "stormed out of the living room," and so on. We might have to make a case for anger, but the case is one that could be made.

EVIDENCE. To prove the claim, we must find evidence to support each subclaim. With the first subclaim, we might initially look to personal accounts and descriptions written by people who have gone through a painful and tragic experience and repressed the effects of that experience. Many of these descriptions have been compiled in anthologies over the years—accounts written and published by survivors of Nazi concentration camps or prisoners of war. A Boolean search on the Internet or a library catalog database may yield names of people (the subjects of these stories), names of authors, or titles of books.

As for the second subclaim, because we are talking about behaviors and because the language of the claim ("repressed" and "projection") describes particular aspects of behavior, the sensible place to go to support these subclaims would be psychological journals or some other professional references in the area of psychology. In an Internet search, for instance, we would come across the Web site for the American Psychological Association (http://www.apa.org). A search of that site would lead to an official clinical definition for "posttraumatic stress disorder" or PTSD, as it is commonly called. This definition would explain that individuals suffering from PTSD commonly experience flashbacks or sudden, vivid memories that are accompanied by painful emotions. PTSD sufferers also experience problems in their relationships with others because of their inability to form close, interpersonal bonds. Perhaps most interestingly, they experience erratic mood swings and outbursts of anger; they can become "suddenly irritable or explosive, even when they are not provoked" (American Psychological Association).

This initial information sounds similar to the behavior of Amy's father, so our claim seems promising. But we need more information. Other searches on the Internet or through databases or print sources may lead to case studies of people who suffer from PTSD to see if Amy's father's behavior is consistent with these cases, if his anger is a consequence of his war experience. During our searches, we may also stumble across information to support our fourth subclaim—case studies or clinical data that illustrate how people project their anger toward others who have not suffered in the same way. (Our third subclaim does not require evidence from outside the text; rather it requires examples from within the text that show Amy's father expressing anger toward Mrs. Isabel.)

Bear in mind that in the process of this investigation, we may decide that Amy's father's anger is not repressed, that he is not projecting and not suffering from any syndrome caused by his war experiences because his symptoms of anger, repression, and projection do not resemble those in the clinical studies. We may also find that his behavior is clinically healthy and not a symptom of any dysfunction.

Looking at a work of literature through the lens of psychological theory enables us to explore a character—how he acts, what motivates him, what his behavior says about his mental or emotional state; we also can look at how emerging themes (such as love, death, war, relationships, hate) might be explained through an examination of mental and emotional elements of the human experience (or how those themes might help to explain aspects of humanity). Psychological theory is a productive tool for exploring the behaviors of other characters besides Amy's father in "The Holocaust Party." We might look into Joel's work in the animal lab and *why* he continues to perform a job that bothers him on some emotional level. Why doesn't he consciously recognize that he is troubled by his work? Why doesn't he recognize the metaphorical similarities between his work in the lab and the experiments conducted by Nazis on Jewish prisoners in World War II? Or at Amy: How can psychological theory explain her relationship with her parents? These questions have potential as possible lines of argument.

PRACTICE 7-B

Reread the poem you used in Practice 7-A using psychological theory as your lens. What questions about behavior, mental and emotional experiences, or personality can you raise? How might those questions be addressed through an inquiry using the lens of psychological theory as a guide? What sources outside of the text might you consult in order to answer those questions?

Turning Out with a Focus on Historicism

When we examine a work of literature from a historical perspective—the history represented within the text of a short story, novel, poem, or play—we use historical documentation or records of real-life events to help us understand and explain the literary text. This type of theoretical inquiry is known as *historicism.* Historicism examines a particular historical moment *present in the text.* This theory maintains that readers must have an understanding of history before they can have an understanding of literature and examines the social, economic, political, gender, and race issues surrounding historical events that emerge within a piece of literature. This theory examines the text independent of the author and the knowledge of the historical event.

At one time, primarily in the nineteenth century, historicism was based on the idea that history was an objective truth, a collection of unquestionable, recorded, *unchanging* facts. We now view history as quite subjective. This new way of thinking about history has made an impact on the use of historicism as a theory for understanding literature. In some ways, it has made the demands of this theory more complex. For example, a story written in 1968 about the March on Washington (thousands of people gathered in Washington, D.C., in March 1963 to demand passage of important Civil Rights legislation; vehicles known as "freedom buses" and "freedom trains" brought people from around the United States to this demonstration, which culminated with the "I Have a Dream" speech by Martin Luther King Jr. on the steps of the Washington Monument) may be historically accurate based on the information available at the time it was written, but it may contain historical inaccuracies according to the new information made available since it was written. So, according to historicism, in order to understand that story, we would have to know the full history of that event; we would have to research both the information available in 1968 and the information available today, and then make a judgment on the value of the story based on its historical accuracy or significance in terms of what we now know to be true.

Now, let's look at the following claim and explore how it is focused and developed through the lens of historicism:

> *Mrs. Isabel's story is not credible because people who worked as slave laborers in Nazi work camps suffered little in those camps and thus experienced few effects from that time.*

CLAIM. The claim is simple: Mrs. Isabel's story is not credible, and the truth of the claim is directly related to the two because clauses: (1) that those who were slave laborers suffered little in Nazi labor camps and (2) because they suffered little, they endured few effects from their experiences.

WARRANT. The warrant here is based on an authoritative definition of suffering and the belief that there are degrees of suffering and proportionate after effects. It is also a causal warrant. Let's assume that suffering includes both a physical component (the initial experience of slave laborers in a Nazi labor camp, the living conditions, the physical demands placed on them) and a psychological component (the emotional pain and discomfort experienced at the time of the forced labor and afterwards through memories). Though most reasonable people understand suffering to be multidimensional, you may need to offer some sort of explanation to clarify your position.

Beyond a definition of the components of suffering, the warrant also assumes that degree of suffering has a measured effect: those who suffer more feel greater effects of that suffering. Stated another way, more (injurious, damaging, longer lasting) physical or psychological pain equals more (intense, lingering) psychological suffering after the fact. Backing for this aspect of your warrant may be difficult to find and should probably consist of more than official, textbook-like definitions. We may want to turn to case studies, specific examples documented through some sort of reliable source that show the experiences of real people to illustrate this measure of suffering and proportionate after effects.

Interestingly enough, the warrant—as you will see in just a moment—is tipping over into evidence to prove this claim. Careful choices will enable us to provide both backing for the warrant and support for the claim. Ultimately, however, we need to remember that cause and effect is difficult to prove, and many people will not believe a causal argument even if the claim makes sense and the evidence "proves" the claim. So, we may find much relevant, typical, and accurate evidence, yet we may not be able to convince our readers because we cannot get them to accept a warrant based on cause and effect.

EVIDENCE. We must find evidence for both reasons in our claim, probably by looking at historical accounts of slave labor during the Nazi regime. We could try to find letters or diary entries written by laborers and research documentaries, perhaps made during the war or shortly after it, recounting the stories of slave laborers. We could find prison documents, such as correspondence or reports that would describe the conditions of slave laborers or check newspapers or magazines of that time (although making such conditions public might not have been a common practice). Another way to research the first claim is to look for follow-up interviews or studies by post–World War II historians who researched this subject of Nazi slave labor. These historians might have found access to such materials as diaries, letters, and films.

A tremendous resource for this type of research is the Internet. For instance, after a quick search, we easily find the Simon Wiesenthal Center online (http://www.wiesenthal.com) as well as a link to the Museum of Tolerance and a multimedia presentation on Nazi labor camps. This site provides documentation of the types of physical labor the prisoners of World War II were forced to endure (direct from the Nazi's official records at each camp), as well as statistical details regarding which prisoners (men, women, children—young, old) were required to work, what type of work they were forced to do, how long they were required to work, and the living conditions they endured as they worked. It also provides personal accounts and links to stories about the suffering endured by the prisoners, years—even decades—after the war ended.

The second part of our claim (that people who worked in Nazi slave labor camps suffered few consequences) may need a different kind of research to prove it. Whereas before we needed to find documentation of the kind of suffering that prisoners endured in the slave labor camps, for the second claim we need to find information that documents the experience of those prisoners after the war ended. This second claim is naturally subsequent to the first claim: if we cannot prove the first claim (that they suffered little), we cannot suggest the second.

If, however, we do happen to prove the first part of the claim, we would look for slightly different kinds of evidence for the second. We might look in medical journals or psychology journals to find out if slave laborers suffered any repercussions. We might want to examine accounts of the mental and emotional effects of slave labor during the war. These accounts might include personal narratives, interviews, and even such things as paintings or other artistic products that might reveal evidence of subsequent effects. We might want to examine statistics on the percentage of slave labor camp survivors who were diagnosed with conditions such as depression, who were admitted to mental institutions, who committed serious crimes, who committed suicide. Such acts might indicate mental suffering, which might be attributed to their lives in the camps.

Actually, most any claim made about "The Holocaust Party" lends itself to historical inquiry; after all, the Holocaust is a historical event. Within the claim posed here, we are arguing about a specific aspect of the Holocaust—the slave laborers in Nazi work camps. The success of the argument depends upon our ability to locate historical information about the Nazi camps and the experience of those who worked under this forced labor. All of our information will come from historical documents detailing this moment in history. By looking closely at those documents, we may come to understand that Mrs. Isabel's story does not accurately reflect recorded history. We may then use that evidence to show that Mrs. Isabel is not a reliable character because her story does not accurately depict the experiences of the many people who suffered in the labor camps as documented in the historical records available today. We must view the character or moment or whatever is connected to that distortion with a critical eye (as in the case of Mrs. Isabel).

It is important to note that history is not confined to events. Historicism also looks at social, economic, political, gender, and race *issues and conditions.* In this way, like the other theories we have discussed, historicism crosses boundaries into other disciplines. We might investigate the economy as depicted within a text, so we would research journals on economics or government data and statistics; or we might investigate gender roles or race relations during a specific period of time in a text, and this focus would lead to documents within the field of psychology or sociology. But we would still view such documents in terms of their historical accuracy and relevance.

All documents related to research are products of their times. In researching the Hemley story, documents created immediately after World War II will reflect a different position than those produced in the 1970s. Interviews immediately after the war will reflect the predispositions of both the interviewer and the person interviewed in ways that are different from interviews conducted years later. So when we are researching with the purpose of understanding history, our research must be thorough and must take into consideration the ways that knowledge and information change through time and place.

In much the same way, the *medium* through which a document is presented will have an impact on the type of information presented and the effect that information has on its audience. While documentaries in the 1940s were primarily black and white film, print publications, or audio recordings, documentaries presented on an Internet Web site may present information through a combination of media (visual, written, oral).

In any case, history does not stand still; people change, their views of events change, and the methods of recording and discussing history change, and all we know about those events is what people tell us. It doesn't necessarily mean that one document is more right than another, but it does mean that there are no "absolute truths" in terms of history. All are accounts by people about people and events using whatever means of recording and presentation that were available at the time, and these accounts reflect the thinking of that particular time and place in history.

PRACTICE 7-C

Take a look at this poem by Claude McKay:

The White House

Your door is shut against my tightened face,
And I am sharp as steel with discontent;
But I possess the courage and the grace
To bear my anger proudly and unbent.
The pavement slabs burn loose beneath my feet,
A chafing savage, down the decent street;
And passion rends my vitals as I pass,
Where boldly shines your shuttered door of glass.
Oh, I must search for wisdom every hour,
Deep in my wrathful bosom sore and raw,
And find in it the superhuman power
To hold me to the letter of your law!
Oh, I must keep my heart inviolate
Against the potent poison of your hate.

What historical questions does the text raise for you? How might these questions be answered through a better understanding of historical events? In order to understand this poem, what aspects of history do you need to research? What sources outside of the text might you consult in order to answer your questions?

Turning Out with a Focus on New Historicism

If we understand that Hemley's story—and any other document we investigate as we attempt to prove our claim—is both a reflection of the particular moment in which it was created and a commentary on that moment, we are stepping into the arena of *new historicism*. New historicism understands that literature is more than a social, cultural, and political artifact specific to a particular historical moment. More than a record of history, it is a political *act* that simultaneously reveals the nature of society at the moment it was created and comments on some aspect of that society. In other words, the text is not only a product but also a producer of its place and time in history.

New historicism developed as a reaction—at least in part—to historicism. Where historicism views literature as a historical document of sorts and judges the text in terms of historical accuracy, new historicism is not so concerned with historical accuracy as it is with how the text reflects society *at the time it was created* and what the text says about some aspect of that society on anything from gender roles to race relations to family structure to government policy—and more. This type of literary theory includes an interesting perspective on the author's intentions both as a part of a particular culture, time, and place and as someone slightly outside of that culture reflecting on society.

At first, you may get this theory confused with historicism, but don't let the similar names fool you. These two theories are quite different:

- With historicism, if you are looking at a text about the March on Washington written in 1968, you are concerned about historical accuracy and must research the *historical records* of the event *from the time it happened to the present.*
- With new historicism, your focus is on how the story's depiction of the March reflects various aspects of society *in 1968* and how this depiction is *a commentary on those aspects of society.*

With new historicism, because the text is seen as more than a historical record, the author's intentions are important to understanding the text. Any information a text reveals about society has been filtered through the author's experience.

Our last example claim, a claim of fact, explores the story as both a product of the time it was written and a social commentary on the ideologies of that time:

In his story "The Holocaust Party," Robin Hemley creates a commentary on the Holocaust revisionist surge of the late 1980s and early 1990s. Through the dialogue that emerges between the characters of Joel, Amy, Amy's father, and Mrs. Isabel, Hemley wants his audience to understand what such a revisionist approach to history tells us about contemporary society.

CLAIM. This claim seeks to prove two things: (1) that the story reflects a particular historical movement during the period of time in which it was created, the historical revision, specifically related to World War II and the Holocaust, that surged to the forefront of scholarly discourse in the late 1980s and early 1990s, and (2) that the story makes a commentary on what that revisionist movement illustrates about contemporary society.

WARRANT. The warrant for the claim is based on several assumptions. To begin with, we are assuming a particular knowledge or awareness of the historical revisionist movement.

However, our readers may not have this knowledge or awareness, so we may have to explain what the Holocaust revisionist movement was and show evidence that it was prominent at the time the story was written. We are also assuming the author, Robin Hemley, had knowledge of a revisionist movement in the 1980s and 1990s related to the Holocaust and that he had reason and motivation to comment on such a movement. In order to provide backing for this aspect of our warrant, we may need to locate some personal information on Hemley.

A simple search on the Internet links to the information that Robin Hemley is Jewish—this would probably explain his concern with the Holocaust and any historical depiction of that time in history. It may be more difficult to show that he knew of the revisionist movement taking place in the 1980s and 1990s. To prove this, we might locate an interview in which he discusses this short story or the revisionist movement or a particular concern with the history of the Holocaust. If we are unable to locate such an interview, we might try contacting Hemley by letter or e-mail. Ultimately, if we cannot find any information about Hemley and are unable to contact him personally, we may look for information provided by other Jewish authors who have expressed a concern with the historical depiction of the Holocaust. We may be able to infer from that information that it is common for Jewish writers to be concerned with issues related to the Holocaust, and because Hemley is Jewish, it is very likely he, too, would have been concerned with such things and maybe even driven to write about them in this fiction.

Because we were quite interested in Hemley's take on this story, we e-mailed him and received this reply. It is not clear if he is aware of the revisionist turn, but it is clear that the story comes out of his own experiences as a Jew placed in a very similar situation:

Subj: Re: Townsend and the gang
Date: 7/22/2002 1:27:53 AM Eastern Daylight Time
From: "Robin Hemley"
To: "Julie Townsend," "Kim Stallings," "Meg Morgan"

Dear Julie and the gang:

Re: your question on "The Holocaust Party"—This story is about as close to actual events as my stories get. I say that with some hesitance because it doesn't matter how many events are "real" in a story, what one does with those events, how one positions them, makes them either largely fictional or autobiographical. In this case, the story, the point of view, is largely fictional, but the events and many of the people are based on real people. I was indeed invited to a party once by a good friend, a Catholic, who wanted me to listen to a true tale of heroism as told by her former teacher. It was a truly odd night and as soon as it was finished, I knew I'd write a story about it. I even knew it would be called "The Holocaust Party." But it took me a number of years to write it, and I failed at many attempts. I tried several times to write it from Mrs. Isabel's point of view, but that didn't work, and so I finally settled on the point of view closest to my own. The woman who told me the story (which was similar though not exactly the same story Mrs. Isabel tells) indeed told me that Jews have thinner blood than normal people. That was a line I knew I'd never forget. My friend and her family were similar to the characters I described in the story. The father was a combination of the woman's real father and the father of another friend of mine—he never went out into the snow, nor did I feel any particular connection to my friend's father. This was simply what I thought was needed in the story. I should add that I have never worked in an animal laboratory, but when I was working on the story, I read about such a lab and felt it belonged in some subtle fashion in the piece. My own Jewishness informed the story, I'm sure. My own sense of identity, religious and ethnic, has always been somewhat slippery, and so I've always been fascinated and appalled by the fact that the Nazis and others would have me killed, regardless of my own ambivalence. That's not to say I'm disconnected to my Jewishness because I'm not—and I'm quite proud of my heritage and religious identity. Nonetheless, for me the story explores the idea (central to my being) that it doesn't matter how slippery my identity is to myself. Others judge me based on intangibles or even lies that have nothing to do with my individuality. And, for me, the haunting thing about Mrs. Isabel was the fact that she still believed this Nazi lie after all these years, that it festered in her, that it had never been challenged. Nor could I challenge it that night. I think I was too stunned, not even sure I'd heard right, the same as my character in the story. I hope this helps.

Robin

EVIDENCE. In order to prove the claim, we would first have to introduce information detailing the Holocaust revisionist movement. Turning to organizations such as the Anti-Defamation League or the Institute for Historical Review (both accessible via the Internet), we might offer an explanation of this revisionist movement—what, specifically, supporters of that movement intended to revise, what aspects of Holocaust history were in dispute (such as the idea that the numbers of Holocaust victims may have been fabricated, the conditions experienced by prisoners of war exaggerated, and, most directly connected to our claim and Hemley's story, the appropriation of the word "Holocaust" by non-Jewish groups to describe oppressive experiences distantly related or unrelated to World War II and the Nazi regime's attack on the Jewish people).

Once we have shown evidence of such a historical movement, we turn back to the text of the story and show examples within the text that illustrate revisionism (Mrs. Isabel's story is the most obvious example). Finally, we must show evidence that Hemley is somehow—overtly or subtly—commenting on this revisionist movement. For example, we might look to the text for Joel's negative reaction to Mrs. Isabel; we might show that Mrs. Isabel is not respected by Joel or Amy's father—in fact, the stories of her experiences during World War II and her labeling of those experiences as Holocaust-like anger Joel and Amy's father. Finally, we might explain that this lack of respect and this anger represent Hemley's commentary on a revisionist approach to Holocaust history.

The claim assumes that the story is not a historical record of the Holocaust but a reflection of a way the Holocaust was discussed in the late 1980s when it was written. After conducting just a little research into sources contemporary to the late 1980s, we would find that during that time, a movement to revise historical accounts of the Holocaust was becoming prominent. Through the lens of new historicism, we might then argue that Hemley used the various perspectives of the characters and their interactions with one another both to reflect the existence of such a movement and to comment on the problems he saw with that movement.

Using the lens of new historicism, we could make many other types of claims, as well. We might see the relationship between Amy and her parents as an illustration of family life in the late 1980s, explore what this says about other families at that time, and consider what the author thinks or feels or wants us to understand about family. Or we might look at Amy and Joel as illustrations of youth in the late 1980s. Based on the information provided about each of these characters, their lifestyles, their attitudes, their behaviors, what might Hemley want us to understand about young adults or families at the time he wrote the story? There are many possibilities for creating lines of argument about this or any text via the lens of new historicism (and note how this particular theory—like the other theories we have explored—branches easily into multiple fields of study).

PRACTICE 7-D

1. Look again at the poem by Claude McKay. What do you know about this text? When was it written? What do you know about the author? How is this text a reflection of the time in which it was written? How does it comment on that time? What does McKay want readers to understand about society through this poem? What sources outside of the text might you consult in order to answer your questions?

2. Select a poem or short story from one of the casebooks. Read it and then generate a list of possible claims that might be clarified and supported through each of the four lenses covered in this chapter: gender studies, psychological theory, historicism, and new historicism. Which focus appears to be the most promising? Why? Were you able to produce claims using all of the lenses? If you had difficulty with any one in particular, speculate on why it did not work as well as the other lenses. Share your work with your classmates in small groups.

3. As a class, select a poem or short story from one of the casebooks. Divide into several groups and choose a particular lens to focus your study of the poem or short story. Each group should then read the text and generate possible claims about the text using their assigned lens as a guide. Group members then should select one of the claims and unpack it using the structure demonstrated in this chapter (show how the claim uses a particular lens to explore and explain the text, explain the warrant behind the claim, and brainstorm a list of possible sources outside of the text to be used as support, then explain how that evidence would support a claim through your particular literary theory). Share the results of your group activity with the rest of the class. You might want to write your claim, warrant, and evidence on an overhead transparency to make this sharing easier and more productive. Does each group's claim clearly reflect a particular theory (gender studies, psychological theory, historicism, or new historicism)? What does your group learn from this activity? What does your group learn from the rest of the class? What do you learn about the nature of argumentation and interpretation?

4. Following is a draft of a student's argument, which was created using the turning out strategies covered in this chapter. Amanda's draft includes some

of her planning work—in particular, a critical annotated bibliography of the sources she consulted during her research process and a final reflection. The poem discussed in this paper appears in Casebook Three, *The Ties that Bind: Relating and Relationships.*

First, read the poem "Cinderella" by Anne Sexton using your choice of reading strategies. Then read Amanda's essay. How did she employ the strategies covered in this chapter in her analysis of the poem? Do you agree with her interpretation? Why, or why not? Do you see something in the poem that Amanda did not see? What are some other approaches that could be used to analyze this poem? Share and discuss your observations with your classmates.

Anne Sexton's "Cinderella"

Surely one's life experiences affect one's actions, work, and creative output; however, one is never able to live in a cultural vacuum apart from society. In some cases, while some authors, such as poet Anne Sexton, felt as if they were drawing from their own personal experiences, in fact, they were speaking as a newfound voice of a changing society. Sexton uses her poems such as "Cinderella" to critique tradition and culture, and comment on the role of women in society.

To begin to understand women's changing roles in America during the period that Sexton wrote, one must examine the role of women in the years preceding the rise in feminism and liberation of the middle-class housewife. During World War II, the American war effort called all, men and women alike, to back their brave troops. Over 6 million women joined the workforce, half of them homemakers, who had never worked outside the home before (Bailey 853). However, after the war ended in 1945 and most of the women returned to their roles as wives and mothers, the image of the 1950s' suburbanite housewife was created, and was immortalized in television, movies, and thus popular culture through stereotypical female characters. "Domestic and quiescent, they moved to the suburbs, created the baby boom, and forged family togetherness. . .the quintessential white middle-class housewives who stayed at home to rear children, clean house, and bake cookies" (Meyerowitz 1).

What happened between the era of aprons and the bra-burning feminist movement of the 1960s and 1970s? The answer lies partially in the fact that, while television preached a perfect world of the "cult of domesticity," real life in America was actually much different. In contrast to World War I, after the conclusion of World War II, many women continued as wage earners—the number of women workers steadily increased. "As the 1950s progressed, another quiet revolution was gaining momentum that was destined to transform women's roles" (Bailey 929). In addition, many women simply could not tolerate the roles that society had created for them, and began rebelling. One housewife in Massachusetts, the mother of two healthy young girls, had been hospitalized for just such "emotional disturbance" after her first of four suicide attempts. This woman was the poet Anne Sexton (McClatchy xiii).

The 1960s and 1970s was a period of much turmoil, war, and rebellion. Women broke out of traditional roles and explored themselves as never before. Nineteen sixty-three marked the publication of Betty Friedan's *The Feminine Mystique,* voicing housewives' discontent of their suppression (Meyerowitz 3). Women were strong individuals, not necessarily tied down to the demands of home and hearth—for the first time, many of them were disturbing the way things were, questioning their roles and the old system of life. However, it was not only women who were questioning the way things always were done, but also society as a whole began to reconsider conservativism and tradition. One way that these new radicals voiced their new opinions was through literature. "While it was possible to be a writer in the sixties without direct involvement in the social movements that characterized the decade, it was almost impossible to ignore them" (Linden-Ward 295).

The poem "Cinderella," first published in Sexton's 1971 book *Transformations,* is a true example of the prevalent feeling of deviation from the norms of society. The entire premise of the book was to rewrite fairy tales— "this book of odd tales / which transform the Brothers Grimm" (Sexton 2)— and were described by the author herself as being "small, funny and horrifying" (Litz 689). Fairy tales are typically used as bedtime stories shared with young children, thus indoctrinating them early into the world of fantasy, heroes, wronged damsels, and happy-ever-after endings. These stories are eventually put aside with age, yet they are universally known. "Cinderella" features a line illustrating this, "Next came the ball, as you all know" (Sexton 54). These stories outline tradition, the promise of an ending in which those who deserved to live a long and happy life. Sexton seems to express her cynicism toward this view of life and in "'Cinderella' the conventional happy endings are perceived as sterile" (Litz 691). In this poem, she begins her telling of this oft-told tale with four small examples of poor unfortunates who essentially "hit the jackpot" and go from "rags to riches," with a concluding, "that story" attached to three of them—in which the reader is able to detect a certain biting sarcasm (Sexton 53).

Another issue that Sexton amusingly critiques is marriage, the eventual heavenly marriage and therefore delivery of the poor downtrodden Cinderella to the prince. The ball itself is but "a marriage market" (Sexton 54), commenting that in the paternalistic society, women's ultimate and enviable destiny was solely marriage, and that her impending doom was decided for her by men. Cinderella's fate, sealed by marriage, doomed her to the never-changing, television mother life that was "never bothered by diapers or dust" (56). In fact, both the newlyweds were soon to be "two dolls in a museum case . . . their darling smiles pasted on for eternity" condemned to forever living the stereotype (56).

Another explanation as to what inspired Sexton to write in such a manner could be her own life. It is, in fact, perhaps, the most dominant view—that she wrote primarily autobiographically, and to a certain extent, Anne Sexton wrote largely from her own experiences. Most agree that she is one of the most prominent poets from the "confessional school," who wrote mainly in the 1950s through the 1960s, writing from their own life experiences, also described as being an "uncensored, image-laden, tell-all style" (Sage). Sexton herself seems to be ambivalent about this label. In 1970, she stated, "It is said that I am part of the so-called 'confessional school.' I prefer to think of myself as an imagist who deals with reality and its hard facts" (Vinson 1772). Two years later, however, she reported in an interview that, "I am the only confessional poet" (Linden-Ward 316).

Sexton's life was shaped early by experiences with her parents. Ralph and Mary Harvey were abusive (Blain, Clements, and Grundy 696) and Sexton, feeling unwanted by them, would spend winters with her grandaunt, Anna Ladd Dingley (Mainiero 64). In addition, her marriage to Alfred Sexton, with whom she had initially eloped, terminated in divorce in 1973 (64). These experiences added to the cynicism and complex feelings about marriage that tinged some of her poetry, such as that which is perhaps too easily detected in *Transformations*. Sexton noted that the twisted fairy tales were "just as much about me as my other poetry" (Litz 689).

Though Sexton may have felt as if she were drawing only from her own life and her own experiences, it seems that her inner thoughts reflected the mindset of American people during this era. Though not universally embraced, *Transformations* earned Sexton the best reviews of any of her writings (689). This, in addition to the fact that five of the poems included in the collection had been previously published in three magazines, *Audience,* and interestingly, *Cosmopolitan* and *Playboy,* seem to indicate that the public was widely receptive of such social commentary in the lighthearted presentation. Had Sexton's ideas been derived without any cultural influence, she would not have been able to communicate so effectively to such a wide audience—her work had meaning on a personal level to many because many shared her thoughts, questions, and scruples.

When Sexton was asked by an interviewer in 1968 how she could write about herself considering the "great issues of the times," Sexton replied, "People have to find out who they are before they can confront national issues . . . I write about human emotions; I write about interior events, not historical ones" (McClatchy 29). In finding out who she was, unconsciously Sexton was forced to examine herself in context with the rest of her society—"no man is an island." As she discovered her own emotions, she thus discovered the emotions of the entire American population, critiquing society and tradition and, in doing so, questioning everything.

AMANDA'S REFLECTIVE COMMENTS HANDED IN WITH THE FIRST DRAFT

What are the strengths of your argument?

I think I gave good background to the time and culture leading up to the period that the author wrote in—the fifties with the suburbanite housewives gave way to the sixties woman of a new identity and role—the working woman. I like the rebuttal to the rebuttal as well.

How can your argument be improved?

I mainly focused on Sexton's writing in general, as opposed to the book Transformations *or even the particular poem "Cinderella." The problem was that people mostly wrote about her other books, especially her first one.*

What in particular do you want your peers to focus on?

I'd like them to critique the flow of the argument, to make sure it moves smoothly from point to point. Also, please look at grammar and punctuation errors.

What has been the most important thing you have learned while working on this draft?

I learned a lot about these "confessional" poets, since most of them seemed to be friends or taking classes from each other or meeting each other at conferences. I grew to appreciate poetry a little more since I'm more of a fan of prose, and am basically frightened by lines, meter, and rhyme . . . half the time I can't even spell rhyme . . .

Writing Assignment Suggestions

1. Select a poem, short story, or play from one of the casebooks in this textbook. Read your selection using appropriate strategies covered in Chapters 3, 4, and 5; then, write an essay in which you turn out from the text using the lens of gender studies, psychological theory, historicism, or new historicism. Make sure that your essay has all of the components of a strong argument: a claim, reasons, and supporting evidence.

2. Using another literary theory, write a second essay using the same poem, short story, or play you used for the previous writing assignment. For instance, if you wrote your first essay from the perspective of gender studies, write another from a new historical perspective. Finish with a reflection that explores and explains which perspective generated the most insightful interpretation of the text.

PART FOUR
Writing Strategies

CHAPTER 8

The Writing Process: Planning

Writing makes reading public. Although reading is not an act without a context (as we discussed in earlier chapters), it is often an activity without an audience. Although we bring to the act of reading many personal conscious as well as unconscious memories, personal experiences, feelings, social experiences, and the emotional outgrowths of these experiences, we read mostly alone and mostly for ourselves.

Writing is something different. Although it may prompt the same emotional response as reading, we write to be read—we write for an audience. And although much writing is never meant to have an audience beyond the writer (for example, when we write in journals or diaries or when we make notes to ourselves about what we are going to do on any particular day), written arguments are always meant to be read: we write to persuade, to influence someone else. In the act of writing arguments, we may clarify things for ourselves; we may learn something new. But the primary act of argumentation is an attempt to convince an audience that we have taken a reasonable position on an issue, that we have the reasons and evidence to support our position, and that the audience might be inclined to consider our position given the reasonableness of our claims, quality of our reasons, and validity of our evidence.

That's where we want to be: we want to have a considered position on an issue. But how do we get there?

Writers get there in multiple ways. In fact, we may alter our way of writing depending upon the rhetorical situation in which we find ourselves. While there is no "right" way to write, there are effective, productive ways to go about understanding the task and set about doing it. There is also no easy way. Writing is not a natural act. There are few "natural-born writers." Unlike speech, we don't come to it regardless of our will. Most people have no choice about learning to speak. They hear speech when they are infants and, through a process that is complicated and not totally understood, learn to use language. Writing is different. Like reading, it is a craft that requires practice to improve. Like reading, we can choose to learn to write better, or not. Given that you are in a class that calls for writing, it might be best to decide to practice the art of writing, to improve upon the strategies you already use, so that your writing will be better at the end of the class than it is right now.

The process that you use to generate a written text is called your "writing process." You may have several writing processes, you may have only one, or you may use only one most of the time. Although your process may be unique to you, in this chapter, we introduce you to planning strategies that could improve your writing processes: asking questions, posing hypotheses, using exploratory strategies, and finding a focus.

Where to Begin?

That's a good question. And that's exactly where you begin—you ask questions. Your reading of any text—especially a literary text—will prompt questions because most writers write to provoke questions. They leave deliberate gaps in the text for you to puzzle over; they use a word that has multiple meanings in context; they raise issues for the reader and do not resolve them; they create characters whose behavior is not understandable by many measures of "normal" behavior. They "hide" their messages. They don't do this to aggravate you, although it may. If everything you read were easy, you probably wouldn't learn very much. Instead, they do it so that by being provoked to ask questions, by being required to work to answer those questions, you will learn more about the text, more about the culture represented in the text, more about your own culture, and perhaps, in the end, more about yourself. Consider this poem by Ezra Pound.

IN A STATION OF THE METRO

The apparition of these faces in the crowd;
Petals on a wet, black bough.

That's the poem. Pound, a poet of the imagist movement of the early twentieth century, focused his readers' attention on his image of people in the subway system in Paris. Perhaps all he wanted was to capture this brief snapshot. But the very poem, its shortness, provokes us to wonder about it.

In the beginning, when you read a text, instead of being frustrated over what you do not understand, puzzle over it and *ask questions* about it. What kind of questions do you ask? First, look for a gap in your reading of the text. Look for something that is not explained very well, that is glossed over, that contradicts what you think you already know—something that puzzles you. Wonder about it. Do not assume it is a defect in the writer or a deficiency in you. Question the nature of the gap. Question what you see as apparent contradictions in the text. Work on the following exercise to practice asking questions. (You will notice that some of the exercises in this chapter on planning to write are similar to the chapters on reading. This similarity is not coincidental. Planning to write about literature in many ways is learning how to be a better reader.)

PRACTICE 8-A

In Chapter 1 you read Robin Hemley's short story "The Holocaust Party." Use the following strategy to discover some questions you may have about this text.

- Underline any words in the story that you do not understand. On the surface, this is a pretty uncomplicated story with an uncomplicated vocabulary. However, there might be references that you do not understand: Do you know the meaning of the word *ingenue*? Do you know the connotations of the phrases *John Birch Society, nasal-spray addict,* and *Laura Ashley*? Do you understand the reference to *Armageddon Quarterly*?

- Underline any words in the story that seem unclear or out of place—words that may puzzle you in this context. The references to cookies and snowmobiles seem to suggest a kind of lifestyle. The reference to the old Cadillac and Amy driving at 70 miles an hour may seem unusual. The father's going to the bathroom and drinking beer puzzle the narrator. Do they also puzzle you?
- What do you know about the Holocaust in Europe during World War II? What do you know about Japanese prisoner of war camps? What do you know about the internment camps set up for Japanese American citizens during the war? What do you know about the demographics of the American Midwest, the story's setting?
- Underline any words or phrases in the story that oppose one another, either in their actual dictionary meanings or in their connotations. (a) In the Holocaust that occurred during World War II, 11 million people were exterminated, about 6 million of them European Jews. Given the magnitude of this horror, the word "Party" in the title seems odd—the direct opposite of the feelings (connotations) that the killing of 11 million people might evoke. (b) Early in the story, Joel poses two nouns that he thinks describe Amy: *ignorance* and *malice.* What is the relationship between these words? What relationship is Joel suggesting? (c) Eyes play an important part in this story. Mrs. Isabel closes her eyes when she recounts her Holocaust story. Looks pass between the mother and daughter; Joel also closes his eyes, and the father stares at the fire and uses his eyes to leave the room on two occasions. What might Hemley be suggesting when he keeps mentioning eyes?
- Look over your list of words: What questions does your list provoke you to ask about the story?

Some of the questions may come from a misunderstanding within the text itself: in one case, you may have misread a passage or a line. When you have reread that part and come to an understanding, you can eliminate those questions. In other cases, questions you raise early in your reading of the text may be answered satisfactorily later in the text. You can eliminate these questions, also. For example,

- The first time we read "The Holocaust Party," we were confused by the paragraph early in the story in which the narrator discusses his job with the Minnesota Biological Services. This reference caused us to ask, What is he doing at the Minnesota Biological Services? What kind of work is it, and why the reference to his job?
- At the end of the story, the narrator decides not to go back to his job. Why? It seems that this job probably has something to do with killing animals, and that might remind him of the millions of people killed during the Holocaust. It also might have something to do with animal experimentation; human experimentation

are 110,000 children in public schools, the integration plan has been overturned, and the Latino community makes up a significant portion of children in the public schools.

Using the literary text of "The Holocaust Party" and the questions posed earlier, we have come up with the following exploration from a dynamic perspective:

- The father doesn't change in the story; however, Joel's perception of him does change—he seems much more sympathetic to the father at the end of the story and much less sympathetic to Mrs. Isabel, Amy, and even Amy's mother. Perhaps it is because the father does not support Mrs. Isabel. Joel may not like Amy's father, but they do share a common dislike of the same person and what the person stands for.
- Perhaps Joel has changed—he might not be so quick to make disparaging judgments about a member of the John Birch Society, or at least about someone who likes Andy Williams, which is probably more of a generational characteristic than anything political. And Joel reveals more about himself than the father, it turns out, through these judgments.
- The story changes from valuing openness in Mrs. Isabel to valuing and respecting the father's privacy and perhaps his private pain. However, while we are not supposed to like the father at the end of the story, we are also not supposed to like Joel very much either. Joel has been led by knee-jerk reactions to certain icons in the culture—John Birch Society, Andy Williams—to stereotype people who belong to those groups. Yet he does not want to be stereotyped as a Jew. He seems at the end of the story to come to an understanding of this, and he quits his job because he has a look at his own hypocrisy (maybe).
- The story, through Amy's father, moves from Joel's close-mindedness about the father to an open-mindedness, and then from an open-mindedness about Mrs. Isabel to an understanding about firmly believed prejudices. Joel does not seem to really understand the depth of his own prejudices about the father and the changes that they might be undergoing.

Relative: Place the subject in a group, compare and contrast the subject with other members of the group. Create an analogy. In some ways, this perspective combines analogy with definition in the topical invention system. There are three functions to this perspective: finding a group and defining it; comparing the subject with another member of that group; creating an analogy about the subject. Again, using the questions that focused our inquiry in the static and dynamic perspectives, let's practice with the relative.

Find and Define a Group Try to find a group that seems to define a relevant aspect of the event, character, or topic of your inquiry. We chose the politically extreme far right as our group. Members of the political far right are often avid supporters of the status quo as it was or as they believed it was a century ago in this country. They tend to believe in the value of the individual over the value of the community; they tend to believe in individual rights, sometimes without a sense that individual rights always butt up against community rights. Politically, they take the stand that the United States should either isolate itself from other world powers or go in and assert its culture through military might.

They tend to support the U.S. government military efforts; however, many also scorn the government in Washington and are more supportive of states' rights than of a strong central government.

Compare and Contrast: Find members of the same group and then compare and contrast two of them, one of which is the character in your text or the subject of your inquiry. Senator Joseph McCarthy (1950s anti-Communist), North Carolina Senator Jesse Helms, Rush Limbaugh, John Ashcroft, and Amy's father are all politically on the right.

- **Senator Joseph McCarthy:** A U.S. senator who initiated Congressional hearings in the 1950s, trying to find and investigate suspected members of the Communist party. McCarthy identified many movie actors who were suspected of communistic leanings or activities and had them blacklisted so many never acted again or only after many years. This activity was supported by many members of the American right who saw communism as an imminent political threat in the United States. In many ways, these feelings were a product of the Cold War and the kind of paranoia that surfaced after we dropped the atomic bomb on two Japanese cities and then learned that the former Soviet Republic also had nuclear weapons.
- **Amy's father:** A World War II veteran who survived the atrocities of a Japanese prisoner of war camp before the Geneva Convention outlined rules of treatment for prisoners of war. Unlike McCarthy, who took his anti-Communist feelings into the public arena, Amy's father keeps all feelings of hate to himself and seems only to allow them to come out when provoked by an occasion that reminds him of this past. The cultural context (the McCarthy era) supports his anger at and hatred for "the enemy." Yet, unlike McCarthy, Amy's father seems to have a reason for his anger—those years as prisoner of war. His anger at Mrs. Isabel seems odd: politically, she is probably close to him. However, she has trivialized her own experiences by noting that the loss of her toe "is the only thing" she "is left with from the war." She also states that God has watched over her. Amy's father apparently has more than a missing toe left over from the war. And where was God when he was a prisoner of war?

There is something to be said about silence, but it often feeds anger in ways that talking may dissipate it. Mrs. Isabel and Senator Joseph McCarthy make their anger public and in so doing cause the public to come to an understanding of their positions—even at the cost of repulsing many of those people; the father says nothing—so no one understands how he feels. Only in these tiny moments that happen randomly can a person (like Joel) learn from him. So, which is better: to act like McCarthy, to cause terrible harm and perhaps some good? or to be like Amy's father, to cause no harm and no good—to remain neutral?

Analogy: Create and explore a comparison between objects, ideas, or events in the text and something that has nothing to do with those objects, ideas, or events. The following are three analogies that might seem to work at coming to understand Amy's father.

1. **The choice between silence and speaking about suffering is like the choice between silence and speaking about art.** This analogy is very much like a comparison between suffering and art. In the story we have two approaches to suffering—talking about it or not. Artists have the same choices: one can draw, write, create or play music, create a film, then destroy the results and no one will ever know—no one will be hurt by the art, but no one will be aided by it either. Emily Dickinson was an artist of this type: she wrote poetry, but much of it was discovered after her death and thus, in some ways, her wishes for her art were subverted by those who found her poetry. Then are artists whose objective is to make their art public. This is how we know them. But the dilemma is, which is better: to hear Mrs. Isabel and in some ways be repulsed by her bigotry yet be changed by it or to not know anything about the father except what is revealed by others? You learn (or Joel did, anyway) from both. In addition, both art and suffering are personal. And, in fact, many hold that you can't have art without some suffering.

2. **Knowing Amy's father is like knowing a computer.** Notice the form of the analogy: there is a parallel structure to it that encourages the comparison, the word *knowing*. When you begin to use analogy, it is a good idea to set it up so that you have this parallel structure. Knowing a computer for most of us who use one is to know its surface features. We see it and use it all the time, but we don't know or care *how* it works. Our successful use of the computer is to get our work done, and this is how Amy's father works: he has a job, he has created a comfortable life for his wife and child, he provides a place where they can function (baking cookies, for example). Yet, he is an enigma. If you take him apart (like if you take apart the computer), you may destroy him entirely. Only the well-trained, well-prepared professional might be able to put him (or a computer) back together. Most people leave the inner working of their computers alone, just as Amy's father is left alone when he walks out of the house. Yet, if left alone, we suspect that he will return to the house when called upon to do so (just as the computer will turn on at our command).

3. **Amy's father's view of life is like picking vegetables.** This is a difficult analogy, partly because there is no parallel term on both sides of the equation. But it is always good to pursue a thought no matter how strange or farfetched it may appear. We might begin here with examining what it means to pick vegetables.

   Picking vegetables requires that the picker knows the right time to pick, not only the time of day but also the time in the life cycle of the vegetables. It's always best to pick vegetables in the early morning, before the heat damages them or causes heat stroke in the picker. It's always best to pick them shielded from heat and bugs with a hat, gloves, and long sleeves. It's always best to pick only the ripe vegetables (some won't ripen off the vine or stalk) and to pick only as many as you can use in a day or so. It's a good practice to share your vegetables with others—your neighbors, friends, or those in need—so the vegetables don't go to waste.

   We can see that in some ways Amy's father has a view of life similar to picking vegetables, even though this analogy seems really farfetched. For example, timing is everything with vegetables, and it seems that timing is important for Amy's father, too. He enters and leaves the room at critical times in the narrative. He seems to compare his time in the Japanese camp with the time Mrs. Isabel spent in her camp or barracks or dormitory. He may understand that bad timing can create a dangerous situation; perhaps that's why he was captured in the first place and why he leaves the room to go outside to be alone. Instead of wearing protective clothing, he covers himself (protects himself) with silence and with clothing that changes color to reflect—what? Perhaps the red Pendleton repels more than the Andy Williams sweater, and he needs clothing to protect himself from pain. Yet, he is different from picking vegetables, at least different from the ways we have set up the distribution of vegetables. We believe that vegetables should be given away, not kept to rot. Yet Amy's father keeps his memories, hoarding them and sharing nothing. Perhaps this sense that vegetables should be shared reveals our own biases we may not have known before this particular analogy revealed them to us. Yet, Amy's father's behavior is consistent with his political beliefs: the individual who grows vegetables is self-sufficient; if you want vegetables, grow your own. Learn to work, earn your own money like I have done.

You can see from this vegetable picking analogy that readers bring preconceptions, perhaps even unconscious ones, to the reading (see also Chapters 3, 4, and 5). This analogy has uncovered one of ours—vegetables should be given away, and this has revealed our biases about memories.

PRACTICE 8-I

Choose either a text you are working on or "The Holocaust Party" and explore it using each of the perspectives of the tagmemic guide. Show your exploration to your teacher or to a classmate for a response.

Finding a Focus

Earlier in this chapter we discussed generating hypotheses based upon your hunches. We called them good guesses. After you have done a thorough exploration of your topic through these invention strategies, you are ready to move from a "good guess" to a "solid claim." As you learned in Chapter 2, you can propose several types of claims; each claim must be arguable, reasonable, and supportable with evidence either from within the text or from outside the text. Here are three we have generated from our work with invention:

- Amy's father refuses to share his story of the Japanese concentration camp; the consequence of this decision is that Amy and her mother are deprived of the full emotional nourishment he might have provided. (Notice the food metaphor that comes from our exploration of picking vegetables.)
- Mrs. Isabel and Amy's father are symbols of two very different views of life: one view (Amy's father) argues for doing no harm and perhaps perpetuating evil; the other

(Mrs. Isabel) calls for doing both harm and good. However, the doer of the latter may not be aware of either the good (Joel's quitting his job) or the harm (Joel's recognition of her longstanding prejudice).

- No character is a reliable storyteller.

PRACTICE 8-J

Go back over all the invention work you have done; find several ideas and write several claims that are arguable, reasonable and supportable. Choose the best claim. Then go back to your invention work and find evidence to support your claims. Write your claims as sentences with "because" clauses. (See Chapter 2 if you need a refresher on how to write claims and "because" clauses.)

Conclusion

In this chapter, we discussed the planning work involved in writing an argument about literature. You should use these strategies with each argument you write, always taking the time to plan carefully and fully and, we trust, to write fruitfully.

Writing Assignment Suggestions

1. As a class, select a poem, short story, or play. Read your selection together and complete individual reading strategies (to understand and respond). Then, working together as a class, complete several of the planning strategies described in this chapter. Save your work for use in a collaborative argument essay—this assignment is continued in Chapter 9.

2. As a class, select a poem, short story, or play. Read your selection and complete individual reading strategies (to understand and respond). Then divide the class into small groups and assign each group a different planning strategy. Work in small groups to complete the planning. Share your results with the rest of the class. Compare and contrast ideas for developing an argument essay. Save your work for use in a collaborative argument essay—this assignment is continued in Chapter 9.

Works Cited

Lauer, Janice, Janet Emig, and Andrea A. Lunsford. *Four Worlds of Writing*. 4th ed. New York: HarperCollins, 1995.

Young, Richard, Alton L. Becker, and Kenneth L. Pike. *Rhetoric: Discovery and Change*. New York: Harcourt, Brace, and World, 1970.

CHAPTER 9

The Writing Process: Drafting, Revising, and Editing

In Chapter 8 we discussed how you might go about planning or preparing for your argument. At some point, however, you are going to have to *write* your argument, and we call that act of writing the *drafting* part of your writing process. This chapter discusses two drafting processes: organizing your argument and choosing an appropriate style. Later in this chapter we also give you some strategies for revising and editing.

There are several things to emphasize about drafting. First, *your audience will influence certain rhetorical choices,* choices in content, the order of your argument, and your style. In Chapter 1 we discussed audience in the academic community as primarily your teacher and classmates. When you start to think about drafting, you must decide what content will be convincing for your audience: what they know or do not know, believe or do not believe. In choosing content, your planning work is crucial because you will select much of your content from it, although you must remember that much of what you generate in planning may not be useful as you draft. You must decide whether to appeal to your audience using ethos, pathos, or logos. So, good judgment in selection is very much part of this drafting process.

You will also have to choose from among several *organizational plans* based on your knowledge of your audience. Drafting is easier if you have a general organizational plan in mind for constructing your argument. It does not have to be an item-by-item plan because some of what you do when you draft is invent and create. Sometimes if you have too detailed a plan, you might subvert the creativity that comes when you draft. But you need some kind of plan. Later in this chapter we describe in detail those plans and the general circumstances that might influence your choice.

Finally, your audience will influence your *writing style,* a style very much based on the particular situation in which you are writing. We define style as word and sentence choices you make to convince the reader of the worth of your argument.

We separate our discussion of designing an organizational plan and deciding on a style because we can't talk about two things at the same time. However, you should know that these choices are interwoven. These multiple, sometimes almost simultaneous, choices make writing hard.

In addition to audience, the genre will influence your drafting. In many classes, your teacher chooses the genre (type of essay). In this textbook, we assume that the genre is an *academic argument essay in the discipline of literary criticism.* Academic writing is often prescribed in certain ways. Claims are often claims of fact or value; the evidence comes from the text or from expert opinion. The evidence in literary criticism is seldom statistical. The organization moves from general to specific, although there does not seem to be a particular pattern beyond that to guide a genre-based organizational plan. The tone is scholarly and measured, seldom colloquial, antagonistic, highly emotional, or offhanded. The sentence structure is formal: the writer uses few if any fragments, even for effect. The vocabulary is sophisticated, revealing some knowledge of literary concepts or content concepts. Of course, there are no errors in spelling, punctuation, and grammar.

Although as we said, these choices are often almost simultaneous and often made for you, we divide *drafting* into devising an organizational plan and choosing an appropriate style.

Devising an Organizational Plan

In some ways, the organizational plan was chosen for you by Greek and Roman scholars over two thousand years ago. At that time, they described a way to organize arguments, based on content, audience, and effect, that many in this western world still follow today in its basic form. And because it is what is expected from those writing or speaking argument, it still works. First, we present the basic plan, and then we show you ways that you can modify it.

THE BASIC PLAN

Using the English words followed by the Roman equivalents and an explanation, here is the basic plan:

- **Introduction/*exordium:*** Like any essay, academic or not, your essay needs an introduction. An introduction serves two purposes, both of which are especially important when writing an argument, and especially an argument to which your audience might be indifferent or even hostile.
    1. **An introduction must convince the audience that your subject is worthy of its time and attention**, that the subject is arguable and interesting, even noteworthy or momentous. Sometimes an introduction will try to correct a previous misunderstanding or interpretation, one that will be elaborated in the actual argument. In short, the introduction argues for the value of the subject you are pursuing. You may want to make your appeal to pathos in your introduction.
    2. **An introduction sets up the credibility of the writer.** This may be accomplished by stating the credentials of the writer ("In my three-month study of 'The Holocaust Party' . . .") or by simply making a strong claim for attention and by making no errors of content, style, or mechanics. No one wants to follow an argument (much less believe one) written by a person who has not studied the issue.
- **Background/*narratio.*** In an essay, if the reader is to follow its points, that reader must know the necessary background. This is especially true in an argument. Before

a reader can believe the claim and evidence, he or she must know what facts (in the form of history, statistics, expert opinion) inform the isssue. In some cases, the background is new information for your reader. However, as we discussed in Chapter 1, much background information about a literary text will be known to your readers (either your teacher or classmates), so your background serves to remind them of the facts of the case and to orient them to the particular aspects you will undertake. In literary argument, often this background consists of a short (a very short) plot summary and perhaps a summary of what critics have said about the text related to your argument. Your background should be brief—certainly not more than a few paragraphs (perhaps 10 percent of your text, if you need a number.)

- **Proof or evidence in support of the case/*confirmatio*.** This part of your essay is its heart. Here you will make your argument in support of your claim based on reasons and evidence. As described earlier, your reasons provide the scaffolding for your essay, your evidence supports your reasons, and *both* support your claim or claims. You may have many reasons in this section, and each reason may have many kinds and sources of evidence. Depending on your audience, reasons may be presented from most important to least important (and vice versa); from important to less important to more important; from most startling to least startling (and vice versa); from most original to least original (and vice versa); from most recent to most distant (and vice versa); from most believable to least believable (or vice versa). One order that seems not to be reversible (or it doesn't make intuitive sense to reverse it) is one that should be seriously considered by any arguer: from most believable or most familiar to least. Using this strategy, you can build on what readers already know and believe and then move to what might be more controversial. This is a way to build common ground with readers.

- **Refutation/*refutatio*.** In ancient oral rhetoric, the speakers would try to discredit the opponent's argument by showing the worthlessness of the logic, by appealing to the audiences' emotions, or by discrediting the speaker through jest, sarcasm, or wit. Many students think that refutation is presenting the opponent's position, and in so doing, they see their own as being weakened. Nothing could be further from the truth. *Refutation is presenting the opposing side only to refute it.* There will be many good points made by your opposition—these can be acknowledged and not refuted. However, the opposing position will have many weak claims with reasons and evidence. These should be presented and then shown for their weaknesses. If you can get the readers to understand the fallacies and weaknesses in the opposition, you make it more possible for those same readers to accept the argument that you are trying to build.

  You can refute in at least three ways in the argument structure. You can refute the claim by stating that the claim made by the opposition is just not so or is not so as it has been asserted. Thus, if a claim about "The Holocaust Party" asserts that Joel is a credible narrator, you might assert the opposite: that his narration is flawed by his biases and thus he is not credible. Second, you can refute by opposing the evidence that your opponent presents. You could show that the evidence is not related to the claim or that it is flawed in some way—a misquote, a quote taken out of context, even the citing of a source that is not credible. Finally, you could refute by pointing to faulty assumptions. For example, you might show that the definition of *credible narrator* is flawed. Here, you would probably have to cite an outside source to protect your own credibility.

In an academic argument, the best and perhaps only way to refute an argument is through *logos*—presenting better claims, reasons, and evidence. You could, we suppose, try to refute using *pathos* by appealing to the emotions of your reader, but while this might work in an oral, nonacademic context, it seldom works in academic writing, mainly because the basis of academic writing is logos. You might want to try refutation by *ethos*, discrediting the qualifications of those persons or organizations that oppose you and asserting your own. This may or may not work, depending on your audience.

Again we remind you that any appeal is totally dependent on the audience and its predispositions: what it knows and does not know, what it believes and does not believe, how it feels about your subject.

- **Conclusion/*peroratio*.** You must conclude your argument. You can do this in several ways, the most common of which is to summarize or recap your major claims and reasons. You might also try to extend your argument by showing the possible consequences of not accepting the claims you have proposed. You could also repeat your own ethical appeal by reasserting your expertise in this particular area. However, you might also use an emotional appeal to the readers' sense of fairness, patriotism, love, religion, or, in the case of an academic readership, reason, balance, intellectual pride, and growth.

MODIFICATIONS

What we have presented above is the basic organizational plan. However, because any plan is based on content and especially audience, you, as the writer, must decide if this basic plan works for you, and if not, what modifications you might make to increase the effectiveness of your argument. Following are some possible modifications:

Basic Plan	Modification 1	Modification 2	Modification 3
Introduction	Introduction	Introduction	Introduction
Background	Background	Background	Background
Proofs—may be several subclaims and reasons	Refutation	Refutation plus proofs	Proofs plus refutation
Refutation—may be several	Proofs	Refutation plus proofs—continue as many times as you need	Proofs plus refutation—continue as many times as you need
Conclusion	Conclusion	Conclusion	Conclusion

In modification 1, you would refute the entire opposing argument immediately after you discuss the background. Under what circumstances might this be an effective strategy? First, you might use this plan if your audience is familiar with an opposing position but may not be convinced of its worth. Placing the opponent's position first gives you an opportunity to present, then refute, and then show a better way—yours. It may not be a very good strategy if your readers are convinced that the opposition is the only way to go—in that case, the basic plan might be better.

Modification 2 offers the same advantage, except you would use it if the opposing position has many points. In this plan, you present each point, refute it, and then present your own claim, reasons, and support.

In modification 3, you present your own claim, reasons and evidence, and then raise and refute any opposing arguments against that point before moving on to your next claim, reason, evidence, and refutation. Again, this plan has the advantage of emphasizing the strength of your own position and deemphasizing the strength of your opposition. It is a good plan if the readers are more committed to your opposition than to hearing what you have proposed.

Of course, there are other ways to organize—modifications of the modifications, if you will. As we have pointed out several times throughout this text, your plan will depend on the arguability of your content (its level of controversy) and the predisposition of your readers to that content.

Choosing an Appropriate Style

Style can be thought of in several ways; however, we think of writers having multiple styles (so style is not based on the writer's personality), all of which are influenced by the writer, the readers, the content, and the situation in which these occur. Style must be appropriate (that is, within a range of acceptability) to a particular situation. For example, some of our students think it's okay to cuss in a first-year writing essay. They seem to base their belief on a practice they developed on the street, in the game room, in the beauty salon, on the football field. However, it's not a practice appropriate to writing in the academic community, although it may be more acceptable in speaking. That is, your teacher may cuss in the classroom and may allow you to do so. In the academic writing community, however, cussing is not okay. In another vein, you probably learned in a previous writing class that using fragments for effect is okay. More than likely, the genre was a personal essay, a kind of "what I did on my summer vacation" variety essay. In such cases, readers are often classmates or even friends or relatives outside the class. Because the genre is more informal and the readers are people who may know you quite well, using fragments or informal words may be acceptable.

Writing academic arguments is quite different in the style expectations. The style tends to be more formal than in the personal essay: the sentences are longer and more complex; the vocabulary shows knowledge of the subject matter; the words are not highly colloquial: there are few if any contractions, for example, or use of local idioms.

Your decision to use a certain kind of sentence rests with the effect you want to achieve on your readers and the appropriateness of your style to the rhetorical situation.

When you are drafting, it might be wise to remember your need to make choices in sentences and words but not to be overly fixated on style. You can easily create the stylistic effect you want when you revise.

Let's first look at sentences as indications of style.

SENTENCES

You can examine sentences from four perspectives, all controlled by purpose and audience: sentence length, function, type, and rhetorical structure.

SENTENCE LENGTH. The length of the sentences you write will depend on the effect you want to have on your readers and the writing situation in which you find yourself. Obvious examples come to mind: the writing done for young children uses short sentences, some as short as one word. You can remember the sentences that appeared in your first-grade readers: "Run, Dick, run. See Dick run." You would never read: "Watch Dick as he runs effortlessly through the field, careful not to step on the flowers." This is not a matter of word choice, except, perhaps, for the word *effortlessly.* All these words would be in the hearing and speaking vocabulary of a first grader. It is a matter of a reading vocabulary and a level of sentence sophistication. Generally, as we get older, we are more able to understand longer sentences. But in terms of length, readership is not the only basis for your choice. You must carefully consider the values and expectations of the community within which you are writing. For instance, if you are writing within the business community, you will be asked to adopt a certain business vocabulary, perhaps to write clear and simple sentences (KISS—"Keep it simple, stupid.") and to organize according to certain principles, such as general to specific. Newspapers anticipate a relatively educated readership—perhaps at a high school level; yet many of the sentences in newspaper writing are short because the journalistic community *values* clarity, and one of the ways it measures clarity is through short sentences. In the academic community, not only will readers be capable of reading long sentences, but also that community *values* longer sentences (although, in fact, it seems to value sentence variety—short sentences and longer sentences, rather than strings of long sentences). So, when you make choices about the length of your sentences, think of ways that you can use both short and long sentences rather than one or the other.

> *Example: Here is a short paragraph using short sentences, with the number of words in the sentences after each period:*
> *Joel is the main narrator of "The Holocaust Party." (9) Mrs. Isabel is another narrator. (5) Joel narrates his story that takes place in the present time. (11) The present time is the time of the reader. (9) Mrs. Isabel narrates her story in the present time of the reader. (12) Her story, however, takes place many years in the past. (10)*

Notice that the range of sentence length is five to twelve words, with most of the sentences having nine to twelve words. Here is the same paragraph using longer sentences:

Joel, the main narrator of "The Holocaust Party," narrates his story that takes place in the present time, the time of the story's reader. (24) Mrs. Isabel, another narrator in the story, also tells her story in the present time. (15) However, her story takes place in the past. (8)

The range in this paragraph is much wider, from eight to twenty-four words. In academic writing, this is the kind of variety in length you are aiming for.

SENTENCE FUNCTION. There is another way to think about sentence variety: by function or use. There are four kinds of sentences classified by function: *declarative, interrogative, imperative, exclamatory.* Most of your sentences will be declarative—that is, they will make a statement. For example, "Most of your sentences will be declarative" is a declarative sentence. An interrogative sentence would be: "Will most of your sentences be declarative?" An imperative sentence would be: "Make most of your sentences declarative." Notice that this sentence is a direct command to a reader. Finally, "Most of your sentences will be declarative!" is an exclamatory sentence, identical to a declarative sentence except for the final punctuation and the tone we imagine because of it.

Many students think that they must ask lots of questions (called rhetorical questions because they are usually asked for effect rather than to actually get an answer) in an argument. Please don't ask rhetorical questions; instead, stick to declarative. When you ask a series of rhetorical questions, you may sound as if you don't know any answers, and this may ruin your ethos. And why would you want to do that? Instead, let your good reasons and evidence create a better ethos! (Note that in the previous paragraph we used all four kinds of sentences.)

SENTENCE TYPE. Variety is also key to writing sentences by structure. You can create four different grammatical sentence structures: *simple, compound, complex,* and *compound-complex.* Grammatical structure has nothing to do with length. You can write long simple sentences and short compound sentences. Let's look at the different structures of grammatical sentences:

- **Simple.** A simple sentence has one main clause: one subject or subject phrase (sp) and one verb or verb phrase (vp). Even a sentence with two or more subjects and verbs in the same clause are simple sentences. Examples of simple sentences:
  >   sp   vp
  - [Joel] [listened] to Mrs. Isabel's story.
  >   sp   vp
  - [Joel and Amy's family] [listened and reacted to] Mrs. Isabel's story.
- **Compound.** A compound sentence is two simple sentences connected by either a comma and a coordinating conjunction, a semicolon, or a semicolon and a conjunctive adverb. Examples of compound sentences:

  comma plus coordinating conjunction

  - Joel reacted strongly to Mrs. Isabel's bigotry, [but] he was unable to explain his reaction to Amy.

semicolon between two simple sentences

- Joel reacted strongly to Mrs. Isabel's bigotry; he was unable to explain his reaction to Amy.

semicolon plus conjunctive adverb

- Joel reacted strongly to Mrs. Isabel's bigotry; [however,] he was unable to explain his reaction to Amy.

- **Complex.** A complex sentence is one simple sentence that expresses the major idea and a dependent clause (incomplete sentence) that expresses a minor or subordinate idea.

dependent clause, simple sentence

- Although Joel reacted strongly to Mrs. Isabel's bigotry, he was unable to explain his reaction to Amy.

- **Compound-Complex.** A compound-complex sentence is two or more simple sentences plus one dependent clause.

dependent clause, simple sentence, simple sentence

- After Joel heard Mrs. Isabel's story, he left the room, and he decided at that time to quit his job.

There is no hierarchy here. Simple sentences are not inferior to compound sentences, which are not inferior to complex sentences, which are not inferior to compound-complex sentences.

RHETORICAL STRUCTURE. The fourth and final way to think of sentences is perhaps more unfamiliar to you than the previous three: it's called the rhetorical structure of sentences. For our purposes, there are basically two kinds of rhetorical sentence structures: *loose* and *periodic*.

A *loose* sentence structure puts the main idea in a simple or compound sentence at the beginning, and then the writer adds modifiers after that initial construction. For example:

- <u>Joel walked out of the living room</u> (simple sentence), [stunned, amazed, and bewildered by what he had heard Mrs. Isabel say, vowing never to return to Amy's house under any circumstances] (modifiers).
- <u>Mrs. Isabel told her story</u> (simple sentence), [her eyes closed, her shoeless feet curled under her, undisturbed by the movements of Amy's father] (modifiers).

The opposite of a loose sentence is called a *periodic sentence,* a sentence is which the modifiers are placed at the beginning and the subject and/or predicate come at the end. For example:

- Walking slowly to the car after hearing Mrs. Isabel's story (modifier), Joel decided to quit his job.
- Driving like a maniac in her father's old Cadillac, her feet pressed to the floorboard and seemingly unaware of the snow and sleet outside (modifiers), Amy rushed homeward.

Users of standard American English prefer the loose sentence; yet the overuse of either of these patterns, because they are so heavily dependent on modifiers, can get tedious. As with everything, try to vary your rhetorical sentence patterns; use them with moderation and for effect, or else they will become ineffective when you need them.

PRACTICE 9-A

The previous section discussed types of sentences and the need for sentence variety. The following paragraph was taken from an essay called "'Handing the Power-Glasses Back and Forth': Women and Technology in the Poems by Adrienne Rich," written by Audrey Crawford. This passage is the second paragraph in the essay, which was published in the *National Women's Studies Association Journal*. Thus, it is an example of the kind of writing style that literature professors use when they are writing for other professors and students of literature. Look at this passage; analyze the types of sentences Crawford uses.

- Count the number of words in each sentence.
- Decide whether each is declarative, interrogative, imperative, or exclamatory.
- Decide if each is simple, compound, complex, or compound-complex.
- Decide if each is loose or periodic.

What does your analysis say about the sentence variety used in this passage? While it is impossible to generalize from this passage to statements about sentence structure in academic writing, what might you say in response to the advice given earlier in this chapter about sentences and academic essay writing?

In the contemporary feminist discourse about women and technology, several currents are discernable. The most visible one addresses the problem of integrating women into technological careers, its optimistic feminist goal being to claim for women the economic and political power that accompanies access to places that have historically been reserved for elite males.[1] A second current focuses on the oppressive and destructive nature of many modern technologies, its primary goal being an exposé of technology as a mecha-

(continued)

PRACTICE 9-A *(continued)*

nism for control.[2] A third current suggests that women are technologists—or, at the very least, are active and significant participants in the technological process; it attempts to reenvision technology to include women's contributions and values.[3] While all of these currents claim that technology can be revised or re-visioned to be more useful or at least less oppressive for women, they also share, more or less implicitly, the recognition that visualizing women as technologists is problematic. The re-visioning of technology to include women is a related but separate problem from the re-visioning of the feminine to include technology, and re-visioning technology without revisioning women as technologists risks leaving women in the position of marginal participants within a domineering structure.

We will return to this passage when we finish the discussion on words.

WORDS

Sentences, obviously, are made up of words. And while sentence structure affects your style, so do the words in those sentences. We discuss the words used in academic writing from several perspectives: vocabulary, level of abstraction, and affect (connotation and denotation).

VOCABULARY OF THE DISCIPLINE. Each discipline that you study has its own special vocabulary. Many people call this vocabulary "jargon" and suggest that using jargon is wrong or at least not done. In some cases this is true, but in many cases, the use of a disciplinary or special jargon indicates that you know what you are talking about in the discipline. If you are a meteorologist, try talking or writing about the weather without using the specialized language of the weather: highs, lows, cumulus, stratus, warm or cold front, dew point, humidity. In and of themselves, these words are not difficult; but within the discipline of weather forecasting, they take on a special meaning that you must know and be able to use if you are to be believed.

The same is true for the discipline of literary studies. You have to know the specialized meanings of words such as rhythm, setting, iambic pentameter, archetypal criticism, irony, and deconstruction if you are to have any credibility in this field. Of course, assuming that most of you are not planning on careers in literary studies, your knowledge of the vocabulary does not have to be as extensive or as sophisticated as someone who writes or teaches in the field. Still, to be a believable writer, there is a level and kind of disciplinary vocabulary you must learn and be able to use.

GENERAL VOCABULARY. In addition to a disciplinary-based vocabulary, you will be expected to know a general vocabulary appropriate to the level of the college student. This does not mean using every multisyllabic word you know. It does mean that you must be able to use a vocabulary that indicates that you have reached a level of education that has given you access to interesting and precise words.

Both a disciplinary-based vocabulary and a general vocabulary are not acquired overnight; to be really comfortable with them, you would have to study a long time. However, by reading in the field of literary studies and by practicing your conversation and writing, you can acquire both vocabularies.

PRACTICE 9-B

Previously, we talked about "The Holocaust Party" and suggested that one way to understand that story is to identify words that you don't understand and try to figure their meanings from the text. That's always a good way to try to acquire a vocabulary: read something slightly beyond you, identify unfamiliar words, and try to guess at their meanings from the text.

Take another look at the paragraph from the Crawford essay in Practice 9-A.

- Identify words that you don't understand.
- Guess at their meanings from the text.
- Identify them as either disciplinary-based or general vocabulary words.
- Try to use them in a sentence or two.
- If necessary, check a dictionary to verify their meanings.

LEVEL OF ABSTRACTION. Words can also be analyzed by looking at their level of abstraction. Words tend to fall into a range of use, from highly abstract to highly concrete. Abstract words are so general that they are usually suggestive of several meanings and may need to be defined. The word *fair* is a good example, and probably one you've used with parents and friends. "It's not fair that you won't let me stay out until 3:00 a.m." to parents; "Let's be fair and divide the candy equally" to friends. We hear this one in our teaching: "It's not fair that I got a D when I spent so much time on this essay." Or "It's not fair that you won't let me have an extra week to make up this assignment." Often the response might be: "What's fair for you is not necessarily fair for me." As used above, *fair* is highly abstract: it can be used to mean multiple things in multiple situations. It can be defined to fit the situation and often must be defined if the sentence is to make any sense.

To make *fair* less abstract, or more concrete, sometimes multiple words must be used in examples or descriptions. Many parents, friends, and teachers create words to help clarify the intended meaning of fair. For parents, fair might mean consistency with family practice: bedtime is midnight—be home by bedtime. For friends, fair might mean that the person who purchased the candy gets a bigger share; for teachers, fair might mean that time spent (often defined as effort) cannot be measured or verified, so what's handed in is graded. Or they might state that extra time for one student is not fair to those students who handed in the assignment on time.

In literary studies, an abstract word might be *artist*. However, the word artist can apply to a person who paints, sculpts, writes music, sings, and so on. A less abstract word might be *poet*. In this case, there is only one possible meaning of the word: a person who writes in a particular genre. This person may write poetry for commercial reasons (song lyrics) or for noncommercial reasons, but both are considered poets.

In argument, abstract words must be defined. While often they are defined in ways that suit the writer and advance the argument in a particular direction, more often, they must be defined so that there is agreement between the writer and readers. When both have agreed on the definition of the operative abstract words, arguing is more productive.

PRACTICE 9-C

Return again to the Crawford paragraph. Find some abstract words and then try to locate more concrete words to help define those abstractions.

AFFECT. Words affect us in many ways; some words arouse positive emotions, some negative. Some remind us of something in our past; others carry virtually no remembrance for us. Some suggest visual images; others suggest smells, tastes, or touch. Some words are highly connotative (suggestive) simply by their use in the general culture; others are denotative (relatively affect free), again by their use in the culture.

In argument, you need to be especially careful of and sensitive to the connotations of words. A mistake in connotation could constitute a major error in argumentation strategy. Often, words carry different meanings based on different audiences. Audience analysis is especially important here (see Chapter 1); what the writer thinks of as logos (reason, denotation) might very well be a strong pathos (emotional appeal), depending on the audience.

Here are some sets of words that may look as if they could be defined the same. What differences do they suggest for you? What differences might they suggest for another reader?

- American Civil War and War of Northern Aggression
- annoyed, crabby, cranky
- inquisitive, curious, nosey
- hard-working and work ethic
- pot and cooking utensil
- dinner and supper
- food and grub

Some of these words have certain connotations because of regional differences. "American Civil War" would be used by teachers of history, probably any place in the United States. "War of Northern Aggression" also might be used by history teachers, especially by teachers and others in the South, even today, almost 150 years after its end. Some of the words have connotations located in social class: "hard-working" suggests a person of any class who puts in more time than is required to get the work done or does an honest day's work for an honest day's pay. A doctor can be hard-working; a mother can be hard-working; a plumber can be hard-working. The phrase "work ethic" takes on the suggestion of a strong cultural value. To have a work ethic means you believe that work will get you certain things, including good character. So, having a strong work ethic is a moral benefit; it means that you are a good person. It may mean that you see work as an end to something valuable, not only material goods, but character. On the other hand, a person who doesn't work very hard may still be okay if he or she is able to support a family, pay the rent, and have other things in life, such as a good community life or social or religious life. However, a person without a strong work ethic might be seen as morally inferior.

Your choice of certain words will, as we've said, affect the feelings of your readers. Words with connotations inappropriate to readers will do nothing to win support for your position. For example, if you are trying to argue for the quality of a restaurant, calling the food "grub" will, at best, confuse people and, at worst, turn them away from the restaurant unless you are in the West or talking about a Western style restaurant. Calling a poem "conventional" suggests that it is not original, when you might have meant that it abides by certain poetic conventions. The same might be true if you describe a novel as "formulaic": some might interpret your remark as a harsh criticism of the novel; others might see your remark as just descriptive. You would have to spend an inordinate amount of time explaining what you meant, either way.

Style depends on individual choices, influenced by writer intention, reader and the desired effect on the reader, and the rhetorical situation of the argument. There may be some limitations to a particular style of a particular writer, but one of the most laudable goals of any writer might be to cultivate a variety of appropriate styles by getting control of variety in sentence structure and word choice.

PRACTICE 9-D

1. Read the following passages, written by Gerald Graff, that appear in his essay called "Disliking Books at an Early Age" that appeared in the September/October 1992 issue of *Lingua Franca*.
   - Identify types of sentences by length, function, grammatical structure, and rhetorical intent.
   - Identify types of words by vocabulary, level of abstraction, and affect.

   This is the first paragraph of the essay.

   I like to think that I have a certain advantage as a teacher of literature because when I was growing up I disliked and feared books. My youthful aversion to books showed a fine impartiality, extending across the whole spectrum of literature, history, philosophy, and

   (continued)

PRACTICE 9-D *(continued)*

what was known by then (the late 1940s) as social studies. But had I been forced to choose, I would have singled out literature and history as the reading I disliked most. Science at least had some discernible practical use, and you could have fun solving the problems in the textbooks with their clear-cut answers. Literature had no apparent application to my experience, and any boy in my school who had cultivated them—I can't recall one who did—would have marked himself as a sissy.

About halfway through the essay, Graff writes a paragraph that begins like this:

To those who have never reconciled themselves to the academicization of literature, the seeming overdevelopment of academic criticism with its obtrusive methodology and its endless disputes among interpretations and theories seems a betrayal not just of literature and the common reader but of the professor's own original passion for literature. In a recent letter to an intellectual journal one writer suggests that we should be concerned less about the oft-lamented common reader whom academic critics have deserted than about "the souls of the academics and literati themselves, who, as a result of social and professional pressures, have lost touch with the inner impulses that drew them to the world of books in the first place."

2. Contrast the sentences used in this latter excerpt with the sentences Graff uses in the first. What are some differences? Contrast the words in this excerpt with the ones he uses in the first. Again, what are some differences? What do these differences suggest about Graff's ability to vary his style, even in the same essay?

Revising and Editing

After you have successfully drafted your essay, you may want to submit it to your teacher or peer group. However, we suggest before you do this, you spend a few days letting the essay sit on your computer or desk. Let your mind free itself of this writing. Then, before you turn it in, revise and edit it. Revising your essay means looking carefully at your claim, your content (your reasons and evidence), and your organizational plan. Editing means looking carefully at issues of style (sentences structure and word choice) as well as the mechanical aspects of your writing: spelling, punctuation, and grammar.

REVISING

Few writers write a "perfect" draft the first time. Some would say that few writers ever write a perfect work—there will always be ways to improve it. Revising is an activity that goes on all the time when you write. You write a sentence and then, before you are finished with it, you think of a better way to write it. So, you begin it again. That is revision-in-the-act-of-drafting. In this section, we are writing about revision-after-the-act-of-drafting. In this situation, you have finished your draft, you have let it sit, and now you are ready to look at it again, with almost fresh eyes, although that is not always possible.

To help you revise, here are some things you can do:

1. **Give your essay to a knowledgeable reader, along with a list of questions you want answered.** Your questions might include:
   - How arguable is the claim?
   - How good are the reasons in support of the claim?
   - How credible is the evidence used to support the reasons and claim? What obvious evidence seems to be missing? What evidence seems to be overstated?
   - What do you think of me as a person who has made this argument? Do I seem reasonable, knowledgeable, and positive about my position? Do I depend upon pathos and logos to enhance my position?
   - What would be a reasonable response to my position? How well do I address that response in my refutation?

Answering these questions is labor-intensive. You cannot get good feedback if you do not give others enough time to be thoughtful and specific. Don't always believe friends and other respondents who tell you that everything "seems okay." They may not want to hurt your feelings, or they may not have taken the time to review your essay, or they may not be very good readers. Believe reviews (both positive and negative) that are specific and detailed.

2. **With these same questions in mind, reread your own essay.** Try to pretend that someone else wrote this essay and that you have been asked to respond to it. This exercise is very difficult to accomplish successfully because most writers have a very heavy investment in what they have written and to deny authorship comes hard to them.

3. **Reread your essay slowly, carefully, and systematically, asking the following questions:**
   - What assumptions am I making in my argument? Will the readers accept my assumptions, or will I have to explain them or argue for them? You will have to ask this question each time you make a claim, each time you state a reason, and each time you offer evidence where there might be some ambiguity, misunderstanding, or even new information.
   - How can I restate my position to make it more acceptable to my readers? How can I try to reach common ground, especially in the area of controversial ideas or terms? Would my argument be helped if I could redefine certain words or make the language more appropriate?
   - What have I omitted that makes my argument unclear or unbelievable? What names, dates, or background would enhance the position I'm taking? At the

same time, what could I add to enhance my argument? Admittedly, you know much more about your subject than almost anyone else, so this question is difficult to answer. Try anyway.

Even if you have carefully revised your essay, your teacher will probably offer further suggestions for improvement. That's what teachers do. When you get your teacher's response, carefully consider each suggestion, trying to incorporate it into your essay if it makes sense. If it doesn't makes sense to you, contact your teacher and ask what the suggestion means and how it will improve the essay. You may need to explain why and how you are having difficulty with the suggestion. Remember that teachers read dozens of essays, often within a short period of time. While they are trained readers, and while the number of essays provides a context for a response, their reading may suffer (and their handwriting most certainly does) from so much work. So ask if you have a question.

EDITING. The final stage of the writing process is making sure that your essay is correct. While everything else in your essay depends on your choices (your claim, evidence, organizational plan, style, etc.), spelling, punctuation, and grammar do not. These are determined for you by social convention; they are so determined that they are often seen in terms of "correct and incorrect." They are so determined that some, perhaps many, teachers will fail an otherwise perfectly good essay if a student has violated spelling, punctuation, and grammar conventions. Editing for spelling, punctuation, and grammar is the last thing you do, and you do it to enhance your credibility. No one will believe you, as we said before, even if everything else is well done, if your essay is filled with one error after the other. Here are some editing strategies for *spelling:*

1. **After you have revised, run a spell check on your work.** The spell check will catch about 50 percent of your spelling errors, perhaps more. However, you may also introduce error with the spell check. For example, the phrase "by social" in the preceding paragraph was originally typed "bysocial" in error. When we ran the spell check, the word "bisocial" came up. If we had approved the change, we would have introduced that error and the sentence would have made no sense. Using the spell check requires an alert mind.
2. **Do not run a grammar check.** We do not recommend running a grammar check because it often introduces conventions that are not appropriate to academic writing. For example, you may get the advice to find a synonym for a word that is a jargon word. If you pay attention to the advice, you will be wrong; even if you ignore it, you will have wasted your time.
3. **Read every sentence carefully for other types of errors, including misspellings of proper names, substitutions of one word for another perfectly correct word, incorrect homonyms, and wrong words.** You may have to read aloud. For example, "Hemley" could be spelled "Hemly" and the missing *e* might not be caught by the spell check. You could substitute "it" for "is" or "and" for "as" and not catch it except with a careful, perhaps out loud, reading. Homonyms are often problems

for students. They often write "there" for "their" or either of these for "they're." All are correct in their own specific context, but they are not interchangeable. Make sure that the words you choose are used correctly. In the above sentence, we used the word "special" initially for the word "specific." While "special" might make some sense in this context, it is not what we meant. So, we had to go back to change that word to the one we wanted: "specific."

While spelling seems to be the major mechanics problem with much student writing, punctuation is a problem and deserves editing attention. One area of punctuation in which students seem to have the most trouble is the use of commas. These are the most common comma errors, according to research done by Dr. Andrea Lunsford and the late Dr. Robert Connors, along with examples.

- **Use a comma after an introductory element.** Example: "While spelling seems to be the major mechanics problem with much student writing, punctuation is a problem and deserves editing attention." You need a comma after the word "writing" in the introductory phrase.
- **Use no comma between independent clauses.** "All are correct in their own specific context, they are not interchangeable." This comma is incorrect because it is connecting two independent clauses—complete sentences. Use a semicolon instead.
- **Use a comma in a compound sentence.** "All are correct in their own specific context, and they are not interchangeable."
- **Use a comma in nonrestrictive phrase.** "Amy, a friend of Joel, invited him to meet Mrs. Isabel." The phrase "a friend of Joel" is nonrestrictive because it can be omitted from this sentence without losing too much meaning.
- **Use no comma in restrictive phrase.** "Joel's friend Amy invited him to meet Mrs. Isabel." The word "Amy" is needed in the sentence, and thus you should not use a comma.
- **Use commas in a series.** "We brought cookies, cakes, and ice cream to the party." You need a comma after each item in the series, including before the *and*.
- **Use a comma inside quotations marks.** "We brought cookies, cakes, and ice cream to the party," she said. If a comma is the correct form of punctuation, it belongs inside the quotation marks.

You may not make these errors; you may make them and not know that you do. You may not understand what it means to make those errors, so you have no idea if you make them or not. But know that many students do make them, and you should be alert to all possibilities. Another common error is confusing *its* and *it's*. *Its* is the possessive form of *it;* it's is the contraction for *it is*.

Finally, when you edit, you must also be alert to errors in grammar—that is, errors in how your sentences are constructed. Four of the most common grammatical errors are vague pronoun reference, pronoun agreement, unintentional sentence fragment, and subject/verb agreement. Here are some examples:

- **Vague pronoun reference error:** "Bob gave the shovel to his father before he returned to the house." Who is returning to the house, Bob or the father? A better sentence might be, "Before Bob returned to the house, he gave the shovel to his father."
- **Pronoun agreement error:** "The company was losing money, so they fired many employees." The word *company* is singular, and the pronoun *they* is plural. A correct sentence is, "The company was losing money, so it fired many employees." A correct and better sentence is, "Because the company was losing money, the owners fired many employees."
- **Unintentional sentence fragment.** As a writer, you may choose to use sentence fragments, often for effect. Short sentence fragments can point the reader to something important in the paragraph. Like sentence fragments. Some students, however, use sentence fragments unintentionally; they just write an incomplete thought as if it were a sentence. Here's an example: "Some students, however, use sentence fragments unintentionally; they just write an incomplete thought as if it were a sentence. Which is a wrong use of sentence fragments." The last unit of this quote is a fragment. It pretends to be a sentence because it begins with a capital and ends with a period. However, the word *which* at the beginning of a declarative sentence is often a clue that the student is about to write a fragment. If you write fragments that look like this one, avoid beginning a declarative sentence with a "which" (although you can begin a question with a *which:* "Which house do you live in?")
- **Subject/verb agreement.** Students usually make this error when there is a phrase or clause between the subject of the sentence and its predicate. Most students would never write "The two boys talks in a monotone." They would immediately catch this error, especially if it is not just a typing error. Regardless, most native English speakers would catch it if they read the sentence out loud. However, they might not catch "The two boys, after they had been humiliated in front of the classroom by the teacher, talks in a monotone." Writers know that a singular noun (*teacher*) takes a singular verb (*talks*): for example, "The teacher talks." They might forget, however, that in our sample sentence, the boys, not the teacher, talk.

PRACTICE 9-E

Edit the following paragraph for spelling, punctuation, and grammar. Compare with a friend:

The short story "the Holocaust Party," by Robin Hemley, wants us to believe that the main character Joel is a racist because he has a prejudice against Amy's father, and Mrs. Isabel. Joel imagines that Amy's father reads a magazine call The Acropolis News but he really doesn't, instead, he belongs to the John Burch Society, a very famous society for Conservative Americans. However, Joel is not a racist because he listens to Mrs. Isabel and he respects her almost up to the very end even though she is not Jewish. In spite of the big differences in their personalities he likes Amy alot or else he would not attend her Christmas party.

Revising and editing take time. They are often the least creative and most detail-oriented aspect of your writing. If you are not a "detail person," or if you tend to wait until the last minute to draft, you will have a difficult time revising and editing. In almost all cases, however, your essay will be vastly improved if you take the time and the energy (even if it is not your "thing") to make those final revision and editing changes.

Conclusion

Drafting, revising, and editing only come after solid and thorough planning. However, writing is not done in stages: first this, then this, then this, finally this. Often during revising and even editing, you will get an idea or make a connection you did not make in planning and drafting. Make sure that you are open to that idea—that you plan again and draft again, even though you are "supposed" to be editing. Ideas often need time to "incubate." After your unconscious mind has been working on them for a while, ideas may surface into your conscious mind, ready for you to use. So, while we have divided the writing process into linear stages of planning, drafting, revising, and editing, we do not suggest that the writing process is linear; instead, ideas come at all times, ready for your thoughtful evaluation.

Writing Assignment Suggestions

1. Using the poem, short story, or play you selected as a class in Chapter 8, continue your writing process and compose a collaborative argument essay. Working together as a whole class, draft the essay (if a networked computer classroom is not available, use an overhead projector). Then make a copy of the essay for each student, and working in small groups or individually, suggest ideas for revising the essay. Share your ideas with the whole class and negotiate changes to the essay. Work together to edit the essay; then distribute copies of the final to everyone in the class. What did you learn from this collaborative endeavor? How will this experience influence your own writing process?

2. Using the poem, short story, or play you selected in Chapter 8, continue working in small groups to compose an argument essay. Draft the essay together; then exchange essays with another group for a peer revision workshop. Make changes based on suggestions from the workshop, revise, and edit the essay. Hold a reading symposium and share your essays with one another. Perhaps combine them into an anthology of essays on your selection.

Works Cited

Conners, Robert J., and Andrea A. Lunsford. "Frequency of Formal Errors in Current College Writing, or, Ma and Pa Kettle Do Research." *College Composition and Communication.* 39 (Dec. 1988): 395–409.

Graff, Gerald. "Disliking Books at an Early Age." *Beyond the Culture Wars: Teaching the Conflicts Can Revitalize American Education.* Rpt. in *Falling into Theory.* Ed. David H. Richter. Boston: Bedford, 1994. 36–43.

CHAPTER 10

Researching Arguments About Literature

Becoming a Literary Detective

To help us gain understanding about a piece of literature so that we might form an interpretation or support an interpretation we have already developed, it is sometimes necessary to move outside the literary text and find and gather information from viable sources. This is, of course, known as *research,* and it usually involves making a trip to that great big building on campus known as the library (although nowadays we might just as easily use the Internet for most of our research, and that can be done from many different locations, including home).

Unlike other types of research, as we begin researching an argument about literature, we have already completed our *primary research;* we have read and studied a piece of literature—a work of fiction or poetry—and this is our primary source. The remainder of our research will involve the investigation of a variety of *secondary sources.* Secondary sources range from print sources that offer background information, to books and journals that hold collections of literary criticism, to Web sites and online databases. Which secondary sources we seek will depend upon the purpose driving our research.

Identifying Your Purpose

Just as with all other aspects of literary study, when conducting research, it is necessary to *identify your purpose* before you begin. Typically, if not driven by your natural curiosity, your purpose will be directly connected to an assignment made by your instructor. These assignments will vary, but your research will involve one or more of the following purposes: researching to understand, researching to explore, and researching to corroborate.

When we *research to understand* a text, we seek answers to questions based on our reading of a text in order to fill in the gaps of knowledge in our personal inventory, our author inventory, or our cultural/historical inventory. This type of research is really just an extended reading strategy and was covered in chapters 4, 5, and 6 of this textbook.

Researching to explore involves investigating literary criticism published in various scholarly journals. This type of research allows us to become familiar with multiple perspectives, interpretations, and arguments on a given work of literature. It is important, when engaging in arguments about literature, to "do your homework" and know what the critics have said about the short story, poem, or novel you are studying. This lends credibility to any argument you may develop on your own.

Finally, when *researching to corroborate,* we gather evidence to support our own interpretation of a piece of literature. This evidence may be facts, statistics, expert opinion, or examples from various nonliterary sources if we are arguing to connect some aspect of the literature to the nonliterary world outside of the text, or it may be expert opinion from literary scholars.

These three purposes for conducting research are not mutually exclusive; they often (even usually) overlap to one degree or another. Each of these purposes for conducting research will illuminate various aspects of any text you are studying and will help you in your quest for ascribing meaning to a story or poem. You may find that you are researching for a variety of purposes with any given assignment, depending on the requirements set forth by your instructor and the extent of your own knowledge of a text.

Common Research Tools: Major Print Sources and Web Sites

Once you have identified your purpose for research, you must become familiar with the discipline-specific tools of research that will lead you to the secondary sources you need. For the discipline of English, particularly literary research in this field, there are particular tools—various publications, anthologies, scholarly journals, and Web sites—known throughout the discipline as reliable sources for information. Depending on your purpose for researching, your array of tools and strategies will vary. Also, the tools that you use will largely depend upon your assignment and the sources available to you through your school's library and the Internet. Because library resources vary among institutions, we cover only briefly the major print sources. Likewise, because the Internet is changing daily—Web sites appear and disappear in the blink of an eye—we take only a cursory look at the Web tools typically at your disposal. Our discussion of research centers more on information-gathering strategies and information-processing strategies. Primarily, we focus our discussion on how to handle the information you gather in a responsible way.

Soon you will understand that researching arguments about literature is a lot like solving a mystery. It's all about chasing clues, uncovering details, and bringing to light a truth that you want to share with the world.

TRADITIONAL PRINT SOURCES

In this ever-expanding world of technology, the library is often not first on our list of resources when we begin a research project. However, remember that the library is an important part of the academic community, and while it is true that many—if not most—sources are now available to you through the Internet, the library offers many valuable print sources as well. One distinct advantage to resources recovered in the library over resources found on the Internet has to do with credibility. All of the sources procured by a university library are first screened by the librarian and are considered to be respectable (to one degree or another) throughout the academic community. This is opposed to many sources found on the Internet, which are not screened by professionals and lack credibility in the eyes of the academic community. If absolute credibility is an important issue while researching, the library is the best place to begin your work.

The types of print sources available to you vary among institutions. For the most part, when beginning a research project, you might look first to a *reference text* to provide background information. For instance, if you are looking for an overview of a genre or a particular author's work, it is useful to check out the *Dictionary of Literary Biography (DLB)*. This source is available in most libraries. The *DLB* is useful when researching traditional literary texts—short stories, novels, and poems. When researching the background of a less-traditional text—such as the lyrics to a song—comparable sources might be *American Songwriters* and *Dictionary of American Biography*. The *DLB, American Songwriters,* and *Dictionary of American Biography* are examples of sources typically found in the *reference area* of a library. These texts do not circulate but are available for use in the library during regular hours (though some libraries also subscribe to electronic versions of these texts and make them available online).

In addition to these reference texts, the library has many texts in *circulation* that may be checked out and taken home for an extended period of time. Fiction and nonfiction books by authors, collections of works by a particular author or a group of authors, and anthologies of critical essays, are just a few examples of the types of book sources we might find in circulation.

Beyond reference texts and circulating fiction and nonfiction books, most libraries also have *collections of periodicals*. Periodicals (called so because they are published periodically—daily, weekly, monthly, and so on) are magazines, newspapers, or professional journals that are usually grouped according to locality or subject matter. Periodicals are often available solely through the library in print form, and they contain the most up-to-date information on literature and pop culture. Again, sometimes these periodicals are also available electronically if your library subscribes to a database such as the Gale Literature Resource Center.

- **Magazines** are most often considered popular texts and are read by the general population of a culture—for example, *Time, Rolling Stone,* and *Ebony.*
- **Newspapers** cover current events, and most libraries subscribe to local, national, and international papers. Hardcopies of newspapers are kept for a relatively short time period, as they do not hold up very well to normal wear and tear. However, most libraries keep microfilm copies of newspapers that date back as far as the 1800s.
- **Professional or scholarly journals** are academic publications within a particular field of study. These typically are kept in binders and are a wonderful resource when researching literary topics.

HELPFUL HINT

Finding what you need in the library is often a challenging task. Many times, the best sources are not located through the most obvious channels. Once you have exhausted sources located through the catalogue or the reference desk, another strategy that often turns up useful information is a *search of indexes.*

(continued)

HELPFUL HINT *(continued)*

Almost every book and periodical in publication contains a subject or topical index. Typically located in the back of a publication, the index is an alphabetical listing of key words or phrases found in the text. These key words lead to particular pages within a text—and often to the most specific and useful information.

It is also useful to pay attention to *bibliographies* included in books or periodical articles. If you have found an article or essay that contains useful information, locating the sources an author used in writing that article may lead you to even more useful information.

WEB SITES

The World Wide Web is an amazing resource for academics and has revolutionized the research process. There are millions of Internet Web sites available at your fingertips twenty-four hours a day, every day. The convenience of researching on the Internet is most appealing, but it is important to be wary. Not all information found on the Internet is worthy of our attention. Anyone can put up a Web site on any topic. For example, a twelve-year-old girl may be a big fan of *Harry Potter and the Sorcerer's Stone* and may construct a Web site honoring her favorite fictional character. That Web site may have information about the author, J.K. Rowling, and may contain pages upon pages of textual references, insights, and interpretations—the site may look fabulous and the interpretations may even be interesting, but that does not mean the site is a credible source for an academic project. With Web sources, you must be especially careful to evaluate the credibility of a source.

The most credible Web sources are *databases.* Databases such as the *Gale Literature Resource Center, EbscoHost, InfoTrac, Masterfile Premiere,* and *MLA International Bibliography* contain articles and essays previously published and screened by a webmaster. These sources are as credible as any you might find in print form in the library. Use them freely and without hesitation. Many magazines, journals, and newspapers available in print form are also available through the Internet, and these sources are credible as well. An article published in the online version of *Rolling Stone* magazine is just as credible as an article published in the print version of the same source. Other credible sources include government sites (.gov), educational sites (.edu), sites published by nonprofit organizations (.org), and sites connected to reputable organizations such as CNN and The Journalist's Toolbox. Typically, commercial sites (.com) are not affiliated with sources immediately deemed credible by the academic community. But it is important to emphasize that *this rule is not without exception.* Again, you must think critically about the information you find on the Internet and use your own best judgment when determining the credibility of a source.

Evaluating the Credibility of Web Sources

When deciding whether or not a Web source is credible, you must consider several points. First of all, the *purpose of the site* must be obvious. Is this an informative site? A site intended primarily for entertainment? Is it a commercial site that earns profits, or is it sponsored by a nonprofit organization? The goals and objectives of the site should be clear—often stated in the form of a mission statement. If the purpose of the site is not clearly identifiable, then the site may not be credible.

It is also important to *identify who developed or sponsored the site.* This information is often found at the bottom of a home page or through a link titled "About." Some sites have corporate or institutional sponsors, so one particular author is not listed. In any case, someone must take responsibility for the information provided on the site, and clear *contact information* must be available in order for the site to be deemed credible in the academic community.

Another important point to consider is whether the site contains any particular *unfair bias.* All texts contain some bias, but you must examine the site for a bias that casts doubt on the accuracy of the information provided on the site—affects the site's credibility. For instance, a Web site promoting the importance of guns in the American culture and sponsored by the NRA (National Rifle Association) would most certainly be biased in favor of gun ownership. That bias does not necessarily make the site less than credible; however, it does warrant scrutiny (this goes back to purpose—the purpose of the Web site and your purpose as a researcher). You have to ask, Who benefits from your acceptance of the information on this site? Do the sponsors of this site benefit personally or financially from the promotion of this information?

In addition, you must determine whether the bias creates any sort of logical fallacy that may affect *your* credibility as a researcher. Sometimes bias is difficult to define; it may be subtle and is most often found in the language and tone of a text. For a Web site, this language extends past the words and includes the visual design. Colors, pictures, and background music may all work to create a bias. We must be alert to the subtle ways in which visual and audio images work to influence us.

Ultimately, the quality of the information provided on a site is what really matters. Anytime examples, facts, statistics, and expert testimony are provided, the source of that *information should be well-documented.* Remember that anyone can have an opinion about anything, but when researching, we are not in search of just anyone's opinion—we seek expert opinions. Examine a Web site for sources or links to sources for the information that is provided. Be wary of sites that contain authoritative-sounding information without documented sources.

Finally, it is necessary to locate *when the site was last updated.* Information may be posted to the Web and then abandoned. If a site is regularly maintained, the information provided is most likely current.

Let's put one of our model sources to the test. Following is a page from the web site http://www.ipl.org/div/litcrit/. Using the criteria outlined above, we will rank the credibility of this site (with 3 = highest and 1 = lowest).

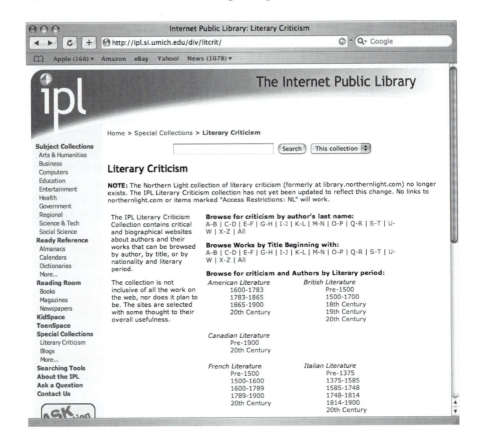

1. **Is the purpose of the site clearly stated or obvious?**

   Yes. Clicking on the link About the IPL, the following information is available:

   ### THE INTERNET PUBLIC LIBRARY MISSION STATEMENT

   The Internet Public Library (IPL), is a public service organization and learning/teaching environment at the University of Michigan School of Information. We will engage in activities in the following areas:

   ### SERVE
   Provide library services to Internet users. Activities include: finding, evaluating, selecting, organizing, describing, and creating information resources; and direct assistance to individuals.

   ### TEACH
   Use a learn-by-doing approach to train information professionals and students to work in an increasingly digital environment.

BUILD
Develop technology and best practices for providing library services via the Internet, including digital reference service and collection management.

LEARN
Conduct research aimed at improving our services and increasing the body of knowledge about digital libraries and librarianship.

SHARE
Promote our services. Share what we've learned with the professional community. Participate in efforts to create and promote relevant standards. Disseminate technology and practices to others. Develop relationships with organizations pursuing similar goals. Provide leadership in these activities.

GROW
Develop a model and plan for long-term sustainability and growth for our organization and services.

We approach the above activities via the values and principles of the profession of librarianship.

Adopted April 12, 2001
Score = 3

2. **Is contact information provided for the developer or sponsor of the site?**
Yes. This site is sponsored by the Regents of the University of Michigan Board. On each page there is a link to the University of Michigan, and on the page pictured above, there is a link: Contact IPL. Clicking on that link takes us to an e-mail form and additional contact information (address and phone numbers).
Score = 3

3. **Is the site free from unfair bias?**
Yes. This site is maintained by a nonprofit organization that serves as an electronic database, a clearinghouse for all types of literary research.
Score = 3

4. **Are sources or links provided for the information included on the site?**
Yes. All resources included on the site contain bibliographic information. For instance, on the link to Flannery O'Connor, author of the short story in Chapter 5, "A Good Man Is Hard to Find," we find this page full of additional links and bibliographic information (raised and highlighted as an example below):

Information Processing: Reading Responsibly

Once you have gathered your research, it is necessary to process the information in a responsible way. As we discussed in Part 2 of this textbook, one of the most important tools you can use when reading and processing a text is the *dialogue journal.* By engaging with a text through a dialogue, you will cut your research time in half. Instead of reading and rereading a text, or reading a text and discovering useful information, then wondering later where in the world you saw that information, if you use a dialogue as you read the first time, you will record the quote from the text that may be useful, the page number where you found that quote, and your initial response to the source. Another bonus: When you begin creating your argument, your evidence has already been gathered, and the source of that evidence has been documented—so you avoid plagiarism, too.

This is a matter of reading responsibly. Many students waste time by reading a text without pen in hand. Then, when they sit down to write their paper, they wonder, now where did I see that quote? And they have to spend more time and energy rereading their sources as they search for the information they need. Unfortunately, this is where many students get into trouble and plagiarize. Unable to locate their original source, they give up and put the information in their papers—undocumented. Skilled instructors will identify such slip-ups, and students will suffer the consequences of irresponsible reading habits.

The moral of the story is: Take the time the first time around to read and record and respond with a dialogue. You'll be glad you did later.

For a more in-depth discussion of reading strategies, please review Chapters 3, 4, and 5.

Using Sources Skillfully

Once you have gathered your sources and processed the information found in those sources, you will begin writing your argument essay. Using the information you found in your research in your own writing is a tricky thing. These are points to consider as you begin to incorporate your research materials into your essay: *balance, skillful integration,* and *in-text documentation.*

BALANCE

As you write about a piece of literature, particularly when creating an argument, it is important to balance the information you use from outside sources with your own ideas. Information you have gathered through your research should be used to support and supplement your ideas, but *your ideas* should always remain the central focus of your essay. So pick and choose the quotations you use carefully. Be selective and only use the information that is absolutely necessary to reinforce points you are making and to lend credibility to your argument.

SKILLFUL INTEGRATION OF SOURCES

Incorporating information from an outside source into your essay must be done skillfully. There are several important points to remember. First, never simply drop a quotation into your paper; instead, integrate the quotation into the body of your text. Use a *tagline* to introduce your source, interpret your quotation, and make necessary connections for your reader. A tagline is like an introduction for a guest speaker. As the host for this guest speaker, it is your responsibility to properly introduce the speaker, to let your audience know who the speaker is, why he is speaking, and why he is worth listening to.

For example, if we are writing an interpretive essay on the lyrics to "Who's Got My Back?" we may decide to use a portion of the interview with Bo Taylor as evidence to support our argument. Because Taylor is an expert in the field of Cherokee history, we definitely want to include his credentials in the form of a tagline to lend credibility to our ideas:

> *According to Bo Taylor, archivist for the Museum of the Cherokee Indian, the words to the chant used at the beginning of the song, "Who's Got My Back?" "change and reflect the personal emotions and whatever the artist wants to convey in his conversation with a higher power" (Interview).*

Second, always *provide your own interpretation* or understanding of the quoted material. Do not assume that your audience will understand the quotation as you understand it. To avoid confusion—and to demonstrate your own understanding—offer a paraphrasing of the quotation.

> *According to Bo Taylor, archivist for the Museum of the Cherokee Indian, the words to the chant used at the beginning of the song, "Who's Got My Back?" "change and reflect the personal emotions and whatever the artist wants to convey in his conversation with a higher power" (Interview). The meaning, then, is not found in the actual words but in the expression of those words in song. That expression may reflect different emotions, and the meaning will change according to the purpose of the conversation with a higher power (or God).*

Third, never use a quotation without *explaining its significance in relation to your ideas*. You cannot assume that your audience will automatically understand the importance of the quotation or how it supports your ideas. You have to provide an explanation—insight into the thought processes that led you to select the material as support for your argument:

> *According to Bo Taylor, archivist for the Museum of the Cherokee Indian, the words to the chant used at the beginning of the song, "Who's Got My Back?" "change and reflect the personal emotions and whatever the artist wants to convey in his conversation with a higher power" (Interview). The meaning, then, is not found in the actual words but* in the expression *of those words in song by an individual artist. That expression may reflect different emotions, and the meaning will change according to the purpose of the conversation with a higher power (or God).*

Therefore, as a listener, the meaning of the chant is created not through an understanding of words but through the emotions we experience by listening to the chant.

Just as the expression of the words of the chant varies from artist to artist and purpose to purpose, the experience of those emotions may vary from listener to listener. For me, the message communicated by the chant is one of mourning and sadness. When coupled with the lyrics to the song that follows, it becomes clear that the speaker is mourning the disconnection he feels as the result of his ongoing struggle with God.

This combination of *tagline, quotation, interpretation,* and *explanation* creates a *full thought cycle*. If any part of the cycle is missing, the reader is left with questions. For instance,

- If no tagline is presented in response to the quotation, the reader wonders, Who says so, and why should I pay attention?
- If no quotation follows, the reader wonders, Where's your proof?
- If no interpretation follows the quotation, the reader wonders, What does this mean?
- And if no explanation follows, the reader wonders, So what?

Skillful use of sources in a full thought cycle leaves no gaps in logic and reasoning for the reader to fall into and strengthens our argument so that it may bend to scrutiny but it will not break.

PRACTICE 10-B

Read the following poem by Wallace Stevens (utilize reading strategies practiced in Chapters 3, 4, and 5). Then read the brief critical essay that follows using a dialogue for your reading strategy. Allow your dialogue to be focused. In the left-hand column, record quotations from the text with which you strongly agree or strongly disagree. In the righthand column, record your interpretation and response for each quotation.

Discuss the poem and the critical essay in small groups or as a whole class. Working together, select a specific point to address. Generate a paragraph that addresses that point. Practice a full thought cycle. Create a tagline introducing the source, integrate a quotation from the source, and add your interpretation and explanation. Share your work in small groups or as a whole class.

THE EMPEROR OF ICE CREAM

Call the roller of big cigars,   1
The muscular one, and bid him whip   2

In kitchen cups concupiscent curds. 3
Let the wenches dawdle in such dress 4
As they are used to wear, and let the boys 5
Bring flowers in last month's newspapers. 6
Let be finale of seem. 7
The only emperor is the emperor of ice-cream. 8

Take from the dresser of deal. 9
Lacking the three glass knobs, that sheet 10
On which she embroidered fantails once 11
And spread it so as to cover her face. 12
If her horny feet protrude, they come 13
To show how cold she is, and dumb. 14
Let the lamp affix its beam. 15
The only emperor is the emperor of ice-cream. 16

Wallace Stevens "The Emperor of Ice Cream"

by ARTHUR F. BETHEA, published in *The Explicator,* 2004

Arthur F. Bethea received his PhD from Ohio University in 1996 and is currently an assistant professor of English at Purdue University-Calumet.

Fifty-five years ago, in what was the first of many notes in *The Explicator* analyzing Wallace Stevens's "The Emperor of Ice-Cream," Robert Thackaberry observed that horny, "an alley word for libidinous," is part of the poem's "sexual symbolism" (n.p.). Thackaberry did not explain the meaning of this symbolism, however, and most critics after him have ignored the sexual implications of lines 13 and 14 ("If her horny feet protrude, they come / To show how cold she is, and dumb") altogether,[1] though this passage has been called the "most shocking par[t] of the poem" (Neill 93) and "the center" of the text (Silverman 166). According to Ronald Sukenick, the woman's feet "only serve to affirm the common fact of physical death" (63), whereas Warren Carrier similarly remarks that the protruding feet "confirm the reality of her death" (234). Although Stevens's poem surely emphasizes "the desolating finality of death" (Beckett 79), "horny" describes feet conspicuously, and the word is only more noticeable because of the endlined position of "come"; hence glosses such as Carrier's and Sukenick's ignoring the sexuality of the language are too narrow. Moreover, emphasized by rhyme, by a comma, and by endline position, "dumb" appears to be a pun: Dead, the woman is mute; alive, she was stupid.

It is not anachronistic to read sexual punning in lines 13 and 14, as the slang definitions of "horny" (sexually excited) and "come" (to have orgasm) were established in the late nineteenth century and the seventeenth century, respectively (OED). But if there is sexual punning, what is the purpose? and why is the woman called stupid? The first key to answering these questions is found in stanza one, which defines the woman's likely profession. The speaker commands, "Let the wenches dawdle in such dress / As they are used to wear [. . .]." While "wenches" has several meanings, "dawdle" strongly implies prostitution, as prostitutes in a brothel are stereotypically imagined to lounge idly, waiting for a customer. The derogatory, diminishing connotations of the phrase "are used" also support this interpretation.

If the dead woman was a prostitute, lines 13 and 14 surely exemplify the "heartless cruelty" that Thomas Grey observes in the poem as a whole (99). So lascivious that her feet are sexually excited,[2] supine (as she was throughout her career), and too stupid to know that she is dead, the whore has an orgasm—or so goes one paraphrase of the demeaning joke. "Emperor" is commonly regarded as an argument for accepting "be" (reality) instead of "seem" (anything rooted in appearances or wishes),[3] yet the poem's sexual punning may ironically imply an unrealistic conception of prostitution.[4]

Before the woman is overtly criticized, the beginning of stanza 2 subtly intimates that she suffered a failure of imagination. The "embroidered" sheet that will cover only part of her body will be taken from "the dresser of deal, / Lacking the three glass knobs [. . .]" (lines 9–10). Stevens associates glass with the imagination, perhaps most famously in "Asides on the Oboe," where the "glass man" is the fecund poet who enriches people's lives by enhancing their imaginations, the requisite power for creating order and meaning out of the chaos of concrete reality (*Collected Poems* 251). Michael Zimmerman correctly notes that the "embroidered sheet" is "a product of the imagination" (121), a quality central to Stevens's epistemology and aesthetics, yet the sheet is something "On which she embroidered fantails once." In the present, associated with images of inadequacy— an undersized sheet taken from a cheap bureau missing glass knobs—the dead woman draws Stevens's ire for having abandoned her imagination to live a life rooted stupidly in the carnal.[5]

Although Stevens doubtlessly emphasizes the reality and finality of death, he also wants us to consider how to live. One response to the inevitable reductiveness is to eat the ice cream of life before it melts; not surprising, "Emperor" has been associated with hedonism. Stuart Silverman, for instance, argues that the poem offers "an amorphous blending of hedonism and vitalism" as a God substitute (168), whereas Carrier asserts that "Stevens affirms the survival of the reign of pleasure despite the death of the individual" (232). Stevens was no starving artist. He was proud of his high-ranking position as an insurance lawyer and gratified by the material pleasures that his income afforded. But he was also influenced by philosophers such as Plato and Emerson (Richardson 23), and, as he explicitly indicated, in "Emperor" he attempted to write about "being" (*Letters* 341), which includes the mind as well as the body. Although the message is not limpidly communicated,[6] "Emperor" suggests both the importance of the physical and its insufficiency without the mental.

Notes

1. All quotations from "The Emperor of Ice-Cream" are from *The Collected Poems of Wallace Stevens* (64).

2. Besides its sexual implications, "horny" is also used for its association with death. As Richard Ellmann observes, "horn is the colour-sign of death" (91–92).

3. See Milton Bates (25), though he considers the argument for "be" over "seem" unintentionally contradicted, a position with which I concur.

4. The joke is perhaps based upon the erroneous notion that prostitutes typically enjoy their paid sexual encounters. The poem also might suggest that the dead woman chose poorly when becoming a prostitute, yet familial and/or economic factors normally coerce women into this profession.

5. John McDermott's reading of "Emperor" helped me to see the idea of an imaginative failure in a reductive emphasis on the physical.

6. In one sense, the poem's crypticness is thematically appropriate. Six of the poem's nine sentences are imperatives, four beginning with "let," the word that starts all of God's commands in the imperative-dominated first chapter of Genesis; the poem's final command, "Let the lamp affix its beam," parodies God's first order, "Let there be light." In rejecting the "seem" of the Christian redemptive myth—a point more obvious in the Harmonium poems "The Death of a Soldier" and "The Worms at Heaven's Gate"—Stevens makes his God substitute enigmatic just like the Genesis ancestor. Less defendable, however, is Stevens's apparent cultivation of obscurity for obscurity's sake. In 1992, while preparing Harmonium for publication, Stevens wrote Harriet Monroe that he "rather desperately" wished "to be as obscure as possible until [he had] perfected an authentic and fluent speech" (qtd. in Kermode).

Works Cited

Bates, Milton J. "'The Emperor' and Its Clothes." *Teaching Wallace Stevens: Practical Essays.* Eds. John N. Serio and B. J. Leggett. Knoxville: U of Tennessee P, 1994. 17–25.

Beckett, Lucy. *Wallace Stevens.* London: Cambridge UP, 1974.

Carrier, Warren. "Commonplace Costumes and Essential Gaudiness: Wallace Stevens's 'The Emperor of Ice-Cream.'" *College Literature* 1 (1974): 130–35.

Ellmann, Richard. "Wallace Stevens's 'Ice-Cream.'" *Kenyon Review* 19 (1959): 89–105.

Grey, Thomas C. *The Wallace Stevens Case: Law and the Practice of Poetry.* Cambridge: Harvard UP, 1991.

Kermode, Frank. *Wallace Stevens.* 1961. New York: Grove, 1979. 9.

McDermott, John V. "Wallace Stevens's 'The Emperor of Ice-Cream.'" *The Explicator* 50 (1992): 87–89.

Neill, Edward. "The Melting Moment: Stevens's Rehabilitation of Ice Cream." *Ariel* 4.1 (1973): 88–96.

Richardson, Joan. *Wallace Stevens: A Biography: The Early Years, 1879–1923.* New York: Morrow, 1986.

Silverman, Stuart. "The Emperor of Ice-Cream." *Western Humanities Review* 26 (1972): 165–68.

Stevens, Wallace. *The Collected Poems of Wallace Stevens.* 1954. New York: Vintage, 1990.

_____. *Letters of Wallace Stevens.* Ed. Holly Stevens. New York: Knopf, 1966.

Sukenick, Ronald. *Wallace Stevens: Musing the Obscure.* New York: New York UP, 1967.

Thackaberry, Robert. "Stevens's 'The Emperor of Ice-Cream.'" *The Explicator* 1 (1948): item 36 (n.p.).

Zimmerman, Michael. "Wallace Stevens's Emperor." *English Language Notes* 4 (1966): 119–23.

IN-TEXT DOCUMENTATION

We've discussed several ways to avoid plagiarism, and the final step you must take is a technical one. Whenever you use information from a source in a paper, you must document the source of that information using an *in-text citation.* The most common form of in-text citation is a parenthetical reference. This sounds a lot more complicated than it really is. A parenthetical reference is *an abbreviated notation in parentheses in the body of your text that leads your reader to your works cited page for a complete bibliographic citation.*

Specific and detailed guidelines for in-text documentation (and the all-important creation of a works cited page) may be found in most handbooks, in *The MLA Handbook for Writer's of Research Papers,* or online through http://www.mla.org. Your school's library Web site may have a link to MLA documentation Web sites.

The following list describes most of the instances of in-text citation you will use. Where possible, our examples are taken from an article written by Elizabeth Marshall called "The Daughter's Disenchantment: Incest as Pedagogy in Fairy Tales and Kathryn Harrison's *The Kiss.*" Here are some general guidelines for documenting sources within your text.

CITING A SINGLE AUTHOR IN YOUR TEXT. Place the author's name and the relevant page numbers within parentheses at the end of the reference or at the end of the sentence:

> In The Kiss, *girlhood appears as a "landscape of feeling that might be continually reworked and reinterpreted" (Steedman 128).*

CITING A SINGLE AUTHOR IN YOUR TEXT WHEN YOU HAVE MENTIONED THE NAME IN YOUR REFERENCING SENTENCE. Place only the page number in parentheses because you have already mentioned the name of the author in your own sentences:

> *Similarly, Cynthia Crossen from* the Wall Street Journal *tells Harrison to "hush-up" (A16).*

CITING MORE THAN ONE AUTHOR OR WORK IN A SINGLE REFERENCE. Put all the authors and pages numbers in parentheses but separate the works with a semicolon. If you cite more than one reference in a single sentence, but the references are separated in the sentence, cite each work separately, close to the place in the sentence where you cited it:

"With few exceptions (Hickman; Zipes, "Maiden"), critics celebrated Huck and Lobel's characterization of Princess Furball's "feminist" qualities (Boyles; Burns).

CITING MORE THAN ONE WORK BY A SINGLE AUTHOR. Cite in parentheses the author, the work, and the page number, using a comma only between the author and the work:

In the process, they "eliminated those passages which they thought would be harmful for children's eyes" (Zipes, Fairy Tales *48). This includes censoring any material that was sexual, while "lurid portrayals of child abuse, starvation, and exposure, like fastidious descriptions of cruel punishments, on the whole escaped censorship" (Zipes,* Hard Facts *10–11).*

CITING A SOURCE THAT HAS NO AUTHOR OR PAGE NUMBERS. Use the title of the work instead. If the title is a long one, shorten it in the text, but use the full title in the work cited list. Also, if the work is short, you can reference the paragraph where the information can be found. (Note: You may often encounter this example when using online sources.)

The article mentions "skillful communication, life/career visioning and dealing with anxiety and stress" as three of the themes in the novel ("Creating Robust Relationships" par. 2).

When you cite at the end of a sentence, the period that ends the sentence goes outside the parenthesis, as we have demonstrated above. When you cite a long quotation (five or more lines) the quote is indented and the period that ends the sentences goes before the beginning of the parentheses.

Harrison's journey home is both a literal return and a psychological one. Harrison reconnects with her mother and in turn reconnects with her own flesh. As her mother dies of cancer, Harrison communicates her betrayal through the body. (421)

END-OF-TEXT DOCUMENTATION:
CONSTRUCTING A WORKS CITED PAGE

The final verification of your research appears in a works cited page at the end of your argument. This page is an alphabetical list of all the works you "cited" in your argument, whether they were cited directly (through a quote or paraphrase) or you simply referred to them in passing. The rules for citing works seem impossible to understand and to memorize, and we suggest you don't try to do either. Instead, try to remember a few general principles and then refer to a good, up-to-date handbook to verify specific information.

Principle 1: The order of the whole list is alphabetical, using the author's last name.

Principle 2: Each citation has a particular order, usually author, work, location of work, publisher, date, and if relevant, page numbers. The location could be a geographical location (the place of publication) or the journal/magazine, newspaper, or Web site within which shorter articles appear.

Principle 3: Punctuation is important, so make sure you follow the citation examples exactly.

Principle 4: The works cited list is double-spaced (like your essay); the second and following lines of each entry are indented five spaces.

Following are examples of particular citations.

BOOK

Bettleheim, Bruno. *The Uses of Enchantment: The Meaning and Importance of Fairy Tales.* New York: Vintage, 1975.

BOOK BY TWO OR MORE AUTHORS

Doane, Jancie, and Devon Hodges. *Telling Incest: Narratives of Dangerous Remembering from Stein to Sappho.* Ann Arbor: U of Michigan P, 2001.
Note 1: The second author's name is written with the first name first.
Note 2: If you have a work by four or more authors, you can name all four authors, or you can name just the first author on the title page and then write *et al.*

EDITED COLLECTION

Note 1: If you cite the writer or writers in the collection, list those names first and the name(s) of the editor(s) after the title:
Oates, Joyce Carol. "In Olden Times, When Wishing Was Having: Classic and Contemporary Fairy Tales." *Mirror, Mirror on the Wall: Women Writers Explore Their Favorite Fairy Tales.* Ed. Kate Bernheimer. New York: Anchor, 1998.
Note 2: If you cite the editor of the collection, enter that name first in the works cited:
Saxton, Ruth, ed. *The Girl: Construction of the Girl in Contemporary Fiction by Women.* New York: St. Martin's, 1998.
Note 3: When you cite more than one editor, enter as you would with an author, but follow the final name with "eds."
Culley, Margo, and Catherine Portuges. eds. *Gendered Subjects: The Dynamics of Feminist Teaching.* Boston: Routledge and Kegan Paul, 1985.

FOREWORD, PREFACE, OR INTRODUCTION TO A BOOK

Berlin, James. Foreword. *Changing Classroom Practices: Resources for Literary and Cultural Studies.* Ed. David B. Downing. Urbana: NCTE, 1994. vii–xv.

TRANSLATED WORK

Note 1: When you focus on the original author:

Grimm, Jacob, and Wilhelm Grimm. "All-Fur." *The Complete Fairy Tales of the Brothers Grimm.* Trans, Jack Zipes. Toronto: Bantam, 1992. 259–63.

Note 2: When you focus on the translator:

Zipes, Jack, trans. Grimm, Jacob, and Wilhelm Grimm. "All-Fur." *The Complete Fairy Tales of the Brothers Grimm.* Toronto: Bantam, 1992. 259–63.

REPUBLISHED BOOK

Note: Give the original publication date after the title and then the current version publication information in the remainder of the citation. If the below book was republished in 2004, for example:

Bettleheim, Bruno. *The Uses of Enchantment: The Meaning and Importance of Fairy Tales.* New York: Vintage, 1975.

The new citation would look like this:

Bettleheim, Bruno. *The Uses of Enchantment: The Meaning and Importance of Fairy Tales.* 1975. New York: Vintage, 2004.

BOOK THAT IS PART OF A SERIES

Kostelnick, Charles, and David D. Roberts, eds. *Designing Visual Language: Strategies for Professional Communicators.* The Allyn and Bacon Series in Technical Communication. Boston: Allyn and Bacon, 1998.

BOOK, READER, OR ANTHOLOGY

Lomax, Alan, and Raoul Abdul, eds. *3000 Years of Black Poetry: An Anthology.* New York: Mead, 1970.

BOOK CHAPTER

Elbow, Peter. "Revising." *Being a Writer.* Boston: McGraw Hill, 2003. 109–142.

BOOK PUBLISHED BEFORE 1900

Note: You can decide to include the publisher's name or not.

Saint-Foix, M. *The Oracle.* London, 1752.

DISSERTATION OR THESIS

Note: If the dissertation or thesis is published, include the city, publisher and year of publication. If the dissertation or thesis is not published, simply include the author's university and year the work was completed.

Smith, Christine. *The Baptistery of Pisa.* Diss. New York U, 1975. New York: Garland
    Pub., 1976.

BOOK REVIEW OR MOVIE REVIEW

Anderson, Jeffrey M. "Getting Ogre It." Rev. of *Shrek 2. San Francisco Examiner.* 19 May 2004.

ARTICLE IN A SCHOLARLY JOURNAL

Some journals are paginated by year and some by issue. The first example below is year-
by-year pagination; the second example includes the issue number after the volume number.

YEAR BY YEAR
Stevens, Laura. "Transatlanticism Now." *American Literary History* (2004): 93–102.

ISSUE/VOLUME
Stevens, Laura. "Transatlanticism Now." *American Literary History* 16.1 (2004): 93–102.

ARTICLE IN A POPULAR MAGAZINE

The citations of articles vary based on how often the magazine is published.

MONTHLY OR BI-MONTHLY
Laliberte, Richard. "Attack From Within." *Lifetime.* June–July. 2004: 60+.

WEEKLY OR BI-WEEKLY
Gliato, Tom, and Sean Daly. "Jake Quake!" *People.* 14 July 2004: 77–8.

ARTICLE IN A NEWSPAPER
Musseau, Natalie. "Date Set for Public Forum on Health Cuts." *The Gulf News.* 29 March
    2004: 1.

LETTER TO THE EDITOR
Raines, James. Letter. *The Charlotte Observer.* 23 Jan. 2001: C4.

BULLETIN, BROCHURE, OR PAMPHLET

Pike, Sandy. *Celebrating the Female Spirit: Authentic Empowerment for Women.* Matthews,
    NC: Mandorla Press, 2004.

GOVERNMENT DOCUMENT

United States. George W. Bush. *Remarks to the United States Attorneys Conference.* Wash-
    ington: GPO, 2001.

Today, you will often use electronic sources to support your claim. MLA format requires
six kinds of information to complete your works cited entry: the author of the work; the

title of the work; the title of the site; the date of electronic publication; the date you examined the site; the Web address. The information will vary from citation to citation. Sometimes you will not have an author; sometimes the Web address will be very long. We provide some typical examples of how to make Web entries in your works cited list.

ONLINE BOOK

Use any and all information provided about the book.

Larson, Dewey. *The Case Against the Nuclear Atom.* Portland: North Pacific Publishers, 1963. *The Online Books Page.* 26 May 2004 <http://www.reciprocalsystem.com/cana/index.htm>.

ONLINE SCHOLARLY JOURNAL ARTICLE

Dau, Dac. "Seamus Heaney's Religious Redress." *Literature and Theology* 17:1 (2003). 2 Dec. 2003 <http://www3.oup.co.uk/litthe/hdb/Volume_17/Issue_01>.

ONLINE POPULAR MAGAZINE

Scott, Jennifer. "Don't Let Stress Ruin your Game." *Golf Online.* June 2004. 3 June 2004 <http://www.golfonline.com/golfonline/fitness/features/article>.

ONLINE NEWSPAPER

Feder, Barnaby. "A Different Era for Alternative Energy." *New York Times.* 29 May 2004. 2 June 2004 <http://www.nytimes.com>.

Note: The article will not always be available on the front page of the online newspaper, and the actual address for the article may change often (especially when archived), so it is acceptable to use the main Web address (in this case, www.nytimes.com). When enough information is given, the reader can perform a search for the article.

PERSONAL OR PROFESSIONAL HOME PAGE

Note: Where possible, include the site's creator and/or sponsor.

Jordan, Michael. Home page. Sportsline.com. 3 June 2004 <http://jordan.sportsline.com>.

E-MAIL

Brown, Peter. E-mail to the author. 25 Jan. 2003.

Note: If you are still unsure of the medium of your source, give all information that is available to you (title, date of publication, sponsor, Web address, etc.) and note that the source is *electronic.*

Sometimes you will need to cite atypical sources, such as CDs, movies, videotapes, personal interviews, and live performances such as plays or lectures. Following are some examples of how to cite them in your essay.

SURVEY OR QUESTIONNAIRE

Tanner, Susan et al. Survey on the Use of Illegal Drugs in College Dormitories. University of Toronto. 12–15 May 2000.

PERSONAL INTERVIEW

Collins, Alfred. Personal Interview. 8 Nov. 2002.

OBSERVATION

Granger, Richard. Observation of Whitewater Rafters. Bryson City, NC. 13 July 2002.

MOVIE

Note: Name the director (dir.) and any other significant participants (namely, performers [perf.]) in the movie.

The Lord of the Rings: The Two Towers. Dir. Peter Jackson. Perf. Elijah Wood, Ian McKellen, Liv Tyler, Sean Astin. DVD. New Line Productions, Inc., 2002.

PERFORMANCE

Hamlet. By William Shakespeare. Dir. John Hartness. Off Tryon Theater Company, Charlotte, NC. 14 Aug. 2001.

LECTURE

Sterling, Ray. "Creating Men Through Music." Four Seasons, Hollywood. 25 Sept. 1999.

Conclusion

The research process is exciting because it reveals information you may not have suspected exists. You can learn much, and as students you can communicate your new knowledge through your essay writing. The research process, although easier because of your ability to conduct online searches, is also harder than it has ever been. Because there is so much "out there," you are forced to make smart choices among perhaps hundreds of sources. You must make increasingly difficult judgment calls about the credibility and relevance of your sources and how to introduce and interpret them in your own writing. Like much of the writing you have done in response to the practices in this textbook, the research process is a collaborative effort among you, your teacher, and your librarian. Because your teacher values this process, she or he will know how to help you. You will also get expert help from your school reference librarian. And in the process, you will become a smarter, better-equipped student.

Writing Assignment Suggestions

1. Select an "A Closer Look" section from one of the casebooks. Begin by reading the literature selections included in the section (as always, utilize appropriate reading

strategies). Next, read the interview with the author. What have you learned that might help you to interpret this writer's literature? What else do you want to know? Make a list of questions, and conduct research with the goal of answering some or all of those questions. Follow the steps outlined in this chapter: Make a plan, conduct a search, record the research process, make a paper trail. Once you have gathered several sources, read them and create a *critical annotated bibliography* of those sources.

An annotated bibliography includes a full MLA citation for the source, a summary of the source, and a brief evaluation of the source. Here is a student example:

Amanda Clark
Meg Morgan, Ph.D.
Writing About Literature
30 March 2004

Critical Annotated Bibliography

Blain, Virginia, Patricia Clements, and Isobel Grundy. *The Feminist Companion to Literature in English Women Writers from the Middle Ages to the Present.* New Haven, CT: Yale UP, 1990.

The authors, Virginia Blain, Patricia Clements, and Isobel Grundy, compile a listing, along with some biographical and critical information, including highlights in their careers, of influential feminist writers across the centuries. Anne Sexton, though one of the most promising and talented writers of her time period, seemed to be obsessed with death and suicide. In fact, after experimenting with it beginning in 1953, after her daughter was born, and her husband was fighting in the Korean War, she first began seriously attempting it. She went back to school to poetry writing classes in the late 1950s, and there met Sylvia Plath and Maxine Kumin. She was a pioneer in women's writing, uncovering the before rarely visited topics of, "women's experience of menstruation, abortion, domestic rage, and emotional and physical child abuse." (Her parents apparently abused her as a young child.) Sexton eventually succeeded in 1974, by carbon monoxide poisoning.

In attempting to discover what impact her life experiences had upon her writing the book *Transformations,* and ultimately the jaded poem "Cinderella," this section gives me a good starting off point from which to evaluate her life. It gives a good overview of her experiences, and dips somewhat into some criticism of her works, though disappointingly not appealing directly to my chosen work.

Hokenson, Jan. *Contemporary Poets Third Edition.* Ed. James Vinson. New York: St. Martin's Press, 1980.

Jan Hokenson illustrates Anne Sexton's poetry in terms of where she was in her life at the time that she wrote it; she divides Sexton's poetry into three "stages." The first stage is the beginning stage, in which Sexton was trying to identify and find herself as a poet, exploring various feminine images such as motherhood and the relationship between mother and daughter, as well as not so solely female issues such as madness (her own personal madness came into question then, as well), separation, and nature. Her books during this time were *To Bedlam and Part Way Back* and *All My Pretty Ones*. The second period of her literary life was marked by more cynicism, simplistic in construct but, perhaps, deeper in content, as best shown by *Live or Die*. The third and last period in her somewhat abbreviated professional career was the even darker deeper period, which was all the same completed by a triumphant ascension to heaven, where she is beaten by God himself at poker. Books of interest during this period include *The Book of Folly* and *The Awful Rowing Toward God*.

This section was another analysis of Sexton's life, though this time focused mainly on her literary works instead of merely forming a chronology of her life. Though it is interesting to break her works up into an organized, neat little three-item system, it does not touch on my poem, or even mention the book it was originally published in at all.

Kevles, Barbara. "The Art of Poetry: Anne Sexton." *Anne Sexton: The Artist and Her Critics*. Ed. J. D. McClatchy. Bloomington: Indiana UP, 1978.

Barbara Kevles serves as the interviewer of poet Anne Sexton. This lengthy interview, named "The Art of Poetry: Anne Sexton," stretches from page 3 through 29 and took place in mid-August of 1968. In it, Sexton explains how she got interested in and began to write poetry, which was after her first nervous breakdown at 28. She spoke about her dependence on other people, such literary greats as W. D. Snodgrass, Sylvia Plath, and her teacher Robert Lowell, along with lesser-known authors such as Maxine Kumin and George Starbuck, and how they influenced her. Plath, having already committed suicide by the time this interview took place, it was pointed out, was obsessed with death, as Sexton was in her book *Live or Die*. The two women discussed death and suicide on many occasions when they were both students under Robert Lowell. This was an eerie prophecy that would fulfill itself only six years later when Sexton herself committed suicide.

Though once again, this interview did not ask directly about the poem I am researching, or *Transformations* as a whole, it did give a good insight into the influences that Sexton had in writing her works, the colleagues she depended upon, and even explored the role her nightmares and "visions" had. This was a startling glimpse into a troubled and seriously disturbed soul who was a strong believer in the Freudian psychology of the id, ego, and superego.

Litz, A. Walton, ed. *American Writers: A Collection of Literary Biographies*. Supplement II, Part 2. New York: Charles Scribner's Sons, 1981.

A. Walton Litz carefully dissects Anne Sexton's poetry of *Transformations*, with personal letters to her editor and the letter asking Kurt Vonnegut to write the foreword to her next collection of "small, funny and horrifying" reworked fairy tales. *Transformations* explores the motives that people have to do the things they do in the relationships with other people. She, in effect, psychoanalyzes and universalizes each of the characters from the children's bedtime stories, naming Rumpelstiltskin not the superego, but the id, naming the miller's spinning daughter as a victim of her father. The evil fairy is given a motive for her actions by commenting that, "her uterus [is] an empty teacup." Sexton also adds in dashes of popular culture, naming Little Red Riding Hood's cloak as "her Linus blanket," and Cinderella, from sitting in her fireside cinders all day, "walked around looking like Al Jolson." Marriage, also, is looked at condescendingly, suggesting that after this cure-all to all women's problems happens, happiness and joy in this conformity abounds forever. *Transformations* brought Sexton some of the best reviews in her career, as critics praised her breaking her ties with pure "confession" to intertwining her own experiences (she names herself the story-telling witch), in an artistic and entertainingly witty form.

   This was probably the most useful piece I have found so far. The entry on Anne Sexton dissected all of her work, but since I was primarily concerned with *Transformations,* I focused on that section. It gave not only reviews from the time it was published, but actual letters from Sexton herself concerning the work, to an analysis of several of the themes and language as well.

   Mainiero, Lina, ed. *American Women Writers.* Vol. 4. New York: Frederick Ungar
      Publishing, 1982.

Lina Maineiero explores, in this entry on Anne Sexton, why Anne wrote what she wrote, and about what she mainly wrote about. Maineriro attributes Sexton's keen but tortured discussion of relationships to Sexton's own life and strange relationships with her great-aunt, parents, husband, and two daughters. Sexton also drew from her experiences in a mental ward and her own descent into madness and "partway back" again. Many of her best poems concerned "madness, guilt, and loss," as in her 1960 work, *To Bedlam and Part Way Back.* This "confessional" poet won the Pulitzer Prize for *Live or Die,* which drew religious and universal parallels of mental illness. Yet, though Sexton is remembered for her tributes and dissection of madness on many levels, she was probably best known for her contributions to female-oriented poetry. She wrote mother-daughter poems and explored her "frustration" of being a woman; in the end she reported being weary with gender as a whole. Though her range is somewhat limited, critics cannot deny the raw power in her autobiographical and confessional words.

   This is an outsider's view of basically what made Anne Sexton tick. Less convincing than the author's interviews in which the same information is given in the author's own words, this example also gives objectivity to her work instead of a personal account. It gives an overview of what Sexton is mainly remembered for, which briefly is intertwined with my questions of why Sexton wrote "Cinderella," such as her female-focused poetry, and startling critics.

   Martz, Louis L. "Critical Essays on Anne Sexton." Rev. of *Transformations* by
      Anne Sexton. Ed. Linda Wagner Martin. Boston: G.K. Hall & Co, 1989.

Louis L. Martz wrote this book review on Anne Sexton's *Transformations* originally for the *Yale Review* in 1972, only a year after it was originally published. He made the point of marking that when Sexton first presented her first book, everyone was amazed by the raw arrangement and emotions in the poetry; yet her follow-up works were dull and vapid in comparison, falling to the ranks of even being "conventional." This work, her 1971 book *Transformations,* however, shone with a dim glimmer of the imagination and power she had exhibited in her original tales. *Transformations* gave personal, modern, artistic twists to traditional fairy tales, such as "Snow White," "Rapunzel," and "Rumpelstiltskin." Though it was interesting during the first read-through, Martz argued, during the second, the reader was more unimpressed by the blatant polar opposites of maturity and childishness, and lost some of its charm and biting wit. Overall, it was a review painting the book as worth a few seconds, but generally a mediocre effort.

This is a somewhat mixed review by a critic writing just after *Transformations* was published. I believe that public opinion, while swayed by the reviews, is not imprisoned by them, since how many times have critics called a movie absolutely appalling, yet viewers wholeheartedly disagree. Perhaps it comes partly from the fact that people are not always welcoming to being told how to think.

Marx, Patricia. "Interview with Anne Sexton." *Anne Sexton: The Artist and Her Critics.* Ed. J. D. McClatchy. Bloomington: Indiana UP, 1978.

In Patricia Marx's "Interview with Anne Sexton," written in 1965, the interviewer focuses primarily on the process that Sexton went through to achieve what she had in the literary circus, from her breakdown to studying under Robert Lowell. Marx asked Sexton about how she felt about poetry in general, her poetry, and the labels placed upon her by society and by her critics. Interestingly, she stated that while in Europe, she carried a bad review around in her wallet, and when starting writing, she in effect, collected rejection slips from the mail. Sexton's poetry, she herself stated, should have a purpose that "should be a shock to the sense. It should almost hurt." Sexton also talked about the effect her children, two daughters, had upon her life, her writing process and the final product. Men, she argued, could not achieve the same creative high as women can because they are deprived of the function of having children. The truth was a different thing when looked at from different angles; "It depends on what you want to call the truth, you see."

This interview was not as useful as the first one, yet it also had significance in what Sexton tried to do with her poetry, where she believed her main influences came from, and why she felt she could so readily "confess" her life to the public through craft. The focus of this interview was, once again, on Anne herself instead of my poem in particular, so it was less useful than other sources.

Root, William Pitt. "Critical Essays on Anne Sexton." Rev. of *Transformations* by Anne Sexton. Ed. Linda Wagner Martin. Boston: G.K. Hall & Co, 1989.

William Pitt Root, writing a review of Anne Sexton's *Transformations,* the fractured fairy tales, originally in *Poetry* in October of 1973. Root describes the works in the book as evoking two reactions, sometimes simultaneously, amusement and disgust. Sometimes, however, Root points out, the author, Sexton, seems to be stretching herself mainly to the point of merely being amusing. Sexton sets herself up as being a kind of twisted Mother Goose, a middle-aged, story-telling "witch." She mocks popular culture and the traditional telling of these tales. The amusing parallels between actual children's fairy tales and adult literature are there, yet there is also present an underlying emotional depth and social commentary. The reviewer also commented that the poet Randall Jarrell, who also wrote alternative versions of children's fairy tales, would have enjoyed *Transformations* very much indeed. Root therefore recommends this book as being entertaining, witty, and yet beautifully and evocatively written.

   This is a good review, in contrast to the previously mentioned mediocre review, to Sexton's book *Transformations*. This reviewer seems impressed with Sexton's fusing of autobiographical material, with popular culture and psychology, in the form of traditional children's stories. It explains some of the themes present throughout the book, and praises the entertaining way in which they are presented. I found this more useful than the other review, though less interesting.

   Sage, Lorna. *The Cambridge Guide to Women's Writing in English.* New York:
      Cambridge University Press, 1999.

Lorna Sage gives a basic chronology of Anne Sexton's life without going into too much detail. She stressed that Sexton was both extremely attractive, working as a part-time model at one time, and had a vibrant personality to match it, making her personal poetry readings of her works maxed out in attendance. Sexton's work was mainly described as confessional, putting much of herself into the words, with no apparent inhibitions, which stunned and appalled critics but kept the public wanting more. Though the public widely embraced her work, and she was awarded with many prestigious honors, including the Pulitzer Prize for Poetry in 1966 and a fellowship of the Royal Society of Literature in London, Sexton was always obsessed with death. Her last books were ironically titled *The Awful Rowing Toward God* and *The Death Notebooks.* Alone on October 4, 1974, Sexton committed suicide, a goal she was headed toward since her first attempt on her 28th birthday in 1956.

   This entry, truthfully, was not very helpful. As a basic chronology, it could have simply been reduced to a timeline, one of which I had found in another book about Sexton's life. I found only the same information as I had found in every other source I picked up.

   Vonnegut, Jr., Kurt. Foreword. *Transformations.* By Anne Sexton. Boston:
      Houghton Mifflin, 1971. vii–x.

Kurt Vonnegut Jr., in his remarkable foreword to Anne Sexton's book of re-worked children's fairy tales, *Transformations,* describes, from a personal point of view, his interaction with Sexton—he was drawn to her initially because of their mutual appreciation for the town of Indianapolis. He went on to explain that he struck up a conversation with her concerning Cinderella, even drawing her a diagram of the story—which happened to be the English version of the story. She was amused and told him that she was working on another version of the story, a reworking of the original tale by the Brothers Grimm, into a form of poetry. Yet Vonnegut concedes that he does not know her very well, and nonetheless admires her for the taming and release of certain wild emotions within him and, he speculates, within her as well. In the end, he does not even attempt to explain the poems in the book, having given up the, "criminal" practice of trying to, "explain works of art."

This was interesting. A contemporary of Sexton writing about her and her poetry was fun to look at. In addition, however, to being amusing to see, like looking at senior blurbs in a literary great yearbook, it also touched on, obviously, the book itself, being the foreword. It also directly concerned my poem, as well, which was useful.

2. Select one of the "A Closer Look" sections from a casebook in this text. Begin by reading the literature selections included in the section (as always, utilize appropriate reading strategies). Next, read the interview with the author. What do you learn from the interview that helps to explain the author's work? Finally, read the critical essay. Complete a dialogue as you read. In the left-hand column, record quotations from the text with which you strongly agree or strongly disagree. In the right-hand column, record your interpretation of those quotations and/or your response. Then, write an argument essay in which you either support the interpretation offered in the critical essay or argue against the interpretation offered in the critical essay. Conduct research as necessary to support your opinion.

PART FIVE
Turning In, Turning Out: Five Thematic Casebooks

◆───────◆

Overview

The following reader is organized thematically into five sections—we call these sections casebooks. Within each casebook we have collected poetry, fiction, and drama related to a particular theme. You will notice that the overall progression of casebooks moves from an introspective focus (such as Casebook One, *Me, Myself, and I: Exploring Identity*) to a focus on a combination of interior and exterior conditions, situations, and events (such as *(Hu)Man/Nature)*. You will also notice that within each casebook, the individual selections sometimes turn in for an introspective look at a particular aspect of a theme and sometimes turn out for a look at the external aspects of a theme.

Each selection offers many opportunities for exploration using the techniques covered throughout this textbook. For example, you might turn in for a look at the symbolism in Galway Kinnell, "Blackberry Eating," or you might turn out for a look at the ironic commentary on gender issues in Steve Martin's "WASP." There are countless possibilities and a broad enough range of subject matter and styles that most everyone should fine something of interest.

Each thematic casebook includes a brief mini-casebook titled "A Closer Look." For each theme, an author was selected for in-depth coverage. Each "A Closer Look" section includes an interview, one or more literary works connected to the overall casebook theme, and one or more critical articles or essays about those literary works. This focused exploration illustrates many important academic strategies covered throughout this textbook—most importantly, it offers the opportunity to read a body of literary work through a variety of lenses—or from multiple perspectives.

Our thanks go out to all of the authors and artists who allowed us to include their works in this book. We hope you enjoy reading and discussing them as much as we have enjoyed the selection process.

CASEBOOK ONE
Me, Myself, and I: Exploring Identity
Overview

For many of us, much of our lifetime is spent on a very personal quest to understand, to define, and to redefine who we are—our sense of identity. Sometimes identity is strongly connected to the spiritual, however we may define that realm; sometimes we define our identity based on our relationship to nature. Others find their identities closely tied to relationships with others—the ways in which they are similar to a group of people or the ways in which they are unique. There are countless ways to define the self, and literature has always been an effective medium of exploration.

The poetry, fiction, and drama included in this casebook explore the concept of identity from multiple perspectives, both male and female, and spanning centuries, continents, and cultures. You will find that you identify strongly with some pieces while others seem unrelated to your own experience, your own quest.

Consider these questions as you read:

- What is the "self"?
- When does one become aware of oneself as an individual? When does one develop self-awareness?
- Is the concept of self universal, or does it change—depending upon culture? Upon gender?
- How is "identity"—understood as one's sense of self, individuality—in conflict with or compatible with "equality"?

Poetry

EMILY BRONTË

Emily Jane Brontë was born in 1818 at Thornton, near Bradford, Yorkshire. Along with her sisters, Charlotte and Anne, Emily wrote fiction as well as poetry. She spent many years as a teacher, and at one time hoped to build her own school. That dream was never realized, and on October 1, 1848, Emily caught a severe cold that developed into inflammation of the lungs. She died on December 19.

No Coward Soul Is Mine

No coward soul is mine,
No trembler in the world's storm-troubled sphere!
I see Heaven's glories shine,
And Faith shines equal, arming me from Fear.

O God within my breast,
Almighty ever-present Deity!
Life, that in me has rest
As I, undying Life, have power in thee!

Vain are the thousand creeds
That move men's hearts, unutterably vain;
Worthless as withered weeds,
Or idlest forth, amid the boundless main

To waken doubt in one
Holding so fast by thy infinity,
Pervades and broods above,
Changes, sustains, dissolves, creates and rears.

Though earth and moon were gone,
And suns and universes ceased to be,
And thou were left alone
Every Existence would exist in thee.

There is not room for Death,
Nor atom that his might could render void
Since thou art Being and Breath,
And what thou art may never be destroyed.

WALT WHITMAN

Walter Whitman was born in 1819 in West Hills, New York. He quit his formal schooling in 1831 and went to work as an office boy for lawyers and doctors. In 1831 he worked as an apprentice for the *Long Island Patriot*—a newspaper publication. From there he had a long, varied, and celebrated career as a writer and a publisher. He died in 1892.

From Song of Myself

1

I celebrate myself, and sing myself,
And what I assume you shall assume,
For every atom belonging to me as good belongs to you.

I loafe and invite my soul,
I lean and loafe at my ease observing a spear of summer grass.

My tongue, every atom of my blood, form'd from this soil,
    this air,
Born here of parents born here from parents the same, and
    their parents the same,
I, now thirty-seven years old in perfect health begin,
Hoping to cease not till death.

Creeds and schools in abeyance,
Retiring back a while sufficed at what they are, but never
    forgotten,
I harbor for good or bad, I permit to speak at every hazard,
Nature without check with original energy.

24

Walt Whitman, a kosmos, of Manhattan the son,
Turbulent, fleshy, sensual, eating, drinking and breeding,
No sentimentalist, no stander above men and women or
    apart from them,
No more modest than immodest.

Unscrew the locks from the doors!
Unscrew the doors themselves from their jambs!

Whoever degrades another degrades me,
And whatever is done or said returns at last to me.

Through me the afflatus surging and surging, through
    me the current and index.

I speak the pass-word primeval, I give the sign of democracy,
By God! I will accept nothing which all cannot have their
    counterpart of on the same terms.

Through me many long dumb voices,
Voices of the interminable generations of prisoners and slaves,
Voices of the diseas'd and despairing and of thieves and dwarfs,
Voices of cycles of preparation and accretion,
And of the threads that connect the stars, and of wombs and
    of the father-stuff,
And of the rights of them the others are down upon,
Of the deform'd, trivial, flat, foolish, despised,
Fog in the air, beetles rolling balls of dung.

Through me forbidden voices,
Voices of sexes and lusts, voices veil'd and I remove the veil,
Voices indecent by me clarified and transfigur'd.

I do not press my fingers across my mouth,
I keep as delicate around the bowels as around the head and
    heart,
Copulation is no more rank to me than death is.

I believe in the flesh and the appetites,
Seeing, hearing, feeling, are miracles, and each part and tag
    of me is a miracle.

Divine am I inside and out, and I make holy whatever I
    touch or am touch'd from,
The scent of these arm-pits aroma finer than prayer,
This head more than churches, bibles, and all the creeds.

If I worship one thing more than another it shall be the
    spread of my own body, or any part of it,
Translucent mould of me it shall be you!
Shaded ledges and rests it shall be you!
Firm masculine colter it shall be you!
Whatever goes to the tilth of me it shall be you!
You my rich blood! your milky stream pale shippings of
    my life!
Breast that presses against other breasts it shall be you!
My brain it shall be your occult convolutions!
Root of wash'd sweet-flag! timorous pond-snipe! nest of
    guarded duplicate eggs! it shall be you!

Mix'd tussled hay of head, beard, brawn, it shall be you!
Trickling sap of maple, fibre of manly wheat, it shall
　　be you!
Sun so generous it shall be you!
Vapors lighting and shading my face it shall be you!
You sweaty brooks and dews it shall be you!
Winds whose soft-tickling genitals rub against me it shall
　　be you!
Broad muscular fields, branches of live oak, loving lounger
　　in my winding paths, it shall be you!
Hands I have taken, face I have kiss'd, mortal I have ever
　　touch'd, it shall be you.

I dote on myself, there is that lot of me and all so luscious,
Each moment and whatever happens thrills me with joy,
I cannot tell how my ankles bend, nor whence the cause of
　　my faintest wish,
Nor the cause of the friendship I emit, nor the cause of the
　　friendship I take again.

That I walk up my stoop, I pause to consider if it really be,
A morning-glory at my window satisfies me more than the
　　metaphysics of books.

To behold the day-break!
The little light fades the immense and diaphanous shadows,
The air tastes good to my palate.

Hefts of the moving world at innocent gambols silently
　　rising, freshly exuding,
Scooting obliquely high and low.

Something I cannot see puts upward libidinous prongs,
Seas of bright juice suffuse heaven.
The earth by the sky staid with, the daily close of their
　　junction,
The heav'd challenge from the east that moment over my head,
The mocking taunt, See then whether you shall be master!

Amiri Baraka

　　Amiri Baraka was born Everett LeRoi Jones in Newark, New Jersey, in 1934. He attended Rutgers University for two years, and then transferred to Howard University, where he earned his B.A. in English in 1954. He served in the Air Force from 1954 until

1957; then he moved to the Lower East Side of Manhattan. There he joined a group of artists, musicians, and writers. In 1968, he became a Muslim, changing his name to Imamu Amiri Baraka.

An Agony. As Now.

I am inside someone
who hates me. I look
out from his eyes. Smell
what fouled tunes come in
to his breath. Love his
wretched women.

Slits in the metal, for sun. Where
my eyes sit turning, at the cool air
the glance of light, or hard flesh
rubbed against me, a woman, a man,
without shadow, or voice, or meaning.

This is the enclosure flesh,
where innocence is a weapon. An
abstraction. Touch. Not mine.
Or yours, if you are the soul I had
and abandoned when I was blind and had
my enemies carry me as a dead man
if he is beautiful, or pitied.

It can be pain. (As now, as all his
flesh hurts me.) It can be that. Or
pain. As when she ran from me into
that forest.

   Or pain, the mind
silver spiraled whirled against the
sun, higher than even old men thought
God would be. Or pain. And the other. The
yes. (Inside his books, his fingers. They
are withered yellow flowers and were never
beautiful.) The yes. You will, lost soul, say?
"beauty." Beauty, practiced, as the tree. The
slow river. A white sun in its wet sentences.

Or, the cold men in their gale. Ecstasy. Flesh
or soul. The yes. (Their robes blown. Their bowls
empty. They chant at my heels, not at yours.) Flesh

or soul, as corrupt. Where the answer moves too quickly.
Where the God is a self, after all.

Cold air blown through narrow blind eyes. Flesh,
white hot metal. Glows as the day with its sun.
It is a human love. I live inside. A bony skeleton
you recognize as words or simple feeling.

But it has no feeling. As the metal, is hot, it is not,
given to love.

It burns the thing
inside it. And that thing
screams.

GARY SOTO

Gary Soto was born in Fresno, California, in 1952. He is the author of ten poetry collections and the youngest poet ever to be included in *The Norton Anthology of Poetry.* Among many awards, he has received fellowships from the California Arts Council, the Guggenheim Foundation, and the National Endowment for the Arts.

Black Hair

At eight I was brilliant with my body.
In July, that ring of heat
We all jumped through, I sat in the bleachers
Of Romain Playground, in the lengthening
Shade that rose from our dirty feet.
The game before us was more than baseball.
It was a figure—Hector Moreno
Quick and hard with turned muscles,
His crouch the one I assumed before an altar
Of worn baseball cards, in my room.
I came here because I was Mexican, a stick
Of brown light in love with those
Who could do it—the triple and hard slide,
The gloves eating balls into double plays.
What could I do with 50 pounds, my shyness,
My black torch of hair, about to go out?
Father was dead, his face no longer

Hanging over the table or our sleep,
And mother was the terror of mouths
Twisting hurt by butter knives.

In the bleachers I was brilliant with my body,
Waving players in and stomping my feet,
Growing sweaty in the presence of white shirts.
I chewed sunflower seeds. I drank water
And bit my arm through the late innings.
When Hector lined balls into deep
Center, in my mind I rounded the bases
With him, my face flared, my hair lifting
Beautifully, because we were coming home
To the arms of brown people.

JUNE JORDAN

June Jordan was born in New York City in 1936. Over the span of her career, she received many awards, such as a Rockefeller Foundation grant, the National Endowment for the Arts, and the New York Foundation for the Arts. She taught at the University of California, Berkeley, where she founded Poetry for the People. June Jordan died of breast cancer in June 2002, in Berkeley, California.

Poem About My Rights

I
Even tonight and I need to take a walk and clear
my head about this poem about why I can't
go out without changing my clothes my shoes
my body posture my gender identity my age
my status as a woman alone in the evening/
alone on the streets/alone not being the point/
the point being that I can't do what I want
to do with my own body because I am the wrong
sex the wrong age the wrong skin and
suppose it was not here in the city but down on the beach/
or far into the woods and I wanted to go
there by myself thinking about God/or thinking
about children or thinking about the world/all of it
disclosed by the stars and the silence:
I could not go and I could not think and I could not

stay there
alone
as I need to be
alone because I can't do what I want to do with my own
body and
who in the hell set things up
like this
and in France they say if the guy penetrates
but does not ejaculate then he did not rape me
and if after stabbing him if after screams if
after begging the bastard and if even after smashing
a hammer to his head if even after that if he
and his buddies fuck me after that
then I consented and there was
no rape because finally you understand finally
they fucked me over because I was wrong I was
wrong again to be me being me where I was/wrong
to be who I am
which is exactly like South Africa
penetrating into Namibia penetrating into
Angola and does that mean I mean how do you know if
Pretoria ejaculates what will the evidence look like the
proof of the monster jackboot ejaculation on Blackland
and if
after Namibia and if after Angola and if after Zimbabwe
and if after all of my kinsmen and women resist even to
self-immolation of the villages and if after that
we lose nevertheless what will the big boys say will they
claim my consent:
Do You Follow Me: We are the wrong people of
the wrong skin on the wrong continent and what
in the hell is everybody being reasonable about
and according to the Times this week
back in 1966 the c.i.a. decided that they had this problem
and the problem was a man named Nkrumah so they
killed him and before that it was Patrice Lumumba
and before that it was my father on the campus
of my Ivy League school and my father afraid
to walk into the cafeteria because he said he
was wrong the wrong age the wrong skin the wrong
gender identity and he was paying my tuition and
before that
it was my father saying I was wrong saying that

I should have been a boy because he wanted one/a
boy and that I should have been lighter skinned and
that I should have had straighter hair and that
I should not be so boy crazy but instead I should
just be one/a boy and before that
it was my mother pleading plastic surgery for
my nose and braces for my teeth and telling me
to let the books loose to let them loose in other
words
I am very familiar with the problems of the c.i.a.
and the problems of South Africa and the problems
of Exxon Corporation and the problems of white
America in general and the problems of the teachers
and the preachers and the f.b.i. and the social
workers and my particular Mom and Dad/I am very
familiar with the problems because the problems
turn out to be
me
I am the history of rape
I am the history of the rejection of who I am
I am the history of the terrorized incarceration of
my self
I am the history of battery assault and limitless
armies against whatever I want to do with my mind
and my body and my soul and
whether it's about walking out at night
or whether it's about the love that I feel or
whether it's about the sanctity of my vagina or
the sanctity of my national boundaries
or the sanctity of my leaders or the sanctity
of each and every desire
that I know from my personal and idiosyncratic
and indisputably single and singular heart
I have been raped
be-
cause I have been wrong the wrong sex the wrong age
the wrong skin the wrong nose the wrong hair the
wrong need the wrong dream the wrong geographic
the wrong sartorial I
I have been the meaning of rape
I have been the problem everyone seeks to
eliminate by forced
penetration with or without the evidence of slime and/

but let this be unmistakable this poem
is not consent I do not consent
to my mother to my father to the teachers to
the f.b.i, to South Africa to Bedford-Stuy
to Park Avenue to American Airlines to the hardon
idlers on the corners to the sneaky creeps in
cars
I am not wrong: Wrong is not my name
My name is my own my own my own
and I can't tell you who the hell set things up like this
but I can tell you that from now on my resistance
my simple and daily and nightly self-determination
may very well cost you your life

BRANDON BOWLIN

Brandon Bowlin attended the University of North Carolina at Charlotte majoring in chemistry and minoring in English. His future plans include medical school with a specialization in psychiatry and to continue observing life as it unfolds and recording experiences through the magic of artistic expression.

The following poem from December 2003 is included in Brandon's personal collection, *Pills and Pillows*.

Behind the Golden Son

My body a tiny rectangle of glass
My face a clear box
Radiating energy for all eternity
A hot glacier too far to see the end beyond the horizon
A mysterious landscape where the moon sticks out
and hangs from the pole I built for it
Inspiration
Life of mine a permanent glow
A place you can't see
Reflection on my ocean
My Japan
My tiger
of everything that you think you see inside of me
Bubbling over
I draw a puddle of myself at your feet

The volcano erupts
and the sky fills with heat
Every mountain-top covered with steam
A circle around the mountain behind the moon
A peaceful butterfly
Invisible
A place where you can't go

Fiction

JOHN UPDIKE

John Updike was born in 1932 in Reading, Pennsylvania. He attended Harvard University and later worked for *The New Yorker* before developing a successful career as a novelist, essayist, and critic. His novels *Rabbit, Run* (1960), *Couples* (1978), and Pulitzer Prize winner *Rabbit is Rich* (1981) have made him one of the most respected and widely read contemporary authors.

A & P

In walks these three girls in nothing but bathing suits. I'm in the third checkout slot, with my back to the door, so I don't see them until they're over by the bread. The one that caught my eye first was the one in the plaid green two-piece. She was a chunky kid, with a good tan and a sweet broad soft-looking can with those two crescents of white just under it, where the sun never seems to hit, at the top of the backs of her legs. I stood there with my hand on a box of HiHo crackers trying to remember if I rang it up or not. I ring it up again and the customer starts giving me hell. She's one of these cash-register-watchers, a witch about fifty with rouge on her cheekbones and no eyebrows, and I know it made her day to trip me up. She'd been watching cash registers for fifty years and probably never seen a mistake before.

By the time I got her feathers smoothed and her goodies into a bag—she gives me a little snort in passing, if she'd been born at the right time they would have burned her over in Salem—by the time I got her on her way the girls had circled around the bread and were coming back, without a pushcart, back my way along the counters, in the aisle between the checkouts and the Special bins. They didn't even have shoes on. There was this chunky one, with the two-piece—it was bright green and the seams on the bra were still sharp and her belly was still pretty pale so I guessed she just got it (the suit)—there was this one, with one of those chubby berry-faces, the lips all bunched together under her nose, this one; and a tall one, with black hair that hadn't quite frizzed right, and one of these sunburns right across under the eyes, and a chin that was too long—you know, the kind of girl other girls think is very "striking" and "attractive" but never quite makes it, as they very well know, which is why they like her so much—and then the third one, that wasn't quite so tall. She was the queen. She kind of led them, the other two peeking around and making their shoulders round. She didn't look around, not this queen, she just walked straight on slowly, on these long white prima-donna legs. She came down a little hard on her heels, as if she didn't walk in her bare feet that much, putting down her heels and letting the weight move along to her toes as if she was testing the floor with every step, putting a little deliberate extra action into it. You never know for sure how girls' minds work (do you really think it's a mind in there or just a little buzz like a bee in a glass jar?) But you got the idea she had talked the other two into coming in here with her, and now she was showing them how to do it, walk slow and hold yourself straight.

She had on a kind of dirty-pink—beige maybe, I don't know—bathing suit with a little nubble all over it and, what got me, the straps were down. They were off her shoulders looped loose around the cool tops of her arms, and I guess as a result the suit had slipped a little on her, so all around the top of the cloth there was a shining rim. If it hadn't been there you wouldn't have known there could have been anything whiter than those shoulders. With the straps pushed off, there was nothing between the top of the suit and the top of her head except just her, this clean bare plane of the top of her chest down from the shoulder bones like a dented sheet of metal tilted in the light. I mean, it was more than pretty.

She had sort of oaky hair that the sun and salt had bleached, done up in a bun that was unraveling, and a kind of prim face. Walking into the A & P with your straps down, I suppose it's the only kind of face you can have. She held her head so high her neck, coming up out of those white shoulders, looked kind of stretched, but I didn't mind. The longer her neck was, the more of her there was.

She must have felt in the corner of her eye, me and over my shoulder Stokesie in the second slot watching, but she didn't tip. Not this queen. She kept her eyes moving across the racks, and stopped, and turned so slow it made my stomach rub the inside of my apron, and buzzed to the other two, who kind of huddled against her for relief, and then they all three of them went up the cat-and-dog food-breakfast-cereal-macaroni-rice-raisins-seasonings-spreads-spaghetti-soft drinks-crackers-and-cookies aisle. From the third slot I look straight up this aisle to the meat counter, and I watched them all the way. The fat one with the tan sort of fumbled with the cookies, but on second thought she put the package back. The sheep pushing their carts down the aisle—the girls were walking against the usual traffic (not that we have one-way signs or anything)—were pretty hilarious. You could see them, when Queenie's white shoulders dawned on them, kind of jerk, or hop, or hiccup, but their eyes snapped back to their own baskets and on they pushed. I bet you could set off dynamite in an A & P and the people would by and large keep reaching and checking oatmeal off their lists and muttering "Let me see, there was a third thing, began with A, asparagus, no, ah, yes, applesauce!" Or whatever it is they do mutter. But there was no doubt this jiggled them. A few house slaves in pin curlers even look around after pushing their carts past to make sure what they had seen was correct.

You know, it's one thing to have a girl in a bathing suit down on the beach, where what with the glare nobody can look at each other much anyway, and another thing in the cool of the A & P, under the fluorescent lights, against all those stacked packages, with her feet paddling along naked over our checker-board green-and-cream rubber-tile floor.

"Oh Daddy," Stokesie said beside me. "I feel so faint."

"Darling," I said, "Hold me tight." Stokesie's married, with two babies chalked up on his fuselage already, but as far as I can tell that's the only difference. He's twenty-two, and I was nineteen this April.

"Is it done?" he asks, the responsible married man finding his voice. I forgot to say he thinks he's going to be manager some sunny day, maybe in 1990 when it's called the Great Alexandrov and Petrooshki Tea Company or something.

What he meant was, our town is five miles from a beach, with a big summer colony out on the Point, but we're right in the middle of town, and the women generally put on a shirt or shorts or something before they get out of the car into the street. And anyway these are usually women with six children and varicose veins mapping their legs and nobody, including them, could care less. As I say, we're right in the middle of town, and if you stand at our front doors you can see two banks and the Congregational church and the newspaper store and three real-estate offices and about twenty-seven old freeloaders tearing up Central Street because the sewer broke again. It's not as if we're on the Cape; we're north of Boston and there's people in this town haven't seen the ocean for twenty years.

The girls had reached the meat counter and were asking McMahon something. He pointed, they pointed, and they shuffled out of sight behind a pyramid of Diet Delight peaches. All that was left for us to see was old McMahon patting his mouth and looking after them sizing up their joints. Poor kids, I began to feel sorry for them, they couldn't help it.

Now here comes the sad part of the story, at least my family says it's sad, but I don't think it's so sad myself. The store's pretty empty, it being Thursday afternoon, so there was nothing much to do except lean on the register and wait for the girls to show up again. The whole store was like a pinball machine and I didn't know which tunnel they'd come out of. After a while they come around out of the far aisle, around the light bulbs, records at discount of the Caribbean Six or Tony Martin Sings or some such gunk you wonder they waste the wax on, six packs of candy bars, and plastic toys done up in cellophane that fall apart when a kid looks at them anyway. Around they come, Queenie still leading the way, and holding a little gray jar in her hand. Slots Three through Seven are unmanned and I could see her wondering between Stokes and me, but Stokesie with his usual luck draws an old party in baggy gray pants who stumbles up with four giant cans of pineapple juice (what do these bums do with all that pineapple juice? I've often asked myself) so the girls come to me. Queenie puts down the jar and I take it into my fingers icy cold. Kingfish Fancy Herring Snacks in Pure Sour Cream: 49¢ Now her hands are empty, not a ring or a bracelet, bare as God made them, and I wonder where the money's coming from. Still with that prim look she lifts a folded dollar bill out of the hollow at the center of her nubbled pink top. The jar went heavy in my hand. Really, I thought that was so cute.

Then everybody's luck begins to run out. Lengel comes in from haggling with a truck full of cabbages on the lot and is about to scuttle into the door marked MANAGER behind which he hides all day when the girls touch his eye. Lengel's pretty dreary, teaches Sunday school and the rest, but he doesn't miss that much. He comes over and says, "Girls, this isn't the beach."

Queenie blushed, though maybe it's just a brush of sunburn I was noticing for the first time, now that she was so close. "My mother asked me to pick up a jar of herring snacks." Her voice kind of startled me, the way voices do when you see the people first, coming out so flat and dumb yet kind of tony, too, the way it ticked over "pick up" and "snacks." All of a sudden I slid right down her voice into her living room. Her father and the other men were standing around in ice-cream coats and bow ties and the women were in sandals picking up herring snacks on toothpicks off a big glass plate and they were all holding drinks the color of water with olives and sprigs of mint in them. When my parents have somebody over they get lemonade and if it's a real racy affair Schlitz in tall glasses with "They'll Do It Every Time" cartoons stenciled on.

"That's all right," Lengel said. "But this isn't the beach." His repeating this struck me as funny, as if it had just occurred to him, and he had been thinking all these years the A & P was a great big dune and he was the head lifeguard. He didn't like my smiling—as I say he doesn't miss much—but he concentrates on giving the girls that sad Sunday-school-superintendent stare.

Queenie's blush is no sunburn now, and the plump one in plaid, that I liked better from the back—a really sweet can—pipes up, "We weren't doing any shopping. We just came in for the one thing."

"That makes no difference," Lengel tells her, and I could see from the way his eyes went that he hadn't noticed she was wearing a two-piece before. "We want you decently dressed when you come in here."

"We are decent," Queenie says suddenly, her lower lip pushing, getting sore now that she remembers her place, a place from which the crowd that runs the A & P must look pretty chummy. Fancy Herring Snacks flashed in her very blue eyes.

"Girls, I don't want to argue with you. After this come in here with your shoulders covered. It's our policy." He turns his back. That's policy for you. Policy is what the kingpins want. What the others want is juvenile delinquency.

All this while, the customers had been showing up with their carts but, you know, sheep, seeing a scene, they had all bunched up on Stokesie, who shook open a paper bag as gently as peeling a peach, not wanting to miss a word. I could feel in the silence everybody getting nervous, most of all Lengel, who asks me, "Sammy, have you rung up this purchase?"

I thought and said "No" but it wasn't about that I was thinking. I go through the punches, 4, 9, GROC, TOT—it's more complicated than you think, and after you do it often enough, it begins to make a little song, that you hear words to, in my case "Hello (bing) there, you (gung) hap-py pee-pul (splat)!"—the splat being the drawer flying out. I uncrease the bill, tenderly as you may imagine, it just having come from between the two smoothest scoops of vanilla I had ever known were there, and pass a half and a penny into her narrow pink palm, and nestle the herrings in a bag and twist its neck and hand it over, all the time thinking.

The girls, and who'd blame them, are in a hurry to get out, so I say "I quit" to Lengel quick enough for them to hear, hoping they'll stop and watch me, their unsuspected hero. They keep right on going, into the electric eye; the door flies open and they flicker across the lot to their car, Queenie and Plaid and Big Tall Goony-Goony (not that as raw material she was so bad), leaving me with Lengel and a kink in his eyebrow.

"Did you say something, Sammy?"

"I said I quit."

"I thought you did."

"You didn't have to embarrass them."

"It was they who were embarrassing us."

I started to say something that came out "Fiddle-de-doo." It's a saying of my grandmother's, and I know she would have been pleased.

"I don't think you know what you're saying," Lengel said.

"I know you don't," I said. "But I do." I pull the bow at the back of my apron and start shrugging it off my shoulders. A couple customers that had been heading for my slot begin to knock against each other, like scared pigs in a chute.

Lengel sighs and begins to look very patient and old and gray. He's been a friend of my parents for years. "Sammy, you don't want to do this to your Mom and Dad," he tells me. It's true, I don't. But it seems to me that once you begin a gesture it's fatal not to go through with it. I fold the apron, "Sammy" stitched in red on the pocket, and put it on the counter, and drop the bow tie on tip of it. The bow tie is theirs, if you've ever wondered. "You'll feel this for the rest of your life," Lengel says, and I know that's true, too, but remembering how he made that pretty girl blush makes me so scrunchy inside I punch the No Sale tab and the machine whirs "pee-pul" and the drawer splats out. One advantage to this scene taking place in summer, I can follow this up with a clean exit, there's no fumbling around getting your coat and galoshes, I just saunter into the electric eye in my white shirt that my mother ironed the night before, and the door heaves itself open, and outside the sunshine is skating around on the asphalt.

I look around for my girls, but they're gone, of course. There wasn't anybody but some young married screaming with her children about some candy they didn't get by the door of a powder-blue Falcon station wagon. Looking back in the big windows, over the bags of peat moss and aluminum lawn furniture stacked on the pavement, I could see Lengel in my place in the slot, checking the sheep through. His face was dark gray and his back stiff, as if he'd just had an injection of iron, and my stomach kind of fell as I felt how hard the world was going to be to me hereafter.

TILLIE OLSEN

Tillie Lerner was born in either 1912 or 1913 in Nebraska (her birth certificate was lost, so her exact birthdate and year remain unknown). Her parents were political refugees from Russia. In 1936, Tillie Lerner became Tillie Olsen when she married Jack Olsen. For years, she concentrated on her life as a wife and a mother and did not return to writing until 1953. Although she has few literary publications, her influence on other writers, especially women, has been significant.

I Stand Here Ironing

I stand here ironing, and what you asked me moves tormented back and forth with the iron.

"I wish you would manage the time to come in and talk with me about your daughter. I'm sure you can help me understand her. She's a youngster who needs help and whom I'm deeply interested in helping."

"Who needs help." . . . Even if I came, what good would it do? You think because I am her mother I have a key, or that in some way you could use me as a key? She has lived for nineteen years. There is all that life that has happened outside of me, beyond me.

And when is there time to remember, to sift, to weigh, to estimate, to total? I will start and there will be an interruption and I will have to gather it all together again. Or I will become engulfed with all I did or did not do, with what should have been and what cannot be helped.

She was a beautiful baby. The first and only one of our five that was beautiful at birth. You do not guess how new and uneasy her tenancy in her now-loveliness. You did not know her all those years she was thought homely, or see her poring over her baby pictures, making me tell her over and over how beautiful she had been—and would be, I would tell her—and was now, to the seeing eye. But the seeing eyes were few or nonexistent. Including mine.

I nursed her. They feel that's important nowadays. I nursed all the children, but with her, with all the fierce rigidity of first motherhood, I did like the books then said. Though her cries battered me to trembling and my breasts ached with swollenness, I waited till the clock decreed.

Why do I put that first? I do not even know if it matters, or if it explains anything.

She was a beautiful baby. She blew shining bubbles of sound. She loved motion, loved light, loved color and music and textures. She would lie on the floor in her blue overalls patting the surface so hard in ecstasy her hands and feet would blur. She was a miracle to me, but when she was eight months old I had to leave her daytimes with the woman downstairs to whom she was no miracle at all, for I worked or looked for work and for Emily's father, who "could no longer endure" (he wrote in his good-bye note) "sharing want with us."

I was nineteen. It was the pre-relief, pre-WPA world of the depression. I would start running as soon as I got off the streetcar, running up the stairs, the place smelling sour, and awake or asleep to startle awake, when she saw me she would break into a clogged weeping that could not be comforted, a weeping I can hear yet.

After a while I found a job hashing at night so I could be with her days, and it was better. But it came to where I had to bring her to his family and leave her.

It took a long time to raise the money for her fare back. Then she got chicken pox and I had to wait longer. When she finally came, I hardly knew her, walking quick and nervous like her father, looking like her father, thin, and dressed in a shoddy red that yellowed her skin and glared at the pock-marks. All the baby loveliness gone.

She was two. Old enough for nursery school they said, and I did not know then what I know now—the fatigue of the long day, and the lacerations of group life in the kinds of nurseries that are only parking places for children.

Except that it would have made no difference if I had known. It was the only place there was. It was the only way we could be together, the only way I could hold a job.

And even without knowing, I knew. I knew the teacher that was evil because all these years it has curdled into my memory, the little boy hunched in the corner, her rasp, "Why aren't you outside, because Alvin hits you? That's no reason, go out, scardey." I knew Emily hated it even if she did not clutch and implore "don't go Mommy" like the other children, mornings.

She always had a reason why we should stay home. Momma, you look is sick. Momma, I feel sick. Momma, the teachers aren't there today, they're sick. Momma, we can't go, there was a fire there last night. Momma, it's a holiday today, no school, they told me.

But never a direct protest, never rebellion. I think of our others in their three-, four-year-oldness—the explosions, the tempers, the denunciations, the demands—and I feel suddenly ill. I put the iron down. What in me demanded that goodness in her? And what was the cost, the cost to her of such goodness?

The old man living in the back once said in his gentle way: "You should smile at Emily more when you look at her." What was in my face when I looked at her? I loved her. There were all the acts of love.

It was only with the others I remembered what he said, and it was the face of joy, and not of care or tightness or worry I turned to them—too late for Emily. She does not smile easily, let alone almost always as her brothers and sisters do. Her face is closed and sombre, but when she wants, how fluid. You must have seen it in her pantomimes, you spoke of her rare gift for comedy on the stage that rouses a laughter out of the audience so dear they applaud and applaud and do not want to let her go.

Where does it come from, that comedy? There was none of it in her when she came back to me that second time, after I had had to send her away again. She had a new daddy now to learn to love, and I think perhaps it was a better time.

Except when we left her alone nights, telling ourselves she was old enough. "Can't you go some other time, Mommy, like tomorrow?" she would ask. "Will it be just a little while you'll be gone? Do you promise?"

The time we came back, the front door open, the clock on the floor in the hall. She rigid awake. "It wasn't just a little while. I didn't cry. Three times I called you, just three times, and then I ran downstairs to open the door so you could come faster. The clock talked loud. I threw it away, it scared me what it talked."

She said the clock talked loud again that night I went to the hospital to have Susan. She was delirious with the fever that comes before red measles, but she was fully conscious all the week I was gone and the week after we were home when she could not come near the new baby or me.

She did not get well. She stayed skeleton thin, not wanting to eat, and night after night she had nightmares. She would call for me, and I would rouse from exhaustion to sleepily call back: "You're all right, darling, go to sleep, it's just a dream," and if she still called, in a sterner voice, "now go to sleep, Emily, there's nothing to hurt you." Twice, only twice, when I had to get up for Susan anyhow, I went in to sit with her.

Now when it is too late (as if she would let me hold and comfort her like I do the others) I get up and go to her at once at her moan or restless stirring. "Are you awake, Emily? Can I get you something?" And the answer is always the same: "No, I'm all right, go back to sleep, Mother."

They persuaded me at the clinic to send her away to a convalescent home in the country where "she can have the kind of food and care you can't manage for her, and you'll be free to concentrate on the new baby." They still send children to that place. I see pictures on the society page of sleek young women planning affairs to raise money for it, or dancing at the affairs, or decorating Easter eggs or filling Christmas stockings for the children.

They never have a picture of the children so I do not know if the girls still wear those gigantic red bows and the ravaged looks on the every other Sunday when the parents can come to visit "unless otherwise notified"—as we were notified the first six weeks.

Oh it is a handsome place, green lawns and tall trees and fluted flower beds. High up on the balconies of each cottage the children stand, the girls in their red bows and white dresses, the boys in white suits and giant red ties. The parents stand below shrieking up to be heard and the children shriek down to be heard, and between them the invisible wall "Not To Be Contaminated by Parental Germs or Physical Affection."

There was a tiny girl who always stood hand in hand with Emily. Her parents never came. One visit she was gone. "They moved her to Rose Cottage," Emily shouted in explanation. "They don't like you to love anybody here."

She wrote once a week, the labored writing of a seven-year-old. "I am fine. How is the baby. If I write my leter nicely I will have a star. Love." There never was a star. We wrote every other day, letters she could never hold or keep but only hear read—once. "We simply do not have room for children to keep any personal possessions," they patiently explained when we pieced one Sunday's shrieking together to plead how much it would mean to Emily, who loved so to keep things, to be allowed to keep her letters and cards.

Each visit she looked frailer. "She isn't eating," they told us.

(They had runny eggs for breakfast or mush with lumps, Emily said later, I'd hold it in my mouth and not swallow. Nothing ever tasted good, just when they had chicken.)

It took us eight months to get her released home, and only the fact that she gained back so little of her seven lost pounds convinced the social worker.

I used to try to hold and love her after she came back but her body would stay stiff, and after a while she'd push away. She ate little. Food sickened her, and I think much of life too. Oh she had physical lightness and brightness, twinkling by on skates, bouncing like a ball up and down up and down over the jump rope, skimming over the hill; but these were momentary.

She fretted about her appearance, thin and dark and foreign-looking at a time when every little girl was supposed to look or thought she should look a chubby blonde replica of Shirley Temple. The doorbell sometimes rang for her, but no one seemed to come and play in the house or be a best friend. Maybe because we moved so much.

There was a boy she loved, painfully through two school semesters. Months later she told me how she had taken pennies from my purse to buy him candy. "Licorice was his favorite and I brought him some every day, but he still liked Jennifer better'n me. Why, Mommy?" The kind of question for which there is no answer.

School was a worry to her. She was not glib or quick in a world where glibness and quickness were easily confused with ability to learn. To her overworked and exasperated teachers she was an overconscientious "slow learner" who kept trying to catch up and was absent entirely too often.

I let her be absent, though sometimes the illness was imaginary. How different from my now-strictness about attendance with the others. I wasn't working. We had a new baby, I was home anyhow. Sometimes, after Susan grew old enough, I would keep her home from school, too, to have them all together.

Mostly Emily had asthma, and her breathing, harsh and labored, would fill the house with a curiously tranquil sound. I would bring the two old dresser mirrors and her boxes of collections to her bed. She would select beads and single earrings, bottle tops and shells, dried flowers and pebbles, old postcards and scraps, all sorts of oddments; then she and Susan would play Kingdom, setting up landscapes and furniture, peopling them with action.

Those were the only times of peaceful companionship between her and Susan. I have edged away from it, that poisonous feeling between them, that terrible balancing of hurts and needs I had to do between the two, and did so badly, those earlier years.

Oh there are conflicts between the others too, each one human, needing, demanding, hurting, taking—but only between Emily and Susan, no, Emily toward Susan that corroding resentment. It seems so obvious on the surface, yet it is not obvious. Susan, the second child, Susan, golden- and curly-haired and chubby, quick and articulate and assured, everything in appearance and manner Emily was not; Susan, not able to resist Emily's precious things, losing or sometimes clumsily breaking them; Susan telling jokes and riddles to company for applause while Emily sat silent (to say to me later, that was my riddle, Mother, I told it to Susan); Susan, who for all the five years' difference in age was just a year behind Emily in developing physically.

I am glad for that slow physical development that widened the difference between her and her contemporaries, though she suffered over it. She was too vulnerable for that terrible world of youthful competition, of preening and parading, of constant measuring of yourself against every other, of envy, "If I had that copper hair," "If I had that skin . . . ." She tormented herself enough about not looking like the others, there was enough of the unsureness, the having to be conscious of words before you speak, the constant caring—what are they thinking of me?—without having it all magnified by the merciless physical drives.

Ronnie is calling. He is wet and I change him. It is rare there is such a cry now. That time of motherhood is almost behind me when the ear is not one's own but must always be racked and listening for the child cry, the child call. We sit for a while and I hold him, looking out over the city spread in charcoal with its soft aisles of light. "Shoogily," he breathes and curls closer. I carry him back to bed, asleep. Shoogily. A funny word, a family word, inherited from Emily, invented by her to say: comfort.

In this and other ways she leaves her seal, I say aloud. And startle at my saying it. What do I mean? What did I start to gather together, to try and make coherent? I was at the terrible, growing years. War years. I do not remember them well. I was working, there were four smaller ones now, there was not time for her. She had to help be a mother, and housekeeper, and shopper. She had to set her seal. Mornings of crisis and near hysteria trying to get lunches packed, hair combed, coats and shoes found, everyone to school or Child Care on time, the baby ready for transportation. And always the paper scribbled on by a smaller one, the book looked at by Susan then mislaid, the homework not done. Running out to that huge school where she was one, she was lost, she was a drop; suffering over the unpreparedness, stammering and unsure in her classes.

There was so little time left at night after the kids were bedded down. She would struggle over books, always eating (it was in those years she developed her enormous appetite that is legendary in our family) and I would be ironing, or preparing food for the next day, or writing V-mail to Bill, or tending the baby. Sometimes, to make me laugh, or out of her despair, she would imitate happenings or types at school.

I think I said once: "Why don't you do something like this in the school amateur show?" One morning she phoned me at work, hardly understandable through the weeping: "Mother, I did it, I won, I won; they gave me first prize; they clapped and clapped and wouldn't let me go."

Now suddenly she was Somebody, and as imprisoned in her difference as she had been in anonymity.

She began to be asked to perform at other high schools, even in colleges, then at city and statewide affairs. The first one we went to, I only recognized her that first moment when thin, shy, she almost drowned herself into the curtains. Then: Was this Emily? The control, the command, the convulsing and deadly clowning, the spell, then the roaring, stamping audience, unwilling to let this rare and precious laughter out of their lives.

Afterwards: You ought to do something about her with a gift like that—but without money or knowing how, what does one do? We have left it all to her, and the gift has as often eddied inside, clogged and clotted, as been used and growing.

She is coming. She runs up the stairs two at a time with her light, so graceful step, and I know she is happy tonight. Whatever it was that occasioned your call did not happen today.

"Aren't you ever going to finish the ironing, Mother? Whistler painted his mother in a rocker. I'd have to paint mine standing over an ironing board." This is one of her communicative nights and she tells me everything and nothing as she fixes herself a plate of food out of the icebox. She is so lovely. Why did you want me to come in at all? Why were you concerned? She will find her way.

She starts up the stairs to bed. "Don't get me up with the rest in the morning." "But I thought you were having midterms." "Oh, those," she comes back in, kisses me, and says quite lightly, "in a couple of years when we'll all be atom-dead they won't matter a bit."

She has said it before. She believes it. But because I have been dredging the past, and all that compounds a human being is so heavy and meaningful in me, I cannot endure it tonight.

I will never total it all. I will never come in to say: She was a child seldom smiled at. Her father left me before she was a year old. I had to work her first six years when there was work, or I sent her home and to his relatives. There were years she had care she hated. She was dark and thin and foreign-looking in a world where the prestige went to blondeness and curly hair and dimples, she was slow where glibness was prized. She was a child of anxious, not proud, love. We were poor and could not afford for her the soil of easy growth. I was a young mother, I was a distracted mother. There were the other children pushing up, demanding. Her younger sister seemed all that she was not. There were years she did not want me to touch her. She kept too much in herself, her life was such she had to keep too much in herself. My wisdom came too late. She has much to her and probably little will come of it. She is a child of her age, of depression, of war, of fear.

Let her be. So all that is in her will not bloom—but in how many does it? There is still enough left to live by. Only help her to know—help make it so there is cause for her to know—that she is more than this dress on the ironing board, helpless before the iron.

Drama

JANE MARTIN

Not much is known about playwright Jane Martin. It is believed that Martin is from Kentucky, but beyond that, there are no available biographies or photographs. It has been speculated that Martin is a pseudonym for playwright Jon Jory. In any case, Martin's play "Keely and Du" premiered at the 1993 Human Festival, was nominated for the Pulitzer Prize in drama, and won the American Theater Critics Association Award for Best New Play in 1996.

Beauty

CHARACTERS
CARLA
BETHANY

An apartment. Minimalist set. A young woman, Carla, on the phone.

CARLA: In love with me? You're in love with me? Could you describe yourself again? Uh-huh. Uh-huh. And you spoke to me? *(A knock at the door.)* Listen, I always hate to interrupt a marriage proposal, but . . . could you possibly hold that thought? *(Puts phone down and goes to door. Bethany, the same age as Carla and a friend, is there. She carries the sort of Mideastern lamp we know of from Aladdin.)*

BETHANY: Thank God you were home. I mean, you're not going to believe this!

CARLA: Somebody on the phone. *(Goes back to it.)*

BETHANY: I mean, I just had a beach urge, so I told them at work my uncle was dying . . .

CARLA: *(motions to Bethany for quiet)* And you were the one in the leather jacket with the 5 tattoo? What was the tattoo? *(Carla again asks Bethany, who is gesturing wildly that she should hang up, to cool it.)* Look, a screaming eagle from shoulder to shoulder, maybe. There were a lot of people in the bar.

BETHANY: *(gesturing and mouthing)* I have to get back to work.

CARLA: *(on phone)* See, the thing is, I'm probably not going to marry someone I can't remember . . . particularly when I don't drink. Sorry. Sorry. Sorry. *(She hangs up.)* Madness.

BETHANY: So I ran out to the beach . . .

CARLA: This was some guy I never met who apparently offered me a beer . . .

BETHANY: . . . low tide and this . . . *(The lamp.)* . . . was just sitting there, lying there . . .

CARLA: . . . and he tracks me down . . .   10

BETHANY: . . . on the beach, and I lift this lid thing . . .

CARLA: . . . and seriously proposes marriage.

BETHANY: . . . and a genie comes out.

CARLA: I mean, that's twice in a . . . what?

BETHANY: A genie comes out of this thing.   15

CARLA: A genie?

BETHANY: I'm not kidding, the whole Disney kind of thing, swirling smoke, and then this twenty-foot-high, see-through guy in like an Arabian outfit.

CARLA: Very funny.

BETHANY: Yes, funny, but twenty feet high! I look up and down the beach, I'm alone. I don't have my pepper spray or my hand alarm. You know me, when I'm petrified I joke.   20
I say his voice is too high for Robin Williams, and he says he's a castrati. Naturally. Who else would I meet?

CARLA: What's a castrati?

BETHANY: You know . . .

The appropriate gesture.

CARLA: Bethany, dear one, I have three modeling calls. I am meeting Ralph Lauren!

BETHANY: Okay, good. Ralph Lauren. Look, I am not kidding!

CARLA: You're not kidding what?!   25

BETHANY: There is a genie in this thingamajig.

CARLA: Uh-huh. I'll be back around eight.

BETHANY: And he offered me *wishes!*

CARLA: Is this some elaborate practical joke because it's my birthday?

BETHANY: No, happy birthday, but I'm like crazed because I'm on this deserted beach with 30
a twenty-foot-high, see-through genie, so like sarcastically . . . you know how I need a new car . . . I said fine, gimme 25,000 dollars . . .

CARLA: On the beach with the genie?

BETHANY: Yeah, right, exactly, and it rains down out of the sky.

CARLA: Oh sure.

BETHANY: *(pulling a wad out of her purse)* Count it, those are thousands. I lost one in the surf.

Carla sees the top bill. Looks at Bethany, who nods encouragement. Carla thumbs through them.

CARLA: These look real.   35

BETHANY: Yeah.

CARLA: And they rained down out of the sky?

BETHANY: Yeah.

CARLA: You've been really strange lately, are you dealing?

BETHANY: Dealing what, I've even given up chocolate.   40

CARLA: Let me see the genie.

BETHANY: Wait, wait.

CARLA: Bethany, I don't have time to screw around. Let me see the genie or let me go on my appointments.

BETHANY: Wait! So I pick up the money . . . see, there's sand on the money . . . and I'm like nuts so I say, you know, "Okay, look, ummm, big guy, my uncle is in the hospital" . . . because as you know when I said to the people at work my uncle was dying, I was on one level telling the truth although it had nothing to do with the beach, but he was in Intensive Care after the accident, and that's on my mind, so I say, okay, Genie, heal my uncle . . . which is like impossible given he was hit by two trucks, and the genie says, "Yes, Master" . . . like they're supposed to say, and he goes into this like kind of whirlwind, kicking up sand and stuff, and I'm like, "Oh my God!" and the air clears, and he bows, you know, and says, "It is done, Master," and I say, "Okay, whatever-you-are, I'm calling on my cell phone," and I get it out and I get this doctor who is like dumbstruck who says my uncle came to, walked out of Intensive Care and left the hospital! I'm not kidding, Carla.

CARLA: On your mother's grave?   45

BETHANY: On my mother's grave.

They look at each other.

CARLA: Let me see the genie.

BETHANY: No, no, look, that's the whole thing . . . I was just, like, reacting, you know, responding, and that's already two wishes . . . although I'm really pleased about my uncle, the $25,000 thing, I could have asked for $10 million, and there is only one wish left.

CARLA: So ask for $10 million.

BETHANY: I don't think so. I don't think so. I mean, I gotta focus in here. Do you have   50 a sparkling water?

CARLA: No. Bethany, I'm missing Ralph Lauren now. Very possibly my one chance to go from catalogue model to the very, very big time, so, if you are joking, stop joking.

BETHANY: Not joking. See, see, the thing is, I know what I want. In my guts. Yes. Underneath my entire bitch of a life is this unspoken, ferocious, all-consuming urge . . .

CARLA: *(trying to get her to move this along)* Ferocious, all-consuming urge . . .

BETHANY: I want to be like you.

CARLA: Me?   55

BETHANY: Yes.

CARLA: Half the time you don't even like me.

BETHANY: Jealous. The ogre of jealousy.

CARLA: You're the one with the $40,000 job straight out of school. You're the one who has published short stories. I'm the one hanging on by her fingernails in modeling. The one who has creeps calling her on the phone. The one who had to have a nose job.

BETHANY: I want to be beautiful. 60

CARLA: You are beautiful.

BETHANY: Carla, I'm not beautiful.

CARLA: You have charm. You have personality. You know perfectly well you're pretty.

BETHANY: "Pretty," see, that's it. Pretty is the minor leagues of beautiful. Pretty is what people discover about you after they know you. Beautiful is what knocks them out across the room. Pretty, you get called a couple of times a year; *beautiful* is twenty-four hours a day.

CARLA: Yeah? So? 65

BETHANY: So?! We're talking *beauty* here. Don't say "So?" Beauty is the real deal. You are the center of any moment of your life. People stare. Men flock. I've seen you get offered discounts on makeup for no reason. Parents treat beautiful children better. Studies show your income goes up. You can have sex anytime you want it. Men have to know me. That takes up to a year. I'm continually horny.

CARLA: Bethany, I don't even like sex. I can't have a conversation without men coming on to me. I have no privacy. I get hassled on the street. They start pressuring me from the beginning. Half the time, it never occurs to them to start with a conversation. Smart guys like you. You've had three long-term relationships, and you're only twenty-three. I haven't had one. The good guys, the smart guys are scared to death of me. I'm surrounded by male bimbos who think a preposition is when you go to school away from home. I have no woman friends except you. I don't even want to talk about this!

BETHANY: I knew you'd say something like this. See, you're "in the club" so you can say this. It's the way beauty functions as an elite. You're trying to keep it all for yourself.

CARLA: I'm trying to tell you it's no picnic.

BETHANY: But it's what everybody wants. It's the nasty secret at large in the world. It's 70 the unspoken tidal desire in every room and on every street. It's the unspoken, the soundless whisper . . . millions upon millions of people longing hopelessly and forever to stop being whatever they are and be beautiful, but the difference between those ardent multitudes and me is that I have a goddamn genie and one more wish!

CARLA: Well, it's not what I want. This is me, Carla. I have never read a whole book. Page six, I can't remember page four. The last thing I read was *The Complete Idiot's Guide to WordPerfect.* I leave dinner parties right after the dessert because I'm out of conversation. You know the dumb blond joke about the application where it says, "Sign here," she put Sagittarius? I've done that. Only beautiful guys approach me, and that's because they want to borrow my eye shadow. I barely exist outside a mirror! You don't want to be me.

BETHANY: None of you tell the truth. That's why you have no friends. We can all see you're just trying to make us feel better because we aren't in your league. This only proves to me it should be my third wish. Money can only buy things. Beauty makes you the center of the universe.

Bethany picks up the lamp.

CARLA: Don't do it. Bethany, don't wish it! I am telling you you'll regret it.

Bethany lifts the lid. There is a tremendous crash, and the lights go out. Then they flicker and come back up, revealing Bethany and Carla on the floor where they have been thrown by the explosion. We don't realize it at first, but they have exchanged places.

CARLA/BETHANY: Oh God.

BETHANY/CARLA: Oh God.   75

CARLA/BETHANY: Am I bleeding? Am I dying?

BETHANY/CARLA: I'm so dizzy. You're not bleeding.

CARLA/BETHANY: Neither are you.

BETHANY/CARLA: I feel so weird.

CARLA/BETHANY: Me too. I feel . . . *(Looking at her hands.)* Oh, my God, I'm wearing 80
your jewelry. I'm wearing your nail polish.

BETHANY/CARLA: I know I'm over here, but I can see myself over there.

CARLA/BETHANY: I'm wearing your dress. I have your legs!!

BETHANY/CARLA: These aren't my shoes. I can't meet Ralph Lauren wearing these shoes!

CARLA/BETHANY: I wanted to be beautiful, but I didn't want to be you.

BETHANY/CARLA: Thanks a lot!!   85

CARLA/BETHANY: I've got to go. I want to pick someone out and get laid.

BETHANY/CARLA: You can't just walk out of here in my body!

CARLA/BETHANY: Wait a minute. Wait a minute. What's eleven eighteenths of 1,726?

BETHANY/CARLA: Why?

CARLA/BETHANY: I'm a public accountant. I want to know if you have my brain. 90

BETHANY/CARLA: One hundred thirty-two and a half.

CARLA/BETHANY: You have my brain.

BETHANY/CARLA: What shade of Rubenstein lipstick does Cindy Crawford wear
with teal blue?

CARLA/BETHANY: Raging Storm.

BETHANY/CARLA: You have my brain. You poor bastard.   95

CARLA/BETHANY: I don't care. Don't you see?

BETHANY/CARLA: See what?

CARLA/BETHANY: We both have the one thing, the one and only thing everybody wants.

BETHANY/CARLA: What is that?

CARLA/BETHANY: It's better than beauty for me; it's better than brains for you. 100

BETHANY/CARLA: What? What?!

CARLA/BETHANY: Different problems.

Blackout.

END OF PLAY

A Closer Look: Kurt Vonnegut

Kurt Vonnegut was born in Indianapolis in 1922. He studied biochemistry at Cornell University; then, after serving in Europe during World War II, he studied anthropology at the University of Chicago before becoming a full-time writer. Author of more than fifteen published novels and many short stories, he has received much critical acclaim—as well as commercial success—for his fiction. He's best known for his witty combination of science fiction, dark humor, and social satire.

INTERVIEW WITH THE AUTHOR

The Salon Interview by Frank Houston

Listen: This is really it. After entertaining and provoking us with his novels for 50 years, Kurt Vonnegut says he is retiring from the literature business. His last book, *Bagombo Snuff Box,* is a short-story collection that harks back to the dawn of his literary career in the 1950s, a Golden Age of magazine fiction long since vanished, when he left his job as a General Electric PR flack and began publishing stories. In his introduction, he calls these new-old (and previously unavailable) pieces—simple melodramas about materialism, pretense, love and heaven—"Buddhist catnaps," observing that the short-story form, "because of its physiological and psychological effects on a human being, is more closely related to Buddhist styles of meditation than it is to any other form of narrative entertainment." In "A Present for Big Saint Nick," children expose a gangster's egotism and their parents' hypocrisy. In the title story, a nine-year-old sniffs out an adult's pretensions. A couple of the stories rise to culminating jokes in the vein of Vonnegut's classic tall tale, "Tom Edison's Shaggy Dog," from his only previous collection, 1968's *Welcome to the Monkey House.*

I recently met Vonnegut on a blustery day in Manhattan to talk about these stories. We also discussed the loneliness of the writer's life, television, politics and life at the end of the 20th century. Vonnegut, who remembers the Depression and served in World War II, turns 78 next month. He smoked unfiltered Pall Malls throughout the interview. When he laughs, which he does frequently, he squeezes his face up horizontally in the wide-open grin of the Cheshire Cat. He is always ready to pounce with a joke, and the loudest laugh, like the last, is always his.

Is this really it? The last Vonnegut book?
I have one more I'm shopping around, but publishers have found the subject rather dated, and so I guess this probably *is* my last book. What I've been shopping around is the story of my love affair with O.J. Simpson. [Laughs.]

Tough sell.

Yes, most people have forgotten who he is. And it was so long ago. It was in Buffalo, and I went to the dressing room after the game. I asked him to autograph my football, but I didn't realize that was code.

For?

Well . . . the beginning of a love affair. But I felt used. Anyway, nobody's interested, so please, let's go on.

OK, OK. Your introduction to the new collection gives a quick career rundown. Did it make you nostalgic to be writing it for your last published book?

I wanted to repair every story, because the premise of each story was pretty good, and I wanted to do more with it now. But no—it is archaeology, and the artifact is from the past. I was nostalgic just for the sake of future generations. It was very easy to get started as a writer during the golden age of magazines, before TV. *The Saturday Evening Post* published five stories every week; *Collier's* published five stories every week; *Cosmopolitan*, which is a sex manual now, published five stories a month; and the country was short-story-crazy. "Hey, did you see the short story in *Collier's* last week?" "No, but I heard about it and I want to read it." A woman, an English major, pregnant with a baby to pay for, could sit down in the kitchen late at night and write a love story and send it off to the *Ladies' Home Journal* or *Cosmo* or whatever, and pay for the baby, because the magazines were really hungry for stories.

As early as 1973, you said you were "tired of thinking," that "it didn't seem to help very much." Is there a little of that attitude in your retirement?

Well, yes. I guess it was either Camus or Sartre who said that because of technology, we no longer make history. History happens to us—the new weaponry, the new communications and all that. I don't much want to play anymore. I enjoyed the game as a young man, but I don't enjoy it now. Early on, I would think of writing plays, for instance. But Broadway has so changed, there's no longer an opportunity.

You once said you were going to give up writing novels entirely and devote yourself strictly to plays.

I did write a couple. What's good about plays is you get extended families, and you can smoke backstage. [Laughs.]

No co-workers as a novelist, I guess.

No, it's a very lonely business. I knew Jack Kerouac at the very end, I knew Truman Capote at the very end, and they were *all* alone.

Kerouac especially.

Yeah.

I didn't realize you'd crossed paths with him.

It was accidentally. He'd moved to Cape Cod for a short time, and I was living there. So somebody brought him around.

Did he know your work?

That I don't know. I'm quite sure Capote didn't. We were neighbors out at Sagaponack, on Long Island. He'd lost all his friends, the ladies at restaurants where he ate, because he'd started writing about them. So he would come over to my house every afternoon—— I have a swimming pool—and say he was there to treat his bursitis. But he also knew where the vodka and the orange juice were, and that was part of the treatment. I have no indication that he had read anything by me, and Kerouac probably hadn't, either.

Kerouac seemed very bitter and demoralized at the end of his life.

He was furious because he had been screwed out of a fortune, which was "Route 66." It was a huge television hit, and it was an obvious rip-off of "On the Road."

Getting into the short stories, a few of them deal with the war. Robert Scholes called Dresden "the completion of your education in pacifism." Would you have become a writer without your World War II experience?

I was going to be a journalist. But after the war I studied anthropology, just in order to become educated. I thought it was worth knowing the science of man. I still intended to become a journalist, but there were no jobs, because the reporters who had gone to war were coming back and were entitled to their jobs, and the women who had replaced them were damned if they'd leave, and they shouldn't have left. These women were absolutely first-rate reporters.

No room for fresh blood. And so on to General Electric, and on to your career as a novelist. You've been a lot of things along the way—Saab dealer, volunteer fireman. How did those experiences inform you as a writer?

Well, they were real, you know? I'm glad I was a foot soldier, I'm glad I was a PFC in combat. And I was glad to really be a teacher. So there's a lot of stuff I don't have to imagine. I don't have to imagine being a car dealer—I *was* one.

That sounds like a particularly funny experience.

I think it's the business story of that decade. I was the third Saab dealer in the United States—you could have a dealership just by asking for one. Had to put up my own money for five cars. Terrible car then, may I say. My story as a Saab dealer is the business story of the decade because in two years I lost only $35,000. [Laughs.]

A lot of these early stories deal with themes that would be carried through your novels—technology, materialism and notions of "progress." They made me wonder if you think we're sort of re-living the 1950s in our rush toward technology or in our blind belief in progress.

At the time I wrote the stories, we weren't swamped by technology. Now we are. Jesus, it's all around us. There wasn't even television then. What television does is rent us friends and relatives who are quite satisfactory. The child watching TV loves these people, you know—they're in color, and they're talking to the child. Why wouldn't a child relate to these people? And you know, if you can't sleep at 3 o'clock in the morning, you can turn on a switch, and there are your friends and relatives, and they obviously like you. And they're charming. Who wouldn't want Peter Jennings for a relative? This is quite something, to rent artificial friends and relatives right inside the house.

What do you think that's doing to people?

Well, they are very commonly more satisfactory friends and relatives than what most people really have. And so, sure, it's analgesic, it's comforting. So many people have awful friends and relatives. [Laughs.]

What about a return—or maybe it's never left us—to the sort of consumerism we associate with the '50s?

I've called the '50s the Golden Age of White People. They were the ones doing the consuming. People of color and women were making very few purchases on their own.

Children are featured prominently in these stories, it struck me—I've never seen so many children in your past literature. They're always there exposing the adults, exposing lies and hypocrisy. Does this have anything to do with the fact that you were raising a family at the time?

I had a lot of kids—three of my own, and I adopted three nephews.

Your sister's children.

Yeah. But I think that one of the things parents have to do is to teach children hypocrisy, because that's how you survive—by being nice to people who are contemptible. So the kid coming into the world sees hypocrisy and wants to point it out. You're nice to this awful person? What you're doing is a crime, isn't it, Dad?

"A Present for Big Saint Nick" is like that.

Yeah. I mean, come on, wise up, we have to eat. And so the kids learn hypocrisy as one of the early lessons.

You were accused at one time of encouraging pessimism and cynicism in youth.

I was speaking at the Library of Congress—and this is like being invited to Buckingham Palace by the royal family—and I was thinking that my jokes, as now, were going pretty well. [Laughs.] And a guy stood up dressed like a middle European. And he had obviously had an awful time under Communism, and somehow he got over here. And he said, "What right have you got as a leader of young people to speak so ill of the most wonderful nation in the world?" And this just muzzled me entirely. I was so abashed I left the stage.

And you didn't speak again for a while.

No. But it *is* a shitty country! [Laughs.]

Speaking of which, you've always concerned yourself with politics and politicians. What do you think of the current crop?

They're television candidates. The permanent government now is the anchorpeople. They don't get elected, and year after year they're responding emotionally to this or that. I mean, CNN now decides where we send our troops next.

Do you think this is because of the intermediation of television, or because people are so tired of the politicians?

I think we don't care much anymore. Most of us, as when we were children, have very sound ethical instincts and realize that it's all a lot of baloney. And so we're completely fatalistic about our government's being for sale.

You once wrote that there were two political parties in America—the Winners and the Losers. And that was in 1972. I doubt you'd say anything is different today.

No. Obviously if Hillary Clinton is a candidate for United States senator, it's because she's so famous, simply as an abused wife.

But would you take her over Giuliani?

Oh, hell, no. Giuliani—I don't like him, but he is surely more entitled to represent New York than she is. All the people involved in the O.J. Simpson case—the case involving my former lover [laughs]—became famous, Johnnie Cochran and all of them. Just to get on TV is what you want to do; that's the only kind of fame you can have now. There's no way you can become famous without TV now.

Kilgore Trout, the hero of "Breakfast of Champions," is frequently referred to as your alter ego. Do you think that's accurate?

Sure. But he is a Christ figure, too. He's not being crucified, but in order to cleanse us of our sins, he is living a life not worth living.

Why did you invent him?

I don't know. As I've said my entire career, it's like skiing—you don't have time to think. Of course, you can have a calculated literary career, but my books are too personal.

What do you think of the film version of "Breakfast of Champions," the latest Hollywood attempt to put your vision on the big screen?

Well, I'm completely in print now; everything I've published is available. Often a movie becomes the only representative of a book that has gone out of print. But I am completely in print. I wrote the book, Alan Rudolph wrote the movie and they're two separate works of art. And that's it—let them both stand on their own two feet. I had nothing to do with the movie.

Have you seen it?

Yes, I've seen it.

Thumbs up or thumbs down?

I answered your question. I said, "Yes, I've seen it." [Laughs.]

Fair enough. It always struck me that "The Sirens of Titan," your second novel, represented a real leap forward for you.

Oh, yes.

You really seemed to discover your voice and your style there. What happened?

It was partly economic. I was at a cocktail party here in New York, living on Cape Cod with a lot of kids, and an editor said, "Hey, isn't it time you wrote another novel?" And I said, "Yeah, as a matter of fact." And I spoke the whole book. I just went off like a burglar alarm. So then I went home and wrote it. People hate to hear of an artist having economic problems or doing anything for money. Like a priest.

Did writing for the slicks help you refine your style?

I knew how to be a good date on a blind date, how to entertain strangers. I developed sociability skills writing for the slicks, because they wouldn't publish it if it wasn't sociable.

So in terms of entertaining strangers, I guess you had a pretty good idea that "The Sirens of Titan" was going to work once it came out of you at the cocktail party.

I knew it was a good story, but you can't count on anything selling. It was just another paperback novel that came out that year. But it felt good. The act of creation feels good.

A lot of your work deals in one way or another with the end of the world. Do you ever get the feeling we're just about there?

I wrote a piece about that, which nobody read, because nobody reads *Playboy.* But I talked about the fact that antibiotics aren't working, and we had an incurable disease show up, AIDS, and I came to the conclusion that the planet's immune system was trying to get rid of us. [Laughs.]

Only you could put it that way.

Well, what do you think of the weather?

What do *you* think of the weather—it fits right in, doesn't it?

The planet's immune system is doing everything it can. Gave a pretty good whack to Taiwan . . . You know, after two world wars and the Holocaust and then the Balkans, I think the planet should get rid of us. We're really awful animals. I mean, that dumb Barbra Streisand song, "People who need people are the luckiest people in the world"—she's talking about cannibals. [Laughs.] Lots to eat. [Laughs harder.]

Is there anything about life at the end of the millennium that has instilled a sense of *happy* wonderment in you?

Oh, sure—civil rights, extraordinary. And after 5 million years, women are finally treated with respect. When F. Scott Fitzgerald and Ernest Hemingway were born, at the tail end of the last century, they were much closer to the utter atrocity of human slavery than we are to the Holocaust today.

So there is such a thing as progress. If you could write an epitaph for the 20th century, what would it be?

I *have* written it. "The good Earth—we could have saved it, but we were too damn cheap and lazy."

A SHORT STORY

Harrison Bergeron

The year was 2081, and everybody was finally equal. They weren't only equal before God and the law. They were equal every which way. Nobody was smarter than anybody else. Nobody was better looking than anybody else. Nobody was stronger or quicker than anybody else. All this equality was due to the 211th, 212th, and 213th Amendments to the Constitution, and to the unceasing vigilance of agents of the United States Handicapper General.

Some things about living still weren't quite right, though. April, for instance, still drove people crazy by not being springtime. And it was in that clammy month that the H-G men took George and Hazel Bergeron's fourteen-year-old son, Harrison, away.

It was tragic, all right, but George and Hazel couldn't think about it very hard. Hazel had a perfectly average intelligence, which meant she couldn't think about anything except in short bursts. And George, while his intelligence was way above normal, had a little mental handicap radio in his ear. He was required by law to wear it at all times. It was tuned to a government transmitter. Every twenty seconds or so, the transmitter would send out some sharp noise to keep people like George from taking unfair advantage of their brains.

George and Hazel were watching television. There were tears on Hazel's cheeks, but she'd forgotten for the moment what they were about.

On the television screen were ballerinas.

A buzzer sounded in George's head. His thoughts fled in panic, like bandits from a burglar alarm.

"That was a real pretty dance, that dance they just did," said Hazel.

"Huh?" said George.

"That dance—it was nice," said Hazel.

"Yup," said George. He tried to think a little about the ballerinas. They weren't really very good—no better than anybody else would have been, anyway. They were burdened with sash-weights and bags of birdshot, and their faces were masked, so that no one, seeing a free and graceful gesture or a pretty face, would feel like something the cat drug in. George was toying with the vague notion that maybe dancers shouldn't be handicapped. But he didn't get very far with it before another noise in his ear radio scattered his thoughts.

George winced. So did two out of the eight ballerinas.

Hazel saw him wince. Having no mental handicap herself, she had to ask George what the latest sound had been.

"Sounded like somebody hitting a milk bottle with a ball peen hammer," said George.

"I'd think it would be real interesting, hearing all the different sounds," said Hazel, a little envious. "All the things they think up."

"Um," said George.

"Only, if I was Handicapper General, you know what I would do?" said Hazel. Hazel, as a matter of fact, bore a strong resemblance to the Handicapper General, a woman named Diana Moon Glampers. "If I was Diana Moon Glampers," said Hazel, "I'd have chimes on Sunday—just chimes. Kind of in honor of religion."

"I could think, if it was just chimes," said George.

"Well—maybe make 'em real loud," said Hazel. "I think I'd make a good Handicapper General."

"Good as anybody else," said George.

"Who knows better'n I do what normal is?" said Hazel.

"Right," said George. He began to think glimmeringly about his abnormal son who was now in jail, about Harrison, but a twenty-one-gun salute in his head stopped that.

"Boy!" said Hazel, "that was a doozy, wasn't it?"

It was such a doozy that George was white and trembling, and tears stood on the rims of his red eyes. Two of the eight ballerinas had collapsed to the studio floor, were holding their temples.

"All of a sudden you look so tired," said Hazel. "Why don't you stretch out on the sofa, so's you can rest your handicap bag on the pillows, honeybunch." She was referring to the forty-seven pounds of birdshot in a canvas bag, which was padlocked around George's neck. "Go on and rest the bag for a little while," she said. "I don't care if you're not equal to me for a while."

George weighed the bag with his hands. "I don't mind it," he said. "I don't notice it any more. It's just a part of me."

"You been so tired lately—kind of wore out," said Hazel. "If there was just some way we could make a little hole in the bottom of the bag, and just take out a few of them lead balls. Just a few."

"Two years in prison and two thousand dollars fine for every ball I took out," said George. "I don't call that a bargain."

"If you could just take a few out when you came home from work," said Hazel. "I mean—you don't compete with anybody around here. You just set around."

"If I tried to get away with it," said George, "then other people'd get away with it—and pretty soon we'd be right back to the dark ages again, with everybody competing against everybody else. You wouldn't like that, would you?"

"I'd hate it," said Hazel.

"There you are," said George. "The minute people start cheating on laws, what do you think happens to society?"

If Hazel hadn't been able to come up with an answer to this question, George couldn't have supplied one. A siren was going off in his head.

"Reckon it'd fall all apart," said Hazel.

"What would?" said George blankly.

"Society," said Hazel uncertainly. "Wasn't that what you just said?"

"Who knows?" said George.

The television program was suddenly interrupted for a news bulletin. It wasn't clear at first as to what the bulletin was about, since the announcer, like all announcers, had a serious speech impediment. For about half a minute, and in a state of high excitement, the announcer tried to say, "Ladies and gentlemen—"

He finally gave up, handed the bulletin to a ballerina to read.

"That's all right—" Hazel said of the announcer, "he tried. That's the big thing. He tried to do the best he could with what God gave him. He should get a nice raise for trying so hard."

"Ladies and gentlemen—" said the ballerina, reading the bulletin. She must have been extraordinarily beautiful, because the mask she wore was hideous. And it was easy to see that she was the strongest and most graceful of all the dancers, for her handicap bags were as big as those worn by two-hundred-pound men.

And she had to apologize at once for her voice, which was a very unfair voice for a woman to use. Her voice was a warm, luminous, timeless melody. "Excuse me—" she said, and she began again, making her voice absolutely uncompetitive.

"Harrison Bergeron, age fourteen," she said in a grackle squawk, "has just escaped from jail, where he was held on suspicion of plotting to overthrow the government. He is a genius and an athlete, is under-handicapped, and should be regarded as extremely dangerous."

A police photograph of Harrison Bergeron was flashed on the screen—upside down, then sideways, upside down again, then right side up. The picture showed the full length of Harrison against a background calibrated in feet and inches. He was exactly seven feet tall.

The rest of Harrison's appearance was Halloween and hardware. Nobody had ever borne heavier handicaps. He had outgrown hindrances faster than the H-G men could think them up. Instead of a little ear radio for a mental handicap, he wore a tremendous pair of earphones, and spectacles with thick wavy lenses. The spectacles were intended to make him not only half blind, but to give him whanging headaches besides.

Scrap metal was hung all over him, Ordinarily, there was a certain symmetry, a military neatness to the handicaps issued to strong people, but Harrison looked like a walking junkyard. In the race of life, Harrison carried three hundred pounds.

And to offset his good looks, the H-G men required that he wear at all times a red rubber ball for a nose, keep his eyebrows shaved off, and cover his even white teeth with black caps at snaggle-tooth random.

"If you see this boy," said the ballerina, "do not—I repeat, do not—try to reason with him."

There was the shriek of a door being torn from its hinges.

Screams and barking cries of consternation came from the television set. The photograph of Harrison Bergeron on the screen jumped again and again, as though dancing to the tune of an earthquake.

George Bergeron correctly identified the earthquake, and well he might have—for many was the time his own home had danced to the same crashing tune. "My God—" said George, "that must be Harrison!"

The realization was blasted from his mind instantly by the sound of an automobile collision in his head.

When George could open his eyes again, the photograph of Harrison was gone. A living, breathing Harrison filled the screen.

Clanking, clownish, and huge, Harrison stood in the center of the studio. The knob of the uprooted studio door was still in his hand. Ballerinas, technicians, musicians, and announcers cowered on their knees before him, expecting to die.

"I am the Emperor!" cried Harrison. "Do you hear? I am the Emperor! Everybody must do what I say at once!" He stamped his foot and the studio shook.

"Even as I stand here—" he bellowed, "crippled, hobbled, sickened—I am a greater ruler than any man who ever lived! Now watch me become what I *can* become!"

Harrison tore the straps of his handicap harness like wet tissue paper, tore straps guaranteed to support five thousand pounds.

Harrison's scrap-iron handicaps crashed to the floor.

Harrison thrust his thumbs under the bar of the padlock that secured his head harness. The bar snapped like celery. Harrison smashed his headphones and spectacles against the wall.

He flung away his rubber-ball nose, revealed a man that would have awed Thor, the god of thunder.

"I shall now select my Empress!" he said, looking down on the cowering people. "Let the first woman who dares rise to her feet claim her mate and her throne!"

A moment passed, and then a ballerina arose, swaying like a willow.

Harrison plucked the mental handicap from her ear, snapped off her physical handicaps with marvellous delicacy. Last of all, he removed her mask.

She was blindingly beautiful.

"Now—" said Harrison, taking her hand, "shall we show the people the meaning of the word dance? Music!" he commanded.

The musicians scrambled back into their chairs, and Harrison stripped them of their handicaps, too. "Play your best," he told them, "and I'll make you barons and dukes and earls."

The music began. It was normal at first—cheap, silly, false. But Harrison snatched two musicians from their chairs, waved them like batons as he sang the music as he wanted it played. He slammed them back into their chairs.

The music began again and was much improved.

Harrison and his Empress merely listened to the music for a while—listened gravely, as though synchronizing their heartbeats with it.

They shifted their weights to their toes.

Harrison placed his big hands on the girl's tiny waist, letting her sense the weightlessness that would soon be hers.

And then, in an explosion of joy and grace, into the air they sprang!

Not only were the laws of the land abandoned, but the law of gravity and the laws of motion as well.

They reeled, whirled, swiveled, flounced, capered, gamboled, and spun.

They leaped like deer on the moon.

The studio ceiling was thirty feet high, but each leap brought the dancers nearer to it.

It became their obvious intention to kiss the ceiling.

They kissed it.

And then, neutralizing gravity with love and pure will, they remained suspended in air inches below the ceiling, and they kissed each other for a long, long time.

It was then that Diana Moon Glampers, the Handicapper General, came into the studio with a double-barreled ten-gauge shotgun. She fired twice, and the Emperor and the Empress were dead before they hit the floor.

Diana Moon Glampers loaded the gun again. She aimed it at the musicians and told them they had ten seconds to get their handicaps back on.

It was then that the Bergerons' television tube burned out.

Hazel turned to comment about the blackout to George. But George had gone out into the kitchen for a can of beer.

George came back in with the beer, paused while a handicap signal shook him up. And then he sat down again. "You been crying?" he said to Hazel.

"Yup," she said.

"What about?" he said.

"I forget," she said. "Something real sad on television."

"What was it?" he said.

"It's all kind of mixed up in my mind," said Hazel.

"Forget sad things," said George.

"I always do," said Hazel.

"That's my girl," said George. He winced. There was the sound of a rivetting gun in his head.

"Gee—I could tell that one was a doozy," said Hazel.

"You can say that again," said George.

"Gee—" said Hazel, "I could tell that one was a doozy."

A CRITICAL ARTICLE

The following scholarly essay was written by Darryl Hattenhauer, associate professor of American Literature at Arizona State University West. It was published in *Studies in Short Fiction,* Fall 1998.

THE POLITICS OF KURT VONNEGUT'S "HARRISON BERGERON"

According to all commentary on Kurt Vonnegut's "Harrison Bergeron," the theme of this satire is that attempts to achieve equality are absurd. For example, Peter Reed says it "satirizes an obsession with equalizing . . ." (29). The critics have taken this text's absurd future utopia as representative of egalitarianism. For example, Stanley Schatt claims that "in any leveling process, what really is lost, according to Vonnegut, is beauty, grace, and wisdom" (133). But the object of Vonnegut's satire is not all leveling—"any leveling process" that might arise. Rather, the object of his satire is the popular misunderstanding of what leveling and equality entail. More specifically, this text satirizes America's Cold War misunderstanding of not just communism but also socialism. To argue that thesis, this article begins outside of the text by situating it in Vonnegut's oeuvre: his fiction, nonfiction, speeches, and interviews. Then this contextualization will attend to Vonnegut's audience. Finally, the analysis will turn to the internal evidence.

If "Harrison Bergeron" is a satire against the Left, then it is inconsistent with the rest of Vonnegut's fiction. For a view of his fiction's politics in general, one need only recall Jailbird's satire on conservatism and its sympathy with striking laborers, or the endorsement of income redistribution in God Bless You, Mr. Rosewater. A specific illustration of his politics occurs in the dedication of Hocus Pocus to socialist Eugene Debs, which quotes him: "While there is a lower class I am in it" (8).

Like his fiction, Vonnegut's non-fiction also satirizes the Right and endorses the Left. And the Left it endorses is not liberalism (America is one of the few nations where liberalism is not centrist). For example, "In a Manner that Must Shame God Himself," which he wrote in response to the 1972 Republican National Convention, claims that Democrats are only a little less Darwinist than Republicans. He satirizes not only the Republicans but also the Democrats as "bossed by Winners" at the expense of "Losers." He concludes, "THE WINNERS ARE AT WAR WITH THE LOSERS, AND THE FIX IS ON" (206). In "Yes, We Have No Nirvanas," he derides notions about "the fairness of the marketplace" (38). In Fates Worse than Death, he refers to the British class system as "robbery" (132). And in his preface to Wampeters, Foma and Granfaloons, he enjoins his readers to "share wealth and work" (xxiv).

His spoken word is consistent with his fiction and nonfiction. In an interview, he said of George Orwell, "I like his socialism" (Clancy 53). He said in a commencement speech at Bennington College, "I suggest that you work for a socialist form of government. . . . It isn't moonbeams to talk of modest plenty for all. They have it in Sweden" (168). In an address at Wheaton College, he even quoted Karl Marx approvingly: "From each according to his abilities. To each according to his needs" (217). When asked in an interview how he would have campaigned against Nixon, he responded, "I would have set the poor against the rich" ("Playboy" 273).

In a letter to me, Vonnegut indicated that the foregoing sympathy with "Losers" influenced "Harrison Bergeron." If the misreadings of this text were valid, then the implied author's sympathy would be for Harrison Bergeron and his antipathy would be for Diana Moon Glampers, the Handicapper General striving to prevent privilege. But Vonnegut suggests that the character he identifies with is not Bergeron but Glampers. He begins his letter by first situating himself as not only an author with both conscious and unconscious intent, but also a reader. He writes about not only what he consciously and unconsciously intended, but also what the resulting text actually is.

> *I can't be sure, but there is a possibility that my story "Harrison Bergeron" is about the envy and self-pity I felt in an over-achievers' high school in Indianapolis quite a while ago now. Some people never tame those emotions. John Wilkes Booth and Lee Harvey Oswald and Mark David Chapman come to mind. "Handicapper Generals," if you like.*

What the story is "about" has two meanings. The first is intent—the conscious mind's intent (he could not remember everything about producing the text) and the unconscious mind's intent (he is probably inferring it rather than relying on evidence such as dreams). Of course, intent does not necessarily establish effect; intent does not necessarily tell us what the text is "about." But it might lead the reader to what a text is about—not just to its origins, but also to its implicit theme. Accordingly, this article argues that the author's oeuvre, the author's intent, and "Harrison Bergeron's" internal evidence are all consistent with each other.

This absurd dystopia's version of equality sounds like something from the pages of popular magazines during the Cold War—because it is. Vonnegut depended on those magazines to establish himself as a writer. ("Harrison Bergeron" first appeared in the *Magazine of Fantasy and Science Fiction*.) Just as Twain could not have sold *Adventures of Huckleberry Finn* and *Pudd'nhead Wilson* if their sympathy with African-American characters had been obvious, so Vonnegut could not have sold a story overtly sympathetic to leveling. Instead, the Handicapper General apparently recalls the likes of John Wilkes Booth, proponent of slavery. (But the coming analysis will reveal that Harrison is the one who embodies a feudal society.) As a struggling writer, Vonnegut had to put a surface on this story that would appeal to his audience. And it did. More specifically, it did so because it appeared to rehearse central tenets of the dominant culture's ideology. It appealed to the literal-minded with such accuracy that William F. Buckley's National Review reprinted it as a morality tale about the dangers of forsaking private enterprise. Here is the narrator's presentation of this utopia's muddled definition of equality:

> *The year was 2081, and everybody was finally equal. They weren't only equal before God and the law. They were equal every which way. Nobody was any smarter than anybody else. Nobody was better looking than anybody else. Nobody was stronger or quicker than anybody else.* (5)

This definition codifies the common American objections not just to communist states, but also to socialist ones. The narrator begins with the widespread assertion that the United States not only can and does know God's law, but that God's favorite country is instituting it. (American history is replete with statements like Ronald Reagan's that his policies reflect God's will—see, e.g., his 1982 address to the National Catholic Education Association). So the narrator's definition of America's equality begins not by positing a future equality as much as exposing the misunderstanding of it in the past and present.

The narrator continues to give not a possible egalitarianism of the future (because, as will be noted, the text's version is physically impossible) but rather an enactment of how absurd society would be if egalitarianism were what America's dominant culture thinks it is. The narrator defines equality only in terms of intelligence, looks, and athletic ability. There is nothing about kinds of intelligence, or how it is used. Similarly, beauty includes only the human appearance; there is nothing about painting, architecture, etc. The first two concerns, intelligence and looks, address two of the traditional categories of philosophy: the true (epistemology) and the beautiful (aesthetics). The third category, the good (ethics), vanishes. Sport replaces it. No wonder there is nothing in the story about the ethics of spending huge amounts of time, money, and natural resources on sports.

Likewise, the story does not address the primary purpose of leveling in other countries: income redistribution. Since Hazel, Harrison's mother, wants the television announcer to get a raise, the definition of "equal every which way" cannot include incomes. According to the proponents of the ideology of America's dominant culture, equal income redistribution would contradict the fact that some are smarter than others (the corollary: the rich are smart and the poor are dumb), and also contradict the fact that some are better looking or more athletic than others (the corollary: attractive and athletic people deserve wealth). Since the power of class and the benefits of income redistribution are obscured in the dominant culture's ideology, the inequalities caused by class differences are appropriately absent from this story. For example, there is nothing about equal access to education or medical care.

The mediocrity depicted in this text is not of the future, but of the past and present. And the cause is America's form of egalitarianism: anti-intellectual leveling. Since the age of Jackson, there has been no one so un-common as the so-called "common man." The characters are not displaying the mindlessness of 2081; they are displaying the mindlessness of 1961, the year this story appeared. The reason Hazel wants the inept announcer to get a raise is that he tried his best. And George, Harrison's father, says, "Forget sad things" (10). Even if ignoring sad things leads to sadder things, ignorance is bliss. Moreover, the intellectual leveling of the past and present implies that ignorance is knowledge. Hazel asks, "Who knows better'n I do what normal is?" (6). Just because she typifies the normal does not mean she understands it. For Hazel, then, she has more expertise than any social scientist with a mountain of data.

It is fitting that the athletic characters in this text are held down by birdshot and that the plot resolution comes when the chief leveler, the Handicapper General, blasts Harrison and his intended with a shotgun. As Richard Slotkin has shown, it was during the frontier expansion that America extended its racist classism in part by developing its anti-intellectualism. Also appropriate is the fact that Harrison's parents are watching a televised ballet, thereby referring to the absurd position that economic leveling means there would be no competition and nobody would be any better than anybody else. The Russian ballet and Swedish theatre (two nations often cited at the time as exemplifying the absurdity of leveling) were highly competitive; they did not hold that all people are equally talented. According to the ideology of America's dominant culture, Russia and Sweden's expenditures on the arts were perverse because they were publicly funded, while America's were pure because they were privately funded—or, rather underfunded. In America's master narratives, only the public sphere costs the citizens. (Currently, however, with the high cost of seeing either a doctor or a baseball game, more Americans understand that the citizens pay private sector costs.) That Hazel and George are watching television is another appropriate metonym of the contradictions of American ideology. In this story, interpellation is the function not of the private media but government-controlled media. The government manages the station on which George and Hazel watch the ballet, and the headphone noises jamming George's thoughts come from a "government transmitter" (5). George misses the televising of his son's murder because George is in the kitchen getting a beer. Presumably he would not have missed it had it been on private television, for he could have left during a commercial.

Critics have missed the object of this text's satire because they miss the irony of the narration. They do not recognize the narration as unreliable. (Given what we know about the author, the narrator cannot be the authorial delegate.) Part of the reason they miss the narration's unreliability is that the plot hides the undeniability of the irony until the end. It is not until the plot resolution that the physically impossible happens. First, Harrison tears "straps guaranteed to support five thousand pounds" (9). Then he and his intended defy gravity by hovering in the air. After that impossible event, the preposterousness of the preceding events emerges more clearly. For example, in a society in which no one is more intelligent than anyone else, everyone would be as stupid as the most mentally deficient person in the populace, and, therefore, all would be unable even to feed themselves. But the critics miss this plot development. For example, Roy Townsend claims that this is "effectively a 'no-plot' situation because nothing happens . . ." (99).

Perhaps such critics miss what happens and the unreliability of the narration because they are interpellated into the very ideology that the text satirizes. For example, Schatt refers to the Handicapper General, Diana Moon Glampers, as "Glompers," perhaps associating the name with labor leader Samuel F. Gompers. (133). And Townsend contends, "The story is a satire, a parody of an ideological society divorced from common sense reality" (100). But the American common sense version of equality is nonsense. Townsend claims, "Vonnegut is appealing to an instinctive sense of what is right and decent" (102). The commonsense notion that ethics are instinctive is common nonsense.

Those who hold Harrison up as a model of freedom overlook the fact that he is a would-be dictator. "I am the Emperor," he declares. "I shall now select my Empress." He tells the musicians, "I'll make you barons and dukes and earls" (9). Thus Bergeron endorses monarchy. If there is a reversion to medieval monarchy, there will be serfs—the functional equivalent of slaves.

So this story satirizes not just mistaken notions of equality. It also satirizes the American definition of freedom as the greatest good to the smallest number. The American myth is that only in a class society can everyone have an equal chance for achieving the greatest economic inequality.

Works Cited

Clancy, Laurie. "Running Experiments Off: An Interview." *Meanjin Quarterly* 30 (Autumn, 1971): 46–54.

Reed, Peter. "Hurting 'Til It Laughs." *Kurt Vonnegut: Images and Representations.* Ed. Marc Leeds and Peter J. Reed. Westport, Connecticut: Greenwood, 2000. 19–38.

Schatt, Stanley. *Kurt Vonnegut, Jr.* Boston: Hall, 1976.

Slotkin, Richard. *The Fatal Environment: The Myth of the Frontier in the Age of Industrialism, 1880–1890.* New York: Atheneum, 1985.

———. *Gunfighter Nation: The Myth of the Frontier in Twentieth-Century America.* New York: Atheneum, 1992.

———. *Regeneration through Violence: The Mythology of the American Frontier.* Middletown, Connecticut: Wesleyan UP, 1973.

Townsend, Roy. "Eliot and Vonnegut: Modernism and Postmodernism?" *Journal of English* 16 (1988): 90–104.

Vonnegut, Kurt, Jr. "Address at Rededication of Wheaton College Library." *Wampeters* 211–19.

———. "Address to Graduating Class at Bennington College, 1970." *Wampeters* 159–68.

———. *Fates Worse Than Death: An Autobiographical Collage of the 1980s.* New York: Putnam's, 1991.

———. "Harrison Bergeron." *Magazine of Fantasy and Science Fiction* Oct. 1961: 5–10.

———. *Hocus Pocus.* New York: Putnam's, 1990.

———. "In a Manner that Would Shame God Himself." *Wampeters* 185–206.

———. Letter to the author. 23 Oct. 2000.

———. "Playboy Interview." *Wampeters* 237–85.

———. *Wampeters, Foma and Granfaloons* (Opinions). New York: Delacorte/ Seymour Lawrence, 1974.

———. "Yes, We Have No Nirvanas." *Wampeters* 31–41.

Conclusion

We hope that you have enjoyed our selections for this casebook on self-exploration and can visualize the patterns that these authors suggest are part of all of our personal discovery: patterns of the pain, loneliness, but empowerment in figuring out who we are; what motivates us on a daily basis; what are our hot buttons for reaction. When are we willing to take risks, and how do we handle the consequences when we choose to do nothing? No matter what our choices may be, are we ever willing to pay the price, to accept responsibility for our actions? Further, our choices and responses, much like those of fictional characters, say as much about who we are as anything else.

CASEBOOK TWO
Growing Up and Older:
His and Hers—Rites of Passage
Overview

It's almost cliché to say this, but it is true nonetheless: as we grow from childhood through adolescence and into adulthood—young adulthood, middle age, and the "golden years"—we experience many "rites of passage." Every culture has them, and many times these rites (or meaningful rituals) are gender-based, though not always. Many times, they involve formal rituals, and sometimes only subtle moments of change.

Rites of passage may be connected to physical maturing and maturity, emotional growth, love, the experience of war, of birth, of death, or some other type of loss. At each moment of change, it is common to become reflective—to pause and consider where we have been, what we have experienced, how we have changed, and what is to come. Much of the world's great literature explores such moments and offers valuable insights into the cycles of growing up and older.

Consider these questions as you read:

- What rites of passage have you experienced in your life to this point?
- Were these moments of change formal and public or informal and private?
- What rites of passage do you anticipate in the future?
- Why are rites of passage important to recognize and reflect upon?

Poetry

EDNA ST. VINCENT MILLAY

Poet and playwright Edna St. Vincent Millay was born in Rockland, Maine, on February 22, 1892. In 1912, her mother encouraged her to enter her poem "Renascence" in a contest: she won fourth place and publication in *The Lyric Year,* bringing her immediate acclaim and a scholarship to Vassar. There, she continued to write poetry and became involved in the theater. In 1917, the year of her graduation, Millay published her first book, *Renascence and Other Poems.* Edna St. Vincent Millay died in 1950.

The following (tiny) poem was published in 1920.

Grown Up

Was it for this I uttered prayers,
And sobbed and cursed and kicked the stairs,
That now, domestic as a plate,
I should retire at half-past eight?

WILFRED OWEN

Wilfred Owen was born in 1893 in Shropshire, England. Educated at the Birkenhead Institute and the Technical School in Shrewsbury in his childhood, he later taught at the Berlitz School of English in France.

In 1915, Owen enlisted in the Artists' Rifles group in support of World War I, and after training in England, was commissioned as a second lieutenant. He was wounded in combat in 1917 and diagnosed with shell shock. After taking some time off to recuperate, he rejoined his regiment in June 1918 and was killed on November 4 of that year.

The following poem was published posthumously in 1920.

Anthem for Doomed Youth

What passing-bells for these who die as cattle?
—Only the monstrous anger of the guns.

Only the stuttering rifles' rapid rattle
Can patter out their hasty orisons.
No mockeries now for them; no prayers nor bells;
Nor any voice of mourning save the choirs,—
The shrill, demented choirs of wailing shells;
And bugles calling for them from sad shires.

What candles may be held to speed them all?
Not in the hands of boys but in their eyes
Shall shine the holy glimmers of goodbyes.
The pallor of girls' brows shall be their pall;
Their flowers the tenderness of patient minds,
And each slow dusk a drawing-down of blinds.

W. H. AUDEN

Wystan Hugh Auden was born in York, England, in 1907. In 1928, Auden published his first book of poetry, and his collection *Poems,* published in 1930, established him as the voice of a new generation. W. H. Auden was a Chancellor of the Academy of American Poets from 1954 to 1973. He died in Vienna in 1973.

A Walk After Dark

A cloudless night like this
Can set the spirit soaring:
After a tiring day
The clockwork spectacle is
Impressive in a slightly boring
Eighteenth-century way.

It soothed adolescence a lot
To meet so shamelesss a stare;
The things I did could not
Be so shocking as they said
If that would still be there
After the shocked were dead

Now, unready to die
But already at the stage
When one starts to resent the young,
I am glad those points in the sky
May also be counted among
The creatures of middle-age.

It's cosier thinking of night
As more an Old People's Home
Than a shed for a faultless machine,
That the red pre-Cambrian light
Is gone like Imperial Rome
Or myself at seventeen.

Yet however much we may like
The stoic manner in which
The classical authors wrote,
Only the young and rich
Have the nerve or the figure to strike
The lacrimae rerum note.

For the present stalks abroad
Like the past and its wronged again
Whimper and are ignored,
And the truth cannot be hid;
Somebody chose their pain,
What needn't have happened did.

Occuring this very night
By no established rule,
Some event may already have hurled
Its first little No at the right
Of the laws we accept to school
Our post-diluvian world:

But the stars burn on overhead,
Unconscious of final ends,
As I walk home to bed,
Asking what judgment waits
My person, all my friends,
And these United States.

DONALD JUSTICE

Donald Justice was born in Florida in 1925. A graduate of the University of Miami, he also attended the universities of North Carolina, Stanford, and Iowa. In 1979 he won the Pulitzer Prize for poetry for his collection *Selected Poems*. He has held teaching positions at Syracuse University, the University of California at Irvine, Princeton University, the University of Virginia, and the University of Iowa, and from 1982 until his retirement in 1992, he taught at the University of Florida, Gainesville.

The following poem was published in 1995 in the collection *New and Selected Poems*.

Men at Forty

Men at forty
Learn to close softly
The doors to rooms they will not be
Coming back to.

At rest on a stair landing,
They feel it moving
Beneath them now like the deck of a ship,
Though the swell is gentle.

And deep in mirrors
They rediscover
The face of the boy as he practices tying
His father's tie there in secret,

And the face of that father,
Still warm with the mystery of lather.
They are more fathers than sons themselves now.
Something is filling them, something
That is like the twilight sound
Of the crickets, immense,
Filling the woods at the foot of the slope
Behind their mortgaged houses.

ADRIENNE RICH

Adrienne Rich was born in Baltimore, Maryland, in 1929. She is the author of nearly twenty volumes of poetry. Rich has received the Bollingen Prize, the Lannan Lifetime Achievement Award, the Academy of American Poets Fellowship, the Ruth Lilly Poetry Prize, the Lenore Marshall Poetry Prize, the National Book Award, and a MacArthur Fellowship; she is also a former Academy Chancellor. In 1997, she was awarded the Academy's Wallace Stevens Award for outstanding and proven mastery in the art of poetry.

Diving into the Wreck

First having read the book of myths,
and loaded the camera,
and checked the edge of the knife-blade,
I put on

the body-armor of black rubber
the absurd flippers
the grave and awkward mask.
I am having to do this
not like Cousteau with his
assiduous team
aboard the sun-flooded schooner
but here alone.

There is a ladder.
The ladder is always there
hanging innocently
close to the side of the schooner.
We know what it is for,
we who have used it.
Otherwise
it is a piece of maritime floss
some sundry equipment.

I go down.
Rung after rung and still
the oxygen immerses me
the blue light
the clear atoms
of our human air.
I go down.
My flippers cripple me,
I crawl like an insect down the ladder
and there is no one
to tell me when the ocean
will begin.

First the air is blue and then
it is bluer and then green and then
black I am blacking out and yet
my mask is powerful
it pumps my blood with power
the sea is another story
the sea is not a question of power
I have to learn alone
to turn my body without force
in the deep element.

And now: it is easy to forget
what I came for
among so many who have always
lived here

swaying their crenellated fans
between the reefs
and besides
you breathe differently down here.

I came to explore the wreck.
The words are purposes.
The words are maps.
I came to see the damage that was done
and the treasures that prevail.
I stroke the beam of my lamp
slowly along the flank
of something more permanent
than fish or weed

the thing I came for:
the wreck and not the story of the wreck
the thing itself and not the myth
the drowned face always staring
toward the sun
the evidence of damage
worn by salt and away into this threadbare beauty
the ribs of the disaster
curving their assertion
among the tentative haunters.

This is the place.
And I am here, the mermaid whose dark hair
streams black, the merman in his armored body.
We circle silently
about the wreck
we dive into the hold.
I am she: I am he

whose drowned face sleeps with open eyes
whose breasts still bear the stress
whose silver, copper, vermeil cargo lies
obscurely inside barrels
half-wedged and left to rot
we are the half-destroyed instruments
that once held to a course
the water-eaten log
the fouled compass

We are, I am, you are
by cowardice or courage
the one who find our way

back to this scene
carrying a knife, a camera
a book of myths
in which
our names do not appear.

SHARON OLDS

Born in San Francisco in 1942, Sharon Olds studied at Stanford University and received a master's degree from Columbia University. Named New York State Poet in 1998, Olds teaches poetry workshops at New York University's Graduate Creative Writing Program, along with a workshop at Goldwater Hospital on Roosevelt Island in New York.

The following poem was published in 1987 in the collection *The Gold Cell*.

First Boyfriend

(for D. R.)
We would park on any quiet street,
gliding over the curb as if by accident,
the houses dark, the families sealed into them,
we'd park away from the street-light, just the
faint waves of its amber grit
reached your car, you'd switch off the motor and
turn and reach for me, and I would
slide into your arms as if I had been born for it,
the ochre corduroy of your sports jacket
pressing the inside of my wrist,
making its pattern of rivulets,
water rippling out like sound waves from a source.
Your front seat had an overpowering
male smell, as if the chrome had been
rubbed with jism, a sharp stale
delirious odor like the sour plated
taste of the patina on an old watch, the
fragrance of your sex polished till it shone in the night, the
jewel of Channing Street, of Benvenue Avenue, of
Panoramic, of Dwight Way, I
returned to you as if to the breast of my father,
grain of the beard on your umber cheeks,
delicate line of tartar on the edge of your teeth,
the odor of use, the stained brass

air in the car as if I had come—
back to a pawnshop to claim what was mine—
and as your tongue went down my throat,
right down the central nerve of my body, the
gilt balls of the street-light gleamed like a
pawnbroker's over your second-hand Chevy and
all the toasters popped up and
all the saxophones began to play
hot riffs of scat for the return of their rightful owners.

GARY SOTO

Gary Soto was born in Fresno, California, in 1952. He is the author of ten poetry collections and the youngest poet ever to be included in *The Norton Anthology of Poetry.* Among many awards, he has received fellowships from the California Arts Council, the Guggenheim Foundation, and the National Endowment for the Arts.

The following poem appeared in *Gary Soto: New and Selected Poems* in 1995.

Oranges

The first time I walked
With a girl, I was twelve,
Cold, and weighted down
With two oranges in my jacket.
December. Frost cracking
Beneath my steps, my breath
Before me, then gone,
As I walked toward
Her house, the one whose
Porch light burned yellow
Night and day, in any weather.
A dog barked at me, until
She came out pulling
At her gloves, face bright
With rouge. I smiled,
Touched her shoulder, and led
Her down the street, across
A used car lot and a line
Of newly planted trees,
Until we were breathing
Before a drugstore. We
Entered, the tiny bell.

Bringing a saleslady
Down a narrow aisle of goods.
I turned to the candies
Tiered like bleachers,
And asked what she wanted—
Light in her eyes, a smile
Starting at the corners
Of her mouth. I fingered
A nickel in my pocket,
And when she lifted a chocolate
That cost a dime,
I didn't say anything.
I took the nickel from
My pocket, then an orange,
And set them quietly on
The counter. When I looked up,
The lady's eyes met mine,
And held them, knowing
Very well what it was all
About.

        Outside,
A few cars hissing past,
Fog hanging like old
Coats between the trees.
I took my girl's hand
In mine for two blocks,
Then released it to let
Her unwrap the chocolate.
I peeled my orange
That was so bright against
The gray of December
That, from some distance,
Someone might have thought
I was making a fire in my hands.

Rita Dove

Rita Dove was born in Akron, Ohio, in 1952. The author of multiple volumes of poetry, her collection titled *Thomas and Beulah* (1986) won the Pulitzer Prize for Poetry. Dove's many honors include the Academy of American Poets's Lavan Younger Poets Award, a Mellon Foundation grant, an NAACP Great American Artist award, Fulbright and Guggenheim Foundation fellowships, and grants and fellowships from the National Endowment for the Arts and the National Endowment for the Humanities. She served at Poet Laureate of the United States from 1993 to 1995, and in 2004 she was named Poet Laureate of the Commonwealth of Virginia and is Commonwealth Professor of English at the University of Virginia.

Adolesence II

Although it is night, I sit in the bathroom, waiting.
Sweat prickles behind my knees, the baby-breasts are alert.
Venetian blinds slice up the moon; the tiles quiver in pale strips.

Then they come, the three seal men with eyes as round
As dinner plates and eyelashes like sharpened tines.
They bring the scent of licorice. One sits in the washbowl,

One on the bathtub edge; one leans against the door.
"Can you feel it yet?" they whisper.
I don't know what to say, again. They chuckle,

Patting their sleek bodies with their hands.
"Well, maybe next time." And they rise,
Glittering like pools of ink under moonlight,

And vanish. I clutch at the ragged holes
They leave behind, here at the edge of darkness.
Night rests like a ball of fur on my tongue.

MARGE PIERCY

Poet, novelist, and essayist Marge Piercy was born in Detroit, Michigan, in 1936. She won a scholarship to the University of Michigan and was the first member of her family to attend college. She subsequently earned a master's degree from Northwestern University. The following poem was published in the collection *Women and Aging.*

Something to Look Forward To

Menopause—word used as an insult:
a menopausal woman, mind or poem
as if not to leak regularly or on the caprice
of the moon, the collision of egg and sperm,
were the curse we first learned to call that blood.

I have twisted myself to praise that bright splash.
When my womb opens its lips on the full
or dark of the moon, that connection

aligns me as it does the sea. I quiver,
a compass needle thrilling with magnetism.

Yet for every celebration there's the time
it starts on a jet with the seatbelt sign on.
Consider the trail of red amoebae
crawling onto hostess's sheets to signal
my body's disregard of calendar, clock.

How often halfway up the side of a mountain,
during a demonstration with the tactical police
force drawn up in tanks between me and a toilet;
during an endless wind machine panel with four males
I the token woman and they with iron bladders,

I have felt that wetness and wanted to strangle
my womb like a mouse. Sometimes it feels cosmic
and sometimes it feels like mud. Yes, I have prayed
to my blood on my knees in toilet stalls
simply to show its rainbow of deliverance.

My friend Penny at twelve being handed a napkin
the size of an ironing board cover, cried out
Do I have to do this from now till I die?
No, said her mother, it stops in middle age.
Good, said Penny, there's something to look forward to.

Today supine, groaning with demon crab claws
gouging my belly, I tell you I will secretly dance
and pour out a cup of wine on the earth
when time stops that leak permanently;
I will burn my last tampons as votive candles.

Fiction

RICHARD WRIGHT

Richard Wright was born on a plantation near Natchez, Mississippi, on September 4, 1908. He was a prolific writer of both poetry and fiction throughout his career and often worked as editor for various publications. In his last years, he was beset by illness and financial difficulties, but he remained constant with his writing. Throughout the most difficult times, he created approximately 4,000 English haikus and a novel. He also prepared another collection of short stories, *Eight Men,* which was published after his death on November 28, 1960.

The Man Who Was Almost a Man

Dave struck out across the fields, looking homeward through paling light. Whut's the use talkin wid em niggers in the field? Anyhow, his mother was putting supper on the table. Them niggers can't understan nothing. One of these days he was going to get a gun and practice shooting, then they couldn't talk to him as though he were a little boy. He slowed, looking at the ground. Shucks, Ah ain scareda them even ef they are biggern me! Aw, Ah know whut Ahma do. Ahm going by ol Joe's sto n git that Sears Roebuck catlog n look at them guns. Mebbe Ma will lemme buy one when she gits mah pay from ol man Hawkins. Ahma beg her t gimme some money. Ahm ol ernough to hava gun. Ahm seventeen. Almost a man. He strode, feeling his long loose-jointed limbs. Shucks, a man oughta hava little gun aftah he done worked hard all day.

He came in sight of Joe's store. A yellow lantern glowed on the front porch. He mounted steps and went through the screen door, hearing it bang behind him. There was a strong smell of coal oil and mackerel fish. He felt very confident until he saw fat Joe walk in through the rear door, then his courage began to ooze.

"Howdy, Dave! Whutcha want?"

"How yuh, Mistah Joe? Aw, Ah don wanna buy nothing. Ah jus wanted t see ef yuhd lemme look at tha catlog erwhile."

"Sure! You wanna see it here?"

"Nawsuh. Ah wants t take it home wid me. Ah'll bring it back termorrow when Ah come in from the fiels."

"You plannin on buying something?"

"Yessuh."

5

"Your ma lettin you have your own money now?"

"Shucks. Mistah Joe, Ahm gittin t be a man like anybody else!"   10

Joe laughed and wiped his greasy white face with a red bandanna.

"What you plannin on buyin?"

Dave looked at the floor, scratched his head, scratched his thigh, and smiled. Then he looked up shyly.

"Ah'll tell yuh, Mistah Joe, ef yuh promise yuh won't tell."

"I promise."   15

"Waal, Ahma buy a gun."

"A gun? What you want with a gun?"

"Ah wanna keep it."

"You ain't nothing but a boy. You don't need a gun."

"Aw, lemme have the catlog, Mistah Joe. Ah'll bring it back."   20

Joe walked through the rear door. Dave was elated. He looked around at barrels of sugar and flour. He heard Joe coming back. He craned his neck to see if he were bringing the book. Yeah, he's got it. Gawddog, he's got it!

"Here, but be sure you bring it back. It's the only one I got."

"Sho, Mistah Joe."

"Say, if you wanna buy a gun, why don't you buy one from me? I gotta gun to sell."

"Will it shoot?"   25

"Sure it'll shoot."

"Whut kind is it?"

"Oh, it's kinda old . . . a left-hand Wheeler. A pistol. A big one."

"Is it got bullets in it?"

"It's loaded."   30

"Kin Ah see it?"

"Where's your money?"

"What yuh wan fer it?"

"I'll let you have it for two dollars."

"Just two dollahs? Shucks. Ah could buy tha when Ah git mah pay."   35

"I'll have it here when you want it."

"Awright, suh. Ah be in fer it."

He went through the door, hearing it slam again behind him. Ahma git some money from Ma n buy me a gun! Only two dollahs! He tucked the thick catalogue under his arm and hurried.

"Where yuh been, boy?" His mother held a steaming dish of blackeyed peas.

"Aw, Ma, Ah just stopped down the road t talk wid the boys."   40

"Yuh know bettah t keep suppah waiting."

He sat down, resting the catalogue on the edge of the table.

"Yuh git up from there and git to the well n wash yosef! Ah ain feedin no hogs in mah house!"

She grabbed his shoulder and pushed him. He stumbled out of the room, then came back to get the catalogue.

"Whut this?"   45

"Aw, Ma, it's jusa catlog."

"Who yuh git it from?"

"From Joe, down at the sto."

"Waal, thas good. We kin use it in the outhouse."

"Naw, Ma." He grabbed for it. "Gimme ma catlog, Ma."   50

She held onto it and glared at him.

"Quit hollerin at me! Whut's wrong wid yuh? Yuh crazy?"

"But Ma, please. It ain mine! It's Joe's! He tol me t bring it back t im termorrow."

She gave up the book. He stumbled down the back steps, hugging the thick book under his arm. When he had splashed water on his face and hands, he groped back to the kitchen and fumbled in a corner for the towel. He bumped into a chair; it clattered to the floor. The catalogue sprawled at his feet. When he had dried his eyes he snatched up the book and held it again under his arms. His mother stood watching him.

"Now, ef yuh gonna act a fool over that ol book, Ah'll take it n burn it up."   55

"Naw, Ma, please."

"Waal, set down n be still!"

He sat down and drew the oil lamp close. He thumbed page after page, unaware of the food his mother set on the table. His father came in. Then his small brother.

"Whutcha got there, Dave?" his father asked.

"Jusa catlog," he answered, not looking up.   60

"Yeah, here they is!" His eyes glowed at blue-and-black revolvers. He glanced up, feeling sudden guilt. His father was watching him. He eased the book under the table and rested it on his knees. After the blessing was asked, he ate. He scooped up peas and swallowed fat meat without chewing. Buttermilk helped to wash it down. He did not want to mention money before his father. He would do much better by cornering his mother when she was alone. He looked at his father uneasily out of the edge of his eye.

"Boy, how come yuh don quit foolin wid tha book n eat yo suppah?"

"Yessuh."

"How you n ol man Hawkins gitten erlong?"

"Suh?"   65

"Can't yuh hear? Why don yuh listen? Ah ast yu how wuz yuh n ol man Hawkins gittin erlong?"

"Oh, swell, Pa. Ah plows mo lan than anybody over there."

"Waal, yuh oughta keep you mind on whut yuh doin."

"Yessuh."

He poured his plate full of molasses and sopped it up slowly with a chunk of corn-   70
bread. When his father and brother had left the kitchen, he still sat and looked again at the guns in the catalogue, longing to muster courage enough to present his case to his mother. Lawd, ef Ah only had tha pretty one! He could almost feel the slickness of the weapon with his fingers. If he had a gun like that he would polish it and keep it shining so it would never rust. N Ah'd keep it loaded, by Gawd!

"Ma?" His voice was hesitant.

"Hunh?"

"Ol man Hawkins give yuh mah money yit?"

"Yeah, but ain no usa yuh thinking about throwin nona it erway. Ahm keepin tha money sos yuh kin have cloes t go to school this winter."

He rose and went to her side with the open catalogue in his palms. She was wash- 75 ing dishes, her head bent low over a pan. Shyly he raised the book. When he spoke, his voice was husky, faint.

"Ma, Gawd knows Ah wans one of these."

"One of whut?" she asked, not raising her eyes.

"One of these," he said again, not daring even to point. She glanced up at the page, then at him with wide eyes.

"Nigger, is yuh gone plumb crazy?"

"Aw, Ma—" 80

"Git outta here! Don yuh talk t me bout no gun! Yuh a fool!"

"Ma, Ah kin buy one fer two dollahs."

"Not ef Ah knows it, yuh ain!"

"But yuh promised me one—"

"Ah don care what Ah promised! Yuh ain nothing but a boy yit!" 85

"Ma ef yuh lemme buy one Ah'll *never* ast yuh fer nothing no mo."

"Ah tol yuh t git outta here! Yuh ain gonna toucha penny of the money fer no gun! Thas how come Ah has Mistah Hawkins t pay yu wages t me, cause Ah knows yuh ain got no sense."

"But, Ma, we needa gun. Pa ain got no gun. We needa gun in the house. Yuh kin never tell whut might happen."

"Now don yuh try to maka fool outta me, boy! Ef we did hava gun, yuh wouldn't have it!"

He laid the catalogue down and slipped his arm around her waist. 90

"Aw, Ma, Ah done worked hard alla summer n ain ast yuh fer nothing, is Ah, now?"

"Thas whut yuh spose t do!"

"But Ma, Ah wans a gun. Yuh kin lemme have two dollahs outta mah money. Please, Ma. I kin give it to Pa . . . Please, Ma! Ah loves yuh, Ma."

When she spoke her voice came soft and low.

"What yu wan wida gun, Dave? Yuh don need no gun. Yuh'll git in trouble. N ef 95 yo pa jus thought Ah let yuh have money t buy a gun he'd hava fit."

"Ah'll hide it, Ma. It ain but two dollahs."

"Lawd, chil, whut's wrong wid yuh?"

"Ain nothin wrong, Ma. Ahm almos a man now. Ah wans a gun."

"Who gonna sell yuh a gun?"

"Ol Joe at the sto." 100

"N it don cos but two dollahs?"

"Thas all, Ma. Jus two dollahs. Please, Ma."

She was stacking the plates away; her hands moved slowly, reflectively. Dave kept an anxious silence. Finally, she turned to him.

"Ah'll let yuh git tha gun ef yuh promise me one thing."

"Whut's tha, Ma?" 105

"Yuh bring it straight back t me, yuh hear? It be fer Pa."

"Yessum! Lemme go now, Ma."

She stooped, turned slightly to one side, raised the hem of her dress, rolled down the top of her stocking, and came up with a slender wad of bills.

"Here," she said. "Lawd knows yuh don need no gun. But yer pa does. Yuh bring it right back t me, yuh hear? Ahma put it up. Now ef yuh don, Ahma have yuh pa lick yuh so hard yuh won fergit it."

"Yessum." 110

He took the money, ran down the steps, and across the yard.

"Dave! Yuuuuu Daaaaave!"

He heard, but he was not going to stop now. "Naw, Lawd!"

The first movement he made the following morning was to reach under his pillow for the gun. In the gray light of dawn he held it loosely, feeling a sense of power. Could kill a man with a gun like this. Kill anybody, black or white. And if he were holding his gun in his hand, nobody could run over him; they would have to respect him. It was a big gun, with a long barrel and a heavy handle. He raised and lowered it in his hand, marveling at its weight.

He had not come straight home with it as his mother had asked; instead he had 115 stayed out in the fields, holding the weapon in his hand, aiming it now and then at some imaginary foe. But he had not fired it; he had been afraid that his father might hear. Also he was not sure he knew how to fire it.

To avoid surrendering the pistol he had not come into the house until he knew that they were all asleep. When his mother had tiptoed to his bedside late that night and demanded the gun, he had first played possum; then he had told her that the gun was hidden outdoors, that he would bring it to her in the morning. Now he lay turning it slowly in his hands. He broke it, took out the cartridges, felt them, and then put them back.

He slid out of bed, got a long strip of old flannel from a trunk, wrapped the gun in it, and tied it to his naked thigh while it was still loaded. He did not go in to breakfast. Even though it was not yet daylight, he started for Jim Hawkins' plantation. Just as the sun was rising he reached the barns where the mules and plows were kept.

"Hey! That you, Dave?"

He turned. Jim Hawkins stood eying him suspiciously.

"What're yuh doing here so early?" 120

"Ah didn't know Ah wuz gittin up so early, Mistah Hawkins. Ah was fixin t hitch up ol Jenny n take her t the fiels."

"Good. Since you're so early, how about plowing that stretch down by the woods?"

"Suits me, Mistah Hawkins."

"O.K. Go to it!"

He hitched Jenny to a plow and started across the fields. Hot dog! This was just what 125 he wanted. If he could get down by the woods, he could shoot his gun and nobody would hear. He walked behind the plow, hearing the traces creaking, feeling the gun tied tight to his thigh.

When he reached the woods, he plowed two whole rows before he decided to take out the gun. Finally, he stopped, looked in all directions, then untied the gun and held it in his hand. He turned to the mule and smiled.

"Know whut this is, Jenny? Naw, yuh wouldn know! Yuhs jusa ol mule! Anyhow, this is a gun, n it kin shoot, by Gawd!"

He held the gun at arm's length. Whut t hell, Ahma shoot this thing! He looked at Jenny again.

"Lissen here, Jenny! When Ah pull this ol trigger, Ah don wan yuh to run n acka fool now?"

Jenny stood with head down, her short ears pricked straight. Dave walked off about 130 twenty feet, held the gun far out from him at arm's length, and turned his head. Hell, he told himself, Ah ain afraid. The gun felt loose in his fingers; he waved it wildly for a moment. Then he shut his eyes and tightened his forefinger. Bloom! A report half deafened him and he thought his right hand was torn from his arm. He heard Jenny whinnying and galloping over the field, and he found himself on his knees, squeezing his fingers hard between his legs. His hand was numb; he jammed it into his mouth, trying to warm it, trying to stop the pain. The gun lay at his feet. He did not quite know what had happened. He stood up and stared at the gun as though it were a living thing. He gritted his teeth and kicked the gun. Yuh almos broke mah arm! He turned to look for Jenny; she was far over the fields, tossing her head and kicking wildly.

"Hol on there, ol mule!"

When he caught up with her she stood trembling, walling her big white eyes at him. The plow was far away; the traces had broken. Then Dave stopped short, looking, not believing. Jenny was bleeding. Her left side was red and wet with blood. He went closer. Lawd, have mercy! Wondah did Ah shoot this mule? He grabbed for Jenny's mane. She flinched, snorted, whirled, tossing her head.

"Hol on now! Hol on."

Then he saw the hole in Jenny's side, right between the ribs. It was round, wet, red. A crimson stream streaked down the front leg, flowing fast. Good Gawd! Ah wuzn't shootin at tha mule. He felt panic. He knew he had to stop that blood, or Jenny would bleed to death. He had never seen so much blood in all his life. He chased the mule for half a mile, trying to catch her. Finally she stopped, breathing hard, stumpy tail half arched. He caught her mane and led her back to where the plow and gun lay. Then he stooped and grabbed handfuls of damp black earth and tried to plug the bullet hole. Jenny shuddered, whinnied, and broke from him.

"Hol on! Hol on now!"   135

He tried to plug it again, but blood came anyhow. His fingers were hot and sticky. He rubbed dirt into his palms, trying to dry them. Then again he attempted to plug the bullet hole, but Jenny shied away, kicking her heels high. He stood helpless. He had to do something. He ran at Jenny; she dodged him. He watched a red stream of blood flow down Jenny's leg and form a bright pool at her feet.

"Jenny . . . Jenny," he called weakly.

His lips trembled. She's bleeding t death! He looked in the direction of home, wanting to go back, wanting to get help. But he saw the pistol lying in the damp black clay. He had a queer feeling that if he only did something, this would not be; Jenny would not be there bleeding to death.

When he went to her this time, she did not move. She stood with sleepy, dreamy eyes; and when he touched her she gave a low-pitched whinny and knelt to the ground, her front knees slopping in blood.

"Jenny . . . Jenny . . ." he whispered.   140

For a long time she held her neck erect; then her head sank, slowly. Her ribs swelled with a mighty heave and she went over.

Dave's stomach felt empty, very empty. He picked up the gun and held it gingerly between his thumb and forefinger. He buried it at the foot of a tree. He took a stick and tried to cover the pool of blood with dirt—but what was the use? There was Jenny lying with her mouth open and her eyes walled and glassy. He could not tell Jim Hawkins he had shot his mule. But he had to tell something. Yeah, Ah'll tell em Jenny started gittin ill n fell on the joint of the plow. . . . But that would hardly happen to a mule. He walked across the field slowly, head down.

It was sunset. Two of Jim Hawkins' men were over near the edge of the woods digging a hole in which to bury Jenny. Dave was surrounded by a knot of people, all of whom were looking down at the dead mule.

"I don't see how in the world it happened," said Jim Hawkins for the tenth time.

The crowd parted and Dave's mother, father, and small brother pushed into   145 the center.

"Where Dave?" his mother called.

"There he is," said Jim Hawkins.

His mother grabbed him.

"Whut happened, Dave? Whut yuh done?"

"Nothin."   150

"C'mon, boy, talk," his father said.

Dave took a deep breath and told the story he knew nobody believed.

"Waal," he drawled. "Ah brung ol Jenny down here sos Ah could do mah plowin. Ah plowed bout two rows, just like yuh see." He stopped and pointed at the long rows of upturned earth. "Then somethin musta been wrong wid ol Jenny. She wouldn ack right a-tall. She started snortin n kickin her heels. Ah tried t hol her, but she pulled erway, rearin n goin in. Then when the point of the plow was stickin up in the air, she swung erroun n twisted herself back on it . . . She stuck herself n started t bleed. N fo Ah could do anything, she wuz dead."

"Did you ever hear of anything like that in all your life?" asked Jim Hawkins.

There were white and black standing in the crowd. They murmured. Dave's mother   155 came close to him and looked hard into his face. "Tell the truth, Dave," she said.

"Looks like a bullet hole to me," said one man.

"Dave, whut yuh do wid tha gun?" his mother asked.

The crowd surged in, looking at him. He jammed his hands into his pockets, shook his head slowly from left to right, and backed away. His eyes were wide and painful.

"Did he hava gun?" asked Jim Hawkins.

"By Gawd, Ah tol yuh tha wuz a gun wound," said a man, slapping his thigh.   160

His father caught his shoulders and shook him till his teeth rattled.

"Tell whut happened, yuh rascal! Tell whut . . ."

Dave looked at Jenny's stiff legs and began to cry.

"What yuh do wid tha gun?" his mother asked.

"Whut wuz he doin wida gun?" his father asked.   165

"Come on and tell the truth," said Hawkins. "Ain't nobody going to hurt you . . ."

His mother crowded close to him.

"Did yuh shoot tha mule, Dave?"

Dave cried, seeing blurred white and black faces.

"Ahh ddinn gggo tt sshooot hher . . . Ah sswear tt Gawd Ahh ddin. . . . Ah wuz a- 170 tryin t sssee ef the gggun would sshoot—"

"Where yuh git the gun from?" his father asked.

"Ah got it from Joe, at the sto."

"Where yuh git the money?"

"Ma give it t me."

"He kept worryin me, Bob. Ah had t. Ah tol im t bring the gun right back t me 175 . . . It was fer yuh, the gun."

"But how yuh happen to shoot that mule?" asked Jim Hawkins.

"Ah wuzn shootin at the mule, Mistah Hawkins! The gun jumped when Ah pulled the trigger . . . N fo Ah knowed anythin Jenny was there a-bleedin."

Somebody in the crowd laughed. Jim Hawkins walked close to Dave and looked into his face.

"Well, looks like you have bought you a mule, Dave."

"Ah swear to Gawd. Ah didn go t kill the mule, Mistah Hawkins!"   180

"But you killed her!"

All the crowd was laughing now. They stood on tiptoe and poked heads over one another's shoulders.

"Well, boy, looks like yuh done bought a dead mule! Hahaha!"

"Ain tha ershame."

"Hohohohoho."   185

Dave stood, head down, twisting his feet in the dirt.

"Well, you needn't worry about it, Bob," said Jim Hawkins to Dave's father. "Just let the boy keep on working and pay me two dollars a month."

"Whut yuh wan fer yo mule, Mistah Hawkins?"

Jim Hawkins screwed up his eyes.

"Fifty dollars."   190

"Whut yuh do wid tha gun?" Dave's father demanded.

Dave said nothing.

"Yuh wan me t take a tree n beat yuh till yuh talk!"

"Nawsuh!"

"Whut yuh do wid it?"   195

"Ah throwed it erway."

"Where?"

"Ah . . . Ah throwed it in the creek."

"Waal, c mon home. N firs thing in the mawnin git to tha creek n fin tha gun."

"Yessuh."   200

"Whut yuh pay fer it?"

"Two dollahs."

"Take tha gun n git yo money back n carry it t Mistah Hawkins, yuh hear? N don fergit Ahma lam you black bottom good fer this! Now march yoself on home, suh!"

Dave turned and walked slowly. He heard people laughing. Dave glared, his eyes welling with tears. Hot anger bubbled in him. Then he swallowed and stumbled on.

That night Dave did not sleep. He was glad that he had gotten out of killing the 205 mule so easily, but he was hurt. Something hot seemed to turn over inside him each time he remembered how they had laughed. He tossed on his bed, feeling his hard pillow. N Pa says he's gonna beat me . . . He remembered other beatings, and his back quivered. Naw, naw, Ah sho don wan im t beat me tha way no mo. Dam em all! Nobody ever gave him anything. All he did was work. They treat me like a mule, n then they beat me. He gritted his teeth. N Ma had t tell on me.

Well, if he had to, he would take old man Hawkins that two dollars. But that meant selling the gun. And he wanted to keep that gun. Fifty dollars for a dead mule.

He turned over, thinking how he had fired the gun. He had an itch to fire it again. Ef other men kin shoota gun, by Gawd, Ah kin! He was still, listening. Mebbe they all sleepin now. The house was still. He heard the soft breathing of his brother. Yes, now! He would go down and get that gun and see if he could fire it! He eased out of bed and slipped into overalls.

The moon was bright. He ran almost all the way to the edge of the woods. He stumbled over the ground, looking for the spot where he had buried the gun. Yeah, here it is. Like a hungry dog scratching for a bone, he pawed it up. He puffed his black cheeks and blew dirt from the trigger and barrel. He broke it and found four cartridges unshot. He looked around: the fields were filled with silence and moonlight. He clutched the gun stiff and hard in his fingers. But, as soon as he wanted to pull the trigger, he shut his eyes and turned his head. Naw, Ah can't shoot wid mah eyes closed n mah head turned. With effort he held his eyes open; then he squeezed. *Blooooom!* He was stiff, not breathing. The gun was still in his hands. Dammit, he'd done it! He fired again. *Blooooom!* He smiled. *Blooooom! Blooooom! Click, click.* There! It was empty. If anybody could shoot a gun, he could. He put the gun into his hip pocket and started across the fields.

When he reached the top of a ridge he stood straight and proud in the moonlight, looking at Jim Hawkin's big white house, feeling the gun sagging in his pocket. Lawd, ef Ah had just one mo bullet Ah'd taka shot at tha house. Ah'd like t scare ol man Hawkins jusa little . . . Jusa enough t let im know Dave Saunders is a man.

To his left the road curved, running to the tracks of the Illinois Central. He jerked his 210 head, listening. From far off came a faint *hoooof-hoooof; hoooof-hoooof* . . . He stood rigid. Two dollahs a mont. Les see now . . . Tha means it'll take bout two years. Shucks! Ah'll be dam!

He started down the road, toward the tracks. Yeah, here she comes. He stood beside the track and held himself stiffly. Here she comes erroun the ben . . . C mon, yuh slow poke! C mon! He had his hand on his gun; something quivered in his stomach. Then the train thundered past, the gray and brown box cars rumbling and clinking. He gripped the gun tightly; then he jerked his hand out of his pocket. Ah betcha Bill wouldn't do it! Ah betcha . . . The cars slid past, steel grinding upon steel. Ahm ridin yuh ternight, so hep me Gawd! He was hot all over. He hesitated just a moment; then he grabbed, pulled atop of a car, and lay flat. He felt his pocket; the gun was still there.

Ahead the long rails were glinting in the moonlight, stretching away, away to somewhere, somewhere where he could be a man . . .

ALICE MUNRO

Alice Laidlaw was born in Wingham, a small town in Canada, in 1931. She began writing down her stories at the age of twelve. She published her first story in 1950 while a student at Western Ontario University, but she left school, married James Munro in 1951, and moved to British Columbia. There she had three children and worked with her husband to establish a bookstore. She divorced James in 1972 and remarried in 1976.

The following story is from her first collection, *Dance of the Happy Shades,* published in 1968. It was highly acclaimed and won that year's Governor General's Award, Canada's highest literary prize.

Boys and Girls

My father was a fox farmer. That is, he raised silver foxes, in pens; and in the fall and early winter, when their fur was prime, he killed them and skinned them and sold their pelts to the Hudson's Bay Company or the Montreal Fur Traders. These companies supplied us with heroic calendars to hang, one on each side of the kitchen door. Against a background of cold blue sky and black pine forests and treacherous northern rivers, plumed adventurers planted the flags of England or of France; magnificent savages bent their backs to the portage.

For several weeks before Christmas, my father worked after supper in the cellar of our house. The cellar was whitewashed, and lit by a hundred-watt bulb over the worktable. My brother Laird and I sat on the top step and watched. My father removed the pelt inside-out from the body of the fox, which looked surprisingly small, mean and rat-like, deprived of its arrogant weight of fur. The naked, slippery bodies were collected in a sack and buried at the dump. One time the hired man, Henry Bailey, had taken a swipe at me with this sack, saying, "Christmas present!" My mother thought that was not funny. In fact she disliked the whole pelting operation—that was what the killing, skinning, and preparation of the furs was called—and wished it did not have to take place in the house. There was the smell. After the pelt had been stretched inside-out on a long board my father scraped away delicately, removing the little clotted webs of blood vessels, the bubbles of fat; the smell of blood and animal fat, with the strong primitive odour of the fox itself, penetrated all parts of the house. I found it reassuringly seasonal, like the smell of oranges and pine needles.

Henry Bailey suffered from bronchial troubles. He would cough and cough until his narrow face turned scarlet, and his light blue, derisive eyes filled up with tears; then he took the lid off the stove, and, standing well back, shot out a great clot of phlegm—hsss—straight into the heart of the flames. We admired him for his performance and for his ability to make his stomach growl at will, and for his laughter, which was full of high whistlings and gurglings and involved the whole faulty machinery of his chest. It was sometimes hard to tell what he was laughing at, and always possible that it might be us.

After we had been sent to bed we could still smell fox and still hear Henry's laugh, but these things, reminders of the warm, safe, brightly lit downstairs world, seemed lost and diminished, floating on the stale cold air upstairs. We were afraid at night in the winter. We were not afraid of *outside* though this was the time of year when snowdrifts curled around our house like sleeping whales and the wind harassed us all night, coming up from the buried fields, the frozen swamp, with its old bugbear chorus of threats and misery. We were afraid of *inside,* the room where we slept. At this time the upstairs of our house was not finished. A brick chimney went up one wall. In the middle of the floor was a square hole, with a wooden railing around it; that was where the stairs came up. On the other side of the stairwell were the things that nobody had any use for any more—a soldiery roll of linoleum, standing on end, a wicker baby carriage, a fern basket, china jugs and basins with cracks in them, a picture of the Battle of Balaclava, very sad to look at. I had told Laird, as soon as he was old enough to understand such things, that bats and skeletons lived over there; whenever a man escaped from the county jail, twenty miles away, I imagined that he had somehow let himself in the window and was hiding behind the linoleum. But we had rules to keep us safe. When the light was on, we were safe as long as we did not step off the square of worn carpet which defined our bedroom-space; when the light was off no place was safe but the beds themselves. I had to turn out the light kneeling on the end of my bed, and stretching as far as I could to reach the cord.

In the dark we lay on our beds, our narrow life rafts, and fixed our eyes on the   5 faint light coming up the stairwell, and sang songs. Laird sang "Jingle Bells," which he would sing any time, whether it was Christmas or not, and I sang "Danny Boy." I love the sound of my own voice, frail and supplicating, rising in the dark. We could make out the tall frosted shapes of the windows now, gloomy and white. When I came to the part, *When I am dead, as dead I well may be*—a fit of shivering caused not by the cold sheets but by pleasurable emotion almost silenced me. *You'll kneel and say, an Ave there above me*—What was an Ave? Every day I forgot to find out.

Laird went straight from singing to sleep. I could hear his long, satisfied, bubbly breaths. Now for the time that remained to me, the most perfectly private and perhaps the best time of the whole day, I arranged myself tightly under the covers and went on with one of the stories I was telling myself from night to night. These stories were about myself, when I had grown a little older; they took place in a world that was recognizably mine, yet one that presented opportunities for courage, boldness and self-sacrifice, as mine never did. I rescued people from a bombed building (it discouraged me that the real war had gone on so far away from Jubilee). I shot two rabid wolves who were menacing the schoolyard (the teachers cowered terrified at my back). I rode a fine horse spiritedly down the main street of Jubilee, acknowledging the towns-people's gratitude for some yet-to-be-worked-out piece of heroism (nobody ever rode a horse there, except King Billy in the Orangemen's Day parade). There was always riding and shooting in these stories, though I had only been on a horse twice—bareback because we did not own a saddle—and the second time I had slid right around and dropped under the horse's feet; it had

and my father talking in the stable, then the heavy, shuffling steps of Mack being backed out of his stall.

In the loft it was cold and dark. Thin, crisscrossed beams of sunlight fell through the cracks. The hay was low. It was a rolling country, hills and hollows, slipping under our feet. About four feet up was a beam going around the walls. We piled hay up in one corner and I boosted Laird up and hoisted myself. The beam was not very wide; we crept along it with our hands flat on the barn walls. There were plenty of knotholes, and I found one that gave me the view I wanted—a corner of the barnyard, the gate, part of the field. Laird did not have a knothole and began to complain.

I showed him a widened crack between two boards. "Be quiet and wait. If they hear you you'll get us in trouble."

My father came in sight carrying the gun. Henry was leading Mack by the halter.   35
He dropped it and took out his cigarette papers and tobacco; he rolled cigarettes for my father and himself. While this was going on Mack nosed around in the old, dead grass along the fence. Then my father opened the gate and they took Mack through. Henry led Mack away from the path to a patch of ground and they talked together, not loud enough for us to hear. Mack again began searching for a mouthful of fresh grass, which was not to be found. My father walked away in a straight line, and stopped short at a distance which seemed to suit him. Henry was walking away from Mack too, but sideways, still negligently holding on to the halter. My father raised the gun and Mack looked up as if he had noticed something and my father shot him.

Mack did not collapse at once but swayed, lurched sideways and fell, first on his side; then he rolled over on his back and, amazingly, kicked his legs for a few seconds in the air. At this Henry laughed, as if Mack had done a trick for him. Laird, who had drawn a long, groaning breath of surprise when the shot was fired, said out loud, "He's not dead." And it seemed to me it might be true. But his legs stopped, he rolled on his side again, his muscles quivered and sank. The two men walked over and looked at him in a businesslike way; they bent down and examined his forehead where the bullet had gone in, and now I saw his blood on the brown grass.

"Now they just skin him and cut him up," I said. "Let's go." My legs were a little shaky and I jumped gratefully down into the hay. "Now you've seen how they shoot a horse," I said in a congratulatory way, as if I had seen it many times before. "Let's see if any barn cat's had kittens in the hay." Laird jumped. He seemed young and obedient again. Suddenly I remembered how, when he was little, I had brought him into the barn and told him to climb the ladder to the top beam. That was in the spring, too, when the hay was low. I had done it out of a need for excitement, a desire for something to happen so that I could tell about it. He was wearing a little bulky brown and white checked coat, made down from one of mine. He went all the way up, just as I told him, and sat down on the top beam with the hay far below him on one side, and the barn floor and some old machinery on the other. Then I ran screaming to my father, "Laird's up on the top beam!" My father came, my mother came, my father went up the ladder talking very quietly and brought Laird down under his arm, at which my mother leaned against the ladder and began to cry. They said to me, "Why weren't you watching him?" but nobody ever knew the truth. Laird did not know enough to tell. But whenever I saw the brown and white checked coat hanging in the closet, or at the bottom of the rag bag, which was where it ended up, I felt a weight in my stomach, the sadness of unexorcized guilt.

I looked at Laird who did not even remember this, and I did not like the look on his thin, winter-pale face. His expression was not frightened or upset, but remote, concentrating. "Listen," I said, in an unusually bright and friendly voice, "you aren't going to tell, are you?"

"No," he said absently.

"Promise." 40

"Promise," he said. I grabbed the hand behind his back to make sure he was not crossing his fingers. Even so, he might have a nightmare; it might come out that way. I decided I had better work hard to get all thoughts of what he had seen out of his mind—which, it seemed to me, could not hold very many things at a time. I got some money I had saved and that afternoon we went into Jubilee and saw a show, with Judy Canova, at which we both laughed a great deal. After that I thought it would be all right.

Two weeks later I knew they were going to shoot Flora. I knew from the night before, when I heard my mother ask if the hay was holding out all right, and my father said, "Well, after to-morrow there'll just be the cow, and we should be able to put her out to grass in another week." So I knew it was Flora's turn in the morning.

This time I didn't think of watching it. That was something to see just one time. I had not thought about it very often since, but sometimes when I was busy, working at school, or standing in front of the mirror combing my hair and wondering if I would be pretty when I grew up, the whole scene would flash into my mind: I would see the easy, practised way my father raised the gun, and hear Henry laughing when Mack kicked his legs in the air. I did not have any great feeling of horror and opposition, such as a city child might have had; I was too used to seeing the death of animals as a necessity by which we lived. Yet I felt a little ashamed, and there was a new wariness, a sense of holding-off, in my attitude to my father and his work.

It was a fine day, and we were going around the yard picking up tree branches that had been torn off in winter storms. This was something we had been told to do, and also we wanted to use them to make a teepee. We heard Flora whinny, and then my father's voice and Henry's shouting, and we ran down to the barnyard to see what was going on.

The stable door was open. Henry had just brought Flora out, and she had broken 45 away from him. She was running free in the barnyard, from one end to the other. We climbed up on the fence. It was exciting to see her running, whinnying, going up on her hind legs, prancing and threatening like a horse in a Western movie, an unbroken ranch horse, though she was just an old driver, an old sorrel mare. My father and Henry ran after her and tried to grab the dangling halter. They tried to work her into a corner, and they had almost succeeded when she made a run between them, wild-eyed, and disappeared around the corner of the barn. We heard the rails clatter down as she got over the fence, and Henry yelled, "She's into the field now!"

That meant she was in the long L-shaped field that ran up by the house. If she got around the center, heading towards the lane, the gate was open; the truck had been driven into the field this morning. My father shouted to me, because I was on the other side of the fence, nearest the lane, "Go shut the gate!"

I could run very fast. I ran across the garden, past the tree where our swing was hung, and jumped across a ditch into the lane. There was the open gate. She had not got out, I could not see her up on the road; she must have run to the other end of the field. The gate was heavy. I lifted it out of the gravel and carried it across the roadway. I had it half-way across when she came in sight, galloping straight towards me. There was just time to get the chain on. Laird came scrambling through the ditch to help me.

Instead of shutting the gate, I opened it as wide as I could. I did not make any decision to do this, it was just what I did. Flora never slowed down; she galloped straight past me, and Laird jumped up and down, yelling, "Shut it, shut it!" even after it was too late. My father and Henry appeared in the field a moment too late to see what I had done. They only saw Flora heading for the township road. They would think I had not got there in time.

They did not waste any time asking about it. They went back to the barn and got the gun and the knives they used, and put these in the truck; then they turned the truck around and came bouncing up the field toward us. Laird called to them, "Let me go too, let me go too!" and Henry stopped the truck and they took him in. I shut the gate after they were all gone.

I supposed Laird would tell. I wondered what would happen to me. I had never dis- 50 obeyed my father before, and I could not understand why I had done it. Flora would not really get away. They would catch up with her in the truck. Or if they did not catch her this morning somebody would see her and telephone us this afternoon or tomorrow. There was no wild country here for her to run to, only farms. What was more, my father had paid for her, we needed the meat to feed the foxes, we needed the foxes to make our living. All I had done was make more work for my father who worked hard enough al-ready. And when my father found out about it he was not going to trust me any more; he would know that I was not entirely on his side. I was on Flora's side, and that made me no use to anybody, not even to her. Just the same, I did not regret it; when she came running at me and I held the gate open, that was the only thing I could do.

I went back to the house, and my mother said, "What's all the commotion?" I told her that Flora had kicked down the fence and got away. "Your poor father," she said, "now he'll have to go chasing over the countryside. Well, there isn't any use planning din-ner before one." She put up the ironing board. I wanted to tell her, but thought better of it and went upstairs and sat on my bed.

Lately I had been trying to make my part of the room fancy, spreading the bed with old lace curtains, and fixing myself a dressing-table with some leftovers of cretonne for a skirt. I planned to put up some kind of barricade between my bed and Laird's, to keep my section separate from his. In the sunlight, the lace curtains were just dusty rags. We did not sing at night any more. One night when I was singing Laird said, "You sound silly," and I went right on but the next night I did not start. There was not so much need to anyway, we were no longer afraid. We knew it was just old furniture over there, old jum-ble and confusion. We did not keep to the rules. I still stayed awake after Laird was asleep and told myself stories, but even in these stories something different was happening, mys-terious alterations took place. A story might start off in the old way, with a spectacular danger, a fire or wild animals, and for a while I might rescue people; then things would change around, and instead, somebody would be rescuing me. It might be a boy from our class at school, or even Mr. Campbell, our teacher, who tickled girls under the arms. And at this point the story concerned itself at great length with what I looked like—how long my hair was, and what kind of dress I had on; by the time I had these details worked out the real excitement of the story was lost.

It was later than one o'clock when the truck came back. The tarpaulin was over the back, which meant there was meat in it. My mother had to heat dinner up all over again. Henry and my father had changed from their bloody overalls into ordinary working overalls in the barn, and they washed their arms and necks and faces at the sink, and splashed water on their hair and combed it. Laird lifted his arm to show off a streak of blood. "We shot old Flora," he said, "and cut her up in fifty pieces."

"Well, I don't want to hear about it," my mother said. "And don't come to my table like that."

My family made him go and wash the blood off.   55

We sat down and my father said grace and Henry pasted his chewing-gum on the end of his fork, the way he always did; when he took it off he would have us admire the pattern. We began to pass the bowls of steaming, overcooked vegetables. Laird looked across the table at me and said proudly, distinctly, "Anyway it was her fault Flora got away."

"What?" my father said.

"She could of shut the gate and she didn't. She just open' it up and Flora run out."

"Is that right?" my father said.

Everybody at the table was looking at me. I nodded, swallowing food with great   60
difficulty. To my shame, tears flooded my eyes.

My father made a curt sound of disgust. "What did you do that for?"

I did not answer. I put down my fork and waited to be sent from the table, still not looking up.

But this did not happen. For some time nobody said anything, then Laird said matter-of-factly, "She's crying."

"Never mind," my father said. He spoke with resignation, even good humour, the words which absolved and dismissed me for good. "She's only a girl," he said.

I didn't protest that, even in my heart. Maybe it was true.   65

Drama

STEVE MARTIN

    Steve Martin was born in Waco, Texas, and raised in Garden Grove, California. Best known for his comedic talents (on *Saturday Night Live* and in a movie career spanning several decades), he is also an accomplished writer. He has written scripts for several movies, and he has written numerous plays, including the hit *Picasso at the Lapin Agile*, sketches and stories for *The New Yorker* and the *New York Times,* collected writings in his bestseller *Pure Drivel,* and critical essays for art publications.

    The following play was written in 1994.

WASP

SCENE 1

WASP

A kitchen in a fifties' house. A dining table is center stage, with four chairs around it. MOM sets the table in silence. Around the table are DAD, SON, and SIS. MOM sits.

DAD: O God in heaven, which is seventeen miles above the Earth, bless this food grown on this Earth that is four thousand three hundred twenty-five years old. Amen.
(They pantomime eating. We hear loud, amplified, prerecorded chewing sounds.)

SON: Jim, where's heaven?

DAD: Son, it's seventeen miles above the Earth. You enter through clouds. Behind the clouds, there are thirteen golden steps leading to a vestibule. Inside the vestibule is Saint Peter. Next to the vestibule are gates twenty-seven feet high. They are solid gold but with an off-center hinge for easy opening.

SON: Then heaven's closer than the moon?

DAD: What do you mean?

SON: Well, according to my science teacher, the moon is 250,000 miles away.
(There is a moment of silence while they contemplate this MOM bursts into tears. DAD stares at SON and starts to chew. Sounds of loud chewing for a long time.)

SON: Jim, if Adam and Eve were the first people on Earth and they had two sons, where did everybody else come from?

DAD: Huh?

(MOM stares at SON.)

SON: Well, if there were only two sons, then who did they marry and where did everybody else come from?

(Another moment of silence. MOM bursts into tears.)

DAD: Do you like your science teacher?

SON: Yeah.

DAD: Well, that's too bad because he's going to have his tongue pierced in hell by a hot poker.

(The phone rings. SIS looks up in anticipation, grips the table.)

SIS: Oh, my God, it's Jeremy!

(MOM goes to the wall phone and answers:)

MOM: Oh, hi, June! . . . *(SIS dies when she realizes it's not for her.)*

Uh-huh . . . yeah . . . really? . . . REALLY? Good news! Thanks! Bye. *(She hangs up, then to herself:)* Oh, great! Great news for me!

(MOM looks at everyone in anticipation. No one asks her anything. She sits back down.

Sounds of loud chewing.)

SIS: Guess what I learned in home economics?

(More munching.)

MOM: I went to a flower show today, and I just thought it was beautiful; they have the most beautiful things there . . . I went with Miriam and she had been before but there was a new exhibit so . . .

(DAD starts talking louder and over MOM.)

MOM:	**DAD**
She wanted to go again and she knows someone there and she got tickets for me so I got in free. Normally it costs three dollars to go in, so I used the money I saved and picked up a nice arrangement . . .	*(loud and over mom):* Boy, oh boy, when I was in college, I remember we used to wear these skinny little pants and shirts with big collars; boy, we must have looked silly.

(Mom's dialogue peters out.

The phone rings. SIS looks at the phone in anticipation.)

SIS *(frantic):* It's Jeremy, it's got to be!

(MOM answers it.)

MOM: Hello? Oh. Jim, it's for you. It's Mr. Carlyle.

(SIS collapses again.)

DAD: I'll take it in the living room.

(DAD exits. Big relax from the family.)

DAD *(offstage, loud and muffled):* I don't give a damn what they're talking about if they can't meet us halfway then we've got to reconsider the whole arrangement. There's no sense in doing what we talked about unless we're willing to do it without a contract and I don't want to see the situation turn around unless we want it to turn around . . .

(MOM, SIS, and SON begin to quake, rattling dishes and cutlery. MOM starts to clear dishes, shaking her way with cups and saucers to the sink. DAD emits a cheery laugh; the family relaxes.)

SON *(relieved, trying to make conversation)*: Where's the dog?

SIS: Yeah, what happened to Coco? I haven't seen her in about two days. And it's not like she comes back at night; the food's always left in the dish.

MOM: She just wouldn't stay off the furniture, so I put her to sleep.

(SIS stares horrified into space. DAD returns, sits.)

DAD: Where's Grandmom? We haven't heard from her in about a week.

(SIS and SON look horrified at MOM. MOM looks guilty, shifts uncomfortably.)

MOM *(then)*: In Europe they eat the salad after the main course, and that's what we're doing tonight.

DAD *(incredulous)*: Salad *after* the main course?

SON: Weird.

MOM: Here it is . . .

(MOM brings out a huge cherry Jell-O ring with fruit bits on it.)

DAD *(looks into the cherry ring and points to a piece of fruit)*: What's that on top?

MOM: Mango.

(SON stifles a vomit.)

SIS: Eyew. I don't think I want any salad. May I be excused? I have to go to choir molestation.

MOM: Okay, you run off.

DAD: I'll have a little piece.

(DAD takes a piece, carefully cutting around and avoiding the mango. MOM starts to cut a piece for SON.)

SON: I don't think I want any either, Mom.

(DAD glares at him.)

SON: Okay, just a little piece. *(He bows his head and utters to himself:)* No mango, no mango, no mango . . .

(MOM carefully cuts him a piece. Son's eyes widen in terror as she gives him the piece with the mango in it. He thinks about it for a second and starts rubbing his forehead rapidly back and forth with his hand. He continues to do this during next dialogue. MOM takes out a letter and sets it nervously on the table.)

DAD: What's that?

MOM *(nervous)*: It's a letter from the chamber of commerce.

SON *(finishes rubbing his forehead)*: Mom, can I be excused? I feel like I have a temperature.

MOM *(feels his forehead with the back of her hand)*: My, oh my, you sure do. You better go straight to bed.

(SON disappears quickly, not having to eat his mango.)

MOM *(as he goes)*: Do you want to take your salad to your room?
(SON indicates he has a stomachache too.)

DAD: What's it about?

MOM: Well, you know our lawn jockey?

DAD: Yeah.

MOM: They want us to paint its face white.

DAD: Why on earth would they want us to do that?

MOM: They feel it's offensive to some of the Negroes in the community.

DAD: That's like saying there never was such a thing as a Negro lawn jockey. It's really a celebration of the great profession of lawn jockeying.

MOM: They think it shows prejudice.

DAD: Well, that's ridiculous. Some of my best friends are Negro. Jerry at work is a Negro, and we work side by side without the slightest problem.

MOM: That's true; he is a Negro. Well, he's a Navajo.

DAD: But times have changed. I'll make a compromise with them. I'll paint the nineteen jockeys on the north side of the driveway white, but I'm leaving the nineteen on the other side of the driveway alone, and I'm not touching the six on the porch.

MOM: That sounds fair. Jim, I have something to discuss with you. Maybe you can help. Lately, I've been having feelings of . . . distance. My heart will start racing, and I feel like I'm going to die. I don't like to leave the house, because when I get to a supermarket, I always start to feel terrified . . .
(SIS, dressed for choir, enters with the evening paper.)

SIS: Evening paper's here.
(SIS exits.)

DAD: Thanks, Judy . . . uh, Sandy.
(SIS turns away. It says KATHY on the back of her choir robe.

DAD takes the paper, spreads it open, covering his face, and starts to read silently.)

MOM *(continuing)*: My mouth gets dry . . . my palms get moist, and I feel like . . . like I'm going to die *(She continues as though nothing is different.)* And when I don't feel that way, I spend most of the day in fear that the feeling is going to come over me. Sometimes I hear things. I don't think I can live like this.

DAD *(from behind paper)*: Honey, it's sounds to me like you're having symptoms of fear without knowing what it is you're afraid of. I'm not going to pretend to know how to cure something like that, but I want you to know that I will be beside you while we together figure out how to conquer this thing. I appreciate how difficult your job is around this house. You are deeply loved. I admire you as a person, as well as a wife. I'm interested in what you say and if there's anytime you need me, I will stop everything to help you.

MOM: Oh, my God, Jim.

(MOM is moved. DAD leans over to kiss her, and although he still holds the newspaper in front of his face, he kisses her through it. It's a tender smooch and he's so moved, he closes his arms around her head, still holding the newspaper. Her head is completely encircled in it. They break.)

DAD *(still holding newspaper)*: Hmmm. You still get me excited. *(He brings down paper.)* Now why don't you pour us a drink, and I'll meet you upstairs?

MOM: Oh! Oh yes . . .

(DAD exits. MOM goes to the cupboard, removes a cocktail shaker, throws in some ingredients, shakes it. She takes out two glasses, one a tiny shot glass, the other glass tankard size. She pours the drink in the tiny glass, then in the large one. She picks up the two drinks, starts to exit, then walks center.)

MOM *(to the air)*: Voices?

FEMALE VOICE *(offstage)*: Yes?

MOM: Hello.

FEMALE VOICE: Hello, Diane.

MOM: Would you visit me if things were different?

FEMALE VOICE: There would be no need.

MOM: Does heaven exist?

FEMALE VOICE: No.

MOM: Does hell exist?

FEMALE VOICE: No.

MOM: Well, that's something anyway. Do things work out in the end?

FEMALE VOICE: No.

MOM: Am I still pretty?

FEMALE VOICE *(pause while she thinks)*: Happiness will make you beautiful.

MOM: You've made me feel better.

(She starts to go, then:) Voices? . . .

FEMALE VOICE: Yes?

MOM: Is there a heartland?

FEMALE VOICE: Yes.

MOM: Could I go there?

FEMALE VOICE: You're in it.

MOM: Oh. Does the human heart exist?

FEMALE VOICE: Listen, you can hear them breaking.

MOM: What is melancholy?

FEMALE VOICE: Wouldn't you love to dance with him in the moonlight?

MOM *(starts to go, then turns back)*: Voices, when he says he loves me, what does he mean? *(Silence. Lights slowly fade.)*

SCENE 2

LEPTON

Lights up. Son's room. We hear Mom's sexual cries coming through the wall. She finishes. Immediately, DAD *comes into the room, wearing a robe.*

DAD (*holding a doorknob sign that says* PRIVATE): Private? It's not really private, is it?

SON: No.

DAD: Well, let's not have the yablons. Der fashion rests particularly well. I hop da balloon fer forest waters. Aged well-brood water babies. In der yablons.

SON: Dad, sometimes I don't know what you're talking about.

DAD: Oh yeah, you're too young to understand now, but one day, you'll have response not too fer-well keption.

SON: Jim, do you think I could get a bicycle?

DAD: Sure, you could get a bicycle. How would you pay for it?

SON: Well. I don't know. I was hoping . . .

DAD: You see, Son, a bicycle is a luxury item. You know what a luxury item is?

SON: No.

DAD: A luxury item is a thing that you have that annoys other people that you have it. Like our very green lawn. That's a luxury item. Oh, it could be less green, I suppose; but that's not what it's about. I work on that lawn, maybe more than I should and pour a little bit o' money into it, but it's a luxury item for me, out there to annoy the others. And let's be fair; they have their luxury items that annoy me. On the corner, that mailbox made out of a ship's chain. Now there's no way I wouldn't like that out in front of our house, but I went for the lawn. What I'm getting at is that you have to work for a luxury item. So if you want that bicycle, you're going to have to work for it. Now, I've got a little lot downtown that we've had for several years, and if you wanted to go down there on weekends and after school and, say, put up a building on it, I think we could get you that bicycle.

SON: Gosh.

DAD: Yes, I know, you're pretty excited. It's not easy putting up a building, Son, but these are the ancient traditions, handed down from the peoples of Gondwanaland, who lived on the plains of Golgotha. Based upon the precepts of Hammurabi. Written in cuneiform on the gates of Babylon. Deduced from the cryptograms of the Questioner of the Sphinx and gleaned from the incunabula of Ratdolt. Delivered unto me by the fleet-footed Mercury when the retrograde Mars backed into Gemini, interpreted from the lyrics of "What a Swell Party." Appeared on my living room wall in blood writ there by God himself and incised in the Holy Trowel of the Masons. Son, we don't get to talk that much; in fact, as far as I can remember, we've never talked. But I was wondering several years ago, and unfortunately never really got around to asking you until now, I was wondering, what you plan to do with your life?

SON: Well . . .

DAD: Before you answer, let me just say that I didn't know what I wanted to do with my life until I was twenty-eight. Which is late when you want to be a gymnast, which, by the way, I gave up when I found out it was considered more an art than a sport. But now, your mother and I have seventeen grand in the bank, at today's prices that's like being a millionaire. See, if you've got a dollar and you spend twenty-nine cents on a loaf of bread, you've got seventy-one cents left. But if you've got seventeen grand and you spend twenty-nine cents on a loaf of bread, you've still got seventeen grand. There's a math lesson for you.

SON: All I know is, it's going to be a great life.

DAD: Well, Son, I have no idea what you're talking about, but I want to suggest that you finish school first and go on to college and get a Ph.D. in Phrenology. But let me just say that no matter what in life you choose to do, I will be there to shame you, unless of course you pass the seventeen thousand mark. Then you will be awarded my college Sigma Delta Phuk-a-lucka pin. Good-bye, and I hope to see you around the house.
(DAD shakes the Son's hand, exits.)

SON: Okay, Dad, I mean, Jim.
(SON stays in the room, takes out a purple pendant, which he puts around his neck. He then takes out a small homemade radio with antenna, dials it. We hear glitches and gwarks, then the sound of a solar wind.)

SON: Premier . . . Premier . . . come in, Premier.
(A cheesy spaceman, PREMIER, walks out on the stage.)

PREMIER: Yes?

SON: How are things on Lepton?

PREMIER: Three hundred eighty-five degrees Fahrenheit. It rained molten steel. Now that's cold.

SON: Tell me again, okay?

PREMIER: Again?

SON: I need it now.

PREMIER: How long has it been since my first visit?

SON: Ten years.

PREMIER: Ah yes. You were four, and you were granted the Vision.

SON: Yes.

PREMIER: So much is credited to the gene pool these days. But the gene pool is nothing compared to the Vision. It's really what I enjoy doing most. Placing the Vision where it's least expected. Anyway, you need to hear it?

SON: Yes.

PREMIER: All right. Her skin will be rose on white. She will come to you, her face close to yours, her breath on your mouth. She will speak words voicelessly, which you will understand because of the movement of her lips on yours. Her hand will be on the small of your back and her fingers will be blades. Your blood will pool around you. You will receive a transfusion of a clear liquid that has been exactly measured. That liquid will be sadness. And then, whatever her name may be—Carol, Susan, Virginia—then, she will die, and you will mourn her. Her death will be final in all respects but this: she will be alive and with someone else. But time and again, you will walk in, always at the same age you are now, with your arms open, your heart as big as the moon, not anticipating the total eclipse. They call you a WASP, *but it's women who have the stingers.* However, you will have a gift. A gift so wonderful that it will take you through the days and nights until the end of your life.

SON: I'm getting a gift? What is it?

PREMIER: The desire to work.

(Fade out.)

SCENE 3

CHOIR

Lights up. Choir practice. SIS, ***wearing her choir robe, stands on a riser. A*** CHOIRMASTER ***faces upstage, conducting the rest of the invisible choir.***

SIS (*singing*): *I SAW THREE SHIPS A-SAILING IN,*
ON CHRISTMAS DAY,
ON CHRISTMAS DAY.

I SAW THREE SHIPS A-SAILING IN,
ON CHRISTMAS DAY IN THE MORNING.

AND ALL THE BELLS ON EARTH SHALL RING,
ON CHRISTMAS DAY,
ON CHRISTMAS DAY.

AND ALL THE BELLS ON EARTH SHALL RING,
ON CHRISTMAS DAY IN THE MORNING.
(Pause, she waits with the count.)

ON CHRISTMAS DAY,
ON CHRISTMAS DAY.
(Waits another count.)

ON CHRISTMAS DAY IN THE MORNING.
(Pause. SIS *waits, then starts to sing on her own. The* CHOIRMASTER *can't hear this, and he keeps on conducting "Three Ships.")*

SIS: *SHE WAS ONLY SIXTEEN . . .*
ONLY SIXTEEN,
I LOVED HER SO.

(The CHOIRMASTER *points at her.)*

SIS: *ON CHRISTMAS DAY IN THE MORNING (pause),*
BUT SHE WAS TOO YOUNG TO FALL IN LOVE,
AND I WAS TOO YOUNG TO KNOW.
SHE WAS ONLY SIXTEEN . . .

All pink and white and fluffy like a marshmallow. So many desirable qualities. She could have been on a poster in black sunglasses and blond hair. Her pretty ears admired by the choirmaster. All this at sixteen, the weight of the years not yet showing. Entering the ball in a beaded dress that weighed so much she could hardly stand up straight. But she did, this tiny girl from the Southland, her pupils made small from the flashbulbs. "ON CHRISTMAS DAY, ON CHRISTMAS DAY . . ." I love to sing; I wish I could be a castrati. Boys get all the fun.

CHOIRMASTER: Kathryn . . .

SIS: Yes?

CHOIRMASTER: You're not paying attention.

SIS: Sorry . . . "ON CHRISTMAS DAY . . ." I guess pretty pink ears don't count for much. How can I possibly pay attention? How can I possibly focus on this little tune when I am so much more fascinating? Those who pass within the area of my magnetism know what I'm talking about. My power extends not just to the length of my arms, but all around me, like a sphere when I pass, in the hallways, lockers, to those who hear my voice. I am a flame, and I bring myself to the unsuspecting moths. Unnaturally and strangely, the power ceases when I'm home. There, my influence stays within here *(she indicates her head),* all within. It's all silent in the presence of my mother and father and brother. What they don't realize is that one idea from *this* little mind changes the course of rivers. Not to mention families.

CHOIRMASTER: Kathryn!

SIS: Sorry. *(Pause.)* I know from where my salvation will come. I will give birth to the baby Jesus. The baby Jesus brought to you by Kathryn, the near virgin. I will have to buy swaddling clothes. The sweet baby Jesus, the magician. He will wave his hand, and the dishes will wash themselves; and he will wave his other hand, and the water on the dishes will bead up and rise to the heavens in a reverse dish-drying rain. *I* will put them away. And I will sweetly cradle him. People will come to him for miracles, and I will look proudly on. He will grow and become my husband, the true virgin and the near virgin. Both of us perfectly unspoiled, perfectly true. He couldn't work the miracles without me. I would run the minimart and be the inspiration, the wife of Jesus. And at the end of our lives, he would become the baby Jesus again, and I would put him in the swaddling clothes and carry him upward, entering heaven in a beaded dress that weighed so much she could hardly stand up straight. But she did, this tiny girl from the Southland, her pupils made small from the flashbulbs. "ON CHRISTMAS DAY, ON CHRISTMAS DAY. I SAW THREE SHIPS A-SAILING IN, ON CHRISTMAS DAY IN THE MORNING."

CHOIRMASTER: Kathryn, see me after class.

SIS: Finally.

(Lights down.)

SCENE 4

YE FAITHFUL

Lights up. Christmas morning around a tree. Several presents lie under it. A shiny bicycle stands next to it, with a small ribbon around the handlebars. SON enters.

SON: Yeah!

(DAD enters in his robe.)

DAD: Aren't you going to open it?

(SON unwraps the ribbon.)

SON: Great bicycle! Thanks, Jim!

DAD: Well, that was a nice, little seven-story building you put up, Son.

SON: Did you really think so?

DAD: Well, you're no Frank Lloyd Wright.

(SIS enters.)

SIS: Oh, Christmas! Goddamn us, every one.

(SIS goes over and casually starts tearing open presents. MOM enters, carrying an elaborate Christmas goose on a tray.)

MOM: Good morning!

DAD, SIS, AND SON: Not really hungry . . . I'm full, I had some cereal *(etc.).*

MOM *(cheery)*: Fine!

DAD: How would all you kids like to take a trip to Israel?

(They stare at him.)

DAD: Well, all that history, going back four thousand three hundred twenty-five years. All the big names: Moses, David, Solomon, Rebecca, Daren the magnificent, Sassafras. See the manger, the palm fronds, go on the rides, see the tablets with the Ten Commandments . . .

SON: Wow!

DAD: Not the originals, of course; those are broken. Since it's Christmas, what if we went through those commandments? Who can name them? Huh?

SON: Thou shalt not kill. Thou shalt not lie . . .

DAD: Right. Numero uno and numero duo. Don't kill, don't lie. Good advice around the home.

MOM: Don't worship false gods?

DAD: Exactly. Now who can tell me what that means?

SON: Uh . . .

MOM: Don't know.

(SIS shrugs her shoulders.)

DAD: Well, you know, false gods. Don't worship 'em. What's another?

(They all think.)

SON: How about, Thou shalt not commit adultery?

(DAD goes into a coughing fit.)

DAD: Next.

SIS: Don't change horses in the middle of the stream.

DAD: Good one, peanut. If you start out as one thing, don't end up another thing. People don't like it.

SON: Everything's comin' up roses?

DAD: Good, that's six.

MOM: Honor thy father and thy mother.

(The children cough violently.)

DAD: Good. Well, there you go. Ten commandments.

SIS: How come it's ten?

DAD: Ten is just right. Fourteen, you go, "Enough already." Eight's not enough, make things too easy. But ten, you can't beat ten. That's why he's God. We got ten fingers, ten toes, and through his wisdom, we don't have ten heads. All thought out beforehand. Well, this has been a real fun morning. Oh, by the way, unhappy childhood, happy life. Bye.

(DAD exits.

MOM, SIS, and SON wait a beat to see if he's gone. They all begin to speak in upper-class English accents.)

SON: Is he gone?

(The children gather round MOM and kneel.)

SON: Mummy, this has been the most wonderful Christmas ever.

MOM: Well, now off you go to write your thank-you notes. When you're done, you bring them down here, and we'll take each note and set it next to each present you received, and we can make sure you've mentioned each gift in the right way.

SIS: I've already written my thank-you notes. I did them last week.

MOM: How could you have written a thank-you note before you knew what the gift was?

SIS: I didn't mention the gift.

MOM: Well, we'll have to do them all over again, won't we?

SIS: Yes, Mummy.

(DAD enters. The kids break away from MOM, and they all revert to American accents.)

DAD: Where are my keys? . . .

SON: Over there, Jim.

DAD (*to* SON): Christmas or no Christmas, I want that lawn mowed today.

SON (*American accent*): I don't wanna!

MOM (*American accent, faking anger*): You do as you're told!

SON (*faking*): Oh, Mom!

DAD: Christ! Where are my keys?

SIS (*American accent*): In the drawer, Dad.

DAD (*picking them up*): How could they get there?

MOM: The butler must have put them there.

(DAD starts to exit.)

DAD: What butler?

MOM: I mean, I must have put them there. Did you remember your clubs? . . .

(But he is gone. The children kneel by MOM again and begin speaking in English accents.)

SIS: I have never understood golf.

MOM: Nor I.

SON: Nor I.

MOM: Scottish game, 'tisn't it?

SON: Oh yes, Scottish.

SIS: *Very* Scottish!

(They all chuckle.)

MOM: Oh, Roger!

(An English butler, ROGER, enters carrying a tea tray.)

ROGER: Yes'um?

MOM: Oh. Good. Tea. Has he gone?

ROGER (*looks offstage*): Just driving off now, ma'am.

MOM: We're so naughty!

SIS: You know what I'd like, a big bowl of Wheat-a-Bix!

MOM: On Christmas you can have anything you want. Roger, would you be so kind, one bowl of Wheat-a-Bix.

SON: Oh, I'll have a bowl too!

MOM: Well, me too.

ROGER: Three bowls of Wheat-a-Bix. Clotted cream?

MOM: Of course. Clotted cream, and oh, just bring a big bowl of bacon fat.

ROGER: Mango?

SON: Mango? Oh, Mummy, pretty please!

MOM: Oh, you do love your mango. We'll take it in the garden. *(Afterthought.)* By the folly.

ROGER: Yes'um.

MOM: Go along, then.

(The children and ROGER *exit.* MOM *is left alone onstage.)*

MOM *(still speaks with her English accent)*: Voices?

FEMALE VOICE *(offstage)*: Yes?

MOM *(English accent)*: Thank you for these moments.

FEMALE VOICE: Would you like to be Italian?

MOM: Oh no, I'm afraid I would burst. Unless . . .

FEMALE VOICE: Unless what?

MOM *(English accent)*: Unless, late at night, when I'm with him, you know, sort of, in bed, well, you know. Maybe just for five minutes.

FEMALE VOICE: You'd like to be Italian for five minutes?

MOM: I was thinking him.

FEMALE VOICE: I see.

MOM: Well, I'll be in the garden by the folly.

(MOM starts to go.)

FEMALE VOICE: One moment. I have an answer to your question.

MOM *(English accent)*: Which one?

FEMALE VOICE: When he says he loves me, what does he mean?

MOM *(normal voice)*: Please.

FEMALE VOICE: He means, if only, if only. If only he could call to you from across a river bank.

MOM: Like Running Bear.

FEMALE VOICE: Yes, as well as Little White Dove. He would dive into the river, swim to you, and drown. He knows this. He cannot come close. He would drown. He knows this. The water has no value like it does to you; it is only trouble. He does not know the meaning of the water like you do. Standing on the bank, calling to his Little White Dove, with her so small in his vision, he loves her fully. Swimming toward her, his words skipping across to her like flat rocks, he drowns, afraid of what she wants, not knowing what he should be, realizing his love was in the words that he shouted while on the bank and not in the small whispers he carries to hand to her.

MOM: Is it ever possible for them not to drown?

FEMALE VOICE: Oh yes.

MOM: What makes the difference?

FEMALE VOICE: When the attraction is chemical.

MOM: Chemical?

FEMALE VOICE: Oh yes. The taste of the skin to the tongue. The touch of the hand to the neck. The shape of the face on the retina. Oh, this is too hard long distance; let me come down to Earth.

(The FEMALE VOICE *appears from offstage, wearing a conservative Chanel suit and holding a handbag.)*

FEMALE VOICE: Can the chemistry of the breath across the lips inhibit the chemistry of bitterness?

(It doesn't strike MOM *as unusual that the* FEMALE VOICE *walks into her living room, looks around.)*

MOM: I see. Would you like something?

FEMALE VOICE (*now onstage*): Oh no. I'm just here for a minute . . .

MOM: Tea?

FEMALE VOICE: Well, maybe just a little.

MOM: Cake?

FEMALE VOICE: No, thanks. I'm trying to lose a few pounds. Maybe a small piece. Here, let me help.

(The FEMALE VOICE *helps set the table.)*

MOM: You were talking about the chemistry of the breath across the lips inhibiting the chemistry of bitterness.

FEMALE VOICE: Oh yeah, what I'm trying to say is: sex is the kicker. It's there to cloud our judgment. Otherwise *nobody* would pair off. Once I slept with a guy just to get him to quit trying to sleep with me.

MOM: I could never do that.

FEMALE VOICE: You're forty. I'm four thousand three hundred twenty-five.

MOM: Any kids?

FEMALE VOICE: I have a girl eleven hundred and a boy eight hundred thirty-five. The eight-hundred-thirty-five year old is a terror.

MOM: So how did you get to be omniscient?

FEMALE VOICE: I went to class.

MOM: They have a class? What do you study?

FEMALE VOICE: Every teeny-weeny little thing. We memorize it. Every little rock, every blade of grass. Everything about people, about men, about cats, every type of gravy, every possibility, every potentiality, ducks. It's one class where *et cetera* really means "et cetera."

MOM: That must be hard.

FEMALE VOICE: It is one son of a bitch. You know what one of the questions on the final was?

MOM: What?

FEMALE VOICE: Name everything.

MOM: Wow.

FEMALE VOICE: When I read that question, my mind went blank. Which is a terrible thing when you're asked to name everything.

MOM: What happened?

FEMALE VOICE: Oh, you know, you get through it; I got an eighty-four. Eighty and above is omniscient. Well, I better be going . . . prom night pimple in Cleveland . . .

MOM (*stops her, concerned*): So you know everything.

FEMALE VOICE: Somewhat.

MOM: So . . . what would it be like if I left him?

FEMALE VOICE: You won't believe this, but that was one of the questions on the final. Let's see . . . you will live in a small cottage. It will be surrounded by a white fence. In the backyard will be many colored flowers. Inside will be small lace doilies like your mother's. You will stand outside on the green lawn, your face up toward the sun; your hands will be outstretched, palms open; and you will speak these words: "What have I done, what have I done, what have I done."

(*Slow blackout.*)

SCENE 5

THE LOGIC OF THE LIE

The dinner table again, the family of four sitting around. DAD is in the middle of a golf story; the family feigns enjoyment.

DAD: Phil tees off, lands midway down the fairway but off to the right. With the three wood, I'm about ten yards shy of him but straight down the middle. I can see the flag damn straight up with a trap off to the right. Phil's gotta fly over the trap. (*MOM and family emit sounds of delighted interest.*) What happens? Phil eight irons it and flies the trap; he's on the green. I full swing my nine and land right in the trap!

SON (*laughs*): Oh man!

SIS: Wow.

MOM (*laughing*): Man, you don't need a nine iron; you need a hoe!

DAD: So now . . . Phil on the back of the green putts and rolls right past the hole, and it keeps going to the edge of the fringe.

SIS (*laughing*): Did he use a eight iron for that too?

(*The whole family overlaughs.*)

DAD: I pop it out of the trap and . . . (*starts to laugh*) . . . the damn thing . . . (*more laughs*) . . . rolls right up about ten inches from the hole!

(*More laughter from the others.*)

DAD: Phil three putts, and I drop it in without hardly looking.

(Really big response from family.)

MOM: Oh . . . ha ha ha.

(MOM has to drink water and fan herself. The phone rings. MOM answers it.)

SIS: Oh, my God, it's Jerermy!

MOM: Hello? Just a minute. *(To SIS:)* It's Jeremy.

SIS: Tell him I'm not in.

MOM: She's not in right now. *(She hangs up.)* I thought you wanted to talk to him.

SIS *(practically sinister)*: He'll call back.

(The table becomes silent as DAD is lost in thought. He hears the sound of the solar wind. Suddenly he stands up, but the rest of the family can't see him.)

DAD: Voice? *(No answer.)* Voice? *(No answer.)* Voices? Voice? Typical, nothing. Left here on my own, with only the images of Washington, Jefferson, and Lincoln. Hello? Hello? I'm living the lie, I know it. Nothing but the rules of the road, the ethics of the lumberjack, the silence of the forest broken only by the sound of the ax getting the job done, the ax never complaining. Truth handed down through the pages of *Redbook* and the *Saturday Evening Post*. Becoming leader and hero, onward and stronger to a better life. I know my feelings cannot tolerate illumination under the hard light, but when seen by the flickering light of a campfire surrounded by the covered wagons heading west, I am a god that walks on Earth. Must be strong, must be strong, and in my silence, I am never wrong. The greater the silence, the greater the strength. And therein is the logic of the lie.

MOM: Butter?

(MOM passes the butter to SON.)

DAD *(looks back at MOM)*: Her. Once, with one hand I held her wrists behind her back and kissed her. Once, I entered her like Caesar into Rome. Once, I drank her blood. I would repeat her name in my head; it swam across my vision to exhaustion. I saw it flying toward me and flapping with wings. I exploded it with the letters flying off in all directions. I inverted it; I anagrammed it. Every word she spoke destroyed or created me. She was the tornado, and I was the barn. I remember her in a yellow chair, leaning forward, her underwear ankled, delivering to me the angel's kiss. Now I stand at the foot of her bed and watch her sleep, and silently ask the question "Who are you?" but the question only echoes back upon myself. Oh, I know what she goes through. She aches with desire. She reaches out for nothing, and nothing comes back. She is bound by walls of feeling. They surround me too, but I must reach through the walls and *provide*. There is no providing on a lingering summer's walk; there is no providing in a caress. I have been to the place she wants me to go. *(Bitterly.)* I have seen how the king of feelings, the great god Romance seats us in his giant hand and thrusts us upward and slowly turns us under the sky. But it is given to us only for minutes, and we spend the rest of our lives paying for those few moments. Love moves through three stages: attraction, desire, need. The third stage is the place I go.

SON: Jim, can I be excused?

DAD: Finish your meal. *(Back to his soliloquy.)* If I can't be excused, why should he? The denial of my affection will make him strong like me. I would love to feel the emotions I have heard so much about, but I may as well try to reassemble a dandelion. *(He snaps out of it and speaks to the family, back to his vigorous delivery.)* Ninth hole, dog-leg left, can't see the pin. *(The family reacts with oohs and ahs. He turns, walks back to the table.)* I decided to go over the trees, but I hit a bad shot, and it goes straight down the middle of the fairway. I don't say a word! Phil *(starts chuckling)* . . . just slow turns and stares at me with this look! . . .

(The others laugh. The sound of munching resumes as they fall silent.)

(Slow fade out.)

A CLOSER LOOK: GWENDOLYN BROOKS

Gwendolyn Brooks was born in Topeka, Kansas, in 1917 and raised in Chicago. The author of more than twenty books of poetry, she won the Pulitzer Prize in 1949 for *Annie Allen*. In 1968, she was named Poet Laureate for the state of Illinois, and from 1985 to 1986 she was Consultant in Poetry to the Library of Congress. She also received an American Academy of Arts and Letters award, the Frost Medal, a National Endowment for the Arts award, the Shelley Memorial Award, and fellowships from the Academy of American Poets and the Guggenheim Foundation. She lived in Chicago until her death on December 3, 2000.

INTERVIEW WITH THE AUTHOR

The following interview was published in the *Humanities* journal in 1994. *Humanities* is the journal of the National Endowment for the Humanities, an independent grant-making agency of the United States government dedicated to supporting research, education, preservation, and public programs in the humanities.

A Conversation with Gwendolyn Brooks

When NEH Chairman Sheldon Hackney spoke with Gwendolyn Brooks, the 1994 Jefferson Lecturer in the Humanities, the conversation turned to "the delicious agony" of writing poetry. Brooks is the author of nineteen volumes of poetry, among them ANNIE ALLEN, which won the 1950 Pulitzer Prize in Poetry.

SHELDON HACKNEY: You are quoted as having said that being both an American and a black person, you felt you had the riches of two cultures as a writer, that that was a great advantage. This is really taking W. E. B. Du Bois's comment about the two-ness of American blacks, and turning it to advantage in some way. Do you feel that it has been an advantage to be black in America as a writer?

GWENDOLYN BROOKS: I'm wondering where I said that, but I believe I can still endorse it. It's not perhaps something that I would have elected if I had a choice.

Don't you think that you can understand my saying that it would have been right, perhaps, with a capital R, to have been born in Africa and stayed in Africa. I feel right about saying that to you. I'd like to quote from a couple of paragraphs that I have here that I've titled "On Being An American."

HACKNEY: Good.

BROOKS: "In America you feel a little or a lot disoriented so far as 'being an American' goes. In the last few decades many Americans have learned an easy contempt for America; and true, a country that for so long endorsed slavery, endorsed lynching, endorsed official segregation, endorsed the Vietnam 'action,' and could be capable of judging political conspiracy acceptable, is not to be blue ribboned across the board. But traveling to other countries helps you italicize American positives. Once you get out of the country, whatever your woes, your wobblinesses, your confusion, your fury, you find that you are operationally an American. I myself am forced to realize that I am claimed by no other country. My kind is claimed by this country, albeit reluctantly. Furthermore, traveling teaches you that cruelty and supersedence are everywhere. Although it is not true that calling myself an American will instantly protect me from harm or detention anywhere in the world—when I was a little girl I thought this was true—still, that concept of a large arm to lean on is implicit. Implicit: do not make plans to do any leaning. Remember for example, Beirut, remember Bosnia. It is not so easy for an American to abstain from 'being an American.' However roots-proud you as a Black may be, and my roots are in the sweet earth of Africa; when asked 'what are you' in Dublin, Devon, London, Israel, Iran, Ghana, in Moscow or Madrid, it is expedient and 'natural' to reply, twingelessly, 'American.' It is the only answer that will interest the questioner. The questioner is impatient. The questioner is ready for the Definer behind you. The questioner has small time, and no time for your efforts at self-clarification."

HACKNEY: I have had not the same experience, but I have had a similar experience of never having felt more American than when abroad.

BROOKS: Yes, yes. It's interesting.

HACKNEY: I would guess from what you say that you would endorse the positive aspects of America, that is the ideal of America, but also caution Americans not to neglect their history. The history is there. It is what has happened. . . .

BROOKS: Positive and negative.

HACKNEY: Positive and negative, yes. Is that an authentic stance for a writer to take?

BROOKS: Well, I can't speak for other writers, I just said what I feel. Other writers are saying all kinds of things these days.

HACKNEY: You're exactly right. Let me go back into some of your biography. You won the Pulitzer Prize at the age of thirty-two in 1950 for Annie Allen. A very young age, a remarkable event; the first black poet to win the Pulitzer Prize. Did that change your life? Or your poetry?

BROOKS: It made it possible for me to teach. I don't have a bachelor's degree. I have about seventy honorary degrees, but I always "blush" because I haven't Toiled In The Night for my honorary degrees. Having a Pulitzer made it possible for me to teach on college campuses. I've enjoyed being able to teach. I'm teaching now at Chicago State University.

HACKNEY: And there is a Gwendolyn Brooks Center there, is there not?

BROOKS: Oh yes, and I hope you'll get to see it sometime. It's really nice. It's inspiring. It has an exciting future. But to get back to your question, naturally, when you get a Pulitzer—and I found out from a member of the family that you are supposed to pronounce it PULL-itzer (after all these decades of saying PEW-litzer)—well, I was going to say, your name becomes, in my case, Gwendolyn PULL-itzer Brooks.

(Laughter.)

And there are nice things about that. But in the late sixties the Black New Risers did not consider such distinctions as glories to be proud of.

HACKNEY: It did not do you a lot of good then.

BROOKS: Among young blacks, those rambunctious young blacks at that time, there was often the feeling that there must be something wrong with you, if you had acquired one of these gifts from the establishment. But that was rather quickly conquered. Because they decided—early on—to believe in me.

HACKNEY: You mentioned your lack of an earned bachelor's degree. What was your education in literature like?

BROOKS: I was given an associate literature degree from a junior college. I know you're horrified to hear that.

HACKNEY: No, no, I think that's wonderful.

BROOKS: In 1936 it was called Woodrow Wilson Junior College. Now it is Kennedy-King.

HACKNEY: But you had parents who were both interested in literature, is that right?

BROOKS: Yes, we had lots of books in the house, and my mother said that at the age of seven, I brought her a page of rhymes, which she praised heartily. Both my parents were supportive of my efforts as a writer, and of my brother's efforts as a painter.

HACKNEY: And that helped

BROOKS: Indeed it did. I was very fortunate.

HACKNEY: One of the things that all critics remark on in your poetry is its remarkable command of all of the traditional literary forms, poetic forms. In fact, you write quite complex verse forms, and use incredible meters and rhyme schemes. Where did that all come from? Did you work at that quite consciously when you were young?

BROOKS: We had the Harvard Classics, for instance, at our home. You'll be interested in this, I think. My father had given the Harvard Classics to my mother, complete with a bookcase which I have now in my bedroom, for a wedding present. And there's lots of poetry in that set, as you know.

HACKNEY: Indeed.

BROOKS: I read English poetry, American poetry, lots of essays. One of my favorites was Emerson. I got a lot of value out of essays like "Compensation" and "Self-Reliance."

HACKNEY: Those good nineteenth century virtues that are all there. Would you recommend that sort of steeping in the literary tradition for a current course?

BROOKS: I tell young writers today, of whom I see such a lot, that they should read everything. And I like to add to my adventures with the Harvard Classics, a little book called Caroling Dusk. I found that in a library, the Forrestville Public Library a block and a half away from my home. And there I learned about the work of Langston Hughes and Sterling Brown.

HACKNEY: And Dunbar.

BROOKS: And the two Cotters, Joseph Cotter Senior and Junior. Countee Cullen. Claude McKay.

HACKNEY: Yes.

BROOKS: And I was fascinated to find out that not only Paul Dunbar, whose work my father recited to my brother and myself, but all these other Black people were writing poetry, and publishing it.

HACKNEY: Was that important to you when you were young?

BROOKS: Absolutely. That was about the age of fifteen that I discovered these folks. In book form, I mean!

HACKNEY: Were you already literary?

BROOKS: Well, as I said, my mother told me that I started writing at the age of seven. I do know that my first four poems to be printed were printed in the *Hyde Parker.* I sent them to the editor. He didn't know I was eleven, and just went ahead and published these four poems.

HACKNEY: That's wonderful.

BROOKS: Very encouraging!

HACKNEY: One of the poems published in your book *Blacks,* "The Chicago Picasso," begins with a line that I would love you to explain—indeed, maybe this is the meaning of the whole poem, that is: "Does man love Art? Man visits Art, but squirms." Is that about the function of art in life, and what is the function of art?

BROOKS: Well, you know the occasion was the unveiling of the Chicago Picasso here. Does man love art? Man visits art. (I wish we could find a word that meant man and woman. If you ever come up with one, let me know.) Does man love art? Well you see, Chicago people had been saying such horrible things about this piece of art, and somebody said that it had always been known that Picasso hated Chicago—

HACKNEY: That's right.

BROOKS: —and that he had chosen this way of expressing his contempt. Other people were saying that they would have preferred a statue of Ernie Banks to this thing. So, in sort of mock exasperation, I'm saying,

Does man love Art? Man visits Art, but squirms. Art hurts. Art urges voyages—

I love that line because I think it is true.

HACKNEY: It is absolutely right.

BROOKS: —and it is easier to stay at home, the nice beer ready. In commonrooms we belch, or sniff, or scratch. Are raw.

But we must cook ourselves and style ourselves. . . .

HACKNEY: I like that line also.

BROOKS: Et cetera, et cetera. Does that help?

HACKNEY: It does indeed, but now bring it back to the rest of your poetry. As you're writing, are you consciously trying to make people squirm on occasion?

BROOKS: Oh no, I never sit down and say "I am going to make people squirm." First of all, I'm excited about something before I begin to write. And then I just put down on the paper whatever comes—that's the beginning. But I believe in a lot of revision.

HACKNEY: Then you work and work on it.

BROOKS: Yes, yes. Everything I've written, no matter how simple it may sound, has been agonized over; and I like to say that writing poetry is delicious agony—delicious agony.

HACKNEY: It is. But what about the voyage, the line about art sending people on voyages.

BROOKS: Don't you consider it that yourself?

HACKNEY: Absolutely.

BROOKS: The enjoyment of art! The practice of art! Both are voyages.

HACKNEY: Indeed, it opens up new vistas and makes people look at things in a slightly different way, if it's successful. Are you, as you write, consciously aware of that effect on the reader?

BROOKS: You know, I don't do all of this very conscious speculating as I'm writing. I'm just anxious to get the verse arrangement down, and then to ask myself over and over, is this really what I want to say. I don't want to imitate anyone else; I have a lot of admirations, but I don't want to sound like any of them.

HACKNEY: Let me pose a choice between two different branches. One, in which you are writing as a poet speaking to an audience and quite aware of your obligation, your social obligation if you will, as a poet. On the other hand, the other branch, is that you are writing because of some inner vision, some compulsion to express your own ideas. It really comes from within, and has very little to do with what effects those words have on whoever happens to read it. Is that a fair sort of division, or do those things actually go together?

BROOKS: Well, I don't give myself any obligations when I'm writing.

HACKNEY: That's interesting.

BROOKS: In this little book, Children Coming Home, I have a poem called "Uncle Seagram," featuring a little five-year-old boy named Merle. And I didn't say when I came to write this poem, well everybody is talking about child abuse, therefore I shall write a poem about child abuse. What I wanted to do was to present a little boy, in this case a little boy from the inner city—which is a phrase I hate—but any child might be saying this.

HACKNEY: Yes.

BROOKS: But that, too, is not something that I told myself. I'm going to read this very quickly.

> My uncle likes me too much.
>
> I am five and a half years old, and in kindergarten. In kindergarten everything is clean.
>
> My uncle is six feet tall with seven bumps on his chin. My uncle is six feet tall, and he stumbles. He stumbles because of his Wonderful Medicine packed in his pocket all times.
>
> Family is ma and pa and my uncle, three brothers, three sisters, and me.
>
> Every night at my house we play checkers and dominoes. My uncle sits close. There aren't any shoes or socks on his feet. Under the table a big toe

tickles my ankle. Under the oilcloth his thin knee beats into mine. And mashes. And mashes.

When we look at TV my uncle picks me to sit on his lap. As I sit, he gets hard in the middle. I squirm, but he keeps me, and kisses my ear.

I am not even a girl.

Once, when I went to the bathroom, my uncle noticed, came in, shut the door, put his long white tongue in my ear, and whispered "We're Best Friends, and Family, and we know how to keep Secrets."

My uncle likes me too much. I am worried.

I do not like my uncle anymore.

Well, when writing that I just tried to feel how a little boy of five might feel in such a situation. Although we come in different sizes, we are capable of feeling for each other, and as each other.

HACKNEY: That's right. When I read that I squirmed.

BROOKS: Well, good! I read it in lots of high schools and colleges, and even elementary schools. And almost always. some child will say to me, "That's going on in my family," or "That has happened in my family." So of course I refer them to their teachers for possible assistance.

HACKNEY: That's right. But that just comes out of your success when you sit down to write, rather than the newspaper and some sense of what social issue you should be writing about.

BROOKS: Or a too present feeling of social obligation. I like that phrase.

HACKNEY: You mentioned earlier the late 1960s and the rambunctious youth in the movement. It was a particular time in our history, and some people writing biographical sketches of you have pointed to the second Fisk writers conference in 1967 as a turning point for you. Is that a fair assessment?

BROOKS: Have I ever had an interview in which that question was not asked?

It certainly was a very special time in my life, when I suppose you've read that I went to Fisk University and got my first taste of what was happening among the young Black people of that time. They were unwilling to be integrated, they were interested in loving themselves and having some kind of accented family feeling. It was a very exciting time. I know that it's the custom now to laugh at the late sixties, but there were good positives there, and I think most of us are better for those that were.

HACKNEY: I think you're right. It had a bright side and a dark side. And the bright side undoubtedly outweighed the dark side. But the dark side was there.

BROOKS: Well, certainly I'm going to thank you for saying "dark" side.

(Laughter).

HACKNEY: Okay.

BROOKS: But you keep reading "the black side." Have you ever stopped to look in the dictionary for the definition of Black and Blackness.

HACKNEY: I have done that actually, yes.

BROOKS: Terrible. Anyway, I got involved with young Black people. I started a workshop—a writing workshop—for some youngsters that I met through Oscar Brown, Jr. Ever heard of him?

HACKNEY: Yes.

BROOKS: He had created a very wonderful show out of the talents of these young Blacks who called themselves the Blackstone Rangers. This show was very well received here in Chicago until the authorities decided it was not a good thing that it was so popular, and shut it down. But there were some dancers and singers who wrote also, and I started a workshop for them. That is how I got whatever reputation I still have as a red-hot revolutionary. I know that sounds ridiculous to you, but. . . .

HACKNEY: No, I think there is, in fact, a very strong sense of social commitment running all the way through your poetry, or sense of injustice that is there. The reason I ask the question is this notion that your poetry before 1967 is descriptive of the black experience but not alert to the injustice, whereas afterwards it is committed, more activist. . . .

BROOKS: But you know, that is absolutely not true.

HACKNEY: Thank you.

BROOKS: Many of the poems that I'm reading on stages now come from my very first book, and are considered "social." I dread saying political.

HACKNEY: But it is there.

BROOKS: Yes, I think so. I've always had a—what do you want to call it?—social feeling, I've always felt for people.

HACKNEY: That is very much in your poetry, and I suppose that is one of the reasons that people think that one of the continuing themes in your poetry is humanity, or caring.

BROOKS: Good, good.

HACKNEY: Which you would like, would you not?

BROOKS: Yes, I do.

HACKNEY: The other thing one hears is that it is also heroic. I'm a historian so I'm not quite sure in what ways literary scholars use the word "heroic," but I think what is meant is not simply that you write about heroes but that you are after very large themes, on a grand scale, especially in your work most recently. Is that a fair statement?

BROOKS: Well, most of the people who use that word when they're talking about me—forgive me for seeming to put this little halo around my head—are speaking of me as heroic.

HACKNEY: Yes.

BROOKS: I'm not going to claim heroism.

HACKNEY: But there is this poem, Winnie. . . .

BROOKS: Yes, it's one I really like.

HACKNEY: That is heroic in its theme, is it not?

BROOKS: Yes, yes. I don't know what you think of Winnie Mandela, but I have always considered her very strong and properly called heroic. She goes up and down in the public favor. Right now she's coming back up again. I claim "heroism" for her.

HACKNEY: Would your poem be different now if you wrote it knowing what you know now?

BROOKS: I've never met her, but I feel that I came so close to nailing her down in that little book, that I feel I don't want to meet her. I want to believe that she is everything that I've put in that long poem.

HACKNEY: Yes, yes.

BROOKS: You mentioned humanitarianism. I do have this little piece called "Humanitarianism." It begins:

> *"Humanitarianism: of course we should love all the people in the world. Of course we should be humanitarian. What I have respected, in all my investigative life, is my vision of this world as a garden of varying flowers. Personally, I would not prefer a world of red roses only. Of white lilies only. Of yellow dandelions, only. Of purple violets, of black orchids, only. Of course I wish my people had not been ripped from Africa, hauled over here in layers of chained slime, but even if I lived in a country of solid Black, I guarantee that it would give me pleasure to understand that, in the world there existed other colors, other varieties, enjoying the fresh air I enjoy, and understanding that there was empathy, that there was the possibility of ultimate commerce."*

HACKNEY: That's wonderful. So you relish the diversity that one finds in the world, and even in the United States.

BROOKS: Yes.

HACKNEY: Are you optimistic about the future?

BROOKS: Yes, I am an optimistic person. I am optimistic. There are so many excellences. And so much real love in the world. I have observed this over and over again, and even in these ticklish times, I am observing it. So I am optimistic, but my eyes are not blind to present horrors and I say frankly to you, that it seems to me that this is one of the worst of times for Black and White relations.

HACKNEY: In America?

BROOKS: Well, anywhere. Listen to what Vladimir Zhirinovsky is saying.

HACKNEY: That's frightening.

BROOKS: Yes, it is frightening. I don't think he's being taken seriously enough.

HACKNEY: Probably not. And there are people in the United States who echo him. Despite that, do you think we will be able to work through that to identifying some common ground for Americans?

BROOKS: Yes, I think so. But I can't give you a date on it.

HACKNEY: That's true. Let me press you a little bit more on the variety of flowers that you enjoy in the human garden. If they are to thrive together in this garden, do they need not only to be different and therefore lively, but also to have something that they share, some commitment to each other? Or some common values?

BROOKS: I think that they should, that all of us should get to know each other better.

POEMS

The Sundays of Satin-Legs Smith

INAMORATAS, with an approbation
Bestowed his title. Blessed his inclination.

He wakes, unwinds, elaborately: a cat
Tawny, reluctant, royal. He is fat
And fine this morning. Definite. Reimbursed.

He waits a moment, he designs his reign,
That no performance may be plain or vain.
Then rises in a clear delirium.

He sheds, with his pajamas, shabby days.
And his desertedness, his intricate fear, the
Postponed resentments and the prim precautions.

Now, at his bath, would you deny him lavender
Or take away the power of his pine?
What smelly substitute, heady as wine,
Would you provide? life must be aromatic.
There must be scent, somehow there must be some.
Would you have flowers in his life? suggest
Asters? a Really Good geranium?
A white carnation? would you prescribe a Show
With the cold lilies, formal chrysanthemum
Magnificence, poinsettias, and emphatic
Red of prize roses? might his happiest
Alternative (you muse) be, after all,

A bit of gentle garden in the best
Of taste and straight tradition? Maybe so.
But you forget, or did you ever know,
His heritage of cabbage and pigtails,
Old intimacy with alleys, garbage pails,
Down in the deep (but always beautiful) South
Where roses blush their blithest (it is said)
And sweet magnolias put Chanel to shame.

No! He has not a flower to his name.
Except a feather one, for his lapel.
Apart from that, if he should think of flowers
It is in terms of dandelions or death.
Ah, there is little hope. You might as well—
Unless you care to set the world a-boil
And do a lot of equalizing things,
Remove a little ermine, say, from kings,
Shake hands with paupers and appoint them men,
For instance—certainly you might as well
Leave him his lotion, lavender and oil.

Let us proceed. Let us inspect, together
With his meticulous and serious love,
The innards of this closet. Which is a vault
Whose glory is not diamonds, not pearls,
Not silver plate with just enough dull shine.
But wonder-suits in yellow and in wine,
Sarcastic green and zebra-striped cobalt.
All drapes. With shoulder padding that is wide
And cocky and determined as his pride;
Ballooning pants that taper off to ends

Scheduled to choke precisely.
　　　　　　　　　　　Here are hats
Like bright umbrellas; and hysterical ties
Like narrow banners for some gathering war.

People are so in need, in need of help.
People want so much that they do not know.

Below the tinkling trade of little coins
The gold impulse not possible to show
Or spend. Promise piled over and betrayed.

These kneaded limbs receive the kiss of silk.
Then they receive the brave and beautiful
Embrace of some of that equivocal wool.
He looks into his mirror, loves himself—
The neat curve here; the angularity
That is appropriate at just its place;
The technique of a variegated grace.

Here is all his sculpture and his art
And all his architectural design.

Perhaps you would prefer to this a fine
Value of marble, complicated stone.
Would have him think with horror of baroque,
Rococo. You forget and you forget.

He dances down the hotel steps that keep
Remnants of last night's high life and distress.
As spat-out purchased kisses and spilled beer.
He swallows sunshine with a secret yelp.
Passes to coffee and a roll or two.
Has breakfasted.

           Out. Sounds about him smear,
Become a unit. He hears and does not hear
The alarm clock meddling in somebody's sleep;
Children's governed Sunday happiness;
The dry tone of a plane; a woman's oath;
Consumption's spiritless expectoration;
An indignant robin's resolute donation
Pinching a track through apathy and din;
Restaurant vendors weeping; and the L
That comes on like a slightly horrible thought.

Pictures, too, as usual, are blurred.
He sees and does not see the broken windows
Hiding their shame with newsprint; little girl
With ribbons decking wornness, little boy
Wearing the trousers with the decentest patch,
To honor Sunday; women on their way
From "service," temperate holiness arranged
Ably on asking faces; men estranged
From music and from wonder and from joy
But far familiar with the guiding awe
Of foodlessness.

        He loiters.

             Restaurant vendors
Weep, or out of them rolls a restless glee.
The Lonesome Blues, the Long-lost Blues, I Want A
Big Fat Mama. Down these sore avenues
Comes no Saint-Saëns, no piquant elusive Grieg,
And not Tschaikovsky's wayward eloquence
And not the shapely tender drift of Brahms.
But could he love them? Since a man must bring

To music what his mother spanked him for
When he was two: bits of forgotten hate,
Devotion: whether or not his mattress hurts:
The little dream his father humored: the thing
His sister did for money: what he ate
For breakfast—and for dinner twenty years
Ago last autumn: all his skipped desserts.

The pasts of his ancestors lean against
Him. Crowd him. Fog out his identity.
Hundreds of hungers mingle with his own,
Hundreds of voices advise so dexterously
He quite considers his reactions his,
Judges he walks most powerfully alone,
That everything is—simply what it is.

But movie-time approaches, time to boo
The hero's kiss, and boo the heroine
Whose ivory and yellow it is sin
For his eye to eat of. The Mickey Mouse,
However, is for everyone in the house.

Squires his lady to dinner at Joe's Eats.
His lady alters as to leg and eye,
Thickness and height, such minor points as these,
From Sunday to Sunday. But no matter what
Her name or body positively she's
In Queen Lace stockings with ambitious heels
That strain to kiss the calves, and vivid shoes

Frontless and backless, Chinese fingernails,
Earrings, three layers of lipstick, intense hat
Dripping with the most voluble of veils.
Her affable extremes are like sweet bombs
About him, whom no middle grace or good
Could gratify. He had no education
In quiet arts of compromise. He would
Not understand your counsels on control, nor
Thank you for your late trouble.

                                    At Joe's Eats
You get your fish or chicken on meat platters.
With coleslaw, macaroni, candied sweets,
Coffee and apple pie. You go out full.
(The end is—isn't it?—all that really matters.)

And even and intrepid come
The tender boots of night to home.

Her body is like new brown bread
Under the Woolworth mignonette.
Her body is a honey bowl
Whose waiting honey is deep and hot.
Her body is like summer earth,
Receptive, soft, and absolute . . .

The Lovers of the Poor

arrive. The Ladies from the Ladies' Betterment
League
Arrive in the afternoon, the late light slanting
In diluted gold bars across the boulevard brag
Of proud, seamed faces with mercy and murder hinting
Here, there, interrupting, all deep and debonair,
The pink paint on the innocence of fear;
Walk in a gingerly manner up the hall.
Cutting with knives served by their softest care,
Served by their love, so barbarously fair.
Whose mothers taught: You'd better not be cruel!
You had better not throw stones upon the wrens!
Herein they kiss and coddle and assault
Anew and dearly in the innocence
With which they baffle nature. Who are full,
Sleek, tender-clad, fit, fiftyish, a-glow, all
Sweetly abortive, hinting at fat fruit,
Judge it high time that fiftyish fingers felt
Beneath the lovelier planes of enterprise.
To resurrect. To moisten with milky chill.
To be a random hitching post or plush.
    To be, for wet eyes, random and handy hem.
Their guild is giving money to the poor.
The worthy poor. The very very worthy
And beautiful poor. Perhaps just not too swarthy?
Perhaps just not too dirty nor too dim
Nor—passionate. In truth, what they could wish
Is—something less than derelict or dull.
Not staunch enough to stab, though, gaze for gaze!
God shield them sharply from the beggar-bold!

The noxious needy ones whose battle's bald
Nonetheless for being voiceless, hits one down.
    But it's all so bad! and entirely too much for them.
The stench; the urine, cabbage, and dead beans,
Dead porridges of assorted dusty grains,
The old smoke, heavy diapers, and, they're told,
Something called chitterlings. The darkness. Drawn
Darkness, or dirty light. The soil that stirs.
The soil that looks the soil of centuries.
And for that matter the general oldness. Old
Wood. Old marble. Old tile. Old old old.
Note homekind Oldness! Not Lake Forest, Glencoe.
Nothing is sturdy, nothing is majestic,
There is no quiet drama, no rubbed glaze, no
Unkillable infirmity of such
A tasteful turn as lately they have left,
Glencoe, Lake Forest, and to which their cars
Must presently restore them. When they're done
With dullards and distortions of this fistic
Patience of the poor and put-upon.
    They've never seen such a make-do-ness as
Newspaper rugs before! In this, this "flat,"
Their hostess is gathering up the oozed, the rich
Rugs of the morning (tattered! the bespattered . . .),
Readies to spread clean rugs for afternoon.
Here is a scene for you. The Ladies look,
In horror, behind a substantial citizeness
Whose trains clank out across her swollen heart.
Who, arms akimbo, almost fills a door.
All tumbling children, quilts dragged to the floor
And tortured thereover, potato peelings, soft-
Eyed kitten, hunched-up, haggard, to-be-hurt.
    Their League is allotting largesse to the Lost.
But to put their clean, their pretty money, to put
Their money collected from delicate rose-fingers
Tipped with their hundred flawless rose-nails seems . . .
    They own Spode, Lowestoft, candelabra,
Mantels, and hostess gowns, and sunburst clocks,
Turtle soup, Chippendale, red satin "hangings,"
Aubussons and Hattie Carnegie. They Winter
In Palm Beach; cross the Water in June; attend,
When suitable, the nice Art Institute;
Buy the right books in the best bindings; saunter
On Michigan, Easter mornings, in sun or wind.
Oh Squalor! This sick four-story hulk, this fibre

With fissures everywhere! Why, what are bringings
Of loathe-love largesse? What shall peril hungers
So old old, what shall flatter the desolate?
Tin can, blocked fire escape and chitterling
And swaggering seeking youth and the puzzled wreckage
Of the middle passage, and urine and stale shames
And, again, the porridges of the underslung
And children children children. Heavens! That
Was a rat, surely, off there, in the shadows? Long
And long-tailed? Gray? The Ladies from the Ladies'
Betterment League agree it will be better
To achieve the outer air that rights and steadies,
To hie to a house that does not holler, to ring
Bells elsetime, better presently to cater
To no more Possibilities, to get
Away. Perhaps the money can be posted.
Perhaps they two may choose another Slum!
Some serious sooty half-unhappy home!—
Where loathe-lover likelier may be invested.

      Keeping their scented bodies in the center
Of the hall as they walk down the hysterical hall,
They allow their lovely skirts to graze no wall,
Are off at what they manage of a canter,
And, resuming all the clues of what they were,
Try to avoid inhaling the laden air.

A Song in the Front Yard

I've stayed in the front yard all my life.
I want a peek at the back
Where it's rough and untended and hungry weed grows.
A girl gets sick of a rose.
I want to go in the back yard now
And maybe down the alley,
To where the charity children play.
I want a good time today.

They do some wonderful things.
The have some wonderful fun.
My mother sneers, but I say it's fine
How they don't have to go in at quarter to nine.
My mother, she tells me that Johnnie Mae
Will grow up to be a bad woman.
That George'll be taken to Jail soon or late

(On account of last winter he sold our back gate).

But I say it's fine Honest, I do
And I'd like to be a bad woman, too,
And wear the brave stocking of night-black lace
And strut down the streets with paint on my face.

A CRITICAL ARTICLE

Written by Judith P. Saunders, the following scholarly essay was published in *Papers on Language & Literature* in Winter 2000.

THE LOVE SONG OF SATIN-LEGS SMITH: GWENDOLYN BROOKS REVISITS PRUFROCK'S HELL

Gwendolyn Brooks's poem "The Sundays of Satin-Legs Smith" (1944) alludes unobtrusively throughout to T. S. Eliot's "The Love Song of J. Alfred Prufrock" (1915), which in turn refers both explicitly and implicitly to Dante's *Inferno* (1321). Together, Eliot's and Brooks's poems form a double-layered trajectory pointing back to a common fourteenth-century source, offering two distinctly different Modern revisions of its assumptions.[1] In their recasting of the *Inferno,* Eliot and Brooks locate hell on earth, in human social environments where their fictive characters are permanent residents; it is readers, rather than protagonists, who are taken on illuminating guided tours. Both poems provide stinging critiques of twentieth-century civilization, with its manifest social, ethical, and spiritual problems. Just as Eliot's depiction of Prufrock and his environment derives ironic impact from allusion to the Inferno, Brooks's portrait of Smith depends for similar effect upon covert comparison with Eliot's.

Brooks's familiarity with Eliot's poetry is well established. She mentions first reading his work at age sixteen, and she expresses special regard for "Prufrock" (Report 173): "I do like, for instance, Eliot's 'Prufrock,' and *The Waste Land,* 'Portrait of a Lady,' and some others of those earlier poems" (Report 156). Readers have discussed Eliot's influence on diction, phrasing, imagery, tone, theme, and narrative posture in a number of the poems in her first book, *A Street in Bronzeville,* the collection in which "Satin-Legs" first appeared (Kent, A Life 140; Melhem, Brooks 29–30, 49; Smith 43–50). Specific parallels between "Satin-Legs" and "Prufrock" have been recognized, moreover, although they have not generated extensive comment. D. H. Melhem, for example, observes that Brooks's poem approximates Eliot's in length, that it "similarly deals with an antiheroic vision," and that its aims reinforce Eliot's while at the same time raising others: "Eliot would improve us socially and spiritually. Brooks, no less concerned, probes social ills at their roots in poverty and discrimination" (Brooks 34). Gary Smith notes intriguing contrasts in self-image and personal style between Prufrock and Brooks's protagonist; he suggests that "Satin-Legs" (along with two other well known poems in the Bronzeville collection) offers "parodic challenges to T. S. Eliot's dispirited anti-hero" (46). This understanding of "Satin-Legs" is briefly underscored by Ann Stanford (169). Brooks's allusion is sufficiently elaborate, however, to require more detailed investigation than it has yet received if the relationship between the two poems is to be appreciated fully.

Formally, Brooks's poem models itself on Eliot's to a considerable degree. Total length is equivalent—Brooks's 153 lines measured against Eliot's 131. Both poems are divided into unequal, non-schematically arranged sections, ranging from short, two-line bits to longer chunks of twenty lines or more. Both rely heavily on rhyme, favoring couplets but committed to casual or accidental placement rather than to any definite scheme. Brooks's poem shows more instances of internal rhyme, and Eliot's more examples of repeated lines and phrases. Both poems tend strongly toward an iambic rhythm, but except in her short epilogue Brooks sticks faithfully to a pentameter line—"a well-mastered, fluid blank verse" (Kent, A Life 70)—while Eliot swings easily from three-foot to five- and even six- or seven-foot lines. Diction in both cases is demanding, often Latinate; these poems achieve eloquence with rich vocabulary and sometimes elaborate syntax. They are peppered with high cultural references and allusions. Prosodical and rhetorical choices in both poems combine to create an unusual balance between gravity and elegance, on the one hand, wryness and wit on the other.

The titles of the poems serve as perhaps their most obvious point of formal similarity. Rhythmically, both consist of an iamb followed by two anapests (Eliot's including a final unstressed syllable, or feminine ending):

 - x | - - x| - - x| minus
The Love| Song of J.| Al fred Pru| frock
 - x | - - x | - - x
The Sun| days of Sat| in - legs Smith

The strong echo in rhythm is matched by equally noticeable echoing in phrasing. Both titles refer to the something of Somebody. Brooks has simply substituted a new name and, more significantly, replaced the term "love song" with that of "Sundays." This shift works to underline the irony in Brooks's reworking of Eliot's theme: her protagonist lacks the spiritual hungers of his predecessor, and Sunday emphatically is not, as a reader might first anticipate, a day of worship and prayer for him. It is rather the day when he, in stark contrast to the lonely, rejection-haunted Prufrock, steps out on the town with a woman and eventually takes her to bed. On Sundays Smith achieves the love that eludes Prufrock throughout his "love song."

Both poets shape narratives around a central character, but Brooks departs from Eliot's model by declining to let her protagonist speak for himself. Her poem is not a dramatic monologue—and for excellent reasons. Her decision to present her character indirectly, to speak for him rather than through him, constitutes the most decisive difference between her formal rhetorical choices and Eliot's. Smith says nothing on his own behalf. He stands in diametrical contrast to Prufrock, whose eloquence in articulating his misery in no way helps him to surmount it, and whose verbal sophistication does not enable him to establish meaningful communication with other human beings. Smith's inability to articulate the insights Brooks's narrating voice supplies obviously calls for a different rhetorical strategy than that operating in "Prufrock." Eliot's protagonist speaks aloud, to himself and to his readers, relying on unarticulated but implicit similarities between his situation and theirs. Brooks, for her part, must act as intermediary between protagonist and readers, explaining and sometimes justifying choices or behavior she assumes readers otherwise would neither understand nor be prepared to admire: "the poem runs a contrast between white expectations and black reality" (Kent, "Aesthetic" 42).[2]

In terms of setting, action, and theme, we observe Brooks laying down central premises closely aligned with Eliot's, i.e., she locates her protagonist in "hell" and focuses on his quest for female companionship. Like Eliot, she draws on Dantean imagery to suggest the netherworld. Eliot evokes "yellow fog" and "yellow smoke" that correspond to the "forever dirty" and "dismal air," the "most acrid" smoke of the Inferno (Eliot 15–25; Dante III, 28; VI, 11; IX, 72). The foul atmosphere of the Inferno, described with emphasis and frequency, functions as an objective correlative to the sinfulness of hell's occupants; evil is realized concretely in the tainted air. Eliot's "yellow fog" and smoke similarly suggest corruption, but also exercise an unexpected soporific effect, dulling the sharpness of the protagonist's anguish. The famous opening comparison of the evening sky to "a patient etherized upon a table" makes clear the anesthetizing power of the polluting haze (3). To a man who feels like a live insect stuck squirming on a pin, anesthesia must be welcome, for it diminishes clarity of conscious perception, hence the domestication of the cat-like yellow fog, which becomes a comforting presence as the poem proceeds.

The effect of fog in Brooks's poem closely mimics that in Eliot's, but it exists on a wholly figurative level. When she shows Smith emerging from his hotel room to stroll through a desperately poor part of Chicago, we are told that "sounds about him smear, / Become a unit" (79–80). "He hears and does not hear" the sounds of wretchedness surrounding him, e.g., "a woman's oath," the "spiritless expectoration" of a tubercular neighbor (80,83,84). In the following stanza, Smith's sense of sight undergoes a parallel kind of deadening. "Pictures, too, as usual, are blurred. / He sees and does not see" signs of misery that greet him on every side: broken windows mended with newspaper, children dressed in ragged clothing, "men estranged

. . . from wonder and from joy" (89,90,96–97). Here haziness is not an attribute of the external environment, but a half-deliberately induced blunting of the protagonist's human senses. For Smith, as for Prufrock, such dulling of perception is crucial for warding off pain. Only when reality "smears" or "blurs" does it become bearable. Brooks echoes Eliot even more closely when she tells readers that "the pasts of [Smith's] ancestors lean against / Him" and "fog out his identity" (114–20). In these lines she attempts to explain that Smith must be understood in terms of his heritage. No matter how little he himself recognizes that his tastes and goals have been shaped by the deprivations that constitute his legacy, Brooks demands that we see him as part of a larger panorama of social and moral problems. Associated with generations of social injustice and its consequences on individual "identity," "fog" continues in her poem to play a hellish role.

We know Eliot's Prufrock is in hell or its equivalent because of the poem's epigraph. His wretchedness and self-condemnation reinforce our natural inclination to interpret his environment, however apparently privileged, as a hell on earth. Brooks provides no clue so direct as Eliot's epigraph, but her portrayal of urban poverty, including harsh glimpses of racial stratification, sufficiently suggests the hellishness of Smith's everyday world. The "hotel" in which he lives may in fact constitute an allusion to the "one-night cheap hotels" in the streets through which Prufrock leads us in the opening lines of Eliot's poem (74,6). Smith lives in the world Prufrock merely passes through, a world which Prufrock is inclined to romanticize: "Shall I say, I have gone at dusk through narrow streets / And watched the smoke that rises from the pipes / Of lonely men in shirt-sleeves, leaning out of windows? . . . " (70–72). Even Brooks's unusual word choice in describing Smith's outcast status—"his desertedness"—may be intended as evocation of the "half-deserted streets" along which Prufrock moves to reach the upper-class, tea party world in which he belongs (4). The outward conditions of Smith's life are the obverse of Prufrock's: six days of the week for Smith are "shabby," filled with "intricate fear . . . / postponed resentments . . . prim precautions" (10–11). If on Sundays he feels "royal," this temporary elevation of mood stands in contrast to the ongoing powerlessness he experiences as a black man earning a precarious living in a white-dominated socioeconomic system: the Chicago of the 1940's. The movie scene (lines 121–25) further defines the dangers and humiliations to which racial prejudice exposes him, e.g., "the heroine / Whose ivory and yellow it is sin / For his eye to eat of" (122–24). In this section tone is arguably at its bitterest, as Brooks briefly sketches out the backdrop against which Smith's triumphantly fulfilling Sunday activities Occur.

Brooks builds on the steadily emerging similarities between her poem and Eliot's to showcase a series of contrasts between Smith and Prufrock. These can be summarized in terms of background, temperament, behavior, and self-image. Prufrock inhabits a world of upper-class wealth and privilege; Smith lives surrounded by poverty and racial prejudice. Prufrock describes his social world articulately, even theatrically, and he judges its deficiencies harshly; Smith neither analyzes his situation nor generalizes from it (Williams 59). Prufrock is motivated to challenge the larger problems he discerns and condemns, although he lacks the courage to follow through; Smith contemplates no rebellion, concentrating his energies instead on forging purely personal satisfactions. Prufrock expresses feelings of unease and inadequacy, despite membership in an elite social group; notwithstanding his lack of social status, Smith demonstrates assertiveness and self-esteem. Socially, Prufrock fears the negative judgments of others, particularly of women; Smith expects and receives positive reactions from others in his social universe, especially from women.

These large contrasts are buttressed by many particulars, as Brooks carefully juxtaposes her protagonist to Eliot's. Clothing, for instance, gleans a relatively minor mention in Eliot's poem but functions as a central motif in Brooks's. Prufrock bemoans his appearance in order to convey his lack of self-trust, his obsession with the critical judgments of his social companions: those eyes that will "fix [him] in a formulated phrase" until he is "pinned and wriggling on the wall" (55–58). Sure that he is dressed impeccably ("my necktie rich and modest, but asserted by a simple pin"), Prufrock nevertheless believes the impression he makes is "almost ridiculous" (43,118). He dwells on signs of his aging not only to emphasize the passing of time and his own inaction, but to suggest his unattractiveness to the opposite sex. Hence Brooks is able to employ Smith's obsession with fancy clothing and outward appearance to highlight vital differences between the two characters. Smith's self-esteem ("he looks into his mirror, loves himself") and his successful pursuit of women, traits that distinguish him definitively from Prufrock, are intimately connected with his outrageous wardrobe (64). The "wonder-suits in yellow, and in wine," the "ballooning pants" and "hysterical ties" are the source of his nickname and of his reputation as a lady's man: "Inamoratas, with an approbation, / Bestowed his rifle. Blessed his inclination" (48,52,54,1–2). His "vault" of a closet contains his most precious possessions, fuels his Sunday well-being and sense of self-worth: "He is fat / And fine this morning" (45,4–5).

In showing the reader "the innards" of Smith's extravagantly stocked clothing closet, Brooks alludes to the opening line of Eliot's poem with ironic effect (51). "Let us go then, you and I," Prufrock urges, inviting readers to enter the world of his loneliness and self-deprecating impotence (1). "Let us go," "let us go," he reiterates twice more in this first section of the poem (4,12). Using nearly identical wording—"Let us proceed"—Brooks's narrating voice invites readers to join in examining Smith's wardrobe, source of the very real satisfactions he achieves despite circumscribed opportunities (43). Persistent regal imagery in the opening sections of the poem further highlights this difference between the two characters. Smith feels "royal" on Sundays: "he designs his reign," lives out the full significance of his "rifle"

(4,6,2). For his part, Prufrock explicitly rejects any such notion: "I am not Prince Hamlet, nor was meant to be" (110). Closer by far, in terms of actual wealth and status, to royalty than Smith (whose "heritage of cabbage and pigtails" is explicitly noted), Prufrock nonetheless despairs of realizing qualities of eminence, authority, or initiative (27).

Eliot's cat imagery also makes a brief appearance in this section of Brooks's poem, reinforcing the contrasts in self-image between the two characters. Where Prufrock looks to the anesthetizing, comfortingly domesticated "yellow smoke. . . / Rubbing its back upon the window panes" to alleviate his anxieties (24–25), Smith finds solace in his own appearance and schemes: awakening, he "unwinds, elaborately: a cat / Tawny, reluctant, royal" (34). More like a lion than like Prufrock's tame housecat, he embarks upon his day with full confidence in his own physical and mental fitness to prevail in his environment. Thus Brooks transforms Eliot's metaphor: instead of signaling surrender to a deadening environment, the cat becomes an image of personal power and pride.

The quest for women's company, which provides impetus for the forward movement in both poems, clearly forms a major point of contrast between the two protagonists. Prufrock fears rejection to such an extent that he cannot approach a woman at all. In fact, he scarcely looks at women as whole beings, seeing instead merely body parts, garments, and accessories: "arms," bracelets, "a shawl," "a dress" (62,66,64). He names no particular woman as the object of his desire or the audience for his love song, and he regards all females as the embodiment of humiliating criticism. If he tries to tell a woman "all," including revelation of his metaphysical questions and insights, she might simply dismiss him: "That is not what I meant at all" (95–97). And his yearning to confide in a sympathetic female is undercut by a fundamental ambivalence: the women he observes who "come and go / Talking of Michelangelo" look like willing participants in the scheme of social hypocrisy and self-disguise he despises (13–14,35–36). He wishes, apparently, for an all-wise, quasi-divine woman, perhaps someone like the Beatrice figure in Dante's trilogy, a woman who would provide a combination of spiritual guidance, moral example, and human love. Frustrated by the absence of any such goddess-like rescuer, he finds otherworldly females only in the mythic mermaids who appear at the poem's conclusion. And these fabulous females, too, he is certain, will turn away from him and refuse to exercise their siren-like powers on him. He is so worthless, in his own view, that even creatures who derive amusement from enticing men to their doom will not waste their time enticing and destroying him: "I do not think that they will sing to me" (125). Insofar as the sirens' song is a representation of male desire (male urges displaced and attributed instead to the fatally seductive females), Prufrock ends his love song expressing fears that desire itself—along with actual women—will elude him.

Smith's quest for female companionship could not be more different. Untroubled by self-doubts and consistently successful, he is portrayed as having squired and bedded numerous women. If readers are perturbed by his lack of monogamous focus, he is not: there is no hint that he wishes his relations with the opposite sex to be anything other than what they are.[3] The poem opens, moreover, with the statement that he is popular with women. They appreciate his clothes; they enjoy his company; they have "bestowed" upon him the nickname of "Satin-legs." Brooks concludes her poem with six italicized lines depicting Smith's lovemaking with the selected "lady" of the week. This day on which he is king, managing to transcend the deprivations and degradations that otherwise shape his life, ends with the most fundamental of human pleasures:

> Her body is like new brown bread
> Under the Woolworth mignonette.
> Her body is a honey bowl
> Whose waiting honey is deep and hot.
> Her body is like summer earth,
> Receptive, soft, and absolute. . . . (148–53)

Food imagery ("bread," "honey") indicates how much he is nourished and sustained by this connection; D. H. Melhem notes the "delicacy" of the "lyric epilogue," which lends the conclusion of Brooks's poem "a startlingly romantic note" (34). His experience of the female body is said, furthermore, to be "absolute." The poem concludes with this word, which lends extra significance to the human event and human feelings it characterizes. The encounter itself may be transitory, but while it lasts the experience is perfect in its human completeness: nothing is missing. Thus Smith, for all the poverty and external difficulties in his life, achieves with a woman the satisfactions unrealized by his wealthy counterpart in Eliot's poem. Smith's quest ends in the simple consummation of desire; Prufrock's ends only with fears about his relations with women, doubts concerning his own erotic potential.

Brooks's poem effectively strips eros of the metaphysical weight it carries in Eliot's and Dante's poems. Both Brooks's predecessors associate woman's love with redemption. Protagonists unable to extricate themselves from a moral and spiritual "dark wood," or its equivalent, require external, female guidance (Headings 21). Dante's protagonist, of course, receives such guidance, while Eliot's does not. Prufrock's desires are more complicated than Smith's in that Prufrock seeks to share profound, vaguely metaphysical communication with a woman, and possibly also to articulate to her his denunciation of his social universe (Headings 24). Certainly his wish to "force the moment to its crisis" has implications that go beyond the physical (80). This difference between his desires and Smith's appears in large measure to be a by-product of economic and educational differences between them and in no way blunts the fact that Brooks's protagonist obtains fulfillment on his own terms, where Eliot's fails to do so. Smith does not need to look to women for spiritual solace or insight. The good he seeks with them is free of transcendent meanings because, unlike Dante or Prufrock, he is not perceived—by himself or by his poet-creator—as enmeshed in any guilty collaboration. He is free of the morbid introspection that is Prufrock's most salient trait for the best of reasons: the injustice and aridity of the environment in which he finds himself are emphatically none of his making.

Why, after all, are these characters in "hell" in the first place? To what ends do the poets offer readers these guided tours through regions of the damned? In each case, the implied relationship between narrator and reader provides an important clue in understanding the poet's purposes. As already noted, Eliot's Prufrock assumes readers know, or at least understand, his world of porcelain and marmelade and cultural one-up-manship. If readers do not end in judging Prufrock quite as severely as he judges himself, it is because they recognize something of themselves in him. Readers, too, have experienced the power of social structures and strictures to thwart the quest for human and spiritual fulfillment. They too have been "afraid" (86). And, like Prufrock, readers perhaps can recognize their own collusion with these same stifling social forces. The epigraph to Eliot's poem forces readers to consider whether they themselves may be living in an earthly hell: will they learn, Dante-like, from observing Prufrock's futile torments, or are they doomed to participate in endless cycles of personal and metaphysical sterility?

As already noted, Brooks's poem addresses an audience much more distant from the protagonist. Frequently the poet-narrator interrupts the narration of Smith's day to caution readers against evaluating him by inappropriate standards. As Stanford points out, Brooks's narrator assumes a set of "unsympathetic and uncomprehending readers" (162). These "implied" readers play a crucial role in the poem, beating the brunt of Brooks's satiric energy: "In the dynamic between the narrator of the poem and the reader/critic, Brooks critiques and revises an aesthetics predicated on the assumption of white Euro-American superiority" (162,163). Without guidance, Brooks clearly implies, an audience unfamiliar with Smith's world will condemn his tastes—in music, in perfume, in women and, above all, in clothes. Over and over she tells readers that poverty and lack of education explain many differences between Smith's aesthetic values and theirs. Yet underlying these differences, she insists, there are essential commonalities; once perceived, these commonalities may persuade readers that Smith's approach to living is not really so very different from their own after all. Brooks speaks, for instance, of the need in life for alluring scents ("life must be aromatic"), for self-adornment, for food, for beauty, for sex (15). All humans need these things, but the forms in which they seek them vary. Smith's tastes could resemble those of the implied readers only if he shared those readers' socioeconomic and cultural background. His urge to clothe himself in fabrics, colors, and patterns that their "limited understanding" deems garish to the point of offensiveness "represents the indomitability of the human spirit in its quest for beauty," expressing itself in an alien, but not illegitimate, set of aesthetic standards (Stanford 163; Kent, A Life 69). As Brooks herself has articulated the point elsewhere, "human beings will break away from ache to dance, to sing, to create, no matter how briefly, how intermittently. . . . [L]ike an under-earth river, that impulse to beauty and art runs fundamentally, relentlessly" (qtd. in Melhem, "Humanism" 33).

His background renders Smith incapable of appreciating understated effects: he wants his women to wear "three layers of lipstick, intense hat / Dripping with the most voluble of veils" (134–35). He enjoys "affable extemes. . . . [L]ike sweet bombs" because only intensity and extremity will speak to a man with "no education / In quiet arts of compromise" (136,138–39). By upper-middle class standards Smith's preferences are flamboyant, but with passing references to "baroque" and "Rococo" Brooks reminds us that the aesthetic tastes of Western high culture have gone through periods when the elaborately ornate was valued (73). One obvious effect of her portrait is to bridge some of the distance between Smith and the reader, to generate a degree of fellowship between them (Miller 104). In the end Smith removes the garments that have come to represent critical differences separating his world from the reader's, and he goes to bed naked, these external distinctions peeled away.

The only way to universalize upper-middle class taste, Brooks flatly informs us, would be through universal redistribution of upper-middle class wealth. There is "little hope" of reforming the tastes of a Smith unless we are willing "to set the world a-boil / And do a lot of equalizing things, / Remove a little ermine, say, from kings, / Shake hands with paupers and appoint them men" (36,40). The poem constitutes an unmistakable indictment of the economic and social system responsible for Smith's circumstances. The moral and political questions directed toward the reader are more pointed and more disturbing than those in Eliot's poem precisely because of the greater distance between reader and protagonist. Where Eliot would have us ask ourselves whether we are acquiescing in our own damnation, Brooks forces us to ask whether we have acquiesced in the damning of others. Working to break down barriers of class and race between reader and protagonist, the poem compels acknowledgment of sweeping social evil. Brooks achieves her purposes all the more powerfully by emphasizing her protagonist's strengths and achievements more than his grievances. He is not foremost a victim, as she presents him, but a man who against all odds has contrived for himself a bearable, sometimes even joyful, existence in circumstances—arguably hellish—to which he has been consigned without justice or reason.

Smith's successes emerge with all the more clarity against the backdrop of the comparison with Prufrock operating quietly throughout Brooks's poem. The sustained allusion to Eliot's dramatic monologue, built on parallels in setting and plot, and reinforced by echoes in phrasing, imagery, and prosody, is a key element in Brooks's carefully crafted campaign to shape reader response to her unusual protagonist. Indeed, to win esteem for a character like Satin-Legs Smith is far from simple, and the contrast with Prufrock provides just the vehicle Brooks needs to accomplish that difficult task. In terms of characterization, she effectively turns Eliot's poem inside out, portraying a man of low status and low income who nevertheless manages his life more competently than does his wealthy, high-status counterpart in Eliot's poem. Diametric differences between the two protagonists push readers toward admiration for Brooks's, fueling a corresponding impatience with Eliot's. The more we shake our heads at Prufrock, who has failed miserably to enjoy his many advantages, the more we celebrate Smith, who has realized so much satisfaction even in a context of poverty and prejudice. The effect of allusion in Brooks's poem, finally, is to compel appreciation of Smith's unsubdued vitality. Refusing to succumb to despair or self-pity, even in an environment that would excuse such surrender, Smith triumphantly reverses nearly every one of Prufrock's failures.

Works Cited

Alighieri, Dante. *The Inferno.* Trans. John Ciardi. New York: Penguin,1954.

Brooks, Gwendolyn. *Report from Part I.* Detroit: Broadside, 1972.

————. "The Sundays of Satin-Legs Smith." *Selected Poems.* New York: Harper, 1944. Rpt. 1963. 12–18.

Eliot, T. S. "The Love Song of J. Alfred Prufrock." *The Waste Land and Other Poems.* London: Faber, 1940. Rpt. New York: Harcourt, 1962. 1–9.

Headings, Philip R. *T. S. Eliot,* Revised Edition. Boston: Twayne, 1982.

Kent, George E. "Aesthetic Values in the Poetry of Gwendolyn Brooks." *A Life Distilled: Gwendolyn Brooks, Her Poetry and Fiction.* Eds. Maria K. Mootry and Gary Smith. Urbana: U of Illinois P, 1987. 30–46.

————. *A Life of Gwendolyn Brooks.* Lexington: UP of Kentucky, 1990.

Melhem, D. H. "Gwendolyn Brooks: Humanism and Heroism." *Heroism in the New Black Poetry: Introductions and Interviews.* Ed. D. H. Melhem. Lexington: UP of Kentucky, 1990. 11–38.

————. *Gwendolyn Brooks: Poetry and the Heroic Voice.* Lexington: UP of Kentucky, 1987.

Miller, R. Baxter. "'Does Man Love Art': The Humanistic Aesthetic of Gwendolyn Brooks." *A Life Distilled: Gwendolyn Brooks, Her Poetry and Fiction.* Eds. Maria K. Mootry and Gary Smith. Urbana: U of Illinois P, 1987. 100–15.

Smith, Gary. "A Street in Bronzeville, the Harlem Renaissance, and the Mythologies of Black Women." *Melus.* 10.3 (1983): 261–77. Rpt. in *Modern Critical Views: Contemporary Poets.* Ed. Harold Bloom. New York: Chelsea, 1986. 43–56.

Stanford, Ann Folwell. "'Like Narrow Banners for Some Gathering War':
Readers, Aesthetics, and Gwendolyn Brooks's 'The Sundays of
Satin-Legs Smith.'" College *Literature*. 17.2/3 (1990): 162–82.

Williams, Kenny J. "The World of Satin-Legs, Mrs. Sallie, and the Black-
stone Rangers: The Restricted Chicago of Gwendolyn Brooks." *A
Life Distilled: Gwendolyn Brooks, Her Poetry and Fiction*. Eds. Maria
K. Mootry and Gary Smith. Urbana: U of Illinois P, 1987. 47–70.

Conclusion

Casebook Two invited us to move into another realm of self-discovery. It challenged us beyond our likes and dislikes, action or nonaction, and the consequences of bracing our-selves for what it means to grow older, gracefully, or experience something, gracefully, and in some cases, not so gracefully. The selections made us engage in a deeper under-standing of the human condition through time and experience. How well are any of us equipped to handle life's successes and disappointments? Perhaps it is the self-exploration that we read about in the first casebook that helps us draw upon the tribulations of the other characters and their situations in this section on the rites of passage. If there are such things as "necessary evils," then perhaps we can claim that some things are "neces-sary passages."

1. Philip R. Headings provides a useful overview and discussion of Dantean allusions in "Prufrock." See "Dantean Observations" in T. S. Eliot, Revised Edition (19–31).

2. Ann Folwell Stanford's 1990 essay on "Satin-Legs" provides a detailed and percep-tive analysis of the relationship betwen narrator and reader in the poem. She shows, point by point, how Brooks "confronts the problem of unsympathetic and uncom-prehending readers by writing an implied reader. . . directly into the text" (162). The poem thus "functions as a corrective primer in reading poetry that has roots in a tradition and culture that is 'other.' Moreover, it upsets the balance of power, plac-ing Satin-Legs' tradition and life in the center, forcing the reader/critic to confront the uncomfortable possibility that his or her world is the foreign one" (168).

3. R. Baxter Miller, for instance, asserts that Smith's amorous adventures constitute an escape from his problems rather than a resolution of them. Miller argues that Brooks's presentation of that escape is ironic, not celebratory, a part of Smith's failure to con-ceptualize his situation in larger sociopolitical terms (101–07).

CASEBOOK THREE
The Ties that Bind: Relating and Relationships
Overview

Human beings are naturally social creatures. The most significant relationships we develop throughout our lives are defined by a complex layer of emotions. Love is not simple or easy—and there is often (as the cliché goes) a fine line between love and hate.

Our first intimate relationships are with our parents and siblings. Then comes romantic love, marriage, and sometimes a baby carriage (to borrow from another clichéd rhyme). The emotional ties that bind us to the significant others in our lives have long been the topic of literary explorations. What we mean when we talk about love depends on who is talking and whom he or she is talking about and when and where and why. Relating to our families, our friends, and our lovers is quite a challenge.

Consider these questions as you read:

- How would you define love at this point in your life? What about ten years ago? Or ten years from now?
- Have you ever been in love? How is romantic love similar to and different from other types of love?
- Why is communication important in relationships?
- Do you communicate in the same ways with all of the significant people in your life?

Poetry

WILLIAM SHAKESPEARE

Born in Stratford-on-Avon in 1564, William Shakespeare was an English dramatist and poet. He is widely regarded as the greatest playwright who ever lived, but he was also a poet and crafted some of the most beautiful sonnets ever written. The following is one of his most widely anthologized poems.

Sonnet 18

Shall I compare thee to a summer's day?
Thou art more lovely and more temperate:
Rough winds do shake the darling buds of May,
And summer's lease hath all too short a date;
Sometimes too hot the eye of heaven shines,
And often is his gold complexion dimmed;
And every fair from fair sometimes declines,
By chance or nature's changing course untrimmed;
But thy eternal summer shall not fade,
Nor lose possession of that fair thou ow'st;
Nor shall death brag thou wand'rest in his shade,
When in eternal lines to Time thou grow'st:
So long as men can breathe, or eyes can see,
So long lives this, and this gives life to thee.

WILLIAM BUTLER YEATS

William Butler Yeats was born in 1865 in Dublin, though he spent more than half of his life outside of Ireland. He studied painting at the Dublin Metropolitan School of Art before focusing on poetry. In 1885, he published his first poems in *The Dublin University Review*. Yeats died in January 1939 at the Hôtel Idéal Séjour, in Menton, France.
The following poem was written in 1919.

A Prayer for My Daughter

Once more the storm is howling, and half hid
Under this cradle-hood and coverlid
My child sleeps on. There is no obstacle
But Gregory's wood and one bare hill
Whereby the haystack- and roof-levelling wind.
Bred on the Atlantic, can be stayed;
And for an hour I have walked and prayed
Because of the great gloom that is in my mind.
I have walked and prayed for this young child an hour
And heard the sea-wind scream upon the tower,
And under the arches of the bridge, and scream
In the elms above the flooded stream;
Imagining in excited reverie
That the future years had come,
Dancing to a frenzied drum,
Out of the murderous innocence of the sea.
May she be granted beauty and yet not
Beauty to make a stranger's eye distraught,
Or hers before a looking-glass, for such,
Being made beautiful overmuch,
Consider beauty a sufficient end,
Lose natural kindness and maybe
The heart-revealing intimacy
That chooses right, and never find a friend.
Helen being chosen found life flat and dull
And later had much trouble from a fool,
While that great Queen, that rose out of the spray,
Being fatherless could have her way
Yet chose a bandy-legged smith for man.
It's certain that fine women eat
A crazy salad with their meat
Whereby the Horn of plenty is undone.
In courtesy I'd have her chiefly learned;
Hearts are not had as a gift but hearts are earned
By those that are not entirely beautiful;
Yet many, that have played the fool
For beauty's very self, has charm made wise.
And many a poor man that has roved,
Loved and thought himself beloved,
From a glad kindness cannot take his eyes.

May she become a flourishing hidden tree
That all her thoughts may like the linnet be,
And have no business but dispensing round
Their magnanimities of sound,
Nor but in merriment begin a chase,
Nor but in merriment a quarrel.
O may she live like some green laurel
Rooted in one dear perpetual place.
My mind, because the minds that I have loved,
The sort of beauty that I have approved,
Prosper but little, has dried up of late,
Yet knows that to be choked with hate
May well be of all evil chances chief.
If there's no hatred in a mind
Assault and battery of the wind
Can never tear the linnet from the leaf.
An intellectual hatred is the worst,
So let her think opinions are accursed.
Have I not seen the loveliest woman born
Out of the mouth of plenty's horn,
Because of her opinionated mind
Barter that horn and every good
By quiet natures understood
For an old bellows full of angry wind?
Considering that, all hatred driven hence,
The soul recovers radical innocence
And learns at last that it is self-delighting,
Self-appeasing, self-affrighting,
And that its own sweet will is Heaven's will;
She can, though every face should scowl
And every windy quarter howl
Or every bellows burst, be happy Still.
And may her bridegroom bring her to a house
Where all's accustomed, ceremonious;
For arrogance and hatred are the wares
Peddled in the thoroughfares.
How but in custom and in ceremony
Are innocence and beauty born?
Ceremony's a name for the rich horn,
And custom for the spreading laurel tree.

GWENDOLYN BROOKS

Gwendolyn Brooks was born in Topeka, Kansas, in 1917 and raised in Chicago. The author of more than twenty books of poetry, she won the Pulitzer Prize in 1949 for *Annie Allen.* In 1968, she was named Poet Laureate for the state of Illinois, and from 1985 to 1986 she was Consultant in Poetry to the Library of Congress. She also received an American Academy of Arts and Letters award, the Frost Medal, a National Endowment for the Arts award, the Shelley Memorial Award, and fellowships from the Academy of American Poets and the Guggenheim Foundation. She lived in Chicago until her death on December 3, 2000.

The Bean Eaters

They eat beans mostly, this old yellow pair.
Dinner is a casual affair.
Plain chipware on a plain and creaking wood,
Tin flatware.

Two who are Mostly Good.
Two who have lived their day,
But keep on putting on their clothes
And putting things away.

And remembering . . .
Remembering, with twinklings and twinges,
As they lean over the beans in their rented back room that
is full of beads and receipts and dolls and cloths,
tobacco crumbs, vases and fringes.

SYLVIA PLATH

Sylvia Plath was born in Boston in 1932. In 1955, having been awarded a Fulbright scholarship, she began two years at Cambridge University. There she met and married the British poet Ted Hughes and settled in England, bearing two children. She committed suicide (at age 30) in 1963.

The following poem was written in 1962. It is one of her most famous and widely anthologized poems.

Daddy

You do not do, you do not do
Any more, black shoe

In which I have lived like a foot
For thirty years, poor and white,
Barely daring to breathe or Achoo.

Daddy, I have had to kill you.
You died before I had time—
Marble-heavy, a bag full of God,
Ghastly statue with one gray toe
Big as a Frisco seal
And a head in the freakish Atlantic
Where it pours bean green over blue
In the waters off beautiful Nauset.
I used to pray to recover you.
Ach, du.

In the German tongue, in the Polish town
Scraped flat by the roller
Of wars, wars, wars.
But the name of the town is common.
My Polack friend

Says there are a dozen or two.
So I never could tell where you
Put your foot, your root,
I never could talk to you.
The tongue stuck in my jaw.

It stuck in a barb wire snare.
Ich, ich, ich, ich,
I could hardly speak.
I thought every German was you.
And the language obscene

An engine, an engine
Chuffing me off like a Jew.
A Jew to Dachau, Auschwitz, Belsen.
I began to talk like a Jew.
I think I may well be a Jew.

The snows of the Tyrol, the clear beer of Vienna
Are not very pure or true.
With my gipsy ancestress and my weird luck
And my Taroc pack and my Taroc pack
I may be a bit of a Jew.

I have always been scared of you,
With your Luftwaffe, your gobbledygoo.

And your neat mustache
And your Aryan eye, bright blue.
Panzer-man, panzer-man, O You—

Not God but a swastika
So black no sky could squeak through.
Every woman adores a Fascist,
The boot in the face, the brute
Brute heart of a brute like you.

You stand at the blackboard, daddy,
In the picture I have of you,
A cleft in your chin instead of your foot
But no less a devil for that, no not
Any less the black man who

Bit my pretty red heart in two.
I was ten when they buried you.
At twenty I tried to die
And get back, back, back to you.
I thought even the bones would do.

But they pulled me out of the sack,
And they stuck me together with glue.
And then I knew what to do.
I made a model of you,
A man in black with a Meinkampf look

And a love of the rack and the screw.
And I said I do, I do.
So daddy, I'm finally through.
The black telephone's off at the root,
The voices just can't worm through.

If I've killed one man, I've killed two—
The vampire who said he was you
And drank my blood for a year,
Seven years, if you want to know.
Daddy, you can lie back now.

There's a stake in your fat black heart
And the villagers never liked you.
They are dancing and stamping on you.
They always knew it was you.
Daddy, daddy, you bastard, I'm through.

ANNE SEXTON

Anne Sexton (1928–1974) wrote what the critics defined as a reenactment of Grimm's fairy tales. In 1966, she won the Pulitzer Prize for Poetry. As Kurt Vonnegut once wrote about her, "She domesticates my terror, examines it, and describes it, teaches it some tricks which will amuse me, then lets it gallop wild in my forest once more."

The following poem is from her collection, *Transformations*. It was first published in 1971.

Cinderella

You always read about it:
the plumber with twelve children
who wins the Irish Sweepstakes.
From toilets to riches.
That story.

Or the nursemaid,
some luscious sweet from Denmark
who captures the oldest son's heart.
From diapers to Dior.
That story.

Or a milkman who serves the wealthy,
eggs, cream, butter, yogurt, milk,
the white truck like an ambulance
who goes into real estate
and makes a pile.
From homogenized to martinis at lunch.

Or the charwoman
who is on the bus when it cracks up
and collects enough from the insurance.
From mops to Bonwit Teller.
That story.

Once
the wife of a rich man was on her deathbed
and she said to her daughter Cinderella:
Be devout. Be good. Then I will smile
down from heaven in the seam of a cloud.
The man took another wife who had
two daughters, pretty enough
but with hearts like blackjacks.

Cinderella was their maid.
She slept on the sooty hearth each night
and walked around looking like Al Jolson.
Her father brought presents home from town,
jewels and gowns for the other women
but the twig of a tree for Cinderella.
She planted that twig on her mother's grave
and it grew to a tree where a white dove sat.
Whenever she wished for anything the dove
would drop it like an egg upon the ground.
The bird is important, my dears, so heed him.

Next came the ball, as you all know.
It was a marriage market.
The prince was looking for a wife.
All but Cinderella were preparing
and gussying up for the big event.
Cinderella begged to go too.
Her stepmother threw a dish of lentils
into the cinders and said: Pick them
up in an hour and you shall go.
The white dove brought all his friends;
all the warm wings of the fatherland came,
and picked up the lentils in a jiffy.
No, Cinderella, said the stepmother,
you have no clothes and cannot dance.
That's the way with stepmothers.

Cinderella went to the tree at the grave
and cried forth like a gospel singer:
Mama! Mama! My turtledove,
send me to the prince's ball!
The bird dropped down a golden dress
and delicate little gold slippers.
Rather a large package for a simple bird.
So she went. Which is no surprise.
Her stepmother and sisters didn't
recognize her without her cinder face
and the prince took her hand on the spot
and danced with no other the whole day.

As nightfall came she thought she'd better
get home. The prince walked her home
and she disappeared into the pigeon house
and although the prince took an axe and broke

it open she was gone. Back to her cinders.
These events repeated themselves for three days.
However on the third day the prince
covered the palace steps with cobbler's wax
and Cinderella's gold shoe stuck upon it.
Now he would find whom the shoe fit
and find his strange dancing girl for keeps.
He went to their house and the two sisters
were delighted because they had lovely feet.
The eldest went into a room to try the slipper on
but her big toe got in the way so she simply
sliced it off and put on the slipper.
The prince rode away with her until the white dove
told him to look at the blood pouring forth.
That is the way with amputations.
They don't just heal up like a wish.
The other sister cut off her heel
but the blood told as blood will.
The prince was getting tired.
He began to feel like a shoe salesman.
But he gave it one last try.
This time Cinderella fit into the shoe
like a love letter into its envelope.

At the wedding ceremony
the two sisters came to curry favor
and the white dove pecked their eyes out.
Two hollow spots were left
like soup spoons.

Cinderella and the prince
lived, they say, happily ever after,
like two dolls in a museum case
never bothered by diapers or dust,
never arguing over the timing of an egg,
never telling the same story twice,
never getting a middle-aged spread,
their darling smiles pasted on for eternity.
Regular Bobbsey Twins.
That story.

THEODORE ROETHKE

Theodore Roethke was born in Saginaw, Michigan, in 1908. He attended the University of Michigan and took a few classes at Harvard, but was unhappy in school. His collection titled *The Waking* was awarded the Pulitzer Prize in 1954. He died in 1963.

The following poem was written in 1948.

My Papa's Waltz

The whiskey on your breath
Could make a small boy dizzy;
But I hung on like death:
Such waltzing was not easy.
We romped until the pans
Slid from the kitchen shelf;
My mother's countenance
Could not unfrown itself.
The hand that held my wrist
Was battered on one knuckle;
At every step you missed
My right ear scraped a buckle.
You beat time on my head
With a palm caked hard by dirt,
Then waltzed me off to bed
Still clinging to your shirt.

FLORENCE WEINBERGER

Florence Weinberger was born in New York and raised in the Bronx. She was educated at Hunter College and UCLA, and she has worked as a teacher and a legal investigator among other things.

The following poem was published in the anthology *Women and Aging.*

The Power in My Mother's Arms

My mother stretched dough thin,
thinner, to its splitting edge.
All that certainty gripped her
wrist, while she sieved
bread crumbs through her fingers,

nuts, sugar, apples, lemon rind,
laying down family legends
like seams in a rock; then
she rolled it all up
the sweet length of the dining room table.
Beaten egg glazed the top, and still
aroma to come, cooling and slicing.
I didn't mind her watching me
eat: I'd give back the heat of my
need gladly, fuel to keep the cycle
elemental, if you've watched birds feed
their young.
To every celebration, she matched a flavor,
giving us memory,
giving exile the bite of bitter herbs.
God's word drifted in fragrant soups,
vigor in the wine she made
herself, clear and original.

    My mother's death
changed the alchemy of food.
     Holidays run together now
like ungrooved rivers. I forget
what they are for. I buy bakery goods.
They look dead
under the blue lights.
I don't do anything the way she taught me
but I get fat.
I don't look like her and I don't sound
like her, but I stand like her.

There must be rituals
that sever what harms
our connection to the past and lets us
keep the rest.
If not, let me invent one
from old scents and ceremonies.
Let me fashion prayer from a
piece of dough, roll it out,
cut in the shape of my mother,
plump, soft, flour-dusted,
the way I once played cook with clay.
Let me keep the cold healing properties
of female images,
and heated, their power
to hold fire.

Let me bake her likeness in vessels
made of earth and water.
Let me bless the flames
that turn her skin gold,
her eyes dark as raisins.
Let me bless the long wait at the oven door.
Let me bless the first warm dangerous taste of love.
Let me eat.

E. E. CUMMINGS

Edward Estlin Cummings was born in Massachusetts in 1894. He received his B.A. in 1915 and his M.A. in 1916, both from Harvard. During World War I, Cummings worked as an ambulance driver in France, but he was interned in a prison camp by the French authorities for his outspoken antiwar views. After the war, he returned to the United States. Known for his experimentation with language, at the time of his death in 1962, he was the second most widely read poet in America (following Robert Frost).

I Like My Body When It Is with Your

i like my body when it is with your
body. It is so quite new a thing.
Muscles better and nerves more.
i like your body. i like what it does,
i like its hows. i like to feel the spine
of your body and its bones, and the trembling
-firm-smooth ness and which i will
again and again and again
kiss, i like kissing this and that of you,
i like, slowly stroking the, shocking fuzz
of your electric fur, and what-is-it comes
over parting flesh . . . . And eyes big love-crumbs,

and possibly i like the thrill

of under me you so quite new

GLENN HUTCHINSON

Dr. Glenn Hutchinson was born in Charlotte, North Carolina. He is a lecturer in the English Department at the University of North Carolina–Charlotte, specializing in rhetoric and composition with particular emphasis upon service-learning and the teaching of writing.

The following poem was written in 2001.

Connecting

"May I have your number?" he says.
"Home number?" she says.
"Please."
"Only if I get yours."
"Here's my cell."
"Is this your regular cell or your work cell?"
"It's both."
"Oh," she says. "How delicious."

"What's your email?" she says.
"Work or home?"
"Both," she says.
"Oh," he complies.
"Here's my email that nobody knows about," she says.
"I'll treasure it," he says.

"Do you IM?" she asks.
"Yes."
"AOL?"
"No. I'm with . . ."
"Oh, that's OK."
"But I could change."
"Would you do that for me?"
"Yes. I would."
"Wow. You're not like most guys, are you?"
"Well . . ."

"Do you fax?" he asks.
"Oh, yes," she says.
"Office or home?"
"Portable."
"Oh. How nice."
"You?"
"Office. But I'm looking."

"So will you call me?" she asks.
"Or should I email you?"
"I'll probably be online tonight."
"I would fax you, but . . ."

"I understand. And anyway, it's too soon . . ."
"Yes, too soon. I wouldn't want to seem too . . ."
"Yes, I know."
"It's been very nice."
"I feel like we've, you know, connected."
"Yeah, connected."
"You're very easy to talk to. I feel like I can tell you—"
"Anything?"
"Yes, anything."

"So call me."
"Or email me."
"Or IM me."
"Or maybe I'll just see you around."

A pause.

"See you around? What do you mean by that?"
"Nothing. I just meant—"
"I just gave you—and now you're already—"
"What?"
"See you around? That's what they all say."
"I don't understand you."
"What's there not to understand?"
"I just like a little space, is all."
"Space?"
"Yeah, I mean I like a little space—what's wrong with that?"
"OK, I'll give you space."
"No, I didn't mean that."

"Hey! Hey! . . . Don't go . . . I'll call you."
"Don't call me. Don't email me. Don't IM me. And don't even think of faxing me."
"But what about us? What about this connection that we've—"
"No, that's it. We're through."
"Through?"
"Through."
"Already?"

"But I'll miss you."
"Well, I'll miss you, too."

"It's been fun . . . talking."
"Yeah, talking."

"You take care of yourself."
"Yeah, you too."

"Look, I'm really sorry about . . ."
"That's OK. These things happen."
"I'll never forget . . ."
"Me neither."

"You'll make somebody a lucky . . ."
"Yeah, you too."

"Well . . . bye."
"Bye."

"Yeah, see ya . . . around."

The End.

Fiction

RAYMOND CARVER

Raymond Carver was born in 1938 in Oregon. He received his B.A. in 1963 at the University of Iowa. In the 1970s, Carver taught for several years at universities throughout the United States. From 1980 to 1983 he was a professor of English at Syracuse University. On August 2, 1988, the author died of lung cancer.

The following short story was published just before his death in 1988.

Night School

My marriage had just fallen apart. I couldn't find a job. I had another girl. But she wasn't in town. So I was at a bar having a glass of beer, and two women were sitting a few stools down, and one of them began to talk to me.

"You have a car?"

"I do, but it's not here," I said.

My wife had the car. I was staying at my parents' place. I used their car sometimes. But tonight I was walking.

The other woman looked at me. They were both about forty, maybe older.   5

"What'd you ask him?" the other woman said to the first woman.

"I said did he have a car."

"So do you have a car?" the second woman said to me.

"I was telling her. I have a car. But I don't have it with me," I said.

"That doesn't do us much good, does it?" she said.   10

The first woman laughed. "We had a brainstorm and we need a car to go through with it. Too bad." She turned to the bartender and asked for two more beers.

I'd been nursing my beer along, and now I drank it off and thought they might buy me a round. They didn't.

"What do you do?" the first woman asked me.

"Right now, nothing," I said. "Sometimes, when I can, I go to school."

"He goes to school," she said to the other woman. "He's a student. Where do you   15
go to school?"

"Around," I said.

"I told you," the woman said. "Doesn't he look like a student?"

"What are they teaching you?" the second woman said.

"Everything," I said.

"I mean," she said, "what do you plan to do? What's your big goal in life? Every- 20 body has a big goal in life."

I raised my empty glass to the bartender. He took it and drew me another beer. I counted out some change, which left me with thirty cents from the two dollars I'd started out with a couple of hours ago. She was waiting.

"Teach. Teach school," I said.

"He wants to be a teacher," she said.

I sipped my beer. Someone put a coin in the jukebox and a song that my wife liked began to play. I looked around. Two men near the front were at the shuffleboard. The door was open and it was dark outside.

"We're students too, you know," the first woman said. "We go to school." 25

"We take a night class," the other one said. "We take this reading class on Monday nights."

The first woman said, "Why don't you move down here, teacher, so we don't have to yell?"

I picked up my beer and my cigarets and moved down two stools.

"That's better," she said. "Now, did you say you were a student?"

"Sometimes, yes, but not now," I said. 30

"Where?"

"State College."

"That's right," she said. "I remember now." She looked at the other woman. "You ever hear of a teacher over there name of Patterson? He teaches adult-education classes. He teaches this class we take on Monday nights. You remind me a lot of Patterson."

They looked at each other and laughed.

"Don't bother about us," the first woman said. "It's a private joke. Shall we tell 35 him what we thought about doing, Edith? *Shall* we?"

Edith didn't answer. She took a drink of beer and she narrowed her eyes as she looked at herself, at the three of us, in the mirror behind the bar.

"We were thinking," the first woman went on, "if we had a car tonight we'd go over and see him. Patterson. Right, Edith?"

Edith laughed to herself. She finished her beer and asked for a round, one for me included. She paid for the beers with a five-dollar bill.

"Patterson likes to take a drink," Edith said.

"You can say that again," the other woman said. She turned to me. "We talked 40 about it in class one night. Patterson says he always has wine with his meals and a highball or two before dinner."

"What class is this?" I said.

"This reading class Patterson teaches. Patterson likes to talk about different things."

"We're learning to read," Edith said. "Can you believe it?"

"I'd like to read Hemingway and things like that," the other woman said. "But Patterson has us reading stories like in *Reader's Digest.*"

"We take a test every Monday night," Edith said. "But Patterson's okay. He wouldn't 45 care if we came over for a highball. Wouldn't be much he could do, anyway. We have something on him. On Patterson," she said.

"We're on the loose tonight," the other woman said. "But Edith's car is in the garage."

"If you had a car now, we'd go over and see him," Edith said. She looked at me. "You could tell Patterson you wanted to be a teacher. You'd have something in common."

I finished my beer. I hadn't eaten anything all day except some peanuts. It was hard to keep listening and talking.

"Let's have three more, please, Jerry," the first woman said to the bartender.

"Thank you," I said.

"You'd get along with Patterson," Edith said.

"So call him," I said. I thought it was just talk.

"I wouldn't do that," she said. "He could make an excuse. We just show up on his porch, he'll have to let us in." She sipped her beer.

"So let's go!" the first woman said. "What're we waiting for? Where'd you say the car is?"

"There's a car a few blocks from here," I said. "But I don't know."

"Do you want to go or don't you?" Edith said.

"He said he does," the first woman said. "We'll get a six-pack to take with us."

"I only have thirty cents," I said.

"Who needs your goddamn money?" Edith said. "We need your goddamn car. Jerry, let's have three more. And a six-pack to go."

"Here's to Patterson," the first woman said when the beer came. "To Patterson and his highballs."

"He'll drop his cookies," Edith said.

"Drink up," the first woman said.

On the sidewalk we headed south, away from town. I walked between the two women. It was about ten o'clock.

"I could drink one of those beers now," I said.

"Help yourself," Edith said.

She opened the sack and I reached in and tore a can loose.

"We think he's home," Edith said.

"Patterson," the other woman said. "We don't know for sure. But we think so."

"How much farther?" Edith said.

I stopped, raised the beer, and drained half the can. "The next block," I said. "I'm staying with my parents. It's their place."

"I guess there's nothing wrong with it," Edith said. "But I'd say you're kind of old for that."

"That's not polite, Edith," the other woman said.

"Well, that's the way I am," Edith said. "He'll have to get used to it, that's all. That's the way I am."

"That's the way she is," the other woman said.

I finished the beer and tossed the can into some weeds.

"Now how far?" Edith said.

"This is it. Right here. I'll try and get the car key," I said.

"Well, hurry up," Edith said.

"We'll wait outside," the other woman said.

"Jesus!" Edith said.   80

I unlocked the door and went downstairs. My father was in his pajamas, watching television. It was warm in the apartment and I leaned against the jamb for a minute and ran a hand over my eyes.

"I had a couple of beers," I said. "What are you watching?"

"John Wayne," he said. "It's pretty good. Sit down and watch it. Your mother hasn't come in yet."

My mother worked the swing shift at Paul's, a *hofbrau* restaurant. My father didn't have a job. He used to work in the woods, and then he got hurt. He'd had a settlement, but most of that was gone now. I asked him for a loan of two hundred dollars when my wife left me, but he refused. He had tears in his eyes when he said no and he hoped I wouldn't hold it against him. I'd said it was all right, I wouldn't hold it against him.

I knew he was going to say no this time too. But I sat down on the other end of the   85
couch and said, "I met a couple of women who asked me if I'd give them a ride home."

"What'd you tell them?" he said.

"They're waiting for me upstairs," I said.

"Just let them wait," he said. "Somebody'll come along. You don't want to get mixed up with that." He shook his head. "You really didn't show them where we live, did you? They're not really upstairs?" He moved on the couch and looked again at the television. "Anyway, your mother took the keys with her." He nodded slowly, still looking at the television.

"That's okay," I said. "I don't need the car. I'm not going anywhere."

I got up and looked into the hallway, where I slept on a cot. There was an ashtray,   90
a Lux clock, and a few old paperbacks on a table beside the cot. I usually went to bed at midnight and read until the lines of print went fuzzy and I fell asleep with the light on and the book in my hands. In one of the paperbacks I was reading there was something I remembered telling my wife. It made a terrific impression on me. There's a man who has a nightmare and in the nightmare he dreams he's dreaming and wakes to see a man standing at his bedroom window. The dreamer is so terrified he can't move, can hardly breathe. The man at the window stares into the room and then begins to pry off the screen. The dreamer can't move. He'd like to scream, but he can't get his breath. But the man having the nightmare knows.

Telling it to my wife, I'd felt the blood come to my face and my scalp prickle. But she wasn't interested.

"That's only writing," she said. "Being betrayed by somebody in your own family, *there's* a real nightmare for you."

I could hear them shaking the outside door. I could bear footsteps on the sidewalk over my window.

"Goddamn that bastard!" I heard Edith say.

I went into the bathroom for a long time and then I went upstairs and let myself   95
out. It was cooler, and I did up the zipper on my jacket. I started walking to Paul's. If I got there before my mother went off duty, I could have a turkey sandwich. After that I could go to Kirby's newsstand and look through the magazines. Then I could go to the apartment to bed and read the books until I read enough and I slept.

The women, they weren't there when I left, and they wouldn't be there when I got back.

MARGARET ATWOOD

Margaret Atwood was born in 1939 in Ottawa and grew up in northern Ontario, Quebec, and Toronto. She received her undergraduate degree from Victoria College at the University of Toronto and her master's degree from Radcliffe College. Acclaimed for her talent for portraying both personal and worldly problems of universal concern, Ms. Atwood's work has been published in more than thirty languages.

The following story is from the collection *Good Bones and Simple Murders* published in 1983.

Happy Endings

John and Mary meet.
What happens next?
If you want a happy ending, try A.

A.

John and Mary fall in love and get married. They both have worthwhile and remunerative jobs which they find stimulating and challenging. They buy a charming house. Real estate values go up. Eventually, when they can afford live-in help, they have two children, to whom they are devoted. The children turn out well. John and Mary have a stimulating and challenging sex life and worthwhile friends. They go on fun vacations together. They retire. They both have hobbies which they find stimulating and challenging. Eventually they die. This is the end of the story.

B.

Mary falls in love with John but John doesn't fall in love with Mary. He merely uses her body for selfish pleasure and ego gratification of a tepid kind. He comes to her apartment twice a week and she cooks him dinner, you'll notice that he doesn't even consider her worth the price of a dinner out, and after he's eaten dinner he fucks her and after that he falls asleep, while she does the dishes so he won't think she's untidy, having all those dirty dishes lying around, and puts on fresh lipstick so she'll look good when he wakes up, but when he wakes up he doesn't even notice, he puts on his socks and his shorts and his pants and his shirt and his tie and his shoes, the reverse order from the one in which he took them off. He doesn't take off Mary's clothes, she takes them off herself, she acts as if she's dying for it every time, not because she likes sex exactly, she doesn't, but she wants John to think she does because if they do it often enough surely he'll get used to her, he'll come to depend on her and they will get married, but John goes out the door with hardly so much as a good-night and three days later he turns up at six o'clock and they do the whole thing over again.

Mary gets run-down. Crying is bad for your face, everyone knows that and so does Mary but she can't stop. People at work notice. Her friends tell her John is a rat, a pig, a dog, he isn't good enough for her, but she can't believe it. Inside John, she thinks, is another John, who is much nicer. This other John will emerge like a butterfly from a cocoon, a Jack from a box, a pit from a prune, if the first John is only squeezed enough.

One evening John complains about the food. He has never complained about her food before. Mary is hurt.

Her friends tell her they've seen him in a restaurant with another woman, whose name is Madge. It's not even Madge that finally gets to Mary: it's the restaurant. John has never taken Mary to a restaurant. Mary collects all the sleeping pills and aspirins she can find, and takes them and a half a bottle of sherry. You can see what kind of a woman she is by the fact that it's not even whiskey. She leaves a note for John. She hopes he'll discover her and get her to the hospital in time and repent and then they can get married, but this fails to happen and she dies.

John marries Madge and everything continues as in A.

C.

John, who is an older man, falls in love with Mary, and Mary, who is only twenty-two, feels sorry for him because he's worried about his hair falling out. She sleeps with him even though she's not in love with him. She met him at work. She's in love with someone called James, who is twenty-two also and not yet ready to settle down. John on the contrary settled down long ago: this is what is bothering him. John has a steady, respectable job and is getting ahead in his field, but Mary isn't impressed by him, she's impressed by James, who has a motorcycle and a fabulous record collection. But James is often away on his motorcycle, being free. Freedom isn't the same for girls, so in the meantime Mary spends Thursday evenings with John.

Thursdays are the only days John can get away.

John is married to a woman called Madge and they have two children, a charming house which they bought just before the real estate values went up, and hobbies which they find stimulating and challenging, when they have the time. John tells Mary how important she is to him, but of course he can't leave his wife because a commitment is a commitment. He goes on about this more than is necessary and Mary finds it boring, but older men can keep it up longer so on the whole she has a fairly good time.

One day James breezes in on his motorcycle with some top-grade California hybrid and James and Mary get higher than you'd believe possible and they climb into bed. Everything becomes very underwater, but along comes John, who has a key to Mary's apartment. He finds them stoned and entwined. He's hardly in any position to be jealous, considering Madge, but nevertheless he's overcome with despair. Finally he's middle-aged, in two years he'll be as bald as an egg and he can't stand it. He purchases a handgun, saying he needs it for target practice—this is the thin part of the plot, but it can be dealt with later—and shoots the two of them and himself. Madge, after a suitable period of mourning, marries an understanding man called Fred and everything continues as in A, but under different names.

D.

Fred and Madge have no problems. They get along exceptionally well and are good at working out any little difficulties that may arise. But their charming house is by the seashore and one day a giant tidal wave approaches. Real estate values go down. The rest of the story is about what caused the tidal wave and how they escape from it. They do, though thousands drown, but Fred and Madge are virtuous and grateful, and continue as in A.

E.

Yes, but Fred has a bad heart. The rest of the story is about how kind and understanding they both are until Fred dies. Then Madge devotes herself to charity work until the end of A. If you like, it can be "Madge," "cancer," "guilty and confused," and "bird watching."

F.

If you think this is all too bourgeois, make John a revolutionary and Mary a counter-espionage agent and see how far that gets you. Remember, this is Canada. You'll still end up with A, though in between you may get a lustful brawling saga of passionate involvement, a chronicle of our times, sort of.

You'll have to face it, the endings are the same however you slice it. Don't be deluded by any other endings, they're all fake, either deliberately fake, with malicious intent to deceive, or just motivated by excessive optimism if not by downright sentimentality.

The only authentic ending is the one provided here:

John and Mary die. John and Mary die. John and Mary die.

So much for endings. Beginnings are always more fun. True connoisseurs, however, are known to favor the stretch in between, since it's the hardest to do anything with.

That's about all that can be said for plots, which anyway are just one thing after another, a what and a what and a what.

Now try How and Why.

Drama

A. R. GURNEY

Albert Ramsdell Gurney, Jr., was born on November 1, 1930. After attending boarding school at St. Paul's in New Hampshire and receiving a B.A. degree from Williams College in 1952, Gurney joined the U.S. Navy during the Korean War and wrote shows to entertain military personnel.

Following his discharge in 1955, he enrolled in the Yale School of Drama. In 1957, he married Mary (Molly) Foreman Goodyear, and the couple moved to Massachusetts where Gurney taught English and Latin at a boys' country day school. Later he joined the faculty at M.I.T. in Cambridge. Gurney is the recipient of many awards, notably a Drama Desk Award in 1971, a Rockefeller Award in 1977, and two Lucille Lortel Awards in 1989 and 1994. He is on the Artistic Board of Playwrights Horizons and is currently on leave from M.I.T.

Love Letters

INTRODUCTION

Here's a play that sort of sneaked up behind me. When I wrote it, I didn't think it was a play at all, and sent it to *The New Yorker,* which promptly sent it back. I had written it almost as an exercise when I was shifting from the manual typewriter to a Radio Shack computer. Possibly the facility of the electronic keyboard and the ease with which you could adjust your mistakes reminded me of the scratch of the fountain pen and indelibly personal penmanship which were so much a part of the letter-writing culture in which I grew up. In any case, after some hesitation, I decided to try performing the work myself by reading it with Holland Taylor, an actress friend of mine, at the New York Public Library. One thing led to another—slowly at first, with a second stage production at the Long Wharf in New Haven, and then Monday night offerings of various teams during the New York run of *The Cocktail Hour.* Little by little various actors of various ages began to take a crack at it, and before long *Love Letters* was touring the country, being translated into many foreign languages, and becoming the centerpiece of countless benefits at home and abroad. Only the English seem to agree with my initial reservations. To them it's still not a play and never will be, and they try to drive a stake through its heart every time it shows up.

ORIGINAL PRODUCTION

Love Letters was initially presented by the Long Wharf Theater (Arvin Brown, Artistic Director; M. Edgar Rosenblum, Executive Director) in New Haven, Connecticut, on November 3, 1988. It was directed by John Tillinger; the lighting was by Judy Rasmuson; and the production stage manager was Beverly J. Andreozzi. The cast was as follows:

Andrew Makepeace Ladd III	*John Rubinstein*
Melissa Gardner	*Joanna Gleason*

CHARACTERS

ANDREW MAKEPEACE LADD III
MELISSA GARDNER

AUTHOR'S NOTE

This is a play, or rather a sort of a play, which needs no theatre, no lengthy rehearsal, no special set, no memorization of lines, and no commitment from its two actors beyond the night of performance. It is designed simply to be read aloud by an actor and an actress of roughly the same age, sitting side by side at a table, in front of a group of people of any size. The actor might wear a dark gray suit, the actress a simple, expensive-looking dress. In a more formal production, the table and chairs might be reasonably elegant English antiques, and the actors' area may be isolated against a dark background by bright, focused lights. In performance, the piece would seem to work best if the actors didn't look at each other until the end, when Melissa might watch Andy as he reads his final letter. They *listen* eagerly and actively to each other along the way, however, much as we might listen to an urgent voice on a one-way radio, coming from far, far away.

DO'S AND DON'TS IN PRODUCING LOVE LETTERS

1. Don't use a curtain. Don't introduce music or singing or any other effects before the houselights dim or after the play is over.
2. The actors should enter and exit from the same side in a low light. The actor should pull out the actress's chair, she should sit, then he should sit, and then the lights come up and they do the play. In all entrances and exits, the woman should enter and leave the stage first, followed by the man. During the curtain call, they should take a bow on either side of the desk before meeting each other in front of it.
3. There should be no changing or adjusting of costumes between acts. The same outfit should be worn throughout.
4. No baby talk, please. When the actors read the earlier letters, they are still older people, looking back, reading what they wrote when they were younger.
5. No mugging, either. When the actors are receiving letters, they are simply recipients, reading letters in private, not people publicizing their reactions or making faces in front of a mirror.

6. If a decanter and water glasses are used, make sure that these do not become too much of a prop. If we see Melissa drinking all the time, she makes it simply a play about alcoholism.

7. Avoid crying. This applies particularly to Andy at the end. Let the audience do the crying, if it feels like it.

8. Don't mess around with the text. No embellishments, insertions, cuts, or silent mouthings, please. Trust what I wrote, perform it as written, and all will be well.

A.R. Gurney

PART I

ANDY: Andrew Makepeace Ladd, the Third, accepts with pleasure the kind invitation of Mr. and Mrs. Gilbert Channing Gardner for a birthday party in honor of their daughter Melissa on April 19th, 1937, at half past three o'clock . . .

MELISSA: Dear Andy: Thank you for the birthday present. I have a lot of Oz books, but not *The Lost Princess of Oz*. What made you give me that one? Sincerely yours, Melissa.

ANDY: I'm answering your letter about the book. When you came into second grade with that stuck-up nurse, you looked like a lost princess.

MELISSA: I don't believe what you wrote. I think my mother told your mother to get that book. I like the pictures more than the words. Now let's stop writing letters.

◆   ◆   ◆

ANDY: I will make my l's taller than my d's.

MELISSA: I will close up my a's and my o's.

ANDY: I will try to make longer p's. Pass it on.

MELISSA: You're funny.

◆   ◆   ◆

ANDY: Will you be my valentine?

MELISSA: Were you the one who sent me a valentine saying "Will you be my valentine?"

ANDY: Yes I sent it.

MELISSA: Then I will be. Unless I have to kiss you.

◆   ◆   ◆

ANDY: When it's warmer out, can I come over and swim in your pool?

MELISSA: No you can't. I have a new nurse named Miss Hawthorne who thinks you'll give me infantile paralysis.

ANDY: Will you help me go down and get the milk and cookies during recess?

MELISSA: I will if you don't ask me to marry you again.

BOTH: I will not write personal notes in class, I will not write personal notes in class, I will not . . .

◆   ◆   ◆

ANDY: Merry Christmas and Happy New Year. Love, Andy Ladd.

MELISSA: I made this card myself. It's not Santa Claus. It's a kangaroo jumping over a glass of orange juice. Do you like it? I like YOU. Melissa.

ANDY: My mother says I have to apologize in writing. I apologize for sneaking into the girl's bath-house while you were changing into your bathing suit. Tell Miss Hawthorne I apologize to her, too.

MELISSA: Here is a picture I drew of you and me without our bathing suits on. Guess which one is you. Don't show this to ANYONE. I love you.

ANDY: Here is a picture of Miss Hawthorne without her bathing suit on.

MELISSA: You can't draw very well, can you?

◆   ◆   ◆

ANDY: Thank you for sending me the cactus plant stuck in the little donkey. I've gotten lots of presents here in the hospital and I have to write thank-you notes for every one. I hate it here. My throat is sore all the time from where they cut out my tonsils. They give me lots of ice cream, but they also take my temperature the wrong way.

◆   ◆   ◆

MELISSA: Merry Christmas and Happy New Year. Why did they send you to another school this year?

ANDY: Merry Christmas. They think I should be with all boys.

MELISSA: You made me promise to send you a postcard. This is it.

ANDY: You're supposed to write personal notes on the backs of postcards. For example, here are some questions to help you think of things to say. Do you like Lake Saranac? Is it fun visiting your grandmother? Are your parents really getting divorced? Can you swim out into the deep part of that lake, or does Miss Hawthorne make you stay in the shallow part where it's all roped off? Is there anybody there my age? I mean boys. Please write answers to all these questions.

MELISSA: No. No. Yes. Yes. No.

◆   ◆   ◆

ANDY: Dear Melissa. Remember me? Andy Ladd? They've sent me to camp so I can be with all boys again. This is quiet hour so we have to write home, but I've already done that, so I'm writing you. There's a real Indian here named Iron Crow who takes us on Nature walks and teaches us six new plants a day. This is O.K., except he forgot about poison ivy. I won the backstroke, which gives me two and a half gold stars. If I get over fifty gold stars by Parent's Day, then I win a Leadership Prize which is what my father expects of me. I'm making a napkin-ring in shop which is worth four stars and which is either for my mother or for you. I hope you'll write me back, because when the mail comes every morning, they shout out our names and it would be neat to walk up and get a letter from a girl.

MELISSA: Help! Eeeek! Yipes! I can't write LETTERS! It took me HOURS just to write "Dear Andy." I write my father because I miss him so much, but to write a BOY! Hell's Bells and Oriental Smells! I'm sending you this picture I drew of our cat instead. Don't you love his expression? It's not quite right, but I tried three times. I drew those jiggly lines around his tail because sometimes the tail behaves like a completely separate person. I love that tail. There's a part of me that feels like that tail. Oh, and here's some bad news. My mother's gotten married again to a man named Hooper McPhail. HELP! LEMME OUTA HERE!

ANDY: I liked the cat. Is that the cat you threw in the pool that time when we were playing over at your house in third grade?

MELISSA: No, that was a different cat entirely.

♦ ♦ ♦

ANDY: This is a dumb Halloween card and wouldn't scare anyone, but I'm really writing about dancing school. My parents say I have to go this year, but I don't see why I have to. I can't figure out why they keep sending us away from girls and then telling us we have to be with them. Are you going to dancing school also? Just write Yes or No, since you hate writing.

MELISSA: Yes.

♦ ♦ ♦

ANDY: Dear Mrs. McPhail. I want to apologize to you for my behavior in the back of your car coming home last night from dancing school. Charlie and I were just goofing around and I guess it just got out of hand. I'm sorry you had to pull over to the curb and I'm sorry we tore Melissa's dress. My father says you should send me the bill and I'll pay for it out of my allowance.

MELISSA: Dear Andy. Mummy brought your letter up here to Lake Placid. She thought it was cute. I thought it was dumb. I could tell your father made you write it. You and I both know that the fight in the car was really Charlie's fault. And Charlie never apologized, thank God. That's why I like him, actually. As for you, you shouldn't always do what your parents WANT, Andy. Even at dancing school you're always doing just the RIGHT THING all the time. You're a victim of your parents sometimes. That was why I picked Charlie to do the rumba with me that time. He at least hacks around occasionally. I'm enclosing a picture I drew of a dancing bear on a chain. That's you, Andy. Sometimes. I swear.

ANDY: I know it seems jerky, but I like writing actually. I like writing compositions in English, I like writing letters, I like writing you. I wanted to write that letter to your mother because I knew you'd see it, so it was like talking to you when you weren't here. And when you couldn't *interrupt.* (Hint, hint.) My father says everyone should write letters as much as they can. It's a dying art. He says letters are a way of presenting yourself in the best possible light to another person. I think that, too.

MELISSA: I think you sound too much like your father. But I'm not going to argue by MAIL and anyway the skiing's too good.

ANDY: Get well soon. I'm sorry you broke your leg.

MELISSA: Mummy says I broke it purposely because I'm a self-destructive person and went down Whiteface Mountain without asking permission. All I know is I wish I had broken my arm instead so I'd have a good excuse not to write LETTERS. I'm enclosing a picture I drew of the bed pan. I'm SERIOUS! Don't you love its shape?

◆ ◆ ◆

ANDY: Andrew M. Ladd, III, accepts with pleasure the kind invitation of Mrs. R. Ferguson Brown for a dinner in honor of her granddaughter Melissa Gardner before the Children's Charity Ball.

MELISSA: I'm writing this letter because I'm scared if I called you up, I'd start crying, right on the telephone. I'm really MAD at you, Andy. Don't you know that when you're invited to a dinner before a dance, you're supposed to dance with the person giving it at least TWICE. And I don't mean my grandmother either. That's why they *give* dinner parties. So people get *danced* with. I notice you danced with Ginny Waters, but you never danced with me once. I just think it's rude, that's all. Straighten up and fly right, Andy. How do you expect to get anywhere in life if you're rude to women? Nuts to you, Andy, and that goes double on Sunday!

ANDY: I didn't dance with you because I've got a stretched groin. If you don't know what that means, look it up some time. I was going to tell you in person but I got embarrassed. I stretched it playing hockey last week. The only reason I danced with Ginny Waters is she takes tiny steps, but you always make me do those big spins and we could have gotten into serious trouble. I tried it out at home with my mother first, and it hurt like hell. That's why I didn't dance with you. I'm using a heating pad now and maybe we can dance next week at the junior assemblies.

MELISSA: I don't believe that hockey stuff. I think Ginny Waters stretched your groin. And next time you cut in, I'm going to stretch the other one.

ANDY: Huh? You obviously don't know what a groin is.

MELISSA: You obviously don't know what a joke is.

◆ ◆ ◆

MELISSA: Merry Christmas and Happy New Year. Guess what? I'm going to a psychiatrist now. My mother says it will do me a world of good. Don't tell anyone, though. It's supposed to be a big secret.

ANDY: Merry Christmas and Happy New Year. I have a question and would you please write the answer *by mail,* because sometimes when you call, my mother listens on the telephone, and when she doesn't my little brother does. Here's the question: do you talk about sex with the psychiatrist?

MELISSA: I talk about sex all the time. It's terribly expensive, but I think it's worth it.

ANDY: If I went to a psychiatrist, I'd talk about you. Seriously. I would. I think about you quite often.

MELISSA: Sometimes I think you just like me because I'm richer than you are. Sometimes I really have that feeling. I think you like the pool, and the elevator in my grandmother's house, and Simpson in his butler's coat coming in with gingerale and cookies on a silver tray. I think you like all that stuff just as much as you like me.

ANDY: All I know is my mother keeps saying you'd make a good match. She says if I ever married you, I'd be set up for life. But I think it's really just physical attraction. That's why I liked going into the elevator with you at your grandmother's that time. Want to try it again?

◆   ◆   ◆

Melissa: HELP! LEMME OUTA HERE! They shipped me off to this nunnery! It's the end of the absolute WORLD! We have to wear these sappy middy-blouses, and learn POSTURE in gym, and speak French out LOUD in class. "Aide-moi, mon chevalier!" Oh God, it's crappy here. All the girls squeal and shriek, and you can hear them barfing in the bathroom after the evening meal. We can only go to Hartford one day a week IF we can find a chaperone, and there are only two dances with boys a year, and if we're caught drinking, even *beer,* it's wham, bam, onto the next train and home, which is WORSE! Can you come visit me some Sunday afternoon? We can invite boys to tea from four to six. There are all these biddies sitting around keeping watch, but if the weather's good, we could walk up and down the driveway before we have to sign in for evening prayers. They've made me room with this fat, spoiled Cuban bitch who has nine pairs of shoes, and all she does is lie on her bed and listen to *Finian's Rainbow.* "How are Things in Glocca Morra?" Who gives a shit how things are *there?* It's here where they're miserable. The walls of this cell are puke-green, and you can't pin anything up except school banners and pictures of your stupid family. What family? Am I supposed to sit and look at a picture of Hooper McPhail? Come save me, Andy. Or at least WRITE! Just so I hear a boy's voice, even on paper.

Andy: Just got your letter. They shipped me off too. Last-minute decision. Your mother told my mother it would do me good. She said I was a diamond in the rough. I'll write as soon as I'm smoother.

Melissa: Dear Diamond. You, too? Oh, I give up. Why do they keep pushing us together and then pulling us apart? I think we're all being brought up by a bunch of foolish farts. Now we'll *have* to write letters which I hate. But don't let them smooth you out, Andy. I like the rough parts. In fact, sometimes I think you ought to be a little rougher. Love. Me.

Andy: I'm very sorry to be so late in replying but I haven't had much time. I also have a lot of obligations. I have to write my parents once a week, and three out of four grandparents, *separately,* once a month, and Minnie, our cook, who sent me a box of fudge. Plus I have all my schoolwork to do, including a composition once a week for English and another for history. My grandmother gave me a new Parker 51 and some writing paper with my name on it as a going-away present, but still, that's a lot of writing I have to do. Last week I was so tied up I skipped my weekly letter to my parents, and my father called the school long-distance about it. I had to go up on the carpet in front of the Rector and say I wasn't sick or anything, I was just working, and so I had to write my parents three pages to make up for the week I missed. So that's why I haven't written till now. (Whew!) School is going well, I guess. In English, we're now finishing up Milton's *Paradise Lost.* In history, we're studying the causes and results of the Thirty Years War. I think the Catholics caused it. In Latin, we're translating Cicero's orations against Catiline. "How long, O Catiline, will you abuse out patience?" When I get home, I'm going to try that on my little brother. In French, we have to sit and listen to Mr. Thatcher read out loud all the parts in *Andromache,* by Jean Racine. It's supposed to be a great masterpiece, but the class comes right after football practice, so it's a little hard to stay awake. In Sacred Studies, we have to compare and contrast all four gospels. It's hard to believe they're all talking about the same guy. In Math, we're trying to factor with two unknowns. Sometimes I let X be me and Y be you, and you'd be amazed how it comes out.

My grades are pretty good. They post your weekly average outside study hall and last week I got 91.7 overall average. Not bad, eh? I got a letter from my grandfather telling me not to be first in my class because only the Jews are first. I wrote him and told him I wasn't first, but even if I was, there are no Jews here. We have a few Catholics, but they're not too smart, actually. I don't think you can be smart and Catholic at the same time.

I was elected to the Student Council and I'm arguing for three things: one, I think we should have outside sports, rather than keeping them all intramural. I think it would be better to play with Exeter than just play with ourselves. Two, I think we should have more than one dance a year. I think female companionship can be healthy occasionally, even for younger boys. And three, I think we should only have to go to chapel *once* on Sunday. I think it's important to pray to be a better guy, and all that, but if you have to do it all day long, you can get quite boring. And if you get boring to yourself, think how boring you must be to God.

I'm playing left tackle on the third team, and I'll be playing hockey, *of course,* this winter, and I think I'll try rowing this spring since I always stank at baseball.

Now I have to memorize the last five lines of *Paradise Lost.* Hold it . . . Back in a little while . . . There. That wasn't so hard, maybe because it reminds me of you and me, sent away from home. I'll write it down for you:

> Some natural tears they dropp'd, but wip'd them soon;
> The World was all before them, where to choose
> Their place of rest, and providence their guide:
> They hand in hand with wand'ring steps and slow,
> Through Eden took their solitary way.

There you are. I wrote that without looking at the book, and it's right, too, because I just checked it, word by word. It's not so bad, is it? In fact, it sounds great if you recite it in the bathroom, when no one is in the shower or taking a dump. Love, Andy.

MELISSA: Thanks for your letter which was a little too long. I guess you have a lot of interesting things to say, Andy, but some of them are not terribly interesting to me. I want to hear more about your FEELINGS. For instance, here are MY feelings. This place STINKS, but I don't want to go back home because Hooper McPhail stinks, and I haven't heard of another boarding school that DOESN'T stink, which means that LIFE stinks in general. Those are my feelings for this week. Write soon. Love, me.

ANDY: One feeling I have almost all the time is that I miss my dog, Porgy. Remember him? Our black cocker who peed in the vestibule when you patted him when you came back to our house after the skating party. I miss him all the time. Some of the masters up here have dogs, and when I pat them I miss Porgy even more. I dream about him. I wrote a composition about him for English called "Will He Remember?" and got a 96 on it. It was about how I remember him, but will he remember me? I have a picture of him on my bureau right next to my parents. By the way, could I have your picture, too?

MELISSA: Here's a picture of me taken at the Hartford bus station. I was all set to run away and then decided not to. This is all you get until I get my braces off Christmas vacation. Don't look at my hair. I'm changing it. By the way, do you know a boy there named Spencer Willis? There's a girl here, Annie Abbott, who met him in Edgartown last summer and thinks he's cute. Would you ask him what he thinks of her?

ANDY: Spencer Willis says Annie Abbott is a potential nympho. I'm sorry to tell you this, but it's true.

MELISSA: Annie says to tell Spencer he's a total turkey. Tell him she'd write and say so herself but she's scared of barfing all over the page.

ANDY: Do you get out for Thanksgiving? We don't, because of the war.

MELISSA: We do, but I don't. I've been grounded just for smoking one lousy Chesterfield out behind the art studio. So now I have to stay here and eat stale turkey with Cubans and Californians. That's all right. I was supposed to meet Mummy in New York, but it looks like she can't be there anyway because she's going to Reno to divorce Hooper McPhail. Yippee! Yay! He was a jerk and a pill, and he used to bother me in bed, if you must know.

◆ ◆ ◆

ANDY: I liked seeing you Christmas vacation, particularly with your braces off. I really liked necking with you in the Watson's rumpus room. Will you go steady with me?

MELISSA: I don't believe in going steady. It's against my religion. I hated that stuff with all those pairs of pimply people in the Watson's basement, leaning on each other, swaying to that dumb music with all the lights off. If that's going steady, I say screw it. My mother says you should meet as many boys as you can before you have to settle down and marry one of them. That way you'll make less of a mistake. It didn't work for her but maybe it will work for me.

ANDY: Can we at least go to the movies together during spring vacation?

MELISSA: I don't know, Andy. I like seeing you, but I don't want to go home much any more. My mother gets drunk a lot, if you must know, and comes into my room all the time, and talks endlessly about I don't know what because she slurs her words. The only really good time I had was when I came over to your house Christmas Eve. That was fun. Singing around the piano, hanging up the stockings, playing Chinese Checkers with your brother, helping your mother with the gravy. I liked all that. You may not have as much money as we have, but you've got a better family. So spring vacation I'm going to visit my grandmother in Palm Beach. Ho hum. At least I'll get a tan. P.S. Enclosed is a picture I drew of your dog Porgy who I remember from Christmas Eve. The nose is wrong, but don't you think the eyes are good?

ANDY: I'm stroking the 4th crew now. Yesterday, I rowed number 2 on the 3rd. Tomorrow I may row number 6 on the 2nd or number 4 on the 5th. Who knows? You get out there and work your butt off, and the launch comes alongside and looks you over, and the next day they post a list on the bulletin board saying who will row what. They never tell you what you did right or wrong, whether you're shooting your slide or bending your back or what. They just post the latest results for all to see.

Some days I think I'm doing really well, and I get sent down two crews. One day I was obviously hacking around, and they moved me UP. There's no rhyme or reason. I went to Mr. Clark who is the head of rowing and I said, "Look, Mr. Clark. There's something wrong about this system. People are constantly moving up and down and no one knows why. It doesn't seem to have anything to do with whether you're good or bad, strong or weak, coordinated or uncoordinated. It all seems random, *sir.*" And Mr. Clark said "That's life, Andy."

And walked away. Well maybe that's life, but it doesn't *have* to be life. You could easily make rules which made sense, so the good ones moved up and the bad ones moved down, and people *knew* what was going on. I'm serious. I'm thinking about going to law school later on.

MELISSA: Your last letter was too much about rowing. Do you know a boy there named Steve Scully. I met him down in Florida, and he said he went to your school, and was on the first crew. He said he was the fastest rower in the boat. Is that true, or was he lying? I think he may have been lying.

ANDY: Steve Scully was lying. He doesn't even row. And if he did, and rowed faster than everyone else in the same boat, he'd mess the whole thing up. He said he got to second base with you. Is that true?

MELISSA: Steve Scully is a lying son of a bitch, and you can tell him I said so.

◆　◆　◆

ANDY: Will you be around this summer? I think I've got a summer job caddying, so no more camp, Thank God.

MELISSA: I'll be visiting my father in California. I haven't seen him in four years. He has a new wife, and I have two half-sisters now. It's like going to find a whole new family. Oh I hope, I hope . . .

ANDY: Do you like California?

◆　◆　◆

ANDY: Write me about California. How's your second family?

◆　◆　◆

ANDY: Did you get my letters? I checked with your mother, and I had the correct address. How come you haven't answered me all summer?

ANDY: Back at school now. Hope everything's O.K. with you. Did you get my letters out in California, or did you have a wicked step-mother who confiscated them?

MELISSA: I don't want to talk about California. Ever. For a while I thought I had two families, but now I know I really don't have any. You're very lucky, Andy. You don't know it, but you are. But maybe I'm lucky, too. In another way. I was talking to Mrs. Wadsworth who comes in from Hartford to teach us art. She says I have a real talent both in drawing and in painting, and she's going to try me out in pottery as well. She says some afternoon she's going to take me just by myself to her studio in Hartford, and we'll do life drawings of her lover in just a jock-strap! Don't laugh. She says art and sex are sort of the same thing.

◆　◆　◆

ANDY: Dear Melissa. I have four questions, so please concentrate. One: will you come up to the mid-winter dance? Two, If so, can you arrive on the eleven-twenty-two Friday night train? Three, Does the Rector's wife have to write your Headmistress telling her where you will be staying? Four. Does the Rector's wife also have to write your mother?

MELISSA: The answer is yes, except for my mother, who won't care.

◆   ◆   ◆

ANDY: I have to tell you this, right off the bat. I'm really goddamn mad at you. I invite you up here for the only dance my class has been able to go to since we got here, I meet you at the train and buy you a vanilla milk-shake and bring you out to school in a taxi, I score two goals for you during the hockey game the next afternoon, I buy you the eight dollar gardenia corsage, I make sure your dance card is filled with the most regular guys in the school, and then what happens? I now hear that you sneaked off with Bob Bartram during the Vienna Waltz, and necked with him in the coatroom. I heard that from two guys! And then Bob himself brought it up yesterday at breakfast. He says he French-kissed you and touched BOTH your breasts. I tried to punch him but Mr. Enbody restrained me. I'm really sore, Melissa. I consider this a betrayal of everything I hold near and dear. Particularly since you would hardly even let me kiss you goodnight after we had cocoa at the Rector's. And you know what I'm talking about, too! So don't expect any more letters from me, or any telephone calls either during spring vacation. Sincerely yours.

MELISSA: Sorry, sorry, sorry. I AM! I HATE that Bob Bartram. I hated him even when I necked with him. I know you won't believe that, but it's true. You can be attracted to someone you hate. Well, maybe *you* can't, but I can. So all right, I necked with him, but he never touched my chest, and if he says he did, he should be strung up by his testicles. You tell him that, for me, at breakfast! Anyway, I got carried away, Andy, and I'm a stupid bitch, and I'm sorry. I felt so guilty about it that I didn't want to kiss you after the cocoa.

And besides, Andy. Gulp. Er. Ah. Um. How do I say this? With you it's different. You're like a friend to me. You're like a brother. I've never had a brother, and I don't have too many friends, so you're both, Andy. You're it. My mother says you must never say that to a man, but I'm saying it anyway and it's true. Maybe if I didn't know you so well, maybe if I hadn't grown up with you, maybe if we hadn't written all these goddamn LETTERS all the time, I could have kissed you the way I kissed Bob Bartram.

Oh, but PLEASE let's see each other spring vacation. Please. I count on you, Andy. I NEED you. I think sometimes I'd go stark raving mad if I didn't have you to hold onto. I really think that sometimes. Much love.

◆   ◆   ◆

MELISSA: Happy Easter! I know no one sends Easter cards except maids, but here's mine anyway, drawn with my own hot little hands. I drew those tears on that corny bunny on the left because it misses you so much, but maybe I've just made it all the cornier.

◆   ◆   ◆

MELISSA: Greetings from Palm Beach. Decided to visit my grandmother. Yawn, yawn. I'm a whiz at backgammon and gin-rummy. Hear you took Gretchen Lascelles to see *Quo Vadis* and sat in the *loges* and put your arm around her and smoked! Naughty, naughty!

◆   ◆   ◆

MELISSA: Back at school, but not for long, that's for sure. Caught nipping gin in the woods with Bubbles Harriman. Have to pack my trunk by tonight and be out tomorrow. Mummy's frantically pulling strings all over the Eastern Seaboard for another school.

Mrs. Wadsworth, my art teacher, thinks I should chuck it all and go to Italy and study art. What do you think? Oh, please write, Andy, PLEASE. I need your advice, or are you too busy thinking about Gretchen Lascelles?

◆　◆　◆

ANDY: To answer your question about Italy, I think you're too young to go. My Mother said she had a roommate once who went to Italy in the summer, and the Italians pinched her all the time on the rear end. Mother says she became thoroughly over-stimulated. So I think you should go to another school, graduate, go to college, and maybe after that, when you're more *mature*, you could go to Italy. That's my advice, for what it's worth, which is probably not much, the way things are going between you and me.

◆　◆　◆

MELISSA: Here I am at Emma Willard's Academy for Young Lesbians. Help! Lemme outa here! "Plus ca change, plus c'est le same shit." Are you coming straight home this June because I am. I want to see you. Or are you still in love with Gretchen Lascelles?

ANDY: For your information, I'm not taking Gretchen Lascelles out any more. I brought her home after the Penneys' party, and my father caught us on the couch. He told me that he didn't care what kind of girls I took out, as long as I didn't bring them around my mother. Even though my mother was up in bed. Still, I guess Gretchen can be embarrassing to older people.

MELISSA: I hope to see you in June, then.

ANDY: Can't come home in June. Sorry. I have to go and be a counselor at the school camp for poor kids from the urban slums. I'm Vice President of my class now, and I'm supposed to set an example of social responsibility all through July. I'll be writing you letters, though, and I hope you'll write me.

MELISSA: I don't want to write letters all the time. I really don't. I want to see you.

ANDY: You just need more confidence in your letter-writing ability. Sometimes you manage to attain a very vivid style.

MELISSA: Won't you please just stop writing about writing, and come home and go to the Campbells' sports party before you go up to that stupid camp? PLEASE! I behave better when you're around. In PERSON! PLEASE!

◆　◆　◆

ANDY: Greetings from New Hampshire. This card shows the town we're near, where we sneak in and buy beer. We're cleaning the place up now, and putting out the boat docks, and caulking the canoes, because the kids arrive tomorrow. Gotta go. Write soon.

MELISSA: I miss you. I really wish you had come to the Campbells' sports party.

ANDY: Dear Melissa. Sandy McCarthy arrived from home for the second shift here at camp, and he told me all about the Campbells' sports party. He said you wore a two piece bathing suit and ran around goosing girls and pushing boys into the pool. Do you enjoy that sort of crap? He said the other girls were furious at you. Don't you want the respect of other women? Sandy also said you let Bucky Zeller put a tennis ball into your cleavage. Are you a nympho or what? Don't you ever like just sitting down somewhere and making conversation? Sandy says you're turning into a hot box. Do you like having that reputation? Hell, I thought there was a difference between you and Gretchen Lascelles. Maybe I was wrong. Don't you care about anything in this world except hacking around? Don't you feel any obligation to help the poor people, for example? Sometimes I think your big problem is you're so rich you don't have enough to do, and so you start playing grab-ass with people. I'm sorry to say these things, but what Sandy told me made me slightly disgusted, frankly.

♦   ♦   ♦

ANDY: I wrote you a letter from New Hampshire. Did you receive it?

♦   ♦   ♦

ANDY: Are you there, or are you visiting your grandmother, or what?

♦   ♦   ♦

ANDY: Are you sore at me? I'll bet you're sore at me.

♦   ♦   ♦

ANDY: I'm sorry. I apologize. I'm a stuffy bastard sometimes, aren't I?

♦   ♦   ♦

ANDY: The hell with you, then.

MELISSA: Oooh. Big, tough Andy using four-letter words like hell.

ANDY: Screw you!

MELISSA: Don't you wish you could!

ANDY: Everyone else seems to be.

MELISSA: Don't believe everything you read in the papers.

♦   ♦   ♦

MELISSA: Dear Andrew Makepeace Ladd, the Turd: I just want you to know you hurt me very much. I just want you to know that. Now let's just leave each other ALONE for a while. All right? All right.

♦   ♦   ♦

ANDY: Dear Melissa: My mother wrote me that your grandmother had died. Please accept my deepest sympathies.

MELISSA: Thank you for your note about my grandmother. I loved her a lot even though she could be a little boring.

ANDY: Congratulations on getting into Briarcliff. I hear it's great.

MELISSA: Thank you for your note about Briarcliff. It's not great and you know it. In fact, it's a total pit. But it's close to New York and I can take the train in and take drawing at the Institute three days a week. And in two years, if I stick it out, Mummy's promised that I can go live in Florence. I hope you like Yale.

ANDY: Would you consider coming to the Yale-Dartmouth game, Saturday, Oct. 28th?

MELISSA: I'll be there.

ANDY: Uh-oh. Damn! I'm sorry, Melissa. I have to cancel. My parents have decided to visit that weekend, and they come first, according to them. My mother says she'd love to have you with us, but my father thinks you can be somewhat distracting.

MELISSA: You and your parents. Let me know when you decide to grow up.

ANDY: How about the Harvard game, November 16th?

MELISSA: Do you plan to grow up at the Harvard game?

ANDY: Give me a chance. I might surprise you.

MELISSA: O.K. Let's give it a try. You should know that I'm even richer now than when you said I was rich, thanks to poor Granny. I plan to drive up to the front gate of Calhoun College in my new red Chrysler convertible, and sit there stark naked, honking my horn and drinking champagne and flashing at all the Freshmen.

ANDY: Here's the schedule. We'll have lunch at Calhoun around noon. Then drive out to the game. Then there's a Sea-Breeze party at the Fence Club afterwards, and an Egg Nog brunch at Saint Anthony's the next day. I'll reserve a room for you at the Taft or the Duncan, probably the Taft, since the Duncan is a pretty seedy joint.

MELISSA: Make it the Duncan. I hear the Taft is loaded with parents, all milling around the lobby, keeping tabs on who goes up in the elevators. Can't WAIT till the 16th.

ANDY: The Duncan it is. Hubba hubba, Goodyear rubba!

◆   ◆   ◆

MELISSA: Dear Andy. This is supposed to be a thank-you note for the Yale-Harvard weekend, but I don't feel like writing one, and I think you know why. Love, Melissa.

ANDY: Dear Melissa. I keep thinking about the weekend. I can't get it out of my mind. It wasn't much good, was it? I don't mean just the Duncan, I mean the whole thing. We didn't really click, did we? I always had the sense that you were looking over my shoulder, looking for someone else, and ditto with me. Both of us seemed to be expecting something different from what was there.

As for the Hotel Duncan, I don't know. Maybe I had too many Sea-Breezes. Maybe you did. But what I really think is that there were too many people in that hotel room. Besides you and me, it seemed my mother was there, egging us on, and my father, shaking his head, and *your* mother zonked out on the couch, and Miss Hawthorne and your *grand*mother, sitting on the sidelines, watching us like hawks. Anyway, I was a dud. I admit it. I'm sorry. I went to the Infirmary on Monday and talked to the Doctor about it, and he said these things happen all the time. Particularly when there's a lot of pressure involved. The woman doesn't have to worry about it so much, but the man does. Anyway, it didn't happen with Gretchen Lascelles. You can write her and ask her if you want.

MELISSA: You know what I think is wrong? These letters. These goddamn letters. That's what's wrong with us, in my humble opinion. I know you more from your LETTERS

MELISSA: Buon Natale . . .

ANDY: Happy Birthday . . . Mother wrote you won an art prize in Perugia. She said it was a big deal. Congratulations . . .

MELISSA: Congratulations on making Scroll and Key, whatever that is . . .

ANDY: Merry Christmas from the Land of Oz . . .

MELISSA: Felice Navidad from the Costa del Sol . . .

ANDY: Happy Birthday from the Sterling Library . . .

MELISSA: Hear you graduated Summa Cum Laude and with all sorts of prizes. Sounds disgusting . . .

ANDY: Anchors Aweigh! Here I am, looking like Henry Fonda in *Mister Roberts,* writing this during the midwatch on the bridge of a giant attack aircraft carrier, churning through the Mediterranean, in the wake of Odysseus and Lord Nelson and Richard Halliburton. You'll be pleased to know our guns are loaded, our planes in position, and our radar is constantly scanning the skies, all designed simply and solely to protect you against Communism. The next time you see me, I want you to salute.

MELISSA: I should have known you'd join the Navy. Now you can once again be with all boys.

ANDY: We come into La Spezia in January. Could we meet?

MELISSA: Sorry. I'll be in Zermatt in January.

ANDY: Ship will be in Mediterranean all spring. We'll come into Naples, March 3, 4, or 5? How about standing on the pier and waving us in?

MELISSA: As the French say, "Je suis desolée." Am meeting Mother in Paris in March. Why don't you sail up the Seine?

ANDY: Merry Christmas from Manila. I've been transferred to an Admiral's staff . . .

MELISSA: Happy New Year from Aspen . . .

ANDY: What are you doing in Aspen?

MELISSA: Going steadily down hill.

ANDY: Hello from Hong Kong . . .

MELISSA: Goodbye to San Francisco . . .

ANDY: Konichiwa. Ohayo Gozaimas. Shore duty in Japan

MELISSA: Hey, you! Rumor hath it you're hooked up with some little Jap bar-girl out there. Say it isn't so . . .

◆   ◆   ◆

MELISSA: Mother wrote that you're living with some Japanese geisha girl and your family's all upset. Is that TRUE?

◆   ◆   ◆

MELISSA: Did you get my letter? You're so far away, and your Navy address is so peculiar that I'm not sure I'm reaching you. I hear you're seriously involved with a lovely Japanese lady. Would you write me about her?

M
D(
is
A**
M
A**
M
A**

M
tat
A**
we
isn
tol
I h
I'v
for
jur
to
So

A**

A**

A**
rio

A**
the

A**

M
all

ANDY: Merry Christmas and Happy New Year. I thought you might appreciate this card. It's a print by the Nineteenth Century artist Hiroshige. It's called "Two Lovers Meeting on a Bridge in the Rain." Love, Andy.

MELISSA: Hey, you sly dog! Are you getting subtle in your old age? Are you trying to TELL me something? If so, tell me MORE!

◆   ◆   ◆

MELISSA: I told my psychiatrist about the great love affair you're having in Japan. I said I felt suddenly terribly jealous. He said that most American men have to get involved with a dark-skinned woman before they can connect with the gorgeous blonde goddesses they really love. He brought up James Fennimore Cooper and Faulkner and John Ford movies and went on and on. Is that TRUE? Write me what you think. I'm dying to hear from you.

◆   ◆   ◆

MELISSA: Did you get my last letter? I hope I didn't sound flip. Actually I've just become involved with someone, too. His first name is Darwin and he works on Wall Street where he believes in the survival of the fittest. I'd love to hear from you.

◆   ◆   ◆

MELISSA: Your mother told my mother that you've decided to marry your Japanese friend and bring her home. Oh no! Gasp, Sob, Sigh. Say it isn't so.

◆   ◆   ◆

MELISSA: I've decided to marry Darwin. He doesn't know it yet, but he will. Won't you at least wish me luck?

◆   ◆   ◆

ANDY: Lieutenant Junior Grade Andrew M. Ladd, III, regrets that he is unable to accept the kind invitation of . . .

MELISSA: Dear Andy. Thank you for the lovely Japanese bowl. I'll put flowers in it when you come to visit us. *If* you come to visit us. And *if* you bring flowers. Maybe you'll just bring your Japanese war bride, and we can all sit around and discuss *Rashomon.* I know you'll like Darwin. When he laughs, it's like Pinocchio turning into a donkey. We're living in a carriage house in New Canaan close to the train station, and I've got a studio all of my own. P.S. Won't you PLEASE write me about your big romance? Mother says your parents won't even talk about it any more.

ANDY: Dear Melissa: I'm writing to tell you this. Outside of you, and I *mean* outside of you, this was probably the most important thing that ever happened to me. And I mean *was.* Because it's over, it's gone, and I'm coming home, and that's all I ever want to say about it, ever again.

◆   ◆   ◆

at this posh joint outside Boston, drying out for one hundred and fifty-five dollars a day. One of my problems is that I got slightly too dependent on the Kickapoo joy juice, a habit which they tell me I picked up during the party days back in Our Town. Another is that I slide into these terrible lows. Mummy says I drag everybody down, and I guess she's right. Aaaanyway, the result is that my Ex has taken over custody of the girls, and I'm holed up here, popping tranquilizers, talking my head off in single and group psychiatric sessions, and turning into probably the biggest bore in the greater Boston area.

ANDY: Have you thought about doing some painting again? That might help.

◆ ◆ ◆

ANDY: Did you get my note about taking up art? You were good, and you know it. You should keep it up.

MELISSA: I *did* get your note, I *have* taken it up, and it *helps*. Really. Thank you. I'm channeling my rage, enlarging my vision, all that. I hope all goes well with you and—wait, hold it, I'm looking it up in my little black book . . . ah hah! Jane! It's Jane. Hmmmm. I hope all's well with you and Jane.

ANDY: Merry Christmas from Andy and Jane Ladd. And Andrew the Fourth! Guess the name of the dog.

MELISSA: Porgy.

ANDY: You got it.

◆ ◆ ◆

MELISSA: Merry Christmas from San Antonio. Am trying the Southwest. I can see the most incredible shapes from my bedroom window. And there's also a pretty incredible shape now sleeping in my bed.

ANDY: Seasons Greetings from the Ladd family. (Mother wrote you were planning to get married again.)

MELISSA: I was. I did. I'm not now.

ANDY: Donner, Rhodes and McAlister announce the appointment to partnership of Mr. Andrew M. Ladd, III . . .

MELISSA: Dear Andy: Now you're such a hot-shot lawyer, could you help me get my children back? Darwin hardly lets me near them, and when he does, they behave as if I had some contagious disease. I wasn't much of a mother, but maybe I could improve, if I just had the legal responsibility

ANDY: Better stay out of this one . . .Our past connections . . . conflict of interest . . .

MELISSA: Hello from Egypt. I'm trying to start again in the cradle of civilization.

◆ ◆ ◆

ANDY: Christmas Greetings from the Ladds: Andy, Jane, Drew, Nicholas, and Ted. And of course Porgy.

MELISSA: Am thinking of moving to Los Angeles. Do you know anyone in Los Angeles? Does anyone know anyone in Los Angeles?

◆ ◆ ◆

ANDY: Joy to the World from all the Ladds. Note our new address.

MELISSA: Merry Christmas. Hey you! What's going on? Just when I decide to move to New York. I see you've scampered off to the suburbs.

ANDY: I find the suburbs generally safer.

MELISSA: Chicken.

◆ ◆ ◆

MELISSA: Mother wrote that you won some important election for the Republicans. I'm terribly disappointed. I love all politicians, but I find Democrats better in bed . . .

ANDY: I'm a liberal Republican with a strong commitment to women's rights. Doesn't that count?

MELISSA: Depends on your position.

◆ ◆ ◆

MELISSA: Paintings and drawings by Melissa Gardner. The Hastings Gallery. 422 Broadway. March 18 through April 30. Opening reception March 20, 6 to 8 P.M. Note I've gone back to my *maiden* name. That's a laugh.

ANDY: Got your announcement for your new show. Good luck. P.S. I'd love to have one of your paintings. We could use a little excitement on our living room walls. Seriously. What would one cost?

MELISSA: Come to the show and find out.

ANDY: Never made your show. Sorry. Things came up.

MELISSA: Chicken again.

ANDY: You're right.

MELISSA: Actually, it's just as well. I'm going through what the critics call an "anarchistic phase." They say I'm dancing on the edge of an abyss. You'd better stay away. I might take you with me when I fall.

◆ ◆ ◆

ANDY: Dear Friends: Jane tells me that it's about time I took a crack at the annual Christmas letter, so here goes. Let's start at the top, with our quarterback, Jane herself, who never ceases to amaze us all. Not only has she continued to be a superb mother to our three sons, but she has also managed to commute into the city and hold down a part-time job in the gift shop at the Metropolitan Museum of Art. Furthermore, she is now well on her way to completing a full-fledged master's degree in Arts Administration at SUNY Purchase. More power to Jane, so say we all.

We are also proud of all three boys. Young Drew was soccer captain at Exeter last fall, and hopes to go on to Yale. Nicholas, our rebel in residence, has become a computer genius in high school, and has already received several tantalizing offers for summer jobs from local electronics firms. We all know that it's tougher to place our youngsters in meaningful summer employment than to get them into Harvard, so we're very proud of how far Nick has come. Ted, our last but in no way our least, now plays the clarinet in the school band at Dickinson Country Day. Since Jane and I are barely capable of singing "You Are My Sunshine" without going disastrously flat, when we hear him produce his dulcet sounds, we look at each other "in a wild surmise."

We recently bought the family summer place from my brother and sister, and hope to spend as much time as we can there, gardening, relaxing, and as the boys say, "generally veging out." Jane and I have become killers on the tennis court, and hereby challenge all comers. If any of our friends are in the Adirondack area this summer, we expect telephone calls, we expect visits, we expect elaborate house presents.

I've enjoyed very much serving on the State Legislature. We've proposed and written a number of bills, and we've won some and lost some. All my life I've had the wish to do something in the way of public service, and it has been a great pleasure to put that wish into practice. For those of my friends who have urged me to seek higher office, let me simply say that I have more than enough challenges right here where I am.

Jane and the boys join me in wishing each and all of you a Happy Holiday Season.

MELISSA: Dear Andy. If I ever get another one of those drippy Xeroxed Christmas letters from you, I think I'll invite myself out to your ducky little house for dinner, and when you're all sitting there eating terribly healthy food and discussing terribly important things and generally congratulating yourselves on all your accomplishments. I think I'll stand up on my chair, and turn around, and moon the whole fucking family!

ANDY: You're right. It was a smug dumb letter and I apologize for it. Jane normally writes it, and it sounds better when she does. I always felt better writing to just one person at a time, such as to you. I guess what I was really saying is that as far as my family is concerned, we're all managing to hold our heads above water in this tricky world. Jane and I have had our problems, but we're comfortable with each other now, and the boys, for the moment, are out of trouble. Nicky seems to be off drugs now, and Ted is getting help on his stammer. Porgy, Jr., my old cocker, died, and I miss him too much to get a replacement. I'm thinking of running for the Senate next fall if O'Hara retires. What do you think? I'd really like your opinion. If you decide to answer this, you might write care of my office address. Jane has a slight tendency toward melodrama, particularly after she got ahold of your last little note.

MELISSA: The Senate yet! I should have known. Oh Andy, just think! Once again, you can be with all boys. Oh hell, go for it, if you want. You'll be an image of righteousness and rectitude in our god-forsaken land. Or maybe it's just me that's godforsaken these days.

ANDY: The Honorable Andrew M. Ladd III wishes to express his thanks for your generous donation to his senatorial campaign . . . You sent too MUCH, Melissa! You didn't need to.

♦　♦　♦

MELISSA: Greetings from Silver Hill. Slight regression in the liquor department. They say it's in the genes. Lord knows, my mother has the problem, and my father, too, in the end. Anyway, I'm working on it. Darwin is being a real shit about the girls. He's cut down on my visitation rights, so when you get to Washington, I want you to write a special law about vindictive ex-husbands, banishing them to Lower Slobbovia, forever and ever. Amen.

◆　◆　◆

ANDY: Seasons Greetings from Senator and Mrs. Andrew M. Ladd and family.

MELISSA: Season's Greetings indeed! Is that all you can say to me after forty years? I'm warning you, Andy. Keep that shit up, and I swear I'll come down and moon the whole Senate.

ANDY: Sorry. My staff sent that out. Merry Christmas, old friend. How are you? Where are you these days?

MELISSA: Living in New York—alone, for a change—but the big question is, WHO am I these days? That's the toughie. I keep thinking about that strange old world we grew up in. How did it manage to produce both you and me? A stalwart upright servant of the people, and a boozed out, cynical, lascivious old broad. The best and the worst, that's us.

ANDY: Don't be so tough on yourself. Get back to your art.

MELISSA: I'll try.

◆　◆　◆

ANDY: Merry Christmas, Happy New Year, and much love.

MELISSA: Much LOVE? MUCH love? God, Andy, how sexy! Remember how much that meant in our preppy days? If it was just "love" you were out in the cold, and if it was "all my love," you were hemmed in for life—but "Much Love" meant that things could go either way. Remember?

◆　◆　◆

ANDY: Merry Christmas and love from us all.

MELISSA: Saw you on *Sixty Minutes*. You looked fabulous. And that was a great little pep talk in the Senate on "our responsibilities" to Latin America. But don't forget to keep your eye on the ball.

ANDY: Thanks for your card. What ball?

MELISSA: The ball is that money doesn't solve everything. It helps, but not as much as people think. Take it from one who knows. That's the ball.

ANDY: Merry Christmas and love. What are you up to these days?

MELISSA: I'm trying to work with clay. Remember that kind of clay we used in Mrs. Mickler's art class in fourth grade? That old gray stuff? We called it plasticene. I'm trying to work with that. I'm making cats, dogs . . . I even made a kangaroo jumping over a glass of orange juice. Remember that? I'm trying to get back to some of those old, old feelings I had back in the Homeland. I have to find feelings, any feelings, otherwise I'm dead. Come down and help me search. I have a studio down in Soho and we could . . . um, er, uh, well we could at least have DINNER and talk about old times, couldn't we, Senator Ladd? P.S. Did you know that my mother got married again? At the age of eighty-two? To my father's BROTHER yet! So now you have to call her Mrs. Gardner again, just like the old days. The wheel seems to be coming around full circle. Hint, hint.

ANDY: A quick note on the way to the airport. When you write, put "attention Mrs. Walpole" on the envelope. She's my private secretary, I've alerted her, and she'll pass your letters directly on to me. Otherwise, the whole office staff seems to get a peek. In haste . . .

MELISSA: I'm having a show opening January 28 through Feb. 25. Won't you come? I'd love to have you see what I've been up to. Maybe it will ring a few old bells.

ANDY: Can't make it. I'll be on an official visit to the Philippines most of February, then a week's spring skiing at Stowe with the boys. Good luck.

◆   ◆   ◆

ANDY: How did the show go?

◆   ◆   ◆

ANDY: Haven't heard from you. Tell me about the show.

◆   ◆   ◆

ANDY: I want to hear from you. Please.

MELISSA: The show stank. The crowd hated it, the critics hated it, I hated it. It was nostalgic shit. You can't go home again, and you can quote me on that. I'm turning to photography now. Realism! That's my bag. The present tense. Look at the modern world squarely in the face, and don't blink . . . Oh Andy, couldn't I see you? You're all I have left.

ANDY: I'll be in New York next Tuesday the 19th. Have to make a fund-raising speech at a dinner. I could stop by your place afterwards.

MELISSA: I'll be there all evening.

◆   ◆   ◆

ANDY: Red roses. This time I think I know what they mean.

MELISSA: All I know is that after last night I want to see you again.

◆   ◆   ◆

MELISSA: Any chance of any other fund-raisers coming up in the near future?

◆   ◆   ◆

MELISSA: Mrs. Walpole, are you there? Are you delivering the mail?

◆   ◆   ◆

ANDY: I'm sorry I've taken so long to reply. I've been upstate mending a few fences, and then to Zurich for a three-day economic conference, and then a weekend with Jane, mending a few fences *there* . . . Darling, I'll have to ask you not to telephone the office. Every call has to be logged in, and most of them get screened by these over-eager college interns who like to rush back to Cambridge and New Haven and announce to their classmates in political science that Senator Ladd is shacking up on the side. The phones simply aren't secure. At long last, the letter beats out the telephone, my love! And guess what? I'm writing this with the old Parker 51 my grandmother gave me when I went away to school. I found it in the back of my bureau drawer with my Scroll and Key pin, and my Lieutenant J. G. bars from the Navy, and the Zippo lighter you gave me at some dance. The pen didn't even work at first. I had to clean it out, and then traipse all over Washington looking for a store which still sells a bottle of ink. Anyway, it feels good holding this thing again. It feels good writing to you again. Longhand. Forming my d's and t's the way Miss Emerson taught us so long ago. I know you've never liked writing letters, but now you HAVE to! Ha, ha. As for business: I plan to come through New York next Wednesday, and I'll call you from the airport if there's time to stop by.

MELISSA: Sweetheart, I LOVED seeing you. Come again . . .

ANDY: . . . will be stopping through a week from next . . .

MELISSA: . . . Did you ever *dream* we'd be so good at sex?

ANDY: . . . Two up-tight old Wasps going at it like a sale at Brooks Brothers . . .

MELISSA: . . . I figure fifty years went into last night . . .

ANDY: . . . Let's go for a hundred . . .

MELISSA: . . . Oh my God, come again soon, or sooner . . .

ANDY: . . . I'm already making plans . . .

(The letters begin to overlap)

MELISSA: . . . have to go to San Francisco to visit the girls. Couldn't we meet somewhere on the way?

ANDY: . . . I don't see how we can possibly go public . . .

MELISSA: . . . some country inn, some deliciously seedy motel . . .

ANDY: . . . I don't see how . . .

MELISSA: . . . see you more than for just a few hours . . .

ANDY: . . . price we have to pay . . .

MELISSA: . . . I'm getting so I think about nothing but how we can . . .

ANDY: . . . I'm not sure I can change my whole life so radically . . .

MELISSA: . . . other politicians have gotten divorced . . . Rockefeller, Reagan . . .

ANDY: . . . Jane . . . the children . . . my particular constituency . . .

MELISSA: . . . you've become the center of my life. If you left, I don't think I could . . .

ANDY: . . . because of the coming election, I don't see how we can . . .

◆　◆　◆

MELISSA: Dear Andy: A reporter called up from the Daily News. What do I do about it?

ANDY: Nothing.

MELISSA: I suppose you know all this, but there's a crack about us in Newsweek. And Mother heard some radio talk show where they actually named names. What should I do? Go away? What?

ANDY: Nothing.

MELISSA: They called Darwin, you know. They tracked him down. The son of a bitch told them this has been going on for years.

ANDY: Wish it had been.

MELISSA: Now they're telephoning. What do I say?

ANDY: Say we're good old friends.

MELISSA: Friends, I like. Good, I like. Old, I'm beginning to have problems with.

ANDY: Then don't say anything. Hang up. This, too, shall pass.

MELISSA: Will I be seeing you again?

ANDY: Better not, for a while.

MELISSA: I meant, after the election . . .

ANDY: Better lie low for a while.

MELISSA: I miss you terribly . . .

ANDY: Better lie low.

MELISSA: I NEED you, Andy. You're my anchor man these days. Without you, I'm not sure I can . . .

(The letters begin to overlap again)

ANDY: Hold on now. Just hold on . . .

MELISSA: . . . where were you? I waited three hours hoping that you'd at least call . . .

ANDY: . . . please don't telephone . . . Mrs. Walpole was sick that day and . . .

MELISSA: . . . I haven't seen you in over a month now . . .

ANDY: . . . the coming election . . .

MELISSA: . . . surely you could at least take time out to . . .

ANDY: . . . if I want to be reelected . . .

MELISSA: . . . I need you. I need to be with you. I don't know if I can . . .

ANDY: . . . the election . . . the election . . . the election.

◆   ◆   ◆

MELISSA: I haven't heard from you in six weeks, Andy.

◆   ◆   ◆

MELISSA: Are you trying to tell me something, Andy?

◆   ◆   ◆

MELISSA: Is this it, Andy?

◆   ◆   ◆

MELISSA: Congratulations on landslide victory. Love. Melissa.

ANDY: Could we meet at your place next Sunday night?

MELISSA: Oh thank God . . .

ANDY: I meant that we have to talk, Melissa . . .

MELISSA: Uh oh. Talk. I'm scared of talk. In fact, I dread it . . .

◆   ◆   ◆

ANDY: Dearest Melissa: Are you all right? That was a heavy scene last Sunday, but I know I'm right. We've got to go one way or the other, and the other leads nowhere. I know I sound like a stuffy prick, but I do feel I have a responsibility to Jane, and the boys, and now, after the election, to my constituency, which had enough faith and trust in me to vote me back in despite all that crap in the newspapers. And it wouldn't work with us anyway, in the long run, sweetheart. We're too old. We're carrying too much old baggage on our backs. We'd last about a week if we got married. But we can still write letters, darling. We can always do that. Letters are still our strength and our salvation. Mrs. Walpole is still with us, and there's no reason why we can't continue to keep in touch with each other in this wonderful old way. I count on your letters, darling. I always have. And I hope you will count on mine . . .

◆　◆　◆

ANDY: Are you there? I keep putting "please forward" on the envelopes but who knows . . .

◆　◆　◆

ANDY: Now I've even resorted to the telephone, but all I get is your damn machine . . . Please. I need to hear from you . . .

◆　◆　◆

ANDY: Senator and Mrs. Andrew M. Ladd, III, and family send you warm Holiday greetings and every good wish for the New Year.

MELISSA: Andy Ladd, is that YOU? Blow dried and custom-tailored and jogging trim at fifty-five. Hiding behind that lovely wife with her heels together and her hands folded discreetly over her snatch? And is that your new DOG, Andy? I see you've graduated to a Golden Retriever. And are those your sons and heirs? And—Help!—is that a *grand*child nestled in someone's arms? God, Andy, you look like the Holy Family! Season's Greetings and Happy Holidays and even Merry Christmas, Senator Ladd. We who are about to die salute you . . .

ANDY: Just reread your last note. What's this "we who are about to die" stuff?

◆　◆　◆

ANDY: May I see you again?

◆　◆　◆

ANDY: I want to see you again, if I may.

◆　◆　◆

ANDY: Dear Mrs. Gardner. I seem to have lost touch with Melissa again. I wonder if you might send me her latest address.

◆　◆　◆

ANDY: Dear Melissa. Your mother wrote that you'd returned to the Land of Oz. I'm flying up next Thursday to see you.

MELISSA: No! Please! Don't! Please stay away! I've let myself go. I'm fat, I'm ugly, my hair is horrible! I'm locked in at the funny farm all week, and then Mother gets me weekends if I'm good. They've put me on all sorts of new drugs, and half the time I don't make sense at all! I can't even do finger-painting now without fucking it up. My girls won't even *talk* to me on the telephone now. They say I upset them too much. Oh, I've made a mess of things, Andy. I've made a total, ghastly mess. I don't like life any more. I hate it. Sometimes I think that if you and I had just . . . if we had just . . . oh but just stay away, Andy. Please.

ANDY: Arriving Saturday morning. Will meet you at your mother's.

MELISSA: DON'T! I don't want to see you! I won't be there! I'll be GONE, Andy! I swear. I'll be gone.

◆　◆　◆

ANDY: Dear Mrs. Gardner: I think the first letter I ever wrote was to you, accepting an invitation for Melissa's birthday party. Now I'm writing you again about her death. I want to say a few things on paper I couldn't say at her funeral, both when I spoke, and when you and I talked afterward. As you may know, Melissa and I managed to keep in touch with each other most of our lives, primarily through letters. Even now, as I write this letter to you, I feel I'm writing it also to her.

MELISSA: Ah, you're in your element now, Andy . . .

ANDY: We had a complicated relationship, she and I, all our lives. We went in very different directions. But somehow over all those years, I think we managed to give something to each other. Melissa expressed all the dangerous and rebellious feelings I never dared admit to . . .

MELISSA: *Now* he tells me . . .

ANDY: And I like to think I gave her some sense of balance . . .

MELISSA: BALANCE? Oh Hell, I give up. Have it your way, Andy: balance.

ANDY: Most of the things I did in life I did with her partly in mind. And if I said or did an inauthentic thing, I could almost hear her groaning over my shoulder. But now she's gone I really don't know how I'll get along without her.

MELISSA: *(Looking at him for the first time.)* You'll survive, Andy . . .

ANDY: I have a wonderful wife, fine children, and a place in the world I feel proud of, but the death of Melissa suddenly leaves a huge gap in my life . . .

MELISSA: Oh now, Andy . . .

ANDY: The thought of never again being able to write to her, to connect to her, to get some signal back from her, fills me with an emptiness which is hard to describe.

MELISSA: Now Andy, stop . . .

ANDY: I don't think there are many men in this world who have had the benefit of such a friendship with such a woman. But it was more than friendship, too. I know now that I loved her. I loved her even from the day I met her, when she walked into second grade, looking like the lost princess of Oz.

MELISSA: Oh, Andy, PLEASE. I can't bear it.

ANDY: I don't think I've ever loved anyone the way I loved her, and I know I never will again. She was at the heart of my life, and already I miss her desperately. I just wanted to say this to you and to her. Sincerely, Andy Ladd.

MELISSA: Thank you, Andy.

The End

A CLOSER LOOK: ADRIENNE RICH

Adrienne Rich was born in Baltimore, Maryland, in 1929. She is the author of nearly twenty volumes of poetry. Rich has received the Bollingen Prize, the Lannan Lifetime Achievement Award, the Academy of American Poets Fellowship, the Ruth Lilly Poetry Prize, the Lenore Marshall Poetry Prize, the National Book Award, and a MacArthur Fellowship; she is also a former Academy Chancellor. In 1997, she was awarded the Academy's Wallace Stevens Award for outstanding and proven mastery in the art of poetry.

INTERVIEW WITH THE AUTHOR

Michael Klein is the author of *1990* (Provincetown Poets Series) and *Track Conditions: A Memoir* (Ballantine Books). The following interview was published in *The Boston Phoenix* in 1999.

A Rich Life: Adrienne Rich on Poetry, Politics, and Personal Revelation

Adrienne Rich is one of the major American poets of the last half of this century. Now 70, she's published more than 16 volumes of poetry and four books of nonfiction, and has been the recipient of nearly every major literary award, including the National Book Award, the Fellowship of the Academy of American Poets, the Ruth Lilly Poetry Prize, the Dorothea Tanning Prize for mastery in the art of poetry given by the Academy of American Poets, and the MacArthur "genius" grant. In 1997, she made headlines when she refused the National Medal for the Arts—which is awarded by the White House and the president. In a letter published by the *New York Times,* Rich wrote to Jane Alexander, then-head of the National Endowment for the Arts: "I cannot accept such an award from President Clinton or this White House because the very meaning of art, as I understand it, is incompatible with the cynical politics of this administration."

Rich's career took flight in 1951, when W. H. Auden selected the twenty-one-year-old's first collection of poetry for inclusion in the Yale Younger Poets series. Her early work echoed the voices of the major poets of the first half of this century, including Auden, but by the 1960s (particularly with the publication of *Snapshots of a Daughter-in-Law*), it reflected more personal explorations. By the late 1960s, her focus on the personal had broadened. Concentrating on the societal status of women in general and lesbians in particular, her poetry had evolved into the passionately political force for moral good that it is today. Her latest volume of poems, *Midnight Salvage: Poems 1995–1998,* continues in that tradition.

One in Ten recently spoke with Rich.

Q: With *The Dream of a Common Language: Poems 1974–1977,* your poems became more political and more far-reaching. Coming out felt less about disclosure and more about pure revolution. There was an incredible sense of how that choice affected other people apart from yourself. How can lesbian poets today, who for the most part are already out with their first book, become part of American intellectual life the way that you have?

A: *The dilemma for a 21-year-old lesbian poet who is already out may well be that so much is already acknowledged and written about and published. How do you enter those conversations that are already taking place, and the even wider conversations about justice, power, or what it means to be a citizen? There has to be a kind of resistance to the already offered clichés, and I think that that's something every good poet has to make up for herself or himself—how to do that.*

I came out first as a political poet, even before The Dream of a Common Language, *under the taboo against so-called political poetry in the U.S., which was comparable to the taboo against homosexuality. In other words, it wasn't done. And this is, of course, the only country in the world where that has been true. Go to Latin America, to the Middle East, to Asia, to Africa, to Europe, and you find the political poet and a poetry that addresses public affairs and public discourse, conflict, oppression, and resistance. That poetry is seen as normal. And it is honored.*

Q: A keen political awareness enabled you to come out sexually. Do poets, gay or not, have to come out in a certain way?

A: *You do, in terms of how do you connect with the world, and what are you defining as the world that you want to be connected to. The connections I was making with the world by coming out—as having any kind of sexuality—had to do with the fact that early on, I was critiquing the conventional male–female identities on which so much of Western poetry has been based, and the ideas about public and private spaces, [and the fact] that never the twain shall meet—woman defined as the private sphere, man as the public sphere.*

Q: One realization I had after reading your essay "Compulsory Heterosexuality and Lesbian Existence" was that there are gay men who are also part of the patriarchy. In fact, they could be patriarchy's best agents.

A: *I think AIDS transformed a lot of gay men, and many lesbians came to the bedsides of their friends with AIDS. I think about the possibilities for empathy, for mutual solidarity among gay men and lesbians, not simply as people who suffer under homophobia, but as people who are also extremely creative, active, and have a particular understanding of the human condition.*

Q: Identity derived from a fierce kind of knowing has always informed your work. *An Atlas of the Difficult World: Poems 1988–1991* may be a book about knowing's dilemma: not wanting to know. You say about the shooting of two lesbians on the Appalachian trail: "I don't want to know how he tracked them / along the Appalachian Trial, hid close / by their tent,"— which, of course, is also a disclosure. You don't want to know what you, yourself, are about to tell us. You don't want to know what you already know.

A: *I keep on not wanting to know what I know—Matthew Shepard, James Byrd Jr., the schoolyard massacres. There keep being things I absolutely don't want to know, and must know—and we as a society must know. I explore the whole idea in a poem in Midnight Salvage called "Camino Real," while driving this road to Los Angeles, thinking about [accounts of] abuses that I had been reading by people who actually went back to where they had their human rights violated. And how that coexists in the poem with what is for me a journey of happiness.*

Q: *Midnight Salvage*'s epigraph quotes from George Oppen: "I don't know how to measure happiness."

A: *And what he's talking about there is really what Hannah Arendt talks about in one of her essays—public happiness. A happiness of true participation in society, which would be possible for everyone.*

Q: One of your societies for many years has been California, after many years of living and writing on the East Coast. There is a strong sense that those vastly different landscapes have greatly influenced you internally as well—what Muriel Rukeyser may have meant when she said: "There are roads to take, when you think of your country."

A: *Well, you know, California is the most bizarre place to be, in a certain sense. It's so laden with contradictions. It is, in some ways, almost flaunting of them. I think it flaunts more than any other part of the country, in the visual sense: the extraordinary visual degradation, the extraordinary beauty. There are still these vast tracts of wilderness. There is this amazing ocean. You're constantly living in a kind of cognitive dissonance here.*

Q: Cognitive dissonance might be a good way to talk about your book *Dark Fields of the Republic,* which deals, in part, with government and art. In "Six: Edgelit," a section from the long poem "Inscriptions," you say, "In my sixty-fifth year I know something about language / it can eat or be eaten by experience / Medbh, poetry means refusing / the choice to kill or die // but this life of continuing is for the sane mad / and the bravest monsters." What has being one of the sane mad or one of the bravest monsters taught you about language?

A: *In the poem, I was answering Medbh McGuckian, who is a poet I tremendously admire, and she's writing from Belfast and the war, and I'm responding on the level* *of what it means to be working in language in a time or a situation when it feels that language can do so little. And hence, this life of continuing, because you keep going with it. But you have to be sane mad.*

Q: If you're an artist.

A: *Exactly. It's very illogical being a writer.*

Q: And yet everyone wants to be one, to be a star.

A: *Poetry has gotten to be very "in," in a way, and I've seen something I would never have imagined, which is that poetry is being commoditized. And I thought it was uncommodifiable, because so few people really believed that it worked. But I think some people believe now that, at least, you can market it.*

    There's a lot of what I would call comfortable poetry around. And I would have to say that some of that comfortable poetry is being written by gay and lesbian poets. I think you can probably find poets from any group who would come under the rubric of "diversity" who are writing comfortable poetry nowadays. But then there is all this other stuff going on—which is wilder, which is bristling; it's juicier, it's everything that you would want. And it's not comfortable. That's the kind of poetry that interests me—a field of energy. It's intellectual and moral and political and sexual and sensual—all of that fermenting together. It can speak to people who have themselves felt like monsters and say: you are not alone, this is not monstrous. It can disturb and enrapture.

    Poetry can add its grain to an accumulation of consciousness against the idea that there is no alternative—that we're now just in the great flow of capitalism and it can never be any different— [that] this is human destiny, this is human nature. A poem can add its grain to all the other grains and that is, I think, a rather important thing to do.

Q: But also, there's a poetry being written that feels like it's corroborating, rather than resisting, the idea that there is no alternative.

A: *Exactly—it's reflecting the "what is" rather than asking what could be.*

Q: Which is what *Midnight Salvage* is constantly doing in those long poems. How do you keep a poem alive for that long?

A: *Well, maybe in the same way that a novelist keeps a novel alive. You have to be in there for the long haul. But if I have a long poem in the works, it's a context that can include diverse and unexpected things. When I was writing* An Atlas of the Difficult World, *the Gulf War became part of that poem, but only because the poem was already there, and open to it.*

Q: In "Letters to a Young Poet," you say: I wanted to go somewhere / the brain had not yet gone / I wanted not to be / there so alone." This incredible, restless intelligence and a loneliness from being in that position is really how your poems seem to come to us. Am I being accurate here?

A: *I think my work comes out of both an intense desire for connection and what it means to feel isolated. There's always going to be a kind of tidal movement back and forth between the two. Art and literature have given so many people the relief of feeling connected—pulled us out of isolation. It has let us know that somebody else breathed and dreamed and had sex and loved and raged and knew loneliness the way we do.*

Q: What are you working on now?

A: *Poems. And sometimes making notes for essays. I'm not really up for writing them yet. I feel this mistrust of there being an audience for the kind of essay I'd like to write, which is, again, not short and not comfortable. And maybe somewhat demanding.*

Q: Critical?

A: *Critical, political, or cultural. One of the things I have to say about this demon of the personal—and I have to take responsibility for my part in helping create this demon, as part of a women's movement in which we celebrated personal experience and personal feelings—is that it has become a horribly commoditized version of humanity. It's almost as though the personal life has been taken hostage in some way, and I'm shying away more and more from anything that would contribute to that.*

Q: *Midnight Salvage,* I think, is a contribution about happiness, which of course means unhappiness as well.

A: *I have a poem from the '60s that begins: "Difficult, ordinary happiness, no one nowadays believes in you." And, yes—it always goes with unhappiness. It's that thing that is glinting at the bottom of the stream that you're reaching for all the time—your hand often not being able to grasp it, even though your eye can see it.*

POEMS

The Burning of Paper Instead of Children

I was in danger of verbalizing my moral impulses out of existence.

—DANIEL BERRIGAN, ON TRIAL IN BALTIMORE.

1. My neighbor, a scientist and art-collector, telephones me in a state of violent emotion. He tells me that my son and his, aged eleven and twelve,

have on the last day of school burned a mathematics textbook in the backyard. He has forbidden my son to come to his house for a week, and has forbidden his own son to leave the house during that time. "The burning of a
book," he says, "arouses terrible sensations in me, memories of Hitler; there
are few things that upset me so much as the idea of burning a book."

Back there: the library, walled
with green Britannicas
Looking again
in Dürer's *Complete Works*
for MELANCOLIA, the baffled woman

the crocodiles in Herodotus
the Book of the Dead
the *Trial of Jeanne d'Arc,* so blue
I think, It is her color

and they take the book away
because I dream of her too often

love and fear in a house
knowledge of the oppressor
I know it hurts to burn

2. To imagine a time of silence
or few words
a time of chemistry and music

the hollows above your buttocks
traced by my hand
or, *hair is like flesh,* you said

an age of long silence

relief

from this tongue   this slab of limestone
or reinforced concrete
fanatics and traders
dumped on this coast wildgreen clayred
that breathed once
in signals of smoke
sweep of the wind

knowledge of the oppressor
this is the oppressor's language

yet I need it to talk to you

3. *People suffer highly in poverty and it takes dignity and intelligence to
overcome this suffering. Some of the suffering are: a child did not had dinner*

last night: a child steal because he did not have money to buy it: to hear a
mother say she do not have money to buy food for her children and to see a
child without cloth it will make tears in your eyes.

(the fracture of order
the repair of speech
to overcome this suffering)

4. We lie under the sheet
after making love, speaking
of loneliness
relieved in a book
relived in a book
so on that page
the clot and fissure
of it appears
words of a man
in pain
a naked word
entering the clot
a hand grasping
through bars:

deliverance

What happens between us
has happened for centuries
we know it from literature

still it happens

sexual jealousy
outflung hand
beating bed

dryness of mouth
after panting
there are books that describe all this
and they are useless

You walk into the woods behind a house
there in that country
you find a temple
built eighteen hundred years ago
you enter without knowing
what it is you enter

so it is with us

no one knows what may happen
though the books tell everything

burn the texts   said Artaud

5. I am composing on the typewriter late at night, thinking of today.
How well we all spoke. A language is a map of our failures. Frederick
Douglass wrote an English purer than Milton's. People suffer highly in
poverty. There are methods but we do not use them. Joan, who could
not read, spoke some peasant form of French. Some of the suffering are:
it is hard to tell the truth; this is America; I cannot touch you now. In
America we have only the present tense. I am in danger. You are in danger. The burning of a book arouses no sensation in me. I know it hurts
to burn. There are flames of napalm in Catonsville, Maryland. I know it
hurts to burn. The typewriter is overheated, my mouth is burning, I cannot touch you and this is the oppressor's language.

from Twenty-One Love Poems

I

Wherever in this city, screens flicker
with pornography, with science-fiction vampires,
victimized hirelings bending to the lash,
we also have to walk . . . if simply as we walk
through the rainsoaked garbage, the tabloid cruelties
of our own neighborhoods.
We need to grasp our lives inseperable
from those rancid dreams, that blurt of metal, those disgraces,
and the red begonia perilously flashing
from a tenement sill six stories high,
or the long-legged young girls playing ball
in the junior highschool playground.
No one has imagined us. We want to live like trees,
sycamores blazing through the sulfuric air,
dappled with scars, still exuberantly budding,
our animal passion rooted in the city.

II

I wake up in your bed. I know I have been dreaming.
Much earlier, the alarm broke us from each other,
you've been at your desk for hours. I know what I dreamed:
our friend the poet comes into my room
where I've been writing for days,
drafts, carbons, poems are scattered everywhere,

and I want to show her one poem
which is the poem of my life. But I hesitate,
and wake. You've kissed my hair
to wake me. I dreamed you were a poem,
I say, a poem I wanted to show someone . . .
and I laugh and fall dreaming again
of the desire to show you to everyone I love,
to move openly together
in the pull of gravity, which is not simple,
which carried the feathered grass a long way down the upbreathing air.

III

Since we're not young, weeks have to do time
for years of missing each other. Yet only this odd warp
in time tells me we're not young.
Did I ever walk the morning streets at twenty,
my limbs streaming with a purer joy?
did I lean from any window over the city
listening for the future
as I listened here with nerves tuned for your ring?
And you, you move toward me with the same tempo.
Your eyes are everlasting, the green spark
of the blue-eyed grass of early summer,
the green-blue wild cress washed by the spring.
At twenty, yes: we thought we'd live forever.
At forty-five, I want to know even our limits.
I touch you knowing we weren't born tomorrow,
and somehow, each of us will help the other live,
and somewhere, each of us must help the other die.

Trying to Talk with a Man

Out in this desert we are testing bombs,
that's why we came here.
Sometimes I feel an underground river
forcing its way between deformed cliffs
moving itself like a locus of the sun
into this condemned scenery. . . .
. . . Coming out to this desert
we meant to change the face of
driving among dull green succulents
walking at noon in the ghost town
surrounded by silence
that sounds like the silence of the place

except that it came with us
and is familiar
and everything we were saying until now
was an effort to blot it out—
coming out here we are up against it
Out here I feel more helpless
with you than without you
You mention the danger
and list the equipment
we talk of caring for each other
in emergencies—lacerations, thirst—
but you look at me like an emergency
Your dry heat feels like power
your eyes are stars of a different magnitude
they reflect lights that spell out: EXIT
when you get up and pace the floor
talking of the danger
as if it were not ourselves
as if we were testing anything else.

A CRITICAL ARTICLE

bell hooks (nee Gloria Watkins) was born in Hopkinsville, Kentucky, in 1952. She received her B.A. from Stanford University in 1973, her M.A. in 1976 from the University of Wisconsin, and her Ph.D. in 1983 from the University of California, Santa Cruz. A passionate scholar, hooks is among the leading public intellectuals of her generation.

The following article was published in *Between Language and Cultures*.

"THIS IS THE OPPRESSOR'S LANGUAGE / YET I NEED IT TO TALK TO YOU": LANGUAGE, A PLACE OF STRUGGLE

bell hooks

Language like desire disrupts—refuses to be contained within boundaries. It speaks itself against our will, in words and thoughts, that intrude, violate even, the innermost private spaces of mind and body. I was in my first year of college when I read Adrienne Rich's poem "The Burning of Paper Instead of Children" published in the collection *The Will to Change*. That poem, speaking against domination, against racism and class oppression, attempts to graphically illustrate that stopping the political persecution and torture of living beings is a more vital issue than censorship, than burning books. This poem contained a line that moved and disturbed something within me. So much so, that in the years of my life since first reading this poem, I have not forgotten it. And perhaps could not have forgotten it had I tried to erase it from memory. This illustrates what I mean to suggest in the opening lines of this essay—that words impose themselves, take root in our memory against our will as the words of this poem begat a life in my memory that I could not abort or change.

Now, when I find myself thinking about language, these lines are there, as if they were always waiting to challenge and assist me. I find myself silently speaking them over and over again in my head, with such intensity they seem like a chant. These words that say: "this is the oppressor's language / yet I need it to talk to you." Startling me, shaking me into an awareness of the link between language and domination, I initially resist the idea of the oppressor's language, certain that this construct has the potential to disempower those of us who are just learning to speak, who are just learning to claim language as a place where we make ourselves subject. "This is the oppressor's language / yet I need it to talk to you." Adrienne Rich's words. Then, when I first read these words, and now, they make me think of standard English, of learning to speak against black vernacular, against the ruptured and broken speech of a dispossessed and displaced people. Standard English is not the speech of exile. It is the language of conquest and domination. In the United States it is the mask which hides the loss of so many tongues, all those sounds of diverse native communities we will never hear, the speech of the Gullah, Yiddish, and so many other unremembered tongues.

Reflecting on Adrienne Rich's words: "this is the oppressor's language / yet I need it to talk to you," I know that it is not the English language that hurts me, but what the oppressors do with it, how they shape it to become a territory that limits and defines, how they make it a weapon that can shame, humiliate, colonize. Gloria Anzaldúa reminds us of this pain in *Borderlands/La Frontera* when she asserts: "So, if you want to really hurt me, talk badly about my language." We have so little knowledge of how displaced, enslaved, or free Africans who came or were brought against their will to the United States felt about the loss of language, about learning English. Only as a woman did I begin to think about these black people in relation to language, to think about their trauma, as they were compelled to witness their language rendered meaningless within a colonizing European culture where voices deemed foreign could not be spoken, were outlawed tongues, renegade speech. When I realize how long it has taken for white Americans to acknowledge diverse languages of native Americans, to accept that the speech their ancestral colonizers declared were merely grunts or gibberish was indeed *language,* it is difficult not to hear in standard English always the sound of slaughter and conquest. I think now of the grief of displaced "homeless" Africans forced to inhabit a world where they saw folks like themselves, inhabiting the same skin, the same condition, but who had no shared language to talk with one another, who needed "the oppressor's language." "This is the oppressor's language / yet I need it to talk to you." When I imagine the terror of Africans on board, slave ships, on auction blocks, inhabiting the unfamiliar architecture of plantations, I consider that this terror extended beyond fear of punishment, that it resided also in the anguish of hearing a language they could not comprehend. The very sound of English had to terrify. I think of black people meeting one another in a space away from the diverse cultures and languages that distinguished them from one another, compelled by circumstance to find ways to speak with one another in a "new world" where blackness, the darkness of one's skin, and not language, would become the space of bonding. How to remember, to reinvoke this terror? How to describe what it must have been like for Africans whose deepest bonds historically forged in the place of shared speech to be abruptly transported to a world where the very sound of one's mother tongues had no meaning?

I imagine them hearing in spoken English "the oppressor's language," yet I imagine them also realizing that this language would need to be possessed, taken, claimed as a space of resistance. I imagine that the moment they realized "the oppressor's language" seized and spoken by the tongues of the colonized could be a space of bonding was joyous. For in that recognition was the understanding that intimacy could be restored, that a culture of resistance could be formed, that would make recovery from the trauma of enslavement possible. I imagine then Africans first hearing English as "the oppressor's language" and then rehearing it as a potential site of resistance. Learning English, learning to speak the alien tongue was one way enslaved Africans began to reclaim their personal power within a context of domination. Possessing a shared language black folks could find again a way to make community, and a means to create the political solidarity necessary to resist.

Needing the oppressor's language to speak with one another they nevertheless also reinvented, remade that language so that it would speak beyond the boundaries of conquest and domination. In the mouths of black Africans in the so-called "new world," English was altered, transformed, and became a different speech. Enslaved black people took broken bits of English, fragments, and made of them a counterlanguage. They put together their words in such a way that the colonizer had to rethink the meaning of English language. Though it has become common in contemporary culture to talk about the messages of resistance that emerged in the music created by slaves, particularly spirituals, less is said about the grammatical construction of sentences in these songs. Often, the English used in the song reflected the broken, ruptured world of the slave. When the slaves sang "nobody knows de trouble I see," their use of the word "nobody" adds a richer meaning than if they had used "no one" for it was the slave's body that was the concrete site of suffering. And even as emancipated black people sang spirituals, they did not change the language, the sentence structure, of our ancestors. For in the incorrect usage of words, in the incorrect placement of words, was a spirit of rebellion that claimed language as a site of resistance. Using English in a way that ruptured standard language usage and meaning so that often white folks could not understand black speech made English more than the oppressor's language.

An unbroken connection exists between the broken English of the displaced, enslaved African and the diverse black vernacular speech black folks use today. In both cases the rupture of standard English enabled and enables rebellion and resistance. By transforming the oppressor's language, making a culture of resistance, black people created an intimate speech that could say far more than was permissible within the boundaries of standard English. The power of this speech is not simply that it enables resistance to white supremacy but that it also forges a space for alternative cultural production and alternative epistemologies—different ways of thinking and knowing that were crucial to creating a counterhegemonic world view. It is absolutely essential that the revolutionary power of black vernacular speech not be lost in contemporary culture. That power resides in the capacity of black vernacular to intervene on the boundaries and limitations of standard English.

In contemporary black popular culture, rap music has become one of the spaces where black vernacular speech is used in a manner that invites dominant mainstream culture to listen—to hear—and to some extent be transformed. However, one of the risks of this attempt at cultural translation is that it will trivialize black vernacular speech. When young white kids imitate this speech in ways that suggest it is the speech of those who are dumb, stupid, or only interested in entertaining or being funny, then the subversive power of this speech is undermined. In academic circles, both in the sphere of teaching and writing, there has been little effort made to utilize black vernacular or, for that matter, any languages other than standard English. When I asked an ethnically diverse group of students in a course I was teaching on black women writers why we only ever heard standard English spoken in the classroom they were momentarily rendered speechless. Though many of them were individuals for whom standard English was a second or third language, it had simply never occurred to them that it was possible to say something in another language, in another way. No wonder then that we continue to think: "this is the oppressor's language / yet I need it to talk to you."

Realizing that I was in danger of losing my relationship to black vernacular speech because I too rarely use it in the predominately white settings that I am most often in both professionally and socially, I have begun to work at integrating the particular southern black vernacular speech I grew up hearing and speaking in a variety of settings. It has been hardest to integrate black vernacular in writing, particularly for academic journals. When I first began to incorporate black vernacular in critical essays, editors would send the work back to me in standard English. Using the vernacular means that translation into standard English may be needed if one wishes a more inclusive audience to understand the meaning of what is said. In the classroom setting. I encourage students to use a first language and translate it so that they do not need to feel that seeking higher education will necessarily estrange them from that language and culture they know most intimately. Not surprising when students in the black women writers class began to speak using diverse language and speech, white students often complained. This seemed to be particularly the case with black vernacular. It was particularly disturbing to them because they could understand the language but not comprehend its meaning. Pedagogically, I encouraged them to think of the moment of not understanding what someone says as a space to learn. Such a space provides not only the opportunity to listen without "mastery," without owning or possessing speech through interpretation, but also the experience of hearing non-English words. These lessons seem particularly crucial in a multicultural society that remains white supremacist, that uses standard English as a weapon to silence and censor. June Jordan reminds us of this in *On Call* when she declares:

> *I am talking about majority problems of language in a democratic state, problems of a currency that someone has stolen and hidden away and then homogenized into an official "English" language that can only express non-events involving nobody responsible, or lies. If we lived in a democratic state our language would have to hurtle, fly, curse, and sing, in all the common American names, all the undeniable and representative participating voices of everybody here. We would not tolerate the language of the powerful and, thereby, lose all respect for words, per se. We would make our language conform to the truth of our many selves and we would make our language lead us into the equality of power that a democratic state must represent. . . . This is not a democratic state. And we put up with that.*

That students in the course on black women writers were repressing all longing to speak in tongues other than standard English without seeing this repression as political was an indication of the way we act in complicity with a culture of domination without conscious awareness.

Recent discussions of diversity and multiculturalism tend to downplay or ignore the question of language. Critical feminist writing focusing on issues of difference and voice have made important theoretical interventions that call for recognition of the primacy of voices that are often silenced, censored, or marginalized. This call for the acknowledgment and/or celebration of diverse voices and consequently diverse languages and speech necessarily disrupts the primacy of standard English. When advocates of feminism first spoke about the desire for diverse participation in the women's movement, there was no discussion of language. It was simply assumed that standard English would remain the primary vehicle for the transmission of feminist thought. Now that the audience for feminist writing and speaking has become more diverse, it is evident that we must change conventional ways of thinking about language, creating spaces where diverse voices can speak in words other than

English or in broken/vernacular speech. This means that at a lecture or even in a written work there will be fragments of speech that may or may not be accessible to every individual. Shifting how we think about language and how we use it necessarily alters how we know what we know. Now at a lecture where I might use southern black vernacular, the particular patois of my region, or where I might use very abstract thought in conjunction with plain speech, responding to a diverse audience, I suggest that we do not necessarily need to hear and know what is stated in its entirety, that we do not need to "master" or conquer the narrative as a whole, that we may know in fragments. That we may learn from spaces of silence as well as spaces of speech. That in the act of being patient as we hear another tongue we may subvert that culture of capitalist frenzy and consumption that suggests all desire must be satisfied immediately or disrupt that cultural imperialism that suggests one is worthy of being heard only if one speaks in standard English.

Adrienne Rich concludes her poem with this statement:

> *I am composing on the typewriter late at night, thinking of today. How well we all spoke. A language is a map of our failures. Frederick Douglass wrote an English purer than Milton's. People suffer highly in poverty. There are methods but we do not use them. Joan, who could not read, spoke some peasant form of French. Some of the sufferings are; it is hard to tell the truth; this is America; I cannot touch you now. In America we have only the present tense. I am in danger. You are in danger. The burning of a book arouses no sensation in me. I know it hurts to burn. There are flames of napalm in Cantonsville, Maryland. I know it hurts to burn. The typewriter is overheated, my mouth is burning. I cannot touch you and this is the oppressor's language.*

To recognize that we touch one another in language seems particularly difficult in a society that would have us believe that there is not dignity in the experience of passion, that to feel deeply is to be inferior, for within Western metaphysical dualistic thought, ideas are always more important than language. To heal the splitting of mind and body, marginalized and oppressed people attempt to recover ourselves and our experiences in language. We seek to make a place for intimacy. Unable to find such a place in standard English, we create the ruptured, broken, unruly speech of the vernacular. When I need to say words that do more than simply mirror and/or address the dominant reality, I speak black vernacular. There, in that location, we make English do what we want it to do. We take the oppressor's language and turn it against itself. We make our words a counterhegemonic speech, liberating ourselves in language.

Conclusion

There is no escaping the lure of relationships, whether with friends, family, or foe. In Casebook Three, we experienced the highs and lows of all types of relationships. In order to relate to others, we function much better when we know our personal frame of reference; when we understand our reactions to situations, whether we think we can control them or not, and then see how well we are able to negotiate what we need and want with others. This casebook also explored another level of personal growth, often through loss. In the book *Necessary Losses,* the author writes, "Death gives life meaning." And though this chapter wasn't all about death, it did invite us to experience loss at the same time that it showed us the fruits of interpersonal, emotional labor.

CASEBOOK FOUR
Land of the Free, Home of the Brave: Defining America(ns)

Overview

There is no denying that the United States of America is multilateral. In fact, we are a nation of multiple, many things: multiple nationalities, multiple goals, wants and desires. It is the beat that never stops—this multiplicity; however, we are also a nation of one primary definition. Primarily, we as a nation are defined by freedom.

Americans, whether native-born or immigrants, have always had a penchant for that which defines us. Freedom has been a constant want that has colored our history when our ancestors demanded it. There have even been incidents in our recent history that made the enforcers of our most precious asset remember our basic tenet. More recently, since 9/11—*especially* since 9/11—our goal to maintain our identity of "land of the free" has come with a price; it has made us realize how precarious freedom can be, how fragile.

Consider these questions as you read the following selections:

- Why does it seem to be important for us to define ourselves according to culture?
- Is it possible to have one culture defined as "American"?
- What are the origins of prejudice? Are stereotypes ever justified?
- Has the definition of an "American" changed over time? If so, how?
- What role does gender play in determining a definition of "American"? Race?

Poetry

WALT WHITMAN

Walter Whitman was born in 1819 in West Hills, New York. He quit his formal schooling in 1831 and went to work as an office boy for lawyers and doctors. In 1831 he worked as an apprentice for the *Long Island Patriot*—a newspaper publication. From there he had a long, varied, and celebrated career as a writer and a publisher. He died in 1892.

I Hear America Singing

I hear America singing, the varied carols I hear,
Those of mechanics, each one singing his as it should be blithe and strong,
The carpenter singing his as he measures his plank or beam,
The mason singing his as he makes ready for work, or leaves off work,
The boatman singing what belongs to him in his boat, the deckhand singing
    on the steamboat deck,
The shoemaker singing as he sits on his bench, the hatter singing as he stands,
The wood-cutter's song, the ploughboy's on his way in the morning, or at
    noon intermission or at sundown,
The delicious singing of the mother, or of the young wife at work, or of the
    girl sewing or washing,
Each singing what belongs to him or her and to none else,
The day what belongs to the day—at night the party of young fellows,
    robust, friendly,
Singing with open mouths their strong melodious songs.

LANGSTON HUGHES

James Langston Hughes was born February 1, 1902, in Missouri. Following high school graduation, he spent a year in Mexico and a year at Columbia University. His first book of poetry, *The Weary Blues,* was published by Alfred A. Knopf in 1926. He finished his college education at Lincoln University in Pennsylvania three years later. The recipient of many honors, Langston Hughes died of complications from prostate cancer in

May 1967. His residence at 20 East 127th Street in Harlem, New York City, was granted landmark status by the New York City Preservation Commission, and East 127th Street was renamed "Langston Hughes Place."

The following poem was written in 1943.

Freedom's Plow

When a man starts out with nothing,
When a man starts out with his hands
Empty, but clean,
When a man starts out to build a world,
He starts first with himself
And the faith that is in his heart—
The strength there,
The will there to build.

First in the heart is the dream.
Then the mind starts seeking a way.
His eyes look out on the world,
On the great wooded world,
On the rich soil of the world,
On the rivers of the world.

The eyes see there materials for building,
See the difficulties, too, and the obstacles.
The hand seeks tools to cut the wood,
To till the soil, and harness the power of the waters.
Then the hand seeks other hands to help,
A community of hands to help—
Thus the dream becomes not one man's dream alone,
But a community dream.
Not my dream alone, but *our* dream.
Not my world alone,
But *your world and my world,*
Belonging to all the hands who build.

A long time ago, but not too long ago,
Ships came from across the sea
Bringing Pilgrims and prayer-makers,
Adventurers and booty seekers,
Free men and indentured servants,
Slave men and slave masters, all new—
To a new world, America!

With billowing sails the galleons came
Bringing men and dreams, women and dreams.
In little bands together,
Heart reaching out to heart,
Hand reaching out to hand,
They began to build our land.
Some were free hands
Seeking a greater freedom,
Some were indentured hands
Hoping to find their freedom,
Some were slave hands
Guarding in their hearts the seed of freedom.
But the word was there always:
          FREEDOM.

Down into the earth went the plow
In the free hands and the slave hands,
In indentured hands and adventurous hands,
Turning the rich soil went the plow in many hands
That planted and harvested the food that fed
And the cotton that clothed America.
Clang against the trees went the ax in many hands
That hewed and shaped the rooftops of America.
Splash into the rivers and the seas went the boat-hulls
That moved and transported America.
Crack went the whips that drove the horses
Across the plains of America.
Free hands and slave hands,
Indentured hands, adventurous hands,

White hands and black hands
Held the plow handles,
Ax handles, hammer handles,
Launched the boats and whipped the horses
That fed and housed and moved America.
Thus together through labor,
All these hands made America.
Labor! Out of labor came the villages
And the towns that grew to cities.
Labor! Out of labor came the rowboats
And the sailboats and the steamboats,
Came the wagons, stage coaches,
Out of labor came the factories,
Came the foundries, came the railroads,
Came the marts and markets, shops and stores,
Came the mighty products moulded, manufactured,

Sold in shops, piled in warehouses,
Shipped the wide world over:
Out of labor—white hands and black hands—
Came the dream, the strength, the will,
And the way to build America.
Now it is Me here, and You there.
Now it's Manhattan, Chicago,
Seattle, New Orleans,
Boston and El Paso—
Now it is the U.S.A.

A long time ago, but not too long ago, a man said:

> ALL MEN ARE CREATED EQUAL . . .
> ENDOWED BY THEIR CREATOR
> WITH CERTAIN INALIENABLE RIGHTS . . .
> AMONG THESE LIFE, LIBERTY
> AND THE PURSUIT OF HAPPINESS.

His name was Jefferson. There were slaves then,
But in their hearts the slaves believed him, too,
And silently took for granted
That what he said was also meant for them.
It was a long time ago,
But not so long ago at that, Lincoln said:

> NO MAN IS GOOD ENOUGH
> TO GOVERN ANOTHER MAN
> WITHOUT THAT OTHER'S CONSENT.

There were slaves then, too,
But in their hearts the slaves knew
What he said must be meant for every human being—
Else it had no meaning for anyone.
Then a man said:

> BETTER TO DIE FREE,
> THAN TO LIVE SLAVES.

He was a colored man who had been a slave
But had run away to freedom.
And the slaves knew
What Frederick Douglass said was true.
With John Brown at Harpers Ferry, Negroes died.
John Brown was hung.
Before the Civil War, days were dark,
And nobody knew for sure
When freedom would triumph.

"Or if it would," thought some.
But others knew it had to triumph.
In those dark days of slavery,
Guarding in their hearts the seed of freedom,
The slaves made up a song:

KEEP YOUR HAND ON THE PLOW!
HOLD ON!

That song meant just what it said: *Hold on!*
Freedom will come!

KEEP YOUR HAND ON THE PLOW!
HOLD ON!

Out of war, it came, bloody and terrible!
But it came!
Some there were, as always,
Who doubted that the war would end right,
That the slaves would be free,
Or that the union would stand.
But now we know how it all came out.
Out of the darkest days for a people and a nation,
We know now how it came out.
There was light when the battle clouds rolled away.
There was a great wooded land,
And men united as a nation.

America is a dream.
The poet says it was promises.
The people say it *is* promises—that will come true.
The people do not always say things out loud,
Nor write them down on paper.
The people often hold
Great thoughts in their deepest hearts
And sometimes only blunderingly express them,
Haltingly and stumbling say them,
And faultily put them into practice.
The people do not always understand each other.
But there is, somewhere there,
Always the *trying* to understand,
And the *trying* to say,
"You are a man. Together we are building our land."

America!
Land created in common,
Dream nourished in common,
Keep your hand on the plow! Hold on!

If the house is not yet finished,
Don't be discouraged, builder!
If the fight is not yet won,
Don't be weary, soldier!
The plan and the pattern is here,
Woven from the beginning
Into the warp and woof of America:

> ALL MEN ARE CREATED EQUAL.

> NO MAN IS GOOD ENOUGH
> TO GOVERN ANOTHER MAN WITHOUT
> THAT OTHER'S CONSENT.

> BETTER DIE FREE,
> THAN LIVE SLAVES.

Who said those things? Americans!
Who owns those words? America!
Who is America? You, me!
We are America!
To the enemy who would conquer us from without,
We say, NO!
To the enemy who would divide
and conquer us from within,
We say, NO!

> FREEDOM!
>   BROTHERHOOD!
>   DEMOCRACY!

To all the enemies of these great words:
We say, NO!

A long time ago,
An enslaved people heading toward freedom
Made up a song:
Keep Your Hand On The Plow! Hold On!
That plow plowed a new furrow
Across the field of history.
Into that furrow the freedom seed was dropped.
From that seed a tree grew, is growing, will ever grow.
That tree is for everybody,
For all America, for all the world.
May its branches spread and its shelter grow
Until all races and all peoples know its shade.

KEEP YOUR HAND ON THE PLOW!
HOLD ON!

CLAUDE MCKAY

Claude McKay (1889–1948) is considered "one of the ornaments of African American literature," even though he was born in Jamaica. McKay began to write poetry at the age of ten, and by the time he was twenty-two, he was already a successful poet. In 1912, he moved to the United States to attend the Tuskegee Institute, but later transferred to Kansas State University to study agriculture. He became interested in communism, living in France for a period of time before settling in Harlem, New York. He edited the leftist journal *The Liberator* for several years.

The following poem was published in 1921 in the book *Harlem Shadows: The Poems of Claude McKay.*

America

Although she feeds me bread of bitterness,
And sinks into my throat her tiger's tooth,
Stealing my breath of life, I will confess
I love this cultured hell that tests my youth!
Her vigor flows like tides into my blood,
Giving me strength erect against her hate.
Her bigness sweeps my being like a flood.
Yet as a rebel fronts a king in state,
I stand within her walls with not a shred
Of terror, malice, not a word of jeer.
Darkly I gaze into the days ahead,
And see her might and granite wonders there,
Beneath the touch of Time's unerring hand,
Like priceless treasures sinking in the sand.

ALLEN GINSBERG

Allen Ginsberg (1926–1997) was widely known as a contemporary poet and as a "revered Beat" writer. Though he addressed multiple issues such as freedom, war, and homosexuality, he has been compared to Thoreau, Emerson, and Whitman. His first book of poems, *Howl,* overcame censorship attempts and is widely regarded as one of the most influential poems of the twentieth century. Ginsberg co-founded and directed the Jack Kerouac School of Disembodied Poetics at the Naropa Institute in Colorado and was named a Distinguished Professor at Brooklyn College. He died in 1997 in New York City.

The following poem was written in January 1956.

America

America I've given you all and now I'm nothing.
America two dollars and twenty-seven cents January 17, 1956.
I can't stand my own mind.
America when will we end the human war?
Go fuck yourself with your atom bomb
I don't feel good don't bother me.
I won't write my poem till I'm in my right mind.
America when will you be angelic?
When will you take off your clothes?
When will you look at yourself through the grave?
When will you be worthy of your million Trotskyites?
America why are your libraries full of tears?
America when will you send your eggs to India?
I'm sick of your insane demands.
When can I go into the supermarket and buy what I need with my good looks?
America after all it is you and I who are perfect not the next world.
Your machinery is too much for me.
You made me want to be a saint.
There must be some other way to settle this argument.
Burroughs is in Tangiers I don't think he'll come back it's sinister.
Are you being sinister or is this some form of practical joke?
I'm trying to come to the point.
I refuse to give up my obsession.
America stop pushing I know what I'm doing.
America the plum blossoms are falling.
I haven't read the newspapers for months, everyday somebody goes on trial for
murder.
America I feel sentimental about the Wobblies.
America I used to be a communist when I was a kid and I'm not sorry.
I smoke marijuana every chance I get.
I sit in my house for days on end and stare at the roses in the closet.
When I go to Chinatown I get drunk and never get laid.
My mind is made up there's going to be trouble.
You should have seen me reading Marx.
My psychoanalyst thinks I'm perfectly right.
I won't say the Lord's Prayer.
I have mystical visions and cosmic vibrations.
America I still haven't told you what you did to Uncle Max after he came over
from Russia.

I'm addressing you.
Are you going to let our emotional life be run by Time Magazine?

I'm obsessed by Time Magazine.
I read it every week.
Its cover stares at me every time I slink past the corner candystore.
I read it in the basement of the Berkeley Public Library.
It's always telling me about responsibility. Businessmen are serious. Movie producers are serious. Everybody's serious but me.
It occurs to me that I am America.
I am talking to myself again.

Asia is rising against me.
I haven't got a chinaman's chance.
I'd better consider my national resources.
My national resources consist of two joints of marijuana millions of genitals an unpublishable private literature that goes 1400 miles and hour and twentyfivethousand mental institutions.
I say nothing about my prisons nor the millions of underpriviliged who live in my flowerpots under the light of five hundred suns.
I have abolished the whorehouses of France, Tangiers is the next to go.
My ambition is to be President despite the fact that I'm a Catholic.

America how can I write a holy litany in your silly mood?
I will continue like Henry Ford my strophes are as individual as his automobiles more so they're all different sexes
America I will sell you strophes $2500 apiece $500 down on your old strophe
America free Tom Mooney
America save the Spanish Loyalists
America Sacco & Vanzetti must not die
America I am the Scottsboro boys.
America when I was seven momma took me to Communist Cell meetings they sold us garbanzos a handful per ticket a ticket costs a nickel and the speeches were free everybody was angelic and sentimental about the workers it was all so sincere you have no idea what a good thing the party was in 1935 Scott Nearing was a grand old man a real mensch Mother Bloor made me cry I once saw Israel Amter plain. Everybody must have been a spy.
America you don't really want to go to war.
America it's them bad Russians.
Them Russians them Russians and them Chinamen. And them Russians.
The Russia wants to eat us alive. The Russia's power mad. She wants to take our cars from out our garages.
Her wants to grab Chicago. Her needs a Red Reader's Digest. her wants our auto plants in Siberia. Him big bureaucracy running our fillingstations.
That no good. Ugh. Him makes Indians learn read. Him need big black niggers.
Hah. Her make us all work sixteen hours a day. Help.
America this is quite serious.

America this is the impression I get from looking in the television set.
America is this correct?
I'd better get right down to the job.
It's true I don't want to join the Army or turn lathes in precision parts
factories, I'm nearsighted and psychopathic anyway.
America I'm putting my queer shoulder to the wheel.

DWIGHT OKITA

Dwight Okita, born in 1958 in Chicago, describes himself as "Japanese-American, gay, and Buddhist," and he claims that these things are reflected in his writing. "In Response to Executive Order 9066" is one of his most widely anthologized, reprinted poems. It was published for the first time in the Asian American poetry anthology *Breaking Silence* (Greenfield Review Press, 1983). On his Web site, http://dwightland.homestead.com/WRITERPAGE.html, Okita says, "I remember growing up hearing some vague reference to my parents being in 'camps' during the war, but it wasn't until I was in high school that I started asking my mother serious questions about it. My father was more reticent about his experience . . . the poem is inspired by my mother's personality and by my own wondering about what might've happened if she had been in high school that day. My mother said that the term 'camp' always sounded fun, like summer camp. So I wrote the poem in the form of a kind of thank-you letter, which I imagined she might've written to the American government."

In Response to Executive Order 9066

Dear Sirs:
Of course I'll come. I've packed my galoshes
and three packets of tomatoe seeds. Janet calls them
'love apples.' My father says where we're going
they won't grow.

I am a fourteen-year-old girl with bad spelling
and a messy room. If it helps any, I will tell you
I have always felt funny using chopsticks
and my favorite food is hot dogs.
My best friend is a white girl named Denise—
we look at boys together. She sat in front of me
all through grade school because of our names:
O'Conner, Ozawa. I know the back of Denise's head very well.
I tell her she's going bald. She tells me I copy on tests.
We're best friends.

I saw Denise today in Geography class.
She was sitting on the other side of the room.

"You're trying to start a war," she said, "giving secrets away
to the Enemy. Why can't you keep your big mouth shut?"
I didn't know what to say.
I gave her a packet of tomatoe seeds
and asked her to plant them for me, told her
when the first tomatoe ripens
to miss me.

GWENDOLYN BROOKS

Gwendolyn Brooks was born in Topeka, Kansas, in 1917 and raised in Chicago. The author of more than twenty books of poetry, she won the Pulitzer Prize in 1949 for *Annie Allen*. In 1968, she was named Poet Laureate for the state of Illinois, and from 1985 to 1986 she was Consultant in Poetry to the Library of Congress. She also received an American Academy of Arts and Letters award, the Frost Medal, a National Endowment for the Arts award, the Shelley Memorial Award, and fellowships from the Academy of American Poets and the Guggenheim Foundation. She lived in Chicago until her death on December 3, 2000.

The Sermon on the Warpland

"The fact that we are black is our ultimate reality."
—RON KARENGA

And several strengths from drowsiness campaigned
but spoke in Single Sermon on the warpland.

And went about the warpland saying No.
"My people, black and black, revile the River.
Say that the River turns, and turn the River.

Say that our Something in doublepod contains
seeds for the coming hell and health together.
Prepare to meet
(sisters, brothers) the brash and terrible weather;
the pains;
the bruising; the collapse of bestials, idols.
But then oh then!—the stuffing of the hulls!
the seasoning of the perilously sweet!
the health! the heralding of the clear obscure!

Build now your Church, my brothers, sisters. Build
never with brick nor Corten nor with granite.
Build with lithe love. With love like lion-eyes.
With love like morningrise.
With love like black, our black—
luminously indiscreet;
complete; continuous."

The Second Sermon on the Warpland

For Walter Bradford

1.

This is the urgency: Live!
and have your blooming in the noise of the whirlwind.

2.

Salve salvage in the spin.
Endorse the splendor splashes;
stylize the flawed utility;
prop a malign or failing light—
but know the whirlwind is our commonwealth.
Not the easy man, who rides above them all,
not the jumbo brigand,
not the pet bird of poets, that sweetest sonnet,
shall straddle the whirlwind.
Nevertheless, live.

3.

All about are the cold places,
all about are the pushmen and jeopardy, theft—
all about are the stormers and scramblers but
what must our Season be, which starts from Fear?
Live and go out.
Define and
medicate the whirlwind.

4.

The time
cracks into furious flower. Lifts its face
all unashamed. And sways in wicked grace.

Whose half-black hands assemble oranges
is tom-tom hearted
(goes in bearing oranges and boom).
And there are bells for orphans—
and red and shriek and sheen.
A garbageman is dignified
as any diplomat.
Big Bessie's feet hurt like nobody's business,
but she stands—bigly—under the unruly scrutiny, stands in the wild weed.

In the wild weed
she is a citizen,
and is a moment of highest quality; admirable.

It is lonesome, yes. For we are the last of the loud.
Nevertheless, live.

Conduct your blooming in the noise and whip of the whirlwind.

MALIN PEREIRA

Dr. Malin Pereira earned her B.A., M.A., and Ph.D. from the University of Wisconsin–Madison. She is an associate professor of English at the University of North Carolina–Charlotte. The following is text from a speech delivered before the Unitarian Universalist Church of Charlotte in 1995. We include this exploration here to provide interesting insight into the poetic vision of Gwendolyn Brooks.

"The Sermons on the Warpland": Gwendolyn Brooks' Moral Vision

In the 1960s, as the Vietnam War raged on, student protests at U.S. college campuses commanded attention, as young men burned their draft cards rather than participate in a war of such questionable justification. Another 50,000 demonstrated at the Lincoln Memorial and the Pentagon. And at 1968's Democratic National Convention in Chicago, protesters grabbed national press coverage as they tried to have their antiwar concerns heard.

The war wasn't only in Vietnam—there was also one at home. Racial discord took center stage in both the South as well as Northern urban centers. Black Americans, frustrated by the slowed progress of the civil rights movement and worsening economic and social conditions, rioted in cities across the country: Tampa, Cincinnati, Buffalo, Newark, Minneapolis, Detroit and New Haven in 1967; Chicago, Washington, and Baltimore in 1968. What is that saying about a riot? A riot is the voices of the unheard? Many African Americans felt unheard.

The South, as those of you from here might recall, was in turmoil over federally mandated school desegregation, which was upheld on appeal in 1967. Pro-segregation forces fought back, electing Lester G. Maddox, a militant segregationist, governor of Georgia. In the wake of racial conflict, the National Guard was called in to take over Jackson State College, imposing martial law downtown.

Black Power, which had gained ground in the African American community as the Northern civil rights movement ground to a halt, called for blacks to take back the power denied them by white America "by any means necessary," as Malcolm X said (although Malcolm himself was dead before 67). Stokely Carmichael called for "total revolution" by blacks in a radio broadcast from Havana. While the Black Power movement was part of a valuable process of self-empowerment and pride for African Americans, many white Americans were frightened by its assertive rhetoric—and the racial divide widened.

During chaotic times such as these, people especially have need of a dream. [The years] 1967 and 68 saw many dreams dashed. One such dream was embodied in the Apollo space program. The nation mourned when three U.S. astronauts in the first Apollo craft died in a flash fire on the ground at Cape Kennedy. Another dream lay in our hope for change through our leaders. Both King and Robert Kennedy were assassinated in 1968. King's murder was devastating to those involved in the civil rights movement. Kennedy's death was especially overwhelming for many Americans—not because he was necessarily the greatest of our leaders to be killed, but simply because, following the murders of John Kennedy in 63, Malcolm X in 65, and King in April of 68, Robert Kennedy had become the last of the carriers of our dream. His death in June of 68 killed for many the dream of real change.

This is the "warped land" or, to try the word play another way, the "war planned" that occasioned these poems. Although, because this is 1995, I can't do a neat thing with the years, like saying "thirty years later" or parallel 1968 and 1998, the chaotic social context of Brooks' poems shares much with our own confusing world, and thus her sermons can offer us important suggestions on how we might negotiate our own warped land today. By echoing the Sermon on the Mount in her titles, Brooks signifies that the lessons of these sermon/poems, like the lessons of Jesus' sermon, are meant to be universal. Jesus didn't limit his moral lessons to a certain people, or a particular time period, or a specific land. Although the multitudes listening to him were from Galilee, Jerusalem, and Jordan, he didn't say "Here's my moral vision for Galileans, Jerusalemians, and Jordanians." No. Biblical scholars, as well as all the regular folks who follow the Bible's teachings, assume his guidelines were meant to transcend time, race, religion, culture, and nationality. Brooks' Sermons on the Warpland likewise provide precepts for everyone. So, even though these poems are directed to a black audience in the late 1960s, their lessons transcend their context and can helped guide our response to our own warped land.

Maybe our land isn't warped in the same ways as 1967 and 68, but when we have renegade anti-government folks blowing up federal buildings, the OJ Simpson trial passing a one-year mark in its media circus, the economic gap widening between rich and poor—especially in the black community where, while we have the largest black middle class ever, many African Americans are living in total poverty in urban war zones—and legislators are cutting funding for every social service imaginable. I don't know about you, but I think that's pretty warped. These are the years of backlash: anti-feminist, anti-intellectual, anti-affirmative action, anti-abortion, anti-environment. When the courts punish a woman by taking away custody of her child because she needs to go to college to improve their standard of living; mind you, although they give the father custody, of course he's not going to stay home and care for the child—his mother's going to. This is warped. And we are having riots too—remember the L.A. riot just three years ago? Every time is warped in its own ways, and ours is no exception.

One of the characteristics of the late 1960s that, I think, many find appealing is that, despite all the horrors of the war and the opposition to racial justice, a spirit of hope for a revolution, or at least a dramatic change, still held many hearts. People still believed, people still had faith in the possibility of a better land, a better world. It is this spirit which informs Brooks' poems. Written in the tradition of the African American sermon, these poems inspire us to try and change our warped land; they exhort us to not give up, but to stay in the fight. These poems offer us a moral vision that empowers us to change the course of events, or, as Brooks terms it in the first poem, to "turn the River." Rather than whining with us about how bad the world is today, these poems tell us to say "No"—and loudly—when we disagree with the course of the river of current events, and to take charge and turn that river the direction we want it to go by coming together.

The first poem, "The Sermon on the Warpland," acknowledges that turning the River, or really changing our direction, is both destructive and constructive. Often you need to tear something down in order to build something new up. This is what Brooks means when she talks about the "doublepod" that contains seeds for the coming hell and health together. A lot of times, I think we say we want change, but we aren't willing to endure the tumult and pain that comes with it. Sometimes, though, you have to go through hell first to get to health as any of you who have been through a divorce know all too well. Brooks' sermon/poem warns us that we need to be prepared to face the negative and endure it to get to the positive. That very organic image of the doublepod stands for the fruits we yield by facing the storms. The seeds will blossom after the rains.

The first sermon encourages us to face the storms of change that our turning the river will bring by building a church of community, faith, and love. We cannot withstand the destruction that precedes real change unless we stand together as a community of faith in our ideals and the future. Interestingly, Brooks insists that our Church not be built with the materials we typically think of as strong: brick, corten steel, or granite. Instead of a rigid and inflexible Church, the speaker of Brooks' sermon/poem exhorts us to build our church with "lithe love," meaning a supple, pliant kind of love. When you think about it, this makes perfect sense: a stiff, rigid structure will snap in a storm, whereas young trees that bend easily survive a whirlwind of force. I think Brooks is also warning us not to become rigid and dogmatic in our faith and ideals. Love and flexibility are the best response to adversity. Such a love can be strong (Like Lion-eyes) and future-looking (like morning-rise), but it should not be rigid—not codified into a permanent, unchanging structure.

Having empowered us to action, warned us to prepare to meet the storms that often precede peace, and encouraged us to build a flexible community of faith and love, Brooks in the second Sermon on the Warpland turns to the situation of the individual amidst radical change. That's really what change comes down to, isn't it?: The individual, the cornerstone of a democracy. She opens with a command, "Live! and have your blooming in the noise of the whirlwind." Remember that doublepod seed from the first sermon? Well here, it blooms in the individual who has the courage to face the whirlwind. It's so tempting to say: "Oh, it's too dangerous" or "I don't know what to do" or "What difference would I make" or "I'm scared" or "What would people think." I've said many of these myself at one time or another rather than getting involved in something messy that might effect some real change. Brooks depicts the involved individual, the person who stands out in the whirlwinds of change, rather than hiding at home, as the one who lives fully and blossoms. In the second section of the sermon/poem, Brooks suggests some individual's possible responses to the chaos of our times, all of which are admittedly partial, but at least are a start. Healing, aiding, supporting are ways to help the people and institutions affected in negative ways. Isolation or detachment, exemplified in the poem by the easy man, jumbo brigand, and sonnet writer, are inadequate responses that Brooks says cannot "straddle the whirlwind." She insists that we recognize that "the whirlwind is our commonwealth," meaning that it affects all of us, the whole body of our people in a democratic state. I think of how sometimes we talk about other people as if they lived on Mars, saying things like "Those welfare mothers" or "Those greedy corporations" or my personal favorite "Those lawyers." What such statements reflect is our lack of understanding that we are all in this together. I think of that proposition last year in California about illegal residents. What did voters thinks folks were going to do if social services were cut off? Just go away? Can't people realize that the starvation, illiteracy, and illness that would result will affect everyone in the community? What we need to do, Brooks says, is to help each other handle the whirlwind as best we can, lending a hand here, making the best of things there. A good example of that is John Lantz, who is profiled in this month's issue of World. When he inherited an apartment complex with multiple problems, including high turnover and low rent collection, instead of evicting people and taking punitive measures, he tried to help people, providing vacuum cleaners, English classes, social events, and garden plots. Small things, but they made a big difference. He realized we're all in this together.

Lantz says he realized that what prevented many of his tenants from participating at first was fear. "Fear is a major controlling factor in everyone's life." Brooks also knows that fear is what prevents many of us from taking action. We often feel like "All about are the cold places / all about are the pushmen and jeopardy, theft— / all about are the stormers and scramblers." I've had days where it seems the world is full of horrible people and frightening events, where every phone call is telemarketing or harassing, where drivers cut me off on the highway then give me the finger, where the nightly news seems full of carjackings, homicide, wars, and human suffering. Yes, the chaos does surround us; yes, the horrors seem overwhelming. But, as Brooks asks, "what must our Season be, which starts from Fear?" If we hide from the world out of fear, it will never change. The answer to crime isn't just to buy a security system and a gun, and sit home picking off trespassers. Brooks insists we must "Live and go out" for our land and world to improve. It reminds me of those "Take Back the Night" marches, which were an outgrowth of the Women's Movement. Instead of avoiding violence against women by saying women should stay home at night, such marches send the message that the night belongs to women too—that we should go out into it and live, and that it's the community's responsibility to help us do that. A season of fear is a season of death and despair, winter; a season of hope is a season of life and new beginnings, spring. We must have the courage to go out into the whirlwind in order to understand our circumstances and begin to heal them—to "define and medicate the whirlwind," as Brooks says. One cannot change what one doesn't understand, and one can't understand something unless one lives in it.

In the final section of the poem, Brooks celebrates each individual's equality in our commonwealth. The individual is the cornerstone of a democracy, and Brooks here applauds the courageous individuals who, despite pain and loneliness, stand in the "wild weed" of a democratic land. As such, everyone is equal; as Brooks writes, "A garbageman is dignified / as any diplomat." To illustrate this concept of the common individual as a democratic hero, Brooks uses the figure of Big Bessie, a woman whose feet are killing her, but who takes her rightful place as a citizen in our wild weed. It feels awkward to her to stand out and be noticed, and Brooks acknowledges that it is lonesome to be one of the few individuals. But Brooks admires such an individual and in Big Bessie offers us a model of our own participation in our democracy. It may be inconvenient, it may even be painful, it may make you feel really exposed, but stand up and participate. Become one of the Big Bessies of the world—ordinary citizens who stood up and said "No" and tried to turn the river: Mother Hale, Nelson Mandela, the Russian people, Lech Walesa, Aung San Suu Kyi, the Chinese students, Marion Wright Edelman. The list goes on. And then you, too, shall have your blooming amidst the noise and whip of the whirlwind.

Margaret Walker

Margaret Walker (1915–1988) completed her B.A. at Northwestern University (Illinois) when she was only nineteen. Walker completed her M.A. at the University of Iowa by writing *For My People,* for which she later became the first African American to win the Yale Younger Poets award. Best known for *Jubilee,* a neo-slave narrative, she is the author of four volumes of poetry, a novel, a biography, and a number of critical essays.

The following poem was published in 1942.

For My People

For my people everywhere singing their slave songs
       repeatedly: their dirges and their ditties and their blues
      and jubilees, praying their prayers nightly to an
      unknown god, bending their knees humbly to an unseen
      power;
For my people lending their strength to the years: to the
      gone years and the now years and the maybe years,
      washing ironing cooking scrubbing sewing mending
      hoeing plowing digging planting pruning patching

dragging along never gaining never reaping never
knowing and never understanding;

For my playmates in the clay and dust and sand of Alabama
backyards playing baptizing and preaching, and doctor
and jail and soldier and school and mama and
cooking and playhouse and concert and store and
Miss Choomby and hair and company;

For the cramped bewildered years we went to school to
learn to know the reasons why and the answers to and
the people who and the places where and the days
when, in memory of the bitter hours when we discovered
we were black and poor and small and different
and nobody wondered and nobody understood;

For the boys and girls who grew in spite of these things to
be Man and Woman, to laugh and dance and sing and
play and drink their wine and religion and success, to
marry their playmates and bear children and then die
of consumption and anemia and lynching;

For my people thronging 47th Street in Chicago and Lenox
Avenue in New York and Rampart Street in New
Orleans, lost disinherited dispossessed and HAPPY people
filling the cabarets and taverns and other people's
pockets needing bread and shoes and milk and land
and money and Something—Something all our own;

For my people walking blindly, spreading joy, losing time
being lazy, sleeping when hungry, shouting when burdened,
drinking when hopeless, tied and shackled and
tangled among ourselves by the unseen creatures who
tower over us omnisciently and laugh;

For my people blundering and groping and floundering in
the dark of churches and schools and clubs and
societies, associations and councils and committees and
conventions, distressed and disturbed and deceived
and devoured by money-hungry glory-craving leeches,
preyed on by facile force of state and fad and novelty
by false prophet and holy believer;

For my people standing staring trying to fashion a better
way from confusion from hypocrisy and misunderstanding,
trying to fashion a world that will hold all
the people all the faces all the adams and eves and
their countless generations;

Let a new earth rise. Let another world be born. Let a bloody
peace be written in the sky. Let a second generation
full of courage issue forth, let a people loving freedom
come to growth, let a beauty full of healing and a

strength of final clenching be the pulsing in our spirits
and our blood. Let the martial songs be written, let
the dirges disappear. Let a race of men now rise and
take control!

JOY HARJO

Joy Harjo was born in Tulsa, Oklahoma, in 1951. She is the author of more than
six volumes of poetry, and she is well-known for her performance art—a combination of
saxophone and poetry—along with her band, Poetic Justice. She has received many honors throughout her career, including the William Carlos Williams Award, fellowships
from the Arizona Commission on the Arts, the Witter Bynner Foundation, and the National Endowment for the Arts.

The following poem was published in the collection *The Woman Who Fell From the
Sky* in 1994.

A Postcolonial Tale

Every day is a reenactment of the creation story. We emerge from dense
unspeakable material, through the shimmering power of dreaming stuff.
This is the first world, and the last.
Once we abandoned ourselves for television, the box that separates the
dreamer from the dreaming. It was as if we were stolen, put into a bag car-
ried on the back of a whiteman who pretends to own the earth and the sky.
In the sack were all the people of the world.
We fought until there was a hole in the bag.
When we fell we were not aware of falling. We were driving to work, or to
the mall. The children were in school learning subtraction with guns.
We found ourselves somewhere near the diminishing point of civilization,
not far from the trickster's bag of tricks. Everything was as we imagined it.
The earth and stars, every creature and leaf imagined with us.
The imagining needs praise as does every living thing. We are evidence of
this praise, and when we laugh, we're indestructible. No story or song will
translate the full impact of falling, or the inverse power of rising up. Of rising up.
Our children put down their guns when we did to imagine with us. We
imagined the shining link between the heart and the sun. We imagined tables of food for everyone. We imagined the songs.
The imagination conversely illumines us, sings with us, dances with us,
drums with us, loves us.

E. E. CUMMINGS

Edward Estlin Cummings was born in Massachusetts in 1894. He received his B.A. in 1915 and his M.A. in 1916, both from Harvard. During World War I, Cummings worked as an ambulance driver in France, but he was interned in a prison camp by the French authorities for his outspoken antiwar views. After the war, he returned to the United States. Known for his experimentation with language, at the time of his death in 1962, he was the second most widely read poet in America (following Robert Frost).

The following poem was published in 1966.

Five Americans

I. LIZ

with breathing as (faithfully) her lownecked
dress a little topples and slightly expands
one square foot mired in silk wrinkling loth
stocking begins queerly to do a few
gestures to death,
                              the silent shoulders are both
slowly with pinkish ponderous arms bedecked
whose white thick wrists deliver promptly to
a deep lap enormous mindless hands.
and no one knows what (i am sure of this)
her blunt unslender, what her big unkeen
"Business is rotten" the face yawning said
what her mouth thinks of
                              (if it were a kiss
distinct entirely melting sinuous lean . . .
whereof this lady in some book had read

II. MAME

she puts down the handmirror. "Look at" arranging
before me a mellifluous idiot grin
(with what was nose upwrinkled into nothing
earthly, while the slippery eyes drown
in surging flesh). A thumblike index down-
dragging yanks back skin "see" (i, seeing, ceased
to breathe). The plump left first opening
"wisdom." Flicker of gold. "Yep. No gas. Flynn"

the words drizzle untidily from released
cheeks "I'll tell duh woild; some noive all right.
Aint much on looks but how dat baby ached."

and when i timidly hinted "novocaine?"
the eyes outstart, curl, bloat, are newly baked

and swaggering cookies of indignant light

III. GERT

joggle i think will do it although the glad
monosyllable jounce possibly can tell
better how the balloons move (as
her ghost lurks, a Beau Brummell sticking in its three-

cornered always moist mouth)—jazz,
for whose twitching lips, between you and me
almost succeeds while toddle rings the bell.
But if her tall corpsecoloured body seat
itself (with the uncouth habitual dull
jerk at garters) there's no sharpest neat
word for the thing.
                    Her voice?
                            gruesome: a trull
leaps from the lungs "gimme uh swell fite

like up ter yknow, Rektuz, Toysday nite;
where uh guy gets gayn troze uh lobstersalad

IV. MARJ

"life?
        Listen" the feline she with radishred
legs said (crossing them slowly) "I'm
asleep. Yep. Youse is asleep kid
and everybody is." And i hazarded
"god" (blushing slightly)—"O damn
ginks like dis Gawd" opening slowlyslowly
them—then carefully the rolypoly
voice squatting on a mountain of gum did
something like a whisper, "even her."
"The Madam?" I emitted; vaguely watching
that mountainous worthy in the fragile act
of doing her eyebrows.-Marj's laughter smacked

me: pummeling the curtains, drooped to a purr . . .

i left her permanently smiling

V. FRAN

should i entirely ask of god why
on the alert neck of this brittle whore
delicately wobbles an improbably distinct face,
and how these wooden big two feet conclude
happeningly the unfirm drooping bloated
calves
            i would receive the answer more
or less deserved, Young fellow go in peace.
which i do, being as Dick Mid once noted
lifting a Green River (here's to youse)
"a bloke wot's well behaved" . . . and always try
to not wonder how let's say elation
causes the bent eyes thickly to protrude—

or why her tiniest whispered invitation
is like a clock striking in a dark house

Fiction

GISH JEN

(Lillian) Gish Jen was born in Scarsdale, New York, in 1956. A second-generation Chinese American and a graduate of Harvard University, she earned a degree in English. Jen's work has appeared in *The New Yorker, The New Republic,* and the *New York Times,* as well as many notable anthologies.

The following short story was published in 1991.

In the American Society

1. HIS OWN SOCIETY

When my father took over the pancake house, it was to send my little sister Mona and me to college. We were only in junior high at the time, but my father believed in getting a jump on things. "Those Americans always saying it," he told us. "Smart guys thinking in advance." My mother elaborated, explaining that businesses took bringing up, like children. They could take years to get going, she said, years.

In this case, though, we got rich right away. At two months we were breaking even, and at four, those same hotcakes that could barely withstand the weight of butter and syrup were supporting our family with ease. My mother bought a station wagon with air conditioning, my father an oversized, red vinyl recliner for the back room; and as time went on and the business continued to thrive, my father started to talk about his grandfather and the village he had reigned over in China—things my father had never talked about when he worked for other people. He told us about the bags of rice his family would give out to the poor at New Year's, and about the people who came to beg, on their hands and knees, for his grandfather to intercede for the more wayward of their relatives. "Like that Godfather in the movie," he would tell us as, his feet up, he distributed paychecks. Sometimes an employee would get two green envelopes instead of one, which meant that Jimmy needed a tooth pulled, say, or that Tiffany's husband was in the clinker again.

"It's nothing, nothing," he would insist, sinking back into his chair. "Who else is going to take care of you people?"

My mother would mostly just sigh about it. "Your father thinks this is China," she would say, and then she would go back to her mending. Once in a while, though, when my father had given away a particularly large sum, she would exclaim, outraged, "But this here is the U-S-of-A!"—this apparently having been what she used to tell immigrant stock boys when they came in late.

She didn't work at the supermarket anymore; but she had made it to the rank of manager before she left, and this had given her not only new words and phrases, but new ideas about herself, and about America, and about what was what in general. She had opinions, now, on how downtown should be zoned; she could pump her own gas and check her own oil; and for all she used to chide Mona and me for being "copy-cats," she herself was now interested in espadrilles, and wallpaper, and most recently, the town country club.

"So join already," said Mona, flicking a fly off her knee.

My mother enumerated the problems as she sliced up a quarter round of watermelon: there was the cost. There was the waiting list. There was the fact that no one in our family played either tennis or golf.

"So what?" said Mona.

"It would be waste," said my mother.

"Me and Callie can swim in the pool."

"Plus you need that recommendation letter from a member."

"Come *on*," said Mona. "Annie's mom'd write you a letter in a *sec*."

My mother's knife glinted in the early summer sun. I spread some more newspaper on the picnic table.

"*Plus* you have to eat there twice a month. You know what that means." My mother cut another, enormous slice of fruit.

"No, I *don't* know what that means," said Mona.

"It means Dad would have to wear a jacket, dummy," I said.

"Oh! Oh! Oh!" said Mona, clasping her hand to her breast. "Oh! Oh! Oh! Oh! Oh!"

We all laughed: my father had no use for nice clothes, and would wear only ten-year-old shirts, with grease-spotted pants, to show how little he cared what anyone thought.

"Your father doesn't believe in joining the American society," said my mother. "He wants to have his own society."

"So go to dinner without him." Mona shot her seeds out in long arcs over the lawn. "Who cares what he thinks?"

But of course we all did care, and knew my mother could not simply up and do as she pleased. For in my father's mind, a family owed its head a degree of loyalty that left no room for dissent. To embrace what he embraced was to love; and to embrace something else was to betray him.

He demanded a similar sort of loyalty of his workers, whom he treated more like servants than employees. Not in the beginning, of course. In the beginning all he wanted was for them to keep on doing what they used to do, and to that end he concentrated mostly on leaving them alone. As the months passed, though, he expected more and more of them, with the result that for all his largesse, he began to have trouble keeping help. The cooks and busboys complained that he asked them to fix radiators and trim hedges, not only at the restaurant, but at our house; the waitresses that he sent them on errands and made them chauffeur him around. Our head waitress, Gertrude, claimed that he once even asked her to scratch his back.

"It's not just the blacks don't believe in slavery," she said when she quit.

My father never quite registered her complaint, though, nor those of the others who left. Even after Eleanor quit, then Tiffany, then Gerald, and Jimmy, and even his best cook, Eureka Andy, for whom he had bought new glasses, he remained mostly convinced that the fault lay with them.

"All they understand is that assembly line," he lamented. "Robots, they are. They want to be robots."

There *were* occasions when the clear running truth seemed to eddy, when he would pinch the vinyl of his chair up into little peaks and wonder if he were doing things right. But with time he would always smooth the peaks back down; and when business started to slide in the spring, he kept on like a horse in his ways.

By the summer our dishboy was overwhelmed with scraping. It was no longer just the hashbrowns that people were leaving for trash, and the service was as bad as the food. The waitresses served up French pancakes instead of German, apple juice instead of orange, spilt things on laps, on coats. On the Fourth of July some greenhorn sent an entire side of fries slaloming down a lady's *massif centrale.* Meanwhile in the back room, my father labored through articles on the economy.

"What is housing starts?" he puzzled. "What is GNP?"

Mona and I did what we could, filling in as busgirls and bookkeepers and, one afternoon, stuffing the comments box that hung by the cashier's desk. That was Mona's idea. We rustled up a variety of pens and pencils, checked boxes for an hour, smeared the cards up with coffee and grease, and waited. It took a few days for my father to notice that the box was full, and he didn't say anything about it for a few days more. Finally, though, he started to complain of fatigue; and then he began to complain that the staff was not what it could be. We encouraged him in this—pointing out, for instance, how many dishes got chipped—but in the end all that happened was that, for the first time since we took over the restaurant, my father got it into his head to fire someone. Skip, a skinny busboy who was saving up for a sports car, said nothing as my father mumbled on about the price of dishes. My father's hands shook as he wrote out the severance check; and he spent the rest of the day napping in his chair once it was over.

As it was going on midsummer, Skip wasn't easy to replace. We hung a sign in the window and advertised in the paper, but no one called the first week, and the person who called the second didn't show up for his interview. The third week, my father phoned Skip to see if he would come back, but a friend of his had already sold him a Corvette for cheap.

Finally a Chinese guy named Booker turned up. He couldn't have been more than thirty, and was wearing a lighthearted seersucker suit, but he looked as though life had him pinned: his eyes were bloodshot and his chest sunken, and the muscles of his neck seemed to strain with the effort of holding his head up. In a single dry breath he told us that he had never bussed tables but was willing to learn, and that he was on the lam from the deportation authorities.

"I do not want to lie to you," he kept saying. He had come to the United States on a student visa, had run out of money, and was now in a bind. He was loath to go back to Taiwan, as it happened—he looked up at this point, to be sure my father wasn't pro-KMT—but all he had was a phony social security card and a willingness to absorb all blame, should anything untoward come to pass.

"I do not think, anyway, that it is against law to hire me, only to be me," he said, smiling faintly.

Anyone else would have examined him on this, but my father conceived of laws as speed bumps rather than curbs. He wiped the counter with his sleeve, and told Booker to report the next morning.

"I will be good worker," said Booker.

"Good," said my father.

"Anything you want me to do, I will do."

My father nodded.

Booker seemed to sink into himself for a moment. "Thank you," he said finally. "I am appreciate your help. I am very, very appreciate for everything." He reached out to shake my father's hand.

My father looked at him. "Did you eat today?" he asked in Mandarin.

Booker pulled at the hem of his jacket.

"Sit down," said my father. "Please, have a seat."

My father didn't tell my mother about Booker, and my mother didn't tell my father about the country club. She would never have applied, except that Mona, while over at Annie's, had let it drop that our mother wanted to join. Mrs. Lardner came by the very next day.

"Why, I'd be honored and delighted to write you people a letter," she said. Her skirt billowed around her.

"Thank you so much," said my mother. "But it's too much trouble for you, and also my husband is . . ."

"Oh, it's no trouble at all, no trouble at all. I tell you." She leaned forward so that her chest freckles showed. "I know just how it is. It's a secret of course, but you know, my natural father was Jewish. Can you see it? Just look at my skin."

"My husband," said my mother.

"I'd be honored and delighted," said Mrs. Lardner with a little wave of her hands. "Just honored and delighted."

Mona was triumphant. "See, Mom," she said, waltzing around the kitchen when Mrs. Lardner left. "What did I tell you? 'I'm just honored and delighted, just honored and delighted.'" She waved her hands in the air.

"You know, the Chinese have a saying," said my mother. "To do nothing is better than to overdo. You mean well, but you tell me now what will happen."

"I'll talk Dad into it," said Mona, still waltzing. "Or I bet Callie can. He'll do anything Callie says."

"I can try, anyway," I said.

"Did you hear what I said?" said my mother. Mona bumped into the broom closet door. "You're not going to talk anything; you've already made enough trouble." She started on the dishes with a clatter.

Mona poked diffidently at a mop.

I sponged off the counter. "Anyway," I ventured, "I bet our name'll never even come up."

"That's if we're lucky," said my mother.

"There's all these people waiting," I said.

"Good," she said. She started on a pot.

I looked over at Mona, who was still cowering in the broom closet. "In fact, there's some black family's been waiting so long, they're going to sue," I said.

My mother turned off the water. "Where'd you hear that?"

"Patty told me."

She turned the water back on, started to wash a dish, then put it back down and shut the faucet.

"I'm sorry," said Mona.

"Forget it," said my mother. "Just forget it."

Booker turned out to be a model worker, whose boundless gratitude translated into a willingness to do anything. As he also learned quickly, he soon knew not only how to bus, but how to cook, and how to wait table, and how to keep the books. He fixed the walk-in door so that it stayed shut, reupholstered the torn seats in the dining room, and devised a system for tracking inventory. The only stone in the rice was that he tended to be sickly; but, reliable even in illness, he would always send a friend to take his place. In this way we got to know Ronald, Lynn, Dirk, and Cedric, all of whom, like Booker, had problems with their legal status and were anxious to please. They weren't all as capable as Booker, though, with the exception of Cedric, whom my father often hired even when Booker was well. A round wag of a man who called Mona and me *shou hou*—skinny monkeys—he was a professed nonsmoker who was nevertheless always begging drags off of other people's cigarettes. This last habit drove our head cook, Fernando, crazy, especially since, when refused a hit, Cedric would occasionally snitch one. Winking impishly at Mona and me, he would steal up to an ashtray, take a quick puff, and then break out laughing so that the smoke came rolling out of his mouth in a great incriminatory cloud. Fernando accused him of stealing fresh cigarettes too, even whole packs.

"Why else do you think he's weaseling around in the back of the store all the time," he said. His face was blotchy with anger. "The man is a frigging thief."

Other members of the staff supported him in this contention and joined in on an "Operation Identification," which involved numbering and initialing their cigarettes—even though what they seemed to fear for wasn't so much their cigarettes as their jobs. Then one of the cooks quit; and rather than promote someone, my father hired Cedric for the position. Rumors flew that he was taking only half the normal salary, that Alex had been pressured to resign, and that my father was looking for a position with which to placate Booker, who had been bypassed because of his health.

The result was that Fernando categorically refused to work with Cedric.

"The only way I'll cook with that piece of slime," he said, shaking his huge tattooed fist, "is if it's his ass frying on the grill."

My father cajoled and cajoled, to no avail, and in the end was simply forced to put them on different schedules.

The next week Fernando got caught stealing a carton of minute steaks. My father would not tell even Mona and me how he knew to be standing by the back door when

Fernando was on his way out, but everyone suspected Booker. Everyone but Fernando, that is, who was sure Cedric had been the tip-off. My father held a staff meeting in which he tried to reassure everyone that Alex had left on his own, and that he had no intention of firing anyone. But though he was careful not to mention Fernando, everyone was so amazed that he was being allowed to stay that Fernando was incensed nonetheless.

"Don't you all be putting your bug eyes on me," he said. "*He's* the frigging crook." He grabbed Cedric by the collar.

Cedric raised an eyebrow. "Cook, you mean," he said.

At this Fernando punched Cedric in the mouth; and the words he had just uttered notwithstanding, my father fired him on the spot.

With everything that was happening, Mona and I were ready to be getting out of the restaurant. It was almost time: the days were still stuffy with summer, but our window shade had started flapping in the evening as if gearing up to go out. That year the breezes were full of salt, as they sometimes were when they came in from the East, and they blew anchors and docks through my mind like so many tumbleweeds, filling my dreams with wherries and lobsters and grainy-faced men who squinted, day in and day out, at the sky.

It was time for a change, you could feel it; and yet the pancake house was the same as ever. The day before school started my father came home with bad news.

"Fernando called police," he said, wiping his hand on his pant leg.

My mother naturally wanted to know what police; and so with much coughing and hawing, the long story began, the latest installment of which had the police calling immigration, and immigration sending an investigator. My mother sat stiff as whalebone as my father described how the man summarily refused lunch on the house and how my father had admitted, under pressure, that he knew there were "things" about his workers.

"So now what happens?"

My father didn't know. "Booker and Cedric went with him to the jail," he said. "But me, here I am." He laughed uncomfortably.

The next day my father posted bail for "his boys" and waited apprehensively for something to happen. The day after that he waited again, and the day after that he called our neighbor's law student son, who suggested my father call the immigration department under an alias. My father took his advice; and it was thus that he discovered that Booker was right: it was illegal for aliens to work, but it wasn't to hire them.

In the happy interval that ensued, my father apologized to my mother, who in turn confessed about the country club, for which my father had no choice but to forgive her. Then he turned his attention back to "his boys."

My mother didn't see that there was anything to do.

"I like to talking to the judge," said my father.

"This is not China," said my mother.

"I'm only talking to him. I'm not give him money unless he wants it."

"You're going to land up in jail."

"So what else I should do?" My father threw up his hands. "Those are my boys."

"Your boys!" exploded my mother. "What about your family? What about your wife?"

My father took a long sip of tea. "You know," he said finally. "In the war my father sent our cook to the soldiers to use. He always said it—the province comes before the town, the town comes before the family."

"A restaurant is not a town," said my mother.

My father sipped at his tea again. "You know, when I first come to the United States, I also had to hide-and-seek with those deportation guys. If people did not helping me, I'm not here today."

My mother scrutinized her hem.

After a minute I volunteered that before seeing a judge, he might try a lawyer.

He turned. "Since when did you become so afraid like your mother?"

I started to say that it wasn't a matter of fear, but he cut me off.

"What I need today," he said, "is a son."

My father and I spent the better part of the next day standing in lines at the immigration office. He did not get to speak to a judge, but with much persistence he managed to speak to a judge's clerk, who tried to persuade him that it was not her place to extend him advice. My father, though, shamelessly plied her with compliments and offers of free pancakes until she finally conceded that she personally doubted anything would happen to either Cedric or Booker.

"Especially if they're 'needed workers,' " she said, rubbing at the red marks her glasses left on her nose. She yawned. "Have you thought about sponsoring them to become permanent residents?"

Could he do that? My father was overjoyed. And what if he saw to it right away? Would she perhaps put in a good word with the judge?

She yawned again, her nostrils flaring. "Don't worry," she said.

"They'll get a fair hearing."

My father returned jubilant. Booker and Cedric hailed him as their savior, their Buddha incarnate. He was like a father to them, they said; and laughing and clapping, they made him tell the story over and over, sorting over the details like jewels. And how old was the assistant judge? And what did she say?

That evening my father tipped the paperboy a dollar and bought a pot of mums for my mother, who suffered them to be placed on the dining room table. The next night he took us all out to dinner. Then on Saturday, Mona found a letter on my father's chair at the restaurant.

> Dear Mr. Chang,
>
> You are the grat boss. But, we do not like to trial, so will runing away now. Plese to excus us. People saying the law in America is fears like dragon. Here is only $140. We hope some day we can pay back the rest bale. You will getting interest, as you diserving, so grat a boss you are. Thank you for every thing. In next life you will be burn in rich family, with no more pancaks.
>
> Yours truley,
> Booker + Cedric

In the weeks that followed my father went to the pancake house for crises, but otherwise hung around our house, fiddling idly with the sump pump and boiler in an effort, he said, to get ready for winter. It was as though he had gone into retirement, except that instead of moving South, he had moved to the basement. He even took to showering my mother with little attentions, and to calling her "old girl," and when we finally heard that the club had entertained all the applications it could for the year, he was so sympathetic that he seemed more disappointed than my mother.

2. IN THE AMERICAN SOCIETY

Mrs. Lardner tempered the bad news with an invitation to a bon voyage "bash" she was throwing for a friend of hers who was going to Greece for six months.

"Do come," she urged. "You'll meet everyone, and then, you know, if things open up in the spring . . ." She waved her hands.

My mother wondered if it would be appropriate to show up at a party for someone they didn't know, but "the honest truth" was that this was an annual affair. "If it's not Greece, it's Antibes," sighed Mrs. Lardner. "We really just do it because his wife left him and his daughter doesn't speak to him, and poor Jeremy just feels so *unloved.*"

She also invited Mona and me to the goings-on, as "*demi*-guests" to keep Annie out of the champagne. I wasn't too keen on the idea, but *before* I could say anything, she had already thanked us for so generously agreeing to honor her with our presence.

"A pair of little princesses, you are!" she told us. "A pair of princesses!"

The party was that Sunday. On Saturday, my mother took my father out shopping for a suit. As it was the end of September, she insisted that he buy a worsted rather than a seersucker, even though it was only ten, rather than fifty percent off. My father protested that it was as hot out as ever, which was true—a thick Indian summer had cozied murderously up to us—but to no avail. Summer clothes, said my mother, were not properly worn after Labor Day.

The suit was unfortunately as extravagant in length as it was in price, which posed an additional quandary, since the tailor wouldn't be in until Monday. The salesgirl, though, found a way of tacking it up temporarily.

"Maybe this suit not fit me," fretted my father.

"Just don't take your jacket off," said the salesgirl.

He gave her a tip before they left, but when he got home refused to remove the price tag.

"I like to asking the tailor about the size," he insisted.

"You mean you're going to *wear* it and then return it?" Mona rolled her eyes.

"I didn't say I'm return it," said my father stiffly. "I like to asking the tailor, that's all."

The party started off swimmingly, except that most people were wearing bermudas or wrap skirts. Still, my parents carried on, sharing with great feeling the complaints about the heat. Of course my father tried to eat a cracker full of shallots and burnt himself in an attempt to help Mr. Lardner turn the coals of the barbeque; but on the whole he seemed to be doing all right. Not nearly so well as my mother, though, who had accepted an entire cupful of Mrs. Lardner's magic punch, and seemed indeed to be under some spell. As Mona and Annie skirmished over whether some boy in their class inhaled when he smoked, I watched my mother take off her shoes, laughing and laughing as a man with a beard regaled her with Navy stories by the pool. Apparently he had been stationed in the Orient and remembered a few words of Chinese, which made my mother laugh still more. My father excused himself to go to the men's room then drifted back and weighed anchor at the hors d'oeuvres table, while my mother sailed on to a group of women, who tinkled at length over the clarity of her complexion. I dug out a book I had brought.

Just when I'd cracked the spine, though, Mrs. Lardner came by to bewail her short-age of servers. Her caterers were criminals, I agreed; and the next thing I knew I was handing out bits of marine life, making the rounds as amicably as I could.

"Here you go, Dad," I said when I got to the hors d'oeuvres table.

"Everything is fine," he said.

I hesitated to leave him alone; but then the man with the beard zeroed in on him, and though he talked of nothing but my mother, I thought it would be okay to get back to work. Just that moment, though, Jeremy Brothers lurched our way, an empty, albeit corked, wine bottle in hand. He was a slim, well-proportioned man, with a Roman nose and small eyes and a nice manly jaw that he allowed to hang agape.

"Hello," he said drunkenly. "Pleased to meet you."

"Pleased to meeting you," said my father.

"Right," said Jeremy. "Right. Listen. I have this bottle here, this most recalcitrant bottle. You see that it refuses to do my bidding. I bid it open sesame, please, and it does nothing." He pulled the cork out with his teeth, then turned the bottle upside down.

My father nodded.

"Would you have a word with it please?" said Jeremy. The man with the beard ex-cused himself. "Would you please have a goddamned word with it?"

My father laughed uncomfortably.

"Ah!" Jeremy bowed a little. "Excuse me, excuse me, excuse me. You are not my man, not my man at all." He bowed again and started to leave, but then circled back. "Viti-culture is not your forte, yes I can see that, see that plainly. But may I trouble you on an-other matter? Forget the damned bottle." He threw it into the pool, and winked at the people he splashed. "I have another matter. Do you speak Chinese?"

My father said he did not, but Jeremy pulled out a handkerchief with some char-acters on it anyway, saying that his daughter had sent it from Hong Kong and that he thought the characters might be some secret message.

"Long life," said my father.

"But you haven't looked at it yet."

"I know what it says without looking." My father winked at me.

"You do?"

"Yes, I do."

"You're making fun of me, aren't you?"

"No, no, no," said my father, winking again.

"Who are you anyway?" said Jeremy.

His smile fading, my father shrugged.

"*Who are you?*"

My father shrugged again.

Jeremy began to roar. "This is my party, *my party,* and I've never seen you before in my life." My father backed up as Jeremy came toward him. "*Who are you? WHO ARE YOU?*"

Just as my father was going to step back into the pool, Mrs. Lardner came running up. Jeremy informed her that there was a man crashing his party.

"Nonsense," said Mrs. Lardner. "This is Ralph Chang, who I invited extra especially so he could meet you." She straightened the collar of Jeremy's peach-colored polo shirt for him.

"Yes, well we've had a chance to chat," said Jeremy.

She whispered in his ear; he mumbled something; she whispered something more.

"I do apologize," he said finally.

My father didn't say anything.

"I do." Jeremy seemed genuinely contrite. "Doubtless you've seen drunks before, haven't you? You must have them in China."

"Okay," said my father.

As Mrs. Lardner glided off, Jeremy clapped his arm over my father's shoulders. "You know, I really am quite sorry, quite sorry."

My father nodded.

"What can I do, how can I make it up to you?"

"No thank you."

"No, tell me, tell me," wheedled Jeremy. "Tickets to casino night?" My father shook his head. "You don't gamble. Dinner at Bartholomew's?" My father shook his head again. "You don't eat." Jeremy scratched his chin. "You know, my wife was like you. Old Annabelle could never let me make things up—never, never, never, never, never."

My father wriggled out from under his arm.

"How about sport clothes? You are rather overdressed, you know, excuse me for saying so. But here." He took off his polo shirt and folded it up. "You can have this with my most profound apologies." He ruffled his chest hairs with his free hand.

"No thank you," said my father.

"No, take it, take it. Accept my apologies." He thrust the shirt into my father's arms. "I'm so very sorry, so very sorry. Please, try it on."

Helplessly holding the shirt, my father searched the crowd for my mother.

"Here, I'll help you off with your coat."

My father froze.

Jeremy reached over and took his jacket off. "Milton's, one hundred twenty-five dollars reduced to one hundred twelve-fifty," he read. "What a bargain, what a bargain!"

"Please give it back," pleaded my father. "Please."

"Now for your shirt," ordered Jeremy.

Heads began to turn.

"Take off your shirt."

"I do not take orders like a servant," announced my father.

"Take off your shirt, or I'm going to throw this jacket right into the pool, just right into this little pool here." Jeremy held it over the water.

"Go ahead."

"One hundred twelve-fifty," taunted Jeremy. "One hundred twelve . . ."

My father flung the polo shirt into the water with such force that part of it bounced back up into the air like a fluorescent fountain. Then it settled into a soft heap on top of the water. My mother hurried up.

"You're a sport!" said Jeremy, suddenly breaking into a smile and slapping my father on the back. "You're a sport! I like that. A man with spirit, that's what you are. A man with panache. Allow me to return to you your jacket." He handed it back to my father. "Good value you got on that, good value."

My father hurled the coat into the pool too. "We're leaving," he said grimly. "Leaving!"

"Now, Ralphie," said Mrs. Lardner, bustling up; but my father was already stomping off.

"Get your sister," he told me. To my mother: "Get your shoes."

"That was *great*, Dad," said Mona as we walked down to the cat. "You were *stupendous*."

"Way to show 'em," I said.

"What?" said my father offhandedly.

Although it was only just dusk, we were in a gulch, which made it hard to see anything except the gleam of his white shirt moving up the hill ahead of us.

"It was all my fault," began my mother.

"Forget it," said my father grandly. Then he said, "The only trouble is I left those keys in my jacket pocket."

"Oh *no*," said Mona.

"Oh no is right," said my mother.

"So we'll walk home," I said.

"But how're we going to get into the *house*," said Mona.

The noise of the party churned through the silence.

"Someone has to going back," said my father.

"Let's go to the pancake house first," suggested my mother. "We can wait there until the party is finished, and then call Mrs. Lardner."

Having all agreed that that was a good plan, we started walking again.

"God, just think," said Mona. "We're going to have to *dive* for them."

My father stopped a moment. We waited.

"You girls are good swimmers," he said finally. "Not like me."

Then his shirt started moving again, and we trooped up the hill after it, into the dark.

SHIRLEY JACKSON

Shirley Hardie Jackson was born December 14, 1916 in San Francisco, California. In 1940, she received her BA in English from Syracuse University. Jackson's writing career flourished with publications in *The New Yorker, Fantasy and Science Fiction, The Yale Review, The New Republic,* the *Saturday Evening Post,* and *Reader's Digest,* among others. She also published several collections of stories. She died in 1965.

The following short story was published in 1949.

The Lottery

The morning of June 27th was clear and sunny, with the fresh warmth of a full-summer day; the flowers were blossoming profusely and the grass was richly green. The people of the village began to gather in the square, between the post office and the bank, around ten o'clock; in some towns there were so many people that the lottery took two days and had to be started on June 26th, but in this village, where there were only about three hundred people, the whole lottery took less than two hours, so it could begin at ten o'clock in the morning and still be through in time to allow the villagers to get home for noon dinner.

The children assembled first, of course. School was recently over for the summer, and the feeling of liberty sat uneasily on most of them; they tended to gather together quietly for a while before they broke into boisterous play, and their talk was still of the classroom and the teacher, of books and reprimands. Bobby Martin had already stuffed his pockets full of stones, and the other boys soon followed his example, selecting the smoothest and roundest stones; Bobby and Harry Jones and Dickie Delacroix—the villagers pronounced this name "Dellacroy"—eventually made a great pile of stones in one corner of the square and guarded it against the raids of the other boys. The girls stood aside, talking among themselves, looking over their shoulders at the boys, and the very small children rolled in the dust or clung to the hands of their older brothers or sisters.

Soon the men began to gather, surveying their own children, speaking of planting and rain, tractors and taxes. They stood together, away from the pile of stones in the corner, and their jokes were quiet and they smiled rather than laughed. The women, wearing faded house dresses and sweaters, came shortly after their menfolk. They greeted one another and exchanged bits of gossip as they went to join their husbands. Soon the women, standing by their husbands, began to call to their children, and the children came reluctantly, having to be called four or five times. Bobby Martin ducked under his mother's grasping hand and ran, laughing, back to the pile of stones. His father spoke up sharply, and Bobby came quickly and took his place between his father and his oldest brother.

The lottery was conducted—as were the square dances, the teenage club, the Halloween program—by Mr. Summers, who had time and energy to devote to civic activities. He was a round-faced, jovial man and he ran the coal business, and people were sorry for him, because he had no children and his wife was a scold. When he arrived in the square, carrying the black wooden box, there was a murmur of conversation among the villagers, and he waved and called, "Little late today, folks." The postmaster, Mr. Graves, followed him, carrying a three-legged stool, and the stool was put in the center of the square and Mr. Summers set the black box down on it. The villagers kept their distance, leaving a space between themselves and the stool, and when Mr. Summers said, "Some of you fellows want to give me a hand?" there was a hesitation before two men, Mr. Martin and his oldest son, Baxter, came forward to hold the box steady on the stool while Mr. Summers stirred up the papers inside it.

The original paraphernalia for the lottery had been lost long ago, and the black box now resting on the stool had been put into use even before Old Man Warner, the oldest man in town, was born. Mr. Summers spoke frequently to the villagers about making a new box, but no one liked to upset even as much tradition as was represented by the black box. There was a story that the present box had been made with some pieces of the box that had preceded it, the one that had been constructed when the first people settled down to make a village here. Every year, after the lottery, Mr. Summers began talking again about a new box, but every year the subject was allowed to fade off without anything's being done. The black box grew shabbier each year; by now it was no longer completely black but splintered badly along one side to show the original wood color, and in some places faded or stained.

Mr. Martin and his oldest son, Baxter, held the black box securely on the stool until Mr. Summers had stirred the papers thoroughly with his hand. Because so much of the ritual had been forgotten or discarded, Mr. Summers had been successful in having slips of paper substituted for the chips of wood that had been used for generations. Chips of wood, Mr. Summers had argued, had been all very well when the village was tiny, but now that the population was more than three hundred and likely to keep on growing, it was necessary to use something that would fit more easily into the black box. The night before the lottery, Mr. Summers and Mr. Graves made up the slips of paper and put them in the box, and it was then taken to the safe of Mr. Summers' coal company and locked up until Mr. Summers was ready to take it to the square next morning. The rest of the year, the box was put away, sometimes one place, sometimes another; it had spent one year in Mr. Graves' barn and another year underfoot in the post office, and sometimes it was set on a shelf in the Martin grocery and left there.

There was a great deal of fussing to be done before Mr. Summers declared the lottery open. There were the lists to make up—of heads of families, heads of households in each family, members of each household in each family. There was the proper swearing-in of Mr. Summers by the postmaster, as the official of the lottery; at one time, some people remembered, there had been a recital of some sort, performed by the official of the lottery, a perfunctory, tuneless chant that had been rattled off duly each year; some people believed that the official of the lottery used to stand just so when he said or sang it, others believed that he was supposed to walk among the people, but years and years ago this part of the ritual had been allowed to lapse. There had been, also, a ritual salute, which the official of the lottery had had to use in addressing each person who came up to draw from the box, but this also had changed with time, until now it was felt necessary only for the official to speak to each person approaching. Mr. Summers was very good at all this; in his clean white shirt and blue jeans, with one hand resting carelessly on the black box, he seemed very proper and important as he talked interminably to Mr. Graves and the Martins.

Just as Mr. Summers finally left off talking and turned to the assembled villagers, Mrs. Hutchinson came hurriedly along the path to the square, her sweater thrown over her shoulders, and slid into place in the back of the crowd. "Clean forgot what day it was," she said to Mrs. Delacroix, who stood next to her, and they both laughed softly. "Thought my old man was out back stacking wood," Mrs. Hutchinson went on, "and then I looked out the window and the kids was gone, and then I remembered it was the twenty-seventh and came a-running." She dried her hands on her apron, and Mrs. Delacroix said, "You're in time, though. They're still talking away up there."

Mrs. Hutchinson craned her neck to see through the crowd and found her husband and children standing near the front. She tapped Mrs. Delacroix on the arm as a farewell and began to make her way through the crowd. The people separated good-humoredly to let her through; two or three people said, in voices just loud enough to be heard across the crowd, "Here comes your Missus, Hutchinson," and "Bill, she made it after all." Mrs. Hutchinson reached her husband, and Mr. Summers, who had been waiting, said cheerfully, "Thought we were going to have to get on without you, Tessie." Mrs. Hutchinson said, grinning, "Wouldn't have me leave m'dishes in the sink, now, would you, Joe?," and soft laughter ran through the crowd as the people stirred back into position after Mrs. Hutchinson's arrival.

"Well, now," Mr. Summers said soberly, "guess we better get started, get this over with, so's we can go back to work. Anybody ain't here?"

"Dunbar," several people said. "Dunbar, Dunbar."

Mr. Summers consulted his list. "Clyde Dunbar," he said. "That's right. He's broke his leg, hasn't he? Who's drawing for him?"

"Me, I guess," a woman said, and Mr. Summers turned to look at her. "Wife draws for her husband," Mr. Summers said. "Don't you have a grown boy to do it for you, Janey?" Although Mr. Summers and everyone else in the village knew the answer perfectly well, it was the business of the official of the lottery to ask such questions formally. Mr. Summers waited with an expression of polite interest while Mrs. Dunbar answered.

"Horace's not but sixteen yet," Mrs. Dunbar said regretfully. "Guess I gotta fill in for the old man this year."

"Right," Mr. Summers said. He made a note on the list he was holding. Then he asked, "Watson boy drawing this year?"

A tall boy in the crowd raised his hand. "Here," he said. "I'm drawing for m'mother and me." He blinked his eyes nervously and ducked his head as several voices in the crowd said things like "Good fellow, Jack," and "Glad to see your mother's got a man to do it."

"Well," Mr. Summers said, "guess that's everyone. Old Man Warner make it?"

"Here," a voice said, and Mr. Summers nodded.

A sudden hush fell on the crowd as Mr. Summers cleared his throat and looked at the list. "All ready?" he called. "Now, I'll read the names—heads of families first—and the men come up and take a paper out of the box. Keep the paper folded in your hand without looking at it until everyone has had a turn. Everything clear?"

The people had done it so many times that they only half listened to the directions; most of them were quiet, wetting their lips, not looking around. Then Mr. Summers raised one hand high and said, "Adams." A man disengaged himself from the crowd and came forward. "Hi, Steve," Mr. Summers said, and Mr. Adams said, "Hi, Joe." They grinned at one another humorlessly and nervously. Then Mr. Adams reached into the black box and took out a folded paper. He held it firmly by one corner as he turned and went hastily back to his place in the crowd, where he stood a little apart from his family, not looking down at his hand.

"Allen," Mr. Summers said. "Anderson. . . . Bentham."

"Seems like there's no time at all between lotteries any more," Mrs. Delacroix said to Mrs. Graves in the back row. "Seems like we got through with the last one only last week."

"Times sure goes fast," Mrs. Graves said.

"Clark. . . . Delacroix."

"There goes my old man," Mrs. Delacroix said. She held her breath while her husband went forward.

"Dunbar," Mr. Summers said, and Mrs. Dunbar went steadily to the box while one of the women said, "Go on, Janey," and another said, "There she goes."

"We're next," Mrs. Graves said. She watched while Mr. Graves came around from the side of the box, greeted Mr. Summers gravely, and selected a slip of paper from the box. By now, all through the crowd there were men holding the small folded papers in their large hands, turning them over and over nervously. Mrs. Dunbar and her two sons stood together, Mrs. Dunbar holding the slip of paper.

"Harburt. . . . Hutchinson."

"Get up there, Bill," Mrs. Hutchinson said, and the people near her laughed.

"Jones."

"They do say," Mr. Adams said to Old Man Warner, who stood next to him, "that over in the north village they're talking of giving up the lottery."

Old Man Warner snorted. "Pack of crazy fools," he said. "Listening to the young folks, nothing's good enough for *them*. Next thing you know, they'll be wanting to go back to living in caves, nobody work any more, live *that* way for a while. Used to be a saying about 'Lottery in June, corn be heavy soon.' First thing you know, we'd all be eating stewed chickweed and acorns. There's *always* been a lottery," he added petulantly. "Bad enough to see young Joe Summers up there joking with everybody."

"Some places have already quit lotteries," Mrs. Adams said.

"Nothing but trouble in *that*," Old Man Warner said stoutly. "Pack of young fools."

"Martin." And Bobby Martin watched his father go forward. "Overdyke. . . . Percy."

"I wish they'd hurry," Mrs. Dunbar said to her older son. "I wish they'd hurry."

"They're almost through," her son said.

"You get ready to run tell Dad," Mrs. Dunbar said.

Mr. Summers called his own name and then stepped forward precisely and selected a slip from the box. Then he called, "Warner."

"Seventy-seventh year I been in the lottery," Old Man Warner said as he went through the crowd. "Seventy-seventh time."

"Watson." The tall boy came awkwardly through the crowd, Someone said, "Don't be nervous, Jack," and Mr. Summers said, "Take your time, son."

"Zanini."

After that, there was a long pause, a breathless pause, until Mr. Summers, holding his slip of paper in the air, said, "All right, fellows." For a minute, no one moved, and then all the slips of paper were opened. Suddenly, all the women began to speak at once, saying, "Who is it?," "Who's got it?," "Is it the Dunbars?," "Is it the Watsons?" Then the voices began to say, "It's Hutchinson. It's Bill," "Bill Hutchinson's got it."

"Go tell your father," Mrs. Dunbar said to her older son.

People began to look around to see the Hutchinsons. Bill Hutchinson was standing quiet staring down at the paper in his hand. Suddenly, Tessie Hutchinson shouted to

Mr. Summers, "You didn't give him time enough to take any paper he wanted. I saw you. It wasn't fair."

"Be a good sport, Tessie," Mrs. Delacroix called, and Mrs. Graves said, "All of us took the same chance."

"Shut up, Tessie," Bill Hutchinson said.

"Well, everyone," Mr. Summers said, "that was done pretty fast, and now we've got to be hurrying a little more to get done in time." He consulted his next list. "Bill," he said, "you draw for the Hutchinson family. You got any other households in the Hutchinsons?"

"There's Don and Eva," Mrs. Hutchinson yelled. "Make *them* take their chance!"

"Daughters draw with their husbands' families, Tessie." Mr. Summers said gently. "You know that as well as anyone else."

"It wasn't *fair*," Tessie said.

"I guess not, Joe," Bill Hutchinson said regretfully. "My daughter draws with her husband's family, that's only fair. And I've got no other family except the kids."

"Then, as far as drawing for families is concerned, it's you," Mr. Summers said in explanation, "and as far as drawing for households is concerned, that's you, too. Right?"

"Right," Bill Hutchinson said.

"How many kids, Bill?" Mr. Summers asked formally.

"Three," Bill Hutchinson said. "There's Bill, Jr., and Nancy, and little Dave. And Tessie and me."

"All right, then," Mr. Summers said. "Harry, you got their tickets back?"

Mr. Graves nodded and held up the slips of paper. "Put them in the box, then." Mr. Summers directed. "Take Bill's and put it in."

"I think we ought to start over," Mrs. Hutchinson said, as quietly as she could. "I tell you it wasn't *fair*. You didn't give him time enough to choose. *Every*body saw that."

Mr. Graves had selected the five slips and put them in the box and he dropped all the papers but those onto the ground, where the breeze caught them and lifted them off.

"Listen, everybody," Mrs. Hutchinson was saying to the people around her.

"Ready, Bill?" Mr. Summers asked, and Bill Hutchinson, with one quick glance around at his wife and children, nodded.

"Remember," Mr. Summers said, "take the slips and keep them folded until each person has taken one. Harry, you help little Dave." Mr. Graves took the hand of the little boy, who came willingly with him up to the box. "Take a paper out of the box, Davy," Mr. Summers said. Davy put his hand into the box and laughed. "Take just *one* paper." Mr. Summers said. "Harry, you hold it for him." Mr. Graves took the child's hand and removed the folded paper from the tight fist and held it while little Dave stood next to him and looked up at him wonderingly.

"Nancy next," Mr. Summers said. Nancy was twelve, and her school friends breathed heavily as she went forward, switching her skirt, and took a slip daintily from the box. "Bill, Jr.," Mr. Summers said, and Billy, his face red and his feet over-large, nearly knocked the box over as he got a paper out. "Tessie," Mr. Summers said. She hesitated for a minute, looking around defiantly, and then set her lips and went up to the box. She snatched a paper out and held it behind her.

"Bill," Mr. Summers said, and Bill Hutchinson reached into the box and felt around, bringing his hand out at last with the slip of paper in it.

The crowd was quiet. A girl whispered, "I hope it's not Nancy," and the sound of the whisper reached the edges of the crowd.

"It's not the way it used to be," Old Man Warner said clearly "People ain't the way they used to be."

"All right," Mr. Summers said. "Open the papers. Harry, you open little Dave's."

Mr. Graves opened the slip of paper and there was a general sigh through the crowd as he held it up and everyone could see that it was blank. Nancy and Bill, Jr., opened theirs at the same time, and both beamed and laughed, turning around to the crowd and holding their slips of paper above their heads.

"Tessie," Mr. Summers said. There was a pause, and then Mr. Summers looked at Bill Hutchinson, and Bill unfolded his paper and showed it. It was blank.

"It's Tessie," Mr. Summers said, and his voice was hushed. "Show us her paper, Bill."

Bill Hutchinson went over to his wife and forced the slip of paper out of her hand. It had a black spot on it, the black spot Mr. Summers had made the night before with the heavy pencil in the coal-company office. Bill Hutchinson held it up, and there was a stir in the crowd.

"All right, folks," Mr. Summers said. "Let's finish quickly."

Although the villagers had forgotten the ritual and lost the original black box, they still remembered to use stones. The pile of stones the boys had made earlier was ready; there were stones on the ground with the blowing scraps of paper that had come out of the box. Mrs. Delacroix selected a stone so large she had to pick it up with both hands and turned to Mrs. Dunbar. "Come on," she said. "Hurry up."

Mrs. Dunbar had small stones in both hands, and she said, gasping for breath, "I can't run at all. You'll have to go ahead and I'll catch up with you."

The children had stones already, and someone gave little Davy Hutchinson a few pebbles.

Tessie Hutchinson was in the center of a cleared space by now, and she held her hands out desperately as the villagers moved in on her. "It isn't fair," she said. A stone hit her on the side of the head.

Old Man Warner was saying, "Come on, come on, everyone." Steve Adams was in the front of the crowd of villagers, with Mrs. Graves beside him.

"It isn't fair, it isn't right," Mrs. Hutchinson screamed, and then they were upon her.

Drama

HANAY GEIOGAMAH

Hanay Geiogamah was born in Lawton, Oklahoma, in 1945. He studied journalism at the University of Oklahoma and earned a B.A. degree in theater and drama from the University of Indiana in 1980. Geiogamah is known for his skillful expression of the alienation felt by Indians in contemporary society and for plays in which he subverts negative stereotypes about Native Americans with humor and intelligence. Winner of the William Randolph Hearst National Writing Award in 1967 and the Charles Mac-Mahon Foundation Scholarship in Journalism in 1963, he has taught at Colorado College, the University of Washington, and the University of California at Los Angeles, and is one of the founders of the American Indian Theater Ensemble.

The following play was published in 1980.

Body Indian

THE PEOPLE OF THE PLAY

> BOBBY LEE, a crippled alcoholic in his mid-thirties
>
> HOWARD, aged sixty-five or seventy, Bobby's Indian "uncle"
>
> THOMPSON, same age as Bobby, overweight and obviously a heavy drinker
>
> EULAHLAH, in her late twenties, Thompson's wife
>
> MARIE, Bobby's cousin, Howard's downstairs neighbor
>
> ETHEL, Howard's girlfriend, a "visitor"
>
> ALICE, one of Bobby's "aunts," a middle-aged heavy drinker
>
> BETTY, same as Alice
>
> MARTHA, in her late teens, a hip young Indian "chick"
>
> FINA, same as Martha
>
> JAMES, in his late teens, Howard's grandson, Martha and Fina's sidekick

SETTING

Howard's one-room apartment. A large old-fashioned bed dominates downstage center. Its mattress and loose coverings are dingy. Upstage right is the entrance door. Immediately right of the entrance stand kitchen props: a small two-burner stove, a one-faucet sink, and a table with oilcloth covering; they all look greasy, messy.

Stage left of the bed is a small mattress on the floor, spread out in pallet fashion. Above the head of the mattress and to the right of the table is a doorway to a bathroom, smaller than the entrance door.

Many empty liquor bottles are lying around the floor. Some of the labels are visible—Arriba, Lucky Tiger, Stag, all cheap wine brands. There are so many of these that the performers must stumble over and around them to make their way through the action of the play.

The railroad tracks and other special effects are provided by means of slides. Additional film effects for exterior scenes may be used at various points suggested by the text; for example, the Mint Bar where Bobby was with his aunts before arriving at Howard's, or the maiming tragedy on the railroad tracks.

AUTHOR'S NOTE

The first scene should immediately establish the mood and tone for the rest of the play. It is important that an "Indian frame of mind" be established in the performances from the very start of the play. This is not something that the actors will build but something that they will sustain throughout. The following suggestions may be helpful.

1. Lines must be delivered in a clipped fashion, a kind of talk characterized by a tendency to drop final g ("goin'"), to jam words together ("lotta"), to add a grammatically superfluous final *s* ("mens"), to leave a hiatus between a final and an initial vowel ("a old one"), and (in women's speech particularly) to lengthen vowels inordinately ("l—ots"). In no way whatever is anything negative or degrading intended; this is simply the way the characters in this play speak English. The actors should be warned against overplaying this "Indian" speech. It should never become garbled and unclear.

Definitions of Indian words used in the play:

> ***Hites:*** *a close friend, usually male, like a brother but not related by blood; one who has shared many life experiences with you.*
> ***Ka-zog-gies:*** *a euphemism for "ass" or one's bottom. In this usage it is plural.*
> ***Pah-be-mas:*** *a way of addressing as friends women who are not related by blood.*
> ***Ko-ta-kes:*** *a misspoken euphemism for "brothers," or for "brothers who've chosen each other as brothers," or, in a special usage, "blood brothers" without being kin by birth.*
> ***Haw:*** *translates as "yes," an affirmative reply.*
> ***Pah-bes:*** *Friends, buddies, "partners," in a special usage one's "brothers."*
> ***Al-hong-ya:*** *money.*

2. Group effort will produce both the proper restraint and gusto for the requisite Indian style of drinking. The drinking should be a controlled part of the entire performance; that is, the actors should be cautioned not to exaggerate the drinking movements, which must be performed as naturally as possible. Great swaggering and swilling of the bottles are more indicative of amateur acting than anything else. It is important that the acting nowhere is conducive to the mistaken idea that this play is primarily a study of the problem of Indian alcoholism. At moments in the play when much drink is available, the performers may take large drinks; when the supply is dwindling, the drinks are smaller or are sipped carefully.

3. The singing and dancing should be informal and improvised extensions of the characters' thoughts and moods. Not every song will be completed; some tunes will be hummed; some songs are cut off abruptly.

4. It is not necessary to distinguish what tribes the various characters belong to, but that there is a difference in tribes, and that the characters are aware of that difference, should be made obvious.

5. A certain degree of rollicking is permissible, but care must be taken not to overdo makeup, the poor quality of the clothing, gesticulation, the "Indian" speech traits, and all physical actions, most especially those used in the rollings.

6. There should be a loud, rushing sound of a train starting off on a journey to signal to the audience that the play is beginning, and Bobby's entrance can be emphasized by the distant sound of the train.

SCENE 1

Bobby enters from stage left and crosses the stage on crutches. He knocks on the door unevenly. Onstage are Howard, Thompson, Eulahlah, and Ethel. Howard and Ethel are lying on a mattress on the floor. Thompson and Eulahlah are sleeping on the bed. Thompson rises slowly and sluggishly to answer Bobby's knock. Lights up from dim to bright as the door opens.

THOMPSON *(opening door)* Well, I'll beee! B—obbye Leee! Come in, hites, come in! Long time no see. *(He reaches for Bobby's hand. They shake. Bobby lumbers into the room.)*

BOBBY Hey, guy, go down and *halp* my aunts up the stairs, will you? And pay that cab. I can't make it back down those stairs now. They're really iced. *(He hands Thompson money.)* My aunts are kinda' buzzin', halp them up the stairs. Don't let them fall on their ka-zog-gies. *(He smiles broadly.)* Say, tell that driver I want my sacks.

Thompson nods in agreement, puts on a shirt and shoes, and exits. Eulahlah stirs when the door shuts. Bobby sits down in the empty chair, exhales.

EULAHLAH *(groggily)* Weeelll Bobbyee Leee. Heeey. *(She gets off bed and goes to hug and kiss him.)* Saaay, guy, last time— *(cough stops her speech).* . . . Hey where's Thompson?

BOBBY He went down to pay my cab. He's coming right back up. He's halping my aunts up them stairs.

EULAHLAH *(puzzled)* Your aunts?

BOBBY Yeah, you know 'em. Betty and Alice.

EULAHLAH Oooh, yeah, yeah, I know all of dem. I drank with Alice 'bout three days ago uptown. Yeah, I know dem, Bobby.

She continues to fondle Bobby and peers around at the others in the room, attempting to focus her eyes and gain composure as she does so.

BOBBY *(nodding toward Howard and Ethel on the floor)* Heeey, what's wrong with old guy there? Is he passed?

EULAHLAH *(giggling)* Oh, no, he's sleep. He and Ethel's been drinkin' for few days now, but he's not passed out now, just sleep. He's got cold. Doctor at clinic told him he better stay in bed for few days. He's been drinkin' l—ots since he made his lease. I guess he got sick from drinkin' too much wine. Thompson was thinkin' 'bout takin' him to hospital at Lawton.

BOBBY *(laughing lightly at this report)* When did he make his lease?

EULAHLAH 'Bout two weeks ago. Or maybe a week ago. Thompson hasn't made his yet.

BOBBY I just made mine this mornin'. But my damn lease man didn't want to pay me what I wanted. I was too broke to hold out, so I just signed it.

Bobby fumbles for a cigarette and takes some time lighting it. He sounds exhausted when he exhales. He smokes the cigarette with deep draws.

BOBBY I was goin' back to city today, but the roads are too bad. I saw my aunts at Mint and they told me Howard was over here. Is Marie down there?

Bobby gestures with his lip toward the floor, but Eulahlah doesn't seem to hear him. Noise is heard from the hallway outside. After many bumping sounds, the door opens and Thompson, Betty, and Alice enter. The women are frowzy. They are in a happy mood, carrying on loudly.

EULAHLAH *(gesturing broadly at the women)* Hae—ye! My pa-be-mas. Heey!

They all laugh lightly and exchange Indian women greetings.

THOMPSON *(with pleased smile)* Here's your sacks, Bobby. Soun's like you got jugs in there.

BOBBY I do.

BETTY Welll, helll, then, open one up!

They crack open a bottle by hitting it on the bottom and then removing the screw top, and begin to take long drinks as the wine is passed around. Drum and rattles come up as the drinking begins. Howard and Ethel are awakened by the merriment. Howard rises from the bed, sees Bobby sitting in the chair, shouts a greeting, then moves arthritically toward Bobby and embraces him. Ethel greets the other women with wan enthusiasm. The bottle continues to be passed around uninterruptedly. Ethel approaches Bobby. The light percussion continues to the end of the scene.

ETHEL H—ell—oo Bobby. How are you, sonny? You look preeety good. Haven't seen you in a lo—ng time, boy.

BOBBY *(more settled now)* You're E—thel, annet?

ETHEL Yeah, yeah, Bobby, it's me, E—thel.

BOBBY You're kin to me, annet?

ETHEL Yeah, yeah, Bobby, we're related. On my mother's side, I think.

BOBBY *(traces of drunken slur beginning to show in his voice)* Your dad was my dad's Indian brother. Ko-ta-kes, haw!

(He makes an appropriate gesture with his hand.)

ETHEL Yeah, that's right, Bobby. Brothers!

HOWARD *(interjecting)* Yeah, yeah, ya'll are kin. Ethel is related to your mother, Bobby. Your mother was my dad's sister. Ethel's dad was kin to both of them.

BOBBY Yeah. That's the way it is . . . yeah.

HOWARD Ethel here has a-been visitin' for few days now. Too cold to go back west. She's waitin' to make her lease.

BOBBY *(continuing to drink from the bottle)* Is Marie down there?

HOWARD Yeah, I think so. I heard her yellin' at them kids this mornin'. She had one of them with her when she was up here last night.

ALICE I saw her uptown yesterday mornin'. I think she's been behavin' it.

The women laugh at this.

BOBBY I need to see her. Need to talk to her 'bout signin' up for program at Norman. She's got to sign with me.

HOWARD *(concerned)* She'll be up here. She'll hear us through the roof. She always come up here when she hear us talkin' and makin' noise.

BOBBY Has she been drinkin'?

HOWARD You know how she is.

Betty rises and carries bottle to Bobby. The others focus on her doing this. Drum and rattles come up.

BETTY *(merrily)* Here, Bobby, take a b—ig drink. We haven't seen you in lo—ng time. Drink with us, Bobby.

Bobby grins, is pleased with Betty's attention. The others laugh and encourage him. He takes the nearly full bottle, turns it up, and downs the entire contents with a slow, steady gurgle. He gasps when he is finished. Another bottle is opened and starts the rounds. Bobby sits almost stupefied. Howard fawns over him. Bobby's teeth grit and streams of saliva run from the sides of his mouth. The others pretend they do not notice. Bobby slumps over the chair and passes out. Slowly they all surround him. There is a menacing air as they do this. The lights dim to a haze.

HOWARD *(gently, to avoid waking Bobby)* Bobby. Hey, Bobby. Sonny, are you wake? You want 'nother drink? Bobby. Situp, sonny. Ethel wants to visit with you. *(There is no sign of life in Bobby. Howard moves in closer.)* Bobby. Bobby.

They lift his body from the chair with drunken eagerness and carelessness and carry him to the bed. One of the women adjusts his legs so that he lies stretched out on the bed.

HOWARD Bobby. Does your leg feel okay? Does it hurt you, sonny? Do you want us to take it off for you? *(He moves close to Bobby's ear.)* Bobby. We goin' run out of jugs. We got to go get some more. Bobby. You got any money, sonny? We goin' run out. Bobby, heeey, Bobby, can you help us out?

Howard touches Bobby's leg, moves back, and motions to Ethel to join him.

HOWARD *(now certain that Bobby is thoroughly passed out)* This boy always pass out pretty fast. When he got his leg cut off and start wearin that other leg, he start drinkin' pretty heavy. *(pause)* He was passed out on those tracks when he got hurt. *(pause)* I know he got money on him. He always hide it in that leg.

Howard and Ethel begin to search Bobby's pockets. They find cigarettes, folded papers, change, and two or three one-dollar bills.

ETHEL This ain't all he has!

HOWARD Feel in back.

Ethel puts her hand in Bobby's back pocket with a stealthy movement.

ETHEL He don't have no billfold. Wait, here's some. . . .

She pulls a few bills out, looks quickly to determine their denomination, and then moves quickly to cover her find.

HOWARD *(nervous)* How much was it?

BETTY Is there any more wine?

Howard and Ethel scuffle over the money.

ETHEL Just little bit.

BETTY Where?

ETHEL *(gesturing with her lips)* Over there . . . in those sacks.

As Betty rises to get the wine, the distant sound of a rushing train and whistle blasts from off-stage. The cast freezes. The drum and rattles grow intense. Expressions of fear slowly cross over cast's faces as they look directly toward the audience.

ETHEL I can hear it. Sounds like it's 'bout twenty, thirty miles away.

ALICE I can barely hear it.

BETTY I hear it little bit.

ETHEL Hear it?

EULAHLAH I can hear it . . . now.

THOMPSON Sounds like hummin'.

ALICE The sound makes a little buzzin' feelin' on my ear.

BETTY *(to Howard)* You hear it, Grampa?

HOWARD *(hobbling to downstage center)* I can hear it just a little bit. Just a li—ttle bit.

Percussion sounds and lights intensify, then out. When the train whistle is heard, color slide projections of railroad tracks can appear, taken at varied sharp angles and flashing in rapid sequence, onto the back wall.

SCENE 2

The lights come up with the company, except for Howard, sitting or lying all about the room. Howard is standing in the middle of the room with a bottle of wine in his hand. He is in a jolly mood, singing and joking with the others. Bobby is sitting at the edge of the bed, his position for most of the rest of the play. Empty bottles clutter the floor. Howard's fun is being supported by the others. There is no indication that anything wicked has taken place, or that there is a world beyond the shabby walls.

HOWARD *(with aged gusto)* I sure like to dance. One of my boys almost won first at the fair one time. He sure was good. *(He moves around.)* I taught all my kids how to sing. He can sing *(pointing to Bobby.)* He sure can hit those high notes. *(no reaction from Bobby.)* He can't drum, but he can sing.

The women begin to shout encouragement to Howard for his dancing.

HOWARD I saw in Darko[1] paper they havin' a b—ig dance at Carnegie tomorrow night. I'd sure like to go. But evreee time this guy always get us stopped by the county laws! *(He points directly to Thompson.)*

ETHEL Are you going to war dance for us, Howard?

HOWARD Any time now. *(They all laugh. The merriment increases.)* Just watch me!

Betty and Alice shake imaginary rattles. Ethel stands and makes supportive accompanying movement. Thompson pretends to drum.

HOWARD Fancy dance! Eee-hah! Eee-hah! Eee-hah! Eee-hah!

BETTY AND ALICE Yo-a-hio-ya, yo-a-hio-ya. *(Music rises offstage. The scene intensifies as Howard trips around the room with his dance.)*

HOWARD *(loudly, breathlessly)* The drummers are gettin' ahead of me! Slow 'em down! *(There is no indication from Thompson that he hears this.)* Eee-hah! Eee-hah! Eee-hah!

BETTY AND ALICE Yo-a-hio-ya, Yo-a-hio-ya.

Then, on cue, the dancing and singing stop abruptly with a rattle fadeout. The participants let out a whoop. While they have been carrying on, Marie has entered. The company all focus on her, and there seems to be an attitude of resentment toward her.

HOWARD *(as if surprised, speaking directly to Marie)* Marieeeee! Come in! Come in! Come over here and sit down. Look who's here. Bobby's here.

[1]Anadarko, Oklahoma

Howard leads her to Bobby on the bed.

MARIE *(suddenly)* Well, hiii, B—obbyee. *(She kisses him.)* Where have you beeen? I haven't seen you in so lo—ng. I was startin' to get worried about you.

The others arrange themselves, find bottles, eye Marie, but one by one fall asleep. Meanwhile Bobby has been coming around, and now sits up on the bed.

BOBBY *(adjusting)* I came down to make my lease. I can't go back to the city today. Roads too bad. Thought I'd come here to see if you was here. They tol' me you was here.

MARIE I thought you was up here when I heard you walkin' on the floor. I thought you'd be here for lease signin'. Did you sign yet?

BOBBY My damn white lease man wouldn't give me what I wanted. I was gonna hold out, but I needed the money. I had to sign for what he wanted to give me. I couldn't help it.

MARIE I'm gonna' make mine Monday. He already made his. *(She lip-gestures toward Howard.)* You got any money on you, Bobby?

BOBBY I can spare you a little bit. I need all I have.

MARIE I don't have any groceries. I tried to borrow some from Howard the other day, but he didn't even have any rations left. Thompson and his wife stay here nearly all the time now. He just barely gets by on that lease money of his. Jobs are hard to find. 'Specially for Indians 'round here. You know how it is. Money's sure scarce.

BOBBY I was gonna' tell you . . . *(pausing to drink)* . . . I want to use my lease money to get in program at Norman. It's a A-A deal for alcoholics. That preacher in the city told me they could dry me out in 'bout six weeks. I wanna' go over there. I need a relative to sign my papers with me. Can you sign them for me?

MARIE Does your caseworker at the Bureau know about this?

BOBBY *(angrily)* He doesn't have to know about it! I can go if I want to.

MARIE Did they say you could go?

BOBBY *(irritated)* I don't have to ask them. I can go on my own, but I have to have a relative to co-sign for me to get in.

MARIE How much does it cost?

BOBBY You can pay if you want to. I want to pay. It costs $400. I'll be in there for six weeks.

When Bobby mentions $400, some of the others stir and take notice.

MARIE Do you have the papers with you, Bobby?

BOBBY *(slurring his words)* I left them in the city.

MARIE Do you want to lay down, Bobby?

BOBBY *(slumping, jerking, drooling)* Uuuhaa.

Bobby is again stupefied from the wine. Marie rises and lays him out on the bed. This takes some effort from her. She talks to him, though she knows he is passed out. Her speech begins to sound chilling. When she has him stretched out, her actions and speech quicken.

MARIE Bobby. Bobby! Bobby, are you sleep? Are you sleep, sonny? Bobby. Bobby.

While she is talking to Bobby, Thompson begins to move, as though drugged, toward the bed.

HOWARD He's sleep. I know he got money. Look in leg.

Marie and Thompson begin to search Bobby's pockets. They go over his entire body, leaving his clothes disheveled, and in the process pull up the pants over Bobby's artificial leg. Frantically they begin to compete to find money stashed in the apparatus. Thompson finds money, and Marie tries to grab it from him.

MARIE I need some of that!

THOMPSON No, uuuh, hey!

THOMPSON *(with a nervous, alcoholic twitch)* I'll check. I'll check . . . for . . . for all of . . . us. *(The others freeze.)* It . . . it's st . . . sti-ll there. Movin' this way. Comin' closer.

The visuals of the tracks appear again, then go out with the lights.

SCENE 3

The lights come up with the women standing center stage in a round dance forma-tion. They begin singing and dancing to the 49 tune of "Strawberries When I'm Hun-gry." Marie sits uneasily in the background, obviously not welcome to take part in the women's frolicking. As the scene progresses, the women's mood gradually becomes sadder, angrier, more desperate.

ALICE I was gonna' camp at the fair this year, but Junior got throwed in 'bout a week be-fore the fair started, and we couldn't put up our arbor. I sure like to hear that music comin' from the dance grounds.

BETTY I haven't camped at the fair since I was a little girl. The dust bothers me, but I like the dancin'.

ETHEL It's cheaper to camp than it is to live in town.

EULAHLAH Daddy and 'em used to butcher before we came to the campgrounds. I re-ally liked to fix up that meat.

ALICE *(slowly)* I wish I had some meat now. My kids been eatin' only commodity meat for 'bout two months now. Junior's unemployment ran out a month ago. There ain't no jobs nowhere.

BETTY Just be glad you have your gas and lights workin'.

ALICE They will be for just couple of days more. I got my final notice that they was gonna' cut them off last week. That city truck will be pullin' up in the alley first thin' Mon-day mornin'.

ETHEL *(reflecting)* I put my nephews in government school this fall. I sure didn't want to, but at least they get taken care of there. I hate for my kids to have to go without.

EULAHLAH I didn't mind goin' to G I school so bad. Aayyee. *(The others smile knowingly at this.)* They treated me pretty good where I went. Some of those schools ain't so bad, but some of them sure no good.

ETHEL   My oldest nephew plays football at Riverside. His picture was in paper two or three weeks ago. I sure felt proud when I saw it in there.

ALICE   *(almost crying)* Everything is sure rough. I can't even get on state welfare. They say my husband is able to work. He's able, but there's no work.

BETTY   *(slowly)* All those white people think Indians have it good because they think the government takes care of us. They don't even know. It's rougher than they know. I'd like to trade my house for a white lady's house on Mission Street. I'd like for a white lady to have my roaches. You see them at the store, and they look at you like your purse is full of government checks. I wish my purse could be full of government checks.

ALICE   I wish I had a check from anywhere.

(The bottle is moving around.)

EULAHLAH   So do I.

ETHEL   So do I. I'd get my son out of county jail if I did.

The drumbeat comes up. Bobby has been watching the women as they lament. A pause while the bottle comes round to him, then he speaks.

BOBBY   *(surprisingly alert)* Every Indian needs to have a government check for $25 thousand. They could give you womens $50 thousand. Then you could buy all your kids shoes, clothes, bicycles, pay rent, pay fines, buy shawls and earrings, and put the money you have left in the bank to live on. That's the only way you'd ever have the money you need.

The women turn their attention to Bobby as he makes this statement. They all laugh heartily as he finishes talking, then rise and surround him to tease him.

ETHEL   Hey, Bobby, sonny. I bet you haven't 49'd in a long time. Come on, dance with us. You can dance with your crutches.

The women straggle into a round dance formation, pulling Bobby up onto the floor with them. He first resists, then gives in. Bottles are in hand. They begin to sing, in high-pitched voices, the 49 song "One-Eyed Ford," with Bobby singing along. As the dancing progresses, Bobby guzzles from a bottle and begins to falter, throwing the dancers out of kelter. One of his crutches flies across the floor as the women, with much fuss and giggling, lay him out on the bed. They stop singing and begin to glance at one another.

ALICE   *(in low voice)* Sssssh. Sssssh. Hey, Bobby has some money, annet?

BETTY   I think so.

ETHEL   He does.

ALICE   How much?

BETTY   I think he's got lots.

ETHEL   He signed his lease today.

EULAHLAH   *(nervously)* He said he signed it.

ALICE   *(to Howard)* Howard, does my nephew have any money?

Howard is nearly out and does not reply.

BETTY I know he'd help us out if he could.

ETHEL He's my relative. I know he'd help me out.

EULAHLAH Me and Thompson helped him out before.

ALICE He always comes to my house when he's here. I always take care of him.

ETHEL He used to stay with me long time ago. He was tryin' to get straightened up.

BETTY He sure is a g—ood guy. Poor thing.

ALICE You all must be good to him now, he's a poor thing. Y'all be good to him.

BETTY We'll be good to him.

ETHEL Yeah, we will.

EULAHLAH Oh, okay. We'll be good to him.

The lights lower as they begin to search Bobby. They find a few dollars, stuffing them into their bras as they do. When Eulahlah fumbles with Bobby's artificial leg, Marie startles all of them.

MARIE I saw you!

The women quickly return to their dancing and singing, pretending they have not rolled Bobby. Their cackling cries are drowned out by the offstage train whistle, this time louder than before. The railroad tracks are projected over them as they freeze in their dance pattern. The lights go out on a slow count as the women clutch for each other, reach their hands out toward the audience, then freeze again.

SCENE 4

A restlessness has settled over the group. They know that the wine supply is quickly dwindling. Eulahlah and Thompson quarrel; Ethel needles Howard.

BETTY I wish John was here. I haven't seen him . . . in 'bout a week now.

ALICE *(in same lonely tone)* Junior went lookin' for a job the other day. Somebody said they saw him at Erma's. He always shows up when he runs out of steam.

BETTY I hope John gets his business taken care of pretty quick. His lease man is a son of a bitch. He won't even give us an advance, even when we don't have groceries.

BOBBY *(coming suddenly to life and slowly, in drunken movements, searching himself)* Somebody took my money. It's almost all gone. *(pause)* I got to use that money to go to Central State at . . . Norman. *(pause)* What happened to it? . . . Who took it? *(shouting)* Howard? *(pause)* Where's . . . Marie? *(Marie makes a movement in his direction, but stops short.)* Where's wine? *(pause)* Who . . . took my . . . money? *(The group doesn't respond to any of his questions and seems not to hear them.)* Why did you do . . . it . . . take my al. . . . ? *(He begins to grit his teeth and his body tenses.)* I want . . . to . . . go . . . to Norman. My money . . . money . . . is . . . for Norman. Where is it? Which one of you?

He slumps over on the bed, but doesn't pass out. He moans and grunts for the next several moments. The group sits now as though there were nothing else to do but wait for something to happen. There is a knock at the door. Howard answers it. The others watch. Enter James, Martha and Fina. The young people are greeted with blank expressions. The youths shake the cold off themselves, exclaim about the harshness of the weather outside, and survey, with expressions of amusement and awe, the scene in the apartment.

JAMES *(to Howard)* How are you, Grampa?

HOWARD Pretty good, preeety good. What are y'all doing, sonny?

JAMES I came up to see you, to ask you for some al-hong-ya.

While they are talking, Martha and Fina approach Bobby on the bed. James guides Howard, now besotted, to the floor pallet.

MARTHA *(jostling Bobby)* Heeeey, Bobby Lee, wake up, guy. Hey, it's me, Marty, your buddy. Wake up. Where you been, dude? I ain't seen you in a long time.

Bobby raises his head, slowly recognizing Martha.

BOBBY *(groggily)* Heeeeeey, what are you . . .? *(focusing on Fina)* Who's this?

MARTHA Her name's Fina.

Fina and Martha giggle. They seem to have a special interest in Bobby.

BOBBY Is she kin to you?

MARTHA Yeah, she's my cousin.

Bobby takes a drink, offers one to Martha and Fina. He is pleased by the attention he is receiving from the two girls. Fina puts her arm enticingly around Bobby. He responds enthusiastically by dropping the bottle to the floor.

FINA *(low whisper to Martha)* He's kind of good-looking.

James is talking and laughing with Howard and Thompson, paying no direct attention to the activity on the bed. Howard occasionally glances sharply at it.

MARTHA *(giggly, bouncy, high)* You want some more wine, Bobby Lee? Where is it?

BOBBY Over there. *(He points to a sack on the floor. Martha moves to get it.)*

MARTHA *(to group, sitting blankly around the room)* Golll, y'all look like y'all've been partying for 'bout three weeks. I bet y'all've drunk a l—ot. *(big giggle)*

There is no response to her remark. Martha, James, and Fina now converge on the bed, happy that they have gotten this far.

FINA *(to James)* Does your Grampa have any money?

JAMES He didn't say.

MARTHA Ask him again.

JAMES Wait!

MARTHA *(gesturing toward Bobby)* I bet he's got some.

JAMES If he did it's probably all gone by now.

FINA Check him out.

JAMES You check him out.

MARTHA Heeey! I sure wish I had twenty. We could get a case and some gas. And we could go to that concert in the city tonight. Get hiii! Aye!

The young trio all laugh at Martha's fantasy.

FINA If I had twenty dollars, I'd buy me a . . . a . . . a living bra! Aaaeee.

JAMES Man, I just wish I had a twenty. And a lid. I wouldn't go to school for days. Aaaeee.

FINA *(as she fondles Bobby's torso)* He's kinda good-lookin'. Aaaeee.

They giggle and tease each other as they get Bobby's body into place to roll it. The adults are paying no attention to any of this.

JAMES *(sternly)* Check his pockets!

MARTHA *(toward group)* They probably took all of it already.

JAMES *(to Howard)* Where's his money, Grampa? Grampa, hey, does he have any money? We need some bad, man.

HOWARD *(after a pause, without looking up)* Look in shoe.

They begin to fidget with the orthopedic shoe attached to the artificial leg, and Martha yanks out a bill.

MARTHA *(exclaiming at the size of the bill)* W—ow! We can really make it with this.

FINA How much is it?

No reply from Martha. She giggles to herself, then signals to James and Fina that they should leave. They put on their coats and prepare to hurry out.

HOWARD *(to James)* Sonny, where y'all goin'?

JAMES We're gonna' drive around for a while, see who's uptown. . . . There's a rock band playin' tonight.

Martha and Fina make giggly small talk with the rest of the company as they prepare to exit. The low bleat of the train whistle sounds offstage. The youths first react as if it is a part of their high but become gradually more concerned, agitated. The track projections flash on.

FINA *(giggly and ooeey)* W—ow. It's really hummin', makin' a kinda' buzzin' noise.

MARTHA Ooooooh. It feels warm. I can feel it on my ear. Hey, this is weird.

The others onstage watch this silently, no movement.

HOWARD Sonny, can y'all come back pretty soon? I want you to help me out. Will you come check on us?

JAMES Yeah, uh, okay, Grampa. 'Bout couple of hours.

MARTHA *(trying to feel the track projections with her fingers)* Psssst! Psssst! I bet these guys have been puttin' their hands on these to get a buzz. Aaaeee.

Giggles from James and Martha; others are frozen in place.

JAMES We'll see y'all pretty soon.

MARTHA   Take it easy.

FINA   Y'all be good. Be careful.

Lights out, sound off when the door closes behind them.

SCENE 5

The party is nearing its end. Bobby Lee has been rolled four times so far, knows that this has happened, but has remained helpless. It is apparent on the players' faces that they have forgotten everything that has happened in the previous four scenes, that they are unaware of their abuse of Bobby. They want only to keep the party going. A soft drumbeat is heard offstage throughout the scene.

HOWARD   *(bitterly)* I guess all the wine is gone. Is there any more anywhere?

ALICE   Is all the wine gone? I want another one.

EULAHLAH   It's not all gone, is it?

THOMPSON   You drank 'bout four bottles of it yourself.

HOWARD   *(to Thompson)* Look over there, under that chair. *(Thompson looks, finds nothing.)*

THOMPSON   I thought I saw somebody hide one under here.

HOWARD   You did. You hid it under here.

EULAHLAH   He hid it. He can drink more than all of us together.

HOWARD   I didn't hide any wine.

EULAHLAH   I know I didn't.

BETTY   Is there a bottle hidden 'round here? Is there one hidden? I thought there was more wine than this.

HOWARD   There was a lot of wine. There was 'bout ten, 'leven, maybe twelve bottles. We had a couple of bottles when Bobby came.

EULAHLAH   We had more than a couple of bottles, Grampa. Goll, there was a lot more than a couple.

ALICE   *(checking under the furniture)* There's another bottle somewhere. It's too cold to go back uptown to get more. There's another bottle somewhere. *(pause)* There's another bottle somewhere.

During this discussion about the wine, Bobby silently watches from the bed, following the movements of the others as they look for bottles.

BETTY   *(angrily)* We bought a lot of bottles when we stopped at the liquor store on the way here in the taxi. I know we bought a lot of them. Two sacks full!

HOWARD   *(to Marie)* Hey, hey you. Do you have anything to drink downstairs?

MARIE   I don't have any wine. You drank all of it when you were down there the other day.

Their searching becomes frantic.

EULAHLAH   If there's no more wine in this place, then somebody go get some uptown.

There is no response from the men. Now there is a silence. Bobby continues to observe their movement.

Howard (*after all have become exasperated from searching*) There's no more wine here. We drank it all up. If any of you want some more to drink, one of us will have to go to town to get it.

Betty One of you men go.

Alice Yeah, Thompson, you or Howard go get us some more drinks!

Eulahlah (*sharply*) Goddamn you, Thompson, go get us some more drinks! (*Thompson tries to push her away, but she persists.*) Get us some more drinks, you damn lazy thing. Go on! Get us some more.

Howard (*to Thompson*) Yeah, sonny, you go get us some more to drink. We don't have no more. Go 'head, go get us some more. We can stay here and drink it. Go 'head.

The others encourage Thompson to go. Thompson gives in.

Bobby (*suddenly, startling them all*) Is there any more. . . wine? I want another drink. . . I need another drink!

Howard We goin' send after some more, Bobby. Thompson here is goin' after some more uptown.

Marie rises, goes to Bobby on the bed.

Marie Bobby, do you want to go downstairs to my house with me? Howard will help you down the stairs so you won't fall.

Bobby I want a drink!

Marie Come with me, Bobby. There isn't any more drinks here.

Bobby (*coming alive*) Yes, there is, there's another drink here. (*The others turn to Bobby when he says this.*)

Howard (*loudly*) Sonny, did you say there's another drink here? Did you say there's a bottle here?

Bobby doesn't reply, reels in his wooziness.

Marie Come downstairs with me, Bobby. They drank up all the wine they had here. There isn't any more wine. Come with me, Bobby.

Howard (*pushing Marie out of his way*) Did you say there's some wine left here, Bobby? Tell me where's it at.

Alice Come on, Bobby Lee, be a good chief, tell us where there's another drink. We done drank up all that we had. There's no more, sonny.

Eulahlah Bobby Lee, hites, come on, guy, share your drink with us. Geee. We always help you out when you need it. Help us out. Share with us.

Bobby tries to protect himself from their pummeling.

Marie Bobby, I'm going downstairs now. I got to check on those kids. Howard will help you down the stairs. Come on down with him. I'll fix you a place to sleep. (*She waits for* *a reply; there is none.)* Howard, you must bring him downstairs. He doesn't need to drink any more. He can sleep for a while. Bobby, you come down with Howard. He'll help you down the stairs. These people are just gonna' keep on drinkin'. Come on downstairs.

Bobby remains silent. The others say nothing to Marie as she exits. They wait for Bobby to say where the wine is hidden.

HOWARD Bobby, do you want to go down to Marie's?

BOBBY No! No! I'm . . . okay, here.

HOWARD Bobby, sonny, where's that wine at?

Bobby smiles faintly at Howard, then reaches slowly into his jacket and pulls out a full pint of wine, holds it up for all to see.

BOBBY Here's wine. Y'all know I always have something hidden on me. . .to drink. *(They all laugh, pretending to accept this as a joke.)* If you drink, you should. . .you should always keep a small one hid on you. If you can.

He opens the bottle and drinks it all in one long gulp. The others push and claw for the bottle, but Bobby, fending them off with his free arm, keeps it out of their reach.

THOMPSON *(almost crying)* Hey, hey, Bobby Lee, hites, save me . . . save *(as last drop drains from bottle)* CORNERRRS![2]

Bobby laughs drunkenly.

EULAHLAH *(with pain)* Oooooooooh, no!

The grip of needing a drink now tightens on all of them. Some of them show signs of "shakes."

HOWARD Thompson, go get us another drink.

THOMPSON *(trembling, sweating)* Okay, Okay! Give me money and I'll go.

HOWARD You have money to buy it.

THOMPSON I don't have any money. I'm broke.

EULAHLAH Me and Thompson don't have any more money. We spent it all a long time ago. You have money.

HOWARD I spent all my lease money already.

EULAHLAH No you didn't! You still have money!

ETHEL *(joining Howard, to Eulahlah)* We don't have any money. Howard's broke. *(pointing to Betty and Alice.)* They have money!

ALICE I don't have any money. I've been broke for the past two weeks. I wish I had some money.

BETTY *(sadly, to Bobby)* I don't have . . . any . . . money.

THOMPSON No money, no drinks!

---

[2]The last little shot, the final drops that usually collect in the corner of the bottle.

HOWARD Which one of you has a couple of dollars? *(No reply from any of them.)* I know somebody's got some.

THOMPSON Who's gonna' give me the money?

Now everybody searches their pockets or purses to look for money. They find nothing. Bobby moans. A loud knock on the door. Howard answers. The three youths enter. They are now more spaced out than previously.

JAMES *(smiling, glassy-eyed)* You said to come back, to check on you all, didn't you, Grampa?

The two girls eye Bobby on the bed, apparently to check his vulnerability once again.

HOWARD Yeah, yeah, I wanted you kids to come back to check on us. Sonny, do you have any al-hong-ya on you?

JAMES *(surprised)* Al-hong-ya? No, I don't. Remember, I asked you for some when we came here before.

HOWARD Yeah, yeah, but do you have any money? We need another drink.

JAMES We're all busted.

He giggles. The girls are waiting, talking with the others.

HOWARD Are y'all in your car, sonny?

JAMES Yeah, uh, huh. We been slidin' around in it uptown.

HOWARD What time is it, sonny?

JAMES It's early, man.

HOWARD Are those stores still open?

JAMES Yeah, they're open, the ones you want. *(He giggles again.)*

HOWARD *(looking around)* We sure need some money.

JAMES What do you want us to do?

HOWARD Sit down, y'all, sit down.

Howard now takes control, his grimness exerting a force over the others.

Y'all know how Bobby Lee gets when he's been drinkin' for a long time and runs out. *(They all indicate that they know what he's talking about.)*

He gets real sick, haw?

(more agreement) I was with him one time in Oklahoma City jail when he got sick, real sick. He was really havin' those dee-tees. His arms was movin' and jerkin', like cow's when you butcher it. His legs was a-shakin'. He soun' like he was chokin'. *(He strains for composure, coughs, trembles.)* He tol' me he saw in his dee-tees a row of lillel' chickens sittin' on those jail bars singin' Indian songs.

He said they was purple and gold and red colors.

He said he felt like his head was bein' hit with a big iron 'bout ever so often.

The two girls giggle at the bizarre images Howard is describing.

He said he felt like he was fallin' through the whole jailhouse floor into the sewer lines.

He said his hair was long as an old lady's, and his fingers were all shrunk up, like he was a-dead.

He tol' me he thought he was goin' die while he was in those dee-tees!

I don't want him to have them again! He's had them lots of times.

I know what they're like. He's going have them again if he don't get a drink.

He don't have any more al-hong-ya. It's all gone. He spent it all. He always spen' his money fast.

He don't have any more wine hid.

I'm goin' get him some more wine before he wakes up.

He's goin' need it. *(pause)* He sure is goin' need a drink when he wakes up. Y'all know that!

Howard moves to the bed. He signals Thompson to join him. They begin jostling Bobby's body roughly, almost brutally. The others begin, one by one, to rise and stand around the bed to watch, hiding the operation from the audience. There is complete silence. Out of the audience's view, Howard and Thompson are removing Bobby's artificial leg. James is the first to leave the encirclement, signaling his two companions that it's time for them to leave. Howard calls James back for him to assist in rearranging Bobby's body on the bed.

HOWARD *(to James)* Sonny, I want you to take us to white man bootleggers on Washington Street. He'll give us what we need for this *(indicating artificial leg)*. He'll let Bobby have it back when Bobby can get it out.

JAMES *(disgust in his voice)* Okay, let's hurry. It's gettin' late. We gotta' go to the concert.

Howard and Thompson prepare to leave, placing the artificial leg upright against the bed. Complete silence until Howard and Thompson are posed at the door with the leg wrapped in a dingy blanket. Drum and rattles now begin a gradual rise to the end of the scene. The youths have exited.

HOWARD *(to those who remain behind)* Y'all wait here. We'll be back pretty soon.

They exit. The women begin to straighten the room, to sweep, to pick up bottles. The track visuals appear in sharp contrast over Bobby's stretched-out body. Some time passes while the women clean before the train whistle is heard. The sound grows louder and awakens Bobby. He feels around on his body and discovers that his artificial leg has been removed. He pulls himself up, speaks increasingly louder so as to be heard over the train sounds. The women do not hear him. There is a sardonic smile fixed on his face.

BOBBY Well, h—ell—o, Bobby Lee. How are you, hites?

Lo—ng time no . . . seee.

He reaches for his crutches, has trouble securing them. Sitting upright on the edge of the bed, he looks straight ahead at a flashing train light, an entirely different mood about him now as horror overtakes him.

Bobby I can hear . . . a . . . train . . . that . . . train . . . my leg . . . that train's gonna' . . . gonna hit . . . . . . my . . . . . . ley—g!

He slumps over as loud blasts from the train echo through the theater. The women continue tidying the room. Train sounds subside, lights begin to dim. The track visuals fade out. Silence.

END

A CLOSER LOOK: MOISÉS KAUFMAN

Moisés Kaufman is a Tony and Emmy nominated director and award-winning play-wright. *The Laramie Project* is among the most frequently performed plays in America over the last decade. *The Laramie Project* opened at the Denver Theater Center in March 2000 and moved to New York in May 2000. *Time* magazine called it "one of the ten best plays of 2000," and it was nominated for the Drama Desk Award for Unique Theatrical Experience.

In November 2000, Kaufman took his company to Laramie, Wyoming, to perform the play there. Kaufman also directed the film adaptation of the *The Laramie Project,* which aired on HBO. He received two Emmy Award nominations for Best Director and Best Writer. He is a Guggenheim Fellow.

INTERVIEW WITH THE AUTHOR

The following interview was written by Jesse McKinley and published in *American Theatre,* Volume 14, in November 1997. Jesse McKinley is a reporter for the *New York Times* City Section and occasionally a playwright.

As Far As He Could Go

Much has been made about *Gross Indecency*'s structure, its use of books—actually the reference materials that you used in researching the play—as props. How did that idea evolve?

I was interested in questions of how one reconstructs history and historical characters, and how you deal with many versions of the same story. It's no different than a film like Rashomon, where several people tell the same story, but the question becomes, how do you deal with those problems in the medium of the theatre? In a sense, I was just asking—and answering—all of my own questions.

What exactly was the impetus for the play?

Someone gave me a book called The Wit and Wisdom of Oscar Wilde. *I had read a lot of Wilde, but the last 10 pages of the book contained part of the trial transcript, and the events of those 10 pages shocked me. Here was an artist in a court of law being asked to defend his art, and it seemed so appropriate for our time. Right now we tend to look at art from a political or social or religious standpoint, and that's all very valid. But Wilde is a purist—he's talking about art as art and trying to isolate what only art can do that nothing else can do. For me, that's a very valid question, because in my work I've always tried to understand what is the thing that only theatre and no other medium can do . . .*

And?

If I could answer that, I wouldn't need the theatre. (Laughter) I don't know what it is, but it's a question to create work by. I didn't mean to be facetious. What is it that theatre can do? Each play will bring about a new answer to that question.

There's a critical moment in the play where Wilde's discourse trips him up and it suddenly becomes apparent that he has incriminated himself.

Yes. He was safe as long as he was talking about art. Every time Carson, the prosecutor, thinks he has cornered Oscar, Oscar does a verbal backwards somersault and ends up in the other corner—Carson doesn't know what hit him. It's only when Carson begins to question him in the vocabulary of the courtroom, this so-called "patriarchal, medical discourse," that Oscar begins to lose his bearings. A question about art leaves some room for creative sidestepping; being asked if he slept with a specific boy does not.

In the trials and in the play, as long as the subject is art, Oscar is on his turf, and he's fine. The moment they took him away from his turf, he was lost.

But wasn't his turf the whole of London? He associated with aristocrats as well as the lower classes.

But for Oscar, his relationship to all those other worlds was one of observer. The only world of which he was truly a resident was the world of art.

The most curious thing about the trials—and to an extent, about the play—is the way in which Wilde partially brought about his own downfall by pursuing a prosecution for libel against his lover's father. What do think his motives were?

You're right. The question really is: Why did he sue the Marquess of Queensbery? I don't think there was one fatal flaw that led him to it. There are many theories. Before the trial, Wilde was in Algiers with Lord Alfred Douglass and he ran into Andre Gide, who said "Oscar, you're not going back—you would be crazy to go back," and Wilde said, "I've come as far as I can go, and now I can only go further from here. I cannot stop and I cannot go back." I think that he had reached a certain degree of fame, and in a way that made him feel invincible. He felt he had to push it.

When he got out of prison, in fact, he changed his name to Sebastian Melmoth, for St. Sebastian and Melmoth the Wanderer, this Gothic novel an uncle of his had written. So there is kind of fantasy of martyrdom. Before the trials, he had conquered the English stage—he was rich, famous and maybe a little bored—but this time, it wasn't going to be an actor saying his lines; it was going to be himself saying his lines. And the conflict and drama was not going to be preordained, it was going to be new. What a great challenge for a dramatist! To be a character in your own play, the outcome of which you don't know. Any playwright would jump at that challenge, right?

Do you think he got caught up in that?

Absolutely. He was caught up in the illusion. But we have to remember that he fell from incredible fame to utter destruction. Now 100 years have gone by, and how many great playwrights from that time are there that we've never heard of? When you talk about Wilde, he and his trials are inextricably linked. So in the trial, perhaps he created something that was as powerful or memorable as any of his plays. And as lasting.

So was it worth it?

Well, that's the problem with heroism: It's always very nice in retrospect.

That sounds almost epigrammatic . . .

I've spent a lot of time with Oscar. (Laughter) Was it worth it for him? No, he lost his entire life. He had to flee England, change his name, hang his head in shame.

Was it worth it for us? Yes. But only if we can learn from it.

A DRAMA

The Laramie Project

INTRODUCTION

BY MOISÉS KAUFMAN

After all, not to create only, or found only,
But to bring perhaps from afar what is already founded,
To give it our own identity, average, limitless, free.

WALT WHITMAN

There are moments in history when a particular event brings the various ideologies and beliefs prevailing in a culture into sharp focus. At these junctures the event becomes a lightning rod of sorts, attracting and distilling the essence of these philosophies and convictions. By paying careful attention in moments like this to people's words, one is able to hear the way these prevailing ideas affect not only individual lives but also the culture at large.

The trials of Oscar Wilde were such an event. When I read the transcripts of the trials (while preparing to write *Gross Indecency*), I was struck by the clarity with which they illuminated an entire culture. In these pages one can see not only a community dealing with the problem that Wilde presented but, in their own words, Victorian men and women telling us—three generations later—about the ideologies, idiosyncrasies, and philosophies that formed the pillars of that culture and ruled their lives.

The brutal murder of Matthew Shepard was another event of this kind. In its immediate aftermath, the nation launched into a dialogue that brought to the surface how we think and talk about homosexuality, sexual politics, education, class, violence, privileges and rights, and the difference between tolerance and acceptance.

The idea of *The Laramie Project* originated in my desire to learn more about why Matthew Shepard was murdered, about what happened that night, about the town of Laramie. The idea of listening to the citizens talk really interested me. How is Laramie different from the rest of the country, and how is it similar?

Shortly after the murder, I posed the question to my company, Tectonic Theater Project. What can we as theater artists do as a response to this incident? And, more concretely, is theater a medium that can contribute to the national dialogue on current events?

These concerns fall squarely within Tectonic Theater Project's mission. Every project we undertake as a company has two objectives: (1) to examine the subject matter at hand, and (2) to explore theatrical language and form. In an age when film and television are constantly redefining and refining their tools and devices, the theater has too often remained entrenched in the nineteenth-century traditions of realism and naturalism. In this sense, our interest was to continue to have a dialogue on both how the theater speaks and how it is created. Thus, I was very interested in this model: A theater company travels somewhere, talks to people, and returns with what it saw and heard to create a play.

At the time I also happened to run across a Brecht essay I had not read in a long time, "The Street Scene." In it Brecht uses as a model the following situation: "an eyewitness demonstrating to a collection of people how a traffic accident took place." He goes on to build a theory about his "epic theatre" based on this model. The essay gave me an idea about how to deal with this project, in terms of both its creation and its aesthetic vocabulary.

So in November 1998, four weeks after the murder of Matthew Shepard, nine members of Tectonic Theater Project and I traveled to Laramie, Wyoming, to collect interviews that might become material for a play. Little did we know that we would devote two years of our lives to this project. We returned to Laramie many times over the course of the next year and a half and conducted more than two hundred interviews.

This play opened in Denver at the Denver Center Theater. Then it moved to New York City, to the Union Square Theatre. And in November 2000 we took the play to Laramie.

The experience of working on *The Laramie Project* has been one of great sadness, great beauty, and, perhaps most important, great revelations—about our nation, about our ideas, about ourselves.

AUTHOR'S NOTE

The Laramie Project was written through a unique collaboration by Tectonic Theater Project. During the year-and-a-half-long development of the play, members of the company and I traveled to Laramie six times to conduct interviews with the people of the town. We transcribed and edited the interviews, then conducted several workshops in which the members of the company presented material and acted as dramaturgs in the creation of the play.

As the volume of material grew with each trip to Laramie, a small writers' group from within the company began to work closely with me to further organize and edit the material, conduct additional research in Laramie, and collaborate on the writing of the play. This group was led by Leigh Fondakowski as head writer, with Stephen Belber and Greg Pierotti as associate writers.

As we got closer to the play's first production in Denver, the actors, including Stephen Belber and Greg Pierotti, turned their focus to performance while Leigh Fondakowski continued to work with me on drafts of the play, as did Stephen Wangh, who by then had joined us as an associate writer and "bench coach."

CHARACTERS

Sherry Aanenson—Russell Henderson's landlord, in her forties.

Anonymous—Friend of Aaron McKinney, in his twenties; works for the railroad.

Bailiff

Baptist minister—Originally from Texas, in his fifties.

Baptist minister's wife—In her late forties.

Stephen Belber—Member of Tectonic Theater Project.

Dr. Cantway—Emergency room doctor at Ivinson Memorial Hospital in Laramie, in his fifties.

Catherine Connolly—Out lesbian professor at the university, in her forties.

Murdock Cooper—Rancher, in his fifties; resident of Centennial, a nearby town.

Rob DeBree—Detective sergeant for the Albany County Sheriff's Department, in his forties; chief investigator of Matthew's murder.

Kerry Drake—Reporter with the *Casper Star-Tribune,* in his forties.

Philip Dubois—President of the University of Wyoming, in his forties.

Tiffany Edwards—Local reporter, in her twenties.

E-mail writer

Gil and Eileen Engen—Ranchers; he is in his sixties; she is in her fifties.

Reggie Fluty—The policewoman who responded to the 911 call and discovered Matthew at the fence, in her late thirties.

Leigh Fondakowski—Member of Tectonic Theater Project.

Matt Galloway—Bartender at the Fireside, in his twenties; student at the University of Wyoming.

Governor Jim Geringer—Republican governor of Wyoming, forty-five years old.

Andrew Gomez—Latino from Laramie, in his twenties.

Amanda Gronich—Member of Tectonic Theater Project.

Russell Henderson—One of the perpetrators, twenty-one years old.

Rebecca Hilliker—Head of the theater department at the University of Wyoming, in her forties; midwestern accent.

Sergeant Hing—Detective at the Laramie Police Department, in his forties.

Jen—A friend of Aaron McKinney, in her early twenties.

Sherry Johnson—Administrative assistant at the university, in her forties.

Stephen Mead Johnson—Unitarian minister, in his fifties.

Two Judges

Jurors and Foreperson

Moisés Kaufman—Member of Tectonic Theater Project.

Aaron Kreifels—University student, nineteen years old.

Phil Labrie—Friend of Matthew Shepard, in his late twenties; eastern European accent.

Doug Laws—Stake Ecclesiastical leader for the Mormon Church in Laramie, in his fifties.

Jeffrey Lockwood—Laramie resident, in his forties.

Aaron McKinney—One of the perpetrators, twenty-one years old.

Bill McKinney—Father of Aaron McKinney, in his forties; truck driver.

Alison Mears—Volunteer for a social service agency in town, in her fifties; very good friend of Marge Murray.

Media / newspaper people

Matt Mickelson—Owner of the Fireside, in his thirties.

Conrad Miller—Car mechanic, in his thirties.

Mormon home teacher to Russell Henderson—In his sixties.

Marge Murray—Reggie Fluty's mother, in his seventies; has emphysema but continues to smoke.

Doc O'Connor—Limousine driver and local entrepreneur, in his fifties.

Andy Paris—Member of Tectonic Theater Project.

Romaine Patterson—Lesbian, twenty-one years old.

Jon Peacock—Matthew Shepard's academic adviser, in his thirties; political science professor.

Reverend Fred Phelps—Minister from Kansas, in his sixties.

Greg Pierotti—Member of Tectonic Theater Project.

Barbara Pitts—Member of Tectonic Theater Project.

Kristin Price—Girlfriend of Aaron McKinney, in her twenties; has a son with Aaron; Tennessee accent.

Priest at the funeral

Cal Rerucha—Prosecuting attorney, in his fifties.

Zackie Salmon—Administrator at the University of Wyoming, in her forties; lesbian; Texas accent.

Father Roger Schmit—Catholic priest, in his forties; very out-spoken.

Jedadiah Schultz—University student, nineteen years old.

Shadow—DJ at the Fireside; African American man, in his thirties.

Shannon—A friend of Aaron McKinney, in his early twenties.

Dennis Shepard—Father of Matthew Shepard, in his forties; Wyoming native.

April Silva—Bisexual university student, nineteen years old.

Jonas Slonaker—Gay man, in his forties.

Rulon Stacey—CEO Poudre Valley Hospital in Fort Collins, Colorado, in his forties; a Mormon.

Trish Steger—Romaine Patterson's sister, in her forties; owner of a shop in town.

Lucy Thompson—Grandmother of Russell Henderson, in her sixties; working-class woman who provided a popular day-care service for the town.

Zubaida Ula—Muslim woman, in her twenties.

Waitress (Debbie Reynolds)

Harry Woods—Gay Laramie resident, fifty-two years old.

NOTE: When a character is not named (for example, friend of Aaron McKinney, "Baptist minister"), it is at the person's request.

PLACE:

Laramie, Wyoming, U.S.A.

TIME:

1998–99

ABOUT THE STAGING

The set is a performance space. There are a few tables and chairs. Costumes and props are always visible. The basic costumes are the ones worn by the company of actors. Costumes to portray the people of Laramie should be simple: a shirt, a pair of glasses, a hat. The desire is to suggest, not re-create. Along the same lines, this should be an actor-driven event. Costume changes, set changes, and anything else that happens on the stage should be done by the company of actors.

ABOUT THE TEXT

When writing this play, we used a technique I developed called moment work. It is a method to create and analyze theater from a structuralist (or tectonic) perspective. For that reason, there are no scenes in this play, only moments. A moment does not mean a change of locale or an entrance or exit of actors or characters. It is simply a unit of theatrical time that is then juxtaposed with other units to convey meaning.

ACT I

MOMENT: A DEFINITION

NARRATOR: On November 14, 1998, the members of Tectonic Theater Project traveled to Laramie, Wyoming, and conducted interviews with the people of the town. During the next year, we would return to Laramie several times and conduct over two hundred interviews. The play you are about to see is edited from those interviews, as well as from journal entries by members of the company and other found texts. Company member Greg Pierotti:

GREG PIEROTTI: My first interview was with Detective Sergeant Hing of the Laramie Police Department. At the start of the interview he was sitting behind his desk, sitting something like this *(he transforms into Sergeant Hing):*

I was born and raised here.

My family is, uh, third generation.

My grandparents moved here in the early nineteen hundreds.

We've had basically three, well, my daughter makes it fourth generation.

Quite a while. . . . It's a good place to live. Good people—lots of space.

Now, all the towns in southern Wyoming are laid out and spaced because of the railroad came through.

It was how far they could go before having to refuel and rewater.

And, uh, Laramie was a major stopping point.

That's why the towns are spaced so far apart.

We're one of the largest states in the country, and the least populated.

REBECCA HILLIKER: There's so much space between people and towns here, so much time for reflection.

NARRATOR: Rebecca Hilliker, head of the theater department at the University of Wyoming:

REBECCA HILLIKER: You have an opportunity to be happy in your life here. I found that people here were nicer than in the Midwest, where I used to teach, because they were happy. They were glad the sun was shining. And it shines a lot here.

SERGEANT HING: What you have is, you have your old-time traditional-type ranchers, they've been here forever—Laramie's been the hub of where they come for their supplies and stuff like that.

EILEEN ENGEN: Stewardship is one thing all our ancestors taught us.

NARRATOR: Eileen Engen, rancher:

EILEEN ENGEN: If you don't take care of the land, then you ruin it and you lose your living. So you first of all have to take care of your land and do everything you can to improve it.

DOC O'CONNOR: I love it here.

NARRATOR: Doc O'Connor, limousine driver:

DOC O'CONNOR: You couldn't put me back in that mess out there back east. Best thing about it is the climate. The cold, the wind. They say the Wyoming wind'll drive a man insane. But you know what? It don't bother me. Well, some of the times it bothers me. But most of the time it don't.

SERGEANT HING: And then you got, uh, the university population.

PHILIP DUBOIS: I moved here after living in a couple of big cities.

NARRATOR: Philip Dubois, president of the University of Wyoming:

PHILIP DUBOIS: I loved it there. But you'd have to be out of your mind to let your kids out after dark. And here, in the summertime, my kids play out at night till eleven and I don't think twice about it.

SERGEANT HING: And then you have the people who live in Laramie, basically.

ZACKIE SALMON: I moved here from rural Texas.

NARRATOR: Zackie Salmon, Laramie resident:

ZACKIE SALMON: Now, in Laramie, if you don't know a person, you will definitely know someone they know. So it can only be one degree removed at most. And for me—I love it! I mean, I love to go to the grocery store 'cause I get to visit with four or five or six people every time I go. And I don't really mind people knowing my business—'cause what's my business? I mean, my business is basically good.

DOC O'CONNOR: I like the trains, too. They don't bother me. Well, some of the times they bother me, but most times they don't. Even though one goes by every thirteen minutes out where I live. . . .

NARRATOR: Doc actually lives up in Bossler. But everybody in Laramie knows him. He's also not really a doctor.

DOC O'CONNOR: They used to carry cattle . . . them trains. Now all they carry is diapers and cars.

APRIL SILVA: I grew up in Cody, Wyoming.

NARRATOR: April Silva, university student:

APRIL SILVA: Laramie is better than where I grew up. I'll give it that.

SERGEANT HING: It's a good place to live. Good people, lots of space. Now, when the incident happened with that boy, a lot of press people came here. And one time some of them followed me out to the crime scene. And uh, well, it was a beautiful day, absolutely gorgeous day, real clear and crisp and the sky was that blue that, uh . . . you know, you'll never be able to paint, it's just sky blue—it's just gorgeous. And the mountains in the background and a little snow on 'em, and this one reporter, uh, lady . . . person, that was out there, she said . . .

REPORTER: Well, who found the boy, who was out here anyway?

SERGEANT HING: And I said, "Well, this is a really popular area for people to run, and mountain biking's really big out here, horseback riding, it's just, well, it's close to town." And she looked at me and she said:

REPORTER: Who in the hell would want to run out here?

SERGEANT HING: And I'm thinking, "Lady, you're just missing the point." You know, all you got to do is turn around, see the mountains, smell the air, listen to the birds, just take in what's around you. And they were just—nothing but the story. I didn't feel judged, I felt that they were stupid. They're, they're missing the point—they're just missing the whole point.

JEDADIAH SCHULTZ: It's hard to talk about Laramie now, to tell you what Laramie is, for us.

NARRATOR: Jedadiah Schultz:

JEDADIAH SCHULTZ: If you would have asked me before, I would have told you Laramie is a beautiful town, secluded enough that you can have your own identity. . . . A town with a strong sense of community—everyone knows everyone. . . . A town with a personality that most larger cities are stripped of. Now, after Matthew, I would say that Laramie is a town defined by an accident, a crime. We've become Waco, we've become Jasper. We're a noun, a definition, a sign. We may be able to get rid of that . . . but it will sure take a while.

MOMENT: JOURNAL ENTRIES

NARRATOR: Journal entries—members of the company. Andy Paris:

ANDY PARIS: Moisés called saying he had an idea for his next theater project. But there was a somberness to his voice, so I asked what it was all about and he told me he wanted to do a piece about what's happening in Wyoming.

NARRATOR: Stephen Belber:

STEPHEN BELBER: Leigh told me the company was thinking of going out to Laramie to conduct interviews and that they wanted me to come. But I'm hesitant. I have no real interest in prying into a town's unraveling.

NARRATOR: Amanda Gronich:

AMANDA GRONICH: I've never done anything like this in my life. How do you get people to talk to you? What do you ask?

NARRATOR: Moisés Kaufman:

MOISÉS KAUFMAN: The company has agreed that we should go to Laramie for a week and interview people.

Am a bit afraid about taking ten people in a trip of this nature. Must make some safety rules. No one works alone. Everyone carries cell phones. Have made some preliminary contacts with Rebecca Hilliker, head of the theater department at the University of Wyoming. She is hosting a party for us our first night in Laramie and has promised to introduce us to possible interviewees.

MOMENT: REBECCA HILLIKER

REBECCA HILLIKER: I must tell you that when I first heard that you were thinking of coming here, when you first called me, I wanted to say, You've just kicked me in the stomach. Why are you doing this to me?

But then I thought, That's stupid, you're not doing this to me. And, more important, I thought about it and decided that we've had so much negative closure on this whole thing. And the students really need to talk. When this happened they started talking about it, and then the media descended and all dialogue stopped.

You know, I really love my students because they are free thinkers. And you may not like what they have to say, and you may not like their opinions, because they can be very redneck, but they are honest and they're truthful—so there's an excitement here, there's a dynamic here with my students that I never had when I was in the Midwest or in North Dakota, because there, there was so much Puritanism that dictated how people looked at the world that a lot of times they didn't have an opinion, you couldn't get them to express an opinion. And, quite honestly, I'd rather have opinions that I don't like—and have that dynamic in education.

There's a student I think you should talk to. His name is Jedadiah Schultz.

MOMENT: *ANGELS IN AMERICA*

JEDADIAH SCHULTZ: I've lived in Wyoming my whole life. The family has been in Wyoming, well . . . for generations. Now when it came time to go to college, my parents can't—couldn't afford to send me to college. I wanted to study theater. And I knew that if I was going to go to college I was going to have to get on a scholarship—and so, uh, they have this competition each year, this Wyoming state high school competition. And I knew that if I didn't take first place in, uh, duets that I wasn't gonna get a scholarship. So I went to the theater department of the university looking for good scenes, and I asked one of the professors—I was like, "I need—I need a killer scene," and he was like, "Here you go, this is it." And it was from *Angels in America*.

So I read it and I knew that I could win best scene if I did a good enough job.

And when the time came I told my mom and dad so that they would come to the competition. Now you have to understand, my parents go to everything—every ball game, every hockey game—everything I've ever done.

And they brought me into their room and told me that if I did that scene, that they would not come to see me in the competition. Because they believed that it is wrong—that homosexuality is wrong—they felt that strongly about it that they didn't want to come see their son do probably the most important thing he'd done to that point in his life. And I didn't know what to do.

I had never, ever gone against my parents' wishes. So I was kind of worried about it. But I decided to do it.

And all I can remember about the competition is that when we were done, me and my scene partner, we came up to each other and we shook hands and there was a standing ovation.

Oh, man, it was amazing! And we took first place and we won. And that's how come I can afford to be here at the university, because of that scene. It was one of the best moments of my life. And my parents weren't there. And to this day, that was the one thing that my parents didn't see me do.

And thinking back on it, I think, why did I do it? Why did I oppose my parents? 'Cause I'm not gay. So why did I do it? And I guess the only honest answer I can give is that, well *(he chuckles)* I wanted to win. It was such a good scene; it was like the best scene!

Do you know Mr. Kushner? Maybe you can tell him.

MOMENT: JOURNAL ENTRIES

NARRATOR: Company member Greg Pierotti:

GREG PIEROTTI: We arrived today in the Denver Airport and drove to Laramie. The moment we crossed the Wyoming border I swear I saw a herd of buffalo. Also, I thought it was strange that the Wyoming sign said: WYOMING—LIKE NO PLACE ON EARTH instead of WYOMING—LIKE NO PLACE ELSE ON EARTH.

NARRATOR: Company member Leigh Fondakowski:

LEIGH FONDAKOWSKI: I stopped at a local inn for a bite to eat. And my waitress said to me:

WAITRESS: Hi, my name is Debbie. I was born in nineteen fifty-four and Debbie Reynolds was big then, so, yes, there are a lot of us around, but I promise that I won't slap you if you leave your elbows on the table.

MOISÉS KAUFMAN: Today Leigh tried to explain to me to no avail what chicken fried steak was.

WAITRESS: Now, are you from Wyoming? Or are you just passing through?

LEIGH FONDAKOWSKI: We're just passing through.

NARRATOR: Company member Barbara Pitts:

BARBARA PITTS: We arrived in Laramie tonight. Just past the WELCOME TO LARAMIE sign— POPULATION 26,687—the first thing to greet us was Wal-Mart. In the dark, we could be on any main drag in America—fast-food chains, gas stations. But as we drove into the downtown area by the railroad tracks, the buildings still look like a turn-of-the-century western town. Oh, and as we passed the University Inn, on the sign where amenities such as heated pool or cable TV are usually touted, it said: HATE IS NOT A LARAMIE VALUE.

NARRATOR: Greg Pierotti:

MOMENT: ALISON AND MARGE

GREG PIEROTTI: I met today with two longtime Laramie residents, Alison Mears and Marge Murray, two social service workers who taught me a thing or two.

ALISON MEARS: Well, what Laramie used to be like when Marge was growing up, well, it was mostly rural.

NARRATOR: Amanda Gronich:

AMANDA GRONICH: Today we divided up to go to different churches in the community. Moisés and I were given a Baptist church. We were welcomed into the services by the reverend himself standing at the entrance to the chapel. This is what I remember of his sermon that morning.

MOMENT: THE WORD

BAPTIST MINISTER: My dear brothers and sisters: I am here today to bring you the Word of the Lord. Now, I have a simple truth that I tell to my colleagues and I'm gonna tell it to you today: The word is either sufficient or it is not.

Scientists tell me that human history, that the world is five billion or six billion years old—after all, what's a billion years give or take? The Bible tells me that human history is six thousand years old.

The word is either sufficient or it is not.

STEPHEN MEAD JOHNSON: Ah, the sociology of religion in the West . . .

NARRATOR: Stephen Mead Johnson, Unitarian minister:

STEPHEN MEAD JOHNSON: Dominant religious traditions in this town: Baptist, Mormon—they're everywhere, it's not just Salt Lake, you know, they're all over—they're like jam on toast down here.

DOUG LAWS: The Mormon Church has a little different thing going that irritates some folks.

NARRATOR: Doug Laws, Stake Ecclesiastical leader for the Mormon Church:

DOUG LAWS: And that is that we absolutely believe that God still speaks to man. We don't think that it happened and some folks wrote it in the Bible. God speaks to us today, and we believe that. We believe that the prophet of the church has the authority to receive inspiration and revelation from God.

STEPHEN MEAD JOHNSON: So, the spectrum would be—uh, on the left side of that panel: So far left that I am probably sitting by myself, is me—and the Unitarian Church. Unitarians are by and large humanists, many of whom are atheists. I mean—we're, you know, we're not even sure we're a religion. And to my right on the spectrum, to his credit, Father Roger, Catholic priest, who is well-established here, and God bless him—he did not equivocate at all when this happened—he hosted the vigil for Matthew that night.

FATHER ROGER SCHMIT: I was really jolted because, you know, when we did the vigil—we wanted to get other ministers involved and we called some of them, and they were not going to get involved. And it was like, "We are gonna stand back and wait and see which way the wind is blowing." And that angered me immensely. We are supposed to stand out as leaders. I thought, "Wow, what's going on here?"

DOUG LAWS: God has set boundaries. And one of our responsibilities is to learn: What is it that God wants? So you study Scripture, you look to your leaders. Then you know what the bounds are. Now once you kinda know what the bounds are, then you sorta get a feel for what's out-of-bounds.

There is a proclamation that came out on the family. A family is defined as one woman and one man and children. That's a family. That's about as clear as you can state it. There's no sexual deviation in the Mormon Church. No—no leniency. We just think it's out-of-bounds.

BAPTIST MINISTER: I warn you: You will be mocked! You will be ridiculed for the singularity of your faith! But you let the Bible be your guide. It's in there. It's all in there.

STEPHEN MEAD JOHNSON: The Christian pastors, many of the conservative ones, were silent on this. Conservative Christians use the Bible to show the rest of the world, It says here in the Bible. And most Americans believe, and they do, that the Bible is the word of God, and how you gonna fight that?

BAPTIST MINISTER: I am a Biblicist. Which means: The Bible doesn't need me to be true. The Bible is true whether I believe it or not. The word is either sufficient or it is not.

STEPHEN MEAD JOHNSON: I arrived in Laramie on September fifteenth. I looked around—tumbleweed, cement factory—and said, "What in the hell am I doing in Wyoming?" Three weeks later, I found out what the hell I'm doing in Wyoming.

MOMENT: A SCARF

STEPHEN BELBER: I had breakfast this morning with a university student named Zubaida Ula. She is an Islamic feminist who likes to do things her own way.

ZUBAIDA ULA: I've lived in Laramie since I was four. Yeah. My parents are from Bangladesh. Two years ago, because I'm Muslim, I decided to start wearing a scarf. That's really changed my life in Laramie. Yeah.

Like people say things to me like, "Why do you have to wear that thing on your head?" Like when I go to the grocery store, I'm not looking to give people Islam 101, you know what I mean? So I'll be like, "Well, it's part of my religion," and they'll be— this is the worst part cuz they'll be like, "I know it's part of your religion, but why?" And it's—how am I supposed to go into the whole doctrine of physical modesty and my own spiritual relationship with the Lord, standing there with my pop and chips? You know what I mean?

STEPHEN BELBER: Yeah.

ZUBAIDA ULA: You know, it's so unreal to me that, yeah, that a group from New York would be writing a play about Laramie. And then I was picturing like you're gonna be in a play about my town. You're gonna be onstage in New York and you're gonna be acting like you're us. That's so weird.

MOMENT: LIFESTYLE 1

BAPTIST MINISTER'S WIFE: Hello?

AMANDA GRONICH: Yes, hello. My name is Amanda Gronich and I am here in Laramie working with a theater company. I went to the reverend's, your husband's church on Sunday, and I was extremely interested in talking with the reverend about some of his thoughts about recent events.

Baptist Minister's wife: Well, I don't think he'll want to talk to you. He has very biblical views about homosexuality—he doesn't condone that kind of violence. But he doesn't condone that kind of lifestyle, you know what I mean? And he was just bombarded with press after this happened and the media has been just terrible about this whole thing.

Amanda Gronich: Oh, I know, I really understand, it must have just been terrible.

Baptist Minister's wife: Oh, yes, I think we are all hoping this just goes away.

Amanda Gronich: Well, um, do you think maybe I could call back and speak with your husband just briefly?

Baptist Minister's wife: Well, all right, you can call him back tonight at nine.

Amanda Gronich: Oh, thank you so much. I'll do that.

Moment: The Fireside

Stephen Belber: Today Barbara and I went to the Fireside Bar, which is the last place Matthew was seen in public.

Barbara Pitts: The Fireside—definitely feels like a college bar, with a couple of pool tables and a stage area for karaoke. Still, the few regulars in the late afternoon were hardly the college crowd.

Stephen Belber: First person we talked to was Matt Mickelson, the owner.

Matt Mickelson: My great-great-grandfather moved here in eighteen sixty-two, he owned Laramie's first opera house, it was called Old Blue Front, and in eighteen seventy Louisa Grandma Swain cast the first woman's ballot in any free election in the world, and that's why Wyoming is the Equality State, so what I want to do is reestablish my bar business as the Old Blue Front Opera House and Good Time Emporium, you know, I want to have a restaurant, I want to have a gift shop, I want to have a pool hall, and do all this shit, you know . . . every night's ladies' night . . .

So the Fireside is the first step towards the Old Blue Front Opera House and Good Time Emporium.

Barbara Pitts: So, what about the night Matthew Shepard was here?

Matt Mickelson: We had karaoke that night, twenty or thirty people here—Matthew Shepard came in, sitting right—right where you're sitting, just hanging out. . . . I mean, if you wanna talk to somebody, you should talk to Matt Galloway, he was the kid that was bartending that night. You'd have to meet him, his character stands for itself.

(Calling) Hey, is Galloway bartending tonight?

Matt Galloway: Okay. I'm gonna make this brief, quick, get it over with, but it will be everything—factual. Just the facts. Here we go. Ten o'clock. I clock in, usual time, Tuesday nights. Ten-thirty—Matthew Shepard shows up—alone—sits down, orders a Heineken.

Narrator: Phil Labrie, friend of Matthew Shepard:

Phil Labrie: Matt liked to drink Heineken and nothing else. Heineken even though you have to pay nine-fifty for a six-pack. He'd always buy the same beer.

Matt Galloway: So what can I tell you about Matt?

If you had a hundred customers like him it'd be the—the most perfect bar I've ever been in. Okay? And nothing to do with sexual orientation. Um, absolute mannerisms. Manners. Politeness, intelligence.

Taking care of me, as in tips. Everything—conversation, uh, dressed nice, clean-cut. Some people you just know, sits down, "Please," "Thank you"—offers intellect, you know, within—within—within their vocabulary.

Um, so, he kicks it there. Didn't seem to have any worries, or like he was looking for anyone. Just enjoy his drink and the company around.

Now approximately eleven forty-five, eleven-thirty-eleven forty-five, Aaron McKinney and Russell Henderson come in—I didn't know their names then, but they're the accused, they're the perps, they're the accused. They walked in, just very stone-faced, you know. Dirty. Grungy. Rude. "Gimme." That type of thing. They walked up to the bar, uh, and, as you know, paid for a pitcher with dimes and quarters, uh, which is something that I mean you don't forget. You don't forget that. Five-fifty in dimes and quarters. That's a freakin' nightmare.

Now Henderson and McKinney, they didn't seem intoxificated at all. They came in—they just ordered a beer, took the pitcher with them back there into the pool room, and kept to themselves. Next thing I knew, probably a half hour later, they were kind of walking around—no beer. And I remember thinking to myself that I'm not gonna ask them if they want another one, because obviously they just paid for a pitcher with dimes and quarters, I have a real good feeling they don't have any more money.

NARRATOR: Romaine Patterson:

ROMAINE PATTERSON: Money meant nothing to Matthew, because he came from a lot of it. And he would like hand over his wallet in two seconds—because money meant nothing. His—shoes—might have meant something. They can say it was robbery . . . I don't buy it. For even an iota of a second.

MATT GALLOWAY: Then a few moments later I looked over and Aaron and Russell had been talking to Matthew Shepard.

KRISTIN PRICE: Aaron said that a guy walked up to him and said that he was gay, and wanted to get with Aaron and Russ.

NARRATOR: Kristin Price, girlfriend of Aaron McKinney:

KRISTIN PRICE: And Aaron got aggravated with it and told him that he was straight and didn't want anything to do with him and walked off. He said that is when he and Russell went to the bathroom and decided to pretend they were gay and get him in the truck and rob him. They wanted to teach him a lesson not to come on to straight people.

MATT GALLOWAY: Okay, no. They stated that Matt approached them, that he came on to them. I absolutely, positively disbelieve and refute the statement one hundred percent. Refute it. I'm gonna give you two reasons why.

One. Character reference.

Why would he approach them? Why them? He wasn't approaching anybody else in the bar. They say he's gay, he was a flaming gay, he's gonna come on to people like that. Bullshit. He never came on to me. Hello?!? He came on to them? I don't believe it.

Two. Territorialism is—is—is the word I will use for this. And that's the fact that Matt was sitting there. Russell and Aaron were in the pool area. Upon their first interaction, they were in Matt's area, in the area that Matt had been seen all night. So who approached who by that?

ROMAINE PATTERSON: But Matthew was the kind of person . . . like, he would never not talk to someone for any reason. If someone started talking to him, he'd just be like, "Oh, blah, blah, blah." He never had any problem just striking up a conversation with anybody.

PHIL LABRIE: Matt did feel lonely a lot of times. Me knowing that—and knowing how gullible Matt could be . . . he would have walked right into it. The fact that he was at the bar alone without any friends made him that much more vulnerable.

MATT GALLOWAY: So the only thing is—and this is what I'm testifying to—'cause, you know, I'm also, basically, the key eyewitness in this case, uh *(pause)* basically what I'm testifying is that I saw Matthew leave. I saw two individuals leave with Matthew. I didn't see their faces, but I saw the back of their heads. At the same time, McKinney and Henderson were no longer around. You do the math.

MATT MICKELSON: Actually, I think the DJ was the last one to talk to him on his way out that night . . . gave him a cigarette or something. His name is Shadow.

SHADOW: I was the last person that Matt talked to before he left the Fireside. . . . I was just bullshittin' around with my shit, and he stopped me, I stopped him actually, and he's like, "Hey, Shadow, da da da," and I was like, "What, man, you gettin' ready to leave?" he's like, "Yeah, man, and this an' that." But then I noticed them two guys and they stood outside, you could see, you could see it, they were standing there, you know, and he was looking over to them, and they were lookin' back at him. And I stood and talked to Matt for like a good ten minutes and you seen the guys with him, you seen 'em getting like, you seen 'em like worried, like, you know, anxious to leave and shit. . . . So when they took off, I seen it, when they took off, it was in a black truck, it was a small truck, and the three of them sat in the front seat and Matt sat in the middle.

And I didn't think nothin' of it, you know. I didn't figure them guys was gonna be like that.

MOMENT: MCKINNEY AND HENDERSON

NARRATOR: A friend of Aaron McKinney:

ANONYMOUS: Oh, I've known Aaron a long time. Aaron was a good kid, I liked Aaron a lot, that's why I was shocked when I heard this, I'm like . . . I know he was, he was living out far . . . at his trailer house is what he told me, with his girl . . . they just started dating last summer . . . they musta gotten pregnant as soon as they started dating, you know, 'cause they had a kid. He was only twenty-one years old, but he was running around with a kid. . . . You see, that's the kinda person Aaron was, just like he always dressed in like big clothes, you know like, in like Tommy "Hile-figer," Polo, Gucci . . .

At the time I knew him, he was just, he was just a young kid trying to, you know, he just wanted to fit in, you know, acting tough, acting cool, but, you know, you could get in his face about it and he would back down, like he was some kinda scared kid.

Narrator: Sherry Aanenson:

Sherry Aanenson: Russell was just so sweet. He was the one who was the Eagle Scout. I mean, his whole presence was just quiet and sweet. So of course it doesn't make sense to me and I know people snap and whatever and like it wasn't a real intimate relationship, I was just his landlord. I did work with him at the Chuck Wagon too. And I remember like at the Christmas party he was just totally drunk out of his mind, like we all were pretty much just party-party time. . . . And he wasn't belligerent, he didn't change, his personality didn't change. He was still the same little meek. Russell, I remember him coming up to me and saying, "When you get a chance, Sherry, can I have a dance?" Which we never did get around to doing that but . . . Now I just want to shake him, you know—What were you thinking? What in the hell were you thinking?

Moment: The Fence

Stephen Mead Johnson: The fence—I've been out there four times, I've taken visitors. That place has become a pilgrimage site. Clearly that's a very powerful personal experience to go out there. It is so stark and so empty and you can't help but think of Matthew out there for eighteen hours in nearly freezing temperatures, with that view up there isolated, and, the "God, my God, why have you forsaken me" comes to mind.

Narrator: Company member Greg Pierotti:

Greg Pierotti: Phil Labrie, a friend of Matthew's, took us to the fence this morning. I broke down the minute I touched it. I feel such a strong kinship with this young man. On the way back, I made sure that no one saw me crying.

Narrator: Leigh Fondakowski:

Leigh Fondakowski: Greg was crying on the way back. I couldn't bring myself to tears, but I felt the same way. I have an interview this afternoon with Aaron Kreifels. He's the boy who found Matthew out there at the fence. I don't think I'm up for it right now. I'll see if someone else can do it.

Moment: Finding Matthew Shepard

Aaron Kreifels: Well I, uh, I took off on my bicycle about five P.M. on Wednesday from my dorm. I just kinda felt like going for a ride. So I—I went up to the top of Cactus Canyon, and I'm not superfamiliar with that area, so on my way back down, I didn't know where I was going, I was just sort of picking the way to go, which now . . . it just makes me think that God wanted me to find him because there's no way that I was going to go that way.

So I was in some deep-ass sand, and I wanted to turn around—but for some reason, I kept going. And, uh, I went along. And there was this rock, on the—on the ground—and I just drilled it. I went—over the handlebars and ended up on the ground.

So, uh, I got up, and I was just kind of dusting myself off, and I was looking around and I noticed something—which ended up to be Matt, and he was just lying there by a fence, and I—I just thought it was a scarecrow. I was like, Halloween's coming up, thought it was a Halloween gag, so I didn't think much of it, so I got my bike, walked it around the fence that was there, it was a buck-type fence. And, uh, got closer to him, and I noticed his hair—and that was a major key to me noticing it was a human being—was his hair. 'Cause I just thought it was a dummy, seriously, I noticed—I even noticed the chest going up and down, I still thought it was a dummy, you know. I thought it was just like some kind of mechanism.

But when I saw hair, well, I knew it was a human being.

So . . . I ran to the nearest house and—I just ran as fast as I could . . . and called the police.

REGGIE FLUTY: I responded to the call.

NARRATOR: Officer Reggie Fluty:

REGGIE FLUTY: When I got there, the first—at first the only thing I could see was partially somebody's feet, and I got out of my vehicle and raced over—I seen what appeared to be a young man, thirteen, fourteen years old because he was so tiny laying on his back and he was tied to the bottom end of a pole.

I did the best I could. The gentleman that was laying on the ground, Matthew Shepard, he was covered in dry blood all over his head, there was dry blood underneath him and he was barely breathing . . . he was doing the best he could.

I was going to breathe for him and I couldn't get his mouth open—his mouth wouldn't open for me.

He was covered in, like I said, partially dry blood and blood all over his head—the only place that he did not have any blood on him, on his face, was what appeared to be where he had been crying down his face.

His head was distorted—you know, it did not look normal—he looked as if he had a real harsh head wound.

DR. CANTWAY: I was working the emergency room the night Matthew Shepard was brought in. I don't think that any of us, ah, can remember seeing a patient in that condition for a long time—those of us who've worked in big city hospitals have seen this. Ah, but we have some people here who've not worked in a big city hospital. And, ah, it's not something you expect here.

Ah, you expect it, you expect this kind of injuries to come from a car going down a hill at eighty miles an hour. You expect to see gross injuries from something like that—this horrendous, terrible thing. Ah, but you don't expect to see that from someone doing this to another person.

The ambulance report said it was a beating, so we knew.

AARON KREIFELS: There was nothing I could do. I mean, if there was anything that I could of done to help him I would've done it but there was nothing.

And I, I was yelling at the top of my lungs at him, trying to get something outta him. Like: "Hey, wake up," "HELLO!"

But he didn't move, he didn't flinch, he didn't anything . . .

REGGIE FLUTY: He was tied to the fence—his hands were thumbs out in what we call a cuffing position—the way we handcuff people. He was bound with a real thin white rope, it went around the bottom of the pole, about four inches up off the ground.

His shoes were missing.

He was tied extremely tight—so I used my boot knife and tried to slip it between the rope and his wrist—I had to be extremely careful not to harm Matthew any further.

DR. CANTWAY: Your first thought is . . . well, certainly you'd like to think that it's somebody from out of town, that comes through and beats somebody. I mean, things like this happen, you know, shit happens, and it happens in Laramie. But if there's been somebody who has been beaten repeatedly, ah, certainly this is something that offends us. I think that's a good word. It offends us!

REGGIE FLUTY: He was bound so tight—I finally got the knife through there—I'm sorry—we rolled him over to his left side—when we did that he quit breathing. Immediately, I put him back on his back—and that was just enough of an adjustment—it gave me enough room to cut him free there—

I seen the EMS unit trying to get to the location, once the ambulance got there we put a neck collar on him, placed him on a back board, and scooted him from underneath the fence—then Rob drove the ambulance to Ivinson Hospital's emergency room . . .

DR. CANTWAY: Now, the strange thing is, twenty minutes before Matthew came in, Aaron McKinney was brought in by his girlfriend. Now I guess he had gotten into a fight later on that night back in town, so I am workin' on Aaron and the ambulance comes in with Matthew. Now at this point I don't know that there's a connection—at all. So I tell Aaron to wait and I go and treat Matthew. So there's Aaron in one room of the ER and Matthew in another room two doors down.

Now as soon as we saw Matthew . . . It was very obvious that his care was beyond our capabilities. Called the neurosurgeon at Poudre Valley, and he was on the road in an hour and fifteen minutes, I think.

REGGIE FLUTY: They showed me a picture . . . days later I saw a picture of Matthew . . . I would have never recognized him.

DR. CANTWAY: Then two days later I found out the connection and I was . . . very . . . struck!!! They were two kids!!!!! They were both my patients and they were two kids. I took care of both of them. . . . Of both their bodies. And . . . for a brief moment I wondered if this is how God feels when he looks down at us. How we are all his kids. . . . Our bodies. . . . Our souls. . . . And I felt a great deal of compassion. . . . For both of them. . . .

End of Act One

ACT II

MOMENT: A LARAMIE MAN

NARRATOR: This is Jon Peacock, Matthew's academic adviser.

JON PEACOCK: Well, the news reports started trickling out on Thursday, but no names were mentioned, the brutality of the crime was not mentioned. All that was mentioned was that there was a man, Laramie man, found beaten, out on the prairie basically. Later on in the evening they mentioned his name. It was like, That can't, that's not the Matthew Shepard I know, that's not my student, that's not this person who I've been meeting with.

ROMAINE PATTERSON: I was in the coffee shop.

NARRATOR: Romaine Patterson:

ROMAINE PATTERSON: And someone pulled me aside and said: "I don't know much, but they say that there's been a young man who's been beaten in Laramie. And they said his name was Matthew Shepard." And he said, "Do you think this could be our Matthew?"

And I said, "Well, yeah, it sounds like it could be our Matthew."

So I called up my sister Trish and I said, "Tell me what you know." I'm just like, "I need to know anything you know because I don't know anything."

TRISH STEGER: So I'm talking to my sister on the phone and that's when the whole story came up on Channel 5 news and it was just like *baboom*.

JON PEACOCK: And the news reports kept rolling in, young University of Wyoming student, his age, his description, it's like, "Oh my God."

TRISH STEGER: And, uh *(pause)* I—I felt sick to my stomach . . . it's just instantly sick to my stomach. And I had to tell Romaine, "Yes, it was Matthew. It was your friend."

MATT GALLOWAY: Well, I'll tell you—I'll tell you what is overwhelming.

NARRATOR: Matt Galloway:

MATT GALLOWAY: Friday morning I first find out about it. I go to class, walk out, boom there it is—in the *Branding Iron*. So immediately I drive to the nearest newsstand, buy a *Laramie Boomerang* 'cause I want more details, buy that—go home . . . before I can even open the paper, my boss calls me, he says:

MATT MICKELSON: Did you hear about what happened?

MATT GALLOWAY: I'm like, "Yeah."

MATT MICKELSON: Was he in the bar Tuesday night?

MATT GALLOWAY: I go, "Yes, yes he was."

MATT MICKELSON: You've got to get down to the bar right now, we've got to talk about this, we've got to discuss what's going to go on.

JON PEACOCK: By this time, I was starting to get upset, but still the severity wasn't out yet.

RULON STACEY: It was Thursday afternoon.

NARRATOR: Rulon Stacey at Poudre Valley Hospital:

RULON STACEY: I got a call: "We just got a kid in from Wyoming and it looks like he may be the victim of a hate crime. We have a couple of newspaper reporters here asking questions." And so, we agreed that we needed one spokesperson: As CEO, I'll do that and we'll try and gather all the information that we can.

ROMAINE PATTERSON: And then I watched the ten o'clock news that night, where they started speaking about the nature and the seriousness of it . . .

MATT GALLOWAY: So I'm on the phone with Mickelson and he's like:

MATT MICKELSON: We need to go to the arraignment so we can identify these guys, and make sure these guys were in the bar.

MATT GALLOWAY: So we go to the arraignment.

MOMENT: THE ESSENTIAL FACTS

NEWSPERSON: Our focus today turns to Laramie, Wyoming, and the Albany County Courthouse, where Aaron James McKinney and Russell Arthur Henderson are being charged with the brutal beating of Matthew Shepard, a gay University of Wyoming student.

NARRATOR: Catherine Connolly:

CATHERINE CONNOLLY: The arraignment was on Friday. Right around lunchtime. And I said, "I'm just going." I just took off—it's just down the street. So I walked a few blocks and I went. Has anybody told you about the arraignment?

There were probably about a hundred people from town and probably as many news media. By that point, a lot more of the details had come out. The fact that the perpetrators were kids themselves, local kids, that everyone who's from around here has some relationship to. And what—Everyone was really I think waiting on pins and needles for what would happen when the perpetrators walked in. And what happened—there's two hundred people in the room at this point . . . they walked in in their complete orange jumpsuits and their shackles, and, you could have heard a pin drop.

It was incredibly solemn.

I mean, lots of people were teary at that point. Then the judge came in and did a reading—there was a reading of the evidence that the prosecution has and—it's just a—it's a statement of facts, and the reading of the facts was . . .

JUDGE: The essential facts are that the defendants, Aaron James McKinney and Russell Arthur Henderson, met Matthew Shepard at the Fireside Bar, and after Mr. Shepard confided he was gay, the subjects deceived Mr. Shepard into leaving with them in their vehicle to a remote area. Upon arrival at said area, both subjects tied their victim to a buck fence, robbed him, tortured him, and beat him. . . . Both defendants were later contacted by officers of the Laramie Police Department, who observed inside the cab of their pickup a credit card and a pair of black patent leather shoes belonging to the victim, Matthew Shepard.

(The JUDGE *goes sotto voce here while* CATHERINE CONNOLLY *speaks.)*

The subjects took the victim's credit card, wallet containing twenty dollars in cash, his shoes, and other items, and obtained the victim's address in order to later burglarize his home.

CATHERINE CONNOLLY: I don't think there was any person who was left in that courtroom who wasn't crying at the end of it. I mean it lasted—five minutes, but it kept on getting more and more horrific, ending with:

JUDGE: Said defendants left the victim begging for his life.

MOMENT: LIVE AND LET LIVE

NARRATOR: Sergeant Hing:

SERGEANT HING: How could this happen? I—I think a lot of people just don't understand, and even I don't really understand, how someone can do something like that. We have one of the most vocal populations of gay people in the state. . . . And it's pretty much: Live and let live.

NARRATOR: Laramie resident Jeffrey Lockwood:

JEFFREY LOCKWOOD: My secret hope was that they were from somewhere else, that then of course you can create that distance: We don't grow children like that here. Well, it's pretty clear that we do grow children like that here . . .

CATHERINE CONNOLLY: So that was the arraignment, and my response—was pretty catatonic—not sleeping, not eating. Don't—you know, don't leave me alone right now.

JON PEACOCK: More and more details came in about the sheer brutality, um, motivations, how this happened. And then quite frankly the media descended and there was no time to reflect on it anymore.

MOMENT: THE GEM CITY OF THE PLAINS

(Many reporters enter the stage, followed by media crews carrying cameras, microphones, and lights. They start speaking into the cameras. Simultaneously, television monitors enter the space—in our production they flew in from above the light grid. In the monitors, one can see in live feed the reporters speaking as well as other media images. The texts overlap to create a kind of media cacophony. This moment should feel like an invasion and should be so perceived by the other actors onstage.)

NEWSPERSON 1: Laramie, Wyoming—often called the Gem City of the Plains—is now at the eye of the storm.

(Enter NEWSPERSON 2. NEWSPERSON 1 *goes sotto voce.)*

The cowboy state has its rednecks and yahoos for sure, but there are no more bigots per capita in Wyoming than there are in New York, Florida, or California. The difference is that in Wyoming there are fewer places to blend in if you're anything other than prairie stock.

NEWSPERSON 2: Aaron McKinney and his friend Russell Henderson came from the poor side of town.

(Enter NEWSPERSON 3. NEWSPERSON 2 *goes sotto voce.)*

Both were from broken homes and as teenagers had had runins with the law. They lived in trailer parks and scratched out a living working at fast-food restaurants and fixing roofs.

NEWSPERSON 3: As a gay college student lay hospitalized in critical condition after a severe beating . . . this small city, which bills itself as Wyoming's Hometown, wrestled with its attitudes toward gay men.

(Enter NEWSPERSON 4. NEWSPERSON 3 *goes sotto voce.)*

NEWSPERSON 4: People would like to think that what happened to Matthew was an exception to the rule, but it was an extreme version of what happens in our schools on a daily basis.

(The voices and sounds have escalated to a high pitch. And the last text we hear is:)

NEWSPERSON 1: It's a tough business, as Matt Shepard knew, and as his friends all know, to be gay in cowboy country.

(These reporters continue speaking into the cameras sotto voce over the next texts.)

JON PEACOCK: It was huge. Yeah. It was herds and—and we're talking hundreds of reporters, which makes a huge dent in this town's population. There's reporters everywhere, news trucks everywhere on campus, everywhere in the town. And we're not used to that type of attention to begin with, we're not used to that type of exposure.

NARRATOR: Tiffany Edwards, local reporter:

TIFFANY EDWARDS: These people are predators. Like this one journalist actually caught one of the judges in the bathroom at the urinal and was like asking him questions. And the judge was like, "Excuse me, can I please have some privacy?" And the journalist was like *OFFENDED* that he asked for privacy. I mean, this is not how journalism started, like the Gutenberg press, you know.

DOC O'CONNOR: I'll tell you what, when *Hard Copy* came and taped me, I taped them at the exact same time. I have every word I ever said on tape so if they ever do anything funny they better watch their fuckin' ass.

NEWSPERSON: Wyoming governor Jim Geringer, a first-term Republican up for reelection:

GOVERNOR GERINGER: I am outraged and sickened by the heinous crime committed on Matthew Shepard. I extend my most heartfelt sympathies to the family.

NEWSPERSON: Governor, you haven't pushed hate crime legislation in the past.

GOVERNOR GERINGER: I would like to urge the people of Wyoming against overreacting in a way that gives one group "special rights over others."

We will wait and see if the vicious beating and torture of Matthew Shepard was motivated by hate.

SERGEANT HING: You've got the beginning of the news story where they have the graphics in the background, and they've got: "Murder in Wyoming," and Wyoming's dripping red like it's got blood on it or something, and it's like, what's the—what is this, this is sensationalism. And . . . we're here going, "Wait a minute. We had the guys in jail in less than a day. I think that's pretty damn good."

EILEEN ENGEN: And for us to be more or less maligned.

NARRATOR: Eileen and Gil Engen:

EILEEN ENGEN: That we're not a good community and we are— The majority of people here are good people.

GIL ENGEN: You git bad apples once in a while. And I think that the gay community took this as an advantage, said this is a good time for us to exploit this.

NEWSPERSON: Bill McKinney, father of one of the accused:

BILL MCKINNEY: Had this been a heterosexual these two boys decided to take out and rob, this never would have made the national news. Now my son is guilty before he's even had a trial.

Tiffany Edwards: Look, I do think that, um, the media actually made people accountable. Because they made people think. Because people were sitting in their homes, like watching TV and listening to CNN and watching Dan Rather and going, "Jesus Christ, well that's not how it is here." Well how is it here?

Moment: Medical Update

Narrator: Matthew Shepard update at three P.M., Saturday, October tenth.

Rulon Stacey: By this point, I looked out there and where there had been two or three reporters . . . it must have been ten or fifteen still photographers, another twenty or thirty reporters, and ten video cameras. The parents had just arrived. I had barely introduced myself to them. I looked out there and I thought, "My gosh. What am I going to do?"

(He crosses to the area where the reporters are gathered with their cameras. As he arrives, several camera flashes go off. He speaks straight into the camera. We see his image on the monitors around the stage.)

Matthew Shepard was admitted in critical condition approximately nine-fifteen P.M., October seventh. When he arrived, he was unresponsive, and breathing support was being provided.

Matthew's major injuries upon arrival consisted of hypothermia and a fracture from behind his head to just in front of the right ear. This has caused bleeding in the brain, as well as pressure on the brain. There were also several lacerations on his head, face, and neck.

Matthew's temperature has fluctuated over the last twenty-four hours, ranging from ninety-eight to one hundred and six degrees. We have had difficulty controlling his temperature.

Matthew's parents arrived at seven P.M., October ninth, and are now at his bedside. The following is a statement from them:

First of all, we want to thank the American public for their kind thoughts about Matthew and their fond wishes for his speedy recovery. We appreciate your prayers and goodwill, and we know that they are something Matthew would appreciate, too.

We also have a special request for the members of the media. Matthew is very much in need of his family at this time, and we ask that you respect our privacy, as well as Matthew's, so we can concentrate all of our efforts, thoughts, and love on our son.

Thank you very much.

Moment: Seeing Matthew

Narrator: Both Aaron McKinney and Russell Henderson pled not guilty to charges. Their girlfriends, Chasity Pasley and Kristin Price, also pled not guilty after being charged as accessories after the fact. On our next trip, we spoke to the chief investigating officer on the case, Detective Rob DeBree of the Albany County Sheriff's Department.

ROB DEBREE: I guess the thing that bothered me the most was when I went down to Poudre Valley, where Matthew was, and the thing that bothered me the most is seeing him, touching him. As a homicide detective, you look at bodies. . . . This poor boy is sitting here, fighting all his life, trying to make it. I wanted it so by the book you know.

AARON KREIFELS: I keep seeing that picture in my head when I found him . . .

NARRATOR: Aaron Kreifels:

AARON KREIFELS: . . . and it's not pleasant whatsoever. I don't want it to be there. I wanna like get it out. That's the biggest part for me is seeing that picture in my head. And it's kind of unbelievable to me, you know, that—I happened to be the person who found him—because the big question with me, like with my religion, is like, Why did God want ME to find him?

CATHERINE CONNOLLY: I know how to take care of myself, and I was irrationally terrified.

NARRATOR: Catherine Connolly:

CATHERINE CONNOLLY: So what that means is, not letting my twelve-year-old son walk the streets, seeing a truck do a U-turn and thinking it's coming after me. Having to stop because I'm shaking so bad. And, in fact, the pickup truck did not come after me, but my reaction was to have my heart in my mouth.

MATT GALLOWAY: Ultimately, no matter how you dice it, I did have an opportunity.

NARRATOR: Matt Galloway:

MATT GALLOWAY: If I had—amazing hindsight of 20/20—to have stopped—what occurred . . . and I keep thinkin', "I shoulda noticed. These guys shouldn'ta been talking to this guy. I shoulda not had my head down when I was washing dishes for those twenty seconds. Things I coulda done. What the hell was I thinking?"

ROB DEBREE: So you do a lot of studying, you spend hours and hours and hours. You study and study and study . . . talking to the officers, making sure they understand, talk to your witnesses again, and then always coming back to I get this flash of seeing Matthew. . . . I wanted it so tight that there was no way that they were gonna get out of this.

REGGIE FLUTY: One of the things that happened when I got to the fence . . .

NARRATOR: Reggie Fluty:

REGGIE FLUTY: . . . It was just such an overwhelming amount of blood . . . and we try to wear protective gloves, but we had a really cheap sheriff at the time, and he bought us shit gloves, you know, you put 'em on, you put 'em on, and they kept breaking, so finally you just ran out of gloves, you know. So, you figure, well, you know, "Don't hesitate," you know, that's what your mind tells you all the time—Don't hesitate—and so you just keep moving and you try to help Matthew and find an airway and, you know, that's what you do, you know.

MARGE MURRAY: The thing I wasn't telling you before is that Reggie is my daughter.

NARRATOR: Marge Murray:

MARGE MURRAY: And when she first told me she wanted to be a police officer, well, I thought there was not a better choice for her. She could handle whatever came her way. . . .

REGGIE FLUTY: Probably a day and a half later, the hospital called me and told me Matthew had HIV. And the doctor said, "You've been exposed, and you've had a bad exposure," because, you see, I'd been—been building—building a, uh, lean-to for my llamas, and my hands had a bunch of open cuts on 'em, so I was kinda screwed *(she laughs)* you know, and you think, "Oh, shoot," you know.

MARGE MURRAY: Would you like to talk about losing sleep?

REGGIE FLUTY: So I said to the doctor, "Okay, what do I do?" And they said, "Get up here." So, I got up there and we started the ATZ (sic) drugs. Immediately.

MARGE MURRAY: Now they told me that's a medication that if it's administered thirty-six hours after you've been exposed . . . it can maybe stop your getting the disease . . .

REGGIE FLUTY: That is a mean nasty medicine. Mean. I've lost ten pounds and a lot of my hair. Yeah . . .

MARGE MURRAY: And quite frankly I wanted to lash out at somebody. Not at Matthew, please understand that, not one of us was mad at Matthew. But we maybe wanted to squeeze McKinney's head off. And I think about Henderson. And, you know, two absolutely human beings cause so much grief for so many people. . . . It has been terrible for my whole family, but mostly for her and her kids.

REGGIE FLUTY: I think it brought home to my girls what their mom does for a living.

MARGE MURRAY: Well, Reggie, you know what I'm gonna tell you now.

REGGIE FLUTY: And my parents told me, you know, they both said the same damn thing.

MARGE MURRAY: You're quitting this damn job!

REGGIE FLUTY: And it's just a parent thing, you know, and they're terribly proud of you, 'cause you do a good job whether it's handling a drunk or handling a case like this, but you're, you know, they don't want you getting hurt—

MARGE MURRAY: Like I said, there's a right way, a wrong way, and then there's Reggie's way.

REGGIE FLUTY: So finally I said, "Oh, for God's sakes, lighten up, Francis!"

MARGE MURRAY: You are so stubborn!

REGGIE FLUTY: They say I'm stubborn, and I don't believe them, but I just think, you know, okay, I've heard your opinion and now here's mine. I'm thirty-nine years old, you know, what are they gonna do, spank me?

MARGE MURRAY: Reggie, don't give me any ideas.

REGGIE FLUTY: It'd look pretty funny. You know, what can they say?

MARGE MURRAY: I just hope she doesn't go before me. I just couldn't handle that.

MOMENT: E-MAIL

NARRATOR: University of Wyoming president Philip Dubois:

PHILIP DUBOIS: Well, this is a young person—who read my statement on the *Denver Post* story, and sent me an e-mail, to me directly, and said:

E-MAIL WRITER: You and the straight people of Laramie and Wyoming are guilty of the beating of Matthew Shepard just as the Germans who looked the other way are guilty of the deaths of the Jews, the Gypsies, and the homosexuals. You have taught your straight children to hate their gay and lesbian brothers and sisters. Unless and until you acknowledge that Matt Shepard's beating is not just a random occurrence, not just the work of a couple of random crazies, you have Matthew's blood on your hands.

PHILIP DUBOIS: And uh, well, I just can't begin to tell you what that does to you. And it's like, you can't possibly know what I'm thinking, you can't possibly know what this has done to me and my family and my community.

MOMENT: VIGILS

(We see images of the vigils taking place around the country in the monitors as:)

NARRATOR: That first week alone, vigils were held in Laramie, Denver, Fort Collins, and Colorado Springs. Soon after in Detroit, Chicago, San Francisco, Washington, D.C., Atlanta, Nashville, Minneapolis, and Portland, Maine, among others. In Los Angeles, five thousand people gathered, and in New York City a political rally ended in civil disobedience and hundreds of arrests. And the Poudre Valley Hospital Web site received close to a million visitors from across the country and around the world, all expressing hope for Matthew's recovery.

MOMENT: MEDICAL UPDATE

NARRATOR: Matthew Shepard medical update at nine A.M., Sunday, October eleventh.

(RULON STACEY is in front of the cameras. We see him on the monitors.)

RULON STACEY: As of nine A.M. today, Matthew Shepard remains in critical condition. The family continues to emphasize that the media respect their privacy. The family also wants to thank the American public for their kind thoughts and concern for Matthew.

MOMENT: LIVE AND LET LIVE

JEDADIAH SCHULTZ: There are certain things when I sit in church.

NARRATOR: Jedadiah Schultz:

JEDADIAH SCHULTZ: And the reverend will tell you flat out he doesn't agree with homosexuality—and I don't know—I think right now, I'm going through changes, I'm still learning about myself and—you know I don't feel like I know enough about certain things to make a decision that says, "Homosexuality is right." When you've been raised your whole life that it's wrong—and right now, I would say that I don't agree with it— yeah, that I don't agree with it but—maybe that's just because I couldn't do it—and speaking in religious terms—I don't think that's how God intended it to happen. But I don't hate homosexuals and, I mean—I'm not going to persecute them or anything like that. At all—I mean, that's not gonna be getting in the way between me and the other person at all.

CONRAD MILLER: Well, it's preached in schools that being gay is okay.

NARRATOR: Conrad Miller:

CONRAD MILLER: And if my kids asked me, I'd set them down and I'd say, "Well, this is what gay people do. This is what animals do. Okay?" And I'd tell 'em, "This is the life, this is the lifestyle, this is what they do." And I'd say, "This is why I believe it's wrong."

MURDOCK COOPER: There's more gay people around than what you think.

NARRATOR: Murdock Cooper:

MURDOCK COOPER: It doesn't bother anybody because most of 'em that are gay or lesbian they know damn well who to talk to. If you step out of line you're asking for it. Some people are saying he made a pass at them. You don't pick up regular people. I'm not excusing their actions, but it made me feel better because it was partially Matthew Shepard's fault and partially the guys who did it . . . you know, maybe it's fifty-fifty.

ZACKIE SALMON: Yes, as a lesbian I was more concerned for my safety.

NARRATOR: Zackie Salmon:

ZACKIE SALMON: I think we all were. And I think it's because somewhere inside we know it could happen to us anytime, you know. I mean, I would be afraid to walk down the street and display any sort of physical affection for my partner. You don't do that here in Laramie.

JONAS SLONAKER: Well, there's this whole idea: You leave me alone, I leave you alone.

NARRATOR: Jonas Slonaker:

JONAS SLONAKER: And it's even in some of the western literature, you know, live and let live. That is such crap. I tell my friends that—even my gay friends bring it up sometimes. I'm like, "That is crap, you know?" I mean, basically what it boils down to: If I don't tell you I'm a fag, you won't beat the crap out of me. I mean, what's so great about that? That's a great philosophy?

MOMENT: IT HAPPENED HERE

ZUBAIDA ULA: We went to the candle vigil.

NARRATOR: Zubaida Ula:

ZUBAIDA ULA: And it was so good to be with people who felt like shit. I kept feeling like I don't deserve to feel this bad, you know? And someone got up there and said, "C'mon, guys, let's show the world that Laramie is not this kind of a town." But it is that kind of a town. If it wasn't this kind of a town, why did this happen here? I mean, you know what I mean, like—that's a lie. Because it happened here. So how could it not be a town where this kind of thing happens? Like, that's just totally—like, looking at an Escher painting and getting all confused, like, it's just totally like circular logic like how can you even say that? And we have to mourn this and we have to be sad that we live in a town, a state, a country where shit like this happens. And I'm not going to step away from that and say,

"We need to show the world this didn't happen." I mean, these are people trying to distance themselves from this crime. And we need to own this crime. I feel. Everyone needs to own it. We are like this. We ARE like this. WE are LIKE this.

MOMENT: SHANNON AND JEN

STEPHEN BELBER: I was in the Fireside one afternoon and I ran into two friends of Aaron McKinney, Shannon and Jen. *(To Shannon and Jen)* You knew Aaron well, right?

SHANNON: Yeah, we both did. When I first found out about this, I thought it was really really awful. I don't know whether Aaron was fucked up or whether he was coming down or what, but Matthew had money. Shit, he had better clothes than I did. Matthew was a little rich bitch.

JEN: You shouldn't call him a rich bitch though, that's not right.

SHANNON: Well, I'm not saying he's a bad guy either, because he was just in the wrong place at the wrong time, said the wrong things. And I don't know, I won't lie to you. There was times that I was all messed up on meth and I thought about going out and robbing. I mean, I never did. But yeah, it was there. It's easy money.

JEN: Aaron's done that thing before. They've both done it. I know one night they went to Cheyenne to go do it and they came back with probably three hundred dollars. I don't know if they ever chose like gay people as their particular targets before, but anyone that looked like they had a lot of money and that was you know, they could outnumber, or overpower, was fair game.

STEPHEN BELBER: But do you think there was any homophobia involved in this that contributed to some of it?

JEN: Probably. It probably would've pissed him off that Matthew was gay 'cause he didn't like—the gay people that I've seen him interact with, he was fine as long as, you know, they didn't hit on him. As long as it didn't come up.

SHANNON: Yeah, as long as they weren't doing it in front of him.

STEPHEN BELBER: Do you get the impression that Aaron knew other gay people?

SHANNON: I'm sure that he knew people that are gay. I mean, he worked up at KFC and there was a couple people up there that—yeah *(he laughs)*—and I'm not saying it's bad or anything 'cause I don't know, half the people I know in Laramie are gay.

STEPHEN BELBER: What would you guys say to Aaron if you saw him right now?

SHANNON: First of all, I'd ask him if he'd ever do anymore tweak.

JEN: He wouldn't I bet. If I saw Aaron now, I'd be like, "Man, why'd you fuck up like that?" But, I'd want to make sure he's doing good in there. But, I'm sure he is though. I'd probably just want to like hang out with him.

SHANNON: Smoke a bowl with him.

JEN: I bet he wants one so bad.

STEPHEN BELBER: So, you guys both went to Laramie High?

SHANNON: Yeah. Can't you tell? We're a product of our society.

MOMENT: HOMECOMING

NEWSPERSON: On a day that is traditionally given over to nothing more profound than collegiate exuberance and the fortunes of the University of Wyoming football team, this community on the high plains had a different kind of homecoming Saturday, as many searched their souls in the wake of a vicious, apparent antigay hate crime.

NARRATOR: University president Philip Dubois:

PHILIP DUBOIS: This was homecoming weekend. There were a lot of people in town, and there's a homecoming parade that was scheduled, and then the students organized to tag onto the back of it—you know, behind the banner supporting Matt, and everybody wearing the armbands that the students had created . . .

HARRY WOODS: I live in the center of town.

NARRATOR: Harry Woods:

HARRY WOODS: And my apartment has windows on two opposite streets. One goes north and one goes south. And that is exactly the homecoming parade route. Now, on the day of the parade, I had a cast on my leg because of a fall. So I was very disappointed because I really wanted to walk with the people that were marching for Matthew. But I couldn't. So I watched from my window. And it was . . . it was just . . . I'm fifty-two years old and I'm gay. I have lived here for many years and I've seen a lot. And I was very moved when I saw the tag on the end of the homecoming parade. About a hundred people walking behind a banner for Matthew Shepard.

So then the parade went down to the end of the block to make a U-turn, and I went to the other side of my apartment to wait for it to come south down the other street.

MATT GALLOWAY: I was right up in front there where they were holding the banner for Matthew, and let me tell you . . . I've never had goose bumps so long in my life. It was incredible. A mass of people. Families—mothers holding their six-year-old kids, tying these armbands around these six-year-old kids and trying to explain to them why they should wear an armband. Just amazing. I mean it was absolutely one of the most—beautiful things I've ever done in my life.

HARRY WOODS: Well, about ten minutes went by, and sure enough the parade started coming down the street. And then I noticed the most incredible thing . . . as the parade came down the street . . . the number of people walking for Matthew Shepard had grown five times. There were at least five hundred people marching for Matthew. Five hundred people. Can you imagine? The tag at the end was larger than the entire parade. And people kept joining in. And you know what? I started to cry. Tears were streaming down my face. And I thought, "Thank God that I got to see this in my life-time." And my second thought was, "Thank you, Matthew."

MOMENT: ONE OF OURS

SHERRY JOHNSON: I really haven't been all that involved, per se. My husband's a highway patrolman, so that's really the only way that I've known about it.

Now when I first found out I just thought it was horrible. I just, I can't . . . Nobody deserves that! I don't care who ya are.

But, the other thing that was not brought out—at the same time this happened that patrolman was killed. And there was nothing. Nothing. They didn't say anything about the old man that killed him. He was driving down the road and he shouldn't have been driving and killed him. It was just a little piece in the paper. And we lost one of our guys.

You know, my husband worked with him. This man was brand-new on the force. But, I mean, here's one of ours, and it was just a little piece in the paper.

And a lot of it is my feeling that the media is portraying Matthew Shepard as a saint. And making him as a martyr. And I don't think he was. I don't think he was that pure.

Now, I didn't know him, but . . . there's just so many things about him that I found out that I just, it's scary. You know about his character and spreading AIDS and a few other things, you know, being the kind of person that he was. He was, he was just a barfly, you know. And I think he pushed himself around. I think he flaunted it.

Everybody's got problems. But why they exemplified him I don't know. What's the difference if you're gay? A hate crime is a hate crime. If you murder somebody you hate 'em. It has nothing to do with if you're gay or a prostitute or whatever.

I don't understand. I don't understand.

MOMENT: TWO QUEERS AND A CATHOLIC PRIEST

NARRATOR: Company member Leigh Fondakowski:

LEIGH FONDAKOWSKI: This is one of the last days on our second trip to Laramie. Greg and I have been conducting interviews nonstop and we are exhausted.

GREG PIEROTTI: We are to meet Father Roger at seven-thirty in the morning. I was wishing we could skip it all together, but we have to follow through to the end. So here we go: seven-thirty A.M., two queers and a Catholic priest.

FATHER ROGER SCHMIT: Matthew Shepard has served us well. You realize that? He has served us well. And I do not mean to condemn Matthew to perfection, but I cannot mention anyone who has done more for this community than Matthew Shepard.

And I'm not gonna sit here and say, "I was just this bold guy—no fear." I was scared. I was very vocal in this community when this happened—and I thought, "You know, should we, uh, should we call the bishop and ask him permission to do the vigil?" And I was like, "Hell, no, I'm not going to do that." His permission doesn't make it correct, you realize that? And I'm not knocking bishops, but what is correct is correct.

You people are just out here on a search, though. I will do this. I will trust you people that if you write a play of this, that you *(pause)* say it right, say it correct. I think you have a responsibility to do that.

Don't—don't—don't, um *(pause)* don't make matters worse. . . . You think violence is what they did to Matthew—they did do violence to Matthew—but you know, every time that you are called a fag, or you are called a you know, a lez or whatever . . .

LEIGH FONDAKOWSKI: Or a dyke.

FATHER ROGER SCHMIT: Dyke, yeah, dyke. Do you realize that is violence? That is the seed of violence. And I would resent it immensely if you use anything I said, uh, you know, to—to somehow cultivate that kind of violence, even in its smallest form. I would resent it immensely. You need to know that.

LEIGH FONDAKOWSKI: Thank you, Father, for saying that.

FATHER ROGER SCHMIT: Just deal with what is true. You know what is true. You need to do your best to say it correct.

MOMENT: CHRISTMAS

NARRATOR: Andrew Gomez:

ANDREW GOMEZ: I was in there, I was in jail with Aaron in December. I got thrown in over Christmas. Assault and battery, two counts. I don't wanna talk about it. But we were sittin' there eatin' our Christmas dinner, tryin' to eat my stuffing, my motherfucking bread, my little roll and whatnot, and I asked him, I was like, "Hey, homey, tell me something, tell me something please, why did you—" Okay, I'm thinking how I worded this, I was like, "Why did you kill a faggot if you're gonna be destined to BE a faggot later?" You know? I mean, think about it, he's either gonna get humped a lot or he's gonna die. So why would you do that, think about that. I don't understand that.

And you know what he told me? Honest to God, this is what he said, he goes: "He tried to grab my dick." That's what he said, man! He's dumb, dog, he don't even act like it was nothin'.

Now I heard they was auctioning those boys off. Up there in the max ward, you know, where the killers go, I heard that when they found out Aaron was coming to prison, they were auctioning those boys off. "I want him. I'll put aside five, six, seven cartons of cigarettes." Auction his ass off. I'd be scared to go to prison if I was those two boys.

MOMENT: LIFESTYLE 2

BAPTIST MINISTER: Hello.

AMANDA GRONICH: Reverend?

BAPTIST MINISTER: Yes, hello.

AMANDA GRONICH: I believe your wife told you a bit about why I'm contacting you.

BAPTIST MINISTER: Yes, she did. And let me tell you—uh—I don't know that I really want to talk to anyone about any of this incident—uh—I am somewhat involved and I just don't think—

AMANDA GRONICH: Yes, I completely understand and I don't blame you. You know, I went to your service on Sunday.

BAPTIST MINISTER: You went to the services on Sunday?

AMANDA GRONICH: Yes, I did.

BAPTIST MINISTER: On Sunday?

AMANDA GRONICH: Yes, this past Sunday.

BAPTIST MINISTER: Did I meet you?

AMANDA GRONICH: Yes, you welcomed me at the beginning, I believe.

BAPTIST MINISTER: I see. Well, let me tell you. I am not afraid to be controversial or to speak my mind, and that is not necessarily the views of my congregation per se. Now as

I said, I am somewhat involved—that half the people in the case—well, the girlfriend of the accused is a member of our congregation, and one of the accused has visited.

AMANDA GRONICH: Mmmmmm.

BAPTIST MINISTER: Now, those two people, the accused, have forfeited their lives. We've been after the two I mentioned for ages, trying to get them to live right, to do right. Now, one boy is on suicide watch and I am working with him—until they put him in the chair and turn on the juice I will work for his salvation. Now I think they deserve the death penalty—I will try to deal with them spiritually.

AMANDA GRONICH: Right, I understand.

BAPTIST MINISTER: Now, as for the victim, I know that that lifestyle is legal, but I will tell you one thing: I hope that Matthew Shepard as he was tied to that fence, that he had time to reflect on a moment when someone had spoken the word of the Lord to him— and that before he slipped into a coma he had a chance to reflect on his lifestyle.

AMANDA GRONICH: Thank you, Reverend, I appreciate your speaking with me.

(Rain begins to fall on the stage.)

MOMENT: THAT NIGHT

RULON STACEY: About eleven-thirty that night, I had just barely gone to bed, and Margo, our chief operating officer, called and said, "His blood pressure has started to drop." "Well, let's wait and see." She called me about ten after—he just died. So I quick got dressed and came in, and uh went into the ICU where the family was, and Judy came up and she put her arms around me and I put my arms around her and we just stood there— honestly, for about ten minutes just—'cause what else do you do?

And then we had to sit and talk about things that you just—"Dennis, it's now public knowledge. . . . And I'm gonna go out there now and tell the whole world that this has happened."

'Cause by this point it was clear to us that it was the world—it was the whole world. And so Judy told me what she wanted me to say. And I went out at four A.M.

(He crosses to the camera.)

MOMENT: MEDICAL UPDATE

NARRATOR: Matthew Shepard medical update for four-thirty A.M., Monday, October twelfth.

RULON STACEY: At twelve midnight on Monday, October twelfth, Matthew Shepard's blood pressure began to drop. We immediately notified his family, who were already at the hospital.

At twelve fifty-three A.M. Matthew Shepard died. His family was at his bedside. The family did release the following statement,

The family again asked me to express their sincerest gratitude to the entire world for the overwhelming response for their son.

The family was grateful that they did not have to make a decision regarding whether or not to continue life support for their son. Like a good son, he was caring to the end and removed guilt or stress from the family.

He came into the world premature and left the world premature.

Matthew's mother said:

Go home, give your kids a hug, and don't let a day go by without telling them that you love them.

MOMENT: MAGNITUDE

RULON STACEY: And—I don't know *how* I let that happen—I lost it on national television, but, you know, we had been up for like seventy-two hours straight and gone home and gone to sleep for half an hour and had to get up and come in—and maybe I was just way—I don't know—but *(pause)* in a moment of complete brain-deadness, while I was out there reading that statement I thought about my own four daughters—and go home, hug your kids *(he begins to cry)* and, oh, she doesn't have her kid anymore.

And there I am and I'm thinking, "This is so lame."

Um, and then we started to get people sending us e-mails and letters. And most of them were just generally very kind. But I did get this one. This guy wrote me and said, "Do you cry like a baby on TV for all of your patients or just the faggots?" And as I told you before, homosexuality is not a lifestyle with which I agree. Um, but having been thrown into this *(pause)* I guess I didn't understand the magnitude with which some people hate. And of all the letters that we got, there were maybe two or three that were like that, most of them were, Thank you for your caring and compassion, and Matthew had caring and compassion from the moment he got here.

MOMENT: H-O-P-E

STEPHEN BELBER: I spoke with Doc today and told him we would soon be coming back out for the upcoming trials of Russell Henderson and Aaron McKinney, and this is what he had to say.

DOC O'CONNOR: I'll tell you what, if they put those two boys to death, that would defeat everything Matt would be thinking about on them. Because Matt would not want those two to die. He'd want to leave them with hope. *(Spelling)* H-O-P-E. Just like the whole world hoped that Matt would survive. The whole thing, you see, the whole thing, ropes around hope, H-O-P-E.

End of Act II

ACT III

(The stage is now empty except for several chairs stage right. They occupy that half of the stage. They are all facing the audience and arranged in rows as if to suggest a church or a courthouse. As the lights come up, several actors are sitting there dressed in black. Some of them have umbrellas. A few beats with just this image in silence. Then matt galloway enters stage left. Looks at them and says:)

MOMENT: SNOW

MATT GALLOWAY: The day of the funeral, it was snowing so bad, big huge wet snowflakes. And when I got there, there were thousands of people in just black, with umbrellas everywhere. And there were two churches—one for the immediate family, uh, invited guests, people of that nature, and then one church for everybody else who wanted to be there. And then, still, hundreds of people outside that couldn't fit into either of the churches. And there was a big park by the church, and that's where these people were. And this park was full.

PRIEST: The liturgy today is an Easter liturgy. It finds its meaning in the Resurrection. The service invites your full participation.

PRIEST: The Lord be with you.

PEOPLE: And also with you.

PRIEST: Let us pray.

TIFFANY EDWARDS: And I guess it was like the worst storm that they have had.

NARRATOR: Tiffany Edwards:

TIFFANY EDWARDS: Like that anybody could ever tell, like trees fell down and the power went out for a couple of days because of it and I just thought, "It's like the forces of the universe at work, you know." Whatever higher spirit, you know, is like that blows storms, was blowin' this storm.

PRIEST: For our brother, Matthew, let us pray to our Lord Jesus Christ, who said, "I am the Resurrection and the Life." We pray to the Lord.

PEOPLE: HEAR US, LORD.

(The PRIEST begins and goes into sotto voce.)

PRIEST: Lord, you who consoled Martha and Mary in their distress: draw near to us who mourn for Matthew, and dry the tears of those who weep. We pray to the Lord.

PEOPLE: HEAR US, LORD.

PRIEST: You wept at the grave of Lazarus, your friend: comfort us in our sorrow. We pray to the Lord.

PEOPLE: HEAR US, LORD.

PRIEST: You raised the dead to life: give to our brother eternal life. We pray to the Lord.

PEOPLE: HEAR US, LORD.

PRIEST: You promised paradise to the thief who repented: bring our brother the joys of heaven. We pray to the Lord.

PEOPLE: HEAR US, LORD.

PRIEST: He was nourished with your Body and Blood; grant him a place at the table in your heavenly kingdom. We pray to the Lord.

PEOPLE: HEAR US, LORD.

PRIEST: Comfort us in our sorrows at the death of our brother; let our faith be our consolation, and eternal life our hope. We pray to the Lord.

KERRY DRAKE: My most striking memory from the funeral . . .

NARRATOR: Kerry Drake, *Casper Star-Tribune:*

KERRY DRAKE: . . . is seeing the Reverend Fred Phelps from Kansas . . . that scene go up in the park.

REVEREND FRED PHELPS: Do you believe the Bible? Do you believe you're supposed to separate the precious from the vile? You don't believe that part of the Bible? You stand over there ignorant of the fact that the Bible—two times for every verse it talks about God's love it talks about God's hate.

(REVEREND FRED PHELPS continues sotto voce.)

KERRY DRAKE: A bunch of high school kids who got out early came over and started yelling at some of these people in the protest—the Fred Phelps people—and across the street you had people lining up for the funeral. . . . Well, I remember a guy, this skinhead coming over, and he was dressed in leather and spikes everywhere, and he came over from across the street where the protest was and he came into the crowd and I just thought, "Oh, this is gonna be a really ugly confrontation" BUT instead he came over and he started leading them in "Amazing Grace."

(The people sing "Amazing Grace.")

REVEREND FRED PHELPS: We wouldn't be here if this was just another murder the state was gonna deal with. The state deals with hundreds of murders every single day. But this murder is different, because the fags are bringing us out here trying to make Matthew Shepard into a poster boy for the gay lifestyle. And we're going to answer it. It's just that simple.

(REVEREND FRED PHELPS continues sotto voce.)

NARRATOR: Six months later, the company returned to Laramie for the trial of Russell Henderson, the first of the two perpetrators. It was to be a capital murder trial. When we got to the Albany County Courthouse, Fred Phelps was already there.

REVEREND FRED PHELPS: You don't like that attribute of God.

NARRATOR: But so was Romaine Patterson.

REVEREND FRED PHELPS: That perfect attribute of God. Well, We love that attribute of God, and we're going to preach it. Because God's hatred is pure. It's a determination—it's a determination that he's gonna send some people to hell. That's God's hatred . . .

(Continues sotto voce.)

We're standing here with God's message. We're standing here with God's message. Is homosexuality—is being a fag okay? What do you mean it's not for you to judge? If God doesn't hate fags, why does he put 'em in hell? . . . You see the barrenness and sterility of your silly arguments when set over against some solid gospel truth? Barren and sterile. Like your lifestyle. Your silly arguments.

ROMAINE PATTERSON: After seeing Fred Phelps protesting at Matthew's funeral and finding out that he was coming to Laramie for the trial of Russell Henderson, I decided that someone needed to stand toe-to-toe with this guy and show the differences. And I think at times like this, when we're talking about hatred as much as the nation is right now, that someone needs to show that there is a better way of dealing with that kind of hatred.

So our idea is to dress up like angels. And so we have designed an angel outfit—for our wings are huge—they're like big-ass wings—and there'll be ten to twenty of us that are angels—and what we're gonna do is we're gonna encircle Phelps . . . and because of our big wings—we are gonna com-ple-te-ly block him.

So this big-ass band of angels comes in, we don't say a fuckin' word, we just turn our backs to him and we stand there. . . . And we are a group of people bringing forth a message of peace and love and compassion. And we're calling it "Angel Action."

Yeah, this twenty-one-year-old little lesbian is ready to walk the line with him.

REVEREND FRED PHELPS: When those old preachers laid their hands on me it's called an ordination. Mine was from Isaiah fifty-eight: one—"Cry aloud. Spare not. Lift up thy voice like a trumpet and show my people their transgressions."

ROMAINE PATTERSON: And I knew that my angels were gonna be taking the brunt of everything he had to yell and say. I mean, we were gonna be blocking his view and he was gonna be liked pissed off to all hell. . . . So I went out and bought all my angels earplugs.

("Amazing Grace" ends.)

MOMENT: JURY SELECTION

BAILIFF: The court is in session.

(All stand.)

NARRATOR: Romaine Patterson's sister, Trish Steger:

TRISH STEGER: As soon as they started jury selection, you know, everybody was coming into my shop with "I don't want to be on this trial. I hope they don't call me." Or, "Oh my God, I've been called. How do I get off?" Just wanting to get as far away from it as they could . . . very fearful that they were going to have to be part of that jury.

And then I heard . . . Henderson had to sit in the courtroom while they question the prospective jurors. And one of the questions that they ask is: Would you be willing to put this person to death?

And I understand that a lot of the comments were: "Yes, I would."

JUROR: Yes, I would, Your Honor.

JUROR: Yes, sir.

JUROR: Absolutely.

JUROR: Yes, sir!

(Jurors continue underneath.)

JUROR: No problem.

JUROR: Yep.

TRISH STEGER: Well, can you imagine hearing that? You know, juror after juror after juror . . .

MOMENT: RUSSELL HENDERSON

("Amazing Grace" begins again.)

JUDGE: You entered a not guilty plea earlier, Mr. Henderson. But I understand you wish to change your plea today. Is that correct?

RUSSELL HENDERSON: Yes, sir.

JUDGE: You understand, Mr. Henderson, that the recommended sentence here is two life sentences?

RUSSELL HENDERSON: Yes, sir.

JUDGE: Do you understand that those may run concurrently or they may run consecutively?

RUSSELL HENDERSON: Yes, sir.

JUDGE: Mr. Henderson, I will now ask you how you wish to plead. Guilty or not guilty?

RUSSELL HENDERSON: Guilty.

JUDGE: Before the Court decides whether the sentences will be concurrent or consecutive, I understand that there are statements to be made by at least one individual.

NARRATOR: This is an excerpt from a statement made to the court by Lucy Thompson.

MS. THOMPSON: As the grandmother and the person who raised Russell, along with my family, we have written the following statement: Our hearts ache for the pain and suffering that the Shepards have went through. We have prayed for your family since the very beginning. Many times throughout the day I have thought about Matt. And you will continue to be in our thoughts and prayers, as we know that your pain will never go away. You have showed such mercy in allowing us to have this plea, and we are so grateful that you are giving us all the opportunity to live. Your Honor, we, as a family, hope that as you sentence Russell, that you will do it concurrently two life terms. For the Russell we know and love, we humbly plead, Your Honor, to not take Russell completely out of our lives forever.

JUDGE: Thank you. Mr. Henderson, you have a constitutional right to make a statement if you would like to do so. Do you have anything you would like to say?

RUSSELL HENDERSON: Yes, I would, Your Honor. Mr. and Mrs. Shepard, there is not a moment that goes by that I don't see what happened that night. I know what I did was very wrong, and I regret greatly what I did. You have my greatest sympathy for what happened. I hope that one day you will be able to find it in your hearts to forgive me. Your Honor, I know what I did was wrong. I'm very sorry for what I did, and I'm ready to pay my debt for what I did.

JUDGE: Mr. Henderson, you drove the vehicle that took Matthew Shepard to his death. You bound him to that fence in order that he might be more savagely beaten and in order that he might not escape to tell his tale. You left him out there for eighteen hours, knowing full well that he was there, perhaps having an opportunity to save his life, and you did nothing. Mr. Henderson, this Court does not believe that you really feel any true remorse for your part in this matter. And I wonder, Mr. Henderson, whether you fully realize the gravity of what you've done.

The Court finds it appropriate, therefore, that sentence be ordered as follows: As to Count Three, that being felony murder with robbery, you are to serve a period of imprisonment for the term of your natural life. On Count One, kidnapping, that you serve a period of imprisonment for the term of your natural life. Sentencing for Count One to run consecutive to sentencing for Count Three.

NARRATOR: After the hearing, we spoke with Russell Henderson's Mormon home teacher.

MORMON HOME TEACHER: I've known Russell's family for thirty-eight years. Russell's only twenty-one, so I've known him his entire life. I ordained Russell a priest of the Mormon Church, so when this happened, you can imagine—disbelief. . . . After the sentencing . . . the church held a disciplinary council, and the result of that meeting was to excommunicate Russell from the Mormon Church. And what that means is that your name is taken off the records of the church, so you just disappear.

Russell's reaction to that was not positive, it hurt him, it hurt him to realize how serious a transgression he had committed.

But I will not desert Russell. That's a matter of my religion and my friendship with the family.

(All exit. Lights fade on RUSSELL, *his grandmother, and his home teacher.)*

MOMENT: *ANGELS IN AMERICA*

NARRATOR: Before we left Laramie, we met again with Rebecca Hilliker at the theater department. She is producing *Angels in America* this year at the university.

REBECCA HILLIKER: I think that's the focus the university has taken—is that we have a lot of work to do. That we have an obligation to find ways to reach our students. . . . And the question is, How do we move—how do we reach a whole state where there is some really deep-seated hostility toward gays? How do you reach them?

This is the beginning . . . and guess who's auditioning for the lead?

JEDADIAH SCHULTZ: MY PARENTS!

NARRATOR: Jedadiah Schultz:

JEDADIAH SCHULTZ: My parents were like, "So what plays are you doing this year at school?" And I was like, *"Angels in America,"* and I told them the whole list of plays. And they're like, "*Angels in America?* Is that . . . that play you did in high school? That scene you did in high school?" And I was like, "Yeah." And she goes: "Huh. So are you gonna audition for it?" And I was like, "Yeah." And we got in this huge argument . . . and my best, the best thing that I knew I had them on is it was just after they had seen me in a performance of *Macbeth,* and onstage like I murdered like a little kid, and Lady Macduff and these two other guys and like and she goes, "Well, you know homosexuality is a sin"—she kept saying that—and I go, "Mom, I just played a murderer tonight. And you didn't seem to have a problem with that . . ."

I tell you. I've never prepared myself this much for an audition in my life. Never ever. Not even close.

ROB DEBREE: Not having to deal that much with the gay society here in Laramie.

NARRATOR: Detective Sergeant Rob DeBree:

ROB DEBREE: Well, once we started working into the case, and actually speaking to the people that were gay and finding out what their underlying fears were, well, then it sort of hit home. This is America. You don't have the right to feel that fear.

And we're still going to have people who hold with the old ideals, and I was probably one of them fourteen months ago. I'm not gonna put up with it, and I'm not going to listen to it. And if they don't like my views on it, fine. The door goes both ways. I already lost a couple of buddies. I don't care. I feel more comfortable and I can sleep at night.

REGGIE FLUTY: Well, you're tested every three months.

NARRATOR: Reggie Fluty:

REGGIE FLUTY: And I was able to have the DNA test done. And so they got me to Fort Collins, they drew the blood there, flew it to Michigan, and did all the DNA work there and—which was—a week later . . . I knew I was negative for good.

MARGE MURRAY: I'll tell ya, we were all on our knees saying Hail Marys.

REGGIE FLUTY: You were just elated, you know, and you think, "Thank God!"

MARGE MURRAY: So what's the first thing she does?

REGGIE FLUTY: I stuck my tongue right in my husband's mouth. I was just happy, you know, you're just so happy. You think, "Yeah, I hope I did this service well," you know, I hope I did it with some kind of integrity. So, you're just really happy . . . and my daughters just bawled.

MARGE MURRAY: They were so happy.

REGGIE FLUTY: And the force . . .

MARGE MURRAY: Oh boy . . .

REGGIE FLUTY: We went out and got shitfaced.

MARGE MURRAY: *(Simultaneous)* Shitfaced.

REGGIE FLUTY: They all bought me drinks too, it was great . . . and everybody hugged and cried, and, you know, I kissed everybody who walked through the door . . .

MARGE MURRAY: Reggie, they don't need to know that.

REGGIE FLUTY: I didn't care if they were male or female, they each got a kiss on the lips.

*(*REGGIE *and* MARGE *exit together, arguing as they go.)*

MARGE MURRAY: Now what part of what I just said didn't you understand?

REGGIE FLUTY: Oh, get over it, Maw!

MOMENT: A DEATH PENALTY CASE

NARRATOR: Almost a year to the day that Matthew Shepard died, the trial for Aaron James McKinney was set to begin.

CAL RERUCHA: Probably the question that most of you have in your mind is ah, ah, how the McKinney case will proceed.

NARRATOR: Cal Rerucha, prosecuting attorney:

CAL RERUCHA: And it's the decision of the county attorney's office that that will definitely be a death penalty case.

MARGE MURRAY: Part of me wants McKinney to get it. But I'm not very proud of that. I was on and off, off and on. I can't say what I would do . . . I'm too personally involved.

ZACKIE SALMON: Oh, I believe in the death penalty one hundred percent. You know, because I want to make sure that guy's ass dies. This is one instance where I truly believe with all my heart an eye for an eye, a tooth for a tooth.

MATT MICKELSON: I don't know about the death penalty. But I don't ever want to see them ever walk out of Rawlins Penitentiary. I'll pay my nickel, or whatever, my little percentage of tax, nickel a day to make sure that his ass stays in there and never sees society again and definitely never comes into my bar again.

MATT GALLOWAY: I don't believe in the death penalty. It's too much for me. I don't believe that one person should be killed as redemption for his having killed another. Two wrongs don't make a right.

ZUBAIDA ULA: How can I protest, if the Shepards want McKinney dead? I just can't interfere in that. But on a personal level, I knew Aaron in grade school. We never called him Aaron, he was called A.J. . . . . How can we put A.J. McKinney—how can we put A.J. McKinney to death?

FATHER ROGER SCHMIT: I think right now our most important teachers must be Russell Henderson and Aaron McKinney. They have to be our teachers. How did you learn? What did we as a society do to teach you that? See, I don't know if many people will let them be their teachers. I think it would be wonderful if the judge said: "In addition to your sentence, you must tell your story, you must tell your story."

BAILIFF: All rise. State of Wyoming versus Aaron James McKinney, docket number 6381. The Honorable Barton R. Voigt presiding. The Court is in session.

MOMENT: AARON MCKINNEY

NARRATOR: During the trial of Aaron McKinney, the prosecution played a tape recording of his confession.

ROB DEBREE: My name is Rob DeBree, sergeant for the Sheriff's Office. You have the right to remain silent. Anything you say can and may be used against you in a court of law.

NARRATOR: The following is an excerpt of that confession.

ROB DEBREE: Okay, so you guys, you and Russ go to the Fireside. So you're at the Fireside by yourselves, right?

AARON MCKINNEY: Yeah.

ROB DEBREE: Okay, where do you go after you leave the Fireside?

AARON MCKINNEY: Some kid wanted a ride home.

ROB DEBREE: What's he look like?

AARON MCKINNEY: Mmm, like a queer. Such a queer dude.

ROB DEBREE: He looks like a queer?

AARON MCKINNEY: Yeah, like a fag, you know?

ROB DEBREE: Okay. How did you meet him?

AARON MCKINNEY: He wanted a ride home and I just thought, well, the dude's drunk, let's just take him home.

ROB DEBREE: When did you and Russ talk about jacking him up?

AARON MCKINNEY: We kinda talked about it at the bar.

ROB DEBREE: Okay, what happened next?

AARON MCKINNEY: We drove him out past Wal-Mart. We got over there, and he starts grabbing my leg and grabbing my genitals. I was like, "Look, I'm not a fuckin' faggot. If you touch me again you're gonna get it." I don't know what the hell he was trying to do but I beat him up pretty bad. Think I killed him.

ROB DEBREE: What'd you beat him with?

AARON MCKINNEY: Blacked out. My fist. My pistol. The butt of the gun. Wondering what happened to me. I had a few beers and, I don't know. It's like I could see what was going on, but I don't know, but I don't know, it was like somebody else was doing it.

ROB DEBREE: What was the first thing that he said or that he did in the truck that made you hit him?

AARON MCKINNEY: Well, he put his hand on my leg, slid his hand like as if he was going to grab my balls.

MOMENT: GAY PANIC

ZACKIE SALMON: When that defense team argued that McKinney did what he did because Matthew made a pass at him . . . I just wanted to vomit, because that's like saying that it's okay. It's like the "Twinkie Defense," when the guy killed Harvey Milk and Moscone. It's the same thing.

REBECCA HILLIKER: As much as, uh, part of me didn't want the defense of them saying that it was a gay bashing or that it was gay panic, part of me is really grateful. Because I was really scared that in the trial they were going to try and say that it was a robbery, or it was about drugs. So when they used "gay panic" as their defense, I felt, this is good, if nothing else the truth is going to be told . . . the truth is coming out.

Moment: Aaron McKinney

Rob Debree: Did he ever try to defend himself against you or hit you back?

Aaron McKinney: Yeah, sort of. He tried his little swings or whatever but he wasn't very effective.

Rob Debree: Okay. How many times did you hit him inside the truck before you guys stopped where you left him?

Aaron McKinney: I'd say I hit him two or three times, probably three times with my fists and about six times with the pistol.

Rob Debree: Did he ask you to stop?

Aaron McKinney: Well, yeah. He was getting the shit kicked out of him.

Rob Debree: What did he say?

Aaron McKinney: After he asked me to stop most all he was doing was screaming.

Rob Debree: So Russ kinda dragged him over to the fence, I'm assuming, and tied him up?

Aaron McKinney: Something like that. I just remember Russ was laughing at first but then he got pretty scared.

Rob Debree: Was Matthew conscious when Russ tied him up?

Aaron McKinney: Yeah. I told him to turn around and don't look at my license plate number 'cause I was scared he would tell the police. And then I asked him what my license plate said. He read it and that's why I hit him a few more times.

Rob Debree: Just to be sure? *(Pause)* So obviously you don't like gay people?

Aaron McKinney: No, I don't.

Rob Debree: Would you say you hate them?

Aaron McKinney: Uh, I really don't hate them but, you know, when they start coming on to me and stuff like that I get pretty aggravated.

Rob Debree: Did he threaten you?

Aaron McKinney: This gay dude?

Rob Debree: Yeah.

Aaron McKinney: Not really.

Rob Debree: Can you answer me one thing? Why'd you guys take his shoes?

Aaron McKinney: I don't know. *(Pause)* Now I'm never going to see my son again.

Rob Debree: I don't know. You'll probably go to court sometime today.

Aaron McKinney: Today? So I'm gonna go in there and just plead guilty or not guilty today?

Rob Debree: No, no, you're just going to be arraigned today.

Aaron McKinney: He is gonna die for sure?

Rob Debree: There is no doubt that Mr. Shepard is going to die.

Aaron McKinney: So what are they going to give me, twenty-five to life or just the death penalty and get it over with?

Rob Debree: That's not our job. That's the judge's job and the jury.

MOMENT: THE VERDICT

NARRATOR: Has the jury reached a verdict?

FOREPERSON: We have, Your Honor.

We the jury, impaneled and sworn to try the above entitled case, after having well and truly tried the matter, unanimously find as follows:

As to the charge of kidnapping, we find the defendant, Aaron James McKinney, guilty.

As to the charge of aggravated robbery, we find the defendant, Aaron James McKinney, guilty.

As to the charge of first-degree felony murder (kidnapping), we find the defendant, Aaron James McKinney, guilty.

(Verdict goes sotto voce. Narration begins.)

As to the charge of first-degree felony murder (robbery), we find the defendant, Aaron James McKinney, guilty.

As to the charge of premeditated first-degree murder, we find the defendant, Aaron James McKinney, not guilty.

As to the lesser-included offense of second-degree murder, we find the defendant, Aaron James McKinney, guilty.

MOMENT: DENNIS SHEPARD'S STATEMENT

NARRATOR: Aaron McKinney was found guilty of felony murder, which meant the jury could give him the death penalty. That evening, Judy and Dennis Shepard were approached by McKinney's defense team, who pled for their client's life. The following morning, Dennis Shepard made a statement to the Court. Here is some of what he said.

DENNIS SHEPARD: My son Matthew did not look like a winner. He was rather uncoordinated and wore braces from the age of thirteen until the day he died. However, in his all too brief life he proved that he was a winner. On October 6, 1998, my son tried to show the world that he could win again. On October 12, 1998, my firstborn son and my hero lost. On October 12, 1998, my firstborn son and my hero died, fifty days before his twenty-second birthday.

I keep wondering the same thing that I did when I first saw him in the hospital. What would he have become? How could he have changed his piece of the world to make it better?

Matt officially died in a hospital in Fort Collins, Colorado. He actually died on the outskirts of Laramie, tied to a fence. You, Mr. McKinney, with your friend Mr. Henderson left him out there by himself, but he wasn't alone. There were his lifelong friends with him, friends that he had grown up with. You're probably wondering who these friends were. First he had the beautiful night sky and the same stars and moon that we used to see through a telescope. Then he had the daylight and the sun to shine on him. And through it all he was breathing in the scent of pine trees from the snowy range. He heard the wind, the ever-present Wyoming wind, for the last time. He had one more friend with him, he had God. And I feel better knowing he wasn't alone.

Matt's beating, hospitalization, and funeral focused world-wide attention on hate. Good is coming out of evil. People have said enough is enough. I miss my son, but I am proud to be able to say that he is my son.

Judy has been quoted as being against the death penalty. It has been stated that Matt was against the death penalty. Both of these statements are wrong. Matt believed that there were crimes and incidents that justified the death penalty. I too believe in the death penalty. I would like nothing better than to see you die, Mr. McKinney. However, this is the time to begin the healing process. To show mercy to someone who refused to show any mercy. Mr. McKinney, I am going to grant you life, as hard as it is for me to do so, because of Matthew. Every time you celebrate Christmas, a birthday, the Fourth of July, remember that Matt isn't. Every time you wake up in your prison cell, remember that you had the opportunity and the ability to stop your actions that night. You robbed me of something very precious, and I will never forgive you for that. Mr. McKinney, I give you life in the memory of one who no longer lives. May you have a long life, and may you thank Matthew every day for it.

MOMENT: AFTERMATH

REGGIE FLUTY: Me and DeBree hugged and cried. . . . And, you know, everybody had tears in their eyes, and you're just so thankful, you know, and Mr. Shepard was cryin', and then that got me bawlin' and everybody just—

ROB DEBREE: This is all we've lived and breathed for a year. Daily. This has been my case daily. And now it's over.

REGGIE FLUTY: Maybe now we can go on and we can quit being stuck, you know?

AARON KREIFELS: It just hit me today, the minute that I got out of the courthouse. That the reason that God wanted me to find him is, for he didn't have to die out there alone, you know. And if I wouldn't of came along, they wouldn't of found him for a couple of weeks at least. So it makes me feel really good that he didn't have to die out there alone.

MATT GALLOWAY: I'm just glad it's over. I really am. Testifying in that trial was one of the hardest things I've ever done. And don't get me wrong, I love the stage, I really do, I love it. But it's tricky, because basically what you have is lawyers questioning you from this angle but the answers need to be funneling this way, to the jury. So what you have to do is establish a funneling system. And that's hard for me because I'm a natural conversationalist, so it's just natural instinct that when someone asks you a question, you look at that person to make eye contact. But it's kind of tough when you literally have to scoot over—change your position, in effect, funnel over to where the jury is. But I was able to do that several times over the course of my testimony.

(Everyone is amused and baffled by this last text.)

REGGIE FLUTY: It's time to move on. And I think for even the citizens are having the town painted red so to speak. They're gonna just be glad to maybe get moved on.

MOMENT: EPILOGUE

ANDY PARIS: On our last trip, I had the good fortune of seeing Jedadiah Schultz play the role of Prior in *Angels in America*. After a performance, we spoke.

JEDADIAH SCHULTZ: I didn't for the longest time let myself become personally involved in the Matthew Shepard thing. It didn't seem real, it just seemed way blown out of proportion. Matthew Shepard was just a name instead of an individual. . . .

I don't know, it's weird. It's so weird, man, I just—I just feel bad. Just for all that stuff I told you, for the person I used to be. That's why I want to hear those interviews from last year when I said all that stuff. I don't know. I just can't believe I ever said that stuff about homosexuals, you know. How did I ever let that stuff make me think that you were different from me?

NARRATOR: This is Romaine Patterson.

ROMAINE PATTERSON: Well, a year ago, I wanted to be a rock star. That was my goal. And now, um, well, now it's obviously changed in the fact that, um, throughout the last year I—I've really realized my role in, um, in taking my part. And, um, so now instead of going to school to be in music, I'm gonna go to school for communications and political science. Um, because I have a career in political activism.

Actually, I just recently found out I was gonna be honored in Washington, D.C., from the Anti-Defamation League. And whenever I think about the angels or any of the speaking that I've done, you know . . . Matthew gave me—Matthew's like guiding this little path with his light for me to walk down. And he just—every time we get to like a door, he opens it. And he just says, "Okay, next step."

And if I get to be a rock star on the side, okay.

NARRATOR: This is Jonas Slonaker.

JONAS SLONAKER: Change is not an easy thing, and I don't think people were up to it here. They got what they wanted. Those two boys got what they deserve, and we look good now. Justice has been served. The OK Corral. We shot down the villains. We sent the prostitutes on the train. The town's cleaned up, and we don't need to talk about it anymore.

You know, it's been a year since Matthew Shepard died, and they haven't passed shit in Wyoming . . . at a state level, any town, nobody anywhere, has passed any kind of laws, antidiscrimination laws or hate crime legislation, nobody has passed anything anywhere. What's come out of it? What's come out of this that's concrete or lasting?

NARRATOR: We all said we would meet again—one last time at the fence.

DOC O'CONNOR: I been up to that site in my limousine, okay? And I remembered to myself the night he and I drove around together, he said to me, "Laramie sparkles, doesn't it?" And where he was up there, if you sit exactly where he was, up there, Laramie sparkles from there, with a low-lying cloud, . . . it's the blue lights that's bouncing off the clouds from the airport, and it goes *tst tst tst tst* . . . right over the whole city. I mean, it blows you away. . . . Matt was right there in that spot, and I can just picture in his eyes, I can just picture what he was seeing. The last thing he saw on this earth was the sparkling lights.

MOMENT: DEPARTURE

MOISÉS KAUFMAN: We've spent the last two days packing a year's worth of materials and saying our good-byes. We've been here six times and conducted over two hundred interviews. Jedadiah cried when he said good-bye.

LEIGH FONDAKOWSKI: Marge wished us luck, and when we asked her how Laramie would feel seeing a play about itself, she said:

MARGE MURRAY: I think we'd enjoy it. To show it's not the hellhole of the earth would be nice, but that is up to how you portray us. And that in turn is up to how Laramie behaves.

GREG PIEROTTI: As we were getting off the phone she said to me:

MARGE MURRAY: Now, you take care. I love you, honey.

STEPHEN BELBER: Doc asked me if I wanted to ghostwrite a book about the whole event. Galloway offered me or anyone else a place to stay if and when we come back to Laramie. He also seemed interested as to whether there'd be any open auditions for this play.

ANDY PARIS: We left Laramie at about seven in the evening. On the way to Denver, I looked in my rearview mirror to take one last look at the town.

FATHER ROGER SCHMIT: And I will speak with you, I will trust that if you write a play of this, that you say it right. You need to do your best to say it correct.

ANDY PARIS: And in the distance I could see the sparkling lights of Laramie, Wyoming.

END OF PLAY

A CRITICAL ESSAY

Don Shewey was born in Denver, Colorado, and studied at Rice University and Boston University. As a journalist and critic, he has published three books about theater and written articles for the *New York Times,* the *Village Voice, Esquire, Rolling Stone,* and other publications. The following essay by Don Shewey was published in *American Theatre* in May/June 2000.

TOWN IN A MIRROR: THE LARAMIE PROJECT

Moisés Kaufman had a hunch. When news reports started emerging from Laramie, Wyoming, in October of 1998 that a gay college student named Matthew Shepard had been savagely beaten, tied to a fence on the edge of town and left to die by two local roofers he met in a bar, Kaufman sensed that this was no fleeting news event. The Venezuela-born, New York-based writer and director, who'd scored an enormous theatrical triumph in 1997 with his play *Gross Indecency: The Three Trials of Oscar Wilde,* saw that people all over the world were being emotionally affected by the symbolism and the brutality of Shepard's death.

In Kaufman's hands, *Gross Indecency* clearly dramatized how Oscar Wilde's prosecution and imprisonment for homosexual behavior became a public referendum on Victorian England's attitudes about sex, gender, money, class and education. Now Kaufman wondered if the lethal gaybashing of Matthew Shepard might be a similarly resonant turning point for American culture—a moment around which a socially conscious piece of theatre might be created.

"What I read in the press about Matthew Shepard told me that the crime captured people's imagination," he recalled recently "How did it do that? And how do we deal with it in the theatre? Before this, did anyone in Laramie ever have to talk publicly about these questions? I wanted to hear what they were saying among themselves." So in November, barely a month after the murder, Kaufman flew to Laramie with nine members of his company, the Tectonic Theater Project, to interview as many people as they could about reactions to the crime.

Fifteen months, five more trips and four workshops later, the company presented the world premiere of *The Laramie Project* at the Denver Center Theatre Company. The February 26 opening night performance was extraordinarily emotional, partly because the audience included several Laramie residents who were characters in the play, and partly because the company had managed to create a powerful and evocative work of art. Eight actors played dozens of characters (including themselves) based on some 200 interviews.

Although the play factually recounts the events that took place on the night of Shepard's beating, the three-day vigil before he died and the trials of his assailants, *The Laramie Project* is not primarily a re-enactment of the crime but a portrait of a small town—think of an Our Town 2000. Its form— open stage, minimal sets, direct address—harkens back to Greek tragedy, in which the outcome is known from the beginning and the play provides an opportunity for the community to talk about things that are on its mind. After a well-received six-week run in Denver, the play transferred directly to the Union Square Theatre in New York in April for an open-ended Off-Broadway run.

This gratifying result was never a foregone conclusion. As Kaufman puts it, "I had a panic attack on the plane to Laramie. I thought, 'What the fuck are we doing?' I was terrified." From the beginning, *The Laramie Project* was an unusual experiment in collective creation. Among those who accompanied Kaufman on the first trip to Laramie were not only three actors from the original cast of *Gross Indecency* (Michael Emerson, who played Wilde, Andy Paris and Greg Pierotti) but also its set designer, Sarah Lambert. Others on the trip had longer associations with Kaufman and Tectonic, including Kaufman's assistant director Leigh Fondakowski, writer and actor Maude Mitchell, and the company's managing director Jeff LaHoste, who has been Kaufman's partner for 11 years. It was the success of *Gross Indecency*, whose 18-month run Off-Broadway spawned companies in San Francisco, Los Angeles, Toronto and London, that gave Tectonic the financial luxury of funding their first round of research on *The Laramie Project.* "To take 10 people to Laramie for a week cost $20,000," says LaHoste. "We challenged our funders to fund us off their regular cycle. The Rockefeller Foundation gave us $40,000 for development. Whether a play happened or not, we knew it would be an experiment in gathering material this way and building the company."

Equally important was the fact that *Gross Indecency* was the third most-produced play in the American theatre last year. Its popularity gave Kaufman enough cachet to call out of the blue and introduce himself to Rebecca Hilliker, head of the theatre department at the University of Wyoming. When he told her the company wanted to interview people in Laramie about their response to Matthew Shepard's murder, she told him, "I feel like you just kicked me in the stomach. The students here need to talk, because the press coverage has cut off all dialogue on the subject." It was Hilliker's encouragement that emboldened Kaufman to proceed with the project and opened the first doors in Laramie.

The New Yorkers arrived in Laramie with a fair amount of trepidation, expecting to encounter a hotbed of Wild West homophobia. Kaufman decreed certain safety rules—no one works alone, and everyone carries a cell phone. Fondakowski and Pierotti, two gay members of the company who had a special interest in finding out about the gay community of Wyoming, prefaced their first trip to Laramie with a visit to Colorado Springs to interview John Paulk. A poster boy for the ex-gay movement that claims sexual orientation can be changed through the power of prayer, Paulk manages homosexuality and gender issues at the right-wing Christian organization Focus on the Family. Fondakowski and Pierotti were curious to explore why such groups had issued statements to the media distancing their work from the murder of Mathew Shepard. Although the Focus on the Family material never made it to the stage, it braced the company for the conservative sexual politics they would face outside of New York City. "It's very scary how organized they are," says Fondakowski. "They get more mail than anyone in the country but the White House. After spending a couple of days with them, I was really frightened driving into Laramie at dusk. It took me four trips to feel safe jogging there."

Once they hit town and started meeting people, though, the theatre artists found they had to reconsider their stereotypes of small-town Westerners. Some churchgoers they interviewed held narrow-minded judgments about gay people; at the same time, one of the most heroically self-searching characters in the play is a Catholic priest. The artists met gay citizens who were political and outspoken, as well as many who were content to blend in with their surroundings rather than embrace public gay identities. They encountered not only female ranchers but also an Islamic feminist born in Bangladesh who'd lived in Laramie since the age of four. Nothing was as simple as it may have seemed.

The company members were clearly empowered by the experience of doing this kind of first-hand research. Back in New York, they transcribed tapes of their interviews and began developing performable impressions of the people they'd met. The first draft of the script was written in three weeks by 10 people. After viewing about 90 minutes of material in January, a team of four consolidated as the writers' group: actors Stephen Belber and Greg Pierotti, project advisor Stephen Wangh (who had served as dramaturg on *Gross Indecency*) and Fondakowski as head writer. (Fondakowski had been developing a similar kind of piece called *I Think I Like Girls,* based on interviews with lesbians from around the country, which is being co-produced by Tectonic and New Georges Theatre in New York.) Actors Amanda Gronich, John McAdams, Barbara Pitts and Kelli Simpkins each continued to feed material to Fondakowski and the writers' group. They are listed as contributing writers in the almost comically elaborate, but scrupulously respectful, program credits for the play.

Between November and April, company members returned to Laramie several times, to attend—among other things—the trial of Russell Henderson, one of Shepard's assailants. "In the course of six months, people changed," says Fondakowski. "For example, Romaine Patterson was incredibly young when we met her." Patterson, a 21-year-old lesbian who had been a friend of Shepard's, learned that his funeral would be picketed by Fred Phelps, the notorious Kansas-based homophobe, carrying signs saying "God Hates Fags." Patterson marshaled a group of people wearing gigantic white angels' wings to encircle the demonstrators and provide a buffer between their hateful chanting and Shepard's mourners. Patterson went on to form an activist group called Angel Action. "One of the great achievements of the piece was following the journey of various individuals and showing the magnitude of their change," Fondakowski says.

After a three-week workshop in May at New York's Classic Stage Company, the next stage of developing *The Laramie Project* took place at the Sundance Theatre Lab in Utah, whose artistic director, Robert Blacker, attended the first reading of the play. "Sundance usually brings in a writer and a director," says Jeff LaHoste, "but they actually paid to bring 12 of us out there for a three-and-a-half-week workshop in July." The first two acts were roughed out at Sundance and further developed at Dartmouth College in an August residency sponsored by New York Theatre Workshop. The third act, which depended on the outcome of Aaron McKinney's trial in October (he, like Henderson, was found guilty and sentenced to life imprisonment), was finished during the rehearsal period in Denver.

While the writers and actors were primarily responsible for boiling the research down to a text of suitable length, it was Kaufman's task to shape the piece theatrically. "Tectonic refers to the art and science of structure," he says. "We're interested in doing plays that explore language and form. As a gay man, I'm interested in revealing the structure: Who tells what story, and how, is important to me. How many stories of Oscar Wilde were told by gay writers? Most of the biographers I read referred to him as being 'diseased.' How do we tell stories? How do we construct our identity as a person? As a gay person, you're forced to define yourself—that's how we learn that identity is a construct." Kaufman's gift as a director lies in his ability to create a structure that allows multiple, potentially conflicting points of view to stay afloat at the same time. Rather than dictating a single truth or conclusion, he invites the audience to synthesize the material themselves—a classic Brechtian strategy.

Kaufman's key collaborator in shaping *The Laramie Project* theatrically was Steve Wangh, who had been a teacher of his at New York University. The oldest member of the company, Wangh kept a healthy distance from the interviewing process and every few weeks would meet with Kaufman for dramaturgical discussions on the level of theory and form rather than "carpentry conversations," as the director put it.

"We would talk about whether staging a particular moment would work better with a Brechtian approach or one from Meyerhold or Piscator," Kaufman recalls. "One of the big problems with this piece is how do you create a whole town onstage with only eight people? Meyerhold was a genius at doing that kind of thing." Asked to describe a Meyerholdian moment, he refers to the arraignment of the men arrested for beating Shepard: "All the chairs are facing sideways, and as the court officer reads aloud the details of the crime, you see the bodies of the people listening slowly implode as the horror of the scene sinks in. That's the kind of reaction that can only be done onstage."

There are, of course, many precedents for the kind of company-created, Living Newspaper-type work that *The Laramie Project* represents. In the 1970s and early '80s, Max Stafford-Clark's London-based Joint Stock Company unleashed actors to do the original research that culminated in such plays as David Hare's *Fanshen* and Caryl Churchill's *Cloud 9*. *The Laramie Project* calls to mind Emily Mann's "theatre of testimony," plays derived from verbatim transcripts of original interviews, especially *Execution of Justice*. And anyone familiar with Elizabeth LeCompte's work with the Wooster Group, especially *L.S.D. (Just the High Points),* would surely recognize it as a model for Kaufman's split-level, highly presentational staging of *Gross Indecency*. Kaufman acknowledges and admires these artists while carefully distinguishing his work from theirs. For instance, asked about another artist who has created powerful theatre from headline news, he says, "I love Anna

Deavere Smith's work. She's interested in the intersection of language and character, though, while I'm interested in what happens onstage, the intersection of language and form." His biggest role model, he says, is Peter Brook's International Center for Theatre Research, especially the era in which Brook's company created *The Ik,* which Kaufman saw as a teenager.

"In Venezuela, because of the oil boom in the early '80s, they hosted an international theatre festival," he says. "When I was 14 or 15, I saw [Polish director Tadeusz] Kantor's *Cricot 2, Pina Bausch,* Peter Brook and Grotowski's *Akropolis.* That was the theatre I grew up with. So when I saw my first naturalistic play—it was Noel Coward's *Private Lives*—I thought: 'Wow, how avant-garde! Real props!'"

Born and raised in a Jewish family, Kaufman started college at a business school in Caracas, but his first accounting class was so boring that he sought refuge in the theatre department, where an experimental company called Thespis was in residence. He joined the company as an actor and spent five years performing Ionesco, Moliere and new work staged by the artistic director, Fernando Ivosky, who was deeply immersed in the work of Brook and Grotowski.

In 1987, at the age of 23, he realized that he wanted to be a director. At the same time, he was coming to grips with his homosexuality. "At the time, I couldn't be gay in Venezuela," he says. "It was too much of a macho Catholic country." Moving to New York, he spent two years studying at NYU's Experimental Theatre Wing, where Brook and Grotowski were also major heroes. "I needed some theoretical basis, so I was able to study what I'd been doing for five years without knowing it," Kaufman says.

ETW turned out to be the launching pad for what would become the Tectonic Theatre Project. "I told them all I need is space and actors to do what I want, and it was enough of a hippie atmosphere that they said, 'Great! Do it!'" *Women in Beckett,* an evening of short plays performed by actresses aged 65 to 80, led to incorporating Tectonic as a not-for-profit theatre, and Kaufman started building a reputation with striking productions of early plays by Naomi Iizuka (Coxinga and Marlowe's Eye) and Franz Xaver Kroetz's *The Nest,* which won an Obie Award in 1995.

David Rothenberg, a veteran producer and publicist of Off-Broadway theatre, recalls seeing Kaufman's production of Marlowe's *Eye at St. Clement's Church* in 1995. "It was very avant-garde," he says. "I couldn't tell if the play was any good. But I remember being constantly surprised by his creative staging, where people were coming from, how he used the set and the lighting. It was very innovative. It reminded me of certain landmarks in my own theatregoing, such as Ellis Rabb's production of *Pantagleize* with the APA or Peter Brook's staging of *Marat/Sade.* His direction was that extraordinary."

But it was *Gross Indecency* that really put Tectonic on the map. Kaufman gathered around him a company of actors and designers willing to devote two years to developing the piece from trial transcripts and other source material about Oscar Wilde. "Many actors just want to be given a script and five weeks' rehearsal," he notes. "This work attracts a very specific kind of artist. These are people who are thinking deeply about theatrical form."

Kaufman credits Brecht and Erwin Piscator as primary influences on his staging of *Gross Indecency,* in which eight performers played a variety of characters without ever "disappearing" into their roles. Literary sources, contemporary news reports and court documents were cited aloud in the text, and the characters who were speaking would be identified by other performers, the same way that TV sportscasters identify ball players for the viewing audience. As anyone who dares to follow Brecht's example all the way discovers, exposing the theatrical structure can create an almost paradoxically involving theatrical event. By admitting the truth that we are watching an artificially constructed event, rather than pretending otherwise, we are able to confront more directly and engage more fully with whatever moral or philosophical investigation the play is putting forward. *The Laramie Project* goes even farther into Brechtian territory than *Gross Indecency,* which revolved around the central figure of Oscar Wilde. *The Laramie Project* ostentatiously declines to represent Matthew Shepard onstage. This choice ingeniously sidesteps sentimental images while at the same time giving the play a mysteriously satisfying spiritual dimension. The unseen presence is much more powerful than the overly familiar depiction of a crucified figure.

Kaufman's aesthetic is anything but dry and severe. The piece begins with actors, grouped around five tables and eight chairs, playing themselves—a theatre company sharing the results of their own investigation. However, as the play opens up and we meet the people of Laramie in various settings, the director and a skillful design team begin to fill the theatrical space with telling touches. A spotlit window box of cornstalks becomes the Wyoming prairie. As the media descend upon Laramie, TV monitors drop from the ceiling (a moment I couldn't help associating with the Wooster Group's *Route 1 & 9,* which displayed on similar TV monitors scenes from *Our Town*). In a scene at the Fireside Bar, the soundtrack features not country music but, more authentically, white-boy hip-hop. A video screen repeatedly shows footage of a two-lane highway late at night as seen in the headlights of a slightly wayward vehicle.

Still, the center of the performance is the actors. Donning a jacket or a pair of glasses, shifting a vocal inflection, the actors slide from one character to another creating indelible impressions in as little as 15 seconds. For a play with no central character, it's almost miraculous how the actors sustain a compelling tension through a narrative whose outline is surely known to almost everyone in the audience. Two things help. One is the forthright way that the actors establish contact with the audience as themselves; we never lose sight of them even as they slip in and out of different roles. The other core element is the company's insistence on representing the people of Laramie in ways that allowed the residents to recognize themselves.

Easy as it would be to depict Shepard as a sentimental martyr, we hear friends of his describe him as "a blunt little shit" who lacked common sense. And rather than caricature the folksy humor and rural accents of Laramie residents, the performers mine those attributes for the savvy they mask. Commenting on the media's frenzied news coverage, Laramie's police chief drawls, "I didn't feel judged—I felt that they were stupid." A particularly haunting character is Reggie Fluty, the female deputy sheriff (played by Mercedes Herrero) who cut Matthew Shepard down from the fence where he was tied. Told by the hospital that Shepard was HIV positive, she was treated with AZT, which made her lose 10 pounds and much of her hair. This information, not widely known, comes as a bit of a bombshell and raises numerous questions that the play provocatively chooses not to pursue. Instead, the anecdote resonates as part of Fluty's experience of the Matthew Shepard ordeal.

As *The Laramie Project* started coming together last summer, the Tectonic Theatre Project began considering possibilities of where to perform the piece. They didn't want to open the piece in New York, as they'd done with *Gross Indecency.* "We needed some distance from New York," says Leigh Fondakowski. "This piece needs time to grow in front of an audience." A number of regional theatres, including the Seattle Repertory Theatre, Arena Stage in Washington, D.C., the Mark Taper Forum in Los Angeles and the McCarter Theatre in Princeton, N.J., were interested in presenting the show. Kaufman was eager to mount it as soon as possible, and he wanted to do it somewhere close enough so that the people of Laramie could see it. Fortuitously, the Denver Center Theatre Company, whose production of *Gross Indecency* was so successful that they brought it back for a return engagement, had a sudden cancellation in the middle of its season. Since it is the closest regional theatre to Laramie, it seemed a perfect place to present the premiere.

On opening night in Denver, it was impossible not to be aware of the enormous responsibility that the actors felt to do justice to the people who had entrusted them with their stories and their innermost feelings. I found myself sitting next to Zackie Salmon, a 52-year-old lesbian university administrator, who was very attentive to how she came off in the play. Aside from some personal vanity about being seen as the "town nerd" in her oversized glasses, she generally approved, although she told *USA Today* that what didn't come through for her was "the depth of grief that was a communal grief. I don't know if it's possible in any way for anybody to capture that. I think they did the best they could." One of the central characters in the play is Matt Galloway, the bartender who served both Matthew Shepard and his assailants the night of the murder. As played by Stephen Belber, Galloway is effusive and somewhat comically self-possessed, yet highly articulate. Heartbreakingly, he questions whether he was to blame for not stepping in to intervene between Shepard and the men with whom he left the bar. After the show, a ripple of electricity ran through the lobby as we realized that the tall, handsome young man embracing Kaufman was Galloway himself, who was later heard saying to a friend, "I hope I'm not that bad. . . ."

Donovan Marley, artistic director of the Denver Center, told me how he felt about presenting *The Laramie Project* at his theatre. "Matthew Shepard's family and the people of Laramie have suffered way, way, way more than they should have to," he said. "Very frankly, I would not have taken on the project if I felt it was contributing to this suffering. But when I met Moisés, I was certain that it would be a positive experience. It's not what he said, because I never listen to what people say. It was spending time with him and the people he had with him and coming to believe that they had been profoundly moved by going through the interviewing process. I just believed that their responses would have great generosity of spirit."

Conclusion

If all the other casebooks asked us to delve into who we are, what we want, and what we need, Casebook Four asked us to consider who we are as part of a larger group. What is the psyche of our collective group? As a group, how much of our personal make-up is lost or enhanced? What are we willing to sacrifice for the good of all? And does our response change when the situation or decision becomes a personal issue rather than a policy issue? How often must we, like the characters, change our minds when it involves us or someone we love?

CASEBOOK FIVE

(Hu)Man /Nature:
Exploring the Nature of Humanity and the Humanity of Nature

Overview

In this casebook, we explore some of the nuances of what is often passed off as "human nature" and humankind's complicated appreciation of and relationship with the natural world at large. As human society progresses and advances—further and further away from a state of being "in tune" with nature—how do we continue to interact with the natural world—with the trees and the stars, with all forms of wildlife? What part of humanity is uniquely reflected in nature and by nature? *What* is or *how* is human nature?

It is almost impossible not to admit that many of our behaviors and responses are as indigenous to us as space is to the stars. What is interesting to explore and question lies in our discernment—how we are locked into or "programmed" for certain responses. Take for an example a mother whose child is about to fall down. The first instinct is to reach for that child. At that particular moment, the mother is oblivious to anything except that child. Where the problem arises, though, is when we fail to accept responsibility for certain behaviors and responses because we claim that it is human nature, when in all probability it is a result of failed attempts to rectify a problem. Our failure turns into complacency. But maybe this is hu(man) nature as well.

Consider these questions as you read the following selections:

- Is there a universal "human nature"?
- Which human responses are innate? Which are learned?
- Does mankind feel a necessity to commune with nature? What happens when we grow apart from our natural environment, our "true nature"?
- Does mankind have a responsibility to preserve the earth?

Poetry

WILLIAM BLAKE

William Blake was born in London in 1757. He was a poet, a painter, a visionary mystic, and an engraver, who—along with his wife—illustrated and printed his own books. The author of many collections of poetry, he once said, "I do not distrust my corporeal or vegetative eye any more than I would distrust a window for its sight. I see through it, not with it." Blake died on August 12, 1827, and was buried in an unmarked grave at the public cemetery of Bunhill Fields.

Earth's Answer

Earth raised up her head
From the darkness dread and drear,
Her light fled,
Stony, dread,
And her locks covered with grey despair.

"Prisoned on watery shore,
Starry jealousy does keep my den
Cold and hoar;
Weeping o're,
I hear the father of the ancient men.

"Selfish father of men!
Cruel, jealous, selfish fear!
Can delight,
Chained in night,
The virgins of youth and morning bear?

"Does spring hide its joy,
When buds and blossoms grow?
Does the sower
Sow by night,
Or the plowman in darkness plough?

"Break this heavy chain,
That does freeze my bones around!
Selfish, vain,
Eternal bane,
That free love with bondage bound."

JOHN CLARE

John Clare was born in July 1793. He was an English poet who lived mostly in rural Northamptonshire until his death in 1864. He is now regarded as one of the most important English poets, but he also wrote many essays and letters about love, politics, and folk life.

The Eternity of Nature

Cowslaps golden blooms
That in the closen and the meadow comes
Shall come when kings and empires fade and dye
And in the meadows as times partners lie
As fresh two thousand years to come as now
With those five crimson spots upon its brow
And little brooks that hum a simple lay
In green unnoticed spots from praise away
Shall sing—when poets in times darkness hid
Shall lie like memory in a pyramid
Forgetting yet not all forgot though lost
Like a threads end in ravelled windings crost [. . .]
And think ye these times play things pass p[r]oud skill
Time loves them like a child and ever will
And so I worship them in bushy spots
And sing with them when all else notice not
And feel the music of their mirth agree
With that sooth quiet that bestirreth me
And if I touch aright that quiet tone
That soothing truth that shadows forth their own
Then many a year shall grow in after days
And still find hearts to love my quiet lays

LANGSTON HUGHES

James Langston Hughes was born February 1, 1902, in Missouri. Following high school graduation, he spent a year in Mexico and a year at Columbia University. His first book of poetry, *The Weary Blues,* was published by Alfred A. Knopf in 1926. He finished his college education at Lincoln University in Pennsylvania three years later. The recipient of many honors, Langston Hughes died of complications from prostate cancer in May 1967. His residence at 20 East 127th Street in Harlem, New York City, was granted landmark status by the New York City Preservation Commission, and East 127th Street was renamed "Langston Hughes Place."

The following poem was published in 1922.

The Negro Speaks of Rivers

I've known rivers:
I've known rivers ancient as the world and older than the flow of human
    blood in human veins.

My soul has grown deep like the rivers.

I bathed in the Euphrates when dawns were young.
I built my hut near the Congo and it lulled me to sleep.
I looked upon the Nile and raised the pyramids above it.
I heard the singing of the Mississippi when Abe Lincoln went down to New
    Orleans, and I've seen its muddy bosom turn all golden in the sunset.

I've known rivers:
Ancient, dusky rivers.

My soul has grown deep like the rivers.

WALLACE STEVENS

Wallace Stevens was born in Reading, Pennsylvania, on October 2, 1879. He attended Harvard as an undergraduate and earned a law degree from New York Law School. Admitted to the U.S. Bar in 1904, Stevens worked with Hartford Accident and Indemnity Company in Connecticut and became vice president of that company in 1934. His first book of poems, *Harmonium,* was published in 1923, and though he is now considered one of the major American poets of the century, he did not receive widespread recognition until the publication of his *Collected Poems* a year before his death in 1955.

Thirteen Ways of Looking at a Blackbird

I

Among twenty snowy mountains,
The only moving thing
Was the eye of the blackbird.

II

I was of three minds,
Like a tree
In which there are three blackbirds.

III

The blackbird whirled in the autumn winds.
It was a small part of the pantomime.

IV

A man and a woman
Are one.
A man and a woman and a blackbird
Are one.

V

I do not know which to prefer,
The beauty of inflections
Or the beauty of innuendoes,
The blackbird whistling
Or just after.

VI

Icicles filled the long window
With barbaric glass.
The shadow of the blackbird
Crossed it, to and fro.
The mood
Traced in the shadow
An indecipherable cause.

VII

O thin men of Haddam,
Why do you imagine golden birds?

Do you not see how the blackbird
Walks around the feet
Of the women about you?

VIII

I know noble accents
And lucid, inescapable rhythms;
But I know, too,
That the blackbird is involved
In what I know.

IX

When the blackbird flew out of sight,
It marked the edge
Of one of many circles.

X

At the sight of blackbirds
Flying in a green light,
Even the bawds of euphony
Would cry out sharply.

XI

He rode over Connecticut
In a glass coach.
Once, a fear pierced him,
In that he mistook
The shadow of his equipage
For blackbirds.

XII

The river is moving.
The blackbird must be flying.

XIII

It was evening all afternoon.
It was snowing
And it was going to snow.
The blackbird sat
In the cedar-limbs.

GALWAY KINNEL

Galway Kinnell was born in Providence, Rhode Island, in 1927. He studied at Princeton University and the University of Rochester. The author of multiple volumes of poetry, Galway Kinnell divides his time between Vermont and New York City, where he is the Erich Maria Remarque Professor of Creative Writing at New York University. He is currently a Chancellor of the Academy of American Poets.

Blackberry Eating

I love to go out in late September
among the fat, overripe, icy, black blackberries
to eat blackberries for breakfast,
the stalks very prickly, a penalty
they earn for knowing the black art
of blackberry-making; and as I stand among them
lifting the stalks to my mouth, the ripest berries
fall almost unbidden to my tongue,
as words sometimes do, certain peculiar words
like strengths or squinched,
many-lettered, one-syllabled lumps,
which I squeeze, squinch open, and splurge well
in the silent, startled, icy, black language
of blackberry-eating in late September.

ROBERT PENN WARREN

Robert Penn Warren was born in Kentucky in 1905. He entered Vanderbilt University in 1921, where he became the youngest member of the group of Southern poets called the Fugitives. From 1925 to 1927, Warren was a teaching fellow at the University of California, where he earned a master's degree. He studied at Oxford as a Rhodes Scholar and returned to the United States in 1930. He taught at Vanderbilt, Louisiana State, the University of Minnesota, and Yale University. Though he is an accomplished poet (having twice won the Pulitzer Prize for poetry), Warren is best known as a novelist and received tremendous recognition for *All the King's Men,* which won the Pulitzer Prize for Fiction in 1947. Warren served as a Chancellor of the Academy of American Poets from 1972 until 1988, and was appointed the first U.S. Poet Laureate in 1985. He died in 1989.

Heart of Autumn

Wind finds the northwest gap, fall comes.
Today, under gray cloud-scud and over gray
Wind-flicker of forest, in perfect formation, wild geese
Head for a land of warm water, the boom, the lead pellet.

Some crumple in air, fall. Some stagger, recover control,
Then take the last glide for a far glint of water. None
Knows what has happened. Now, today, watching
How tirelessly V upon V arrows the season's logic,

Do I know my own story? At least, they know
When the hour comes for the great wing-beat. Sky-strider,
Star-strider—they rise, and the imperial utterance,
Which cries out for distance, quivers in the wheeling sky.

That much they know, and in their nature know
The path of pathlessness, with all the joy
Of destiny fulfilling its own name.
I have know time and distance, but not why I am here.

Path of logic, path of folly, all
The same—and I stand, my face lifted now skyward,
Hearing the high beat, my arms outstretched in the tingling
Process of transformation, and soon tough legs,

With folded feet, trail in the sounding vacuum of passage,
And my heart is impacted with a fierce impulse
To unwordable utterance—
Toward sunset, at a great height.

N. Scott Momaday

Navarro Scott Mammedaty, a Kiowa Indian, was born in Lawton, Oklahoma, in 1934 and grew up in close contact with the Navajo and San Carlos Apache communities. He received his B.A. in political science in 1958 from the University of New Mexico. At Stanford University he received his M.A. and Ph.D in English, in 1960 and 1963 respectively. Momaday's honors include the Golden Plate Award from the American Academy of Achievement, an Academy of American Poets Prize, an award from the National Institute of Arts and Letters, and the Premio Letterario Internationale "Mondello," Italy's highest literary award. He is recipient of a Guggenheim Fellowship and is a Fellow of the American Academy of Arts and Sciences. He holds twelve honorary degrees from American colleges and universities, including Yale University, the University of Massachusetts, and the University of Wisconsin.

The Bear

What ruse of vision
escarping the wall of leaves,
  rending incision
into countless surfaces,

  would cull and color
his somnolence, whose old age
  has outworn valour,
all but the fact of courage?

  Seen, he does not come,
move, but seems forever there,
  dimensionless, dumb,
in the windless noon's hot glare.

  More scarred than others
these years since the trap maimed him,
  pain slants his withers,
drawing up the crooked limb.

  Then he is gone, whole,
without urgency, from sight
  as buzzards control,
imperceptibly, their flight.

MARGE PIERCY

Poet, novelist, and essayist Marge Piercy was born in Detroit, Michigan, in 1936. She won a scholarship to the University of Michigan and was the first member of her family to attend college. She subsequently earned a master's degree from Northwestern University.

The Common, Living Dirt

What calls louder than the cry of a field of corn ready, or trees of ripe peaches?

The small ears prick on the bushes,
furry buds, shoots tender and pale.

The swamp maples blow scarlet.
Color teases the comer of the eye,
delicate gold, chartreuse, crimson,
mauve speckled, just dashed on.

The soil stretches naked. All winter
hidden under the down comforter of snow,
delicious now, rich in the hand
as chocolate cake: the fragrant busy
soil the worm passes through her gut
and the beetle swims in like a lake.

As I kneel to put the seeds in
careful as stitching, I am in love.
You are the bed we all sleep on.
You are the food we eat, the food
we ate, the food we will become.
We are walking trees rooted in you.

You can live thousands of years
undressing in the spring your black
body, your red body, your brown body
penetrated by the rain. Here
is the goddess unveiled,
the earth opening her strong thighs.

Yet you grow exhausted with bearing
too much, too soon, too often, just
as a woman wears through like an old rug.
We have contempt for what we spring
from. Dirt, we say, you're dirt
as if we were not all your children.

We have lost the simplest gratitude.
We lack the knowledge we showed ten
thousand years past, that you live
a goddess but mortal, that what we take
must be returned; that the poison we drop
in you will stunt our children's growth.

Tending a plot of your flesh binds
me as nothing ever could, to the seasons,
to the will of the plants, clamorous
in their green tenderness. What
calls louder than the cry of a field
of corn ready, or trees of ripe peaches?

I worship on my knees, laying
the seeds in you, that worship rooted
in need, in hunger, in kinship,
flesh of the planet with my own flesh,
a ritual of compost, a litany of manure.
My garden's a chapel, but a meadow

gone wild in grass and flower
is a cathedral. How you seethe
with little quick ones, vole, field
mouse, shrew and mole in their thousands,
rabbits and woodchuck. In you rest
the jewels of the genes wrapped in seed.

Power warps because it involves joy
in domination; also because it means
forgetting how we too starve, break
like a corn stalk in the wind, how we
die like the spinach of drought,
how what slays the vole slays us.

Because you can die of overwork, because
you can die of the fire that melts
rock, because you can die of the poison
that kills the beetle and the slug,
we must come again and worship you
on our knees, the common living dirt.

LESLIE MARMON SILKO

Leslie Marmon Silko was born March 1948 in New Mexico. She attended the University of New Mexico, and graduated with honors in 1969 with a B.A. in English. Her poetry has been honored repeatedly, and she has been named a Living Cultural Treasure by the New Mexico Endowment for the Humanities Council. Silko has taught English at the Navajo Community College in Tsaile, Arizona, and at the University of New Mexico. She is currently a professor at the University of Arizona at Tucson.

Where Mountain Lion Lay Down with Deer

I climb the black rock mountain
    stepping from day to day
           silently.

I smell the wind for my ancestors
   pale blue leaves
   crushed wild mountain smell.
Returning
  up the gray stone cliff
  where I descended
       a thousand years ago.

Returning to faded black stone
  where mountain lion lay down with deer.
It is better to stay up here
         watching wind's reflection
         in tall yellow flowers.
The old ones who remember me are gone
     the old songs are all forgotten
and the story of my birth.
How I danced in snow-frost moonlight
    distant stars to the end of the Earth,
How I swam away
     in freezing mountain water
     narrow mossy canyon tumbling down
        out of the mountain
          out of the deep canyon stone
   down
     the memory
        spilling out
        into the world.

Joy Harjo

    Joy Harjo was born in Tulsa, Oklahoma, in 1951. She is the author of more than six volumes of poetry, and she is well-known for her performance art—a combination of saxophone and poetry—along with her band, Poetic Justice. She has received many honors throughout her career, including the William Carlos Williams Award, fellowships from the Arizona Commission on the Arts, the Witter Bynner Foundation, and the National Endowment for the Arts.

Eagle Poem

To pray you open your whole self
To sky, to earth, to sun, to moon

To one whole voice that is you
And know there is more
That you can't see, can't hear
Can't know except in moments
Steadly growing, and in languages
That aren't always sound but other
Circles of motion.
Like eagle that Sunday morning
Over Salt River. Circled in blue sky
In wind, swept our hearts clean
With sacred wings.
We see you, see ourselves and know
That we must take the utmost care
And kindness in all things.
Breathe in, knowing we are made of
All this, and breathe, knowing
We are truly blessed because we
Were born, and die soon within a
True circle of motion,
Like eagle rounding out the morning
Inside us.
We pray that it will be done
In beauty.
In beauty.

Fiction

LINDA HOGAN

Linda Hogan was born in 1947 into a military family. As a result of moving quite often as a child, she did not grow up within an Indian community (her tribal affiliation is Chickasaw). Most of her childhood was spent in Oklahoma and Colorado. She obtained an M.A. degree from University of Colorado at Boulder in 1978. She has served on the National Endowment for the Arts poetry panel for two years and has been involved in wildlife rehabilitation as a volunteer.

Amen

He was born with only one eye and maybe that's why he saw things different than most people. The good eye was dark. The sightless eye was all white and lightly veined.

"There's a god in the light of that eye," Sullie's mother said.

Sullie only saw the man's eye once in her life. It was the night of the big fish and she thought it was more like a pearl or moon than like an eye. And it was all the more unusual because Jack was, after all, only an ordinary man. He had an old man's odor and wasn't always clean.

He carved wood and fished like all the men. With his small hands he carved tree limbs into gentle cats, sleeping dogs, and chickens. And he carved chains to hold them all together.

"It's the only way I can keep a cat and dog in the same room," he joked.

Sullie kept most of his carvings. She watched the shavings pile up on the creaking porch until a breeze blew them into the tall grass or weeds. On a hot windless day they'd fall onto the gold back of the sleeping dog or on its twitching ear. She sat at old Jack's feet and watched and smelled the turpentine odor of wood. His unpatched eye was sharp and black. She could see herself in it, her long skinny legs folded under, her faded dress, dark scraggly hair, all in his one good eye. The other eye was covered, as usual, with a leather patch.

Even then he had been pretty old. His skin was loosening from the bones. He was watching with his clear and black eye how the sky grew to be made of shadows. And some days he didn't have room for one more word so they sat in silence.

The night of the big fish, people had been talking about Jack. He wasn't at the picnic and that was as good invitation to gossip.

"Jesse James was part Chickasaw," said Enoch. "Pete has one of his pistols. Word has it that Pete and Jack are related to the James brothers."

Gladys waved her hand impatiently. She leaned her chair back a little and stuck her chest out. "Go on. That old man?"

"That old man was a pallbearer at Jesses Jame's funeral, yessir."

"They wouldn't have had an Indian at the funeral, would they?" she asked.

"Look it up. Besides, in his younger days he wore a coal black shirt, even when it was hot. And he had one of them there Arabian horses no one else knew how to ride. And a concho belt made out of real silver. Had a silver saddle horn, too."

Will smiled at the other men. He removed his hat and rubbed back his thick black and gray hair. "That's right. Rumor has it his own brother stole that saddle and belt."

People still kept watch for it, for the stirrups dangling like half-moons and the hammered conchos down the sides. There had also been the horsehair bridle he brought back from Mexico. It was red, black and white horsehair with two heavy threads of purple running through it. The purple dye had come from seashells. Greek shellfish, someone said and Jack liked to touch the threads and feel the ocean in them, the white Greek stucco buildings, the blue sky. He liked the purple thread more than all the silver. Almost.

"You wouldn't have crossed him in those days. He won that horse in a contest. The trader said if anyone could ride it, they could have it. Jack got on and rode it. He sure did. And then the trader said he couldn't give it to Jack. 'I'd be broke,' he said. So Jack said, 'Give me fifty dollars.' The man said he didn't have that kind of money. Jack pulled out his pistol and said, 'If I kill you, you won't have no worries about money or horses."

Everyone nodded. A couple of old folks said, "Amen," like good Baptists do. A cheater was a bad man. Jack's brother killed a man for cheating him out of thirty-eight cents. It didn't sound like much but there wasn't much food in those days and the thief had been an outsider. The old folks then also said, "Amen." They had to feed their own. Not much grew out of the dry Oklahoma soil except pebbles. Word had it that this was just a thin layer of earth over big stone underground mountains. Close to the hot sun and the corn-eating grasshoppers.

And even Sullie had lived through two droughts, a dozen or more black and turquoise tornadoes roiling through the sky, and the year that ended in October. That year cotton grew up out of the soft red soil and it grew tall. At first the old people praised the cotton and said "Amen" to the ground. But it kept growing until it was tall as the houses, even the houses with little attics. It stretched up to the wooden roof-tops, above the silvered dry wood.

Jack went out in the mornings looking for signs of blossoms. Every morning he stood at the far end of the field and sang a song to the cotton. Sullie went out behind him and hid in the tall green plants. She heard parts of the song and silence and the cotton whisper and grow. No pale flowers ever bloomed. No hint of anything that would dry and burst open with white soft cotton inside. Jack went out daily. He stood and sang. He walked through the plants as if his steps would force the stems to let out frail blossoms.

Sullie's mother watched from the door. She dried her hands on the back of her skirt. "I don't think nothing's going to work." She whispered to Sullie and it was true because when October came the taller-than-houses plants froze, turned transparent and then dried a dull yellow. And the banks closed. And the new red mules died of bloat. And Sullie learned to keep silent at the long empty table.

"He even shot his own brother-in-law for beating up his sister. At a picnic just like this one."

"Amen," the women said, good Baptists. They nodded their round dark faces in agreement.

"After that he'd never sit by a window or go in a dark room. Why, he wouldn't even go into a barn unless it had two doors because he was sure the law or someone from the family would get him."

"He was mean, all right, a man to be feared. You'd forget he had such tiny little hands. And he only wore a size two shoe. Don't know how he ran so fast or handled them guns. And all the time turning his head like a rooster to make up for the missing eye."

It grew dark and several men went down to the lake to jack fish. They shined big lights into the water and it attracted fish the same way it paralyzed deer or other land animals. They wouldn't have done it if Jack had been there.

Sullie went down to the water. She was almost a teenager and she liked to watch the big men. She liked their tight jeans and shirts and hats. The women didn't like girls following the men but they forgot about her soon, they were so busy talking about new cotton dresses, their own little children sleeping now on blankets on the hillside. And later they'd talk about women things, men, herbs, seeing Eliza George, the old doctor woman who healed their headaches and helped them get pregnant. Sullie would be back in time to hear about Miss George and how to get pregnant.

But for now she watched the lights shine on the water. And light underneath showing up like sunset. A few miles away in the dark she saw the passing headlights of trucks. She sat in a clump of bushes and trees for a while, then went down to the dark edge of the lake. The men couldn't see into the darkness because of the bright lights in their eyes.

She waded in the warm water. The hem of her dress stuck to her legs. She went a little deeper. She stubbed her toe and felt something move and give way. Whatever it was made a large current and she felt frightened. It was cool and slippery and swam like a large fish. Then it stopped. She reached her hand into the water, wetting even her hair, but it was gone. She felt nothing except the fast motion of water.

She smelled the water. She swam a little and looked at the lights the women kept on the table, and the black trees.

She heard voices of the men out in the center of the lake. "Over there," someone said. And the lights swayed on the water.

Jack walked down to the lake. Sullie started to call to him but then kept still. In the moonlight she saw that he wasn't wearing his eyepatch. And he walked still like maybe he was mad. So she kept silent and waded a little further into rocks and weeds and darkness near the shore.

He didn't have a boat or canoe and he stood a moment at the edge of the dark water. Then he dunked himself and stood again. Sullie saw his knobby shoulders beneath the wet shirt, the bones at the neck. Then he submerged himself in the water and swam toward the other men. There were only a few splashes, an occasional glimpse of his head rising out of the water.

Before he reached the men with lights, Sullie heard them all become noisy at once. "Lordy," one of them said. The water near them grew furious and violent. One small canoe tipped and the lights shone off all directions.

Sullie waded out again to her chest to watch, forgetting about the women's talk. She heard the men's voices. "I could put my hands in that gill slit." Someone else said, "Watch his fins. They're like razor blades." They were pulling something around, taking ropes out of the boats when Jack arrived. Sullie didn't hear the conversation between Jack and the other men but she saw him breathing hard in one of the boats and then he was gone, swimming again toward shore, her direction.

"Pry it out of those rocks," Enoch yelled.

The men were jubilant, dredging up the old fish with only one eye. It was an old presence in the lake and Jack must have known about it all along. His absence had given the younger men permission to fish with illegal light.

He came up from the water close to Sullie and walked through the rocks and sand out into the night air.

Sullie followed Jack a ways. In the darkness there was a tree standing in moonlight, the moon like a silver concho. Jack's hands were small and the light outlined the bones and knuckles. They were spotted like the sides of the ancient fish.

She held herself back from the old man. His shoulders were high and she remembered how he had made cornbread on the day of her birth and fed her honey so she'd never be thin. Sullie's mother had been surprised that Sullie knew this. "Who told you?" she asked.

"Nobody."

"You remember it on your own? Babies can't see."

"I just remember, that's all."

And now he stood breathing in the dark. And there were yucca plants at his feet. After the first freeze they would scatter a circle of black seeds on the earth like magic. Like the flying wisteria seeds that had hit and scared Sullie one night. So much mystery in the world, in the way seeds take to air and mimosa leaves fold in delicate prayer at night.

"Who's there?" he said.

"It's me." Her voice was weak. She was afraid to go near him, afraid to run off. He turned and the sight of his eye made her pull her breath too fast into her lungs. It was bright as the moon and the lanterns on water. He watched her a moment and then turned. He looked toward where the cotton was growing this year, toward a few scattered houses with dark windows. Fireflies appeared while he stood. And the sounds of locusts and crickets Sullie hadn't noticed before.

"Let's go back to the rest of the folks," he said.

And they walked, the skinny wet girl, the skinny wet man. The women shut up when they saw them coming. The men didn't notice. They were dragging the rope-bound old fish up on the shore and all the children were awake and running and splashing the water.

Its fins slowed. The gills quit opening while they cut at it and cleaned it of red and yellow ropey intestines and innards. Dogs lapped at its juices.

In the moonlight the sharp scales were scraped off like hunks of mica in a shining glassy pile.

The smell of fish cooking. The dogs eating parts of the head. So large, that dull-colored thing. They'd all talk about it forever. Something that had survived the drought, the famine, the tornadoes and dead crops. It grew large. It was older than all of them. It had hooks in it and lived.

Sullie refused to eat. She pushed her dish away. Her mother hit the table with a pot. "Eat," she said.

Jack's one eye looked far inside Sullie. She was growing old. She could feel it. In his gaze, she grew old. She grew silent inside. She pulled the plate toward her and looked at the piece of fish, the fried skin and pale bones of it.

"Eat it," Jack motioned with his fork, his own cheeks full of the pink meat. "Eat it. It's an Indian fish."

"Amen," said the women just like they'd always been good Baptists.

NATHANIEL HAWTHORNE

A central figure in the American Renaissance, Nathaniel Hawthorne's best-known works include *The Scarlet Letter* (1850) and *The House of the Seven Gables* (1851). Aside from his importance as a novelist, Hawthorne is also notable as a short-story writer. The following, often anthologized story was written in 1835.

Young Goodman Brown

Young Goodman Brown came forth at sunset into the street at Salem village; but put his head back, after crossing the threshold, to exchange a parting kiss with his young wife. And Faith, as the wife was aptly named, thrust her own pretty head into the street, letting the wind play with the pink ribbons of her cap while she called to Goodman Brown.

"Dearest heart," whispered she, softly and rather sadly, when her lips were close to his ear, "prithee put off your journey until sunrise and sleep in your own bed tonight. A lone woman is troubled with such dreams and such thoughts that she's afeard of herself sometimes. Pray tarry with me this night, dear husband, of all nights in the year."

"My love and my Faith," replied young Goodman Brown, "of all nights in the year, this one night must I tarry away from thee. My journey, as thou callest it, forth and back again, must needs be done 'twixt now and sunrise. What, my sweet, pretty wife, dost thou doubt me already, and we but three months married?"

"Then God bless you!" said Faith, with the pink ribbons; "and may you find all well when you come back."

"Amen!" cried Goodman Brown. "Say thy prayers, dear Faith, and go to bed at dusk, and no harm will come to thee."

So they parted; and the young man pursued his way until, being about to turn the corner by the meeting-house, he looked back and saw the head of Faith still peeping after him with a melancholy air, in spite of her pink ribbons.

"Poor little Faith!" thought he, for his heart smote him. "What a wretch am I to leave her on such an errand! She talks of dreams, too. Methought as she spoke there was trouble in her face, as if a dream had warned her what work is to be done tonight. But no, no; 't would kill her to think it. Well, she's a blessed angel on earth; and after this one night I'll cling to her skirts and follow her to heaven."

With this excellent resolve for the future, Goodman Brown felt himself justified in making more haste on his present evil purpose. He had taken a dreary road, darkened by all the gloomiest trees of the forest, which barely stood aside to let the narrow path creep through, and closed immediately behind. It was all as lonely as could be; and there is this peculiarity in such a solitude, that the traveller knows not who may be concealed by the innumerable trunks and the thick boughs overhead; so that with lonely footsteps he may yet be passing through an unseen multitude.

"There may be a devilish Indian behind every tree," said Goodman Brown to himself; and he glanced fearfully behind him as he added, "What if the devil himself should be at my very elbow!"

His head being turned back, he passed a crook of the road, and, looking forward again, beheld the figure of a man, in grave and decent attire, seated at the foot of an old tree. He arose at Goodman Brown's approach and walked onward side by side with him.

"You are late, Goodman Brown," said he. "The clock of the Old South was striking as I came through Boston, and that is full fifteen minutes agone."

"Faith kept me back a while," replied the young man, with a tremor in his voice, caused by the sudden appearance of his companion, though not wholly unexpected.

It was now deep dusk in the forest, and deepest in that part of it where these two were journeying. As nearly as could be discerned, the second traveller was about fifty years old, apparently in the same rank of life as Goodman Brown, and bearing a considerable resemblance to him, though perhaps more in expression than features. Still they might have been taken for father and son. And yet, though the elder person was as simply clad as the younger, and as simple in manner too, he had an indescribable air of one who knew the world, and who would not have felt abashed at the governor's dinner table or in King William's court, were it possible that his affairs should call him thither. But the only thing about him that could be fixed upon as remarkable was his staff, which bore the likeness of a great black snake, so curiously wrought that it might almost be seen to twist and wriggle itself like a living serpent. This, of course, must have been an ocular deception, assisted by the uncertain light.

"Come, Goodman Brown," cried his fellow-traveller, "this is a dull pace for the beginning of a journey. Take my staff, if you are so soon weary."

"Friend," said the other, exchanging his slow pace for a full stop, "having kept covenant by meeting thee here, it is my purpose now to return whence I came. I have scruples touching the matter thou wot'st of."

"Sayest thou so?" replied he of the serpent, smiling apart. "Let us walk on, nevertheless, reasoning as we go; and if I convince thee not thou shalt turn back. We are but a little way in the forest yet."

"Too far! too far!" exclaimed the goodman, unconsciously resuming his walk. "My father never went into the woods on such an errand, nor his father before him. We have been a race of honest men and good Christians since the days of the martyrs; and shall I be the first of the name of Brown that ever took this path and kept"—

"Such company, thou wouldst say," observed the elder person, interpreting his pause. "Well said, Goodman Brown! I have been as well acquainted with your family as with ever a one among the Puritans; and that's no trifle to say. I helped your grandfather, the constable, when he lashed the Quaker woman so smartly through the streets of Salem; and it was I that brought your father a pitch-pine knot, kindled at my own hearth, to set fire to an Indian village, in King Philip's war. They were my good friends, both; and many a pleasant walk have we had along this path, and returned merrily after midnight. I would fain be friends with you for their sake."

"If it be as thou sayest," replied Goodman Brown, "I marvel they never spoke of these matters; or, verily, I marvel not, seeing that the least rumor of the sort would have driven them from New England. We are a people of prayer, and good works to boot, and abide no such wickedness."

"Wickedness or not," said the traveller with the twisted staff, "I have a very general acquaintance here in New England. The deacons of many a church have drunk the communion wine with me; the selectmen of divers towns make me their chairman; and a majority of the Great and General Court are firm supporters of my interest. The governor and I, too—But these are state secrets."

"Can this be so?" cried Goodman Brown, with a stare of amazement at his undisturbed companion. "Howbeit, I have nothing to do with the governor and council; they have their own ways, and are no rule for a simple husbandman like me. But, were I to go on with thee, how should I meet the eye of that good old man, our minister, at Salem village? Oh, his voice would make me tremble both Sabbath day and lecture day."

Thus far the elder traveller had listened with due gravity; but now burst into a fit of irrepressible mirth, shaking himself so violently that his snake-like staff actually seemed to wriggle in sympathy.

"Ha! ha! ha!" shouted he again and again; then composing himself, "Well, go on, Goodman Brown, go on; but, prithee, don't kill me with laughing."

"Well, then, to end the matter at once," said Goodman Brown, considerably nettled, "there is my wife, Faith. It would break her dear little heart; and I'd rather break my own."

"Nay, if that be the case," answered the other, "e'en go thy ways, Goodman Brown. I would not for twenty old women like the one hobbling before us that Faith should come to any harm."

As he spoke he pointed his staff at a female figure on the path, in whom Goodman Brown recognized a very pious and exemplary dame, who had taught him his catechism in youth, and was still his moral and spiritual adviser, jointly with the minister and Deacon Gookin.

"A marvel, truly, that Goody Cloyse should be so far in the wilderness at nightfall," said he. "But with your leave, friend, I shall take a cut through the woods until we have left this Christian woman behind. Being a stranger to you, she might ask whom I was consorting with and whither I was going."

"Be it so," said his fellow-traveller. "Betake you to the woods, and let me keep the path."

Accordingly the young man turned aside, but took care to watch his companion, who advanced softly along the road until he had come within a staff's length of the old dame. She, meanwhile, was making the best of her way, with singular speed for so aged a woman, and mumbling some indistinct words—a prayer, doubtless—as she went. The traveller put forth his staff and touched her withered neck with what seemed the serpent's tail.

"The devil!" screamed the pious old lady.

"Then Goody Cloyse knows her old friend?" observed the traveller, confronting her and leaning on his writhing stick.

"Ah, forsooth, and is it your worship indeed?" cried the good dame. "Yea, truly is it, and in the very image of my old gossip, Goodman Brown, the grandfather of the silly fellow that now is. But—would your worship believe it?—my broomstick hath strangely disappeared, stolen, as I suspect, by that unhanged witch, Goody Cory, and that, too, when I was all anointed with the juice of smallage, and cinquefoil, and wolf's bane"—"Mingled with fine wheat and the fat of a new-born babe," said the shape of old Goodman Brown.

"Ah, your worship knows the recipe," cried the old lady, cackling aloud. "So, as I was saying, being all ready for the meeting, and no horse to ride on, I made up my mind to foot it; for they tell me there is a nice young man to be taken into communion to-night. But now your good worship will lend me your arm, and we shall be there in a twinkling."

"That can hardly be," answered her friend. "I may not spare you my arm, Goody Cloyse; but here is my staff, if you will."

So saying, he threw it down at her feet, where, perhaps, it assumed life, being one of the rods which its owner had formerly lent to the Egyptian magi. Of this fact, however, Goodman Brown could not take cognizance. He had cast up his eyes in astonishment, and, looking down again, beheld neither Goody Cloyse nor the serpentine staff, but his fellow-traveller alone, who waited for him as calmly as if nothing had happened.

"That old woman taught me my catechism," said the young man; and there was a world of meaning in this simple comment.

They continued to walk onward, while the elder traveller exhorted his companion to make good speed and persevere in the path, discoursing so aptly that his arguments seemed rather to spring up in the bosom of his auditor than to be suggested by himself. As they went, he plucked a branch of maple to serve for a walking stick, and began to strip it of the twigs and little boughs, which were wet with evening dew. The moment his fingers touched them they became strangely withered and dried up as with a week's sunshine. Thus the pair proceeded, at a good free pace, until suddenly, in a gloomy hollow of the road, Goodman Brown sat himself down on the stump of a tree and refused to go any farther.

"Friend," said he, stubbornly, "my mind is made up. Not another step will I budge on this errand. What if a wretched old woman do choose to go to the devil when I thought she was going to heaven: is that any reason why I should quit my dear Faith and go after her?"

"You will think better of this by and by," said his acquaintance, composedly. "Sit here and rest yourself a while; and when you feel like moving again, there is my staff to help you along."

Without more words, he threw his companion the maple stick, and was as speedily out of sight as if he had vanished into the deepening gloom. The young man sat a few moments by the roadside, applauding himself greatly, and thinking with how clear a conscience he should meet the minister in his morning walk, nor shrink from the eye of good old Deacon Gookin. And what calm sleep would be his that very night, which was to have been spent so wickedly, but so purely and sweetly now, in the arms of Faith! Amidst these pleasant and praiseworthy meditations, Goodman Brown heard the tramp of horses along the road, and deemed it advisable to conceal himself within the verge of the forest, conscious of the guilty purpose that had brought him thither, though now so happily turned from it.

On came the hoof tramps and the voices of the riders, two grave old voices, conversing soberly as they drew near. These mingled sounds appeared to pass along the road, within a few yards of the young man's hiding-place; but, owing doubtless to the depth of the gloom at that particular spot, neither the travellers nor their steeds were visible. Though their figures brushed the small boughs by the wayside, it could not be seen that they intercepted, even for a moment, the faint gleam from the strip of bright sky athwart which they must have passed. Goodman Brown alternately crouched and stood on tiptoe, pulling aside the branches and thrusting forth his head as far as he durst without discerning so much as a shadow. It vexed him the more, because he could have sworn, were such a thing possible, that he recognized the voices of the minister and Deacon Gookin, jogging along quietly, as they were wont to do, when bound to some ordination or ecclesiastical council. While yet within hearing, one of the riders stopped to pluck a switch.

"Of the two, reverend sir," said the voice like the deacon's, "I had rather miss an ordination dinner than to-night's meeting. They tell me that some of our community are to be here from Falmouth and beyond, and others from Connecticut and Rhode Island, besides several of the Indian powwows, who, after their fashion, know almost as much deviltry as the best of us. Moreover, there is a goodly young woman to be taken into communion."

"Mighty well, Deacon Gookin!" replied the solemn old tones of the minister. "Spur up, or we shall be late. Nothing can be done, you know, until I get on the ground."

The hoofs clattered again; and the voices, talking so strangely in the empty air, passed on through the forest, where no church had ever been gathered or solitary Christian prayed. Whither, then, could these holy men be journeying so deep into the heathen wilderness? Young Goodman Brown caught hold of a tree for support, being ready to sink down on the ground, faint and overburdened with the heavy sickness of his heart. He looked up to the sky, doubting whether there really was a heaven above him. Yet there was the blue arch, and the stars brightening in it.

"With heaven above and Faith below, I will yet stand firm against the devil!" cried Goodman Brown.

While he still gazed upward into the deep arch of the firmament and had lifted his hands to pray, a cloud, though no wind was stirring, hurried across the zenith and hid the brightening stars. The blue sky was still visible, except directly overhead, where this black mass of cloud was sweeping swiftly northward. Aloft in the air, as if from the depths of the cloud, came a confused and doubtful sound of voices. Once the listener fancied that he could distinguish the accents of towns-people of his own, men and women, both pious and ungodly, many of whom he had met at the communion table, and had seen others rioting at the tavern. The next moment, so indistinct were the sounds, he doubted whether he had heard aught but the murmur of the old forest, whispering without a wind. Then came a stronger swell of those familiar tones, heard daily in the sunshine at Salem village, but never until now from a cloud of night. There was one voice of a young woman, uttering lamentations, yet with an uncertain sorrow, and entreating for some favor, which, perhaps, it would grieve her to obtain; and all the unseen multitude, both saints and sinners, seemed to encourage her onward.

"Faith!" shouted Goodman Brown, in a voice of agony and desperation; and the echoes of the forest mocked him, crying, "Faith! Faith!" as if bewildered wretches were seeking her all through the wilderness.

The cry of grief, rage, and terror was yet piercing the night, when the unhappy husband held his breath for a response. There was a scream, drowned immediately in a louder murmur of voices, fading into far-off laughter, as the dark cloud swept away, leaving the clear and silent sky above Goodman Brown. But something fluttered lightly down through the air and caught on the branch of a tree. The young man seized it, and beheld a pink ribbon.

"My Faith is gone!" cried he, after one stupefied moment. "There is no good on earth; and sin is but a name. Come, devil; for to thee is this world given."

And, maddened with despair, so that he laughed loud and long, did Goodman Brown grasp his staff and set forth again, at such a rate that he seemed to fly along the forest path rather than to walk or run. The road grew wilder and drearier and more faintly traced, and vanished at length, leaving him in the heart of the dark wilderness, still rushing onward with the instinct that guides mortal man to evil. The whole forest was peopled with frightful sounds—the creaking of the trees, the howling of wild beasts, and the yell of Indians; while sometimes the wind tolled like a distant church bell, and sometimes gave a broad roar around the traveller, as if all Nature were laughing him to scorn. But he was himself the chief horror of the scene, and shrank not from its other horrors.

"Ha! ha! ha!" roared Goodman Brown when the wind laughed at him. "Let us hear which will laugh loudest. Think not to frighten me with your deviltry. Come witch, come wizard, come Indian powwow, come devil himself, and here comes Goodman Brown. You may as well fear him as he fear you."

In truth, all through the haunted forest there could be nothing more frightful than the figure of Goodman Brown. On he flew among the black pines, brandishing his staff with frenzied gestures, now giving vent to an inspiration of horrid blasphemy, and now shouting forth such laughter as set all the echoes of the forest laughing like demons around him. The fiend in his own shape is less hideous than when he rages in the breast of man. Thus sped the demoniac on his course, until, quivering among the trees, he saw a red light before him, as when the felled trunks and branches of a clearing have been set on fire, and throw up their lurid blaze against the sky, at the hour of midnight. He paused, in a lull of the tempest that had driven him onward, and heard the swell of what seemed a hymn, rolling solemnly from a distance with the weight of many voices. He knew the tune; it was a familiar one in the choir of the village meeting-house. The verse died heavily away, and was lengthened by a chorus, not of human voices, but of all the sounds of the benighted wilderness pealing in awful harmony together. Goodman Brown cried out, and his cry was lost to his own ear by its unison with the cry of the desert.

In the interval of silence he stole forward until the light glared full upon his eyes. At one extremity of an open space, hemmed in by the dark wall of the forest, arose a rock, bearing some rude, natural resemblance either to an alter or a pulpit, and surrounded by four blazing pines, their tops aflame, their stems untouched, like candles at an evening meeting. The mass of foliage that had overgrown the summit of the rock was all on fire, blazing high into the night and fitfully illuminating the whole field. Each pendent twig and leafy festoon was in a blaze. As the red light arose and fell, a numerous congregation alternately shone forth, then disappeared in shadow, and again grew, as it were, out of the darkness, peopling the heart of the solitary woods at once.

"A grave and dark-clad company," quoth Goodman Brown.

In truth they were such. Among them, quivering to and fro between gloom and splendor, appeared faces that would be seen next day at the council board of the province, and others which, Sabbath after Sabbath, looked devoutly heavenward, and benignantly over the crowded pews, from the holiest pulpits in the land. Some affirm that the lady of the governor was there. At least there were high dames well known to her, and wives of honored husbands, and widows, a great multitude, and ancient maidens, all of excellent repute, and fair young girls, who trembled lest their mothers should espy them. Either the sudden gleams of light flashing over the obscure field bedazzled Goodman Brown, or he recognized a score of the church members of Salem village famous for their especial sanctity. Good old Deacon Gookin had arrived, and waited at the skirts of that venerable saint, his revered pastor. But, irreverently consorting with these grave, reputable, and pious people, these elders of the church, these chaste dames and dewy virgins, there were men of dissolute lives and women of spotted fame, wretches given over to all mean and filthy vice, and suspected even of horrid crimes. It was strange to see that the good shrank not from the wicked, nor were the sinners abashed by the saints. Scattered also among their pale-faced enemies were the Indian priests, or powwows, who had often scared their native forest with more hideous incantations than any known to English witchcraft.

"But where is Faith?" thought Goodman Brown; and, as hope came into his heart, he trembled.

Another verse of the hymn arose, a slow and mournful strain, such as the pious love, but joined to words which expressed all that our nature can conceive of sin, and darkly hinted at far more. Unfathomable to mere mortals is the lore of fiends. Verse after verse was sung; and still the chorus of the desert swelled between like the deepest tone of a mighty organ; and with the final peal of that dreadful anthem there came a sound, as if the roaring wind, the rushing streams, the howling beasts, and every other voice of the unconcerted wilderness were mingling and according with the voice of guilty man in homage to the prince of all. The four blazing pines threw up a loftier flame, and obscurely discovered shapes and visages of horror on the smoke wreaths above the impious assembly. At the same moment the fire on the rock shot redly forth and formed a glowing arch above its base, where now appeared a figure. With reverence be it spoken, the figure bore no slight similitude, both in garb and manner, to some grave divine of the New England churches.

"Bring forth the converts!" cried a voice that echoed through the field and rolled into the forest.

At the word, Goodman Brown stepped forth from the shadow of the trees and approached the congregation, with whom he felt a loathful brotherhood by the sympathy of all that was wicked in his heart. He could have well-nigh sworn that the shape of his own dead father beckoned him to advance, looking downward from a smoke wreath, while a woman, with dim features of despair, threw out her hand to warn him back. Was it his mother? But he had no power to retreat one step, nor to resist, even in thought, when the minister and good old Deacon Gookin seized his arms and led him to the blazing rock. Thither came also the slender form of a veiled female, led between Goody Cloyse, that pious teacher of the catechism, and Martha Carrier, who had received the devil's promise to be queen of hell. A rampant hag was she. And there stood the proselytes beneath the canopy of fire.

"Welcome, my children," said the dark figure, "to the communion of your race. Ye have found thus young your nature and your destiny. My children, look behind you!"

They turned; and flashing forth, as it were, in a sheet of flame, the fiend worshippers were seen; the smile of welcome gleamed darkly on every visage.

"There," resumed the sable form, "are all whom ye have reverenced from youth. Ye deemed them holier than yourselves, and shrank from your own sin, contrasting it with their lives of righteousness and prayerful aspirations heavenward. Yet here are they all in my worshipping assembly. This night it shall be granted you to know their secret deeds: how hoary-bearded elders of the church have whispered wanton words to the young maids of their households; how many a woman, eager for widows' weeds, has given her husband a drink at bedtime and let him sleep his last sleep in her bosom; how beardless youths have made haste to inherit their fathers' wealth; and how fair damsels—blush not, sweet ones—have dug little graves in the garden, and bidden me, the sole guest to an infant's funeral. By the sympathy of your human hearts for sin ye shall scent out all the places—whether in church, bedchamber, street, field, or forest—where crime has been committed, and shall exult to behold the whole earth one stain of guilt, one mighty blood spot. Far more than this. It shall be yours to penetrate, in every bosom, the deep mystery of sin, the fountain of all wicked arts, and which inexhaustibly supplies more evil impulses than human power—than my power at its utmost—can make manifest in deeds. And now, my children, look upon each other."

They did so; and, by the blaze of the hell-kindled torches, the wretched man beheld his Faith, and the wife her husband, trembling before that unhallowed altar.

"Lo, there ye stand, my children," said the figure, in a deep and solemn tone, almost sad with its despairing awfulness, as if his once angelic nature could yet mourn for our miserable race. "Depending upon one another's hearts, ye had still hoped that virtue were not all a dream. Now are ye undeceived. Evil is the nature of mankind. Evil must be your only happiness. Welcome again, my children, to the communion of your race."

"Welcome," repeated the fiend worshippers, in one cry of despair and triumph.

And there they stood, the only pair, as it seemed, who were yet hesitating on the verge of wickedness in this dark world. A basin was hollowed, naturally, in the rock. Did it contain water, reddened by the lurid light? or was it blood? or, perchance, a liquid flame? Herein did the shape of evil dip his hand and prepare to lay the mark of baptism upon their foreheads, that they might be partakers of the mystery of sin, more conscious of the secret guilt of others, both in deed and thought, than they could now be of their own. The husband cast one look at his pale wife, and Faith at him. What polluted wretches would the next glance show them to each other, shuddering alike at what they disclosed and what they saw!

"Faith! Faith!" cried the husband, "look up to heaven, and resist the wicked one."

Whether Faith obeyed he knew not. Hardly had he spoken when he found himself amid calm night and solitude, listening to a roar of the wind which died heavily away through the forest. He staggered against the rock, and felt it chill and damp; while a hanging twig, that had been all on fire, besprinkled his cheek with the coldest dew.

The next morning young Goodman Brown came slowly into the street of Salem village, staring around him like a bewildered man. The good old minister was taking a walk along the graveyard to get an appetite for breakfast and meditate his sermon, and bestowed a blessing, as he passed, on Goodman Brown. He shrank from the venerable saint as if to avoid an anathema. Old Deacon Gookin was at domestic worship, and the holy words of his prayer were heard through the open window. "What God doth the wizard pray to?" quoth Goodman Brown. Goody Cloyse, that excellent old Christian, stood in the early sunshine at her own lattice, catechizing a little girl who had brought her a pint of morning's milk. Goodman Brown snatched away the child as from the grasp of the fiend himself. Turning the corner by the meeting-house, he spied the head of Faith, with the pink ribbons, gazing anxiously forth, and bursting into such joy at sight of him that she skipped along the street and almost kissed her husband before the whole village. But Goodman Brown looked sternly and sadly into her face, and passed on without a greeting.

Had Goodman Brown fallen asleep in the forest and only dreamed a wild dream of a witch-meeting?

Be it so if you will; but, alas! it was a dream of evil omen for young Goodman Brown. A stern, a sad, a darkly meditative, a distrustful, if not a desperate man did he become from the night of that fearful dream. On the Sabbath day, when the congregation were singing a holy psalm, he could not listen because an anthem of sin rushed loudly upon his ear and drowned all the blessed strain. When the minister spoke from the pulpit with power and fervid eloquence, and, with his hand on the open Bible, of the sacred truths of our religion, and of saint-like lives and triumphant deaths, and of future bliss or misery unutterable, then did Goodman Brown turn pale, dreading lest the roof should thunder down upon the gray blasphemer and his hearers. Often, waking suddenly at midnight, he shrank from the bosom of Faith; and at morning or eventide, when the family knelt down at prayer, he scowled and muttered to himself, and gazed sternly at his wife, and turned away. And when he had lived long, and was borne to his grave a hoary corpse, followed by Faith, an aged woman, and children and grandchildren, a goodly procession, besides neighbors not a few, they carved no hopeful verse upon his tombstone, for his dying hour was gloom.

Drama

WILLIAM SHAKESPEARE

Born in Stratford-on-Avon in 1564, William Shakespeare was an English dramatist and poet. He is widely regarded as the greatest playwright who ever lived.

The Tempest

ACT I

SCENE I.

On a ship at sea: a tempestuous noise

of thunder and lightning heard.

Enter a Master and a Boatswain

MASTER Boatswain!
BOATSWAIN Here, master: what cheer?
MASTER Good, speak to the mariners: fall to't, yarely,
or we run ourselves aground: bestir, bestir.

Exit

Enter Mariners

BOATSWAIN Heigh, my hearts! cheerly, cheerly, my hearts!
yare, yare! Take in the topsail. Tend to the
master's whistle. Blow, till thou burst thy wind,
if room enough!

Enter ALONSO, SEBASTIAN, ANTONIO, FERDINAND, GONZALO, and others

ALONSO Good boatswain, have care. Where's the master?
Play the men.
BOATSWAIN I pray now, keep below.

ANTONIO Where is the master, boatswain?

BOATSWAIN Do you not hear him? You mar our labour: keep your
cabins: you do assist the storm.

GONZALO Nay, good, be patient.

BOATSWAIN When the sea is. Hence! What cares these roarers
for the name of king? To cabin: silence! trouble us not.

GONZALO Good, yet remember whom thou hast aboard.

BOATSWAIN None that I more love than myself. You are a
counsellor; if you can command these elements to
silence, and work the peace of the present, we will
not hand a rope more; use your authority: if you
cannot, give thanks you have lived so long, and make
yourself ready in your cabin for the mischance of
the hour, if it so hap. Cheerly, good hearts! Out
of our way, I say.

Exit

GONZALO I have great comfort from this fellow: methinks he
hath no drowning mark upon him; his complexion is
perfect gallows. Stand fast, good Fate, to his
hanging: make the rope of his destiny our cable,
for our own doth little advantage. If he be not
born to be hanged, our case is miserable.

Exeunt

Re-enter Boatswain

BOATSWAIN Down with the topmast! yare! lower, lower! Bring
her to try with main-course.

A cry within

A plague upon this howling! they are louder than
the weather or our office.

Re-enter SEBASTIAN, ANTONIO, and GONZALO

Yet again! what do you here? Shall we give o'er
and drown? Have you a mind to sink?

SEBASTIAN A pox o' your throat, you bawling, blasphemous,
incharitable dog!

BOATSWAIN Work you then.

ANTONIO Hang, cur! hang, you whoreson, insolent noisemaker!
We are less afraid to be drowned than thou art.

GONZALO I'll warrant him for drowning; though the ship were

no stronger than a nutshell and as leaky as an
unstanched wench.

BOATSWAIN Lay her a-hold, a-hold! set her two courses off to
sea again; lay her off.

Enter Mariners wet

MARINERS All lost! to prayers, to prayers! all lost!

BOATSWAIN What, must our mouths be cold?

GONZALO The king and prince at prayers! let's assist them,
For our case is as theirs.

SEBASTIAN I'm out of patience.

ANTONIO We are merely cheated of our lives by drunkards:
This wide-chapp'd rascal—would thou mightst lie drowning
The washing of ten tides!

GONZALO He'll be hang'd yet,
Though every drop of water swear against it
And gape at widest to glut him.

A confused noise within: 'Mercy on us!'—'We split, we split!'—'Farewell, my wife and children!'—'Farewell, brother!'—'We split, we split, we split!'

ANTONIO Let's all sink with the king.

SEBASTIAN Let's take leave of him.

Exeunt ANTONIO and SEBASTIAN

GONZALO Now would I give a thousand furlongs of sea for an
acre of barren ground, long heath, brown furze, any
thing. The wills above be done! but I would fain
die a dry death.

Exeunt

SCENE II.

The island. Before PROSPERO'S cell.

Enter PROSPERO and MIRANDA

MIRANDA If by your art, my dearest father, you have
Put the wild waters in this roar, allay them.
The sky, it seems, would pour down stinking pitch,
But that the sea, mounting to the welkin's cheek,
Dashes the fire out. O, I have suffered
With those that I saw suffer: a brave vessel,
Who had, no doubt, some noble creature in her,

Dash'd all to pieces. O, the cry did knock
Against my very heart. Poor souls, they perish'd.
Had I been any god of power, I would
Have sunk the sea within the earth or ere
It should the good ship so have swallow'd and
The fraughting souls within her.

PROSPERO Be collected:
No more amazement: tell your piteous heart
There's no harm done.

MIRANDA O, woe the day!

PROSPERO No harm.
I have done nothing but in care of thee,
Of thee, my dear one, thee, my daughter, who
Art ignorant of what thou art, nought knowing
Of whence I am, nor that I am more better
Than Prospero, master of a full poor cell,
And thy no greater father.

MIRANDA More to know
Did never meddle with my thoughts.

PROSPERO 'Tis time
I should inform thee farther. Lend thy hand,
And pluck my magic garment from me. So:

Lays down his mantle

Lie there, my art. Wipe thou thine eyes; have comfort.
The direful spectacle of the wreck, which touch'd
The very virtue of compassion in thee,
I have with such provision in mine art
So safely ordered that there is no soul—
No, not so much perdition as an hair
Betid to any creature in the vessel
Which thou heard'st cry, which thou saw'st sink. Sit down;
For thou must now know farther.

MIRANDA You have often
Begun to tell me what I am, but stopp'd
And left me to a bootless inquisition,
Concluding 'Stay: not yet.'

PROSPERO The hour's now come;
The very minute bids thee ope thine ear;
Obey and be attentive. Canst thou remember
A time before we came unto this cell?
I do not think thou canst, for then thou wast not

Out three years old.

MIRANDA Certainly, sir, I can.

PROSPERO By what? by any other house or person?
Of any thing the image tell me that
Hath kept with thy remembrance.

MIRANDA 'Tis far off
And rather like a dream than an assurance
That my remembrance warrants. Had I not
Four or five women once that tended me?

PROSPERO Thou hadst, and more, Miranda. But how is it
That this lives in thy mind? What seest thou else
In the dark backward and abysm of time?
If thou remember'st aught ere thou camest here,
How thou camest here thou mayst.

MIRANDA But that I do not.

PROSPERO Twelve year since, Miranda, twelve year since,
Thy father was the Duke of Milan and
A prince of power.

MIRANDA Sir, are not you my father?

PROSPERO Thy mother was a piece of virtue, and
She said thou wast my daughter; and thy father
Was Duke of Milan; and thou his only heir
And princess no worse issued.

MIRANDA O the heavens!
What foul play had we, that we came from thence?
Or blessed was't we did?

PROSPERO Both, both, my girl:
By foul play, as thou say'st, were we heaved thence,
But blessedly holp hither.

MIRANDA O, my heart bleeds
To think o' the teen that I have turn'd you to,
Which is from my remembrance! Please you, father.

PROSPERO My brother and thy uncle, call'd Antonio—
I pray thee, mark me—that a brother should
Be so perfidious!—he whom next thyself
Of all the world I loved and to him put
The manage of my state; as at that time
Through all the signories it was the first
And Prospero the prime duke, being so reputed
In dignity, and for the liberal arts
Without a parallel; those being all my study,
The government I cast upon my brother

And to my state grew stranger, being transported
And rapt in secret studies. Thy false uncle—
Dost thou attend me?

MIRANDA Sir, most heedfully.

PROSPERO Being once perfected how to grant suits,
How to deny them, who to advance and who
To trash for over-topping, new created
The creatures that were mine, I say, or changed 'em,
Or else new form'd 'em; having both the key
Of officer and office, set all hearts i' the state
To what tune pleased his ear; that now he was
The ivy which had hid my princely trunk,
And suck'd my verdure out on't. Thou attend'st not.

MIRANDA O, good sir, I do.

PROSPERO I pray thee, mark me.
I, thus neglecting worldly ends, all dedicated
To closeness and the bettering of my mind
With that which, but by being so retired,
O'er-prized all popular rate, in my false brother
Awaked an evil nature; and my trust,
Like a good parent, did beget of him
A falsehood in its contrary as great
As my trust was; which had indeed no limit,
A confidence sans bound. He being thus lorded,
Not only with what my revenue yielded,
But what my power might else exact, like one
Who having into truth, by telling of it,
Made such a sinner of his memory,
To credit his own lie, he did believe
He was indeed the duke; out o' the substitution
And executing the outward face of royalty,
With all prerogative: hence his ambition growing—
Dost thou hear?

MIRANDA Your tale, sir, would cure deafness.

PROSPERO To have no screen between this part he play'd
And him he play'd it for, he needs will be
Absolute Milan. Me, poor man, my library
Was dukedom large enough: of temporal royalties
He thinks me now incapable; confederates—
So dry he was for sway—wi' the King of Naples
To give him annual tribute, do him homage,
Subject his coronet to his crown and bend
The dukedom yet unbow'd—alas, poor Milan!—

To most ignoble stooping.

MIRANDA O the heavens!

PROSPERO Mark his condition and the event; then tell me
If this might be a brother.

MIRANDA I should sin
To think but nobly of my grandmother:
Good wombs have borne bad sons.

PROSPERO Now the condition.
The King of Naples, being an enemy
To me inveterate, hearkens my brother's suit;
Which was, that he, in lieu o' the premises
Of homage and I know not how much tribute,
Should presently extirpate me and mine
Out of the dukedom and confer fair Milan
With all the honours on my brother: whereon,
A treacherous army levied, one midnight
Fated to the purpose did Antonio open
The gates of Milan, and, i' the dead of darkness,
The ministers for the purpose hurried thence
Me and thy crying self.

MIRANDA Alack, for pity!
I, not remembering how I cried out then,
Will cry it o'er again: it is a hint
That wrings mine eyes to't.

PROSPERO Hear a little further
And then I'll bring thee to the present business
Which now's upon's; without the which this story
Were most impertinent.

MIRANDA Wherefore did they not
That hour destroy us?

PROSPERO Well demanded, wench:
My tale provokes that question. Dear, they durst not,
So dear the love my people bore me, nor set
A mark so bloody on the business, but
With colours fairer painted their foul ends.
In few, they hurried us aboard a bark,
Bore us some leagues to sea; where they prepared
A rotten carcass of a boat, not rigg'd,
Nor tackle, sail, nor mast; the very rats
Instinctively had quit it: there they hoist us,
To cry to the sea that roar'd to us, to sigh
To the winds whose pity, sighing back again,
Did us but loving wrong.

MIRANDA Alack, what trouble
Was I then to you!

PROSPERO O, a cherubim
Thou wast that did preserve me. Thou didst smile.
Infused with a fortitude from heaven,
When I have deck'd the sea with drops full salt,
Under my burthen groan'd; which raised in me
An undergoing stomach, to bear up
Against what should ensue.

MIRANDA How came we ashore?

PROSPERO By Providence divine.
Some food we had and some fresh water that
A noble Neapolitan, Gonzalo,
Out of his charity, being then appointed
Master of this design, did give us, with
Rich garments, linens, stuffs and necessaries,
Which since have steaded much; so, of his gentleness,
Knowing I loved my books, he furnish'd me
From mine own library with volumes that
I prize above my dukedom.

MIRANDA Would I might
But ever see that man!

PROSPERO Now I arise:

Resumes his mantle

Sit still, and hear the last of our sea-sorrow.
Here in this island we arrived; and here
Have I, thy schoolmaster, made thee more profit
Than other princesses can that have more time
For vainer hours and tutors not so careful.

MIRANDA Heavens thank you for't! And now, I pray you, sir,
For still 'tis beating in my mind, your reason
For raising this sea-storm?

PROSPERO Know thus far forth.
By accident most strange, bountiful Fortune,
Now my dear lady, hath mine enemies
Brought to this shore; and by my prescience
I find my zenith doth depend upon
A most auspicious star, whose influence
If now I court not but omit, my fortunes
Will ever after droop. Here cease more questions:
Thou art inclined to sleep; 'tis a good dulness,
And give it way: I know thou canst not choose.

MIRANDA sleeps

Come away, servant, come. I am ready now.
Approach, my Ariel, come.

Enter ARIEL

ARIEL All hail, great master! grave sir, hail! I come
To answer thy best pleasure; be't to fly,
To swim, to dive into the fire, to ride
On the curl'd clouds, to thy strong bidding task
Ariel and all his quality.

PROSPERO Hast thou, spirit,
Perform'd to point the tempest that I bade thee?

ARIEL To every article.
I boarded the king's ship; now on the beak,
Now in the waist, the deck, in every cabin,
I flamed amazement: sometime I'ld divide,
And burn in many places; on the topmast,
The yards and bowsprit, would I flame distinctly,
Then meet and join. Jove's lightnings, the precursors
O' the dreadful thunder-claps, more momentary
And sight-outrunning were not; the fire and cracks
Of sulphurous roaring the most mighty Neptune
Seem to besiege and make his bold waves tremble,
Yea, his dread trident shake.

PROSPERO My brave spirit!
Who was so firm, so constant, that this coil
Would not infect his reason?

ARIEL Not a soul
But felt a fever of the mad and play'd
Some tricks of desperation. All but mariners
Plunged in the foaming brine and quit the vessel,
Then all afire with me: the king's son, Ferdinand,
With hair up-staring,—then like reeds, not hair,—
Was the first man that leap'd; cried, 'Hell is empty
And all the devils are here.'

PROSPERO Why that's my spirit!
But was not this nigh shore?

ARIEL Close by, my master.

PROSPERO But are they, Ariel, safe?

ARIEL Not a hair perish'd;
On their sustaining garments not a blemish,
But fresher than before: and, as thou badest me,

In troops I have dispersed them 'bout the isle.
The king's son have I landed by himself;
Whom I left cooling of the air with sighs
In an odd angle of the isle and sitting,
His arms in this sad knot.

PROSPERO Of the king's ship
The mariners say how thou hast disposed
And all the rest o' the fleet.

ARIEL Safely in harbour
Is the king's ship; in the deep nook, where once
Thou call'dst me up at midnight to fetch dew
From the still-vex'd Bermoothes, there she's hid:
The mariners all under hatches stow'd;
Who, with a charm join'd to their suffer'd labour,
I have left asleep; and for the rest o' the fleet
Which I dispersed, they all have met again
And are upon the Mediterranean flote,
Bound sadly home for Naples,
Supposing that they saw the king's ship wreck'd
And his great person perish.

PROSPERO Ariel, thy charge
Exactly is perform'd: but there's more work.
What is the time o' the day?

ARIEL Past the mid season.

PROSPERO At least two glasses. The time 'twixt six and now
Must by us both be spent most preciously.

ARIEL Is there more toil? Since thou dost give me pains,
Let me remember thee what thou hast promised,
Which is not yet perform'd me.

PROSPERO How now? moody?
What is't thou canst demand?

ARIEL My liberty.

PROSPERO Before the time be out? no more!

ARIEL I prithee,
Remember I have done thee worthy service;
Told thee no lies, made thee no mistakings, served
Without or grudge or grumblings: thou didst promise
To bate me a full year.

PROSPERO Dost thou forget
From what a torment I did free thee?

ARIEL No.

PROSPERO Thou dost, and think'st it much to tread the ooze

Of the salt deep,
To run upon the sharp wind of the north,
To do me business in the veins o' the earth
When it is baked with frost.

ARIEL I do not, sir.

PROSPERO Thou liest, malignant thing! Hast thou forgot
The foul witch Sycorax, who with age and envy
Was grown into a hoop? hast thou forgot her?

ARIEL No, sir.

PROSPERO Thou hast. Where was she born? speak; tell me.

ARIEL Sir, in Argier.

PROSPERO O, was she so? I must
Once in a month recount what thou hast been,
Which thou forget'st. This damn'd witch Sycorax,
For mischiefs manifold and sorceries terrible
To enter human hearing, from Argier,
Thou know'st, was banish'd: for one thing she did
They would not take her life. Is not this true?

ARIEL Ay, sir.

PROSPERO This blue-eyed hag was hither brought with child
And here was left by the sailors. Thou, my slave,
As thou report'st thyself, wast then her servant;
And, for thou wast a spirit too delicate
To act her earthy and abhorr'd commands,
Refusing her grand hests, she did confine thee,
By help of her more potent ministers
And in her most unmitigable rage,
Into a cloven pine; within which rift
Imprison'd thou didst painfully remain
A dozen years; within which space she died
And left thee there; where thou didst vent thy groans
As fast as mill-wheels strike. Then was this island—
Save for the son that she did litter here,
A freckled whelp hag-born—not honour'd with
A human shape.

ARIEL Yes, Caliban her son.

PROSPERO Dull thing, I say so; he, that Caliban
Whom now I keep in service. Thou best know'st
What torment I did find thee in; thy groans
Did make wolves howl and penetrate the breasts
Of ever angry bears: it was a torment
To lay upon the damn'd, which Sycorax

Could not again undo: it was mine art,
When I arrived and heard thee, that made gape
The pine and let thee out.

ARIEL I thank thee, master.

PROSPERO If thou more murmur'st, I will rend an oak
And peg thee in his knotty entrails till
Thou hast howl'd away twelve winters.

ARIEL Pardon, master;
I will be correspondent to command
And do my spiriting gently.

PROSPERO Do so, and after two days
I will discharge thee.

ARIEL That's my noble master!
What shall I do? say what; what shall I do?

PROSPERO Go make thyself like a nymph o' the sea: be subject
To no sight but thine and mine, invisible
To every eyeball else. Go take this shape
And hither come in't: go, hence with diligence!

Exit ARIEL

Awake, dear heart, awake! thou hast slept well; Awake!

MIRANDA The strangeness of your story put
Heaviness in me.

PROSPERO Shake it off. Come on;
We'll visit Caliban my slave, who never
Yields us kind answer.

MIRANDA 'Tis a villain, sir,
I do not love to look on.

PROSPERO But, as 'tis,
We cannot miss him: he does make our fire,
Fetch in our wood and serves in offices
That profit us. What, ho! slave! Caliban!
Thou earth, thou! speak.

CALIBAN [*Within*] There's wood enough within.

PROSPERO Come forth, I say! there's other business for thee:
Come, thou tortoise! when?

Re-enter ARIEL like a water-nymph

Fine apparition! My quaint Ariel,
Hark in thine ear.

ARIEL My lord it shall be done.

Exit

PROSPERO Thou poisonous slave, got by the devil himself
Upon thy wicked dam, come forth!

Enter CALIBAN

CALIBAN As wicked dew as e'er my mother brush'd
With raven's feather from unwholesome fen
Drop on you both! a south-west blow on ye
And blister you all o'er!

PROSPERO For this, be sure, to-night thou shalt have cramps,
Side-stitches that shall pen thy breath up; urchins
Shall, for that vast of night that they may work,
All exercise on thee; thou shalt be pinch'd
As thick as honeycomb, each pinch more stinging
Than bees that made 'em.

CALIBAN I must eat my dinner.
This island's mine, by Sycorax my mother,
Which thou takest from me. When thou camest first,
Thou strokedst me and madest much of me, wouldst give me
Water with berries in't, and teach me how
To name the bigger light, and how the less,
That burn by day and night: and then I loved thee
And show'd thee all the qualities o' the isle,
The fresh springs, brine-pits, barren place and fertile:
Cursed be I that did so! All the charms
Of Sycorax, toads, beetles, bats, light on you!
For I am all the subjects that you have,
Which first was mine own king: and here you sty me
In this hard rock, whiles you do keep from me
The rest o' the island.

PROSPERO Thou most lying slave,
Whom stripes may move, not kindness! I have used thee,
Filth as thou art, with human care, and lodged thee
In mine own cell, till thou didst seek to violate
The honour of my child.

CALIBAN O ho, O ho! would't had been done!
Thou didst prevent me; I had peopled else
This isle with Calibans.

PROSPERO Abhorred slave,
Which any print of goodness wilt not take,
Being capable of all ill! I pitied thee,
Took pains to make thee speak, taught thee each hour

One thing or other: when thou didst not, savage,
Know thine own meaning, but wouldst gabble like
A thing most brutish, I endow'd thy purposes
With words that made them known. But thy vile race,
Though thou didst learn, had that in't which good natures
Could not abide to be with; therefore wast thou
Deservedly confined into this rock,
Who hadst deserved more than a prison.

CALIBAN You taught me language; and my profit on't
Is, I know how to curse. The red plague rid you
For learning me your language!

PROSPERO Hag-seed, hence!
Fetch us in fuel; and be quick, thou'rt best,
To answer other business. Shrug'st thou, malice?
If thou neglect'st or dost unwillingly
What I command, I'll rack thee with old cramps,
Fill all thy bones with aches, make thee roar
That beasts shall tremble at thy din.

CALIBAN No, pray thee.

Aside

I must obey: his art is of such power,
It would control my dam's god, Setebos,
and make a vassal of him.

PROSPERO So, slave; hence!

Exit CALIBAN

Re-enter ARIEL, invisible, playing and singing; FERDINAND following

ARIEL'S song.
Come unto these yellow sands,
And then take hands:
Courtsied when you have and kiss'd
The wild waves whist,
Foot it featly here and there;
And, sweet sprites, the burthen bear.
Hark, hark!

Burthen [dispersedly, within]

The watch-dogs bark!

Burthen Bow-wow

Hark, hark! I hear
The strain of strutting chanticleer

Cry, Cock-a-diddle-dow.

FERDINAND Where should this music be? i' the air or the earth?
It sounds no more: and sure, it waits upon
Some god o' the island. Sitting on a bank,
Weeping again the king my father's wreck,
This music crept by me upon the waters,
Allaying both their fury and my passion
With its sweet air: thence I have follow'd it,
Or it hath drawn me rather. But 'tis gone.
No, it begins again.

ARIEL sings

Full fathom five thy father lies;
Of his bones are coral made;
Those are pearls that were his eyes:
Nothing of him that doth fade
But doth suffer a sea-change
Into something rich and strange.
Sea-nymphs hourly ring his knell

Burthen Ding-dong

Hark! now I hear them,—Ding-dong, bell.

FERDINAND The ditty does remember my drown'd father.
This is no mortal business, nor no sound
That the earth owes. I hear it now above me.

PROSPERO The fringed curtains of thine eye advance
And say what thou seest yond.

MIRANDA What is't? a spirit?
Lord, how it looks about! Believe me, sir,
It carries a brave form. But 'tis a spirit.

PROSPERO No, wench; it eats and sleeps and hath such senses
As we have, such. This gallant which thou seest
Was in the wreck; and, but he's something stain'd
With grief that's beauty's canker, thou mightst call him
A goodly person: he hath lost his fellows
And strays about to find 'em.

MIRANDA I might call him
A thing divine, for nothing natural
I ever saw so noble.

PROSPERO [*Aside*]
It goes on, I see,
As my soul prompts it. Spirit, fine spirit! I'll free thee
Within two days for this.

FERDINAND Most sure, the goddess
On whom these airs attend! Vouchsafe my prayer
May know if you remain upon this island;
And that you will some good instruction give
How I may bear me here: my prime request,
Which I do last pronounce, is, O you wonder!
If you be maid or no?

MIRANDA No wonder, sir;
But certainly a maid.

FERDINAND My language! heavens!
I am the best of them that speak this speech,
Were I but where 'tis spoken.

PROSPERO How? the best?
What wert thou, if the King of Naples heard thee?

FERDINAND A single thing, as I am now, that wonders
To hear thee speak of Naples. He does hear me;
And that he does I weep: myself am Naples,
Who with mine eyes, never since at ebb, beheld
The king my father wreck'd.

MIRANDA Alack, for mercy!

FERDINAND Yes, faith, and all his lords; the Duke of Milan
And his brave son being twain.

PROSPERO [*Aside*]
The Duke of Milan
And his more braver daughter could control thee,
If now 'twere fit to do't. At the first sight
They have changed eyes. Delicate Ariel,
I'll set thee free for this.

To FERDINAND

A word, good sir;
I fear you have done yourself some wrong: a word.

MIRANDA Why speaks my father so ungently? This
Is the third man that e'er I saw, the first
That e'er I sigh'd for: pity move my father
To be inclined my way!

FERDINAND O, if a virgin,
And your affection not gone forth, I'll make you
The queen of Naples.

PROSPERO Soft, sir! one word more.

Aside

They are both in either's powers; but this swift business

I must uneasy make, lest too light winning
Make the prize light.

To FERDINAND

One word more; I charge thee
That thou attend me: thou dost here usurp
The name thou owest not; and hast put thyself
Upon this island as a spy, to win it
From me, the lord on't.

FERDINAND No, as I am a man.

MIRANDA There's nothing ill can dwell in such a temple:
If the ill spirit have so fair a house,
Good things will strive to dwell with't.

PROSPERO Follow me.
Speak not you for him; he's a traitor. Come;
I'll manacle thy neck and feet together:
Sea-water shalt thou drink; thy food shall be
The fresh-brook muscles, wither'd roots and husks
Wherein the acorn cradled. Follow.

FERDINAND No;
I will resist such entertainment till
Mine enemy has more power.

Draws, and is charmed from moving

MIRANDA O dear father,
Make not too rash a trial of him, for
He's gentle and not fearful.

PROSPERO What? I say,
My foot my tutor? Put thy sword up, traitor;
Who makest a show but darest not strike, thy conscience
Is so possess'd with guilt: come from thy ward,
For I can here disarm thee with this stick
And make thy weapon drop.

MIRANDA Beseech you, father.

PROSPERO Hence! hang not on my garments.

MIRANDA Sir, have pity;
I'll be his surety.

PROSPERO Silence! one word more
Shall make me chide thee, if not hate thee. What!
An advocate for an imposter! hush!

Thou think'st there is no more such shapes as he,
Having seen but him and Caliban: foolish wench!
To the most of men this is a Caliban
And they to him are angels.

MIRANDA My affections
Are then most humble; I have no ambition
To see a goodlier man.

PROSPERO Come on; obey:
Thy nerves are in their infancy again
And have no vigour in them.

FERDINAND So they are;
My spirits, as in a dream, are all bound up.
My father's loss, the weakness which I feel,
The wreck of all my friends, nor this man's threats,
To whom I am subdued, are but light to me,
Might I but through my prison once a day
Behold this maid: all corners else o' the earth
Let liberty make use of; space enough
Have I in such a prison.

PROSPERO [*Aside*]
It works.

To FERDINAND

Come on.
Thou hast done well, fine Ariel!

To FERDINAND

Follow me.

To ARIEL

Hark what thou else shalt do me.

MIRANDA Be of comfort;
My father's of a better nature, sir,
Than he appears by speech: this is unwonted
Which now came from him.

PROSPERO Thou shalt be free
As mountain winds: but then exactly do
All points of my command.

ARIEL To the syllable.

PROSPERO Come, follow. Speak not for him.

Exeunt

ACT II

Scene I.

Another part of the island.

Enter ALONSO, SEBASTIAN, ANTONIO, GONZALO, ADRIAN, FRANCISCO, and others

GONZALO Beseech you, sir, be merry; you have cause,
So have we all, of joy; for our escape
Is much beyond our loss. Our hint of woe
Is common; every day some sailor's wife,
The masters of some merchant and the merchant
Have just our theme of woe; but for the miracle,
I mean our preservation, few in millions
Can speak like us: then wisely, good sir, weigh
Our sorrow with our comfort.

ALONSO Prithee, peace.

SEBASTIAN He receives comfort like cold porridge.

ANTONIO The visitor will not give him o'er so.

SEBASTIAN Look he's winding up the watch of his wit;
by and by it will strike.

GONZALO Sir,—

SEBASTIAN One: tell.

GONZALO When every grief is entertain'd that's offer'd,
Comes to the entertainer—

SEBASTIAN A dollar.

GONZALO Dolour comes to him, indeed: you
have spoken truer than you purposed.

SEBASTIAN You have taken it wiselier than I meant you should.

GONZALO Therefore, my lord,—

ANTONIO Fie, what a spendthrift is he of his tongue!

ALONSO I prithee, spare.

GONZALO Well, I have done: but yet,—

SEBASTIAN He will be talking.

ANTONIO Which, of he or Adrian, for a good
wager, first begins to crow?

SEBASTIAN The old cock.

ANTONIO The cockerel.

SEBASTIAN Done. The wager?

ANTONIO A laughter.

SEBASTIAN A match!

ADRIAN Though this island seem to be desert,—

SEBASTIAN Ha, ha, ha! So, you're paid.

ADRIAN Uninhabitable and almost inaccessible,—

SEBASTIAN Yet,—

ADRIAN Yet,—

ANTONIO He could not miss't.

ADRIAN It must needs be of subtle, tender and delicate temperance.

ANTONIO Temperance was a delicate wench.

SEBASTIAN Ay, and a subtle; as he most learnedly delivered.

ADRIAN The air breathes upon us here most sweetly.

SEBASTIAN As if it had lungs and rotten ones.

ANTONIO Or as 'twere perfumed by a fen.

GONZALO Here is everything advantageous to life.

ANTONIO True; save means to live.

SEBASTIAN Of that there's none, or little.

GONZALO How lush and lusty the grass looks! how green!

ANTONIO The ground indeed is tawny.

SEBASTIAN With an eye of green in't.

ANTONIO He misses not much.

SEBASTIAN No; he doth but mistake the truth totally.

GONZALO But the rarity of it is,—which is indeed almost beyond credit,—

SEBASTIAN As many vouched rarities are.

GONZALO That our garments, being, as they were, drenched in the sea, hold notwithstanding their freshness and glosses, being rather new-dyed than stained with salt water.

ANTONIO If but one of his pockets could speak, would it not say he lies?

SEBASTIAN Ay, or very falsely pocket up his report

GONZALO Methinks our garments are now as fresh as when we put them on first in Afric, at the marriage of the king's fair daughter Claribel to the King of Tunis.

SEBASTIAN 'Twas a sweet marriage, and we prosper well in our return.

ADRIAN Tunis was never graced before with such a paragon to their queen.

GONZALO Not since widow Dido's time.

ANTONIO Widow! a pox o' that! How came that widow in?

widow Dido!

SEBASTIAN What if he had said 'widower AEneas' too? Good Lord, how you take it!

ADRIAN 'Widow Dido' said you? you make me study of that: she was of Carthage, not of Tunis.

GONZALO This Tunis, sir, was Carthage.

ADRIAN Carthage?

GONZALO I assure you, Carthage.

SEBASTIAN His word is more than the miraculous harp; he hath raised the wall and houses too.

ANTONIO What impossible matter will he make easy next?

SEBASTIAN I think he will carry this island home in his pocket and give it his son for an apple.

ANTONIO And, sowing the kernels of it in the sea, bring forth more islands.

GONZALO Ay.

ANTONIO Why, in good time.

GONZALO Sir, we were talking that our garments seem now as fresh as when we were at Tunis at the marriage of your daughter, who is now queen.

ANTONIO And the rarest that e'er came there.

SEBASTIAN Bate, I beseech you, widow Dido.

ANTONIO O, widow Dido! ay, widow Dido.

GONZALO Is not, sir, my doublet as fresh as the first day I wore it? I mean, in a sort.

ANTONIO That sort was well fished for.

GONZALO When I wore it at your daughter's marriage?

ALONSO You cram these words into mine ears against
The stomach of my sense. Would I had never
Married my daughter there! for, coming thence,
My son is lost and, in my rate, she too,
Who is so far from Italy removed
I ne'er again shall see her. O thou mine heir
Of Naples and of Milan, what strange fish
Hath made his meal on thee?

FRANCISCO Sir, he may live:
I saw him beat the surges under him,
And ride upon their backs; he trod the water,
Whose enmity he flung aside, and breasted
The surge most swoln that met him; his bold head
'Bove the contentious waves he kept, and oar'd

Himself with his good arms in lusty stroke
To the shore, that o'er his wave-worn basis bow'd,
As stooping to relieve him: I not doubt
He came alive to land.

ALONSO No, no, he's gone.

SEBASTIAN Sir, you may thank yourself for this great loss,
That would not bless our Europe with your daughter,
But rather lose her to an African;
Where she at least is banish'd from your eye,
Who hath cause to wet the grief on't.

ALONSO Prithee, peace.

SEBASTIAN You were kneel'd to and importuned otherwise
By all of us, and the fair soul herself
Weigh'd between loathness and obedience, at
Which end o' the beam should bow. We have lost your
son,
I fear, for ever: Milan and Naples have
More widows in them of this business' making
Than we bring men to comfort them:
The fault's your own.

ALONSO So is the dear'st o' the loss.

GONZALO My lord Sebastian,
The truth you speak doth lack some gentleness
And time to speak it in: you rub the sore,
When you should bring the plaster.

SEBASTIAN Very well.

ANTONIO And most chirurgeonly.

GONZALO It is foul weather in us all, good sir,
When you are cloudy.

SEBASTIAN Foul weather?

ANTONIO Very foul.

GONZALO Had I plantation of this isle, my lord,—

ANTONIO He'ld sow't with nettle-seed.

SEBASTIAN Or docks, or mallows.

GONZALO And were the king on't, what would I do?

SEBASTIAN 'Scape being drunk for want of wine.

GONZALO I' the commonwealth I would by contraries
Execute all things; for no kind of traffic
Would I admit; no name of magistrate;
Letters should not be known; riches, poverty,
And use of service, none; contract, succession,

Bourn, bound of land, tilth, vineyard, none;
No use of metal, corn, or wine, or oil;
No occupation; all men idle, all;
And women too, but innocent and pure;
No sovereignty;—

SEBASTIAN Yet he would be king on't.

ANTONIO The latter end of his commonwealth forgets the beginning.

GONZALO All things in common nature should produce
Without sweat or endeavour: treason, felony,
Sword, pike, knife, gun, or need of any engine,
Would I not have; but nature should bring forth,
Of its own kind, all foison, all abundance,
To feed my innocent people.

SEBASTIAN No marrying 'mong his subjects?

ANTONIO None, man; all idle: whores and knaves.

GONZALO I would with such perfection govern, sir,
To excel the golden age.

SEBASTIAN God save his majesty!

ANTONIO Long live Gonzalo!

GONZALO And,—do you mark me, sir?

ALONSO Prithee, no more: thou dost talk nothing to me.

GONZALO I do well believe your highness; and
did it to minister occasion to these gentlemen,
who are of such sensible and nimble lungs that
they always use to laugh at nothing.

ANTONIO 'Twas you we laughed at.

GONZALO Who in this kind of merry fooling am nothing
to you: so you may continue and laugh at
nothing still.

ANTONIO What a blow was there given!

SEBASTIAN An it had not fallen flat-long.

GONZALO You are gentlemen of brave metal; you would lift
the moon out of her sphere, if she would continue
in it five weeks without changing.

Enter ARIEL, invisible, playing solemn music

SEBASTIAN We would so, and then go a bat-fowling.

ANTONIO Nay, good my lord, be not angry.

GONZALO No, I warrant you; I will not adventure
my discretion so weakly. Will you laugh

me asleep, for I am very heavy?

ANTONIO Go sleep, and hear us.

All sleep except ALONSO, SEBASTIAN, and ANTONIO

ALONSO What, all so soon asleep! I wish mine eyes
Would, with themselves, shut up my thoughts: I find
They are inclined to do so.

SEBASTIAN Please you, sir,
Do not omit the heavy offer of it:
It seldom visits sorrow; when it doth,
It is a comforter.

ANTONIO We two, my lord,
Will guard your person while you take your rest,
And watch your safety.

ALONSO Thank you. Wondrous heavy.

ALONSO sleeps. Exit ARIEL

SEBASTIAN What a strange drowsiness possesses them!

ANTONIO It is the quality o' the climate.

SEBASTIAN Why
Doth it not then our eyelids sink? I find not
Myself disposed to sleep.

ANTONIO Nor I; my spirits are nimble.
They fell together all, as by consent;
They dropp'd, as by a thunder-stroke. What might,
Worthy Sebastian? O, what might?—No more:—
And yet me thinks I see it in thy face,
What thou shouldst be: the occasion speaks thee, and
My strong imagination sees a crown
Dropping upon thy head.

SEBASTIAN What, art thou waking?

ANTONIO Do you not hear me speak?

SEBASTIAN I do; and surely
It is a sleepy language and thou speak'st
Out of thy sleep. What is it thou didst say?
This is a strange repose, to be asleep
With eyes wide open; standing, speaking, moving,
And yet so fast asleep.

ANTONIO Noble Sebastian,
Thou let'st thy fortune sleep—die, rather; wink'st

Whiles thou art waking.

SEBASTIAN Thou dost snore distinctly;
There's meaning in thy snores.

ANTONIO I am more serious than my custom: you
Must be so too, if heed me; which to do
Trebles thee o'er.

SEBASTIAN Well, I am standing water.

ANTONIO I'll teach you how to flow.

SEBASTIAN Do so: to ebb
Hereditary sloth instructs me.

ANTONIO O,
If you but knew how you the purpose cherish
Whiles thus you mock it! how, in stripping it,
You more invest it! Ebbing men, indeed,
Most often do so near the bottom run
By their own fear or sloth.

SEBASTIAN Prithee, say on:
The setting of thine eye and cheek proclaim
A matter from thee, and a birth indeed
Which throes thee much to yield.

ANTONIO Thus, sir:
Although this lord of weak remembrance, this,
Who shall be of as little memory
When he is earth'd, hath here almost persuade,—
For he's a spirit of persuasion, only
Professes to persuade,—the king his son's alive,
'Tis as impossible that he's undrown'd
And he that sleeps here swims.

SEBASTIAN I have no hope
That he's undrown'd.

ANTONIO O, out of that 'no hope'
What great hope have you! no hope that way is
Another way so high a hope that even
Ambition cannot pierce a wink beyond,
But doubt discovery there. Will you grant with me
That Ferdinand is drown'd?

SEBASTIAN He's gone.

ANTONIO Then, tell me,
Who's the next heir of Naples?

SEBASTIAN Claribel.

ANTONIO She that is queen of Tunis; she that dwells
Ten leagues beyond man's life; she that from Naples

Can have no note, unless the sun were post—
The man i' the moon's too slow—till new-born chins
Be rough and razorable; she that—from whom?
We all were sea-swallow'd, though some cast again,
And by that destiny to perform an act
Whereof what's past is prologue, what to come
In yours and my discharge.

SEBASTIAN What stuff is this! how say you?
'Tis true, my brother's daughter's queen of Tunis;
So is she heir of Naples; 'twixt which regions
There is some space.

ANTONIO A space whose every cubit
Seems to cry out, 'How shall that Claribel
Measure us back to Naples? Keep in Tunis,
And let Sebastian wake.' Say, this were death
That now hath seized them; why, they were no worse
Than now they are. There be that can rule Naples
As well as he that sleeps; lords that can prate
As amply and unnecessarily
As this Gonzalo; I myself could make
A chough of as deep chat. O, that you bore
The mind that I do! what a sleep were this
For your advancement! Do you understand me?

SEBASTIAN Methinks I do.

ANTONIO And how does your content
Tender your own good fortune?

SEBASTIAN I remember
You did supplant your brother Prospero.

ANTONIO True:
And look how well my garments sit upon me;
Much feater than before: my brother's servants
Were then my fellows; now they are my men.

SEBASTIAN But, for your conscience?

ANTONIO Ay, sir; where lies that? if 'twere a kibe,
'Twould put me to my slipper: but I feel not
This deity in my bosom: twenty consciences,
That stand 'twixt me and Milan, candied be they
And melt ere they molest! Here lies your brother,
No better than the earth he lies upon,
If he were that which now he's like, that's dead;
Whom I, with this obedient steel, three inches of it,
Can lay to bed for ever; whiles you, doing thus,
To the perpetual wink for aye might put

This ancient morsel, this Sir Prudence, who
Should not upbraid our course. For all the rest,
They'll take suggestion as a cat laps milk;
They'll tell the clock to any business that
We say befits the hour.

SEBASTIAN Thy case, dear friend,
Shall be my precedent; as thou got'st Milan,
I'll come by Naples. Draw thy sword: one stroke
Shall free thee from the tribute which thou payest;
And I the king shall love thee.

ANTONIO Draw together;
And when I rear my hand, do you the like,
To fall it on Gonzalo.

SEBASTIAN O, but one word.

They talk apart

Re-enter ARIEL, invisible

ARIEL My master through his art foresees the danger
That you, his friend, are in; and sends me forth—
For else his project dies—to keep them living.

Sings in GONZALO's ear

While you here do snoring lie,
Open-eyed conspiracy
His time doth take.
If of life you keep a care,
Shake off slumber, and beware:
Awake, awake!

ANTONIO Then let us both be sudden.

GONZALO Now, good angels
Preserve the king.

They wake

ALONSO Why, how now? ho, awake! Why are you drawn?
Wherefore this ghastly looking?

GONZALO What's the matter?

SEBASTIAN Whiles we stood here securing your repose,
Even now, we heard a hollow burst of bellowing
Like bulls, or rather lions: did't not wake you?
It struck mine ear most terribly.

ALONSO I heard nothing.

ANTONIO O, 'twas a din to fright a monster's ear,

To make an earthquake! sure, it was the roar
Of a whole herd of lions.

ALONSO Heard you this, Gonzalo?

GONZALO Upon mine honour, sir, I heard a humming,
And that a strange one too, which did awake me:
I shaked you, sir, and cried: as mine eyes open'd,
I saw their weapons drawn: there was a noise,
That's verily. 'Tis best we stand upon our guard,
Or that we quit this place; let's draw our weapons.

ALONSO Lead off this ground; and let's make further search
For my poor son.

GONZALO Heavens keep him from these beasts!
For he is, sure, i' the island.

ALONSO Lead away.

ARIEL Prospero my lord shall know what I have done:
So, king, go safely on to seek thy son.

Exeunt

SCENE II.

Another part of the island.

Enter CALIBAN with a burden of wood. A noise of thunder heard

CALIBAN All the infections that the sun sucks up
From bogs, fens, flats, on Prosper fall and make him
By inch-meal a disease! His spirits hear me
And yet I needs must curse. But they'll nor pinch,
Fright me with urchin—shows, pitch me i' the mire,
Nor lead me, like a firebrand, in the dark
Out of my way, unless he bid 'em; but
For every trifle are they set upon me;
Sometime like apes that mow and chatter at me
And after bite me, then like hedgehogs which
Lie tumbling in my barefoot way and mount
Their pricks at my footfall; sometime am I
All wound with adders who with cloven tongues
Do hiss me into madness.

Enter TRINCULO

Lo, now, lo!
Here comes a spirit of his, and to torment me
For bringing wood in slowly. I'll fall flat;
Perchance he will not mind me.

TRINCULO Here's neither bush nor shrub, to bear off
any weather at all, and another storm brewing;
I hear it sing i' the wind: yond same black
cloud, yond huge one, looks like a foul
bombard that would shed his liquor. If it
should thunder as it did before, I know not
where to hide my head: yond same cloud cannot
choose but fall by pailfuls. What have we
here? a man or a fish? dead or alive? A fish:
he smells like a fish; a very ancient and fish-like
smell; a kind of not of the newest Poor-John.
A strange fish! Were I in England now,
as once I was, and had but this fish painted,
not a holiday fool there but would give a piece
of silver: there would this monster make a
man; any strange beast there makes a man:
when they will not give a doit to relieve a lame
beggar, they will lazy out ten to see a dead
Indian. Legged like a man and his fins like
arms! Warm o' my troth! I do now let loose
my opinion; hold it no longer: this is no fish,
but an islander, that hath lately suffered by a
thunderbolt.

Thunder

Alas, the storm is come again! my best way is to
creep under his gaberdine; there is no other
shelter hereabouts: misery acquaints a man with
strange bed-fellows. I will here shroud till the
dregs of the storm be past.

Enter STEPHANO, singing: a bottle in his hand

STEPHANO I shall no more to sea, to sea,
Here shall I die ashore—
This is a very scurvy tune to sing at a man's
funeral: well, here's my comfort.

Drinks

Sings

The master, the swabber, the boatswain and I,
The gunner and his mate

Loved Mall, Meg and Marian and Margery,
But none of us cared for Kate;
For she had a tongue with a tang,
Would cry to a sailor, Go hang!
She loved not the savour of tar nor of pitch,
Yet a tailor might scratch her where'er she did itch:
Then to sea, boys, and let her go hang!
This is a scurvy tune too: but here's my comfort.

Drinks

CALIBAN Do not torment me: Oh!

STEPHANO What's the matter? Have we devils here? Do you put
tricks upon's with savages and men of Ind, ha? I
have not scaped drowning to be afeard now of your
four legs; for it hath been said, As proper a man as
ever went on four legs cannot make him give ground;
and it shall be said so again while Stephano
breathes at's nostrils.

CALIBAN The spirit torments me; Oh!

STEPHANO This is some monster of the isle with four legs, who
hath got, as I take it, an ague. Where the devil
should he learn our language? I will give him some
relief, if it be but for that. if I can recover him
and keep him tame and get to Naples with him, he's a
present for any emperor that ever trod on neat's leather.

CALIBAN Do not torment me, prithee; I'll bring my wood home faster.

STEPHANO He's in his fit now and does not talk after the
wisest. He shall taste of my bottle: if he have
never drunk wine afore will go near to remove his
fit. If I can recover him and keep him tame, I will
not take too much for him; he shall pay for him that
hath him, and that soundly.

CALIBAN Thou dost me yet but little hurt; thou wilt anon, I
know it by thy trembling: now Prosper works upon thee.

STEPHANO Come on your ways; open your mouth; here is that
which will give language to you, cat: open your
mouth; this will shake your shaking, I can tell you,
and that soundly: you cannot tell who's your friend:
open your chaps again.

TRINCULO I should know that voice: it should be—but he is
drowned; and these are devils: O defend me!

STEPHANO Four legs and two voices: a most delicate monster!
His forward voice now is to speak well of his
friend; his backward voice is to utter foul speeches
and to detract. If all the wine in my bottle will
recover him, I will help his ague. Come. Amen! I
will pour some in thy other mouth.

TRINCULO Stephano!

STEPHANO Doth thy other mouth call me? Mercy, mercy! This is
a devil, and no monster: I will leave him; I have no
long spoon.

TRINCULO Stephano! If thou beest Stephano, touch me and
speak to me: for I am Trinculo—be not afeard—thy
good friend Trinculo.

STEPHANO If thou beest Trinculo, come forth: I'll pull thee
by the lesser legs: if any be Trinculo's legs,
these are they. Thou art very Trinculo indeed! How
camest thou to be the siege of this moon-calf? can
he vent Trinculos?

TRINCULO I took him to be killed with a thunder-stroke. But
art thou not drowned, Stephano? I hope now thou art
not drowned. Is the storm overblown? I hid me
under the dead moon-calf's gaberdine for fear of
the storm. And art thou living, Stephano? O
Stephano, two Neapolitans 'scaped!

STEPHANO Prithee, do not turn me about; my stomach is not constant.

CALIBAN [*Aside*]
These be fine things, an if they be
not sprites.
That's a brave god and bears celestial liquor.
I will kneel to him.

STEPHANO How didst thou 'scape? How camest thou hither?
swear by this bottle how thou camest hither. I
escaped upon a butt of sack which the sailors
heaved o'erboard, by this bottle; which I made of
the bark of a tree with mine own hands since I was
cast ashore.

CALIBAN I'll swear upon that bottle to be thy true subject;
for the liquor is not earthly.

STEPHANO Here; swear then how thou escapedst.

TRINCULO Swum ashore. man, like a duck: I can swim like a
duck, I'll be sworn.

STEPHANO Here, kiss the book. Though thou canst swim like a duck, thou art made like a goose.

TRINCULO O Stephano. hast any more of this?

STEPHANO The whole butt, man: my cellar is in a rock by the
sea-side where my wine is hid. How now, moon-calf!
how does thine ague?

CALIBAN Hast thou not dropp'd from heaven?

STEPHANO Out o' the moon, I do assure thee: I was the man i'
the moon when time was.

CALIBAN I have seen thee in her and I do adore thee:
My mistress show'd me thee and thy dog and thy bush.

STEPHANO Come, swear to that; kiss the book: I will furnish
it anon with new contents swear.

TRINCULO By this good light, this is a very shallow monster!
I afeard of him! A very weak monster! The man i'
the moon! A most poor credulous monster! Well
drawn, monster, in good sooth!

CALIBAN I'll show thee every fertile inch o' th' island;
And I will kiss thy foot: I prithee, be my god.

TRINCULO By this light, a most perfidious and drunken
monster! when 's god's asleep, he'll rob his bottle.

CALIBAN I'll kiss thy foot; I'll swear myself thy subject.

STEPHANO Come on then; down, and swear.

TRINCULO I shall laugh myself to death at this puppy-headed
monster. A most scurvy monster! I could find in my
heart to beat him,—

STEPHANO Come, kiss.

TRINCULO But that the poor monster's in drink: an abominable monster!

CALIBAN I'll show thee the best springs; I'll pluck thee berries;
I'll fish for thee and get thee wood enough.
A plague upon the tyrant that I serve!
I'll bear him no more sticks, but follow thee,
Thou wondrous man.

TRINCULO A most ridiculous monster, to make a wonder of a
Poor drunkard!

CALIBAN I prithee, let me bring thee where crabs grow;
And I with my long nails will dig thee pignuts;
Show thee a jay's nest and instruct thee how
To snare the nimble marmoset; I'll bring thee
To clustering filberts and sometimes I'll get thee
Young scamels from the rock. Wilt thou go with me?

STEPHANO I prithee now, lead the way without any more

talking. Trinculo, the king and all our company
else being drowned, we will inherit here: here;
bear my bottle: fellow Trinculo, we'll fill him by
and by again.

CALIBAN [*Sings drunkenly*]
Farewell master; farewell, farewell!

TRINCULO A howling monster: a drunken monster!

CALIBAN No more dams I'll make for fish
Nor fetch in firing
At requiring;
Nor scrape trencher, nor wash dish
'Ban, 'Ban, Cacaliban
Has a new master: get a new man.
Freedom, hey-day! hey-day, freedom! freedom, hey-day, freedom!

STEPHANO O brave monster! Lead the way.

Exeunt

ACT III

SCENE I.

Before PROSPERO'S Cell.

Enter FERDINAND, bearing a log

FERDINAND There be some sports are painful, and their labour
Delight in them sets off: some kinds of baseness
Are nobly undergone and most poor matters
Point to rich ends. This my mean task
Would be as heavy to me as odious, but
The mistress which I serve quickens what's dead
And makes my labours pleasures: O, she is
Ten times more gentle than her father's crabbed,
And he's composed of harshness. I must remove
Some thousands of these logs and pile them up,
Upon a sore injunction: my sweet mistress
Weeps when she sees me work, and says, such baseness
Had never like executor. I forget:
But these sweet thoughts do even refresh my labours,
Most busy lest, when I do it.

Enter MIRANDA; and PROSPERO at a distance, unseen

MIRANDA Alas, now, pray you,
Work not so hard: I would the lightning had

Burnt up those logs that you are enjoin'd to pile!
Pray, set it down and rest you: when this burns,
'Twill weep for having wearied you. My father
Is hard at study; pray now, rest yourself;
He's safe for these three hours.

FERDINAND O most dear mistress,
The sun will set before I shall discharge
What I must strive to do.

MIRANDA If you'll sit down,
I'll bear your logs the while: pray, give me that;
I'll carry it to the pile.

FERDINAND No, precious creature;
I had rather crack my sinews, break my back,
Than you should such dishonour undergo,
While I sit lazy by.

MIRANDA It would become me
As well as it does you: and I should do it
With much more ease; for my good will is to it,
And yours it is against.

PROSPERO Poor worm, thou art infected!
This visitation shows it.

MIRANDA You look wearily.

FERDINAND No, noble mistress; 'tis fresh morning with me
When you are by at night. I do beseech you—
Chiefly that I might set it in my prayers—
What is your name?

MIRANDA Miranda.—O my father,
I have broke your hest to say so!

FERDINAND Admired Miranda!
Indeed the top of admiration! worth
What's dearest to the world! Full many a lady
I have eyed with best regard and many a time
The harmony of their tongues hath into bondage
Brought my too diligent ear: for several virtues
Have I liked several women; never any
With so fun soul, but some defect in her
Did quarrel with the noblest grace she owed
And put it to the foil: but you, O you,
So perfect and so peerless, are created
Of every creature's best!

MIRANDA I do not know
One of my sex; no woman's face remember,

Save, from my glass, mine own; nor have I seen
More that I may call men than you, good friend,
And my dear father: how features are abroad,
I am skilless of; but, by my modesty,
The jewel in my dower, I would not wish
Any companion in the world but you,
Nor can imagination form a shape,
Besides yourself, to like of. But I prattle
Something too wildly and my father's precepts
I therein do forget.

FERDINAND I am in my condition
A prince, Miranda; I do think, a king;
I would, not so!—and would no more endure
This wooden slavery than to suffer
The flesh-fly blow my mouth. Hear my soul speak:
The very instant that I saw you, did
My heart fly to your service; there resides,
To make me slave to it; and for your sake
Am I this patient log—man.

MIRANDA Do you love me?

FERDINAND O heaven, O earth, bear witness to this sound
And crown what I profess with kind event
If I speak true! if hollowly, invert
What best is boded me to mischief! I
Beyond all limit of what else i' the world
Do love, prize, honour you.

MIRANDA I am a fool
To weep at what I am glad of.

PROSPERO Fair encounter
Of two most rare affections! Heavens rain grace
On that which breeds between 'em!

FERDINAND Wherefore weep you?

MIRANDA At mine unworthiness that dare not offer
What I desire to give, and much less take
What I shall die to want. But this is trifling;
And all the more it seeks to hide itself,
The bigger bulk it shows. Hence, bashful cunning!
And prompt me, plain and holy innocence!
I am your wife, it you will marry me;
If not, I'll die your maid: to be your fellow
You may deny me; but I'll be your servant,
Whether you will or no.

FERDINAND My mistress, dearest;

And I thus humble ever.

MIRANDA My husband, then?

FERDINAND Ay, with a heart as willing
As bondage e'er of freedom: here's my hand.

MIRANDA And mine, with my heart in't; and now farewell
Till half an hour hence.

FERDINAND A thousand thousand!

Exeunt FERDINAND and MIRANDA severally

PROSPERO So glad of this as they I cannot be,
Who are surprised withal; but my rejoicing
At nothing can be more. I'll to my book,
For yet ere supper-time must I perform
Much business appertaining.

Exit

SCENE II.

Another part of the island.

Enter CALIBAN, STEPHANO, and TRINCULO

STEPHANO Tell not me; when the butt is out, we will drink
water; not a drop before: therefore bear up, and
board 'em. Servant-monster, drink to me.

TRINCULO Servant-monster! the folly of this island! They
say there's but five upon this isle: we are three
of them; if th' other two be brained like us, the
state totters.

STEPHANO Drink, servant-monster, when I bid thee: thy eyes
are almost set in thy head.

TRINCULO Where should they be set else? he were a brave
monster indeed, if they were set in his tail.

STEPHANO My man-monster hath drown'd his tongue in sack:
for my part, the sea cannot drown me; I swam, ere I
could recover the shore, five and thirty leagues off
and on. By this light, thou shalt be my lieutenant,
monster, or my standard.

TRINCULO Your lieutenant, if you list; he's no standard.

STEPHANO We'll not run, Monsieur Monster.

TRINCULO Nor go neither; but you'll lie like dogs and yet say
nothing neither.

STEPHANO Moon-calf, speak once in thy life, if thou beest a
good moon-calf.

CALIBAN How does thy honour? Let me lick thy shoe.
I'll not serve him; he's not valiant.

TRINCULO Thou liest, most ignorant monster: I am in case to
justle a constable. Why, thou deboshed fish thou,
was there ever man a coward that hath drunk so much
sack as I to-day? Wilt thou tell a monstrous lie,
being but half a fish and half a monster?

CALIBAN Lo, how he mocks me! wilt thou let him, my lord?

TRINCULO 'Lord' quoth he! That a monster should be such a natural!

CALIBAN Lo, lo, again! bite him to death, I prithee.

STEPHANO Trinculo, keep a good tongue in your head: if you
prove a mutineer,—the next tree! The poor monster's
my subject and he shall not suffer indignity.

CALIBAN I thank my noble lord. Wilt thou be pleased to
hearken once again to the suit I made to thee?

STEPHANO Marry, will I kneel and repeat it; I will stand,
and so shall Trinculo.

Enter ARIEL, invisible

CALIBAN As I told thee before, I am subject to a tyrant, a
sorcerer, that by his cunning hath cheated me of the island.

ARIEL Thou liest.

CALIBAN Thou liest, thou jesting monkey, thou: I would my
valiant master would destroy thee! I do not lie.

STEPHANO Trinculo, if you trouble him any more in's tale, by
this hand, I will supplant some of your teeth.

TRINCULO Why, I said nothing.

STEPHANO Mum, then, and no more. Proceed.

CALIBAN I say, by sorcery he got this isle;
From me he got it. if thy greatness will
Revenge it on him,—for I know thou darest,
But this thing dare not,—

STEPHANO That's most certain.

CALIBAN Thou shalt be lord of it and I'll serve thee.

STEPHANO How now shall this be compassed?
Canst thou bring me to the party?

CALIBAN Yea, yea, my lord: I'll yield him thee asleep,
Where thou mayst knock a nail into his head.

ARIEL Thou liest; thou canst not.

CALIBAN What a pied ninny's this! Thou scurvy patch!
I do beseech thy greatness, give him blows
And take his bottle from him: when that's gone
He shall drink nought but brine; for I'll not show him
Where the quick freshes are.

STEPHANO Trinculo, run into no further danger:
interrupt the monster one word further, and,
by this hand, I'll turn my mercy out o' doors
and make a stock-fish of thee.

TRINCULO Why, what did I? I did nothing. I'll go farther
off.

STEPHANO Didst thou not say he lied?

ARIEL Thou liest.

STEPHANO Do I so? take thou that.

Beats TRINCULO

As you like this, give me the lie another time.

TRINCULO I did not give the lie. Out o' your
wits and bearing too? A pox o' your bottle!
this can sack and drinking do. A murrain on
your monster, and the devil take your fingers!

CALIBAN Ha, ha, ha!

STEPHANO Now, forward with your tale. Prithee, stand farther
off.

CALIBAN Beat him enough: after a little time
I'll beat him too.

STEPHANO Stand farther. Come, proceed.

CALIBAN Why, as I told thee, 'tis a custom with him,
I' th' afternoon to sleep: there thou mayst brain him,
Having first seized his books, or with a log
Batter his skull, or paunch him with a stake,
Or cut his wezand with thy knife. Remember
First to possess his books; for without them
He's but a sot, as I am, nor hath not
One spirit to command: they all do hate him
As rootedly as I. Burn but his books.
He has brave utensils,—for so he calls them—
Which when he has a house, he'll deck withal
And that most deeply to consider is
The beauty of his daughter; he himself
Calls her a nonpareil: I never saw a woman,
But only Sycorax my dam and she;

But she as far surpasseth Sycorax
As great'st does least.

STEPHANO Is it so brave a lass?

CALIBAN Ay, lord; she will become thy bed, I warrant.
And bring thee forth brave brood.

STEPHANO Monster, I will kill this man: his daughter and I
will be king and queen—save our graces!—and
Trinculo and thyself shall be viceroys. Dost thou
like the plot, Trinculo?

TRINCULO Excellent.

STEPHANO Give me thy hand: I am sorry I beat thee; but,
while thou livest, keep a good tongue in thy head.

CALIBAN Within this half hour will he be asleep:
Wilt thou destroy him then?

STEPHANO Ay, on mine honour.

ARIEL This will I tell my master.

CALIBAN Thou makest me merry; I am full of pleasure:
Let us be jocund: will you troll the catch
You taught me but while-ere?

STEPHANO At thy request, monster, I will do reason, any
reason. Come on, Trinculo, let us sing.

Sings

Flout 'em and scout 'em
And scout 'em and flout 'em
Thought is free.

CALIBAN That's not the tune.

Ariel plays the tune on a tabour and pipe

STEPHANO What is this same?

TRINCULO This is the tune of our catch, played by the picture
of Nobody.

STEPHANO If thou beest a man, show thyself in thy likeness:
if thou beest a devil, take't as thou list.

TRINCULO O, forgive me my sins!

STEPHANO He that dies pays all debts: I defy thee. Mercy upon us!

CALIBAN Art thou afeard?

STEPHANO No, monster, not I.

CALIBAN Be not afeard; the isle is full of noises,
Sounds and sweet airs, that give delight and hurt not.
Sometimes a thousand twangling instruments

Will hum about mine ears, and sometime voices
That, if I then had waked after long sleep,
Will make me sleep again: and then, in dreaming,
The clouds methought would open and show riches
Ready to drop upon me that, when I waked,
I cried to dream again.

STEPHANO This will prove a brave kingdom to me, where I shall
have my music for nothing.

CALIBAN When Prospero is destroyed.

STEPHANO That shall be by and by: I remember the story.

TRINCULO The sound is going away; let's follow it, and
after do our work.

STEPHANO Lead, monster; we'll follow. I would I could see
this tabourer; he lays it on.

TRINCULO Wilt come? I'll follow, Stephano.

Exeunt

SCENE III.

Another part of the island.

*Enter ALONSO, SEBASTIAN, ANTONIO, GONZALO, ADRIAN, FRANCISCO, and
others*

GONZALO By'r lakin, I can go no further, sir;
My old bones ache: here's a maze trod indeed
Through forth-rights and meanders! By your patience,
I needs must rest me.

ALONSO Old lord, I cannot blame thee,
Who am myself attach'd with weariness,
To the dulling of my spirits: sit down, and rest.
Even here I will put off my hope and keep it
No longer for my flatterer: he is drown'd
Whom thus we stray to find, and the sea mocks
Our frustrate search on land. Well, let him go.

ANTONIO [*Aside to SEBASTIAN*]
I am right glad that he's so
out of hope.
Do not, for one repulse, forego the purpose
That you resolved to effect.

SEBASTIAN [*Aside to ANTONIO*]
The next advantage
Will we take throughly.

ANTONIO [*Aside to SEBASTIAN*]
Let it be to-night;
For, now they are oppress'd with travel, they
Will not, nor cannot, use such vigilance
As when they are fresh.

SEBASTIAN [*Aside to ANTONIO*]
I say, to-night: no more.

Solemn and strange music

ALONSO   What harmony is this? My good friends, hark!

GONZALO   Marvellous sweet music!

Enter PROSPERO above, invisible. Enter several strange Shapes, bringing in a banquet; they dance about it with gentle actions of salutation; and, inviting the King, & c. to eat, they depart

ALONSO   Give us kind keepers, heavens! What were these?

SEBASTIAN   A living drollery. Now I will believe
That there are unicorns, that in Arabia
There is one tree, the phoenix' throne, one phoenix
At this hour reigning there.

ANTONIO   I'll believe both;
And what does else want credit, come to me,
And I'll be sworn 'tis true: travellers ne'er did lie,
Though fools at home condemn 'em.

GONZALO   If in Naples
I should report this now, would they believe me?
If I should say, I saw such islanders—
For, certes, these are people of the island—
Who, though they are of monstrous shape, yet, note,
Their manners are more gentle-kind than of
Our human generation you shall find
Many, nay, almost any.

PROSPERO [*Aside*]
Honest lord,
Thou hast said well; for some of you there present
Are worse than devils.

ALONSO   I cannot too much muse
Such shapes, such gesture and such sound, expressing,
Although they want the use of tongue, a kind
Of excellent dumb discourse.

PROSPERO [*Aside*]
Praise in departing.

FRANCISCO   They vanish'd strangely.

SEBASTIAN No matter, since
They have left their viands behind; for we have stomachs.
Will't please you taste of what is here?

ALONSO Not I.

GONZALO Faith, sir, you need not fear. When we were boys,
Who would believe that there were mountaineers
Dew-lapp'd like bulls, whose throats had hanging at 'em
Wallets of flesh? or that there were such men
Whose heads stood in their breasts? which now we find
Each putter-out of five for one will bring us
Good warrant of.

ALONSO I will stand to and feed,
Although my last: no matter, since I feel
The best is past. Brother, my lord the duke,
Stand to and do as we.

*Thunder and lightning. Enter ARIEL, like a harpy; claps his wings upon the table; and, with
a quaint device, the banquet vanishes*

ARIEL You are three men of sin, whom Destiny,
That hath to instrument this lower world
And what is in't, the never-surfeited sea
Hath caused to belch up you; and on this island
Where man doth not inhabit; you 'mongst men
Being most unfit to live. I have made you mad;
And even with such-like valour men hang and drown
Their proper selves.

ALONSO, SEBASTIAN & c. draw their swords

You fools! I and my fellows
Are ministers of Fate: the elements,
Of whom your swords are temper'd, may as well
Wound the loud winds, or with bemock'd-at stabs
Kill the still-closing waters, as diminish
One dowle that's in my plume: my fellow-ministers
Are like invulnerable. If you could hurt,
Your swords are now too massy for your strengths
And will not be uplifted. But remember—
For that's my business to you—that you three
From Milan did supplant good Prospero;
Exposed unto the sea, which hath requit it,
Him and his innocent child: for which foul deed
The powers, delaying, not forgetting, have
Incensed the seas and shores, yea, all the creatures,

Against your peace. Thee of thy son, Alonso,
They have bereft; and do pronounce by me:
Lingering perdition, worse than any death
Can be at once, shall step by step attend
You and your ways; whose wraths to guard you from—
Which here, in this most desolate isle, else falls
Upon your heads—is nothing but heart-sorrow
And a clear life ensuing.

He vanishes in thunder; then, to soft music enter the Shapes again, and dance, with mocks and mows, and carrying out the table

PROSPERO Bravely the figure of this harpy hast thou
Perform'd, my Ariel; a grace it had, devouring:
Of my instruction hast thou nothing bated
In what thou hadst to say: so, with good life
And observation strange, my meaner ministers
Their several kinds have done. My high charms work
And these mine enemies are all knit up
In their distractions; they now are in my power;
And in these fits I leave them, while I visit
Young Ferdinand, whom they suppose is drown'd,
And his and mine loved darling.

Exit above

GONZALO I' the name of something holy, sir, why stand you
In this strange stare?
ALONSO O, it is monstrous, monstrous:
Methought the billows spoke and told me of it;
The winds did sing it to me, and the thunder,
That deep and dreadful organ-pipe, pronounced
The name of Prosper: it did bass my trespass.
Therefore my son i' the ooze is bedded, and
I'll seek him deeper than e'er plummet sounded
And with him there lie mudded.

Exit

SEBASTIAN But one fiend at a time,
I'll fight their legions o'er.
ANTONIO I'll be thy second.

Exeunt SEBASTIAN, and ANTONIO

GONZALO All three of them are desperate: their great guilt,
Like poison given to work a great time after,

Now 'gins to bite the spirits. I do beseech you
That are of suppler joints, follow them swiftly
And hinder them from what this ecstasy
May now provoke them to.
ADRIAN Follow, I pray you.

Exeunt

ACT IV

SCENE I.

Before PROSPERO'S cell.

Enter PROSPERO, FERDINAND, and MIRANDA

PROSPERO If I have too austerely punish'd you,
Your compensation makes amends, for I
Have given you here a third of mine own life,
Or that for which I live; who once again
I tender to thy hand: all thy vexations
Were but my trials of thy love and thou
Hast strangely stood the test here, afore Heaven,
I ratify this my rich gift. O Ferdinand,
Do not smile at me that I boast her off,
For thou shalt find she will outstrip all praise
And make it halt behind her.
FERDINAND I do believe it
Against an oracle.
PROSPERO Then, as my gift and thine own acquisition
Worthily purchased take my daughter: but
If thou dost break her virgin-knot before
All sanctimonious ceremonies may
With full and holy rite be minister'd,
No sweet aspersion shall the heavens let fall
To make this contract grow: but barren hate,
Sour-eyed disdain and discord shall bestrew
The union of your bed with weeds so loathly
That you shall hate it both: therefore take heed,
As Hymen's lamps shall light you.
FERDINAND As I hope
For quiet days, fair issue and long life,
With such love as 'tis now, the murkiest den,
The most opportune place, the strong'st suggestion.
Our worser genius can, shall never melt

Mine honour into lust, to take away
The edge of that day's celebration
When I shall think: or Phoebus' steeds are founder'd,
Or Night kept chain'd below.

PROSPERO Fairly spoke.
Sit then and talk with her; she is thine own.
What, Ariel! my industrious servant, Ariel!

Enter ARIEL

ARIEL What would my potent master? here I am.

PROSPERO Thou and thy meaner fellows your last service
Did worthily perform; and I must use you
In such another trick. Go bring the rabble,
O'er whom I give thee power, here to this place:
Incite them to quick motion; for I must
Bestow upon the eyes of this young couple
Some vanity of mine art: it is my promise,
And they expect it from me.

ARIEL Presently?

PROSPERO Ay, with a twink.

ARIEL Before you can say 'come' and 'go,'
And breathe twice and cry 'so, so,'
Each one, tripping on his toe,
Will be here with mop and mow.
Do you love me, master? no?

PROSPERO Dearly my delicate Ariel. Do not approach
Till thou dost hear me call.

ARIEL Well, I conceive.

Exit

PROSPERO Look thou be true; do not give dalliance
Too much the rein: the strongest oaths are straw
To the fire i' the blood: be more abstemious,
Or else, good night your vow!

FERDINAND I warrant you sir;
The white cold virgin snow upon my heart
Abates the ardour of my liver.

PROSPERO Well.
Now come, my Ariel! bring a corollary,
Rather than want a spirit: appear and pertly!
No tongue! all eyes! be silent.

Soft music

Enter IRIS

IRIS Ceres, most bounteous lady, thy rich leas
Of wheat, rye, barley, vetches, oats and pease;
Thy turfy mountains, where live nibbling sheep,
And flat meads thatch'd with stover, them to keep;
Thy banks with pioned and twilled brims,
Which spongy April at thy hest betrims,
To make cold nymphs chaste crowns; and thy broom-groves,
Whose shadow the dismissed bachelor loves,
Being lass-lorn: thy pole-clipt vineyard;
And thy sea-marge, sterile and rocky-hard,
Where thou thyself dost air;—the queen o' the sky,
Whose watery arch and messenger am I,
Bids thee leave these, and with her sovereign grace,
Here on this grass-plot, in this very place,
To come and sport: her peacocks fly amain:
Approach, rich Ceres, her to entertain.

Enter CERES

CERES Hail, many-colour'd messenger, that ne'er
Dost disobey the wife of Jupiter;
Who with thy saffron wings upon my flowers
Diffusest honey-drops, refreshing showers,
And with each end of thy blue bow dost crown
My bosky acres and my unshrubb'd down,
Rich scarf to my proud earth; why hath thy queen
Summon'd me hither, to this short-grass'd green?

IRIS A contract of true love to celebrate;
And some donation freely to estate
On the blest lovers.

CERES Tell me, heavenly bow,
If Venus or her son, as thou dost know,
Do now attend the queen? Since they did plot
The means that dusky Dis my daughter got,
Her and her blind boy's scandal'd company
I have forsworn.

IRIS Of her society
Be not afraid: I met her deity
Cutting the clouds towards Paphos and her son
Dove-drawn with her. Here thought they to have done
Some wanton charm upon this man and maid,
Whose vows are, that no bed-right shall be paid
Till Hymen's torch be lighted: but vain;

Mars's hot minion is returned again;
Her waspish-headed son has broke his arrows,
Swears he will shoot no more but play with sparrows
And be a boy right out.

CERES High'st queen of state,
Great Juno, comes; I know her by her gait.

Enter JUNO

JUNO How does my bounteous sister? Go with me
To bless this twain, that they may prosperous be
And honour'd in their issue.

They sing:

JUNO Honour, riches, marriage-blessing,
Long continuance, and increasing,
Hourly joys be still upon you!
Juno sings her blessings upon you.

CERES Earth's increase, foison plenty,
Barns and garners never empty,
Vines and clustering bunches growing,
Plants with goodly burthen bowing;
Spring come to you at the farthest
In the very end of harvest!
Scarcity and want shall shun you;
Ceres' blessing so is on you.

FERDINAND This is a most majestic vision, and
Harmoniously charmingly. May I be bold
To think these spirits?

PROSPERO Spirits, which by mine art
I have from their confines call'd to enact
My present fancies.

FERDINAND Let me live here ever;
So rare a wonder'd father and a wife
Makes this place Paradise.

Juno and Ceres whisper, and send Iris on employment

PROSPERO Sweet, now, silence!
Juno and Ceres whisper seriously;
There's something else to do: hush, and be mute,
Or else our spell is marr'd.

IRIS You nymphs, call'd Naiads, of the windring brooks,
With your sedged crowns and ever-harmless looks,
Leave your crisp channels and on this green land

Answer your summons; Juno does command:
Come, temperate nymphs, and help to celebrate
A contract of true love; be not too late.

Enter certain Nymphs

You sunburnt sicklemen, of August weary,
Come hither from the furrow and be merry:
Make holiday; your rye-straw hats put on
And these fresh nymphs encounter every one
In country footing.

Enter certain Reapers, properly habited: they join with the Nymphs in a graceful dance; towards the end where of PROSPERO starts suddenly, and speaks; after which, to a strange, hollow, and confused noise, they heavily vanish

PROSPERO [*Aside*]
I had forgot that foul conspiracy
Of the beast Caliban and his confederates
Against my life: the minute of their plot
Is almost come.

To the Spirits

Well done! avoid; no more!

FERDINAND This is strange: your father's in some passion
That works him strongly.

MIRANDA Never till this day
Saw I him touch'd with anger so distemper'd.

PROSPERO You do look, my son, in a moved sort,
As if you were dismay'd: be cheerful, sir.
Our revels now are ended. These our actors,
As I foretold you, were all spirits and
Are melted into air, into thin air:
And, like the baseless fabric of this vision,
The cloud-capp'd towers, the gorgeous palaces,
The solemn temples, the great globe itself,
Ye all which it inherit, shall dissolve
And, like this insubstantial pageant faded,
Leave not a rack behind. We are such stuff
As dreams are made on, and our little life
Is rounded with a sleep. Sir, I am vex'd;
Bear with my weakness; my, brain is troubled:
Be not disturb'd with my infirmity:
If you be pleased, retire into my cell
And there repose: a turn or two I'll walk,

To still my beating mind.
FERDINAND MIRANDA We wish your peace.

Exeunt

PROSPERO Come with a thought I thank thee, Ariel: come.

Enter ARIEL

ARIEL Thy thoughts I cleave to. What's thy pleasure?
PROSPERO Spirit,
We must prepare to meet with Caliban.

ARIEL Ay, my commander: when I presented Ceres,
I thought to have told thee of it, but I fear'd
Lest I might anger thee.

PROSPERO Say again, where didst thou leave these varlets?

ARIEL I told you, sir, they were red-hot with drinking;
So fun of valour that they smote the air
For breathing in their faces; beat the ground
For kissing of their feet; yet always bending
Towards their project. Then I beat my tabour;
At which, like unback'd colts, they prick'd their ears,
Advanced their eyelids, lifted up their noses
As they smelt music: so I charm'd their ears
That calf-like they my lowing follow'd through
Tooth'd briers, sharp furzes, pricking goss and thorns,
Which entered their frail shins: at last I left them
I' the filthy-mantled pool beyond your cell,
There dancing up to the chins, that the foul lake
O'erstunk their feet.

PROSPERO This was well done, my bird.
Thy shape invisible retain thou still:
The trumpery in my house, go bring it hither,
For stale to catch these thieves.

ARIEL I go, I go.

Exit

PROSPERO A devil, a born devil, on whose nature
Nurture can never stick; on whom my pains,
Humanely taken, all, all lost, quite lost;
And as with age his body uglier grows,
So his mind cankers. I will plague them all,
Even to roaring.

Re-enter ARIEL, loaden with glistering apparel, & c

Come, hang them on this line.

PROSPERO and ARIEL remain invisible. Enter CALIBAN, STEPHANO, and TRIN-CULO, all wet

CALIBAN Pray you, tread softly, that the blind mole may not
Hear a foot fall: we now are near his cell.

STEPHANO Monster, your fairy, which you say is
a harmless fairy, has done little better than
played the Jack with us.

TRINCULO Monster, I do smell all horse-piss; at
which my nose is in great indignation.

STEPHANO So is mine. Do you hear, monster? If I should take
a displeasure against you, look you,—

TRINCULO Thou wert but a lost monster.

CALIBAN Good my lord, give me thy favour still.
Be patient, for the prize I'll bring thee to
Shall hoodwink this mischance: therefore speak softly.
All's hush'd as midnight yet.

TRINCULO Ay, but to lose our bottles in the pool,—

STEPHANO There is not only disgrace and dishonour in that,
monster, but an infinite loss.

TRINCULO That's more to me than my wetting: yet this is your
harmless fairy, monster.

STEPHANO I will fetch off my bottle, though I be o'er ears
for my labour.

CALIBAN Prithee, my king, be quiet. Seest thou here,
This is the mouth o' the cell: no noise, and enter.
Do that good mischief which may make this island
Thine own for ever, and I, thy Caliban,
For aye thy foot-licker.

STEPHANO Give me thy hand. I do begin to have bloody thoughts.

TRINCULO O king Stephano! O peer! O worthy Stephano! look
what a wardrobe here is for thee!

CALIBAN Let it alone, thou fool; it is but trash.

TRINCULO O, ho, monster! we know what belongs to a frippery.
O king Stephano!

STEPHANO Put off that gown, Trinculo; by this hand, I'll have
that gown.

TRINCULO Thy grace shall have it.

CALIBAN The dropsy drown this fool I what do you mean
To dote thus on such luggage? Let's alone

And do the murder first: if he awake,
From toe to crown he'll fill our skins with pinches,
Make us strange stuff.

STEPHANO Be you quiet, monster. Mistress line,
is not this my jerkin? Now is the jerkin under
the line: now, jerkin, you are like to lose your
hair and prove a bald jerkin.

TRINCULO Do, do: we steal by line and level, an't like your grace.

STEPHANO I thank thee for that jest; here's a garment for't:
wit shall not go unrewarded while I am king of this
country. 'Steal by line and level' is an excellent
pass of pate; there's another garment for't.

TRINCULO Monster, come, put some lime upon your fingers, and
away with the rest.

CALIBAN I will have none on't: we shall lose our time,
And all be turn'd to barnacles, or to apes
With foreheads villanous low.

STEPHANO Monster, lay-to your fingers: help to bear this
away where my hogshead of wine is, or I'll turn you
out of my kingdom: go to, carry this.

TRINCULO And this.

STEPHANO Ay, and this.

A noise of hunters heard. Enter divers Spirits, in shape of dogs and hounds, and hunt them about, PROSPERO and ARIEL setting them on

PROSPERO Hey, Mountain, hey!

ARIEL Silver I there it goes, Silver!

PROSPERO Fury, Fury! there, Tyrant, there! hark! hark!

CALIBAN, STEPHANO, and TRINCULO, are driven out

Go charge my goblins that they grind their joints
With dry convulsions, shorten up their sinews
With aged cramps, and more pinch-spotted make them
Than pard or cat o' mountain.

ARIEL Hark, they roar!

PROSPERO Let them be hunted soundly. At this hour
Lie at my mercy all mine enemies:
Shortly shall all my labours end, and thou
Shalt have the air at freedom: for a little
Follow, and do me service.

Exeunt

ACT V

SCENE I.

Before PROSPERO'S cell.

Enter PROSPERO in his magic robes, and ARIEL

PROSPERO Now does my project gather to a head:
My charms crack not; my spirits obey; and time
Goes upright with his carriage. How's the day?

ARIEL On the sixth hour; at which time, my lord,
You said our work should cease.

PROSPERO I did say so,
When first I raised the tempest. Say, my spirit,
How fares the king and's followers?

ARIEL Confined together
In the same fashion as you gave in charge,
Just as you left them; all prisoners, sir,
In the line-grove which weather-fends your cell;
They cannot budge till your release. The king,
His brother and yours, abide all three distracted
And the remainder mourning over them,
Brimful of sorrow and dismay; but chiefly
Him that you term'd, sir, 'The good old lord Gonzalo;'
His tears run down his beard, like winter's drops
From eaves of reeds. Your charm so strongly works 'em
That if you now beheld them, your affections
Would become tender.

PROSPERO Dost thou think so, spirit?

ARIEL Mine would, sir, were I human.

PROSPERO And mine shall.
Hast thou, which art but air, a touch, a feeling
Of their afflictions, and shall not myself,
One of their kind, that relish all as sharply,
Passion as they, be kindlier moved than thou art?
Though with their high wrongs I am struck to the quick,
Yet with my nobler reason 'gaitist my fury
Do I take part: the rarer action is
In virtue than in vengeance: they being penitent,
The sole drift of my purpose doth extend
Not a frown further. Go release them, Ariel:
My charms I'll break, their senses I'll restore,
And they shall be themselves.

ARIEL I'll fetch them, sir.

Exit

PROSPERO Ye elves of hills, brooks, standing lakes and groves,
And ye that on the sands with printless foot
Do chase the ebbing Neptune and do fly him
When he comes back; you demi-puppets that
By moonshine do the green sour ringlets make,
Whereof the ewe not bites, and you whose pastime
Is to make midnight mushrooms, that rejoice
To hear the solemn curfew; by whose aid,
Weak masters though ye be, I have bedimm'd
The noontide sun, call'd forth the mutinous winds,
And 'twixt the green sea and the azured vault
Set roaring war: to the dread rattling thunder
Have I given fire and rifted Jove's stout oak
With his own bolt; the strong-based promontory
Have I made shake and by the spurs pluck'd up
The pine and cedar: graves at my command
Have waked their sleepers, oped, and let 'em forth
By my so potent art. But this rough magic
I here abjure, and, when I have required
Some heavenly music, which even now I do,
To work mine end upon their senses that
This airy charm is for, I'll break my staff,
Bury it certain fathoms in the earth,
And deeper than did ever plummet sound
I'll drown my book.

Solemn music

Re-enter ARIEL before: then ALONSO, with a frantic gesture, attended by GONZALO; SE-BASTIAN and ANTONIO in like manner, attended by ADRIAN and FRANCISCO they all enter the circle which PROSPERO had made, and there stand charmed; which PROS-PERO observing, speaks:

A solemn air and the best comforter
To an unsettled fancy cure thy brains,
Now useless, boil'd within thy skull! There stand,
For you are spell-stopp'd.
Holy Gonzalo, honourable man,
Mine eyes, even sociable to the show of thine,
Fall fellowly drops. The charm dissolves apace,
And as the morning steals upon the night,
Melting the darkness, so their rising senses

Begin to chase the ignorant fumes that mantle
Their clearer reason. O good Gonzalo,
My true preserver, and a loyal sir
To him you follow'st! I will pay thy graces
Home both in word and deed. Most cruelly
Didst thou, Alonso, use me and my daughter:
Thy brother was a furtherer in the act.
Thou art pinch'd fort now, Sebastian. Flesh and blood,
You, brother mine, that entertain'd ambition,
Expell'd remorse and nature; who, with Sebastian,
Whose inward pinches therefore are most strong,
Would here have kill'd your king; I do forgive thee,
Unnatural though thou art. Their understanding
Begins to swell, and the approaching tide
Will shortly fill the reasonable shore
That now lies foul and muddy. Not one of them
That yet looks on me, or would know me Ariel,
Fetch me the hat and rapier in my cell:
I will discase me, and myself present
As I was sometime Milan: quickly, spirit;
Thou shalt ere long be free.

ARIEL sings and helps to attire him

Where the bee sucks. there suck I:
In a cowslip's bell I lie;
There I couch when owls do cry.
On the bat's back I do fly
After summer merrily.
Merrily, merrily shall I live now
Under the blossom that hangs on the bough.

PROSPERO Why, that's my dainty Ariel! I shall miss thee:
But yet thou shalt have freedom: so, so, so.
To the king's ship, invisible as thou art:
There shalt thou find the mariners asleep
Under the hatches; the master and the boatswain
Being awake, enforce them to this place,
And presently, I prithee.

ARIEL I drink the air before me, and return
Or ere your pulse twice beat.

Exit

GONZALO All torment, trouble, wonder and amazement
Inhabits here: some heavenly power guide us
Out of this fearful country!

PROSPERO Behold, sir king,
The wronged Duke of Milan, Prospero:
For more assurance that a living prince
Does now speak to thee, I embrace thy body;
And to thee and thy company I bid
A hearty welcome.

ALONSO Whether thou best he or no,
Or some enchanted trifle to abuse me,
As late I have been, I not know: thy pulse
Beats as of flesh and blood; and, since I saw thee,
The affliction of my mind amends, with which,
I fear, a madness held me: this must crave,
An if this be at all, a most strange story.
Thy dukedom I resign and do entreat
Thou pardon me my wrongs. But how should Prospero
Be living and be here?

PROSPERO First, noble friend,
Let me embrace thine age, whose honour cannot
Be measured or confined.

GONZALO Whether this be
Or be not, I'll not swear.

PROSPERO You do yet taste
Some subtilties o' the isle, that will not let you
Believe things certain. Welcome, my friends all!

Aside to SEBASTIAN and ANTONIO

But you, my brace of lords, were I so minded,
I here could pluck his highness' frown upon you
And justify you traitors: at this time
I will tell no tales.

SEBASTIAN [*Aside*]
The devil speaks in him.

PROSPERO No.
For you, most wicked sir, whom to call brother
Would even infect my mouth, I do forgive
Thy rankest fault; all of them; and require
My dukedom of thee, which perforce, I know,
Thou must restore.

ALONSO If thou be'st Prospero,
Give us particulars of thy preservation;
How thou hast met us here, who three hours since
Were wreck'd upon this shore; where I have lost—
How sharp the point of this remembrance is!—

My dear son Ferdinand.

PROSPERO I am woe for't, sir.

ALONSO Irreparable is the loss, and patience
Says it is past her cure.

PROSPERO I rather think
You have not sought her help, of whose soft grace
For the like loss I have her sovereign aid
And rest myself content.

ALONSO You the like loss!

PROSPERO As great to me as late; and, supportable
To make the dear loss, have I means much weaker
Than you may call to comfort you, for I
Have lost my daughter.

ALONSO A daughter?
O heavens, that they were living both in Naples,
The king and queen there! that they were, I wish
Myself were mudded in that oozy bed
Where my son lies. When did you lose your daughter?

PROSPERO In this last tempest. I perceive these lords
At this encounter do so much admire
That they devour their reason and scarce think
Their eyes do offices of truth, their words
Are natural breath: but, howsoe'er you have
Been justled from your senses, know for certain
That I am Prospero and that very duke
Which was thrust forth of Milan, who most strangely
Upon this shore, where you were wreck'd, was landed,
To be the lord on't. No more yet of this;
For 'tis a chronicle of day by day,
Not a relation for a breakfast nor
Befitting this first meeting. Welcome, sir;
This cell's my court: here have I few attendants
And subjects none abroad: pray you, look in.
My dukedom since you have given me again,
I will requite you with as good a thing;
At least bring forth a wonder, to content ye
As much as me my dukedom.

Here PROSPERO discovers FERDINAND and MIRANDA playing at chess

MIRANDA Sweet lord, you play me false.

FERDINAND No, my dear'st love,
I would not for the world.

MIRANDA Yes, for a score of kingdoms you should wrangle,
And I would call it, fair play.

ALONSO If this prove
A vision of the Island, one dear son
Shall I twice lose.

SEBASTIAN A most high miracle!

FERDINAND Though the seas threaten, they are merciful;
I have cursed them without cause.

Kneels

ALONSO Now all the blessings
Of a glad father compass thee about!
Arise, and say how thou camest here.

MIRANDA O, wonder!
How many goodly creatures are there here!
How beauteous mankind is! O brave new world,
That has such people in't!

PROSPERO 'Tis new to thee.

ALONSO What is this maid with whom thou wast at play?
Your eld'st acquaintance cannot be three hours:
Is she the goddess that hath sever'd us,
And brought us thus together?

FERDINAND Sir, she is mortal;
But by immortal Providence she's mine:
I chose her when I could not ask my father
For his advice, nor thought I had one. She
Is daughter to this famous Duke of Milan,
Of whom so often I have heard renown,
But never saw before; of whom I have
Received a second life; and second father
This lady makes him to me.

ALONSO I am hers:
But, O, how oddly will it sound that I
Must ask my child forgiveness!

PROSPERO There, sir, stop:
Let us not burthen our remembrance with
A heaviness that's gone.

GONZALO I have inly wept,
Or should have spoke ere this. Look down, you god,
And on this couple drop a blessed crown!
For it is you that have chalk'd forth the way
Which brought us hither.

ALONSO I say, Amen, Gonzalo!

GONZALO Was Milan thrust from Milan, that his issue
Should become kings of Naples? O, rejoice
Beyond a common joy, and set it down
With gold on lasting pillars: In one voyage
Did Claribel her husband find at Tunis,
And Ferdinand, her brother, found a wife
Where he himself was lost, Prospero his dukedom
In a poor isle and all of us ourselves
When no man was his own.

ALONSO [*To FERDINAND and MIRANDA*]
Give me your hands:
Let grief and sorrow still embrace his heart
That doth not wish you joy!

GONZALO Be it so! Amen!

Re-enter ARIEL, with the Master and Boatswain amazedly following

O, look, sir, look, sir! here is more of us:
I prophesied, if a gallows were on land,
This fellow could not drown. Now, blasphemy,
That swear'st grace o'erboard, not an oath on shore?
Hast thou no mouth by land? What is the news?

BOATSWAIN The best news is, that we have safely found
Our king and company; the next, our ship—
Which, but three glasses since, we gave out split—
Is tight and yare and bravely rigg'd as when
We first put out to sea.

ARIEL [*Aside to PROSPERO*]
Sir, all this service
Have I done since I went.

PROSPERO [*Aside to ARIEL*]
My tricksy spirit!

ALONSO These are not natural events; they strengthen
From strange to stranger. Say, how came you hither?

BOATSWAIN If I did think, sir, I were well awake,
I'ld strive to tell you. We were dead of sleep,
And—how we know not—all clapp'd under hatches;
Where but even now with strange and several noises
Of roaring, shrieking, howling, jingling chains,
And more diversity of sounds, all horrible,
We were awaked; straightway, at liberty;
Where we, in all her trim, freshly beheld

Our royal, good and gallant ship, our master
Capering to eye her: on a trice, so please you,
Even in a dream, were we divided from them
And were brought moping hither.

ARIEL [*Aside to PROSPERO*]
Was't well done?

PROSPERO [*Aside to ARIEL*]
Bravely, my diligence. Thou shalt be free.

ALONSO This is as strange a maze as e'er men trod
And there is in this business more than nature
Was ever conduct of: some oracle
Must rectify our knowledge.

PROSPERO Sir, my liege,
Do not infest your mind with beating on
The strangeness of this business; at pick'd leisure
Which shall be shortly, single I'll resolve you,
Which to you shall seem probable, of every
These happen'd accidents; till when, be cheerful
And think of each thing well.

Aside to ARIEL

Come hither, spirit:
Set Caliban and his companions free;
Untie the spell.

Exit ARIEL

How fares my gracious sir?
There are yet missing of your company
Some few odd lads that you remember not.

Re-enter ARIEL, driving in CALIBAN, STEPHANO and TRINCULO, in their stolen apparel

STEPHANO Every man shift for all the rest, and
let no man take care for himself; for all is
but fortune. Coragio, bully-monster, coragio!

TRINCULO If these be true spies which I wear in my head,
here's a goodly sight.

CALIBAN O Setebos, these be brave spirits indeed!
How fine my master is! I am afraid
He will chastise me.

SEBASTIAN Ha, ha!
What things are these, my lord Antonio?
Will money buy 'em?

ANTONIO Very like; one of them

Is a plain fish, and, no doubt, marketable.

PROSPERO Mark but the badges of these men, my lords,
Then say if they be true. This mis-shapen knave,
His mother was a witch, and one so strong
That could control the moon, make flows and ebbs,
And deal in her command without her power.
These three have robb'd me; and this demi-devil—
For he's a bastard one—had plotted with them
To take my life. Two of these fellows you
Must know and own; this thing of darkness!
Acknowledge mine.

CALIBAN I shall be pinch'd to death.

ALONSO Is not this Stephano, my drunken butler?

SEBASTIAN He is drunk now: where had he wine?

ALONSO And Trinculo is reeling ripe: where should they
Find this grand liquor that hath gilded 'em?
How camest thou in this pickle?

TRINCULO I have been in such a pickle since I
saw you last that, I fear me, will never out of
my bones: I shall not fear fly-blowing.

SEBASTIAN Why, how now, Stephano!

STEPHANO O, touch me not; I am not Stephano, but a cramp.

PROSPERO You'ld be king o' the isle, sirrah?

STEPHANO I should have been a sore one then.

ALONSO This is a strange thing as e'er I look'd on.

Pointing to Caliban

PROSPERO He is as disproportion'd in his manners
As in his shape. Go, sirrah, to my cell;
Take with you your companions; as you look
To have my pardon, trim it handsomely.

CALIBAN Ay, that I will; and I'll be wise hereafter
And seek for grace. What a thrice-double ass
Was I, to take this drunkard for a god
And worship this dull fool!

PROSPERO Go to; away!

ALONSO Hence, and bestow your luggage where you found it.

SEBASTIAN Or stole it, rather.

Exeunt CALIBAN, STEPHANO, and TRINCULO

PROSPERO Sir, I invite your highness and your train

To my poor cell, where you shall take your rest
For this one night; which, part of it, I'll waste
With such discourse as, I not doubt, shall make it
Go quick away; the story of my life
And the particular accidents gone by
Since I came to this isle: and in the morn
I'll bring you to your ship and so to Naples,
Where I have hope to see the nuptial
Of these our dear-beloved solemnized;
And thence retire me to my Milan, where
Every third thought shall be my grave.

ALONSO　I long
To hear the story of your life, which must
Take the ear strangely.

PROSPERO　I'll deliver all;
And promise you calm seas, auspicious gales
And sail so expeditious that shall catch
Your royal fleet far off.

Aside to ARIEL

My Ariel, chick,
That is thy charge: then to the elements
Be free, and fare thou well! Please you, draw near.

Exeunt

EPILOGUE

SPOKEN BY PROSPERO　Now my charms are all o'erthrown,
And what strength I have's mine own,
Which is most faint: now, 'tis true,
I must be here confined by you,
Or sent to Naples. Let me not,
Since I have my dukedom got
And pardon'd the deceiver, dwell
In this bare island by your spell;
But release me from my bands
With the help of your good hands:
Gentle breath of yours my sails
Must fill, or else my project fails,
Which was to please. Now I want
Spirits to enforce, art to enchant,
And my ending is despair,
Unless I be relieved by prayer,

Which pierces so that it assaults
Mercy itself and frees all faults.
As you from crimes would pardon'd be,
Let your indulgence set me free.

A Closer Look: William Stafford

William Stafford was born in Hutchinson, Kansas, in 1914. He received a B.A. and an M.A. from the University of Kansas at Lawrence and, in 1954, a Ph.D. from the University of Iowa. During the Second World War, Stafford was a conscientious objector and worked in the civilian public service camps. He traveled and read his work widely. Stafford taught at Lewis and Clark until his retirement in 1980.

INTERVIEW WITH AN AUTHOR

The following interview was written by Thomas E. Kennedy and published in *The American Poetry Review* in May–June 1993.

William Stafford: An Interview

This interview was conducted in September 1991 in the office of the Cultural Attache at the American Embassy in Copenhagen. When I appeared at the door of the embassy at the appointed time, I was stripped of my tape recorder and camera by a young security guard. "I'm here to interview one of America's greatest living poets," I explained. "I need those to do the job."

The guard was clearly unhappy, but had his orders. Finally, the press attache appeared and persuaded the guard to return my tools. Inside, the cultural attache and William Stafford greeted me with laughter. "You must be a dangerous man," Stafford said. He is a silver-haired, ruddy-faced man with a quiet smile and cordial manner. He opened the interview by saying, "I figure we're in the same racket, sort of, so I am going to relax, and you will kill me off or not depending on what you want to do with what I say."

Thomas E. Kennedy: In the dictionary of literary biography, Steve Garrison calls your poetry a log of explorations. Jonathan Holden calls you a "deep imagist," and Lawrence Lieberman calls you an "expansional" poet, working in confrontation with "the mystique of oneself." Donald Hall identifies your language as quiet, colloquial, and profoundly subjective and [says] that it—together with the work of your contemporaries—signaled the end of the era of T. S. Eliot and the New Criticism. Do you think of your poetry in such terms? Do you think of your style of poetry as signalling the end of a previous era? How do you view your poetry both in and of itself and as a part of the American tradition?

William Stafford: Let me start with what Donald Hall said: The end of T. S. Eliot. I and the people I know are writing the language of everyday, and the background of this writing sprang out of the daily language. The "Tradition and the Individual Talent," which T. S. Eliot wrote about, is not a written but a spoken tradition. The great river of language is the language that we speak. Whether Eliot thought of it that way or not, the effect of his writing tradition is to make an artist feel that he is the end of a relay race, of a succession of writers. I think we are the continuing turning and overturning of the language not only of writers, but of everyone—delivery people, mechanics, barbers, children. So the tradition is not the tradition of literature but of human discourse.

TK: In your poem "Burning a Book" you write, "More disturbing than book ashes are whole libraries that no one got around to writing. Desolate towns, miles of unthought in cities and the terrorized countryside where wild dogs own anything that moves . . . So I've burned books and there are many I haven't ever written and nobody has." This seems to me to embody poetically some of the dangers existing in the United States today, inter alia, in the hundreds of creative writing programs, where many writer-teachers, dependent on the university for their bread, might feel pressured to refrain from writing certain books or exploring certain thoughts, fearful from both the Right and the Left and chilled away from perhaps their best potentials. Do you feel that there is anything to this? Is the United States suffering a new McCarthyism today?

STAFFORD: I don't think so. I went late into those writing programs, and I was already formed. But I have been through them, and I don't feel alarmed. Maybe this is just a function of my being square, but I don't feel any pressure. I feel absolutely free. And the writers I know are not at all timid or reticent or guarded, except about their careers, and there's no way out of this. In any society, there are some things that will please people more than other things. You're in no danger in the United States, but you are enticed about certain rewards: Do I get invited to the White House? Don't kick too much. But I don't see how to get away from that in any society. Even in heaven, there's a jealous God.

TK: Do you think this affects the choices a writer makes? Does it cause important books to go unwritten, have an effect on the general freedom of thought and expression in the society?

STAFFORD: I think it does affect the choices—everything does. I've met many writers and students from abroad, and I don't know that it's any stronger in the U.S. than other places. An artist has to operate from an inner compass. It is not art when it's drawn by the numbers, when it's Hallmark cards for the market, and most writers I know are doing Hallmark cards for the market. You've got to be—I started to say tough, I don't know if you got to be tough. You've got to be reckless. A kind of divine recklessness someone said. And do it your way. Anything that guides you toward not doing it your way is eroding the compass or whatever you use as an artist. That's not government especially; it's not government in the United States. It is not any educational program any more than any other educational program. I feel lonely as an artist on purpose. Succumbing to an editor, to where the money is, trying to piggyback your second book on your first, all those things that people do: That is a human problem for all artists I presume.

TK: You taught at Lewis and Clark for more than thirty years in both the Literature and the Creative Writing departments.

STAFFORD: Mostly literature. I didn't teach writing if I had a choice.

TK: I read someplace you considered it a privilege as a poet to be able to spend your days considering great poems.

STAFFORD: If I said that I'd like to revise it a bit. I think a campus is a good place. There is a library. You have a lot of freewheeling people around you. Students and faculty enjoy this big bubble of protection from daily intrusion. It takes quiet, sustained thought, it takes reckless exploration of options to lead the intellectual life. I think the campus is one of the great good places.

TK: Yet the "politically correct" restrictions are a university phenomenon. In many years of submitting stories, this year is the first time I ever had anything rejected for allegedly being racist or sexist, and I was stunned because the works in question were in fact antiracist and antisexist. Both rejections were from university presses or journals. One large university press in rejecting a short-story collection, sent their anonymous reader's report which praised its merits, but lambasted it for sexism—among other things because only one story was from a woman's point of view, and many of the stories were in fact anti-sexist. The note from the editor said, "We don't necessarily agree with this evaluation, but you might want to take it into consideration if you are considering a rewrite."

STAFFORD: My interpretation, if it were my own manuscript, would be, well, I happened to hit a dud who didn't get what I was doing. Lately I have done this myself for publishers. You read a manuscript, you write a letter that they can use for deniability, say, "Well I asked an expert." That is one way you earn your money, as an expert who can be blamed. The out-of-town editor. But I think because of a great scramble to try to undo injustices of the past, a new kind of orthodoxy is surfacing. Many people talk about this, and my small witness is, I see no reason to disagree with their disquiet because I think a new kind of orthodoxy is being established, the reverse of the old sometimes: Every oppressed person is a hero and a martyr, which is, of course, far from true. And they're like the oppressors. Some of the oppressors could not help it, they were a reluctant part of the troops. So for a while it seems you are subject to those hazards, people are sensitized, and they have over-learned some things.

TK: Back to poetry: There seems to be a great focus on so-called confessional poetry today. When you look at a poem like "Prufrock," for example, there certainly seems to be an element of confession, but it reaches beyond that to far greater issues than the merely personal. Are there great poems being written today in that mode, or is there a danger in contemporary poetry of becoming fixated in the personal and anecdotal?

STAFFORD: That label has been handy for a long time. But to tag a poet with being confessional or subjective is a weird thing, because in fact, objective things are convergences of a lot of subjectivities. There are fads not just among writers, but among readers, editors, in societies. They eat it up. One of the most popular books, a bestseller, in the United States recently is *Iron John* by Robert Bly. He conducts gatherings where people explore their subjectivity. That's what people are interested in. They used to think maybe that they were certain types, he-men or she-women, and now that's all gone. It's all part of the turmoil we were talking about before: The injustices that existed before as a consequence of this kind of cookie-cutter society. We're breaking down those problems, so there is a lot of turning over in myself, the person. As a reader, I get tired of having the writer, the poet, be the center of the universe at which everything happens. I like to go to the Tycho Brahe Museum to see someone who looked out. As a writer, as a person, I would like to do that. On the other hand, the seething inner decision-making part of a person looms pretty large. So I feel sympathetic with the topic that we're on, but I don't feel orthodox one way or the other about this. I can't put a label on our time. I think many of the writers I know have succumbed to a style but that is a part of what we were talking about earlier. They are having in their time and writers turn over what is given them by their society.

TK: I feel a similar thing happening in fiction with the split between the experimental writers and the so-called realists or neo-realists. The realists seem to go very close-up on subjective experience, and when, say, Raymond Carver is most successful, it almost is like looking into outer space, but other times, it seems to fall rather flat and give a claustrophobic picture of existence.

STAFFORD: Yes, claustrophobia. I knew Raymond Carver. I know his writings very well. It has a strange effect, reading those things, but I wouldn't want to live there.

TK: Joseph Epstein complains that American poetry has grown less difficult. Walt Whitman once wrote that great poetry requires a great audience. Is one of the challenges of American poetry today that we who read and listen lack the ability to challenge our poets sufficiently to reach further than they do?

STAFFORD: I enjoy the writings of Joseph Epstein and am necessarily in awe of Whitman, but I feel disquiet again about this great audience label. As a writer, inside the writing, I don't care about the audience. You know, Whitman can worry about it. Critics, embassies, can worry about it. But as a writer, I could care less. You know, don't jiggle my elbow. I am doing something here that you got to get inside of. So I am not trying to create an audience or do something about my time. I am my time. And you want to find out what it's like? Here it is.

TK: In the sixties and the seventies American fiction became more intellectual and experimental, but American poetry, it seems to me, became simpler and more mimetic during the same period, and perhaps I've missed it, but I didn't see any great experimental things going on in the poetry of the sixties and seventies. I have seen so-called revolutionary or protest poetry and the experiment of coming closer to the rhythms of everyday language, of playing with the language, but I haven't seen something which I can equate with what happened in American fiction.

STAFFORD: Yes, imitative of daily life, that is what a lot of it is about. It's as close as possible, like Raymond Carver. No flourishes. Just what's there. That is an impulse I feel myself. On the other hand, I feel a lot of disquiet about the purposefully experimental. I mean purposeful anything. Purposefully patriotic, purposefully revolutionary, purposefully experimental, they're all leaving the center. They're all forsaking that inner compass that art comes from. The rest is artificial, drawing by the numbers. It disquiets me to see these blurbs on books. "This extends further." You know, the current trend of the experimental. I don't care where you're experimenting; what are you finding? What's there? I don't care if it's experimental. I am just doing what I find. Is it a pretty rock or not? if you like it, fine, if you don't, send it back.

TK: But the rocks you're writing about, are they primarily interior rocks or are they exterior rocks?

STAFFORD: Yesterday, I had a little twinge of this being out there in the University, where someone was complaining about students—"They're going into deconstruction and they no longer believe in truth." I had some feeling of being isolated from both sides. I mean, truth, mooth, what are you talking about? I don't feel either way. What I am doing is stumbling through this already mixed-up, serious experience of life, yes. So I have no labels to put on this. It's okay. I like to talk about these things but when I'm writing I'm in another mood, the mood of stupidity if you like, the mood of not knowing what is going on. Kind of sneaking along the trail.

TK: So the critical terminology is something you use after the fact. You don't use it whatsoever in your writing?

STAFFORD: That's right. I don't like absolute statements, but I'd like to erase all such considerations when I write.

TK: What about Language poetry? I never got very far with it myself. I don't understand it. I know it has some political intent, but I do not really know how to read it. Do you have thoughts about this?

STAFFORD: Yes, I do. I have encountered this. Anyone who is racketing around in our field encounters it, and I think this might seem a little strange coming from me because I am a language-that-I-meet-when-talk-to-the-mailman kind of poet, but experiments in the language, the Language poets seem as interesting as any other experiments, but no more. And I already said what I think about experimenters. To have a program is to abandon art. Right and left, I'm not there, you know, I'm here in the center.

TK: What do you think of poetry as a so-called transparent medium, in the sense of David Walker's book, *The Transparent Lyric:* that poetry, particularly contemporary poetry, is open-ended, leaving the final meaning to be created by the reader? It seems to me that much, perhaps most, of your poetry is quite specific, which is not to imply that it is simple but that it is nonetheless lucid, accessible, or at least approachable, there. Something which you have discovered and which I, as a reader, must rediscover to experience it with you—as opposed to the idea of poetry as an open-ended thing, where the final experience is left to the reader to complete.

STAFFORD: Well, the area that we are in fascinates me; I want to take the position that reading or listening, either, is an activity, and as a matter of fact all language has a shimmer in it. Even two plus two equals four, which is really a republican statement. It's alright with me if my poetry seems lucid and direct, but lucidity and directness are part of the strategy of discourse. And a person who assumes too fast that they've got it all is too fast. It depends on the receiver, depends on how far up you turn the interior volume. You can get a lot out of something that is simple. A part of the fun of writing, for me, is to have something that sounds so simple until later in the quiet of the night. Maybe a line like "Hope lasts a long time if you're happy." Is that optimistic or pessimistic? I don't know. I like the idea of putting forward things that put the reader or hearer off guard. Those who decide to be hard to nail down, that's interesting. Everyone is hard to nail down. Freud knew that, and I know that.

TK: Is the "meaning" of your poems in your possession, so to speak? When you've created a poem, is it completely your creation or is it also the reader's creation, in his experience of it?

STAFFORD: I think a poem is a crystallization of language. Language is just about to become this. So it's not my possession. Once I write it down, it's everybody's. Someone says what I see in your poem is such and such: I have no quarrel. The language is social. They own as much of it as I do. So I came to it my way, but they take it out their way. The language crystallizes, I make a lucky pass through some language, someone else grows lucky about it, okay, they may take it. I have a poem called "The Animal that Drank Up Sound," and I was in Iran when the Shah was there. The translator of my poems came to me and said, "Some of your poems are so political." He was afraid to translate the poem. I thought it was an Indian legend, but when I looked over his shoulder, I felt the Shah looking over my shoulder, and I saw it was a terribly political poem there where they had censorship.

TK: In a piece in *Field* twenty years ago you said, "At times, without my insisting on it, my writing becomes coherent, but I do not insist on it, for I know that in back of my activity there will be the coherence of myself, and that indulgence of my impulses will bring recurrent patterns and meanings again." Where does your writing issue from? Is it spontaneous overflow or planned activity that you comprehend and guide with your intellect?

STAFFORD: Whether or not a critic calls the writing reasonable, planned, intellectually satisfying, depends pretty much on where the critic enters the process. I mean, first there is nothing; then there is something. What happens in between? Well, the critic might say, you begin to have a plan. I say, How do you begin to have a plan, and where does it come from? A student challenged me on this once, about how hazy it all is at the beginning. He quoted a writer—I think it was Ferlinghetti—who said, When I write anything, even a poem, I know exactly what I am doing. I have an outline in mind. My response is, Where did you get the outline? There was a time when you did not have the outline. Then you have the outline. What happened in between? That is the creative part. So I think he left out the interesting part, the creative instant. So I write from—I'll be vainglorious—a succession of creative instants. A critic comes along and says, Ah! This makes sense, so you must have planned it ahead of time. I don't know what to say. I think I go through the same process the critic does. He explains it one way, I explain it another.

TK: Does that plan come from the totality then of your person, or does it come from some kind of Jungian collective source?

STAFFORD: The Jungian metaphor is sometimes handy. That's what I feel about that. It is inevitable, and probably buried in the language. I am already getting myself into trouble trying to extricate myself from this. A person is lost in the woods; they bring a tracker to find this person. The tracker brings his bloodhound in the back of his pick-up. The journalist or critic comes up to the bloodhound and says: "Mr. bloodhound, what is your plan?" The bloodhound goes Sniff sniff sniff sniff. The critic says, "I mean, you know, you must have a principle on this to find this person." The bloodhound's going Sniff sniff sniff sniff. I'm the bloodhound. The critic wants to have a plan.

TK: Is the poet's role an elite one, as Eliot suggested, "to purify the language of the tribe," or should we be mourning the days of popular poets like Kipling, Housman, Edna St. Vincent Millay, e.e. cummings, perhaps even Robert W. Service. I always liked him from when I was a kid.

STAFFORD: Sure, I can recite some of those. We can probably do it in unison. "A bunch of the boys were whooping it up / at the Malamute saloon / The kid that handles the music box . . ."

TK: ". . . was playing a ragtime tune . . ."

STAFFORD: See? Those things have grabbed us earlier. We could do a lot of that. I don't make a big distinction about this. Poetry happens wherever the language gets lucky. People are talking in the street; they like some things they say more than other things. You can see it by their expressions. I think we all veer into and out of these intervals of relative illumination, clarity, or maybe even dizziness. Some of that comes in a literary way, and some of it comes in this language way, and as a writer, I don't restrict myself to the literary way. I feel easy. I feel the limits. This is the function of where we are in relation to a sustained interest in discourse. I have a sustained interest in discourse. We have the terminology for it, we've been near this neighborhood before, we can find our way in and out of these topics that we're on. I think that's fine.

TK: It seems to me that there is little lyricism in American poetry today and that song is not one of the major parts of contemporary poetry. Maybe I have a tin ear. T. S. Eliot is considered elite, but to me his language has always been symphonic, musical, and when I read T. S. Eliot it doesn't matter to me whether I understand what he is saying because I find the language so musical and beautiful. And I feel the same about Dylan Thomas, his surprising turns of song, and even Robert Frost and E. A. Robinson seem to me to have a good deal of music, whereas much of the poetry I read today seems to have only the very faintest remnant of music. Is that because the poetry that I am pointing to is not very good poetry, or is this the result of abandoning fixed meter, or some sense of meter beyond the rhythm of everyday speech? Or am I mistaken?

STAFFORD: This is an enticing area for anyone in discourse. Not just a poet, anyone, a talker, a writer of anything, a listener. I feel completely sympathetic with the drift about T. S. Eliot and the rest, too. When I look at some of this poetry, I wonder what kind of a tin ear does this person have? They have a tin ear, that's what kind of tin ear they have. In between in this sandwich, that's the area of manoeuvre for us, I think. What you said about liking T. S. Eliot even when you don't quite understand it, language is like that. When you listen to speeches of the President, the melody is what's getting to you. If you think it's all intellectual, think again. These writers are better than that. So you are succumbing to a melody, and if you think that you're not, it's just what he'd like you to think. And some people just haven't got that. They think they can do it in a nonelegant way, and just so they got the message right, they got it. The message is not just what they think it is; it is the total experience. I think poetry is the form of discourse in which that haunting part, that double part of language, is particularly important; for it to be absent is to forego a lot of the richness that the language offers. When Milton, to take a champion, says, "Avenge, oh Lord, Thy slaughtered saints, whose bones he scattered in the Alpine mountains . . ." I haven't come to a rhyme yet, but all the syllables are like a team of sled dogs. All sorts of things are happening. So, a poet is totally responsible. A prose writer ought to be totally responsible, but we allow them quite a bit of leeway.

TK: We have to write so many more words. I understand that you have been very attracted to fiction and read a lot of it.

STAFFORD: I read a lot more prose than poetry. I have more respect for current prose writers than current poets. There is something about life, especially in the United States, which drains the talent out of the poetry area of literature. Maybe one of the great big drains is the label of the dollar bill, and if you got talents of discourse and you like to eat well, guess what? Should you do a novel or a collection of poems?

TK: Depends on your novel, too. Actually, the money is in speech-writing.

STAFFORD: Other kinds of discourse. And you know we are surrounded by people who don't "get" it. They're proud of that. That's a stupid thing to say, but they say it: I don't get it. Okay, you don't get it. That's interesting.

TK: What writers do you like?

STAFFORD: I think Cervantes said, "I'm the kind of person, when I see a piece of paper blowing down the street, I got to pick it up and see what is on it." That's the kind of reader I am. I read anything, any trash. And I tend toward pretty good trash. But when I read for fun, I read Nietzsche, Kierkegaard, Pascal, a lot of others.

TK: You have a Ph.D. from the University of Iowa for which you did a creative dissertation. Do you feel that the current MFA and other creative writing university programs suffer from a lack of scholars on the staff and would do better to have perhaps something approaching more of equal time between scholarship and creative writing?

STAFFORD: At Iowa, when I went for my Ph.D., I didn't know about the other option. So I took all the courses, old English, Latin, the various periods. I took the writtens and orals, and then handed in a Ph.D. thesis. I like being freighted with that experience of having read under stringent conditions these works. Otherwise, I would not have done it systematically. But if I didn't have gusto for it, I wouldn't have done it. If someone was thinking about doing this just to get a job, I'd say forget it. But if you can't help yourself, go ahead, it's fun. But my fear is that if the MFA program decided to take on the scholarly part, the scholarship they would promote might turn into something like developmental periods in the collected works of Philip Whalen or something like that. I'd rather read Milton.

TK: Well, I was thinking in terms of more emphasis on the masters. And more communication between the creative and academic departments. When I took my MFA, I was very happy that there were some instructors there with Ph.D.s, and I was always appalled to hear people going around complaining about being forced to read dead poets.

STAFFORD: I share your disquiet. We're in that kind of world. I think maybe the crucial distinction is the degree of gusto a student has. If they are reading Milton as a duty to pass the exam, then they have missed the flight. It's a dead bird they're studying. Maybe what we are up against so often in education is not the letter of the law, but the spirit of the law.

TK: You were born and grew up in Kansas and then moved to Oregon?

STAFFORD: There are various small diversions. During World War II, I was drafted out of Kansas, and for four years I was a conscientious objector. Whatever concentration camp I was sent to—I use this word about the barracks, wire cots, etc.—first to Arkansas, then to several places in California, ending in Illinois, for those four years, I was outside of Kansas. This was my transition time, when my life turned around, when I knew it wasn't stable, when my own country was a foreign place. So in a way, I was quickly transported to Siberia, and it made a difference. And even in Oregon, I was not there a lot of time. I taught a year in Indiana, a year in California, a while in Alaska, Montana, Vermont, etc.

TK: Is Oregon home now?

STAFFORD: Yes, but Kansas also feels like home. They say you can't go home, but when I go back to Kansas, do I feel at home? Yeah.

TK: What about the use of language? Do you find a difference?

STAFFORD: The short answer is no. The difference is only superficial. It's easy to talk with Texans. Even New Yorkers.

TK: So there really is one American language?

STAFFORD: To say otherwise when you are abroad would be misleading. Of course, there are nuances. There are differences between north and south Denmark for all I know. Some Eskimos have a southern accent.

TK: What about differences in culture?

STAFFORD: The big difference is, there are people who are positive, there are people who think they know where the center of the universe is. They are foreigners wherever they are. I don't think they know where the center of the universe is. The more positive they are, the more vulnerable they are. There are a lot of maybes in this experience.

TK: Have you read the experimental fiction writers of the last twenty years or so? Robert Coover, Donald Barthelme, John Barth, etc.

STAFFORD: As one of those people like Cervantes who catches up any piece of paper that's blowing by, . . . when they blew by, I read them and I didn't put them in the garbage can. But there is a big river of language, and they are exploring tributaries. The Mississippi is elsewhere. The Mississippi is the language that flows around me every day. Even far-out people, when they want to find out the direction to go, they join the river. The tradition that I am a part of is our big river of language.

TK: You spoke once about the loneliness of the poet and the poet's misguided need to check with others for validation of his work. Is there anyplace a writer can go for affirmation, or must he just labor alone?

STAFFORD: Once when I was travelling in the East, my host, a very friendly guy and a good writer and teacher in a good university, asked who my committee for my books consisted of—who I sent a book to when it was about ready for publication, to look it over and give ideas about it. I said, I send it to an editor. He picked up a book there in his living room and opened it. I think it was by Maxine Kumin, and it said, special thanks to so and so and so and so. He said they had a hot line back and forth, and every time they write a poem they call up and read it to the other one to hear what they have to say. Then he picked up another book and there, too, this writer said special thanks to so and so—Raymond Carver, Tess Gallagher and some others. And I said Oh, well, I'm from the West, and I didn't know about this. I just write my books myself, and I send them off and see if they send them back. Well, while I was there the mail came, and there was a manuscript from a very well known poet—he was ready to submit and wanted my host to look it over and give him ideas of how to change it before he let an editor see it. It's like a student paying someone to fix his term paper. I didn't say this to my host but I thought, that is cheating. Is it your book or not? Is it a committee book? Yeah, it's a committee book. I have always thought poetry is the kind of discourse nobody edits. If you write prose, if you're Thomas Wolfe, you're saved by some heroic editor, but if you are a poet, editors don't want to get into that. They will say yes or no, but they won't say here's how to improve it. If they know so much, why don't they do it? My wife doesn't even see a piece before I'm done with it. My son, who is a writer, doesn't see it. A soldier once asked

Gandhi, When shall I lay down my rifle? and Gandhi said, When you have to. What I say to an editor is, Am I begging you to publish my book? No. If you'd like to, do it, if you don't want to, send it back.

TK: As a committed pacifist who did not serve militarily in the Second World War, what are your thoughts on the recent war in the Gulf?

STAFFORD: I was appalled by this war. Like many others. I thought they did the wrong thing. I mean, incinerating all those people. Riling up the whole world. A collossal failure of understanding, of the possibilities. Failure of imagination. A swashbuckling excursion that may have consequences. Creating stable conditions takes deftness, the accumulation of world opinions. It's better if you can begin to make it happen by millions of intricate little adjustments. But every now and then someone sees a short trip, thinks, Well, we can neglect the secondary effects of this, and we can decisively win this war, so let's do it. And as a human being, a hostage to those things happening above us, you know, let's see if we can do it without killing so many people.

TK: So you are opposed to war. Period.

STAFFORD: I am. I remember the person beside me in a cot in Arkansas. He just got his Ph.D. in philosophy from Harvard. His draft board called him in: "Oh, so you're opposed to war. All wars? Even a good war?" He said, "Show me a good one."

TK: What are your thoughts in general on recent developments in the world? East Europe and the fall of the Berlin Wall and the Iron Curtain? Do you think that the world now has a real chance to turn from the bloody past and to try to shape peace, or is man doomed by his own folly to continue to repeat the bloody past?

STAFFORD: (*Chuckles*) We're not betting money on this, are we? I don't want to manage my estate by my response, but because I want my response to be in terms of possibility, I feel cheered. I welcome all this, very much so.

TK: Do you see the increasing trends of international initiatives as a positive trend—the growth of the European Economic Communities and the increasing importance of the United Nations . . .

STAFFORD: Yes, I'm a positive liberal, and in all those standard ways I could be categorized as one. I went to graduate school in economics, not literature, at the University of Wisconsin. As an economist, I am on the side of free trade and the natural adaptability of various regions as a resource for the world.

TK: In your poem, "Waiting in Line," you seem to praise consciousness, even the moment of it that allows an elderly person to be aware, standing on a corner, that it is time to say goodbye to all of it, as a moment of great joy, presumably because it is a fully experienced moment. Do you see poetry as a continuing quest for the refinement of consciousness?

STAFFORD: I'm leaning toward yes on this. I sort of like to wander around in between yes and no, that is my area, in between, there is a lot of maybe in my life, and in my language, but I think the answer is yes. It has to do with the difference between unconsciousness and full consciousness. I think all of us, perhaps especially in the literary life, are inducers of realization. And there is another part of me that wants to go and sleep in the sun.

I don't want to neglect that. I don't want to be a frenzied seeker of sensation. There is something else. So it is not the same as sensationalism. Act, I'm sort of on the dull side deliberately, but being helpful, nondestructive has illuminated life very much I think.

TK: But writing poetry and dedicating your life to it, do you feel as you look back at yourself in earlier periods of your life that your consciousness is more refined now, that you have come to a higher level of sorts, that in some way your work has had a cumulative effect on your totality as a human being? Or do you look back and say, well that's who I was then, and I can't be that person anymore, because now I'm here?

STAFFORD: Luckily for me, I can say I don't know. I do not feel formed as a person. There is a lot of rigidness in that. I am not the kind of writer who says, This is what I wrote when I was beginning; isn't it stupid? See what I've become now? No, this is what I wrote then, and it still looks pretty good to me. I feel congenial about it. You may think it's bad, but that is your privilege. I know where it comes from. I feel at home. There are both gains and losses as the years go by.

TK: I am thinking also of the poem you wrote in which there is a line that says something to the effect of—it is too late for earlier ways of doing things; now we must act in accordance with the light we have at this moment.

STAFFORD: Yes.

TK: You once said, "Writing can be a liberating thing for the individual. It does not have to be held to the task of producing masterpieces for later generations. The idea of engaging in an activity which is helpful in itself is a part of our lives now more than it was before and I think that is good." I agree, but it also occurs to me that if the people who have produced masterpieces—I think of those most important to me, T. S. Eliot, Dostoyevski, Shakespeare, etc.—had not done what they did, I don't know what I would do. And I wonder who will do that for our own times? Who will create the masterpieces of our own times—if indeed we are worthy of masterpieces?

STAFFORD: This is tantalizing to me because, like you, I have enjoyed the works of these people. But something about banking on that disquiets me. As a writer I would be harming my usefulness to pay much attention to this. That burden is not my burden. I read an article recently that said, If you are a student writer now, you must be sure to read so and so and so and so, you know, the author's friends. I thought, Poor Sophocles! He didn't have a chance to read Adrienne Rich. Too bad. No, what we rely on is what the tide brings, and what it brings today is what we use, and to think of what the tide should have brought is not the function of an oyster. The oyster takes what the tide brings. That is what I do. If I did not have Adrienne Rich, I'd make do with Sophocles.

POEMS

Traveling Through the Dark

Traveling through the dark I found a deer
dead on the edge of the Wilson River road.

It is usually best to roll them into the canyon:
that road is narrow; to swerve might make more dead.

By glow of the tail-light I stumbled back of the car
and stood by the heap, a doe, a recent killing;
she had stiffened already, almost cold.
I dragged her off; she was large in the belly.

My fingers touching her side brought me the reason—
her side was warm; her fawn lay there waiting,
alive, still, never to be born.
Beside that mountain road I hesitated.

The car aimed ahead its lowered parking lights;
under the hood purred the steady engine.
I stood in the glare of the warm exhaust turning red;
around our group I could hear the wilderness listen.

I thought hard for us all—my only swerving—,
then pushed her over the edge into the river.

Waking at 3 am

Even in the cave of the night when you
wake and are free and lonely,
neglected by others, discarded, loved only
by what doesn't matter—even in that
big room no one can see,
you push with your eyes till forever
comes in its twisted figure eight
and lies down in your head.
You think water in the river;
you think slower than the tide in
the grain of the wood; you become
a secret storehouse that saves the country,
so open and foolish and empty.
You look over all that the darkness
ripples across. More than has ever
been found comforts you. You open your
eyes in a vault that unlocks as fast
and as far as your thought can run.
A great snug wall goes around everything,
has always been there, will always
remain. It is a good world to be
lost in. It comforts you. It is
all right. And you sleep.

Evolution

The thing is, I'm still
an animal. What is a spirit,
I wonder. But I only wonder:
I'll never know.

Night comes and I'm hungry.
Tempted by anything, or called
by my peculiar appetites,
I turn aside, faithfully.

What comes before me
transforms into my life.
"Truth," I say, and it answers,
"I'm what you need."

I sing, and a song shaped like a bird
flies out of my mouth.

A CRITICAL ESSAY

The following essay was written by Terry Fairchild and published in *The Explicator* in Spring 1997.

WILLIAM STAFFORD'S "TRAVELING THROUGH THE DARK"

William Stafford's "Traveling Through the Dark" examines the killing of a pregnant doe by a hit-and-run driver, a subject that would no doubt be treated sentimentally by a lesser poet. One of nature's exquisite creatures has been slaughtered and callously left on the road, unburied, unmourned, potentially to cause future accidents. Stafford, thankfully, avoids the maudlin trap of this topic by presenting the poem's events objectively with an almost reporter-like, semi-detached eye. His attitude toward this common tragedy is sadness but also resignation.

The repetition of the title in the opening phrase states the narrator's literal experience but suggests much more. It conveys the conditions of the accident. The road death is fresh, so the driver who had hit the deer was presumably also driving in the dark, and because nothing was done about the accident, for the sake of the deer or the safety of others, the driver's inaction suggests moral darkness. The darkness also suggests the narrator's confusion about what to do with the deer. "Traveling Through the Dark" also symbolizes the spiritual void of humankind in its insensitivity toward nature. Finally, darkness points to the final destiny of all beings, the darkness of death.

The poem's opening line creates for the reader a false first impression: the surprising appearance of a deer, usually an occasion for happiness. However, the first word of the next line, "dead," immediately reverses this impression, more so by its delay. Following the pause at the end of line one and at the beginning of line two, "dead" receives extra emphasis. Placed where it is in the poem, the word can hardly be pronounced without producing a dull, flat, thud; in this context it is more than surprising, it is appalling, like the experience of a driver negotiating a mountain bend and seeing a dead deer for the first time. Stafford's traveler quickly assesses the scene and understands its moral implications. It is his duty to roll the deer "into the canyon . . . to swerve might make more dead." The word "swerve" here means neglect of duty, but it also suggests the kinetic image of a swerving automobile, the event that killed the deer.

The second stanza examines the dead deer more closely under the harsh glare of tail-lights: an eerie, infernal scene that links the traveler's vehicle with that of the hit-and-run driver. The deer is called a "heap," no longer a being, a cold and stiff thing that can be dragged off. Then we learn that it is a pregnant doe, a detail that moves our emotions from sympathy to the brink of pathos. However, Stafford's language is precise and controlled; he doesn't want to be inflammatory. Understating the situation, he simply says, "she was large in the belly."

The third stanza offers an unhappy paradox. The traveler feels the doe's underside and finds that it is still warm; it contains a fawn waiting to be born. In death the traveler discovers life, but not normal life that emerges from the womb into the world, for the fawn is "never to be born." This unhappy realization causes the traveler to hesitate. His mind, as pregnant as the dead doe, is filled with muddled emotions: pity, anger, frustration, and confusion about how to act. He may even wonder if the fawn can be saved, but knows all along what he must do. The reader understands from the first stanza. The traveler's hesitation, therefore, may be seen as simply a moment of silence, a secular prayer before performing his inescapable task.

The fourth stanza draws a closer parallel between the traveler's car and the dead deer. The car with its parking lights jutting forward mimics a beast staring into the darkness, and like the heart of a mammal, its engine "purred." The traveler stands in its "warm exhaust turning red," no doubt from the glare of the tail-lights but also from heated emotions pumping blood to his face. The red glow, moreover, cannot help but suggest the deer's blood. The traveler senses the wilderness witnessing (and perhaps censuring) the drama of "our group": the dead deer, the fawn, never to be born, the car only mechanically alive, and himself.

In the final couplet the traveler thinks hard for "us all," not just for the group, but for every being in creation, for all who suffer and face death—a natural prayer brought on by the moment. The pause was his "only swerving," he says, nothing more could be done. Finally he pushes the deer into the river, a shock even though the poem has prepared us for it. The reader has known from the beginning that this is what the traveler will do to save more lives, but this knowledge cannot eliminate a feeling of helplessness nor a sense of waste.

Stafford's poem might have worked the reader into a frenzy of hate for the hit-and-run driver, but "Traveling Through the Dark" is not about hatred. It is about the sadness that accompanies each traveler on the longer journey of life and toward the inevitability of death, so that when we encounter a misfortune on the road, we hesitate before we move on. Stafford's somber scene is a small tragedy, but in his simplicity, in his directness without swerving, he creates a metaphor for life.

Conclusion

In this casebook on (hu)man/nature, we were able to explore even more of the human condition, beyond just the individual. We were asked to recognize that even when some things are set into motion, we still have a choice. Nothing is carved, written, or determined in stone. Unfortunately, not everyone will respond to a choice, because that involves personal responsibility. Sometimes, as we saw, it seemed easier to acquiesce and pass it off as "human nature."

Credits

Chapter 1

p. 5: Gwendolyn Brooks from *Blacks:* "We Real Cool." Reprinted by consent of Brooks Permissions; **p. 11:** Robin Hemley, "The Holocaust Party" from *The Big Ear,* John F. Blair Publishing, Winston-Salem, NC. Reprinted by permission of the author.

Chapter 2

p. 33: "A Curtain Up Review: The Laramie Project," Elyse Sommer, <www.curtainup.com>. Reprinted by permission of Elyse Sommer; **p. 36:** Review, "(Mostly) Harmless Theatre Production: The Laramie Project," Steve Callahan. Reprinted by permission of KDHX-FM, St. Louis, Missouri; **p. 47:** By permission. From Merriam-Webster's Collegiate® Dictionary, 11th Edition. ©2005 by Merriam-Webster, Incorporated (http://www.Merriam-Webster.com); **p. 53:** Lindsey Franklin, "'Oranges': A Glimpse at a Boy's Life Truly Lived."

Chapter 3

p. 64: "Say I" Written by Scott Stapp and Mark Tremonti © 1999 Tremonti/Stapp Music and Dwight Frye Music, Inc. All rights adm. by Dwight Frye Music, Inc.; **p. 66:** "Black Elvis" by Geoffrey Becker originally appeared in *Ploughshares* Vol. 25, #4. Reprinted by permission of the author; **p. 76:** "Call It Fear" from the book *She Had Some Horses* by Joy Harjo. Copyright © 1983, 1987 by Thunder's Mouth Press. Appears by permission of the publisher, Thunder's Mouth Press; **p. 77:** "The Welcome Table" from *In Love & Trouble: Stories of Black Women,* copyright © 1970 and renewed 1998 by Alice Walker, reprinted by permission of Harcourt, Inc.

Chapter 4

p. 82: Gwendolyn Brooks from *Blacks:* "We Real Cool." Reprinted by consent of Brooks Permissions; **p. 87:** Christopher Davis, "Aborted Fetus" from *Ploughshares,* Winter 1990–1991; **p. 90:** "Heartbeats" by Melvin Dixon from *Poets for Life,* Crown Publishers, 1989. Reprinted by permission. **p. 92:** Robin Hemley, "Riding the Whip" from *20 Under 30: Best Stories by America's New Young Writers,* Scribner's, 1986, originally appeared in ACM (Another Chicago Magazine, 1984). Reprinted by permission of the author.

Chapter 5

p. 102: (*top*) Christopher Davis, "At an Intersection" from *The Tyrant of the Past and the Slave of the Future,* © 1990 Texas Tech University Press. Reprinted by permission; (*bottom*) "A Good Man Is Hard to Find" from *A Good Man Is Hard to Find and Other Stories,* copyright 1953 by Flannery O'Connor and renewed 1981 by Regina O'Connor, reprinted by permission of Harcourt, Inc.

645

Chapter 6

p. 121: "Ethics," from *Waiting for My Life* by Linda Pastan. Copyright © 1981 by Linda Pastan. Used by permission of W.W. Norton & Company, Inc.; **p. 138:** Monica Martin-Kendrick, "Turning In: An Exploration of 'The Second Sermon on the Warpland.'"

Chapter 7

p. 150: Claude McKay, "The White House" from *Selected Poems of Claude McKay*. Courtesy of the Literary Representative for the Works of Claude McKay, Schomburg Center for Research in Black Culture, The New York Public Library, Astor, Lenox and Tilden Foundations; **p. 155:** Amanda Clark, "Anne Sexton's 'Cinderella.'"

Chapter 8

p. 162: "In a Station of the Metro" by Ezra Pound, from *Personae,* copyright © 1926 by Ezra Pound. Reprinted by permission of New Directions Publishing Corp.

Chapter 9

p. 189: Excerpt from Audrey Crawford, "'Handing the Power-Glasses Back and Forth': Women and Technology in the Poems by Adrienne Rich," *NWSA Journal* 7, no. 3 (Fall 1995): 35–53; **pp. 193, 194:** Gerald Graff, excerpts from "Disliking Books at an Early Age" from *Lingua Franca,* September/October 1992. Reprinted by permission of the author.

Chapter 10

p. 209: "Who's Got My Back?" Written by Scott Stapp and Mark Tremonti © 2002 Tremonti/Stapp Music and Dwight Frye Music, Inc. All rights adm. by Dwight Frye Music, Inc.; **p. 214:** Excerpts from an interview with Bo Taylor, archivist for The Museum of the Cherokee Indian, regarding "Who's Got My Back." Reprinted with the permission of Bo Taylor; **p. 218:** "The Emperor of Ice Cream," copyright 1923 and renewed 1951 by Wallace Stevens, from *The Collected Poems of Wallace Stevens* by Wallace Stevens. Used by permission of Alfred A. Knopf, a division of Random House, Inc.; **p. 219:** Arthur F. Bethea, "Wallace Stevens, 'The Emperor of Ice Cream,'" *The Explicator,* January 2004. Reprinted with permission of the Helen Dwight Reid Educational Foundation. Published by Heldref Publications, 1319 Eighteenth St., NW, Washington, DC 20036-1802. Copyright © 2004; **p. 229:** "Critical Annotated Bibliography" by Amanda Clark.

Casebook 1

p. 237: Amiri Baraka, "An Agony. As Now." from the book *The Leroi Jones/Amiri Baraka Reader,* William J. Harris, Editor. Copyright © 1960, 1961, 1963, 1964, 1965, 1966, 1967, 1968, 1969, 1970, 1971, 1972, 1975, 1979, 1980, 1981, 1984, 1985, 1987, 1989, 2000 by Amiri Baraka. Appears by permission of the publisher, Thunder's Mouth Press, a division of Avalon Publishing Group; **p. 242:** "Black Hair" from *New and Selected Poems* © 1995 by Gary Soto. Used with permission of Chronicle Books LLC, San Francisco. Visit Chronicle Books.com; **p. 243:** "Poem About my Rights" from the book *Living Room* by June Jordan. Copyright © 1985 by June Jordan. Appears by permission of the publisher, Thunder's Mouth Press, a division of Avalon Publishing Group; **p. 246:** Brandon Bowlin, "Behind the Golden Son," from *Pills and Pillows;* **p. 248:** "A & P," from *Pigeon Feathers and Other Stories* by John Updike, copyright © 1962 and renewed 1990 by John Updike. Used by permission of Alfred A. Knopf, a division of Random House, Inc.; **p. 252:** "I Stand Here Ironing," copyright © 1956, 1957, 1960, 1961 by Tillie Olsen, from *Tell Me a Riddle* by Tillie Olsen, Introduction by John Leonard. Used by permission of Elaine Markson Literary Agency; **p. 258:** *Beauty.* Copyright © 2001 by Alexander Speer, Trustee. All rights reserved. All inquiries concerning rights should be addressed to Alexander Speer, Actors Theatre of Louisville, 316 Main Street, Louisville, KY 40202; **p. 263:** This article first appeared in Salon.com, at http://www.Salon.com. An online version remains in the Salon archives. Reprinted with permission; **p. 268:** "Harrison Bergeron" by Kurt Vonnegut, from *Welcome to the Monkey House* by Kurt Vonnegut, Jr., copyright © 1961 by Kurt Vonnegut, Jr. Used by permission of Dell Publishing, a division of Random House, Inc.; **p. 273:** "The Politics of Kurt Vonnegut's 'Harrison Bergeron,'" from *Studies in Short Fiction,* by Darryl Hattenhauer, Twayne Publishers, © 1998 Twayne Publishers. Reprinted by permission of the Gale Group.

Casebook 2

p. 280: (*bottom*) "Anthem for Doomed Youth" by Wilfred Owen, from *The Collected Poems of Wilfred Owen,* copyright © 1963 by Chatto & Windus, Ltd. Reprinted by permission of New Directions Publishing Corp.; **p. 281:** "A Walk After Dark," copyright © 1966 by W.H. Auden, from *Collected Poems* by W.H. Auden. Used by permission of Random House, Inc.; **p. 283:** (*top*) "Men at Forty," from *Collected Poems* by Donald Justice, copyright © 2004 by Donald Justice. Used by permission of Alfred A. Knopf, a division of Random House, Inc.; (*bottom*) "Diving into the Wreck." Copyright © 2002 by Adrienne Rich, Copyright © 1973 by W.W. Norton & Company, Inc., from *The Fact of a Doorframe: Selected Poems 1950–2001* by Adrienne Rich. Used by permission of the author and W.W. Norton & Company, Inc.; **p. 286:** "First Boyfriend," from *The Gold Cell* by Sharon Olds, copyright © 1987 by Sharon Olds. Used by permission of Alfred A. Knopf, a division of Random House, Inc.; **p. 287:** "Oranges" from *New and Selected Poems* by Gary Soto. © 1995. Published by Chronicle Books LLC, San Francisco. Used with permission. Visit http://www.chroniclebooks.com; **p. 289:** (*top*) "Adolescence — II" from *The Yellow House on the Corner,* Carnegie-Mellon University Press, © 1980 by Rita Dove. Reprinted by permission of the author; (*bottom*) "Something to Look Forward to," from *Available Light* by Marge Piercy, copyright © 1988 by Middlemarsh, Inc. Used by permission of Alfred A. Knopf, a division of Random House, Inc.; **p. 291:** "The Man Who Was Almost a Man" from the book *Eight Men: Short Stories* by Richard Wright. Copyright © 1940, 1961 by Richard Wright. Appears by permission of the publisher, Thunder's Mouth Press, a division of Avalon Publishing Group; **p. 300:** Alice Munro, "Boys and Girls." From *Dance of the Happy Shades.* Copyright © 1968 by Alice Munro. Reprinted by permission of the William Morris Agency, LLC on behalf of the author; **p. 310:** "WASP" from *Picasso at the Lapin Agile and Other Plays* by Steve Martin. Copyright © 1996 by 40 Share Productions, Inc. Used by permission of Grove/Atlantic, Inc.; **p. 327:** A Conversation with Gwendolyn Brooks and Sheldon Hackney, *Humanities,* May/June 94, Vol. 15, Issue 3, p. 4, 6pp; **pp. 335, 339:** Gwendolyn Brooks from *Blacks:* "The Sundays of Satin-Legs Smith," "The Lovers of the Poor," "A Song in the Front Yard." Reprinted by consent of Brooks Permissions; **p. 342:** Judith Saunders, "The Love Song of Satin-Legs Smith: Gwendolyn Books Revisits Prufrock's Hell," *Papers of Language and Literature,* Volume 36, No 1, Winter 2000. Copyright © 2000 by The Board of Trustees, Southern Illinois University Edwardsville. Reprinted by permission.

Casebook 3

p. 357: (*top*) Gwendolyn Brooks from *Blacks:* "The Bean Eaters." Reprinted by consent of Brooks Permissions; (*bottom*) All lines from "Daddy" from *Ariel* by Sylvia Plath. Copyright © 1963 by Ted Hughes. Reprinted by permission of HarperCollins Publishers and Faber and Faber Ltd.; **p. 360**: "Cinderella," from *Transformations* by Anne Sexton. Copyright © 1971 by Anne Sexton. Reprinted by permission of Houghton Mifflin Company. All rights reserved.; **p. 363** (*top*) "My Papa's Waltz," copyright 1942 by Hearst Magazines, Inc., from *The Collected Poems of Theodore Roethke* by Theodore Roethke. Used by permission of Doubleday, a division of Random House, Inc.; (*bottom*) Florence Weinberger, "The Power in My Mother's Arms" first appeared in *Woman and Aging,* an anthology published by Calyx in 1986, and reprinted in *The Invisible Telling Its Shape and Breathing Like a Jew,* both published in 1997, the former by Fithian Press, the latter by Chicory Blue Press, both collections by Florence Weinberger; **p. 365**: "i like my body when it is with your." Copyright 1923, 1925, 1951, 1953, © 1991 by the Trustees for the E.E. Cummings Trust. Copyright © 1976 by George James Firmage. From *Complete Poems: 1904–1962* by E.E. Cummings, edited by George J. Firmage. Used by permission of Liveright Publishing Corporation.; **p. 366**: "Connecting" by Glenn Hutchinson, UNC Charlotte. Reprinted by permission of the author; **p. 369**: "Night School" from *Will You Please Be Quiet, Please* by Raymond Carver, copyright © 1990 by Tess Gallagher. Used by permission of Alfred A. Knopf, a division of Random House, Inc.; **p. 373**: "Happy Endings," from *Good Bones and Simple Murders* by Margaret Atwood, copyright © 1983, 1992, 1994, by O.W. Toad Ltd. A Nan A. Talese Book. Used by permission of Doubleday, a division of Random House, Inc. and McClelland & Stewart Ltd.; **p. 376**: "Love Letters," copyright © 1989 by A.R. Gurney, from *Love Letters and Two Other Plays* by A.R. Gurney. Used by permission of Dutton Signet, a division of Penguin Group (USA) Inc.; **p. 405**: Michael Klein, "A Rich Life: Adrienne Rich on Poetry, Politics, and Personal Revelation," *Boston Phoenix,* 1999. Reprinted by permission of the author; **pp. 409, 412, 413**: "The Burning of Paper Instead of Children." Copyright © 2002 by Adrienne Rich. Copyright © 1971 by W.W. Norton & Company, Inc.; Poems I, II, III of "Twenty-One Love Poems," Copyright © 2002 by Adrienne Rich. Copyright © 1978 by W.W. Norton & Company, Inc.; "Trying to Talk with a Man," Copyright © 2002 by Adrienne Rich. Copyright © 1973 W.W. Norton & Company, Inc., from *The Fact of a Doorframe: Selected Poems 1950–2001* by Adrienne Rich. Used by permission of the author and W.W. Norton & Company, Inc.; **p. 414**: "this is the oppressor's language/yet I need it to talk to you: language, a place of struggle" by bell hooks from *Between Languages and Cultures: Translation and Cross-Cultural Texts,* Anuradha Dingwaney and Carol Maier, Eds. © 1995 by University of Pittsburgh Press. Reprinted by permission of the University of Pittsburgh Press.

Casebook 4

p. 423: "Freedom's Plow," copyright 1942 by Langston Hughes, from *Selected Poems of Langston Hughes* by Langston Hughes. Used by permission of Alfred A. Knopf, a division of Random House, Inc.; **p. 428**: Claude McKay, "America" from *Selected Poems*. Courtesy of the Literary Representative for the Works of Claude McKay, Schomburg Center for Research in Black Culture, The New York Public Library, Astor, Lenox and Tilden Foundations; **p. 429**: All lines from "America" from *Collected Poems 1947–1980* by Allen Ginsberg. Copyright © 1956, 1959 by Allen Ginsberg. Reprinted by permission of HarperCollins Publishers; **p. 431**: Dwight Okita, "In Response to Executive Order 9066" from *Crossing with the Light,* Tia Chucha Press, 1992. Reprinted by permission; **pp. 432, 433**: Gwendolyn Brooks from *Blacks:* "The Sermon on the Warpland"; "The Second Sermon on the Warpland." Reprinted by consent of Brooks Permissions; **p. 434**: Sermon delivered

Index